HOW TO FIX JUST ABOUT ANYTHING

R E A D E R ' S   D I G E S T

HOW TO FIX JUST ABOUT ANYTHING

QUICK AND EASY WAYS TO SOLVE THE MOST COMMON PROBLEMS IN YOUR HOUSE, GARAGE AND GARDEN

Published by The Reader's Digest Association Limited · LONDON · NEW YORK · SYDNEY · CAPE TOWN · MONTREAL

QUICK-FIND GUIDE

ALL THE SUBJECTS in this book are arranged alphabetically. If you want to know how to shorten a belt, for example, you will find it under BELT; if you need to repair a chip in a bath, look it up under BATHS & BASINS. But in case you are unsure where to look for a particular subject, the Quick-find Guide that follows groups all entries according to their subject areas. Under CLEANING METHODS you will find all the entries on cleaning, from Brass to Upholstery; PESTS covers everything from Ants to Woodworm. An even more detailed list of contents appears in the index at the end of the book.

Continued overleaf

IN THE GARAGE

IN THE GARDEN

TOOLS & GADGETS

MATERIALS

EDITOR
Noel Buchanan

ART EDITOR
Joanna Walker

CONSULTANT EDITORS
Cassandra Kent Tony Wilkins

ASSISTANT EDITORS
Jill Steed Jo Wells

SENIOR DESIGNER
Jane McKenna

DESIGNERS
Emma Gilbert Austin Taylor

RESEARCHERS
Alistair McDermott Lucy Berridge
Gisèle Edwards

READER'S DIGEST GENERAL BOOKS

EDITORIAL DIRECTOR
Cortina Butler

ART DIRECTOR
Nick Clark

EXECUTIVE EDITOR
Julian Browne

MANAGING EDITOR
Paul Middleton

EDITORIAL GROUP HEADS
Ruth Binney Noel Buchanan

STYLE EDITOR
Ron Pankhurst

RESEARCH EDITOR
Prue Grice

PICTURE RESEARCH EDITOR
Martin Smith

WRITERS
Mike Baldock Chris Bowers
Anthony Byers Francesca Greenoak
Ernest Hall Cassandra Kent
Derek Smith Kate Smith
David Tucker Tony Wilkins

CHECKERS & TECHNICAL CONSULTANTS

ABC Music Shop
Geoff Apps
Peter Bateman FRES
Richard Bell
Roger Bisby
British Adhesives & Sealants
  Association
British Association of Landscape
  Industries
British Decorators Association
British Gas North Thames
John Burgess: Heating & Ventilating
  Contractors' Association
Camping & Outdoor Centre
Ivor Carrol
Terry Cooper Tennis
Electricity Association
The English Table Tennis Association
Evansport of Purley
Ever Ready Ltd
Cliff Forrest
Simon Gilham
Hire Association Europe
Colin Kinloch
Keith & Melissa Hunt
Ivor Mairants Musicentre
Janome (UK) Ltd
John Jaques & Son
Lillywhites
Low Pressure Surf of London
John McGowan
McLaren Ltd
Paul Magan

Lon Moir
Ocean Leisure Ltd
Prestige Group UK plc
Purley Downs Golf Club
E.J. Riley
Royal Photographic Society
Tricia Schofield BSc, FIHEc
Servis UK Ltd
Gary Shipman
Skate Attack Ltd
Snow & Rock Sports Ltd
Soccer Scene
Streatham Skates
Pauline Swaine FIHEc
Philip Swindells MIHort. MISTC FLS
Whyteleafe Football Club
Woodbridge Violins

PHOTOGRAPHERS

Martin Cameron
Features: Vernon Morgan

ILLUSTRATORS

Andrew Bezear
Ray Burrows
Kuo Kang Chen
Tony Graham
Mike Grey
Nicholas Hall
King & King
Janos Marffy
Sandra Pond & Will Giles
Precision Illustration
Mike Shoebridge
John Spencer (Garden Studio)
Raymond Turvey

INDEXER

Indexing Specialists, Hove,
  East Sussex

1998 REPRINT
Axis Design

ART DIRECTOR
Siân Keogh
MANAGING EDITOR
Jo Wells

The publishers wish to
thank the following
organisations for the
special help they gave to
the editors of
**HOW TO FIX JUST
ABOUT ANYTHING**

AFS Ltd
Buck & Ryan Ltd
Electrolux
Hoover plc
Robert Mullis: Rocking Horse Maker
Multi-Sharp Tools
Neill Tools Ltd
W.H. Newson & Sons Ltd
RAC (Royal Automobile Club)
Stanley Tools
Thames Water Utilities plc
Vax Ltd

Other organisations which
provided assistance and
advice are listed on
page 416.

Adhesives: SEE GLUES

Air bed

If the bed deflates, first make sure the plug is clean and firmly in place. Sand may have prevented it sealing.

Repairing a puncture   Time: 1 hour or less

> YOU WILL NEED Repair kit appropriate to the type of air bed.
> Possibly: bowl of water.

If the puncture is visible, clean away any sand or grease and dry the surface thoroughly.

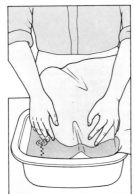

If you cannot see the puncture, inflate the bed and hold likely areas close to your cheek. You should be able to feel air escaping.

If not, as a last resort, hold suspect areas under water and watch for bubbles; then mark the spot. Dry the fabric thoroughly.

Having found the puncture, deflate the bed before making any repair, otherwise pressure of air inside can push off the patch before the adhesive has set.

RUBBERISED AIR BED If the bed is made of a rubberised fabric, buy a repair kit that contains rubber adhesive and repair patches.

Roughen the surface around the puncture with the abrasive paper supplied with the kit, and spread adhesive on both the area to be repaired and the patch.

Allow the adhesive to become touch-dry, then apply a second coat. Allow this to become touch-dry, then press the two parts firmly together.

PVC AIR BED If the bed is made of PVC, buy a kit containing a solvent adhesive which softens the plastic to form a bond. Spread the adhesive on both the PVC and the patch. While they are still tacky, press them firmly together. Leave the repair to dry completely before reinflating.

In an emergency, dry the surface and use strips of PVC household repair tape to cover the puncture.

Air brick

The most common air bricks are those which allow air into the underfloor area of a timber-floored house. Air bricks are also used high up a wall to provide room ventilation; they have a louvred internal face.

Covering a broken air brick

If an air brick gets broken, don't block it up; you will prevent ventilation, which could lead to rot in the floor. To make sure that rodents or birds don't creep in, cover the damaged area with chicken wire or plastic netting, until the brick can be replaced.

Replacing a broken air brick   Time: ½ a day or less

> YOU WILL NEED Club hammer, cold chisel, heavy-duty gloves, safety spectacles, dustpan and stiff brush, small trowel, new air brick, small bag of dry mortar mix, piece of board for mixing. Possibly: short piece of bent 15 mm copper pipe.

Before removing the damaged brick, carefully measure it so that you get a replacement of the same size.

Wearing gloves and safety spectacles, use a cold chisel and club hammer to remove the surrounding mortar. Break the brick from the centre out, and remove all debris.

With a cavity wall, you will probably find some form of liner bridging the gap between the two wall surfaces. Be careful not to damage it. The liner ensures that air passes through to the interior of the underfloor, and it also prevents debris from entering the air space in the wall.

Make up a small amount of mortar on a board, keeping the mix on the dry side to prevent it from spreading and staining the surrounding brickwork.

Dampen the wall opening and the new air brick, then 'butter' them both with mortar and insert the new brick in the hole.

Tap it in place with the handle end of the club hammer (never with metal which could break it).

Wipe away all surplus mortar, and point the joint around the air brick (see *Brickwork*). Use either the trowel or a short piece of copper pipe bent to a curve – depending on the shape of the adjacent pointing.

9

Replacing a damaged louvre Time: ½ a day or less

> YOU WILL NEED Cold chisel, club hammer, heavy-duty gloves, safety spectacles, dustpan and stiff brush, new plastic louvre. Possibly: contact adhesive (or wall plugs, screws, power drill and masonry bit in place of the adhesive).

The damaged louvre may be made of brick or plaster. Wearing gloves and safety spectacles, carefully chip it away with the cold chisel and club hammer. Take care not to damage any lining behind it. Brush out the debris.

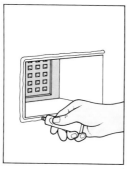 

FIXING WITH ADHESIVE If the new louvre has no screw holes, apply contact adhesive to its inner rim and round the hole. Allow both surfaces to become touch-dry. Then, making sure that the new louvre is level, press it firmly onto the wall.

FIXING WITH SCREWS If the new louvre has screw holes, hold it in position, mark through the holes onto the wall, then drill and plug the wall (see *Wall fixings*).

If screws are not provided with the new louvre, use rustproof round-headed screws (or countersunk screws if the holes are countersunk). Do not overtighten the screws or you might crack the plastic.

Air lock

An air lock in a tap Time: 1 hour or less

When the flow of water from a tap – usually a hot-water tap – slows to a trickle or stops altogether, the most probable cause is an air bubble, or 'air lock' in the pipe.

> YOU WILL NEED Length of 13 mm (½ in) garden hose, hose connectors to fit your taps (see *Hose*).

Connect one end of the hose to the tap that is giving you trouble, and the other end to the cold-water tap over the kitchen sink. The kitchen cold-water tap is supplied direct from the water main.

First, turn on the tap giving trouble and then the sink cold-water tap. The mains pressure will force the air bubble out of the system.

TROUBLE AT A KITCHEN MIXER TAP If the air lock is in the pipe supplying the hot water to a kitchen sink mixer you will need just a short length of garden hose. Connect one end of the hose to the outlet of the mixer.

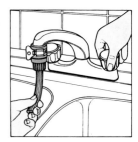

Then squeeze the free end with your fingers or a hose clip to prevent water escaping, and turn on both the hot and the cold water. The cold water under mains pressure will flow up the hot-water outlet and force out the air lock.

FINDING THE CAUSE OF AIR LOCKS Air locks occur when the water level in the cold-water storage tank (which is usually in the loft) falls more quickly than it can be replaced through the ball-valve inlet from the rising main. Eventually the tank empties and air enters the pipes. If air locks occur often, investigate three possible causes:

- The cold-water storage tank is too small.
- The pipe to the hot-water cylinder from the cold-water tank is too narrow. It should be at least $\frac{3}{4}$ in.
- The ball valve in the tank is giving too weak a flow.

You will probably need to call in a plumber to deal with the first two, but see *Ball valves* for the third.

Refilling a hot-water system 'upwards'

Air locks are likely to occur when a hot-water system is refilled after it has been emptied.

To prevent this happening, fill the system 'upwards' by connecting one end of a hose to the cold tap over the sink and the other end to the lowest drain cock in the system. This may be beside the boiler, or at the base of the hot-water cylinder.

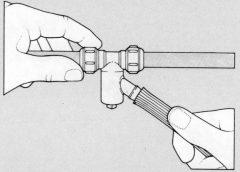

Open the drain cock and then turn on the cold tap slowly. Water will flow into the hot-water system, driving trapped air in front of it as it rises. If the pressure of the water should force the hose off the drain cock, fix it on again with a hose clip.

Ants

Ants enter homes in search of food. The most common species in Britain is the black garden ant which, despite its name, is actually dark brown.

Destroying ants   Time: a few minutes

> YOU WILL NEED Ant powder or a proprietary ant bait based on boric acid. Possibly: insecticidal lacquer.

The short-term method of disposing of ants is to pour boiling water over them as they march past, but this won't kill the queen ant.

To eradicate the ants' nest puff ant powder into the hole at the entrance of the nest. Lay more powder a day or so later if stragglers continue to emerge.

An alternative method is to use an ant bait which is available in the form of a gel based on boric acid. Following the manufacturer's instructions, squeeze a small amount out of the tube, positioning it where the ants will find it and take it back to their nest.

INSECTICIDAL BARRIER To stop ants from entering your home, buy an insecticidal lacquer designed to kill ants. Paint it across door thresholds and along any join between walls and floors where you have seen the ants. The lacquer is available in both aerosols and tins.

PHARAOH ANTS Places that are kept very hot, such as blocks of flats with centrally controlled central heating, may be invaded by tropical pharaoh ants. These small, yellowish ants nest in the building itself and can spread disease to food, especially their preferred savoury foods. If you see these ants, call a specialist pest-control company.

Asphalt path

Repairing sunken and missing areas

> YOU WILL NEED Garden fork, spade, rubble and stones, earth rammer, black bitumen primer, cheap brush, bagged repair macadam, rake. Possibly: garden roller.

Hollows and holes in the surface of the path, which collect puddles, are usually the result of poor preparation of the foundations. Dig out the sunken or damaged areas of asphalt to expose the undersoil. Dig out some of the soil and then ram in rubble and stones, tamping them down firmly with a earth rammer.

Coat the area with black bitumen primer, using a cheap brush that you can throw away afterwards.

Then apply new repair macadam. Rake it out so that it is just above the level of the path. Tamp it down and roll it with a garden roller if the area is large.

Recoating a dry, crumbling surface

> YOU WILL NEED Cold-applied bitumen, old watering can, gloves.

As asphalt dries out over the years, it loses its adhesion and becomes crumbly. You can correct this by applying a coating of cold-applied bitumen as a binder. The bitumen flows like treacle and finds its own level.

An old watering can is ideal for pouring on the bitumen, but you will have to throw the can away afterwards. This can be a messy job, so protect your hands with an old pair of gloves.

Keep the path out of service until the bitumen has hardened completely. Usually, this takes about 24 hours, depending on the weather.

Repairing collapsed path edges

The edges of an asphalt path can crumble and collapse with constant use, but they can be patched successfully.

> YOU WILL NEED Spade, timber battens (about 2.5 cm (1 in) thick and as wide as the path height), wooden pegs, club hammer, black bitumen primer, bagged repair macadam, rake, macadam rammer. Possibly: builder's line or string and sticks.

Dig away the edge that has collapsed and make sure that the foundation that is exposed is firm. Remove any loose, or crumbling pieces of asphalt.

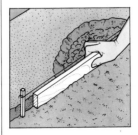

Hold the batten on edge and align it with the rest of the path. For a long run of path, establish a straight line by using a builder's line or a length of garden string tied to two sticks.

Fix the batten firmly in place by driving in wooden pegs with a club hammer. Then coat the area to be repaired (but not the timber) with black bitumen primer, using a cheap brush that can be thrown away afterwards.

Fill in up to the batten with repair macadam. Tamp until firm, then carefully remove the batten. Do not walk on the path for 24 hours.

REINFORCING AN ASPHALT PATH

Because macadam has no great structural strength, it helps to have some form of edging to the path, such as concrete edging blocks.

COMBATING STICKINESS

Macadam is very sticky when fresh. To prevent it from sticking to tools, have a watering can handy and keep the working surfaces wet at all times.

Ball valve

Stopping a constantly dripping overflow
Time: ½ hour or less

A constant drip, or a steady stream, of water from an overflow pipe indicates that there is a fault in the ball valve which regulates the water supply to the lavatory cistern or the cold-water storage tank.

If the water is dripping down a wall, it needs to be stopped fairly quickly, otherwise a damp patch is likely to appear on the inside of the house. This could damage the decoration or lead to serious structural problems.

If the ball valve has jammed open, the overflow pipe will not be able to cope with the volume of water, and eventually the tank will overflow.

To stop the overflow temporarily, you will need to cut off the water supply to the ball valve. There may be a servicing valve in the supply pipe near the ball-valve inlet. If there is, turn it off with a screwdriver or a coin.

Otherwise you will need to tie up the ball-valve float arm in either the lavatory cistern or the cold-water tank.

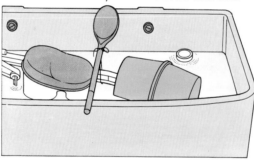

On a lavatory cistern, a wooden spoon should be about the right length to lay across the top to support the float arm. However, on a cold-water tank, which is larger, you will probably have to lay a timber batten across the tank.

Now investigate the cause of the trouble. The ball float may have sprung a leak, the valve washer may need replacing or there may be grit in the valve.

Fixing a leaky ball float   Time: 1 hour or less

A leaking ball float will sink in the water and produce a steady stream from the overflow pipe.

YOU WILL NEED Plastic bag for a temporary repair, a sharp pocket knife or an old-fashioned tin-opener, string.

Unscrew the leaking float from the end of the float arm. With your knife or tin-opener, enlarge the leak or make a fresh hole. Empty out the water. Screw the float back onto the arm and slip the plastic bag over it, tying the mouth securely around the float arm. Restore the water supply.

Buy a new ball float from a DIY store as soon as possible and screw it onto the float arm.

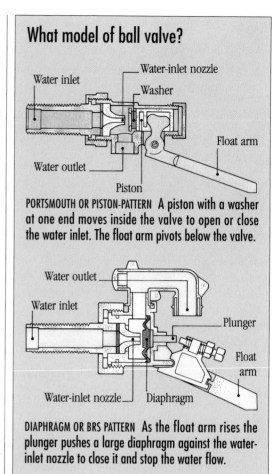

What model of ball valve?

PORTSMOUTH OR PISTON-PATTERN A piston with a washer at one end moves inside the valve to open or close the water inlet. The float arm pivots below the valve.

DIAPHRAGM OR BRS PATTERN As the float arm rises the plunger pushes a large diaphragm against the water-inlet nozzle to close it and stop the water flow.

Replacing the washer in a Portsmouth valve
Time: ½ a day or less

A worn washer on a Portsmouth ball valve can cause the valve to leak, and a build-up of limescale or bad corrosion can cause it to jam open or closed.

YOU WILL NEED Screwdriver, pliers, fine abrasive paper, ball-valve washer, pencil, petroleum jelly, replacement split pin.

First, cut off the water supply (see next page, margin). Steady the float arm and use pliers to close the split pin on which it pivots. Pull out the pin – which may break.

Insert the blade of the screwdriver into the slot beneath the valve, from which you withdrew the float arm. Push out the piston. If you have trouble doing this try putting the screwdriver up the water outlet.

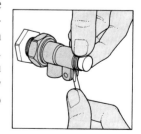

The washer is held in the piston by a screw-on cap. Insert the screwdriver into the slot in the piston and unscrew the cap with the pliers. If it won't move, pick out the old washer from the end of the piston with the point of a penknife and force the new one into its place. Make sure that it lies flat on its seating.

Clean the outside of the plug with fine abrasive paper. Wrap some abrasive paper around a pencil and clean the inside of the valve in the same way. Apply a light smear of petroleum jelly to the plug and reassemble the valve. Fit a new split pin if necessary. Restore the water supply.

Poor flow from a diaphragm valve Time: 1 hour or less

Poor water flow from a diaphragm ball valve can be caused by debris becoming trapped behind the diaphragm.

> YOU WILL NEED Screwdriver.

Cut off the water supply to the valve (see margin) and unscrew the large knurled nut.

Pull the nut away from the valve, taking with it the valve's front plate, the plunger and the float arm.

Use the screwdriver to prise out the diaphragm, then clean the space behind it. Replace the diaphragm and reassemble the valve.

There is a tiny projection in the front plate which must be fitted into a small slot at the top of the valve body in order to make a tight seal.

Adjusting the water level Time: 1 hour or less

An overflow may occur if the height of the ball float is wrongly adjusted. Modern ball valves are easy to adjust.

> YOU WILL NEED Possibly: a pair of pliers.

A ball valve with a metal float arm has a vertical section at the float end. The ball can be moved up or down to raise or lower the water level, and then screwed tight.

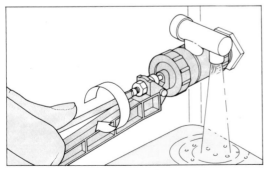

A ball valve with a plastic arm has an adjusting screw. Turning it clockwise lowers the water level.

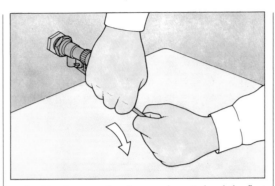

With older Portsmouth valves you have to bend the float arm to adjust the water level. First unscrew the ball float and remove it, otherwise you might break it off. Now take the float arm in both hands and bend the float end downwards to lower the water level, or upwards to raise it. Screw the ball back on.

Curing a noisy ball valve Time: a day or less

If your plumbing makes a banging noise or a persistent hum it probably comes from the ball valve in the cold-water storage tank.

As water flows into the tank it creates ripples which may make the ball valve bounce on its seating. The movement is transmitted to the rising main, producing the noise.

> YOU WILL NEED An empty yoghurt or cottage cheese pot, about 60 cm (2 ft) of nylon string. Possibly: some 15 mm pipe clips, screwdriver, bradawl.

Make sure that the rising main, which supplies water to the cold-water tank, is supported by roof timbers near the tank. Fit pipe clips to secure the pipe, if necessary.

If this does not cure the noise, make two small holes opposite each other near the rim of a yoghurt pot. Thread some nylon string through the holes and hang the loop over the float arm, near the float, so that the pot is suspended in the water below the ball float.

It will stabilise the float and prevent it from bouncing.

Replacing an old ball valve Time: 2 hours or less

Modern diaphragm ball valves with overhead outlets are quieter and less prone to limescale and corrosion problems than old Portsmouth valves. If you have persistent trouble with an old ball valve, replace it with a modern one.

> YOU WILL NEED A new diaphragm ball valve with overhead outlet, a new ball float, one or two adjustable spanners. Possibly: penetrating oil.

Cut off the water supply to the ball valve (see margin).

Cutting off the water supply to a valve

Look for a servicing valve in the supply pipe near the inlet to the ball valve and turn it off with a screwdriver.
If there isn't one, turn off the appropriate stopcock in the following manner.
If the faulty valve is in the cold-water storage tank, turn off (clockwise) the main stopcock, which is probably under the kitchen sink or in the cellar if you have one.
If the faulty valve is in a lavatory cistern, turn off the circular gate valve on the supply pipe from the cold-water tank to the lavatory. It will probably be near the bottom of the cold-water tank.
To make sure you have turned off the right gate valve, flush the lavatory; it shouldn't refill.
Once you have identified the gate valve, label it for the next time.
If no gate valve is fitted, tie the ball-valve arm to a batten across the top of the cold-water tank, and turn on the bathroom cold taps to empty the tank.

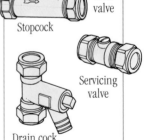

Gate valve

Stopcock

Servicing valve

Drain cock

In many houses there are two cold-water tanks in the loft. As well as the main storage tank, there is a much smaller one which is the feed-and-expansion tank of the central heating system.

Dripping from its overflow does not necessarily mean a fault in the ball valve – simply that the tank was overfilled.

When the system is cold there should be only a small amount of water in the feed-and-expansion tank. As the central heating heats up the water expands, flowing back into the tank. If the tank was too full when the system was cold, the water will drip out through the overflow pipe.

If the overflow drips, try taking about four pints of water out of the tank.

KEEPING SCREWS IN A SAFE PLACE

As you remove screws, nuts and bolts while doing a job, keep them safe and in the order they were removed, by sticking them down somewhere close at hand with insulating tape.

REMOVING THE OLD VALVE Unscrew the connector nut, which joins the water-supply pipe to the inlet of the valve. Pull the connector away from the valve inlet (left).

Unscrew the large back nut outside the wall of the tank that holds the ball valve in place. This could be the most difficult part of the job. Apply penetrating oil if necessary.

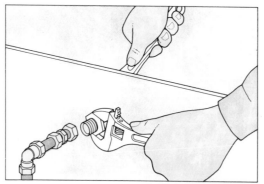

Hold the valve with one hand as you use the spanner to turn the nut. You might find it easier to hold the valve – or the nut inside the cistern – with another spanner (above).

Take out the old ball valve.

INSTALLING THE NEW VALVE You will notice that the new ball valve has two large plastic nuts screwed onto its tail. Unscrew and remove one of them.

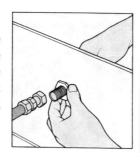

Then push the tail of the new ball valve through the hole in the cistern from the inside. Screw the plastic nut back onto the protruding tail (right).

Do not tighten it until you have used the nut inside the tank to ensure that the tail protrudes just enough to join up with the connector of the water-supply pipe.

Once the tail is correctly positioned, tighten the nut outside the tank wall by hand while holding the ball valve upright inside the tank with the other hand.

Push the lining of the connector into the ball-valve inlet, move the connector nut up to the threaded tail of the ball valve and screw it up as tightly as possible.

Restore the water supply and test for leaks. If there is a leak, tighten the connector nut as tightly as it will go until the flow of water stops.

High-pressure and low-pressure valves

Ball valves are classified as either 'high-pressure' or 'low-pressure' according to the diameter of their nozzle openings.

HIGH-PRESSURE VALVES They have a smaller opening and are normally used in cold-water tanks where they are under pressure from the main water supply.

Narrow nozzle

LOW-PRESSURE VALVES They have a larger opening and are used for lavatory cisterns which are fed from the cold-water tank under lower pressure.

Wide nozzle

If a high-pressure valve is fitted where a low-pressure one is needed, the cistern will fill extremely slowly. If a low-pressure one is fitted where a high-pressure is needed, it will probably leak.

Some modern ball valves are fitted with screw-in high-pressure nozzles, but they are also supplied with a low-pressure nozzle that can be substituted, should it appear necessary.

Balusters

Refitting loose balusters Time: parts of two days

If a nail holding the baluster works loose, replace it with a longer, thicker nail. If the dry warmth of the central heating cause balusters to shrink, and become loose in their sockets, they will have to be wedged more firmly in place.

YOU WILL NEED Tenon saw, 12 mm ($\frac{1}{2}$ in) chisel, scrap softwood, PVA wood adhesive, hammer, mallet, damp cloth, small paint brush, varnish or paint. Possibly: wood stain.

To make wedges from softwood saw off pieces 6 mm ($\frac{1}{4}$ in) thick, then pare them down with a chisel.

If the balusters are varnished, stain the wedges to match the surrounding wood, then coat them with PVA adhesive. Tap them in with the hammer round the loose baluster, ensuring that the baluster is kept central.

While the adhesive is still wet trim away any excess from the wedges with a chisel and mallet. Wipe off excess adhesive with a damp cloth. Stain any raw wooden edges. When the adhesive is dry, varnish or paint the repair.

Repairing a broken baluster Time: parts of two days

Moving large pieces of furniture up and down stairs is a common cause of breakages to balusters.

> YOU WILL NEED Pincers, means of clamping (see box), sandpaper, hammer, 12 mm ($\frac{1}{2}$ in) chisel, wedges, PVA wood adhesive. Possibly: fine round nails, hand or power drill, twist drill, nail punch, wood filler.

If the baluster is not completely broken you may be able to repair it in position using a rubber bandage and glue (see 'Two ways of clamping a baluster', right).

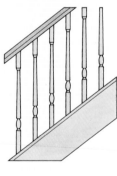

On a cut string (see 'What shape of staircase?', below) lever off the moulding at the side of the step with a chisel. This will release the bottom piece of the baluster.

The baluster may be nailed in place at both top and bottom, so don't use force. Use the baluster to lever the nail out far enough to grip with pincers.

What shape of staircase?

Balusters are fixed at the bottom to a length of wood which may be either a closed string or a cut string.

CLOSED STRING The string is a straight piece of timber with the top and bottom edges parallel, running diagonally across the profile of the stairs. The bottoms of the balusters are either slotted into sockets or simply nailed.

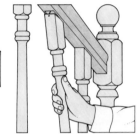

CUT STRING The string is cut in a zig-zag profile, that follows the shape of the stairs, with the bottoms of the balusters fitted in the horizontal sections. Pieces of wood moulding usually hold the balusters in place.

Two ways of clamping a baluster

If the baluster has broken diagonally, glue it and bind it with an old bicycle inner tube. Split the tube open to form one wide or two narrow bandages. Then bind a strip tightly around the baluster, tucking the end under one of the layers. It will apply considerable pressure to the join but won't bruise the wood.

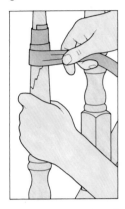

If the baluster has broken straight across, you will need to apply pressure from each end while the glue sets. Tie a piece of strong string in a loose loop around the ends. To protect the ends of the baluster from damage insert pieces of card under the string. Insert a short piece of dowel into the loop and twist until it tightens the string, applying pressure.

If the baluster on a closed string has snapped, ease out the two pieces. Check that the pieces mate. If they don't, see 'Finding a replacement baluster'. If they do, apply plenty of PVA wood adhesive to both parts and press them firmly together. Wipe away surplus adhesive with a damp cloth.

REPLACING THE BALUSTER The following day, when the glue has set, smooth the baluster with sandpaper, and remove any old adhesive from the ends.

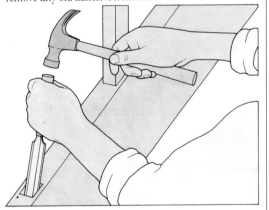

Deepen the socket on a closed string, using a hammer and chisel, until you can wiggle the baluster down far enough to get it back into the handrail.

Apply adhesive to the baluster and the staircase where they meet, then put the baluster in place. If necessary, wedge the lower end in place as described under 'Refitting loose balusters' (facing page).

FINDING A REPLACEMENT BALUSTER

If the baluster is damaged beyond repair, it may be possible to find a matching one in a yard that sells reclaimed materials from old houses. You can find them in *Yellow Pages* under 'Architectural Antiques' or 'Demolition'.
Failing that, a local carpenter should be able to make a new one on a lathe, but he will need an old baluster as a pattern.

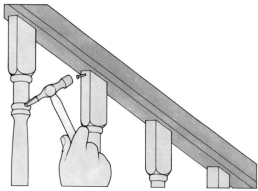

FIXING WITH NAILS If the top of the baluster was originally fixed to the handrail with a nail, replace it with an oval-head nail or a panel pin.

If you can't use the original hole, make a new one with a fine drill to avoid splitting the wood. Use a nail punch to sink the head just below the surface, and fill the hole with filler. Use matching wood filler if the baluster is varnished.

Bamboo furniture:

SEE CANE FURNITURE

Barbecue

Cleaning stains on concrete Time: ½ an hour or less

Spilled grease can leave nasty marks on concrete paving.

Dissolve about a cupful of washing soda in a bucket of warm water and rub hard at the mark using a tough cloth or pan scourer dipped in the solution.

Alternatively, use a specialist concrete cleaner.

SEALING THE SURFACE If you regularly barbecue food over concrete surfaces it may be worth using a special concrete sealer, so that future marks can be wiped away with a damp cloth (see *Concrete floor*).

Baths & basins (SEE ALSO SEALANTS)

Repairing a scratched plastic bath Time: 1 hour or less

YOU WILL NEED Fine wire wool, metal polish, cloth. Possibly: wet-and-dry abrasive paper.

Most modern plastic baths are tough and hard-wearing, but their appearance may be marred by surface scratches.

To remove shallow scratches from the bath's surface, rub them with fine wire wool (but not with abrasive paper or an abrasive cleaner). Finish off and restore the shine by polishing the repaired area with a metal polish.

For a deeper scratch, try gentle rubbing with a very fine grade of wet-and-dry abrasive paper, used wet. Don't replace it as it wears smooth, but do keep it wet. Finish with metal polish to restore the sheen.

Removing stains from a bath Time: 1 hour or less

Brown and green stains, which are caused by iron and copper dissolved in the water, can appear below the taps in soft-water areas. In hard-water areas, grey limescale can build up. Both are the likely result of a dripping tap, so first stop the drip (see *Taps*).

A bath-stain remover, used following the instructions, will usually remove these stains. Make sure that it is designed for use on your bath type — enamel or plastic. Don't leave it on any longer than recommended as it could damage the bath surface.

Repairing a chipped enamel bath Time: depends on area

If the damage to the bath is extensive you can get it professionally renovated. Look in *Yellow Pages* under 'Bathroom Equipment'. It is possible to repair small chips yourself.

YOU WILL NEED Household cleaner, fine wire wool, epoxy-resin repair kit such as Plastic Padding, fine abrasive paper, matching bath enamel, small paint brush. Possibly: rust stabiliser.

Clean the area thoroughly with a powerful household cleaner, and then rinse. If the chip shows any sign of rust, apply rust stabiliser, following the maker's instructions.

After about three hours clean off the stabiliser with wire wool, then rinse and dry the area.

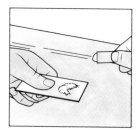

Following the manufacturer's instructions, mix up a small amount of epoxy-resin filler and fill the hole. Wipe away any surplus filler while it is still moist.

When the filler has set, after about 30 minutes, smooth it down with fine abrasive paper, avoiding the surrounding enamel. Then touch it up with matching bath enamel.

A partly blocked bath or basin Time: 1 hour or less

YOU WILL NEED Paperclip or piece of stiff wire, petroleum jelly, rubber gloves, plastic spoon, chemical drain cleaner.

First, check to see if hair, clinging below the plughole, is the culprit. If so, remove it with a piece of bent wire — such as a paperclip or hairpin.

Once the water has drained away completely, smear petroleum jelly over the plughole to protect the chrome.

Then, wearing rubber gloves, spoon chemical drain cleaner down the hole with a plastic spoon. Pour in boiling water to flush it into the waste pipe. Repeat as necessary.

A completely blocked bath or basin Time: 1 hour or less

YOU WILL NEED Sink plunger, damp cloth, chemical drain cleaner, rubber gloves. Possibly: bucket, screwdriver, expanding curtain wire or sink auger, adjustable spanner, length of wood.

Press a damp cloth firmly against the overflow. Then place the rubber cup of the sink plunger over the plughole and press down firmly and sharply with the handle four or five times. Repeat a few times until the water flows away.

Once the blockage is cleared, clean the waste pipe thoroughly with a chemical drain cleaner (see above).

CLEANING THE TRAP If the water does not run out, the pipe or trap may be blocked by an object such as a hairclip.

To get to the waste pipe, unscrew and remove the side panel of the bath or the basin pedestal. Basins are not supported by the pedestal but by the plumbing pipes and a wall bracket. The bath panel is usually held in place with dome-head screws which have caps that are removed to reveal the screw slot.

If you have been using a chemical cleaner to clear a partially blocked waste, pour two or three pints of water down the plughole before attempting to remove the trap and wear rubber gloves to protect your hands.

The waste outlet pipe may have either a conventional U-bend made of brass or plastic, or a plastic bottle trap. To undo the access nut of an old U-bend trap with a spanner, steady the joint with a piece of wood held in the bend to prevent the pipe buckling as you turn the spanner.

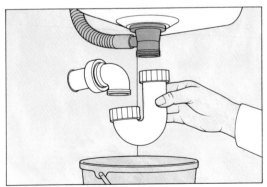

To remove a plastic trap place a bucket beneath the trap and unscrew it by hand. Clean and replace it.

CLEANING THE PIPE If the trap proved to be clear, examine the waste pipe for a possible blockage. Use a sink auger or expanding curtain wire to probe the pipe and locate and then dislodge the obstruction.

Replace the trap and test the system. Then replace the pedestal or side panel and clean the pipes with a chemical drain cleaner (see 'A partly blocked bath or basin'). Protect your hands when using a chemical cleaner.

Finally, if the drain remains blocked, call a plumber.

Finding a plumber

There is a lot to be said for listening to the personal recommendations of friends or relatives. Remember, though, that a tradesman who might be perfectly competent to carry out a simple job like renewing a tap may be less competent with a more complex task.

If you have to rely on advertisements or *Yellow Pages* look for plumbers with AIP or MIP (Associate or Member of the Institute of Plumbing) or RP (a plumber registered by the Institute of Plumbing) after their names.

Plumbers who also carry out gas central heating installation have to be CORGI registered and this implies an expertise in all plumbing fields. The address of the Institute of Plumbing is 64 Station Lane, Hornchurch, Essex RM12 6NB (Tel. 01708 472791).

Bees

Bees are not pests and won't sting unless provoked, but if they are swarming around your house, they may be dangerous to someone who is allergic to their stings. Stay well clear and keep children and animals indoors until the bees have been removed.

Call in an expert to remove them – don't attempt to remove the bees yourself. A list of beekeepers is available from the local authority pest-control office, the police and public libraries. Some will collect swarms as a free service.

HEAT AND ACRYLIC BATHS

Acrylic baths are easily damaged by extreme heat, and the marks cannot be removed. So never rest a lighted cigarette on the bath rim, and take great care if you are using a blow torch in the bathroom to do plumbing work.

A sink auger

A flexible spiral of wire, up to 4.6 m (15 ft) long, also called a sink clearer. Use it to dislodge blockages from pipework by inserting it into the waste pipe and rotating the handle. Sink augers can be hired by the day.

CURING A SMELLY OVERFLOW

A musty smell, or tiny black flies, in the bathroom are likely to come from the basin overflow. Soapy water builds up a deposit in the overflow which may smell unpleasant as it dries. Wearing rubber gloves, spoon drain cleaner into the overflow, then pour in boiling water. After about ten minutes, push a wire bottle brush down the overflow, and vigorously clean the interior. Rinse out afterwards.

Belt

When a belt needs fixing it is usually because the buckle has come off, or you have lost or gained weight and need to make a new hole because the belt no longer fits.

Fixing a detached buckle Time: ½ an hour or less

YOU WILL NEED Strong needle, strong thread, scissors.

If a buckle on a fabric belt has become loose or detached, simply sew it back on again, provided that the piece of belt to which it was attached is undamaged. If it is damaged, cut off as short a piece as possible and fix the buckle to the undamaged section. Use a strong needle and thread.

Making a new hole Time: a few minutes

YOU WILL NEED Ball-point pen, thin awl or thick darning needle. Possibly: eyelets and fixing tool, fabric glue or nail varnish.

With the belt on, mark the spot with a ball-point pen and then take off the belt. Use a thin awl or a thick darning needle to make the hole. Take care not to make it too big or the point of the buckle may work loose.

It is unnecessary to finish the hole on a leather or plastic belt unless it has to match other holes. In this case, buy matching eyelets, in a kit, from a haberdashery department. Follow the instructions on the pack.

On a stiff fabric belt which does not have eyelets, use a touch of fabric glue or clear nail varnish, or a fine buttonhole stitch (see *Stitches*) round the hole to stop the fabric from fraying when it is washed.

Shortening a belt Time: ½ an hour or less

YOU WILL NEED Craft knife or scissors. Possibly: jeweller's screwdriver or spectacle-repair screwdriver, sewing machine.

An overlong belt is best altered at the buckle end so that the alterations will be covered when the belt is worn. Take off the buckle (see box, above right), and cut the leather to the required length. Then replace the buckle.

Belts can also be cut shorter at the unbuckled end, although changes will be visible when it is worn. Simple leather and plastic belts can be cut and left as they are, but stitched leather belts will need to be machine-stitched. A little shoe polish rubbed along the cut edge will help it match the surface, but rub it in well so that it doesn't come off on your clothes.

When machining plastic or very thin leather, be sure to use a needle that is strong enough and suitable for the material (see *Sewing machine*).

USING MOLE GRIPS

When using Mole grips to hold a metal surface avoid damaging the metal by wrapping it in some card or cloth.

Taking off a buckle

Some buckles can be removed easily if you want to shorten the belt. Shortening at the buckle end avoids spoiling the stitching at the other end. Fabric belts can also be easily shortened from the buckle end.

SCREW-ON BUCKLE Use a spectacle-repair or jeweller's screwdriver to loosen the screws. Cut the belt to length. Make a new central slot in the leather and reassemble the belt.

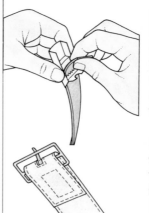

QUICK-RELEASE BUCKLE Undo the tooth-edged clamp and release the belt. Cut it to the right length and replace the end of the belt in the clamp.

FABRIC BELT Unpick the stitching and shorten the belt. Make a new hole for the belt prong. Reassemble the belt and fasten it in place with a large rectangle of stitching.

Bicycle bearings

Adjusting wheel bearings Time: 1 hour or less

If a wheel does not turn freely or if it can be moved from side to side, the bearings need adjusting. This is most easily done with the wheel removed (see *Bicycle wheels*).

YOU WILL NEED Open-ended spanners, cone spanner, adjustable spanner or Mole grips.

On the rear wheel the adjustment is done on the side opposite the gear cogs. The front wheel bearings can be adjusted on either side.

The bearings are held round the axle by a cone-shaped nut at each end of the axle, and each cone is held in place by a locknut. Undo the locknut with an open-ended spanner, holding the axle with an adjustable spanner if it has a flat side, or with Mole grips if not. Take care not to damage the axle threads (see margin).

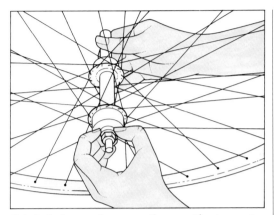

With the locknut undone, screw the cone either in or out as necessary, using your fingers so as not to over-tighten it.

If the bicycle wheel is not spinning easily, unscrew the cone slightly to release it.

If there is side-to-side movement, screw the cone in far enough to stop play in the axle, but leave it slightly loose.

Retighten the locknut while holding the cone in place with a cone spanner. This will tighten the bearings, so twist the axle with your finger to check that it turns freely.

Replace the wheel.

Replacing or greasing wheel bearings
Time: ½ a day or less

If a wheel will not turn freely and makes a grating noise the ball bearings may need replacing, or cleaning and regreasing – or the axle may be bent, which may also have damaged the bearings. The procedure is the same.

First remove the wheel (see *Bicycle wheels*). If it is the rear wheel of a mountain or racing bike, also remove the freewheel (see *Bicycle gears*: 'Removing a freewheel').

> **YOU WILL NEED** Open-ended spanners, cone spanner, adjustable spanner or Mole grips, old jar or dish to hold bearings, white spirit and rag, grease.

Hold the axle at one side of the wheel, using an adjustable spanner or Mole grips, and undo the cone lock-nut on the opposite side.

Remove the lock washer and cone. If the threads are in good condition the cone will unscrew by hand; otherwise use a cone spanner.

 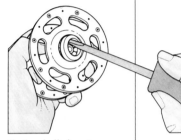

Withdraw the axle enough to expose the ball bearings on the side from which you removed the cone.

If the ball bearings are hidden by a dust cover, carefully prise it out, then remove the bearings.

Some dust covers are too fine to remove so use a toothbrush to clean out any dirt from behind the cover.

If the grease has dried up the bearings may fall out. Do not lose any as they may be reusable. Even if they

Cone spanner
The tool needed to adjust the cone is a specially thin open-ended spanner. Sometimes a multipurpose spanner (which often comes with a new bike) incorporates a cone spanner.

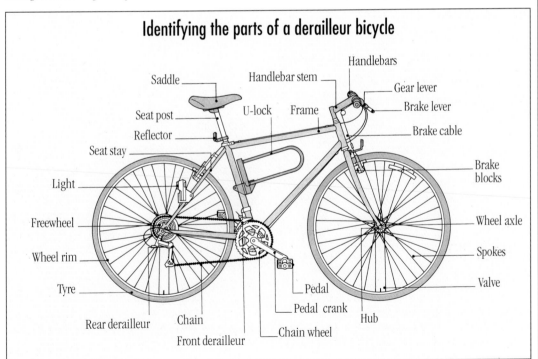

Identifying the parts of a derailleur bicycle

- Saddle
- Handlebar stem
- Handlebars
- Gear lever
- Brake lever
- Seat post
- U-lock
- Frame
- Brake cable
- Reflector
- Seat stay
- Brake blocks
- Light
- Freewheel
- Wheel axle
- Spokes
- Wheel rim
- Valve
- Tyre
- Pedal
- Rear derailleur
- Chain
- Pedal crank
- Hub
- Front derailleur
- Chain wheel

are not reusable you will need to count them to know how many new ball bearings to buy.

Withdraw the axle completely to expose the ball bearings on the other side. Remove these too.

CLEANING THE PARTS Use white spirit on a rag to clean the recess in the hub where the bearings sit. Then clean the ball bearings and the cone and replace any with badly pitted surfaces or dullness.

If you suspect that the axle is bent, check it by removing the remaining locknut and cone and rolling the axle along a flat surface. If the axle is straight it will roll smoothly, otherwise it will wobble.

Take the old ball bearings, cones or axles, to the bicycle shop to make sure that you buy new ones the correct size, as nonstandard sizes are used on some bikes.

Pack waterproof or motor grease into the recesses which hold the ball bearings. Then reassemble the wheel.

REASSEMBLING THE WHEEL Push the ball bearings into the grease, which will hold them in place. Replace any dust covers. Put a cone onto the axle and push the axle back into the hub, taking care not to dislodge the ball bearings.

Replace the second cone and loosely fit the locknuts and washers (which fit between the cone and the locknut).

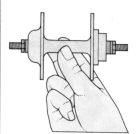

Make sure you have an equal length of axle showing beyond each locknut.

Adjust the bearings (see 'Adjusting wheel bearings') and retighten the locknuts.

If you removed the freewheel, screw it back by hand then replace the wheel.

Adjusting bottom-bracket axle bearings
Time: 1 hour or less

If the pedal cranks do not turn freely or have play in them, the axle bearings in the bottom bracket may need adjusting. Work on the side opposite the chain wheel.

The bearings are contained in a cup which screws into the frame and is held in place by a lockring. Some new bicycles are fitted with a maintenance-free sealed unit and cannot be adjusted.

> YOU WILL NEED Bottom-bracket lockring spanner and pin spanner (bottom-bracket cup spanner), or large adjustable spanner and open-ended spanner, depending on type.

Undo the lockring with a lockring spanner. A multi-purpose bicycle spanner often includes one. The usual type of lockring has a number of notches in its outer edge that the spanner fits into.

Then use a pin spanner, (also called a bottom-bracket cup spanner) to adjust the bearing cup.

If you don't have the correct tool, it may be possible to turn the cup by wedging a nail into one of the small holes in its surface and tap it with a hammer if it is tight.

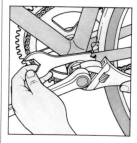

Alternatively, the bearing cup may have a raised section with two flat sides that an adjustable spanner or an open-ended spanner will fit.

Screw the bearing cup in enough to let it turn freely, but tight enough to prevent up-or-down play in the axle.

Hold the cup in place with the tool used to turn it while you retighten the lockring. Screw the lockring on quite tightly so that it does not work loose.

Adjusting headset bearings Time: 1 hour or less

Correct adjustment of the bicycle headset is necessary for safe steering and braking.

Test the headset for looseness by standing beside the bike, applying the front brake and pushing the bike forward. If the headset is loose the wheel and forks will move slightly backwards towards the frame.

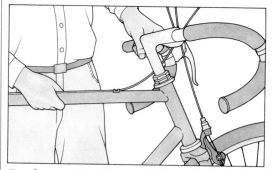

Test for excessive tightness by lifting the front wheel off the ground and turning the steering. It should turn freely without any stiffness.

> YOU WILL NEED Large adjustable spanner, headset spanner.

Use an adjustable spanner to undo the locknut where the handlebar stem enters the frame. The headset cup is below the locknut, but there may be a washer or brake-cable hanger between them. To adjust it you may need a special thin spanner; some multipurpose bicycle spanners fit. Some cups can be held by hand or with pliers; a few accept a normal or adjustable spanner.

Turn the headset cup clockwise to tighten it and anticlockwise to loosen it.

Tighten it sufficiently to prevent any play, but not so much that the handlebars will not turn freely.

After making the adjustment, hold the cup in place while you retighten the locknut. Tighten it quite firmly.

If the headset is stiff, loosen the headset cup slightly.

Check after riding the bike that the cup has not worked loose again and tighten if necessary.

Adjusting or replacing pedal bearings
Time: 1 hour or less

Pedals sometimes develop excessive sideways play. Many modern pedals do not contain adjustable bearings, so the whole pedal must be replaced. However, some better quality and older pedals can be adjusted.

> YOU WILL NEED Open-ended spanners, small screwdriver.
> Possibly: pliers, new bearings, white spirit rag, jar and grease.

Remove the dust cap from the outer end of the pedal. It usually unscrews by hand or with pliers. Some dust caps prise off; a few screw off with a spanner.

Beneath the dust cap there is a locknut. Use an open-ended spanner to undo and remove it.

Adjust the cone underneath the locknut with a small screwdriver. The pedal must be able to spin freely but it must not move from side to side.

Retighten the locknut while holding the cone in place with a screwdriver.

GREASING THE BEARINGS To replace or regrease the bearings, remove the locknut, cone and washers. The pedal will then pull off and the ball bearings will drop out.

Thoroughly clean the ball bearings and the surfaces they run against with a rag dipped in white spirit. Inspect the bearings for pitting and, if necessary, buy new ones.

Pack the recesses where the bearings sit with grease and reassemble the pedal. Adjust the bearings as described above and replace the dust cap.

Bicycle brakes

When the brakes are not being applied, the brake blocks should be positioned so that they are close to the wheel rims without actually touching them.

Minor brake adjustment Time: a few minutes

You can usually make minor adjustments by turning the barrel adjuster. Adjusters have a locknut which must be undone before the adjustment can be made, and retightened afterwards.

On side-pull brakes the adjuster is situated where the cable enters the brake. On centre-pulls and cantilevers it is on the brake lever or cable hanger.

If your brakes have a brake-release button, make sure it is not engaged when you begin adjusting your brakes.

What model of brake?

Bicycle brakes come in four main designs. These are side-pull, centre-pull and two types of cantilever.

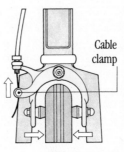

Cable clamp

SIDE-PULL The most common type, fitted to most utility and racing bikes. Each of the two main parts, called calipers, hold a brake block and move on a central pivot on the attachment bolt.

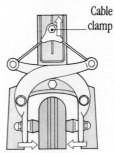

Cable clamp

CENTRE-PULL Now less common and most often seen on racing bikes. It consists of two calipers which are joined by a short straddle wire. Each caliper moves on a separate pivot when the brakes are activated.

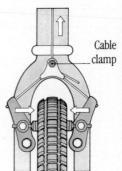

Cable clamp

CANTILEVER Each brake block is attached to a cantilever arm which pivots on a boss brazed onto the frame or forks. Depending on the design, the brake cable is either tightened at a central clamp (as shown) or at the side, on a cantilever arm.

Select the right brake cable

Brake cables are sold in different lengths.

The inner wire has a nipple at one end that fits into the brake lever. Dropped, straight and flat handlebars each require a different type of nipple.

A 'universal' replacement cable has a nipple of each type at opposite ends. Use cable cutters to adjust the length of the cable, removing the unwanted nipple. Alternatively, take the old cable to a cycle shop and ask them to cut the new cable to length.

Major brake adjustment   Time: 1 hour or less

If the adjustment is beyond the scope of the barrel adjuster, you will need to tighten the brake cable.

> YOU WILL NEED Open-ended or ring spanners, pliers, 'third hand', Allen keys.

Screw the barrel adjuster almost fully home so that the cable slackens. (This will allow you to compensate for future wear in the blocks, by turning the barrel adjuster anticlockwise to move the blocks towards the wheel rims.)

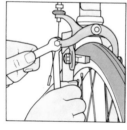

Use a spanner or Allen key to unfasten the brake-cable clamp. Loosen it just enough to let the cable slide through. On side-pulls the clamp is on the end of one of the calipers.

On centre-pulls and some cantilevers, the clamp is on the straddle yoke, directly above the brake. On most cantilevers it is on the end of one of the cantilever arms. Some types of clamp need two spanners to undo them.

Push the brake blocks onto the rim and hold them there. It is much easier if a helper does this, or you can use a purpose-made tool called a third hand (see margin).

With the blocks held against the rims, grip the end of the cable and pull it through the clamp until it is tight. Use a spanner to tighten the clamp enough to hold the cable in place.

Then fit a second spanner to the other nut to do the final tightening. If the brake blocks now touch the rim, adjust the barrel adjuster slightly.

Check the tightness of the clamp to ensure that the cable doesn't pull through when the brakes are applied.

'Third hand'

A tool specially designed to make brake adjustment easier is called a 'third hand'. It passes between the spokes, holding the two brake blocks against the wheel rims. This leaves both your hands free to work on the brake cable.

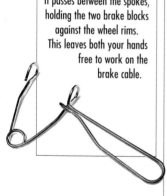

Fitting new brake blocks   Time: 1 hour or less

When the brake blocks have worn right down, they must be replaced. Always replace them in pairs.

> YOU WILL NEED New brake blocks, open-ended or ring spanners, pliers. Possibly: 'third hand' and Allen keys.

Unfasten the brake-cable clamp (see 'Major brake adjustment', left). Then undo the single nut that holds the brake block to the brake. It will be either a standard hexagonal nut or an Allen-key type.

Fit the new brake blocks and screw on the securing nuts so they are finger-tight.

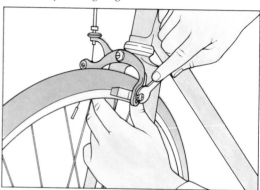

Push the brakes against the wheel rim and align each block so that the whole of its surface meets the flat surface of the rim. Fully tighten the securing nuts.

Adjust the brakes.

Fitting a new brake cable   Time: 1 hour or less

A brake cable normally consists of an inner cable sliding inside an outer casing. When a cable breaks or becomes frayed, you need only replace the inner cable, unless the problem has occurred because of the poor condition of the casing, in which case replace both.

> YOU WILL NEED New cable of correct type, open-ended or ring spanners, pliers, grease. Possibly: Allen keys, 'third hand', cable cutters.

REMOVING THE OLD CABLE Start removing the old inner wire by unfastening the brake-cable clamp bolt at the brake (see 'Major brake adjustment').

Pull the brake lever and disengage the nipple at the end of the lever. Remove the inner wire from the outer casing by pulling it from the lever end with pliers or your fingers. Throw it away.

Before fitting the new inner wire, apply a little grease along its whole length. Also grease the nipple, which will allow it to rotate slightly in the lever as the cable twists during braking. Without grease, the cable may eventually fray and break near the nipple.

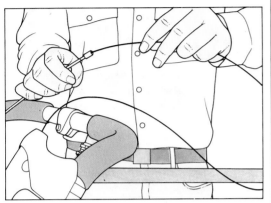

PUTTING IN THE NEW WIRE Feed the replacement inner wire through the lever and through the outer casing.

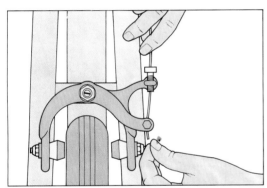

When the wire emerges at the brake, feed it through the loosened brake-cable clamp.

Check that the nipple is fully seated in the lever and that the outer casing is seated correctly at the lever and in any barrel adjusters or guides.

Finally, adjust the brake (see 'Major brake adjustment', facing page) and test it before riding the bike.

What model brake block?

Side-pull   Cantilever

STYLE OF BRAKE-BLOCK FITTING There are two types of brake-block fitting — one for side-pull brakes, the other for cantilevers. Centre-pull brakes may have holders of either design.

Bicycle chain

Removing a link on a derailleur bike
Time: 1 hour or less

On bikes with derailleur gears, the chain tension is maintained by a spring in the rear gear mechanism.

If a single link becomes bent, or damaged in some other way, you can usually remove it and rejoin the chain without spoiling the tension. Separate links are not normally available; if several links get damaged you will have to replace the whole chain, unless you kept some spare ones when the chain was originally fitted.

YOU WILL NEED Chain-rivet extractor.

To remove a link you need a chain-rivet extractor.

Locate the chain in the guides so that the point of the tool is centred on the rivet you are removing and the plate at the back of the link is supported by the tool.

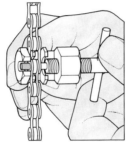 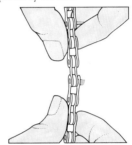

Gradually screw in the rivet pusher, but stop when the end of the rivet is flush with the outside face of the chain-rivet extractor.

Now remove the tool and flex the chain slightly to separate the two links. Take care that the rivet does not come right out.

To join the chain up again once you have taken out the necessary number of links, place the link with the protruding rivet in the guides of the extractor so that the tool's point is centred on the rivet and the link's rear plate is supported by the tool.

Screw the tool gently to push the rivet back in place, making sure that an equal amount of rivet protrudes from each side of the chain.

CURING A STIFF LINK Sometimes the new join is stiff because the rivet has been pushed too far out. Push it back slightly from the other side. To do this the tool has a second guide slot where the rear plate is not supported.

Fitting a new chain on a derailleur bike
Time: 1 hour or less

Even under ideal conditions bicycle chains last only a few months before they become badly worn, and a worn chain can cause wear in more expensive parts such as the chain wheels and gear cogs.

Chain-rivet extractor

An inexpensive addition to your tool kit is a chain-rivet extractor (also called a chain tool). It is essential for removing links in the chain of a bike with derailleur gears.

To check for excessive wear, try to pull the chain away from the teeth at the front of the chain wheel. The more a tooth can be exposed, the greater the wear.

The time has come for a replacement chain when you can see almost all of the tooth.

YOU WILL NEED Chain-rivet extractor, new derailleur chain.

Take out a rivet from one of the links (see 'Removing a link on a derailleur bike', previous page). Then pull the chain off the bike, but don't let the end with the protruding rivet pass through the rear gear mechanism; it might jam.

The new chain will almost certainly be too long, so you will have to shorten it.

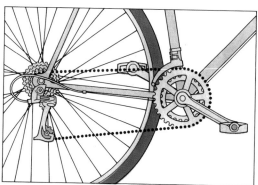

Thread the chain around the cogs and derailleur at the back and the chain wheel at the front and rejoin the chain, using the chain-rivet extractor (see 'Removing a link on a derailleur bike', previous page).

Make sure that the chain is only just long enough to accommodate the combination of the largest rear gear cog and the largest front chain wheel.

Remove any surplus links, using the chain-rivet extractor, and keep the discarded links for spares in case you need to replace a bent link in the future.

Join the two ends of the chain together, using the chain-rivet extractor as before.

Adjusting the chain on a non-derailleur bike
Time: 1 hour or less

YOU WILL NEED Spanners. Possibly: chain-rivet extractor.

On single-speed and hub-gear bikes the correct tension in the chain is achieved by moving the back wheel forwards or backwards until there is only a small amount of slack left in the chain. You should not be able to push the chain down or up more than 1.3 cm ($\frac{1}{2}$ in).

If the wheel is as far back as it will go, it probably

means that the chain has stretched. Some cyclists then shorten the chain to obtain the correct tension. However, the chain usually needs replacing (see 'Fitting a new chain on a non-derailleur bike', below).

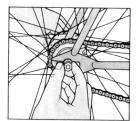

Undo the wheel nuts on the rear wheel and move it either forwards or backwards until you have the correct tension.

Then tighten the wheel nuts, ensuring that the wheel is central between the forks. Turn the pedals backwards to see if the chain is running freely.

Fitting a new chain on a non-derailleur bike
Time: 1 hour or less

Even under ideal conditions a chain on a non-derailleur bike will last a year or so. The easiest way to check for excessive wear is to try to pull the chain away from the teeth at the front of the chain wheel. The more a tooth can be exposed, the greater the wear. When you can see most of the tooth, the chain needs replacing.

YOU WILL NEED New chain, chain-rivet extractor, small screwdriver, pliers, spanners.

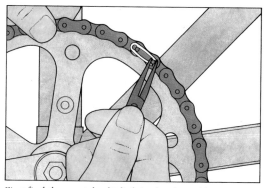

First find the special split-link in the chain. The two rivets in the link are gripped on the outer side by a spring clip. Prise it off with pliers.

Pull the link out and remove the chain from the bike.

When fitting a new chain you may need to shorten it. Thread it around the rear cogs and chain wheel, then undo the rear wheel so that you can move it backwards and forwards to judge the length needed.

Using a chain-rivet extractor, remove the necessary number of links (see 'Removing a link on a derailleur bike', previous page). When the length is right, replace the split-link and refit the retaining clip with pliers. Then adjust the tension by moving the wheel backwards or forwards, and tighten the wheel nuts.

REPLACING A 'JUMPED' CHAIN

A derailleur chain will occasionally jump off while you are riding. To put it back, first make sure it is located properly on the rear cogs, using a stick or a screwdriver to protect your hands from grease. Then replace it on the top of the front chain wheel. If it is jammed in the cogs, pull it out or prise it out with a screwdriver or spanner. Lift the back wheel off the ground and turn the pedal crank forwards.

If the chain comes off frequently, the gears may need adjusting (see *Bicycle gears*) or there may be a stiff link (see 'Removing a link on a derailleur bike', previous page).

Bicycle gears

The gears regulate the transmission of power from your legs to the bicycle wheels, evening out the effort needed to keep the bike moving. It should take the same effort to slowly climb a steep hill as to whizz along on the flat.

What model of gear?

Nearly all racers and mountain bikes are fitted with derailleur gears; utility bikes may have hub gears. Derailleurs have between 5 and 24 gears. Two types of derailleurs are available – indexed and friction – and adjustment methods differ slightly.

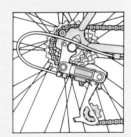

INDEXED DERAILLEURS The lever clicks into preset positions, each click moving the derailleur arm a fixed distance.

FRICTION DERAILLEURS The lever does not click; the rider has to decide the best position for each gear.

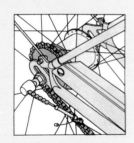

THREE-SPEED HUB GEARS Many utility bikes are fitted with three-speed hub gears, which are largely trouble-free, although occasionally the cable may need to be adjusted.

Adjusting a front derailleur Time: 1 hour or less

The front derailleur, if one is fitted, rarely needs adjusting unless it is knocked. But if your bike throws the chain off to the left or right at the front, or if you cannot select one of the chain rings, adjustment is possible.

YOU WILL NEED Small screwdriver, set of small open-ended spanners or Allen keys. Possibly: pliers.

Remove any slack from the cable (see 'Adjusting a rear derailleur'). Then adjust the two small screws on top of the front derailleur, which limit how far it moves from side to side, until the gears are selected smoothly.

If you still have a problem selecting gears, check that the derailleur is at the right height over the largest chain ring. It should be about 2 mm ($\frac{1}{16}$ in) above it.

Also, look at the mechanism from above to check that the derailleur is in line with the chain wheel.

If it needs moving, unclamp the cable and undo the bolt that holds the derailleur to the frame. Make the adjustment, then retighten the bolt. Connect the cable and readjust the limiter screws and cable tension.

Adjusting a rear derailleur Time: $\frac{1}{2}$ a day or less

If changing gear on the bike becomes difficult or unreliable, and the chain keeps coming off, the derailleur gears probably need to be adjusted.

YOU WILL NEED Small straight-headed or cross-headed screwdriver. Possibly: pliers, small open-ended spanners or Allen keys.

TIGHTENING A SLACK CABLE Position the chain on the smallest rear sprocket and check whether there is any slack in the rear gear cable. Any slack in an indexed system will make the gears malfunction, but a small amount in a friction system should not matter.

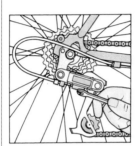

To take up the cable slack, first make sure that the chain is on the smallest sprocket with the gear lever set in the correct position. Then undo the cable clamp on the rear derailleur using a spanner or an Allen key depending on the model.

Pull the cable tight, either by hand or with a pair of pliers, and retighten the clamp.

ADJUSTING A DERAILLEUR LIMITER On indexed and friction systems, two small screws on the derailleur limit how far it moves from side to side. They are usually marked 'L' for the lowest gear (the largest sprocket), and 'H' for the highest gear (the smallest sprocket).

If the chain overshoots the sprockets and moves into the spokes when you try to change to the largest sprocket, screw in (or unscrew) the L screw slightly to stop the derailleur moving too far.

If you cannot engage the largest sprocket, turn the L screw slightly to allow the derailleur to travel far enough.

The same principles apply when adjusting the H screw to allow selection of the smallest sprocket.

Now make sure that both the smallest and largest cogs can be engaged without the chain coming off.

EXTRA ADJUSTER FOR INDEXED GEARS On indexed systems there is also a barrel adjuster on the cable where it enters the rear derailleur. If the derailleur is not moving far enough to engage the next gear, turn the adjuster anti-clockwise slightly and try again.

Repeat this gradual adjustment until the gear selection is working correctly. If the derailleur is overshooting the next gear, screw the barrel adjuster slightly clockwise.

Replacing a broken derailleur cable Time: 2 hours or less

Derailleur cables can fray and snap because of wear or rust. When you buy a replacement cable specify the type of bike and gears. Unless the outer casing is damaged, you can replace just the inner cable.

> YOU WILL NEED New cable, pliers, set of open-ended spanners or Allen keys.

Before replacing a rear gear cable, put the bicycle into the highest gear (the chain should be on the smallest rear cog). And to replace the cable on the front gears, select the smallest front chain wheel.

Then use an open-ended spanner or Allen key to unfasten the cable clamp on the derailleur.

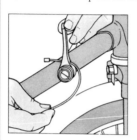

To remove the inner cable, push it through the lever a little until the cable nipple appears. You may have to move the lever as you push. Pull the cable out through the gear lever.

Thread the new cable through the lever, making sure that the nipple is correctly seated. Then double-check that the lever is in the correct position to select the smallest rear cog if you are changing a rear cable, or the smallest chain wheel for a front cable.

Refasten the cable clamp and make sure there is no slack by holding the cable with pliers as you tighten.

Finally, adjust the gears (see previous page).

Adjusting hub gears Time: 1 hour or less

This section is aimed at three-speed hub gears, which are a common type. If the selection of hub gears becomes less positive and the gears frequently slip into neutral, the problem is likely to be due to a slack gear cable.

> YOU WILL NEED Pliers. Possibly: screwdriver, bicycle oil, penetrating oil.

A cable runs from the gear selector down to the rear wheel, where it joins a little chain via a barrel adjuster with a lockring. The chain enters the hub and is attached to a rod to operate the gearing system inside the hub.

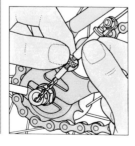

Put the gear lever in the position for second gear. Then unscrew the lockring on the barrel adjuster.

The hub nut that the little chain enters has an inspection hole. Look through this hole at the chain, which is attached to a rod. The end of the rod should be level with the end of the axle. If it is not, adjust the barrel adjuster by turning it until the rod is correctly positioned.

Check the gears again and lock the barrel adjuster in position with the lockring.

MOVING THE CABLE CLAMP If you cannot tighten the cable enough with the barrel adjuster, move the clamp that holds the gear cable to the frame. Undo the screw on the clamp and move the clamp away from the gears to take up any slack. Tighten the screw and make any minor adjustments with the barrel adjuster. Test the gears.

ADJUSTING THE LITTLE CHAIN If you still have trouble, disconnect the little chain from the barrel adjuster by unscrewing the adjuster until it comes away. Using your fingers make sure that the chain is screwed clockwise fully into the hub. Reconnect the barrel adjuster and readjust.

OILING ALL THE PARTS If the gears still do not work properly, oil the gear lever and cable and any pulleys that it passes through and put some oil in the gear hub to help free any jammed parts.

Replacing a hub-gear cable Time: 2 hours or less

Cables on hub gears sometimes break because of wear and corrosion. Another common problem is that the outer cable rusts on the inside, making it difficult for the inner cable to slide within it, and affecting the gear change.

The cable is replaced as a whole, both inner and outer. Take the old cable with you when buying a replacement so that you get the right length.

> YOU WILL NEED New cable, open-ended spanners, screwdriver.

First put the gear trigger in the correct position to select the highest gear (third on 3-speed models).

Then unscrew the lockring and barrel adjuster at the hub-end of the cable in order to disconnect the gear cable from the little chain.

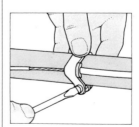

Loosen the clamp that holds the outer cable to the cycle frame just far enough for the plastic cable stop to slide out. Then pull the cable away from the frame to give it some slack.

REMOVING THE OLD CABLE To free the old cable from the trigger, put the trigger in the position to select the highest gear. Some gear triggers have a small ratchet spring that must be lifted up to allow the nipple to be released.

To free the cable, push the trigger up slightly past the high gear position while you push the cable into the trigger body until the cable nipple comes free.

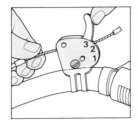

On other models push the cable in until it comes free.

Pull the whole cable out of the trigger and remove it from the bike. Keep the plastic stop that fits on the cable where it is clamped to the frame.

PUTTING ON THE NEW CABLE Put the trigger into third gear and feed the inner wire of the new cable into the trigger body until it hooks into the nipple holder.

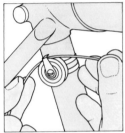 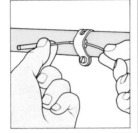

Place the cable over the pulleys fitted on some models. Reconnect it to the little chain with the barrel adjuster and lockring.

Thread the other end of the new gear cable through the plastic stop and the clamp that holds it onto the bicycle frame.

With the trigger still in third gear move the clamp until the inner cable has just a little slack, and tighten the clamp again. Put the cycle into second gear and adjust the cable (see 'Adjusting hub gears').

Test the bike and adjust the gears if necessary.

Removing a freewheel Time: 1 hour or less

The freewheel is the cluster of sprockets on the rear wheel. Some jobs, such as replacing a spoke on the freewheel side of the wheel, need the freewheel to be taken off first.

YOU WILL NEED Freewheel remover (see margin, right), large adjustable spanner.

Most freewheels screw onto a thread on the hub. The more expensive 'cassette hubs', which are also called free-hubs, should be taken to a cycle shop to be replaced.

For other models, first take off the back wheel. Then remove the wheel nut from the freewheel side of the bicycle (if the bicycle has a quick-release wheel, unscrew and remove the finger nut).

Fit the freewheel remover in the notches of the freewheel, replace the wheel nut (or finger nut minus its springs) and screw it onto the axle so that it is hand-tight.

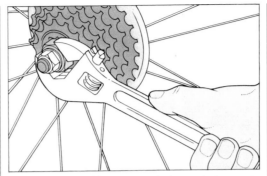

Use a large adjustable spanner – the longer the better – to unscrew the remover and the freewheel anticlockwise. It will take quite a lot of effort to shift it.

As soon as it starts to move, remove the wheel nut (or finger nut) and continue to unscrew the remover by hand. The freewheel will come off in one piece.

Replace the freewheel by hand so as not to damage the threads. Riding the bike will do the final tightening.

Removing the back wheel from a bike with derailleur gears

Put the bike into top gear (the smallest gear cog).

Check that the tyre will pass through the brake blocks. If the tyre is wider than the rim, the blocks will have to be moved apart. Some centre-pull brakes have a small release lever where the cable enters the brake which moves the blocks apart.

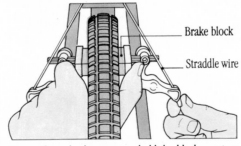

Brake block

Straddle wire

On cantilever brakes you can hold the blocks against the rim and disconnect the brake straddle wire from one side – or let some air out of the tyre.

Undo the wheel nuts or quick-release mechanism. Then pull the rear derailleur away from the sprockets (towards the rear), and lift the back of the bike off the ground to let the wheel drop out.

If necessary push the wheel forward so that the axle clears the rear fork ends. To replace the wheel, reverse the procedure.

Pull the rear derailleur back to let the sprocket mesh with the chain as you replace the wheel.

Freewheel remover

To take off the freewheel, you will have to buy a freewheel remover to match the model fitted to your bike. It is not expensive, but take the bike to the shop to make sure you get the right tool.

Bicycle handlebars

Adjusting the height Time: 1 hour or less

Handlebars are usually set at the same height as the saddle, but it is a matter of personal comfort.

> YOU WILL NEED Spanner or Allen key, wooden mallet or hammer and piece of wood.

The handlebar stem which enters the frame is secured by an expander bolt. The head of the bolt may be an Allen-key type or hexagonal. Unscrew the bolt a couple of turns so that it rises above the top of the stem.

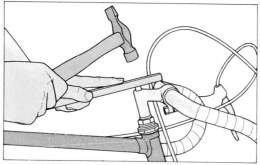

Now hit the bolt firmly with a wooden mallet, or protect it with a piece of wood and use a hammer. This will release the expander hidden inside the base of the stem.

Grip the wheel between your legs and turn the handlebars from side to side, adjusting their height as necessary.

Replacing handlebar grips Time: 1 hour or less

The plastic grips fitted to the ends of flat handlebars become brittle with age and crack. Replacing them is an easy job if you buy new ones of the same length and width.

> YOU WILL NEED New handlebar grips, craft knife. Possibly: talcum powder, lighter fuel.

Either pull off the old grips or cut them away with a craft knife. Clean the handlebars, then push the new grips on. Lubricate them with talcum powder or lighter fuel if they will not slip on easily. Don't use grease or oil because the grips will not stay in position.

Replacing handlebar tape Time: 1 hour or less

Three types of tape are used to cover handlebars: thin cloth or plastic tape, padded tape or foam-rubber sleeving.

> YOU WILL NEED New covering, scissors. Possibly: screwdriver, Allen key, new end-stops, talcum powder, lighter fuel.

THIN HANDLEBAR TAPE Thin adhesive tape is easiest to fit. Discard the old tape but reuse the old end-plugs.

Fold back the rubber hoods on the brake levers and then start taping from the top, about a hand's width from the handlebar stem. Wind the adhesive tape around the handlebar, overlapping the first turn so that the end of the tape does not show and the start is secure.

Work down the bar keeping an even tension and over-lapping the tape slightly. Don't worry about the bar showing behind the brake lever. It is covered later.

At the end of each bar cut the tape, leaving about 1.6 cm ($\frac{5}{8}$ in) surplus. Tuck the surplus into the bar and insert the end-plug. Some push in, but others also have an expander screw which is turned to secure the stop fully.

Cut small pieces of tape to cover the bar behind each brake lever. Stick each on the side of the brake lever, pass it around the back of the bar, then secure it the other side of the lever. Fold the lever hood back in place.

PADDED TAPE The tape usually comes in two pieces and is accompanied by two pieces of adhesive trim or, in some cases, two plastic clips for securing it near the stem.

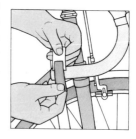

Start at one end of the handlebars. If the tape is not adhesive, fix the end to the bar with masking tape or something similar. Wind the padded tape over the masking tape to conceal it, then go on winding around the bar, working upwards.

Treat the brake levers as recommended for thin tape (see above). When you get within a hand's breadth of the stem, cut the tape so that the cut end is underneath the bar. Secure the end with the adhesive trim or retaining clip. Fit the end-plug in the same way as for thin handlebar tape, except that no tape is tucked into the bars.

Then repeat the whole process on the other side.

FOAM-RUBBER SLEEVING Remove the brake levers. The brake cables may have to be disconnected to get at the fixing bolts. Pull on the lever and you will see the fixing bolt under the cable. Some are Allen key bolts, others have a screw head. Partly unscrew the bolt.

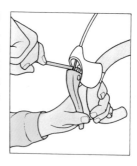

Twist the lever from side to side and slide it off. The foam rubber comes in four pieces; two fit above the brake levers and two fit below. Some makers include a lubricant to ease the sleeving onto the bars; if not, use talcum powder or lighter fuel inside the sleeving or on the bars. Work one piece of sleeving onto each side of the handlebars.

Refit the brake levers in the most comfortable position. Fit the last sections and replace the end-plugs. Slide the remaining pieces onto the bars and fit the end-stops.

Bicycle lighting

What model of light?

BATTERY LAMPS A bracket is fitted to the bicycle frame and the lamp slots into place. They are easy to fit and easily transferable from one bike to another. But the cost of batteries makes them relatively expensive to run. However, they are also easy to steal, so take them with you when you leave your bike locked up.

LED LAMPS Light-emitting diodes are used in the lamps instead of filament bulbs. They run for many hours on small batteries. They are currently illegal in Britain as sole sources of bicycle lighting, but are useful as a supplement to your main lights.

DYNAMO LIGHTING More difficult and costly to fit than battery lamps, but costs nothing to run. However, the lights go out when the bike stops and you have to pedal much harder when they are working.

HYBRID SYSTEM Combined dynamo and rechargeable batteries. Expensive to install, but the lights don't go out when you stop. Some come with rechargeable packs that plug directly into a mains socket.

Fitting battery lamps Time: 1 hour or less

YOU WILL NEED Set of front and rear lamps. Possibly: mounting brackets, spanners.

If your bike already has a front-lamp bracket – near the headset or on the forks – take it with you when you buy your lamps to make sure you get the right type.

You should be able to push the lamp straight onto the bracket, although some types have small nuts which are tightened with a spanner for added security. If your bike does not have a front-lamp bracket, buy a lamp that

comes with a universal bracket. It can be fitted onto either the handlebars or the handlebar stem, usually without the need for tools. Mount it as high as possible for best results.

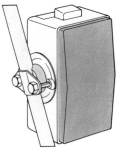

Rear lights are of two main types: this one can be fitted to the seat stay with bolts.

This can be fixed to the seat pillar or the seat stay with a universal mounting bracket.

Fit your lights either centrally or slightly to the right-hand side when viewed from the rear.

Fitting bottle dynamo lights Time: ½ a day or less

A bottle dynamo – which is so called because of its shape – is usually mounted on the seat stay or front fork and is driven by a small serrated wheel in contact with the tyre wall. Because the rear lamp is also mounted on the seat stay it usually shares its mounting bracket with the dynamo. Dynamo sets include full fitting instructions, but what follows are the basics, plus some tips.

YOU WILL NEED Bottle-dynamo lighting set, spanners, screwdriver. Possibly: front-mounting bracket.

The mounting bracket for the dynamo and the rear lamp has two nuts and bolts to clamp it to the seat stay. The dynamo and the rear lamp then bolt onto the bracket (see left). Make sure that the dynamo drive wheel meets the tyre wall square on, and presses against it with the right amount of pressure. It should press just hard enough not to slip when the tyre gets wet. If it presses too hard it will act as a brake and also wear out the tyre.

A screw with a sharp point goes through the dynamo mounting bracket and pierces the paint on the frame to make a good electrical contact, so that the frame acts as an earth and completes the circuit.

Two leads emerge from the bottom of the dynamo to supply the power – one to the front lamp and one to the rear. The dynamo set usually includes small plastic ties to attach the leads to the frame, but you can thread the lead to the front lamp through existing brake-cable eyes, or twist it around the brake cable, or secure it with PVC insulating tape. There should be just enough slack in the lead to allow the handlebars to turn fully.

You may have to buy a separate bracket to mount the front lamp. Not all kits include one, and a bracket that is already fitted to the bike may be the wrong size.

LAMPS FOR LUGGAGE RACKS

When buying lamps take account of any luggage racks fitted to your bike. Rear panniers will obscure a light fitted to the rear seat stay, for example, and a front basket may cover the usual mounting points. Special lamp brackets are available for luggage racks.

Chain cleaner

A brushing device is fitted to the top of a can of cleaning solvent. The chain can be run through the brush without being taken off the bike. Chain cleaners are fairly expensive but they save time.

High-visibility accessories

A common cause of accidents is car drivers not seeing cyclists, so make sure that both you and your bike are highly visible both day and night.

- Fluorescent waterproofs, jerseys and bibs all improve your visibility while cycling during the day.
- Night-time cycling clothing should include reflective bands such as Sam Browne belts, which go round the waist and diagonally across the body. The bands can be worn over normal clothing then put in your pocket at the end of a journey. Make sure that they are reflective and not just fluorescent.
- Reflective anklebands draw attention to a cyclist effectively because they move up and down as you pedal. They also serve as trouser-clips, protecting your trousers from oil on the chain.
- Reflective armbands are useful for hand signals, and some helmets carry reflectors.

Fitting reflectors   Time: 1 hour or less

YOU WILL NEED Reflectors. Possibly: screwdriver, small open-ended spanners.

All new bicycles in Britain must be sold with reflectors fitted facing the front and the rear, as well as on the spokes of both wheels and on both pedals.

Many types of reflector can be bought separately either to replace broken ones or to increase your night time visibility. By law rear reflectors on a bicycle must be red, and front ones white. Pedal reflectors and the reflectors on wheels may be either white or amber.

REAR REFLECTOR New rear reflectors are most easily fitted to the mudguard, which will probably already have a hole drilled near the end. The reflector is held in position by a single bolt or screw. You may have to remove the rear wheel (see *Bicycle tyres*) to tighten the bolt or screw.

If you do not have full-length mudguards fitted on your bike, you can buy a rear reflector which fits onto the mounting bolt of either side-pull or centre-pull brakes.

Bicycles which have cantilever brakes, including most mountain bikes, will usually have a suitable hole drilled in the position where a side-pull brake would go. Reflectors are also available that fit onto the rear luggage carrier.

FRONT REFLECTOR There is only one commonly available type of front reflector. It is fitted onto the brake mounting bolt in the same way as a rear reflector.

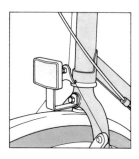

WHEEL REFLECTORS Clear or amber plastic reflectors which snap onto the spokes make the bike more visible at night when seen side-on. Tyres with reflective walls do the same job, but they are quite hard to find in Britain.

PEDAL REFLECTORS Reflectors moulded into the pedals appear to dance up and down in car headlights. Bolt-on or snap-on types of reflector can sometimes be found, but they often do not stand up to wear and tear.

REFLECTIVE ADHESIVE TAPE Short lengths of reflective tape can be applied to the bike's frame, mudguards or any other reasonably flat surface, to make the bicycle more visible.

Bicycle lubrication

Cleaning a dirty chain   Time: 1 hour or less

A dirty or excessively oily bicycle chain should be cleaned before it is lubricated.

The most thorough way to clean it is to remove the chain (see *Bicycle chain*) and soak it in a large metal tray containing white spirit or degreaser.

Wear rubber gloves to protect your hands and brush the chain with an old toothbrush.

You can give the bike chain a fairly good clean without removing it by using a specially designed chain cleaner (see margin, left), available from bicycle shops.

The chain can be run through the brush on the chain cleaner without removing it from the bike.

Lubrication programme

Fortnightly and monthly oiling is easy to do yourself, but yearly regreasing jobs could be part of an annual service carried out by a bike shop.

FORTNIGHTLY Oil the chain.

MONTHLY Oil the gears, freewheel, cables, brakes and, in some models, the bottom bracket axle and the hubs.

YEARLY Grease the bottom bracket axle (ball-bearing type), hubs, headset and pedals containing ball bearings.

Where your bike needs oil and grease

Any bicycle that is ridden frequently needs regular lubrication to prevent unnecessary wear on the parts and to keep them running smoothly. Consult the previous page in order to determine how often each part needs to be oiled or greased. The illustration below shows where the parts on the bike are that need lubrication.

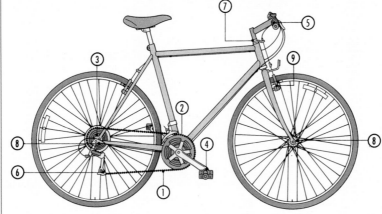

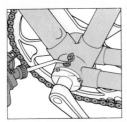

1 CHAIN Oil the chain lightly. Too much oil picks up dirt which causes wear to the chain and cogs.

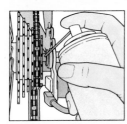

2 BOTTOM BRACKET AXLE On most bikes this does not need oiling, but get a bike shop to grease it yearly. If it has a flip-up cap, squirt in oil once a month.

3 FREEWHEEL About once a month spray lubricant between the revolving part of the freewheel and the stationary part.

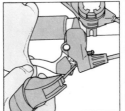

4 PEDALS Traditional pedals with ball bearings should be repacked with grease once a year (see *Bicycle bearings*). Some pedals have a plastic bearing that should not need oiling, but if the bearing starts to squeak spray it with lubricant.

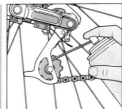

5 CABLES Exposed inner cables on brakes and gears need a coat of grease or spray-on lubricant about once a month. To lubricate them, depress the brake levers and expose the inner cables. Then spray on aerosol lubricant.

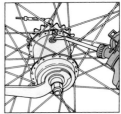

6 DERAILLEUR GEARS Oil the pivots, the operating levers and all the other moving parts with spray-on lubricant about once a month, paying particular attention to the small guide jockey wheels that the chain runs over on the rear derailleur.

7 HEADSET The headset should be repacked with grease. Get it done annually by a bike shop.

8 HUBS Repack both hubs with grease annually. If there is a small cap for oiling, open it and give the hub a good squirt of oil about once a month.

9 BRAKES Apply a drop of oil or a quick squirt with spray-on lubricant to all pivot points. Don't get oil on the brake blocks.

Bicycle mudguards

Adjusting a mudguard Time: 1 hour or less

YOU WILL NEED Possibly: screwdriver or open-ended spanner (usually 8 mm).

BENDING THE STAYS Sometimes a mudguard begins to rub against the tyre – usually because it has been knocked or the bike has been leant against a wall.

With your hands, gently bend the stays (the wire rods holding the mudguards to the fixings) until the mudguard is positioned so that it no longer touches the tyre.

TIGHTENING THE FIXINGS If a mudguard rattles, the fixing screws on the front or rear forks have probably come loose or fallen out. Depending on the fixing, use a screwdriver or small spanner to tighten or replace them.

Then tighten the fixings at the other end of the stays.

The pair of stays may be attached to the underside of the mudguard with a screw or a small nut and bolt – or sometimes with rivets.

Alternatively, metal plates may be fixed to the mudguard holding bolts which, in turn, hold the stays. This allows some degree of up-and-down adjustment, but the bolts are more likely to come loose.

QUICK FIX FOR LOOSE MUDGUARDS

If you lose the bolt that fixes the mudguard stay to the frame, fix it temporarily by passing garden wire through the stay and the hole in the frame. Twist it together with pliers.

Bicycle pedals

Fitting new pedals Time: 1 hour or less

Damaged pedals need to be replaced. Or you might want to change your pedals for others you like better – such as wide pedals for boots or rubber pedals for slippery soles. It's an easy job; the only quirk is that the left-hand pedal has a left-hand thread.

When you buy new pedals say whether they are to fit steel or alloy cranks, or take your bike to the shop. On some pedals, the threaded section that screws into the crank is too short for an alloy crank and may crack it.

> YOU WILL NEED Pedals, open-ended spanner.

Move the right-hand crank (attached to the chain-wheel) so that it is pointing forwards, and is horizontal.

Fit an open-ended spanner (usually 15 mm) to the part of the spindle that screws into the crank. Hold the pedal firmly with one hand. Unscrew the pedal by pushing down on the spanner with your other hand.

Remove the left-hand pedal in the same way, but use your right hand to push down on the spanner.

Before you fit the new pedals, check which is the left and which the right. They are marked with an R or an L, usually near the threads that enter the crank.

FINDING THE RIGHT SADDLE HEIGHT

Getting the saddle to the right height is crucial for comfort, safety and efficient riding. To check the height, stand your bike on flat ground near a wall (or get someone to hold it for you). Climb aboard, hold onto the wall and put your heels on the pedals. Then get the cranks in line with the seat tube. With your heels on the pedals, one leg should be almost straight. This is the best height for efficient pedalling. However, for safety you may have to lower the saddle slightly in order to touch the ground while cycling in traffic.

Bicycle pump

Mending a faulty pump Time: 1 hour or less

> YOU WILL NEED Possibly: new adapter, washer, screwdriver.

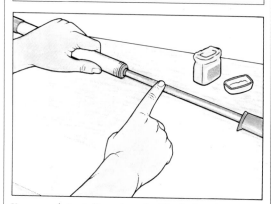

You can substantially prolong the life of a bicycle pump by greasing the plunger (which is the rod that goes in and out of the barrel) with petroleum jelly.

If the barrel or plunger of a pump is damaged, you will have to throw it away, but other problems can be fixed.

REPLACING THE ADAPTER If the pump has a small hose, called an adapter, that screws onto the tyre valve, it may perish with age until it leaks air. You can buy replacement adapters cheaply. They are a standard fit at the pump end, but have different fittings at the other end to fit onto different types of valves (see *Bicycle tyres*).

REPLACING A VALVE WASHER If you have the kind of pump that connects directly onto the valve, the rubber washer that fits on the valve may wear out. It can be replaced, although spares may be hard to find. The washer housing simply unscrews by hand.

REPLACING A PLUNGER WASHER The washer which forms the end of the plunger can wear out, resulting in reduced pressure. If you can find a replacement washer, it is not difficult to fit. Unscrew the cap on the barrel by hand and pull the plunger completely out of the pump's barrel.

Loosen the screw which holds the washer in place on the plunger. On some models the washer simply pulls off. Fit a new washer and push the plunger into the pump barrel, ensuring that the washer fits snugly. Finally, replace the cap of the barrel by hand.

Bicycle saddle

Adjusting the saddle position Time: ½ an hour or less

> YOU WILL NEED Possibly: Allen keys, spanners, penetrating oil.

CHANGING THE HEIGHT To alter the height of a bicycle saddle undo the bolt where the seat post enters the frame. Some bolts have normal hexagonal nuts, others have Allen key holes. Some bikes are fitted with a quick-release bolt that you loosen with a lever.

Push the saddle down or pull it up as required. If it is a tight fit, twist it from side to side as you do so. If it is stuck, squirt it with penetrating oil and leave it for a few hours. Grease the seat post to ensure it does not get stuck again.

• Line up the saddle with the crossbar (or down-tube on a woman's frame), then tighten the seat bolt securely.

CHANGING THE ANGLE Saddles are normally horizontal, but some people prefer a slight downward or upward tilt. You can also move the saddle forwards or backwards.

The exact position is a matter of taste, but as a rough guide the centre of your leading knee should be above the pedal spindle when the cranks are horizontal.

Both these adjustments are made at the saddle clamp, which attaches the saddle to the seat post. Two types of saddle clamp are most commonly used on bikes.

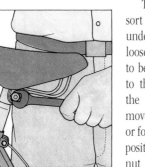

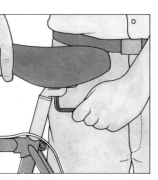

The traditional steel sort has a nut on each side, under the saddle. You need loosen only one nut slightly to be able to tilt the saddle to the angle you want. At the same time, you can move the saddle backwards or forwards to find the ideal position. Then tighten the nut firmly.

An alloy seat post and clamp is found on many racers and mountain bikes. It is usually secured by a single Allen key bolt underneath the rear of the saddle. Slacken the bolt, to allow you to make forward and backward adjustments, as well as changes to the tilt of the seat. Retighten firmly.

What model of saddle?

MAN'S MODEL Designs of saddle differ between sexes. A man's saddle is long and narrow.

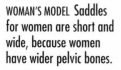

WOMAN'S MODEL Saddles for women are short and wide, because women have wider pelvic bones.

PLASTIC SADDLE Inexpensive and not affected by rain. Some have foam under the top for comfort.

LEATHER SADDLE Popular, but can take time to mould to your shape. Very comfortable when finally 'broken in'. Needs regular treatment with saddle dressing.

GEL SADDLE For extra comfort, a layer of synthetic gel is inserted between a firm base and a Lycra or plastic top.

More tips for greater comfort

If you do not want to buy a new saddle, consider one or more of the following suggestions for greater comfort.

- Wear cycling shorts that have a towelling or synthetic chamois pad sewn on the inside. They can be worn under normal clothing in cooler weather.
- Wear shorts liners – a sort of cyclist's underwear with the same sort of padding as Lycra shorts.
- A cheaper but possibly less effective answer is a slip-on saddle cover made from sheepskin or gel and Lycra.
- Replace your existing saddle with one fitted with springs. Extra suspension is particularly useful on mountain bikes.

Bicycle security

What model of bicycle lock?

CABLE LOCK Plastic-coated steel cable. It may deter casual theft but it can be cut off fairly easily by a determined or skilled thief. A long one can be used to secure parts of the bike that are easy to remove, such as quick-release wheels.

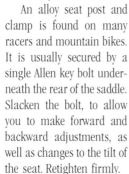

CHAIN AND PADLOCK The stronger the chain and padlock the heavier they are to carry on the bike. A long chain can be passed through all the easily removed parts of the bike, making them more difficult to steal.

U-LOCK (SHACKLE LOCK) A hardened-steel U with a bar that locks across the ends. This is a very strong type of lock, and some makes offer a guarantee if the bike is stolen. The lock is heavy, but most come with a carrying bracket that fits onto the bicycle.

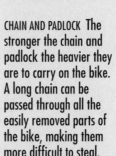

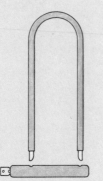

POSTCODING YOUR BIKE

A stolen bike is more likely to be returned if your postcode and house number are stamped into the frame. Some police stations can arrange free postcoding. Call the local crime prevention officer. If you don't have it postcoded, at least make a note of the frame number (usually stamped under the bottom of the frame).

How to lock your bike

Always try to lock your bike to a fixed object such as a metal post or iron railings, but don't use a short post, because the bike could be lifted clear quite easily.

Pass the lock through the frame and at least one of the wheels, preferably the front because it is easier to remove. If you have a chain or cable long enough, pass it through both wheels and the frame and around the fixed object.

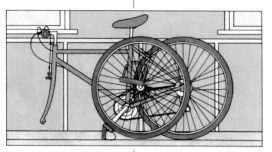

If your bike has a quick-release front wheel and you have a short security chain or a U-lock, take off the front wheel and line it up with the rear wheel. Then pass your lock or chain through both wheels and the frame before fixing it to a rail or post.

Some mountain bikes have a quick-release saddle; remove it and pass the lock through it, or take it with you.

Bicycle tyres

Fixing a flat tyre Time: $\frac{1}{2}$ an hour or less

When you discover a flat tyre, first check that the valve is attached tightly. Then put saliva on the end of the valve and watch it for a few seconds, for air bubbles.

If air leaks out, either replace the valve or fit a new inner tube (see 'What model of valve?', above right).

If the valve is not faulty, assume the tyre is punctured.

YOU WILL NEED Puncture repair kit, 3 tyre levers, pump, bowl of water, wheel-nut spanner.

REMOVING THE WHEEL If the bike has derailleur gears, put it in the highest gear. Then remove the wheel, either by undoing the wheel nuts or with the quick-release lever.

TAKING OUT THE TUBE Remove the valve dust cap and then unscrew the collar that holds the valve against the rim.

Squeeze the tyre all the way round the rim to pull the bead away from the rim. Then push the flat end of a tyre lever under the tyre about a spoke away from the valve and leave it sticking up. Take care not to snag the inner tube.

Repeat with a second lever, inserting it about two more spokes away from the valve. Then put a third lever on the other side of the valve.

What model of valve?

There are three types of valve commonly found on bicycle tyres – Schraeder, Presta and Woods.

For some sizes of tyre, you can buy inner tubes fitted with alternative types of valve. For rarer sizes there is no choice. The tyres on most 3-speeds and on all mountain bikes are fitted with Schraeder valves. Most bicycle pumps can be modified to fit all valves.

SCHRAEDER VALVE Schraeder valves look like the valves on car tyres. If they become faulty, most of them can be replaced either by using a special tool or by reversing the dust cap and using it.

PRESTA VALVE Prestas are narrow with a small knurled collar on the top which must be undone to inflate or deflate. You can use a special pump which has no adapter or a standard pump with the appropriate adapter. Prestas cannot usually be replaced.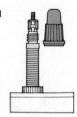

WOODS VALVE A traditional British valve, it can easily be replaced without tools. Use a standard pump with the appropriate adapter. The modern valve core is better than the valve-rubber type.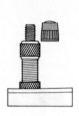

Push down each lever, one after the other, and hook it behind the spoke that is nearest to it. Once the third and final lever is in position, the centre lever will drop out.

Leave one lever in position and carefully run the second lever all the way around the wheel to prise the tyre loose and lift it over the edge of the wheel rim.

REPAIRING THE PUNCTURE Pull out the inner tube and inflate it. If the puncture is not obvious, put the inflated tube into a bowl of water and look for bubbles.

If they come from where the valve stem meets the tube, you will almost certainly have to buy a new tube because most modern valve stems are not replaceable.

When you have found the puncture, mark it with a cross, using the crayon provided in the puncture repair kit.

Dry the tube and roughen the area around the puncture with the glasspaper supplied with the kit.

Spread an even coating of rubber solution over the puncture, covering an area slightly bigger than the repair patch. Leave it for a few minutes to dry.

There are two kinds of repair patch: one type of patch has foil backing on one side and paper backing on the reverse; the other type has paper on only one side.

If you have a foil-backed patch, remove the foil and press the patch firmly onto the rubber solution, making sure the edges are well stuck down. Leave for a few minutes, and then remove the paper backing.

With the paper-only type of patch, remove the paper backing and press the patch firmly in place, making sure that the edges are stuck down all round.

The kit contains either powdered chalk or a stick of chalk that can be powdered with the grater. Dust the area with chalk to prevent the tube sticking to the tyre. If you've lost the chalk, use ordinary talcum powder.

REPLACING THE TUBE Carefully check inside the tyre to see if there is anything, such as a thorn or a piece of glass, that caused the puncture. If you find anything, remove it.

Also check that the puncture was not caused by a spoke poking through the rim tape. If it was, fit a new rim tape (see 'Replacing the rim tape', margin, right).

Put the inner tube back inside the tyre, starting with the valve. Pump a little air into the tube in order to stiffen it and make it much easier to fit back into the tyre.

With your hands opposite the valve, push the tyre back onto the rim, working round towards the valve.

Make sure that the valve is properly seated in the rim. Replace the fixing collar on the valve, if one was fitted.

Take care not to pinch the inner tube as you replace the tyre. It is best not to use tyre levers because they can puncture the tube; some tyres are so tight that you may have to resort to levers, but take great care in doing so.

REPLACING THE WHEEL Check around the rim again to make sure that the tyre is not pinching the tube, then partially inflate the tyre and replace the wheel.

Some types of tyre will not pass through the brake blocks while they are fully inflated, so leave the final inflation until the wheel is back on the bike.

Make sure that the wheel is centrally situated between the forks and brake blocks when you replace it, and also check that the wheel nuts are tight.

Fitting a new tyre Time: 2 hours or less

Check the size of your tyres before buying a replacement. It is printed on the tyre wall and may be in metric or Imperial measurements. If you are unsure, take the old wheel with you when you go to buy the replacement. If you do a lot of cycling, it is wise to keep a spare handy.

You can buy tyres in some sizes that have a puncture-resistant band; it might be worth paying the extra. The quality of a tyre is usually reflected in its price. Always choose a well-known brand if possible.

> YOU WILL NEED New tyre, 3 tyre levers, pump, wheel-nut spanner.

REMOVING A WHEEL AND TYRE Remove the wheel by undoing the wheel nuts or quick-release lever. If the tyre is on the rear wheel of a derailleur-geared bike, first put it in the highest gear (the smallest rear sprocket).

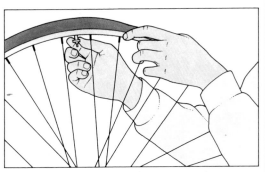

Let the air out of the tyre, then unscrew the retaining collar that holds the valve to the rim, if one is fitted.

Use the tyre levers to prise one side of the tyre over the edge of the rim (see facing page). Remove the inner tube and then pull the old tyre off the rim. If it is a tight fit you may need to lever it off with the tyre levers.

Take the opportunity to check the state of the rim tape which protects the inner tube from the ends of the spokes. If a spoke has pierced it, or it is worn, fit a new one (see 'Replacing the rim tape', margin).

PUTTING ON THE NEW TYRE Some tyre designs are meant to be fitted one way round only because of the tread pattern. Check the walls of your new tyre. If it has a horizontal arrow, it has been designed to revolve in the direction the arrow is pointing, when you are moving forward.

REPLACING THE RIM TAPE

The rim tape covers the rim to protect the tube from the ends of the spokes. If it rots, the spokes may pierce the tube. The tape will need to be replaced when you fix the puncture. Remove the tyre and pull off the old tape. If it is rubber it will pull off. If it is cloth there will be a buckle by the valve hole. Replace the rim tape with a rubber one if possible. It gives better protection and is easier to fit. Slip it on the rim like a rubber band, making sure its hole is lined up with the valve hole in the rim. It must cover all the spoke ends.
If you fit the cloth type, place it around the rim, covering the ends of the spokes. Line the buckle up with the valve hole, thread the end of the tape through the buckle, and tuck it neatly under the tape.

Push one side of the tyre onto the rim. Then pump a little air into the tube to make it firmer and easier to fit back into the tyre, and make sure it is not twisted.

With your hands opposite the valve, push the tyre back onto the rim making sure it does not pinch the tube. See that the valve is properly seated in the rim and is straight. Replace the fixing collar on the valve if one was fitted originally.

Ideally, you should not use levers to replace the tyre because they may puncture the tube, but some tyres are so tight that it may be necessary. Take great care with them.

Check round the rim again to make sure that the tyre is not pinching the inner tube, then inflate the tube a bit more and replace the wheel. Some tyres will not pass through the brake blocks fully inflated, so leave the final, complete inflation until the wheel is on the bike.

Make sure that the wheel is central between the forks and brake blocks and, finally, tighten the wheel nuts.

Bicycle wheels

Replacing broken spokes Time: $\frac{1}{2}$ a day or less

If more than a couple of spokes have broken, the wheel is likely to be badly out of true and should be fixed by a bike shop. It might even have to be replaced. If only one or two spokes are broken and the wheel itself seems reasonably straight, you can try fixing it yourself.

Buy replacement spokes of exactly the same length as the spokes in the wheel. Measure the existing spokes from the centre of the head at the wheel hub to where the spoke enters the nipple. Then add an extra 1.3 cm ($\frac{1}{2}$ in) to allow for the ends which are out of sight.

> YOU WILL NEED New spokes, screwdriver, spoke key, tyre levers, wheel-nut spanner. Possibly: small file, freewheel remover.

TAKING OUT THE BROKEN SPOKE If you are repairing the rear wheel on a derailleur bike, put it into top gear (that is, on the smallest sprocket). Remove the tyre, tube and rim tape (see *Bicycle tyres*).

If the broken spoke is on the freewheel side of the bicycle's rear wheel, remove the freewheel (see *Bicycle gears*: 'Removing a freewheel'). Pull out the bits of broken spoke and dispose of them carefully as they can be dangerous.

INSTALLING THE NEW SPOKE Start by unscrewing the nipple from the end of the new spoke and removing it.

Look at the pattern of spokes at the hub flange to decide whether it should be inserted from inside the flange or from outside.

Then thread it through the hole so the bent and flattened end of the new spoke fits inside the hub.

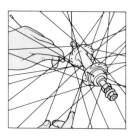

Thread it through the spokes alongside, again checking their pattern to see which it goes over or under.

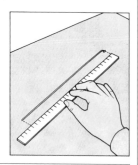

Insert the threaded end of the spoke through the rim and screw the nipple onto it with a screwdriver to begin with. Then use the spoke key (left) to tension the spoke. Just take up the tension at this stage.

ADJUSTING THE WHEEL When you have replaced the broken spokes, straighten the wheel (see below). This is best done on the bike, but with the tyre off, so you can see whether any spokes are protruding. If the new spokes protrude through the rim more than the others, file the ends down.

Replace rim tape, tyre and tube and refit the wheel.

Straightening a wheel Time: $\frac{1}{2}$ a day or less

If a wheel has a slight sideways wobble, you can straighten it yourself. If the wobble is more than about 1.3 cm ($\frac{1}{2}$ in) or is an up-down wobble, take it to a bike shop. Even they may not be able to fix it, and you will need a new wheel.

> YOU WILL NEED Spoke key, chalk. Possibly: maintenance spray

The wheel must be able to turn while you work on it, so stand the bike upside-down or suspend it from a garage or shed roof and let a little air out of the tyre.

Use the brake blocks as guides to find which part of the rim is out of true. Hold a piece of chalk by the side of the brake block so the part of the rim which is out of true is marked by the chalk as you turn the wheel.

Mark the point where the rim wobbles most, in order to find the spoke that needs adjusting. Loosen the spoke if it is on the same side as the chalk mark, or tighten if it is on the other. If the spoke nipples are rusted onto the spokes, apply a little maintenance spray and leave for at least ten minutes before trying again to loosen it.

Spin the wheel to check its trueness, again using the brake blocks as a guide. Repeat the process by half turns, tightening or loosening spokes, until the wheel is true.

The process may take some time, but do not be tempted to turn the spoke nipples more than half a turn at a time.

Blinds

Replacing a slat on a venetian blind Time: 1 hour or less

Order a new slat for a venetian blind through your retailer, providing the measurements and the maker's name.

When the slat arrives, check that the colour matches the rest of the blind. If the new slat is a slightly different shade, put it in at the top, where it will be less noticeable.

To take the blind apart, remove the cap from one end of the bottom rail. (You may need to prise it off with a screwdriver.) A slat fits along the bottom of the rail; slide it out of its grooves.

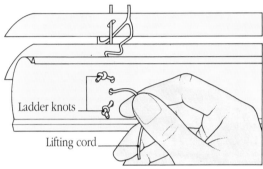

Undo the knots in the lifting cord below the bottom rail. Don't undo the ladder knots on either side.

Pull the lifting cord out of the slats. Leave the lifting cord dangling from the top rail.

Take a handful of slats in the middle of the blind. Hold them together and gently lift them out of the side ladders.

Repeat throughout the whole blind, and then give the slats a good clean, if necessary (see overleaf).

Beginning at the top, replace the slats one by one in the side ladders, with the curved side up. Thread the lifting cord through the hole in each slat as you go, making sure that it weaves down alternate sides of the rungs of the ladder.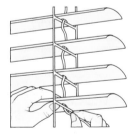

Reknot the lifting cord at each end, and let the blind down to check that it hangs evenly. If the slats are not aligned, adjust the cord equaliser until they are straight.

Renewing cords on a venetian blind Time: ½ hour or less

Frayed lifting cord on a venetian blind can be replaced without taking down the blind.

> **YOU WILL NEED** Cord, scissors, adhesive tape or masking tape or thin string.

Measure the old cord in position to estimate the length of new cord needed. Buy new cord from a haberdashers.

What model of blind?

ROLLER BLIND A single length of stiffened fabric is attached to a sprung roller.

FESTOON BLIND Lightweight silk or fine cotton, forms puffy yet elegant scalloped shapes.

VENETIAN BLIND Horizontal slats tilt to control the amount of light in a room.

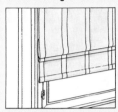 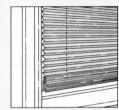

ROMAN BLIND Constructed like a festoon blind, a Roman blind draws up in neat, crisp pleats.

PLEATED PAPER BLIND Made from thick paper, a series of even, horizontal pleats give a concertina effect.

Pull up the blind then remove the looped end of the cord from the equaliser and, with sharp scissors, cut through both lengths of cord about 20 cm (8 in) from the end.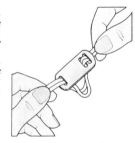

Attach both ends of the new cord to the cut ends of the old cord with adhesive tape, masking tape or thin string, creating a large loop. Make sure that it is firmly secured.

Remove the cap from one end of the bottom rail and slide out the bottom slat.

Use the lifting cord to release the lock and lower the blind. Pull the joined cords through the lock until the new cord has taken the place of the old.

Grasp the looped end of the new cord and pull it through the bottom rail. As each join in the cord is pulled through the bottom rail, separate them and discard the old cord. Knot the ends of the new one and fit the loop into the equaliser. Adjust the blind if it does not hang straight.

Fixing roller blind tension Time: ½ hour or less

If the tension fails in a roller blind, the blind won't roll up.

Pull the blind down to two-thirds of its full length and lift it off the brackets. Roll it up by hand and put it back in position. Pull right down and then see if it rolls up properly when released. Keep repeating the procedure until it runs smoothly, but if this doesn't restore tension, it is likely that the ratchet is broken.

MENDING PLEATED PAPER BLINDS

Mend small tears with transparent sticky tape on the wrong side of the blind. Use the type recommended for mending book pages, such as Filmoplast or document repair tape. It is almost impossible to camouflage a mend in a badly torn paper blind, so in this case the entire blind should be replaced.

REPLACING A ROLLER BLIND RATCHET Ratchets cannot be mended, so you will have to buy a new one. However, you may have to buy an entire blind kit, and replace the roller.

Ease off or carefully unstaple the fabric. Cut the new roller to length, and refix the fabric (see below).

Fitting new fabric to a roller blind Time: 1 hour or less

> YOU WILL NEED Fabric, antifray spray, sewing machine, tin tacks, small hammer. Possibly: iron-on hemming tape, iron.

Cut the new fabric to size allowing for side seams and top and bottom pockets for the roller and slat to fit into. If you treat the edges with an antifray spray, the side seams will only need to be folded once before hemming.

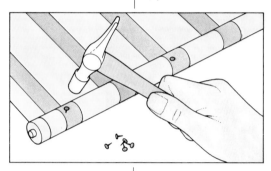

Machine stitch the side seams or seal them with iron-on hemming tape, and iron them down. Machine stitch the top and bottom pockets that will carry the roller and slat. Then use tin tacks and a small hammer to tack the material to the roller (left).

If the fabric is too limp to roll up and down properly, stiffen it with blind-stiffening spray. Ideally, choose a still day, peg the fabric to a clothes line and spray thoroughly. If you have to spray indoors, take the blind down and lay it on an old sheet. Ensure the ventilation is adequate.

How to clean blinds

VENETIAN BLIND Vacuum clean the slats regularly. Lower the blind, and use the dusting-brush attachment.

Alternatively, use a two or three-pronged brush specially designed for cleaning venetian blinds, or wear soft gloves and run your hand along both sides of each slat (left). Gently wipe the cords with a duster when the blind is pulled up.

Or wash the slats in the bath (on a towel to protect the bath's surface) in a solution of warm, soapy water.

ROLLER BLIND Sponge the blind gently. Use a very weak solution of washing-up liquid, and wring out the sponge. Never wash a roller blind in a washing machine – the fabric will wrinkle, distort and shrink.

PLEATED PAPER BLIND Spread the blind over a table and vacuum very gently with the dusting-brush attachment. A soft pencil rubber should remove ingrained marks.

FESTOON BLIND Vacuum festoon blinds regularly fold by fold, using either the upholstery brush or crevice tool of the vacuum cleaner.

Shake the blind as you raise and lower it to dislodge dust.

Occasionally let the blind right down to its full length and vacuum the whole surface with the upholstery brush.

Some blinds should only be dry-cleaned, but if the fabric is washable, wash it by hand in a soapflake or handwashing-detergent solution. Don't put the blind in a washing machine and don't tumble dry it.

ROMAN BLIND Provided Roman blinds are raised and lowered daily, dust should not accumulate in the folds. Vacuum the blind gently when it is down, using the vacuum cleaner's upholstery attachment.

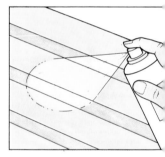

If the blind is lightly soiled, take it down and spread it out flat. Then use a sponge or dry-cleaning spray to clean the fabric. Ensure that there is good ventilation when spraying.

If the blind is heavily soiled, it is safer to take it to a specialist cleaner.

Bluebottles

If bluebottles are too numerous to swat, buy an insecticidal spray, a vapourising insecticidal strip or an electric insect killer. To keep bluebottles down, use an insecticidal dustbin powder to kill eggs or maggots. If you are severely plagued, fit fly screens over your windows.

Boiler: SEE CENTRAL-HEATING BOILER

Book

Avoid damage to books by keeping them dry and clean. If they do not have dust jackets of their own, it is worth covering them with clear film, either self-adhesive or the type that takes a fold without cracking.

Replacing a loose or lost spine Time: parts of 2 days

Sometimes the spine will come off a much-handled hard-cover book, spoiling the look of it and shortening its life. It is possible to replace the spine or make a new one.

PROTECTING A BOOK'S SPINE

Try to avoid damaging a book by pulling it from the shelf by the top of its spine; grip it halfway down instead. This is easier if the books are not too tightly packed on the shelf.

> **YOU WILL NEED** Fine sandpaper, firm card, matching bookcloth or fabric, craft knife or scissors, blunt knife or a plastic spatula, PVA wood glue, brown paper, two pieces of board slightly larger than the book, strong cord, heavy weight.

Clean the spine of the book very carefully, dusting off crumbly paper and old bits of glue. Rub down with fine sandpaper to achieve a smooth finish.

MAKING THE NEW SPINE Cut a piece of card to fit the spine, matching its length to the front and back coverboards – not to the spine, which is slightly shorter.

Then use the card as a template to cut a piece of matching bookcloth fabric, allowing an extra 2.5 cm (1 in) all round, to make flaps. Cut the flaps so that they taper slightly at each end, for a neat finish.

If there is a 'wrong' side to the cloth, have it facing upwards. Apply glue to the card and lay it in the centre of the cloth, folding over the top and bottom flaps. Then smooth them down with a knife or spatula.

ATTACHING THE NEW SPINE Cut a piece of brown paper to match the spine area, glue it well and place it in position on the exposed spine, rubbing it down firmly.

Use the knife or spatula to gently ease away the fabric on the exposed edges of the front and back covers to a depth of about 2.5 cm (1 in).

Using a piece of card, insert glue into the space between the cover and the board, in readiness for the new flap.

Insert the flap and use the knife to push the cloth home well. Then insert the second, on the other side.

Lay the book on its side and run the knife along the crease, making a firm edge at each side.

Place a smooth board on the upper surface of the book, aligning it to reach almost to the edge of the spine, and place a heavy weight on it. Leave overnight.

REGLUING THE SPINE COVER If the original spine cover is reusable, clean it off and, after checking you have it the right way up, glue it into position on top of the new spine.

To make sure the bond is really strong, place a wad of paper over the repaired area and another over the opening edges of the cover. Bind the whole book round and round with cord, so that it applies pressure to the glued section but does not damage or cut into the cover. Allow it to dry thoroughly before undoing it.

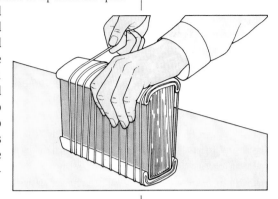

Quick fixes for books

- If a book has got wet, put it into a frost-free freezer – one that does not ice up and uses a dry fan system. It will draw the moisture out of the paper. If the pages look wrinkled, press them with a warm iron.

- Books kept in a damp room may develop mould and mildew. A dusting of cornflour, left on for a few hours and then brushed off, will clean and dry them.

- Rows of books can be cleaned quickly, using the upholstery brush attachment on your vacuum cleaner, or you can use a large, soft, clean paintbrush.

- Leather bindings can be cleaned with saddle soap, neat's-foot oil or petroleum jelly, applied gently with your fingers or a soft cloth. Give a second application several hours later.

Replacing a detached hard cover   Time: parts of 2 days

When the front or back cover has come right off a book it is possible to fix it back in place. The repair involves making a cloth hinge that will be inserted under the original spine.

STORING BOOKS

Avoid extremes of temperature when storing books. Cold damp areas, such as cellars or garages are unsuitable, because they may foster damp and mildew. Too much sun will fade the spines of books, so keep them away from a sunny window. Storing them above a radiator can dry them out so much that coverboards buckle and small brown spots appear on the pages. Glass-fronted cabinets starve books of fresh air, making the pages discolour and smell stale.

Book (cont.)

HOW TO PROTECT A DUST JACKET

Cut a piece of polypropylene sheet larger than the depth of the jacket. Lay the dust jacket on top, unprinted side uppermost, and fold the polypropylene over the top and bottom edges. When the folds are correct, make a sharp crease with a fingernail or the back of a pair of scissors. The polypropylene can be bought from suppliers of art materials. Do not use sticky tape to secure the front or back edges of a dust jacket, as this will eventually turn yellow and drop off, leaving a stain on the paper.

BOOK REPAIR TAPE

Book repair tape is made from paper tissue which has been coated with adhesive. It is thin and transparent, and is a useful short cut when mending tears in paper (see *Tape*).

YOU WILL NEED Bookcloth such as jaconet, scissors, needle, linen thread, sharp knife, PVA wood glue, spatula, heavy weight.

Carefully ease away the original spine of the book on the side where the cover has come off. Do not detach it completely. Clean the exposed area right back to the paper and tapes. Do not damage the threads.

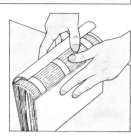

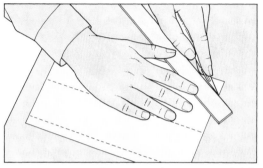

MAKING THE HINGE Cut a piece of jaconet just slightly shorter than the length of the spine and twice its width plus an extra 1.9 cm ($\frac{3}{4}$ in) each side. Taper the corners.

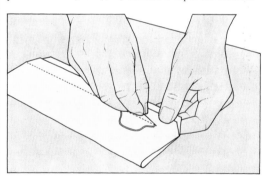

Stitch the jaconet to make a tube the same width as the spine, with both loose edges to one side, one protruding twice as far as the other.

ATTACHING THE HINGE Spread adhesive evenly along the exposed spine, making sure to cover the entire area.

Lay the jaconet tube in place, along the spine of the book, with the loose edges protruding on the side of the detached cover.

Rub the cover down well, all over, to make sure that it has made good contact with the spine.

Take the loose cover and stand it with the raw edge uppermost. Using a sharp knife, make a 2.5 cm (1 in) split in the cover, to accommodate the jaconet flaps.

Use a spatula or a piece of cardboard to spread adhesive evenly inside the split, taking particular care not to get any on the surface of the cover.

Slide the jaconet flaps into the slit, making sure that they go in to the same depth and that the cover is aligned with the rest of the book. Then allow it to dry under a weight, preferably overnight.

ATTACHING THE LOOSE SPINE Next day, cover the outer side of the jaconet tube with adhesive and press the flapping spine cover into place. Support the book, spine side up, and pad the spine area with a cloth or wad of newspaper. Bind it firmly with cord, distributing the pressure evenly.

Once it is dry, trim away or glue down any loose threads of cloth. Using a felt-tip pen of an appropriate colour, touch up any areas of jaconet that are exposed.

Repairing a paperback Time: about 1 hour

YOU WILL NEED Knife, vice or book press, mini-hacksaw, support cards, PVA wood glue, spatula or scrap of card. Possibly: tissue paper or document repair paper.

To repair a broken-up paperback, first remove the cover by holding the pages firmly with one hand and easing the cover off with the other, exposing the spine. Do this carefully, both at the front and the back.

Try not to damage the cover. Check that all sections of the book are in the right order and the right way up.

PREPARING THE SPINE Place a piece of stiff card on each side of the book and then clamp it in a vice or book press, with the spine uppermost. Scrape off all the old glue and any crumbly bits of paper.

With a mini-hacksaw, make shallow cuts across the exposed spine to prepare the surface to absorb adhesive. Using the spatula or a piece of scrap card, spread glue down the full length of the spine. Allow it to dry.

REPLACING THE COVER If the cover or its hinges have been damaged, glue a piece of tissue paper over any torn area and smooth it down carefully.

Remove the support cards, put the book back into the vice and apply a second coat of glue to the spine. Lay the cover over the glued spine, making sure it is the right way up. Press the cover down onto the spine firmly, smoothing out all the air bubbles.

As further strengthening, spread a layer of glue along the outer cover of the spine. Allow to dry thoroughly.

Repairing a tear in a page   Time: 1 hour

Sometimes old books are spoiled by a torn page. Tears and holes can be mended, but if part of the page is missing, try to match the weight and colour of the paper. Old books at jumble sales are a good source of suitably aged paper.

> YOU WILL NEED Tissue paper, PVA wood glue, mirror or piece of glass, grease-proof paper, craft knife or scissors. Possibly: iron, matching paper, very sharp pencil.

Make sure the torn edges will join up once they have been smoothed down. Use a warm iron, if necessary, to flatten the damaged edges.

Tear a piece of tissue paper slightly larger than the tear, creating a soft, fibrous edge. Spread adhesive on a piece of glass or a mirror. Lay the tissue over the glue, patting it gently so that it picks up the glue.

Carefully lift the glued tissue paper off the glass or mirror and lay it, glued side downwards, over the torn area, smoothing it down with your fingers. Make sure the torn edges have been brought as close to one another as possible.

Insert grease-proof paper between the repaired page and its neighbours. Allow the repair to dry. Then trim off any excess tissue paper with a craft knife or sharp scissors.

FILLING A GAP If there is a gap in the damaged area, patch it before applying the glued tissue paper.

Lay a sheet of matching paper under the page. With a very sharp, fine pencil, mark the shape of the hole onto the loose sheet. Make sure the patch matches the hole perfectly.

Tear or cut the shape out of the loose sheet and fit it in the hole. Then secure it with glued tissue paper, as above.

Replacing a single loose page   Time: a few minutes

> YOU WILL NEED Tissue paper or fine plain paper, ruler, sharp craft knife, PVA wood glue, waxed paper.

Cut a strip of tissue paper to the same length as the loose page and slightly less than twice the width of the margin.

Fold the paper down the middle lengthways, and then apply wood glue to the convex (outer) side of it.

Carefully position one half of the folded, glued strip along the loose page, lining up the raw edge of the page with the fold in the strip. Check that the strip does not overlap either the top or bottom of the page.

Make sure the page is the right way up and in the right place, then position it in the book. Check that the replaced page is tucked as far into the gutter as possible and that the page lines up with the rest of the pages in the book. Smooth down the other half of the glued strip.

Slip a piece of waxed paper into the fold, close the book and allow it to dry under pressure.

Booklice

Booklice, or psocids, can be identified by their tiny, soft bodies and rapid running movements. Not only do they eat mould that grows on the glue in the bindings of books, but also the mould that grows on damp foods (especially cereals) and porous surfaces such as leather, plaster and wood.

To eliminate booklice, remove all infested food, wipe away any visible mould and try to create a dry atmosphere. Booklice are very susceptible to heat, so it may be necessary to heat a room to above 24°C and keep the relative humidity below 50 per cent for 24 hours to kill them.

As a last resort try using an insecticide that contains organophosphorus compounds or synthetic pyrethroids.

Bottles, decanters & jars

Cleaning bottles and decanters

To clean wine stains from the inside of a decanter or a bottle, fill it with a warm solution of biological detergent, such as Biotex, or plastic tableware cleaner such as Chempro T. Alternatively, use denture cleaner and leave it to soak, preferably overnight. Then rinse and dry well.

To get rid of extremely stubborn stains on the inside of a decanter, pour in a little vinegar and add some dishwasher salt granules, coarse cooking salt or fine sand (available from pet shops and garden centres).

If you can't get the lid off a jar, place a wide rubber band round the cap and try again. Alternatively, wrap a tea towel around the jar lid. Then turn the jar upside-down and tap it on the floor. A metal lid will loosen if you turn the jar upside-down on a warm surface for a few seconds. Protect your hand from the heat with a cloth, when you loosen the lid.

SMOOTHING A CHIP

If a glass decanter or stopper chips, you may be able to smooth it with a crystal engraver (see *Glassware*). If the decanter is valuable, contact your local antique-glass dealer for information.

Every half-hour, for up to 5 or 6 hours, swirl it around until the stain vanishes. Rinse thoroughly in warm water.

Alternatively, send your decanter to a glass specialist to be cleaned in a pickle bath. Although this process is an effective way of removing cloudy marks from the inside of a decanter it does carry a risk of breaking the glass. Contact your local antique-glass dealer for information.

Rinse the decanter out thoroughly after cleaning and shake out as much water as possible.

To dry the inside of a decanter with a narrow neck, roll up a dry J-cloth or a length of paper towel and push it through the neck as far down inside the decanter as possible. Leave part of the cloth protruding from the decanter so that you can pull it out again.

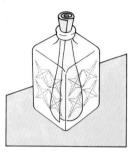

Then stand the decanter in a warm place overnight so that the cloth can absorb all the moisture inside.

Opening wine without a corkscrew

Even if you have lost your corkscrew there are still ways of opening a bottle of wine.

SCREW HOOK Screw a large screw hook into the cork, and fit the handle of a wooden spoon or stick into the hook to pull the cork out.

SCREW AND PLIERS Drive a plain screw into the cork and pull the head of the screw firmly with a pair of pliers.

PRESS IN THE CORK Push the cork into the bottle with the handle of a wooden spoon, but do it carefully, over the kitchen sink, to avoid spilling wine on your clothes or the carpet. Also, try not to get small pieces of cork in the wine.

Unstopping a jammed decanter

If a stopper is stuck fast in a decanter, wrap a hot, wet cloth round the neck of the decanter. Then use the handle of a wooden spoon to tap gently on opposite sides of the stopper, in order to loosen it.

If this fails pour two or three drops of cooking oil around the rim and leave the decanter in a warm place until the oil has seeped down between stopper and neck, and eased the stopper. Then try again with the hot cloth.

Brass

Stain removal and polishing

Brass tarnishes easily and should be polished regularly with brass polish or impregnated wadding. If you clean infrequently, use a 'long-term' polish which will put a tarnish-reducing finish on the brass. Alternatively, apply a clear lacquer after polishing to prevent tarnishing. The lacquer will break down after some time and should be removed with cellulose thinner or nail varnish remover before being renewed.

Slightly tarnished brass will respond to being rubbed with a paste made from salt and lemon juice. More than one application may be needed.

BRASS IN POOR CONDITION For badly tarnished brass and green corrosion, use a corrosion remover such as Dax Chemical Brass Tarnish & Verdigris Remover.

To avoid making a mess, do the cleaning in an old washing-up bowl or a bucket. Use an old toothbrush to clean crevices or intricate areas.

Alternatively, use metal polish that does not contain a tarnish inhibitor.

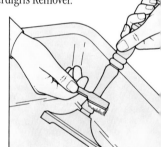

Soak the piece for several hours in a strong, warm washing-soda solution to remove the green corrosion. Rub the surface with an old brush or cloth. Rinse, dry and polish.

Brickwork

Cleaning dirty brickwork Time: depends on area

Smoke, dust and algae can all make house walls grubby. To smarten up your house you can scrub the brickwork.

YOU WILL NEED Stiff scrubbing brush, bucket, piece of matching brick, safety spectacles, gardening gloves. Possibly: purpose-made masonry cleaner.

Use warm water and a scrubbing brush to remove dust and grime. Do not use soap or detergent in the water; they cause stains that cannot be removed. It is possible to buy a special masonry cleaner that will not leave a stain.

To get rid of stubborn dirt, try to find a matching brick, break it and use a piece as an abrasive block. It will wear the dirt away without marking the brickwork. Wear safety spectacles and gardening gloves to protect you while you work.

Do not use a high-pressure jet hose: the water may dislodge soft pointing. Water can be also be forced into gaps around windows and doors, causing the wood to rot.

White deposits on brickwork Time: depends on area

The white fluffy deposit often found on brickwork is called efflorescence. Moisture causes salts in the bricks and the pointing to be drawn out, forming fine white crystals.

> YOU WILL NEED Stiff dustpan brush and dustpan, cheap 100 mm (4 in) paintbrush, clear waterproofing fluid, safety spectacles, gardening gloves.

When the wall is as dry as possible, brush away all the surface crystals. Then coat the wall with a clear waterproofing fluid. Apply it liberally, so it flows down the wall – but keep it off window ledges and glass.

The coating prevents water from penetrating the brickwork, but still allows the wall to 'breathe'.

Protect yourself by wearing safety spectacles and gardening gloves as you work and protect pathways and drives as splashes will stain them.

Mould and algae Time: parts of 2 days

Dampness and lack of sunlight encourage the growth of the fungal and algal spores that always float in the air.

> YOU WILL NEED Paint scraper, stiff brush, exterior fungicidal solution, cheap 100 mm (4 in) paintbrush, safety spectacles, face mask, gardening gloves.

Start by removing larger growths, such as clumps of moss, with a paint-stripping knife, then use a stiff brush to dispose of any remaining growth on the brickwork.

Dilute an exterior fungicide according to the instructions, and brush it liberally onto the wall. (It is usually north-facing walls that are most severely affected.)

Allow time for the fungicide to kill off algae, lichen or moss. You will see it darken over several days as it dies.

Brush away the dead material, then recoat the wall with fungicide to discourage further attacks.

When applying fungicide or brushing off dead growths, wear safety spectacles, a face mask and gardening gloves.

Unwanted paint on brickwork Time: depends on area

Paint is extremely difficult to remove from bricks because it enters the pores. It is possible to clean small areas, but do not use chemical paint stripper; it makes a mess which is impossible to remove.

> YOU WILL NEED Stripping knife (paint scraper), piece of matching brick or a power drill with wire cup brush, safety spectacles, face mask, gardening gloves. Possibly: a needle gun from a hire shop.

SMALL AREAS Remove drips of paint by lifting off as much as possible with a stripping knife, then rub off the rest with a piece of matching brick. Or use a wire cup brush in a power drill. Wear safety spectacles, a face mask and gardening gloves when using abrasives.

LARGE AREAS A tool called a needle gun can be hired – or more expensively, a sandblaster – but the job is likely to be long and tedious. An alternative would be to repaint.

Cracks in brickwork Time: depends on area

Small cracks along the line of the mortar joints can occur through a slight settling of foundations. They should be filled to prevent rain seeping into the fabric of the house.

> YOU WILL NEED Small trowel, old paintbrush, small bag of dry mortar mix, a board for mixing, old stiff dustpan brush.

Clean out any loose material from the cracks in the wall with the point of a small trowel, then brush them clean with an old paintbrush.

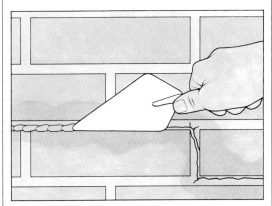

Make up a dryish mortar mix, which will bind in the hand like a sand pie. Damp the cracks with clean water, then fill them with the mortar, using the trowel. Brush away surplus mortar with an old stiff dustpan brush.

GETTING ADVICE ABOUT SERIOUS CRACKS

If you notice cracking in the walls of your house – possibly running across bricks – or if cracks reappear after being filled, get professional advice from a surveyor or through the planning department of your local authority. There may be serious subsidence.

BRICKWORK: TO PAINT OR NOT TO PAINT?

Think very carefully before painting brickwork. It rarely looks smart, and the paint is practically impossible to clean off because it soaks into the pores of the bricks. To give your house a new look, have it rendered first, and then painted.

What style of pointing?

FLUSH POINTING The mortar is flush with the brickwork. Allow the new mortar to become almost dry, then rub over the joints with coarse sacking. Lightly brush away any mortar remaining on the brickwork.

WEATHERED POINTING A slope ensures that rain runs off. On vertical joints, press the trowel into one side of the mortar, then draw it down, angling it to match the surrounding pointing.

On horizontal joints, hold a wooden straightedge below the joint and use it to guide the trowel, held at the appropriate angle. Trim off surplus mortar.

When the mortar is almost dry, lightly rub over the surface with a soft brush.

KEYED POINTING To achieve a concave finish to the pointing draw a piece of bent 12 mm ($\frac{1}{2}$ in) copper tubing along the mortar in the joints.
Then brush away any surplus mortar.

Replacing missing pointing Time: depends on area

If the mortar between rows of bricks (called pointing) becomes loose and falls out, it can provide a route for damp to seep into the house and damage the wall on the inside. The area should be repointed.

YOU WILL NEED 12 mm ($\frac{1}{2}$ in) cold chisel, club hammer, safety spectacles, gardening gloves, old paintbrush, bag of dry mortar mix, board for mixing, small trowel, soft dusting brush, some coarse sacking or a short piece of copper pipe or a timber straightedge.

Use a cold chisel and a club hammer to dig out all the loose and crumbling pointing to a depth of about 1 cm ($\frac{3}{8}$ in). Then clean out all the debris from the joints with an old paintbrush.

Add a little water to the mortar to make up a dryish mix which will compact in the hand like a sand pie.

Dampen the joints with an old brush and a little water. Press the mortar into the gaps with the trowel, bringing it just proud of the surface. Deal with the vertical joints first, starting at the top of the area. Then do the horizontal joints.

As you work, finish the surface of the pointing to match the style used on the surrounding brickwork (see left). Pointing is designed to shed rainwater and to look neat. Most exposed brickwork will have been done in the style known as 'weathered pointing' as it sheds water best.

Broom

Joining a new head and handle

Broom heads and handles are often sold separately and have to be joined with glue and a screw. Or you may want to replace a broken handle.

YOU WILL NEED Chisel or trimming knife, steel tape measure, pencil, PVA waterproof wood glue, nail, power drill or hand drill and fine twist bit, screwdriver, screw.

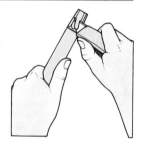

Measure the depth of the hole in the broom head. Transfer the measurement to the non-rounded end of the broom handle and draw a line around it. Then use a chisel or trimming knife to pare away a little wood to form a gentle taper.

Keep trying the stick in the hole, to get a good tight fit.

Apply PVA glue around the inside rim of the hole, then insert the handle in the broom head. Holding the head in both hands, tap the handle on the floor to force it right in.

The broom head will have a screw hole already drilled in it. Check that the handle is fully inserted by poking a nail into it. You should feel the resistance of the handle.

Put a fine twist bit into the hole and drill a pilot hole in the handle. Insert a screw and tighten.

Tightening a loose handle

A broom handle may wobble because the holding screw is missing or has come loose. Alternatively, the end of the broomstick might have shrunk.

YOU WILL NEED PVA wood glue, power drill or hand drill and fine twist bit, screwdriver.

Start either repair job by removing the handle.

LOST SCREW Apply PVA wood glue to the inner rim of the socket in the broom head, and replace the handle so that new wood appears in line with the screw hole. With a fine bit make a pilot hole in the handle. Drive in a screw.

SHRUNKEN HANDLE Cut off a small amount of the tapered end of the handle with a tenon saw and push it in until it is a tighter fit. Then fix with glue and a screw.

Builders

(SEE ALSO ELECTRICIANS AND PLUMBERS)

Hiring the wrong people to do building work can waste a lot of money and cause a great deal of inconvenience. By following a few general rules you should be able to avoid making an expensive mistake.

- Never give work to door-to-door callers. If they seem reputable, ask them the address of their company's head office and send for information.
- When possible employ people on personal recommendation from friends or relatives. Alternatively ask the company that you are considering employing to give you referees in the area who have had similar work done. Contact them and ask if they were satisfied with the work.
- If no one can give you a recommendation, choose companies affiliated to recognised associations or federations. This will guarantee the standard of work. Builders usually display the symbols of any associations of which they are members. Ring the body to confirm membership.
- Contact two or three companies for quotations before deciding which to use. Prices can vary according to the size of a company, or how busy they are.
- Don't use an unknown company just because it offers a 'Ten year guarantee'. If the company goes bust, the guarantee is worthless. Look for underwritten or insurance-backed guarantees.

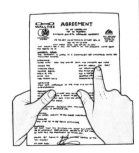

- Get an agreement in writing, spelling out exactly what is to be done, what materials will be used, how long the job will take and how much it will cost. This protects you as well as the builder. Verbal agreements can often go wrong.

- On large projects, consider employing a local architect or surveyor, who will be responsible for ensuring that only reputable tradesmen are involved. Because of their training and experience, architects and surveyors can often save you more than the cost of their fees.

Regulatory bodies for builders

British Wood Preserving and Damp-proofing Association (BWPDA), Building 6, The Office Village, 4 Romford Road, Stratford, London E15 4EA Tel. 0181 519 2588

Federation of Master Builders, Gordon Fisher House, 14/15 Great James Street, London WC1N 3DP Tel. 0171 242 7583

Guild of Master Craftsmen, 166 High Street, Lewes, East Sussex BN7 1XU Tel. 01273 478449

National Cavity Insulation Association (NCIA), P.O. Box 12, Haslemere, Surrey GU27 3AH Tel. 01428 654011

Electrical Contractors' Association, ESCA House, 34 Palace Court, London W2 4HY Tel. 0171 229 1266

National Inspection Council for Electrical Installation Contracting (NICEIC), Vintage House, 37 Albert Embankment, London SE1 7UJ Tel. 0171 582 7746

National Housebuilding Council (NHBC), Buildmark House, Chiltern Avenue, Amersham, Buckinghamshire HP6 5AP Tel. 01494 434477

Burst pipes: SEE PIPES

Buttonholes

Mending a worn buttonhole

A worn buttonhole can ruin the look of a garment, and if left the buttonhole could tear. It is worth paying to have expensive clothing repaired professionally, so consult a dry-cleaner with a repair service. Alternatively, you could do it yourself, by hand or using a sewing machine.

> YOU WILL NEED Small piece of iron-on hemming tape, needle, thread, scissors, seam ripper. Possibly: sewing machine.

First pin a small piece of iron-on hemming tape to the back of the buttonhole, aligning both edges of the buttonhole so that they touch. Iron on the tape, following the instructions that come with the tape for iron temperature.

BY MACHINE Use the buttonhole foot and thread which matches the other buttonholes. Make a test buttonhole on a piece of spare fabric of similar weight to the garment.

To prevent fraying, work a buttonhole over the existing buttonhole threads, making sure that you will be able to cut through the iron-on backing when you have finished.

Using a seam ripper cut through the new buttonhole, working carefully out from the centre (see below). Enlarge the buttonhole gradually and keep testing it to see if the button will fit through snugly.

BY HAND Use a needle and a thread that matches the fabric, and buttonhole stitch neatly around the original buttonhole (see *Stitches*), covering the old stitching.

Opening a machine-stitched buttonhole

Always use a seam ripper – never use scissors. Position a pin at each end of the new buttonhole to prevent the seam ripper slipping and cutting through the bar tacks.

Buttons

Replacing a button Time: a few minutes

Always replace a button as soon as possible. Most clothes are designed with the correct number of buttons for closing gaps, so when one falls off strain is put on the others and heavier fabrics may become distorted.

Replace a button before the garment is dry-cleaned or washed, unless the buttons are made of a delicate material such as mother-of-pearl. In that case, remove the buttons before cleaning, and sew them on again afterwards. If in doubt, take advice from a dry-cleaner.

Use a strong needle and strong thread for durable fabrics, and a thin needle and thin thread for delicate fabrics. Don't use nylon thread to sew on a button – it may be strong but it is also hard to knot, and there is a chance you will lose the button if the thread works loose.

> YOU WILL NEED Needle, thread, scissors. Possibly: matching button or piece of strong fabric.

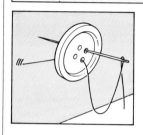

MAKING THE SHANK Take three small backstitches (see *Stitches*) to anchor the thread securely. Draw the needle up through one of the holes in the button, then down through another and back into the fabric.

Hold the button a little way above the fabric to create a shank. The shank should be long enough to allow the fabric surrounding the buttonhole to lie flat.

Make it the same length as the shanks on the garment's other buttons; if there aren't any others, it should be fractionally longer than the thickness of the fabric that the button will pass through when it is being done up.

With four-hole buttons, work the stitching in the same pattern as the other buttons on the garment. They may be sewn either diagonally across the four holes or in two straight sets of stitches.

Make as many stitches as necessary to secure the button without allowing the shank to become too thick.

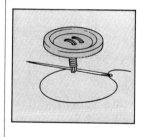

Wind the thread round the shank several times so that it is firm. Then take it through to the inside of the garment and finish off with a few small stitches on top of one another. Snip off any surplus thread.

REINFORCING A BUTTON With soft fabrics such as jersey, it may be difficult to anchor a button securely.

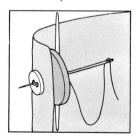

In this case, stitch a much smaller button, with the same number of holes, onto the inside of the fabric. Stitch through both the buttons, creating a shank on the right side of the fabric by stitching over a toothpick or matchstick.

Remove the toothpick and finish off by winding the thread round the shank and fastening it off securely.

Alternatively, use a piece of stronger fabric or iron-on tape to reinforce the area, especially if you are sewing a button to an area which is torn, such as on a child's shirt.

Calculator

Battery model won't light up Time: a few minutes

> YOU WILL NEED Battery tester. Possibly: new batteries.

Make sure that the batteries are the right way round and check that the calculator is switched on.

If it still won't work, the batteries may be run down. Use a check unit on the battery packaging or a battery tester to test them, or fit new batteries straight away.

If the calculator still won't work and it is under guarantee, return it to the supplier. Otherwise it will probably be cheaper to buy a new one than have it repaired.

Mains model won't light up Time: 1 hour or less

> YOU WILL NEED Possibly: table lamp, screwdriver, new fuse, new batteries.

Make sure that the calculator is plugged in and that the socket and the calculator are both switched on.

If it still won't come on, test the socket by plugging in an electrical appliance such as a table lamp. If the socket is supplying power, check the wiring in the calculator's plug and replace the fuse (see *Electric plug*).

If the calculator still doesn't work, and it is still under guarantee, return it to the supplier. Otherwise, take it to an electrical shop or write to the makers for advice.

Fails to show complete numbers Time: 1 hour or less

Sometimes a calculator's display screen fails to show all the segments in the numbers.

Use a battery tester to check the batteries.

If the batteries are working properly, the cause of the problem may be that the calculator has been exposed to heat, from sunlight or a radiator. Move it so it can cool.

If the problem persists, there is probably a fault with the display. If it is under guarantee, return it to the supplier. Otherwise it will probably be cheaper to buy a new calculator than to have it repaired.

Camcorder

Cleaning a camcorder Time: 1 hour or less

Camcorders need little cleaning if they are treated carefully and if good-quality cassettes are used.

> YOU WILL NEED Clean soft cloth or antistatic cloth, household spray cleaner, blower brush, cotton bud, head-cleaning tape.

Do not try to clean inside a camcorder, apart from the video head and the area of the tape compartment that is visible when the tape door is open.

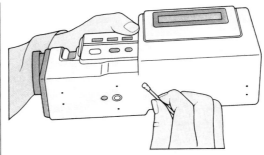

THE CASING Test cleaning liquid on a small area of the casing to make sure that it does not cause a mark. Don't get cleaner on the viewfinder or lens, or into controls.

Never use a cleaner containing bleach or ammonia and do not spray or pour the cleaner onto the camcorder. Instead put it onto a cloth first, then rub the casing all over and polish it off with a dry cloth.

VIEWFINDER AND LENS Clean the viewfinder and lens with a blower brush or rub the glass with a soft cloth.

If the mark remains, breathe on the glass and clean off. An antistatic lens cloth, available from photographic shops, should remove stubborn marks.

THE TAPE COMPARTMENT Open the tape door and tip out any large particles of dirt. Then use the blower brush or a cotton bud to remove any remaining dust.

THE VIDEO HEAD Only clean the video head if there is poor picture playback or sound.

Look at the owner's manual before using a head-cleaning tape. If the camcorder is still under guarantee, and there is nothing in the manual about head-cleaning tapes, contact the manufacturer to make sure that using one will not invalidate the guarantee. The manufacturer may be able to supply a head-cleaning tape or recommend a head-cleaning kit (see margin, overleaf).

Carry a spare battery

To make sure that your camcorder does not run out of power when you go on a long filming session, take a spare, fully charged battery.

Camcorder (cont.)

HEAD-CLEANING KIT

Head-cleaning kits are available for camcorders.

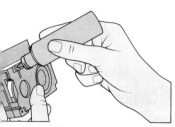

The most common type consists of a cassette case with a pad which you impregnate with cleaner and load into the camcorder.

Faultfinder guide: Camcorders

Picture quality poor

- The video head might be dirty. Try cleaning it (see 'Cleaning a camcorder', previous page).
- If the video tape is worn or inferior, the picture quality will be poor. Use a new, good-quality tape.
- If there is no improvement, try adjusting the tracking as described in your manual.
- If the fault persists, return the camcorder for repair.

Video tape sticks

- One of the biggest problems with camcorders is condensation. It occurs when the camera is moved from warm air to cold, or vice versa.

    Condensation can cause the tape to stick to the video head, resulting in damage to both tape and camcorder when the tape is removed.
- Try to ensure that temperature change is as gradual as possible. When going from a warm room into cold air, put the camcorder in a bag and leave it for about 20 minutes to adjust to the colder temperature. Do the same when coming indoors from the cold.
- If the tape gets stuck and you suspect it may be due to condensation, leave the camcorder in a warm room for several hours until it has dried out.

Camcorder won't operate

- Make sure that a tape is loaded and rewound.
- Some camcorders have a shutter lock to prevent accidental use. Check that it is not in the locked position.
- If it fails to work on battery power try mains power. If it operates, recharge the battery as described in the manual (see also 'Recharging a camcorder battery', below). If the power light still won't light up, the fault is likely to be in the camcorder. Take it in for repair.

Power light goes off quickly

- If the power light comes on, but then goes out again within a few minutes, the battery is probably flat.
- Recharge the battery as described in the manual. If the fault persists, the battery may be suffering from 'battery memory effect' (see 'Recharging a camcorder battery', below and page 71) or need replacing.
- If the power light comes on but goes out again when using the mains, the camcorder is probably faulty. Return it for repair.

Autofocus fails to operate or works slowly

- The autofocus sensor may be covered or obstructed by your fingers, clothing or the camera case. Remove any obstruction. Make sure that the sensor is not dirty.
- The camcorder batteries may need recharging (see 'Recharging a camcorder battery', below).
- The camcorder might be focusing close by on a lamppost, tree, person or car while you are trying to take a picture of a distant object. Try moving it a few degrees to left or right.
- If the autofocus still fails to work, return the camcorder for repair.

Power zoom fails or operates slowly

- The camcorder batteries may need recharging (see 'Recharging a camcorder battery', below).
- Make sure that the lens and operating button are clean. If the fault persists, return the camcorder to the maker for repair.

Picture in viewfinder blurred

- The eyepiece may not be adjusted correctly. Adjust it until you get a clear picture through the viewfinder.

FILMING ON THE BEACH

A camcorder can suffer severe internal damage from sand or water, particularly salt water. Never put a camcorder down on the sand or allow it to get wet. To protect it keep it in a clear plastic bag inside its case when it is not being used and make sure that your hands are clean when you are filming.

Recharging a camcorder battery

When rechargeable batteries are charged before being fully discharged they can suffer from 'battery memory effect' (see page 71). This problem results in the battery only partially recharging. To avoid battery memory effect ensure that the battery is fully discharged before recharging it. Leave a tape playing until the battery goes flat. Speed up the discharge of power by rewinding the video tape or zooming repeatedly in and out.

Many camcorders have a battery symbol that will either appear, disappear or flash when the battery is low. Others display 'Bat' or 'Battery'.

If any of these symbols appears, it indicates that it is almost time for the battery to be recharged.

Protecting a camcorder

Replace the lens cap when not using the camcorder.

Keep the camcorder in a camera bag or case to protect it from knocks and dirt.

If you don't plan to use the camcorder for a long time, remove the battery and the video cassette.

Quick-fix cleaning

In an emergency you can use a cotton bud dipped in methylated spirit to clean the video head.

Never use methylated spirit near a naked flame or a lit cigarette as it could ignite.

Camera

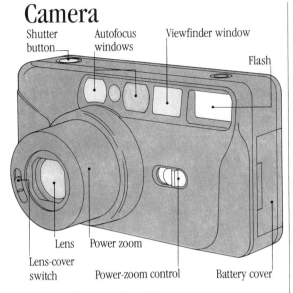

Shutter button — Autofocus windows — Viewfinder window — Flash

Lens — Power zoom

Lens-cover switch — Power-zoom control — Battery cover

Cleaning the camera and lens

Cameras need very little cleaning if they are treated carefully (see margin). Avoid cleaning the inside unless there is a build-up of dirt. Unexplained marks on your photographs might be caused by dust or sand in the camera.

YOU WILL NEED Clean soft cloth, household spray cleaner, blower brush (also called a puffer brush).

Before using any cleaning liquid, test it on a small area to check that it will not stain or mark the finish. Never use bleach or ammonia-based cleaner. Do not apply the cleaner directly, instead transfer a little onto a cloth.

THE CAMERA BODY Clean the camera body with the damp cloth. Avoid overwetting and do not get any of the cleaner on the camera lens or viewfinder.

Make sure that no cleaner enters any switches or controls. Polish off the cleaner with a dry cloth.

VIEWFINDER AND LENS Clean dust from the viewfinder and lens with a blower brush, which can be bought at camera shops. Rub off any marks with a soft clean cloth, used dry. Breathe on the viewfinder or lens and rub it clean if the mark persists. An antistatic cloth that will remove stubborn stains can be bought from camera shops.

THE INTERIOR Take out the film and use a blower brush to get rid of any dirt. If the camera has a removable lens, also clean the area that is exposed when the lens is taken off.

Faultfinder guide: Camera

Camera will not take a picture

- Wind the film on. Most cameras won't take another picture until the film is moved on to the next frame.
- Many cameras wind the film forward automatically. Check that the camera batteries are charged, or put in some new ones, if necessary.
- If the camera has a shutter lock to prevent accidental use, make sure it is not in the locked position.
- If the camera has a separate automatic winder or motor drive, clean the connections between the winder and the camera. Try taking a picture without the winder fitted. If the camera works, the fault probably lies with the winder. Take the winder and camera to a repair shop.

Flash won't work, or operates intermittently

- If the flash only works every few minutes, the batteries are nearly flat. Replace them.
- Many automatic flash units will not work if the amount of light is above a certain level. Try taking a photograph in a darkened room.
- If the camera has a separate flash unit, check that the batteries are charged, or change them. Make sure the connections between the flash unit and the camera are clean and dry.
- Some separate flash units are triggered by the camera when the available light is too dim. Make sure that any flash-operating switch on the camera is switched on. If there is an override or test button, use it to see if the flash works. Try taking a picture in a darkened room.
- Use another flash unit that you know will work. If it operates on your camera, the fault probably lies with your flash unit. If it fails to operate, the fault is probably in the camera. Take the flash unit and camera to a repair shop.

Camera fails to focus or power zoom fails to operate

- Replace the batteries if they are not fully charged.
- Make sure that your fingers, the camera case or a piece of clothing is not covering the autofocus sensor and that dirt has not accumulated on it.
- Make sure the camera is not focusing on a near object when you are trying to take a long-distance shot. If a lamppost or tree is in the foreground, move the camera slightly to the left or right to refocus.
- If the camera has a zoom button, check that dirt is not obstructing either the lens or the operation of the button. Clean if necessary.

CHANGING BATTERIES IN MID FILM

If the camera's battery goes flat in mid film, you can change it – but remember that the film counter may go back to nought. So you will need to keep count.

LOOKING AFTER YOUR CAMERA

- Keep the camera in a bag or case when it is not in use.
- Brush sand or dirt off the camera case before opening it.
- Always replace the lens cap after taking pictures.
- To use your camera in the rain, put it in a plastic bag. Make a hole for the lens to poke through. Seal the bag round the lens with an elastic band.
- Check the battery with a battery tester once a year and replace it if necessary.
- If you don't intend to use the camera for a long time, take out the battery.

49

Cane furniture

Cleaning unpainted cane furniture
Time: depends on amount

> **YOU WILL NEED** Soft brush, sponge or scrubbing brush, bowl, soapless cleanser or saltwater solution.

Brush cane furniture regularly with a soft brush.

Make a saltwater solution of one tablespoon of salt in 1 litre ($1\frac{3}{4}$ pints) of water and lightly sponge unpainted cane furniture with it. As it dries it will bleach and stiffen the cane.

Scrub very dirty cane with a soapless cleanser, such as sugar soap, and leave it to dry naturally. Do not use a detergent as it could discolour the cane.

Fitting new cane to a chair seat   Time: a weekend or less

Cane can be found in craft shops and if you measure the chair seat before ordering the cane, the supplier will be able to advise on the amount needed.

> **YOU WILL NEED** Trimming knife, hammer, bradawl, hand drill, about 20 golf tees or pieces of wooden dowel to fit the holes, cane in sizes 2, 4 and 12, bucket of water, bodkin or heavy needle, sharp scissors.

PREPARATION Using a trimming knife, remove the old seat and save it in case you need to refer to it later.

Knock out the old pegs with a hammer and remove any bits of cane from the holes with a bradawl. If any pegs are stubborn drill them out with a hand drill, taking care not to damage the chair frame. This is a good time to do any other necessary renovation to the chair frame (see *Chair*).

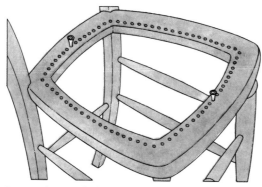

Start working with the chair facing you, and peg dowels or tees into the centre holes, front and back.

Put another peg in the back left corner hole. Count the number of holes between it and the centre, and mark the corresponding hole on the front row with a peg. (The front row will probably have more holes than the back.)

Soak the No.2 cane in water for about five minutes before starting the next stage, and put it into a plastic bag to keep it damp and flexible while you are working with it.

FIRST LAYER OF CANE Start working at the back left corner of the chair. Remove the peg that you had inserted earlier.

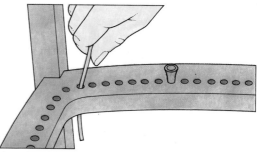

Thread a piece of No.2 cane down through the hole until about 10 cm (4 in) is protruding. Secure it with the peg.

With its shiny side up, pull the cane towards the front left hand peg without stretching it. Remove the peg, and take the cane down through the hole. Pull it taut, secure it with the peg, and bring the cane up through the hole to its right. Pull this tight and move the peg to secure it.

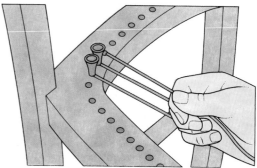

Take the cane to the back of the seat and down through the opposite hole at the back. Take a new peg to secure it and lead it under the seat to come up in the hole beside it.

Repeat this process, keeping the cane taut and parallel, working backwards and forwards until all the holes in the back of the seat have been used. When you come to the end of a piece of cane, secure it with a peg. Start the next piece in the adjoining hole, securing it with another peg.

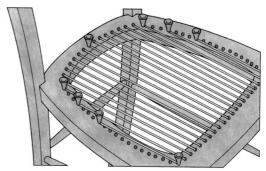

Complete both sides of the seat, using the outer holes on the front row and matching them with side holes, making sure that the cane lies parallel to the existing lines.

Bodkins

Bodkins are strong, blunt needles with large eyes — some have two eyes of different sizes. They can be either flat or round and come in many forms. They are used for threading coarse materials such as twine or string through sacking or carpeting, or elastic through a waistband.

DRYING CANE FURNITURE

Newly cleaned cane furniture is best dried slowly, outdoors in the sunshine. Avoid drying it in front of a fire or radiator, because the intense heat may cause the cane to buckle.

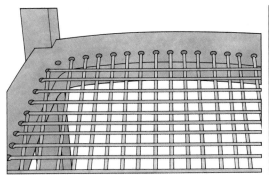

FITTING THE SECOND LAYER OF CANE The second layer lies on top of the first and runs from side to side. Fit it in the same way as the first layer, and do not interweave it.

FITTING THE THIRD LAYER OF CANE Create another layer of cane, running in the same direction as the first layer, but start working at the front this time.

Make sure that when the cane is taken beneath the seat from one hole to the next, it is running across the spaces not covered when you fitted the first layer of cane.

FITTING THE FOURTH LAYER OF CANE Soak the No.4 cane for a few minutes before starting to make it flexible. This layer will be woven through the other three layers of cane.

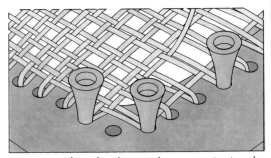

Start at one side, and work across the seat, weaving it under the first layer and over the third layer. Make sure that the cane runs across the spaces not covered by the second layer, when it runs from one hole to the next, under the seat.

Fasten off and secure as before. You may need to use a bodkin or heavy, blunt needle to push the cane through the holes as they begin to fill (see margin, facing page).

FITTING A FIFTH AND SIXTH LAYER When the entire seat has been interwoven, and still using the No.4 cane, run a fifth layer that travels diagonally across the seat, going over one intersection of the first four layers, and under the next.

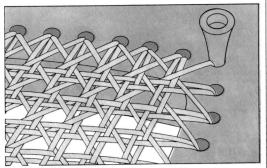

For the sixth layer, work in the opposite diagonal direction and reverse the weaving at the intersections.

SECURING THE CANE From the No.12 cane, cut a plug for each hole, each plug slightly shorter than the depth of the hole. Taper one end a little with the trimming knife.

Tap a plug into each hole, taking care not to damage the cane. When the peg is almost level with the chair seat, use the handle of a bradawl to knock it below the surface. Trim off the cane ends underneath the seat with sharp scissors.

Car aerial

Fitting an internally mounted aerial

Time: ½ an hour or less

> YOU WILL NEED Internally mounted aerial kit.
> Possibly: screwdriver.

Press the new aerial onto the window, where it will not impede the driver's view.

If the aerial cable plugs into a socket on a cable leading from the radio, there is no need to remove the radio. But if the aerial cable plugs directly into the radio, you may have to remove the radio in order to connect it.

It may be possible to use a screwdriver to remove the screws holding the radio in place and pull it out, but in some cars the radio requires a specially designed tool to

QUICK FIX FOR CANE SEATS

Small, badly damaged patches on any woven cane chair can be fixed by weaving similar sized cane into the original, almost like darning. Dampen a length of cane to make it flexible, introduce it from below and weave it into the chair, following the pattern. Begin the patching at least 2.5 cm (1 in) away from the damage to make it stronger. Tuck in loose ends and trim away any excess underneath.

RADIO CODING

If your car is fitted with a security-coded radio, make sure that you know the code before disconnecting either the battery or the radio's power lead. You will need the code to reset the radio once the power is reconnected.

remove it. If so, get the radio aerial replaced by a garage.

Run the new cable along a convenient route, unfastening trim at the sills and floor to conceal it if necessary.

What model of aerial?

ROOF MOUNTED An aerial above the windscreen is protected from vandals to some extent. If it gets damaged, buy a new one from a dealer that specialises in your make of car. Screw the new one in place.

INTERNALLY MOUNTED Most internal aerials consist of a thin metal strip in a plastic casing that sticks to the inside of a window. A device is available that allows you to use the rear-window heater as an aerial.

Internal aerials are vandal proof and need no hole drilled in the bodywork.

WING MOUNTED If a telescopic aerial is sited on the front wing, the route for the cable – from the aerial to the radio – is short. But aerials sited on the wings are vulnerable to damage.

Replacing a wing-mounted aerial (non-electric)
Time: ½ day or less

YOU WILL NEED Spanner, adjustable spanner, screwdriver, strong scissors or wire cutters. Possibly: hosepipe.

Put the handbrake full-on then look underneath the wheel arch to see if you can get to the aerial mounting base. If you can, brush down the area to clean off the dirt.

REMOVING A WING LINER Some modern cars have an extra plastic layer under the wheel arch to protect the metal of the wing from dirt and stones – this is called a wing liner. If you cannot see the aerial base, it is probably located between the wing liner and outer wing.

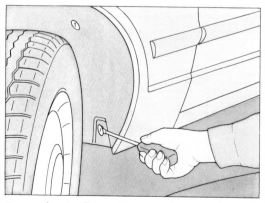

Remove the wing liner, using a screwdriver to either undo the screws which are holding it in place or to gently prise out the plastic studs holding it onto the wing.

Using a hydrometer to test a battery

A battery hydrometer consists of a glass tube with a rubber bulb on the end. The tube is inserted in each battery cell and the rubber bulb squeezed to draw electrolyte into the tube. A float in the tube indicates the strength of the electrolyte. When the scale is marked in volts, about 1.25 V is right. Other types simply show green and red for fully charged and flat.

WHAT IS IN A BATTERY?

The metal plates in a battery sit in electrolyte – which is sulphuric acid, diluted with distilled water. When you top up the electrolyte in a battery you only need to add distilled water.

You may need to turn the steering to one side, or even remove the wheel, to gain access to the wing liner.

INSTALLING THE NEW AERIAL Once you have access to the mounting base, use a spanner to undo the nut securing it. You may have to hold the rest of the mount in place with an adjustable spanner as you turn the nut.

Take off any washers and withdraw the aerial. Then, cut the old aerial off its cable with a strong pair of scissors or wire cutters – the new aerial will have its own cable.

Clean the area around the hole in the wing. Then push the new aerial through the hole ensuring the parts are fitted according to the instructions, and secure it in place.

FITTING THE CABLE Follow the route of the old aerial cable and find the hole where it enters the car. Pull out the old cable. Feed in the new cable, making sure that the rubber grommet seals the hole. Then replace the old cable with the new, following the same route.

If the old cable plugs directly into the back of the radio, you may have to remove the radio from its mounting to connect the cable. Otherwise the aerial cable will plug into a socket on a cable leading from the radio, in which case there is no need to remove the radio.

Replace the wing liner by pushing the plastic studs firmly back into their hole or by replacing the screws.

Car battery
(SEE ALSO CAR EMERGENCIES)

The car battery provides the power to start the engine. It should last a few years, but eventually it will lose its ability to hold a charge.

How long the battery lasts depends partly on how it is treated. Keep the battery connections free of dirt and deposits, and the battery secure on its tray. Letting it go flat repeatedly will shorten the battery's life.

Recharging a battery Time: 1 day or less

If the battery is flat you can usually recharge it.

If you have a garage with a convenient mains socket and adequate ventilation, the battery can be charged while it is still in the car. Otherwise, remove it (see 'Replacing a battery', facing page).

YOU WILL NEED Mains battery charger. Possibly: spanners.

Disconnect the leads from the battery terminals – earth terminal first. Usually this is the negative (black) lead, but if in doubt it is the lead connecting the battery to the car body. Unless it is a sealed battery, remove or loosen the plastic tops that cover the openings to allow the explosive gas to escape as the battery recharges.

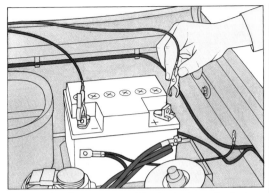

Connect the charger's crocodile-clip leads to the battery. The black lead goes to the negative (– or black) terminal and the red lead goes to the positive (+ or red) terminal. Plug the charger into the mains and switch on.

Most chargers have a gauge on the front to show that the battery is charging. If the needle doesn't move when you switch on, turn off the charger and check that the connections to the battery terminals are good.

It takes 7-12 hours to fully charge an ordinary battery and no more than 7 hours for a sealed battery. A few hours of recharging may be enough to start the car.

When the battery is charged, unplug the charger then remove the crocodile clips from the battery terminals. Do not remove the clips while the charger is still switched on, as there is the risk of an explosion.

Replace the battery tops and reconnect the leads.

TESTING A BATTERY If the battery goes flat again quickly, recharge it fully then use a hydrometer (see facing page, margin) to check that it can maintain a charge or take it to a garage to be checked. If it can no longer hold a charge, replace it (see 'Replacing a battery', right).

Topping up electrolyte Time: a few minutes

Sealed batteries do not need topping-up. Batteries that do need topping up usually have a see-through body with a minimum-level marker or a plastic bar visible through the cell opening. The electrolyte should reach the mark.

Remove the battery's snap-on cover or the plastic screw-in tops. Then top up the electrolyte with distilled water so it reaches the minimum mark or covers the metal plates inside.

Do not use tap water in place of distilled water because impurities in it will considerably shorten the battery's life. Electrolyte is corrosive, so take care not to spill it.

Replacing a battery Time: 1 hour or less

If a battery is at the end of its life, replace it. Battery capacity and terminal types differ, so get the correct one for your model of car. Batteries are sold fully charged and the box normally has a sell-by date stamped on it.

REMOVING THE OLD BATTERY First note which way round the battery goes and which lead goes to which terminal. Then slip the plastic covers off the terminals (if fitted).

Use a spanner to disconnect the earth lead from the battery. The earth lead is usually attached to the negative terminal (if in doubt it is the lead attached to the car body). Then disconnect the other lead.

Undo any nuts and bolts holding the battery in place and lift it out upright, to avoid spilling the electrolyte.

FITTING THE NEW BATTERY Put the new battery in place and fasten the clamps that hold it. Connect the positive lead (red) and tighten it with a spanner. Connect the negative lead, then leave the battery to stand for a couple of minutes. This 'resting period' will allow the electrolyte to settle. Start the car to see if the battery is working.

Car body

Repairing minor rust damage Time: 1 day

If minor rust damage is left untreated it can spread quickly. So deal with rust as soon as you notice it.

> YOU WILL NEED Wire brush, wet-and-dry abrasive paper, rust killer, body filler, touch-up paint.

Use a wire brush to scrape off loose or damaged paint from an area slightly larger than that affected by the rust.

Scrape off the worst of the rust and sand down the bodywork with wet-and-dry abrasive paper, used dry.

Treat the area with paint-on rust killer to prevent any remaining rust from spreading. Some brands need to be washed off after a few minutes.

SAFETY WITH BATTERIES

- Never charge a maintenance-free (sealed) battery for more than seven hours, unless your charger reduces the current as the charge increases.
- Car batteries give off explosive gases. Keep away from flames and sparks, and charge in a well-ventilated place.
- Batteries contain highly corrosive acid. Keep it away from your skin and eyes. Keep the battery upright to prevent spills.
- To avoid a short circuit remove jewellery while working on the battery and never rest tools on the battery.
- Remove the earth lead first and replace it last.

SPRAYING ON PAINT

Spray on aerosol only in very thin layers or it will sag. Use only very brief spurts from the aerosol can. To prevent the nozzle clogging, up-end the can and depress the nozzle when you finish painting. When only propellant emerges the nozzle is clear and it can be safely stored.

CHOOSING TOUCH-UP PAINT

Touch-up paint must be an exact match. The name and serial number of the paint will be found on a plate somewhere on the car or in the owner's handbook.

USING BRAKE FLUID SAFELY

Brake-and-clutch fluid is extremely toxic. Do not let it make contact with skin or eyes. If you spill any on car paintwork wipe it off immediately with a rag. Dispose of the rag. Buy brake-and-clutch fluid only when you need it, and keep the top on tightly. Fluid in half-empty cans goes off because it absorbs moisture from the air.

Use body filler to raise the level of the damaged area so it is a little higher than the surrounding bodywork. When it is set, use wet wet-and-dry abrasive paper to sand it down until it is smooth and flush with the good paintwork.

Wash off any dust and dry the area thoroughly.

If the affected area is small, you can get a reasonable finish using brush-on touch-up paint, applied in two thin coats. Let the first coat dry then sand it lightly with a fine grade of wet-and-dry, used dry. Then apply a second coat.

For a larger area use aerosol primer, followed by aerosol touch-up paint. Apply it in several thin coats, lightly sanding it down between coats.

Repairing small dents   Time: 1 day or less

> YOU WILL NEED Wet-and-dry abrasive paper, body filler, sanding block or electric sander, aerosol primer, touch-up paint, masking tape, newspaper. Possibly: screwdriver, rust killer.

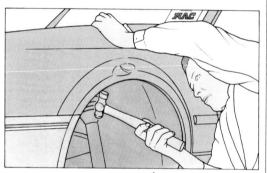

Dents deeper than about 1.3 cm ($\frac{1}{2}$ in) should be partially knocked out from behind with a hammer, or filled with two or more separate layers of filler.

If the dent has rusted because the paint has cracked, treat the rust (see previous page). Then roughen the paint inside the dent with coarse wet-and-dry paper, used dry, so the filler has something to stick to.

Mix the filler paste, according to the instructions. Press it into the dent with the spatula supplied and level it off so that it stands just proud of the surrounding paintwork.

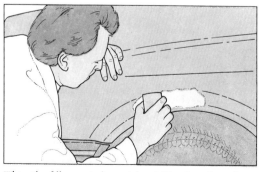

When the filler paste has set hard (the time depends on the product and the air temperature) sand it down until it is level with the surrounding area.

Do the final sanding by hand with a fine grade of wet-and-dry, used dry. Wash and dry the area afterwards.

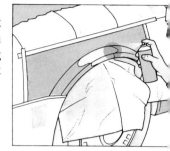

PAINTING THE PATCH Protect the surrounding area with newspaper and masking tape. Spray primer paint over the repair.

If you notice any minor holes in the surface of the filler at this stage, patch them with fresh filler.

Spray the area with the finishing colour. This is best done in several thin coats. Lightly sand with fine-grade abrasive paper between each coat.

Touching up scratches   Time: 1 hour or less

> YOU WILL NEED Methylated spirit, touch-up paint.

If a chip or scratch has not penetrated as far as the metal, it can be fixed quickly and easily. Clean the area with methylated spirit on a clean rag, then apply a very small amount of touch-up paint to the centre of the chip or scratch and carefully use the brush to work it to the edge.

Car brakes

If the level of brake fluid drops suddenly, the brakes may feel spongy, or the pedal will go down farther than usual and the brakes won't work. If the level drops gradually, you may not notice it until it has become dangerous. If you suspect a leak, get it checked by a garage immediately.

Topping up brake fluid   Time: a few minutes

Check the brake fluid weekly and top it up if necessary. Most reservoirs have an external minimum-level mark.

> YOU WILL NEED Brake-and-clutch fluid.

To avoid getting brake-and-clutch fluid on your skin, wrap a cloth round the lid of the brake-and-clutch-fluid reservoir before you unscrew it. Then pour the fresh fluid very carefully into the reservoir.

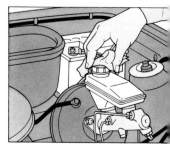

Wipe up any spills immediately with an old rag and dispose of the rag. Screw the lid back on.

Car cooling system

(SEE ALSO CAR EMERGENCIES)

Looking after the cooling system

The car cooling system prevents the engine from overheating. Some cars rely simply on the passage of air through the engine compartment, but the most common cooling system is a network of water passages carrying a mixture of water and antifreeze, known as coolant.

As the coolant circulates it absorbs the heat that is generated by the engine and disperses it via the radiator.

Antifreeze prevents the water from freezing and damaging the engine. It also prevents the cooling system corroding and so most car manufacturers recommend that you use antifreeze or their own brand of coolant all year round. Check in the car owner's manual. Coolant must be renewed at certain intervals (refer to the owner's manual) to remain effective.

Check the coolant level weekly when the engine is cold. Some cars have a small expansion tank marked with MIN and MAX where extra water and antifreeze are added to the engine. Otherwise, remove the radiator cap to inspect the level of coolant inside. It should be about 2.5cm (1in) below the neck. Top it up if necessary.

Check the engine hoses regularly, especially before a long journey. Allow the engine to cool, then flex the hoses with your hands. This should expose any hidden cracks. Pay particular attention to any areas of the hoses which have been discoloured by deposits, and those parts near to clips, where failure most often occurs.

Then, with the engine running, see if there are any leaks from the hoses, especially at the joins.

If you see any leaks, turn off the engine and allow it to cool down for about a quarter of an hour.

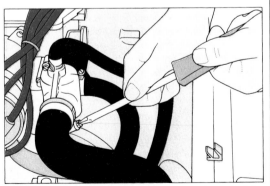

Once it is cool tighten the clip that secures the end of the leaking hose and restart the engine and take another look.

Topping up car coolant Time: a few minutes

After repairing a leak, and as part of regular maintenance, check the level of coolant (the mixture of antifreeze and water) in the engine and top it up if necessary.

For temperatures as low as −16°C (3°F) the coolant in a car engine should be at least one-third antifreeze in order to protect against frost damage. A mixture of half antifreeze and half water should be adequate to cope with temperatures falling as low as −32°C (−26°F).

Add the mixture of water and antifreeze either to the radiator or to the expansion tank (if one is fitted).

Replacing a cracked or perished hose
Time: 1 hour or less

Dripping coolant and overheating of the engine can both result from cracked or perished hoses. But by checking the hoses regularly you should avoid these situations.

> YOU WILL NEED Screwdriver, new hose, spanner, hose clips.

Most hoses are specific to the model of car, but general spares shops should stock them. You can also buy replacements from dealers specialising in your make of car.

When the engine is cool note the position and route of the old hose (it may help to make a quick sketch). Remove it and clean any deposits from the stub to which it fits.

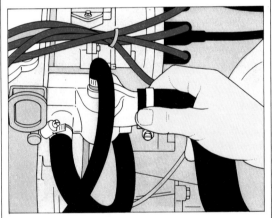

Place the new clips over the new hose. Push the hose into place and slide each clip round until the tightening bolt is in the most convenient position, then tighten them firmly.

Refill the system with coolant either into the radiator or the expansion tank. Then start the engine and let it run for about five minutes to get up to normal operating temperature and check that the new hose is not leaking.

Replacing a hose clip

The old hose will be secured by a clip (also known as a Jubilee clip) at each end. Remove the old clips with either a screwdriver or spanner.

The old clips are often difficult to refit and some are designed to be used only once. It is usually easier to replace them with standard Jubilee clips sold in various sizes at motorists' shops and hardware stores.

SAFETY WITH RADIATORS

Never remove the radiator cap on a hot engine. The hot water inside is under great pressure and will spurt out. Wait for at least 20 minutes to allow the engine to cool and stop hissing – the longer you can wait the better. Protect your hand and wrist with a large cloth and keep your head out of the way when removing the radiator cap. If possible wait until the engine is cold to add more water. Never put cold water into a hot engine as it will cause damage.

Car drive belt

(SEE ALSO CAR EMERGENCIES)

Most cars have one drive belt; a few car models have two. They are often also referred to as fan belts.

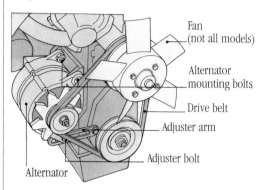

Fan
(not all models)

Alternator
mounting bolts

Drive belt

Adjuster arm

Adjuster bolt

Alternator

Most modern cars have a belt to drive the alternator (which provides electricity for the car) and the water pump (which circulates coolant round the cooling system).

Replacing a drive belt Time: 1 hour or less

Check the drive belt regularly, and before long journeys. On most models of car it should move no more than 1.3 cm ($\frac{1}{2}$ in) at a point halfway between the pulleys (check the owner's handbook). Adjust it by moving the alternator towards or away from the engine.

A squealing noise when you start the engine or accelerate quickly may indicate a loose drive belt. If a belt is loose or has snapped, a warning light should come on. The engine may also overheat and the alternator may not provide power. A diesel car can become difficult to brake.

Renew a belt if it breaks or stretches, or looks worn.

YOU WILL NEED New belt, spanners.

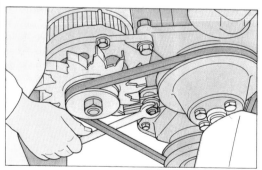

Slacken the bolts holding the alternator to the engine and the one holding the adjuster arm in place.

Remove the old drive belt and fit the new one. Adjust the new drive belt until it is correctly tensioned (see above) by moving the alternator towards or away from the engine.

Then tighten the bolts on the generator and the adjuster arm. Readjust the belt after about 250 miles.

BREAKDOWN
SAFETY

If your car breaks down, try to get it off the road. Switch on your hazard warning lights. Place a warning triangle about 50 m (55 yd) behind your car to warn approaching traffic. If you are on a motorway, place the triangle 100 m (110 yd) away.
If you break down on a motorway don't wait in the car for help as vehicles on the hard shoulder can be hit by traffic.

TAKING SPARES
ON TRIPS
ABROAD

The national motoring organisations will rent out kits, including spares, to take when driving abroad. In some countries it is a legal requirement to carry certain items such as spare bulbs, warning triangle, first-aid kit and fire extinguisher. Check before you go.

Car emergencies

Spares to carry in your car

If your car is more than five years old, it is wise to carry a few basic spares in a bag in the boot, even if you are a member of a national motoring organisation. It may be quicker to make minor repairs yourself by the roadside rather than wait for help.

- Water-repellent spray (WD 40)
- Emergency drive belt (also called fan belt)
- Fuses
- Temporary hose-repair kit or waterproof tape
- Insulating tape
- Oil
- Petrol can (empty)
- Radiator sealer such as Radweld
- Set of spare bulbs
- String or garden wire
- Temporary windscreen (available as a roll of plastic, which you can fit if your windscreen shatters)
- Tow rope
- Warning triangle
- Water container

A basic tool kit

You will also need to carry a basic tool kit to make use of the spares and to make minor repairs.

- Craft knife
- Torch (preferably a free-standing one)
- Jump leads
- Jack and wheelbrace
- Pliers
- Rags
- Screwdrivers (flat and cross-head in a variety of sizes)
- Spanner set to fit your car
- Tyre-pressure gauge and pump

Working on a car safely
- Never go under a car that is jacked up.
- Place the spare wheel half under a jacked-up car to cushion the car if it falls, and to prevent anyone becoming trapped underneath it.
- Only use the proper jacking points given in the owner's handbook. They are specially strengthened.
- If the ground is not firm, support the jack on a plank of wood to spread the load.
- Remove all jewellery and keep your hair and any loose clothing well out of the way while you are working on the car engine.

Changing a wheel Time: ½ hour or less

Position the car safely on firm, level ground where it will not be hit by other vehicles. Put the handbrake on, put the car in second gear and chock the wheels if possible.

> **YOU WILL NEED** Wheelbrace, jack, spare wheel, adjustable spanner or socket. Possibly: plank of wood, screwdriver.

Get the spare wheel, jack and wheelbrace out of the car. They are usually in the boot, possibly under a false floor or side panel. The spare wheel may be under the bonnet, under the car or behind the front seat.

Prise or pull off the wheeltrim or hub cap if there is one – by hand or with a screwdriver or the flat end of the wheelbrace. Loosen the nuts on the wheel by half a turn.

JACKING UP THE CAR Find the jacking points. Some cars have one on each side; others have two. (The details will be given in the owner's handbook). Some jacks fit into a hole at the jacking point, others fit underneath the point.

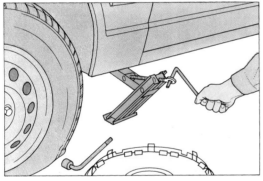

Attach the jack and work it until the wheel that you need to change is at least 2.5 cm (1 in) off the ground.

Unscrew the wheel nuts or bolts with an adjustable spanner or a socket, and lift the wheel off the hub (above).

If your wheel is fixed on with nuts, place the spare wheel onto the studs sticking out of the hub and replace the nuts. If the wheel is fixed with bolts, line up the spare wheel with the boltholes in the hub.

A car wheel is heavy and it is awkward to hold in position against the car so if possible get a helper to hold it in place while you screw in the fixing bolts.

If you have no help, try to position the wheel so that the bolts line up as illustrated and screw the top bolt in place first to hold the wheel while you fit the remaining bolts (see also margin, right).

TIGHTEN THE NUTS OR BOLTS Tighten each nut or bolt a few turns at a time to keep the wheel centred on the hub. Tighten them as much as possible without moving the car.

Lower the jack, remove it and stow it away.

Fully tighten the wheel nuts or bolts. They must be as secure as possible, so put your foot on the wheelbrace and use your full weight to tighten them if necessary.

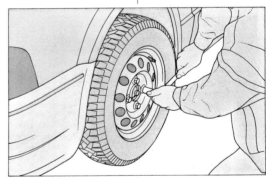

Push the wheeltrim back on to the new wheel and stow away the old wheel and brace.

Check and adjust the pressure of the replacement tyre at the earliest opportunity and do not forget to have the old tyre repaired or replaced as soon as possible.

Repairing a broken drive belt
Time: ½ hour or less

> **YOU WILL NEED** Emergency drive belt.

If a drive belt works loose or snaps on a journey, the car will overheat and at least one warning light will come on. On diesel cars the brakes may become difficult to apply.

If you do not have an emergency drive belt you may be able to buy one from the nearest filling station.

Cut the emergency belt to size and clip, or stick, the ends together. The emergency belt should get you home, where you can fit a proper new belt (see *Car drive belt*).

FITTING WHEEL-BOLTS THE EASY WAY

To help fit car wheels which are held in place with bolts, cut off the heads of two spare fixing bolts and keep them in your spares kit.
When the wheel needs changing you can use the headless bolts, screwed lightly into place, to hold the wheel in position while you fit the proper fixing bolts.

REMOVING TIGHT WHEEL NUTS

You may need to use your body weight to shift the wheel nuts. Stand on the wheel brace with one foot. Remember it is always easier to push than to pull.
When you buy a new car loosen and retighten the wheel nuts at home. This should ensure that you can get them off if you ever have to change a wheel by the roadside.

Car emergencies (cont.)

SAFETY WITH RADIATORS

Never remove the radiator cap on a hot engine. The hot water inside is under great pressure and will spurt out. Wait for at least 20 minutes to allow the engine to cool and stop hissing – the longer you can wait the better. Protect your hand and wrist with a large cloth and keep your head out of the way when removing the radiator cap. If possible wait until the engine is cold to add more water. Never put cold water into a hot engine as it will cause damage.

WHAT VOLTAGE IS YOUR VEHICLE?

Most cars, except very old VW Beetles, are 12 V. But commercial vehicles such as lorries and vans can have different voltages. The battery is usually marked with the voltage, or you can look in the owner's handbook.

Faultfinder guide: Engine overheats

Electrical system or temperature warning lights on, gauge in the red or steam from the bonnet

POSSIBLE CAUSE Leaking hose.
SOLUTION Fix leak or replace hose (see below).

POSSIBLE CAUSE Leaking radiator.
SOLUTION Fix the leak (see 'Repairing a leaking radiator', right).

POSSIBLE CAUSE Loose or broken drive belt.
SOLUTION Replace or tighten the drive belt (see 'Repairing a broken drive belt').

Temporary repair to a leaking hose

Time: $\frac{1}{2}$ hour or less

If the car overheats and the temperature gauge is in the red zone, or the temperature warning light comes on, and coolant drips from the engine, one of the hoses which carry coolant around the engine may be leaking.

If you have a new hose, you can replace the leaking hose (see *Car cooling system*).

A hose-repair kit should get you to a garage. Kits usually consist of a thin strip of rubber or hose with ties.

YOU WILL NEED Hose-repair kit or waterproof tape, pliers.

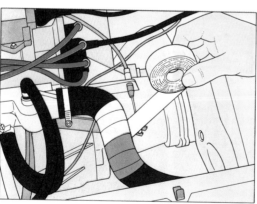

Switch off the engine and let the water temperature and pressure drop. Once the leak slows, wrap a strip of rubber around the split. Hold it in place with waterproof tape or wire or plastic ties, tightened with pliers if necessary.

Waterproof tape can be used as a temporary repair for a leaking hose. Wrap the tape as tightly as possible around the split hose, using several overlapping layers.

Top up the coolant mixture before restarting the engine. Then drive slowly and keep an eye on the temperature gauge or warning light.

Repairing a leaking radiator Time: a few minutes

If the level of the coolant in the engine drops and there are no leaking hoses, or if there are stains on the radiator fins, the radiator may be leaking.

Small leaks can be temporarily cured by adding a liquid radiator sealant to the coolant.

Faultfinder guide: Car won't start

No response at all or engine turns over slowly

CAUSE Poor battery connections or flat battery.
ACTION Clean battery connections (see 'Cleaning battery connections'). Jump or push start the car. (see 'Jump starting a car' or 'Push starting a car').

Engine clicks or whirrs but does not turn over

CAUSE Poor battery connections, flat battery or a jammed starter motor.
ACTION As above or free jammed starter motor (see 'Freeing a jammed starter motor', facing page).

Turns properly but does not fire

CAUSE No fuel.
ACTION Put fuel in the tank.

CAUSE Loose ignition cables.
ACTION Secure cables.

CAUSE Damp ignition system.
ACTION Dry ignition system (see 'Drying out a damp ignition system').

Engine turns properly but doesn't fire (smells of petrol)

CAUSE Flooded engine.
ACTION Dry engine (see 'Drying a flooded engine').

Drying out a damp ignition system Time: a few minutes

If the car was running normally when it was last used, but it won't start in wet or foggy weather, the fault is probably dampness or condensation in the ignition.

Use water-repellent spray on the ignition coil, the distributor, and the leads to the distributor and spark plugs. But do not spray inside the distributor cap because it could affect the engine's timing.

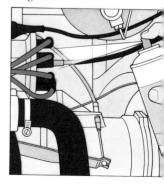

After spraying the ignition give the engine a few minutes to recover before trying to start it again, otherwise you will flatten the battery.

Cleaning battery connections Time: ½ an hour or less

If the connections to the battery are faulty, not enough power will reach the starter motor.

You can easily fix this problem yourself.

> **YOU WILL NEED** Spanners, glasspaper or a metal file, copper grease or petroleum jelly, stiff scrubbing brush.

Turn off the engine and remove the plastic covers over the battery terminals. Clean off any white deposits from the terminals and clamps with hot water and a stiff brush.

Unfasten the clamps that attach the cables to the terminals with a spanner, starting with the earth terminal. The earth is connected to the car body. It is usually the negative, marked '–', and has a black wire attached to it.

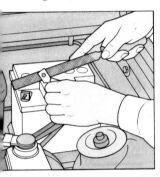

Clean the battery terminals with a metal file or glasspaper, until they are shiny, then lightly coat them with copper grease or petroleum jelly.

Clean the clamps with glasspaper, then attach them to the terminals. Attach the earth terminal last.

Make sure that the nuts and bolts are tight. Then lightly coat the clamps with petroleum jelly and replace the plastic cover on the battery (if fitted).

Jump starting a car Time: ½ an hour or less

If the car headlights are very dim or won't come on at all, and there is no response when you turn the ignition key, the battery is probably flat. You can start the car with the help of another car's battery.

! First make sure (from the owner's handbook) that your model of car will not be damaged by a jump start.

Most cars are earthed through their negative battery terminal and lead: all the following instructions assume a negative earth. To check, look to see which battery terminal is connected to the car body – if the negative terminal is connected to the body then the car has a negative earth.

> **YOU WILL NEED** Jump leads, another car with an electrical system of the same voltage.

! Position the two vehicles close enough for the jump leads to reach between them, but do not allow them to touch.

Make sure that the ignition and all accessories are turned off on both cars and that both are out of gear.

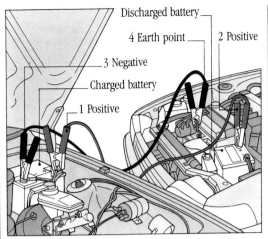

Discharged battery

4 Earth point 2 Positive

3 Negative

Charged battery

1 Positive

Connect the jump leads to the car batteries as illustrated above, and in the numbered order shown.

Make the final connection to a piece of bare metal on the car, such as the engine block. Do not connect the jump lead to any part of the car with paint on it, as the paint will burn. Make the connection as far as possible from the discharged battery and route the leads so that they will not be caught by any moving parts once the engine starts.

Start the engine of the car with the good battery, then start the car with the flat battery. Once it is running smoothly, disconnect the jump leads, in reverse order.

Drive the car for about half an hour before parking it, so that the battery has time to recharge. Charge the battery with a battery charger at the first opportunity.

Push starting a car (not automatic) Time: a few minutes

If a jump start is not possible, get someone to give you a push start, but do not use this method on a petrol-engined car fitted with a catalytic convertor or on an automatic car.

Use the choke if the engine is cold. Turn the ignition on. Then put the car in second gear and depress the clutch. Keep the clutch down as the helper starts to push. When the car is rolling at about jogging speed release the clutch sharply and press the accelerator at the same time. Repeat the process if necessary.

Freeing a jammed starter motor Time: a few minutes

If you turn the ignition key to start the car and all you get is a click, the starter motor may be jammed.

> **YOU WILL NEED** Possibly: spanner.

There are two ways to deal with a jammed starter motor: Turn the ignition off and put the car in second or third gear. Then get out and rock the car backwards and forwards. Take the car out of gear and try to start it again.

Locate the starter motor (look in the car handbook). Some types have a square pin in the centre of one end. Turn this with a spanner then try the starter again.

Drying a flooded engine

Sometimes during repeated attempts to start a car, the engine becomes flooded with petrol (there is also often a strong smell of petrol inside the car).

When an engine is flooded it will not start until the petrol evaporates, which could take a long time. But you can usually clear the excess fuel easily.

First push the choke in. Then press the accelerator pedal all the way down and keep it there. Turn the ignition key and let the engine turn over for about ten seconds.

Dealing with a broken windscreen

If a windscreen is broken, perhaps by a stone flying up from the road, it will craze rather than break into pieces.

If the windscreen breaks be careful not to swerve to the left or right. To keep the car in a straight line, look out of the driver's side window at a solid line – such as a kerb or solid lines on the road – to gauge your position on the road. Gently brake, indicate left and pull over.

Freeing a frozen door lock Time: a few minutes

YOU WILL NEED Lighter or matches, de-icer or hot water.

If the door lock freezes during icy weather, heat the key with matches or a lighter before you insert it.

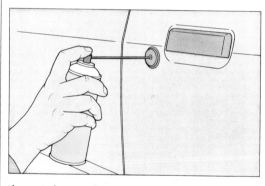

Alternatively, spray de-icer into the lock or pour a little hot water over it. It is also possible to buy a battery powered de-icer which you insert into the lock.

Car fuse

Checking a suspect fuse Time: ½ an hour or less

Fuses are designed to be the weak link in an electrical circuit, so that if a fault occurs the fuse burns out before any more serious damage is done to the electrical equipment.

Cars have several fuses. Each one protects a single item, such as the main headlamp beam, or else a group of items. When something electrical in the car stops working, first check the relevant fuse.

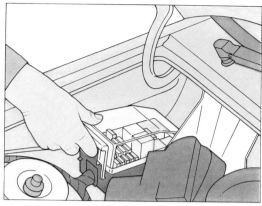

The car fuses are normally located in the engine compartment or under the dashboard. Check in the owner's handbook if you cannot find them.

If there is no indication which fuse corresponds to which piece of electrical equipment in the car or the owner's manual you will have to check all the fuses one by one.

Pull the fuse out to inspect it properly. You should be able to remove it with your fingers; if not, prise it out with a pair of long-nosed pliers or the tool provided in the fuse box.

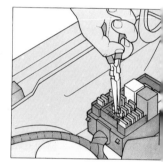

Be careful not to touch the contacts of one of the adjoining fuseholders if you are using a metal tool such as pliers, as the metal will cause a short circuit.

Take out the fuses one by one to check them (see below) and replace any that have blown.

What model of fuse?

CYLINDRICAL PLASTIC BODY The metal strip along the side of the plastic body melts when the fuse has blown.

FLAT PLASTIC BODY Two metal 'legs' hold the fuse in position. The wire melts when the fuse has blown.

GLASS BODY The fine wire strip running along inside the glass body melts when the fuse has blown.

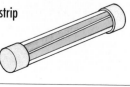

Replacing a blown fuse Time: a few minutes

YOU WILL NEED New fuse, screwdriver.

Fuses are rated in amps; it is essential that a blown fuse is replaced with one of the same amp rating.

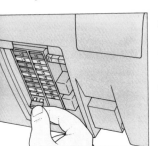

Some fuse boxes hold a set of spare fuses.

Push the new fuse into the holder. Then switch on the affected equipment. If several items were involved, turn them on one item at a time in order to trace the source of the fault.

If the fuse blows again immediately, there is a fault in the electrical circuit or equipment which should be dealt with by an automobile electrician.

Turning on the equipment item by item should enable you to isolate which appliance is faulty.

Car horn

Motor vehicles must by law have an effective horn. The horn will be checked in the MOT test and the car could fail if the horn is not working properly.

Fixing a broken or feeble horn Time: 1 hour or less

YOU WILL NEED Glasspaper. Possibly: spanner, voltmeter.

SOUNDLESS HORN Check that the relevant fuse has not blown (see *Car fuses*). If not, check with a voltmeter that current is reaching the horn. If not, make sure that the connectors attaching the wiring to the horn are secure. If they are, clean the contact points with glasspaper. Some horns also earth through the fixing bolt.

If the fixing bolt becomes dirty or corroded, it will give a bad connection so clean or replace it as necessary.

Replace the connectors and try the horn.

FEEBLE HORN If the horn sounds feeble, check the connections. If they are clean and secure, see if you can adjust the horn. Some have a small nut in the centre which you turn with a spanner to alter the sound produced.

Stopping a car horn sounding

Stop a constantly sounding horn by pulling out the fuses in the fuse box one at a time until the horn stops, then disconnect the wire from the back of the horn and replace the fuses.

Car lights

Replacing blown lamps Time: $\frac{1}{2}$ an hour or less

All car lamps must work by law, even during the day. Check them at least once a week and carry spare bulbs.

HEADLAMP BULBS On most cars the headlamp bulbs are replaced from inside the engine compartment.

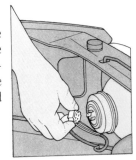

Remove any protective cover over the back of the lamp. Then grasp the connector block that joins the wiring to the headlamp and disconnect it.

Remove the old bulb by either unclipping or rotating the retainer that holds it in place, if it is fitted. Then fit the new bulb and replace the retaining clip.

Push the connector block back on and replace any protective cover. Finally, test the lights. If the lamp still does not work there may be a faulty connection.

SEALED HEADLAMP UNITS Old cars with round headlamps, such as Minis, may use sealed-beam units.

If one of this type blows the whole headlamp must be replaced. Remove it from outside the car.

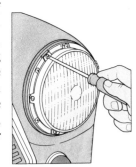

There is often a strip of metal or plastic trim concealing the fixing screws, which hold the retaining ring in place around the lamp. Remove it and loosen the screws. Do not confuse the beam alignment screws, which have springs under them, with fixing screws.

Pull out the lamp to expose the wiring behind it. Disconnect the connector block and remove the sidelight (if fitted). Push the connector onto the new headlamp and replace the sidelight. Test the lamp then replace the retaining ring and trim. Realign the lamp if necessary.

OTHER LAMPS On most car models other lamps (indicators, stoplights, sidelights) are reached from inside the boot or engine compartment. In this case the replacement method is the same as for headlamps (see above).

In a boot they will probably be fitted with a protective plastic or fibreboard covering that pulls off by hand.

Voltmeter

A voltmeter will show if any electrical current is flowing through a wire.

HANDLING HALOGEN BULBS

If the lamps use halogen bulbs take care not to touch the glass or the bulb will fail. Handle them with a cloth or the sleeve they are normally packed in. If you do touch the glass clean it with methylated spirit.

REMOVING A BROKEN BULB

If the bulb is broken, press a wine cork onto the jagged edge to push the bulb in and turn it.

Car mirrors

REARVIEW MIRROR If the rearview mirror comes unstuck, you can buy a double-sided adhesive pad or a kit to stick it back on. The kit contains a tube of adhesive and a piece of mesh. Follow the instructions on the pack.

EXTERNAL MIRROR You must have at least one effective external mirror. Replacing a whole external mirror can be expensive. If the glass is just tarnished rather than broken, you can buy thin replacement 'glass' (actually made of plastic) that sticks on top of the old one. Use a hacksaw to saw it to the right size and shape.

You may be able to use a clear tape, designed for outdoor use, to fix a cracked external mirror temporarily.

Car MOT test

All cars over three years old must pass an MOT safety test every 12 months. Many vehicles fail because of faults that could easily be spotted by their owners before the test.

What to check before a test

LIGHTS Check that all the lights are working and that the lenses are clean. Don't forget the fog lamps, the hazard warning lights and the headlamp main beams.

WIPERS Change wiper blades if they are worn (see *Car windows*) and clean the windscreen.

WINDSCREEN WASHERS Make sure there is water in the bottle and that the jets are neither blocked nor positioned so that they spray water in the wrong direction.

HORN Ensure that the horn is working properly.

MIRRORS The rearview mirror and the external mirror on the driver's side must be clean and in good condition.

SEATS The seats should stay locked in position.

SEATBELTS Make sure the seatbelts are not frayed, and are properly anchored. Also, check that the buckles and any inertia-reel mechanisms work as they should.

WINDSCREEN A cracked windscreen will fail the test.
Chips out of the screen may fail the test. Those directly in front of the driver are the most serious, and any chip larger than a small fingernail will probably fail.

DOORS, BOOTS AND BONNETS You must be able to open doors from inside and outside (with the exception of doors with child locks). Doors, boots and bonnets must stay shut.

BRAKES The tester will inspect the brake pipes and flexible hoses, and look for leaking cylinders.

You are unlikely to notice gradual deterioration in the brakes because you compensate for it in your driving. The tester will use special equipment to check that the brakes work effectively and evenly around the car.

Make sure that the handbrake works effectively.

BODY STRUCTURE Major rust in any load-bearing part of the structure will fail the car. This includes suspension, shock absorber and steering mounting points, main frame members, floor, sills, and inner wings.

FUEL TANK The filler cap must be secure. The tank is rarely a problem, unless the car has been in an accident, although corrosion can occur in older cars.

TYRES Look for any bulges or cuts in the tyres. Remember to check both sides. The tyres must have tread at least 1.6 mm deep over the central three-quarters around their total circumference. On a 10p coin the top of the letters in the word pence are 2 mm from the edge. Check the tyre pressures. Don't forget the spare tyre.

WHEELS Dented wheel rims can fail the test. But damaged wheel trims or hub caps are only a problem if they have sharp edges which could damage the tyre.

Car oil

Checking the level

Engine oil is replaced as part of the car's regular service, but check the level weekly and before a long journey.

Make sure the car is on level ground with the engine turned off. If it has been running, wait 5 minutes for all the oil to drain back into the sump.

Open the bonnet and find the dipstick. Check the owner's handbook if the position isn't obvious. The dipstick is a rod that fits into the sump – where the oil is held.

Pull out the dipstick and wipe it clean, then push it all the way back in and pull it out again.

The dipstick has two marks at the end, showing the minimum and maximum oil level. If the oil is near or below the minimum mark, top it up (see margin, left).

BUYING THE RIGHT OIL

The owner's handbook will list the types of oil that are suitable for your car. Any multigrade engine oil should be suitable for most cars, although turbo-charged and diesel engines may have special requirements. Oil sold at filling stations may be as much as twice the price of that sold at supermarkets or car accessory shops.

TOPPING UP THE OIL

You probably won't need more than a litre can of oil for topping up. Remove the oil filler cap on the engine (check the owner's manual if you aren't sure where it is). Pour in about half a litre of oil. Give it a couple of minutes to get down to the sump then check the level again.

Car radio

Tuning the aerial Time: a few minutes

For the best reception on the AM radio bands (medium and long wave) tune the aerial to match the radio. Do this by selecting a weak radio station towards the upper end of the medium wave band (about 200 m or 1500 kHz), then adjust the aerial tuner screw on the radio until you find the best reception. Refer to the instruction booklet to find out where the screw is located.

Aerials for FM reception do not need tuning. In practice, mounting an aerial between 45° and 90° to the car body gives good reception on all bands.

Faultfinder guide: Radio interference

Most cars built after about 1980 are fitted with suppressors to stop electrical equipment from interfering with radio reception. If you get radio interference on a modern car a suppressor might need replacing. On an older car suppressors may not have been fitted.

PROBLEM Generally bad reception and interference that happens or gets worse over bumpy ground.

CAUSE If the car-radio aerial is damaged it will give bad reception.

An aerial that is not properly earthed to the body of the vehicle can also give problems with reception (see *Car aerial*).

SOLUTION If the aerial is poorly earthed, release the earth wire from the car body and clean up the place where it fits, then replace it. If the aerial is damaged, replace it. See *Car aerial* for both repair tasks.

PROBLEM Radio interference happens whenever the engine is running and the noise rises in tone in proportion to the increase in the engine's revs.
CAUSE The ignition system is causing interference because it has not been properly suppressed.
SOLUTION This is usually cured by fitting a 2µF (pronounced '2 micro farad') suppressor to the ignition coil in the engine.

PROBLEM Interference happens when you turn on a piece of equipment such as the windscreen wipers.
CAUSE Electrical equipment is not suppressed.
SOLUTION The item concerned needs to be fitted with a suppressor (see 'Fitting a suppressor', right).

Fitting a suppressor Time: ½ hour or less

Fit a new suppressor on a piece of electrical equipment that is causing radio interference. Test to see what is causing it; the ignition coil, alternator and windscreen-wiper motor are the most likely sources of interference.

Suppressors range from 1µF to 3µF (pronounced '1 to 3 micro farad'). Check which size is suitable at the shop.

YOU WILL NEED Suppressor, spanner.

Connect the suppressor lead to the power supply terminal on the equipment. It will usually be an eyelet or push-on spade connector.

Connect the outer casing of the suppressor to the car body (earth). It may be possible to secure the suppressor with the bolt holding the equipment to the car, or you may have to find an alternative earthing point.

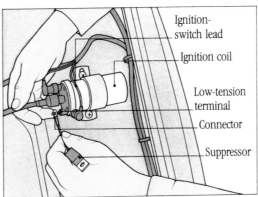

Ignition-switch lead
Ignition coil
Low-tension terminal
Connector
Suppressor

SUPPRESSING AN IGNITION COIL Connect the suppressor lead to the positive (low-tension) terminal on the ignition coil, where the lead from the ignition switch is connected.

The outer casing of the suppressor will have an earthing bracket attached for fixing it to the car body. Use one of the bolts that attach the ignition coil to the car body as the earth connection for the suppressor.

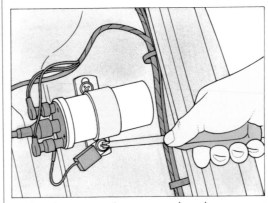

Slacken the screw so that you can place the suppressor casing over the screw hole. Then push the screw through the hole and tighten it with a screwdriver.

Car security

A car is stolen every 2 minutes in Britain. Standard door locks and ignition switches do little to deter thieves.

Alarms and immobilisers

When an alarm detects a theft it may set off a siren or sound the horn, and flash the lights. It may also cut off the fuel supply or disable the ignition.

It is best to get an alarm fitted professionally.

Etching windows and lights

Etching the car's registration number on all the windows, the sunroof and possibly the headlamps may deter some professional car thieves who steal for profit, but it will be ineffective against joy riders.

Etching is a cheap additional security measure and some insurance companies and national motoring organisations will arrange for it to be done free.

Steering wheel and other locks

Steering-wheel locks are popular and fairly cheap. Some lock the clutch pedal or brake pedal to the steering wheel; others have a long projection which makes it impossible to turn the steering wheel. Some locks hook over the steering wheel, but they can be forced off by bending the wheel. It is better to buy one that locks round the steering wheel.

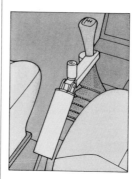

Another device locks the handbrake and gear lever together, making it impossible to drive the car.

Before you buy this type of security device, make sure that the knob on top of the gear lever does not screw or pull off easily.

Wheel clamp

For the ultimate in security fit a wheel clamp, like the ones used on illegally parked cars. They are quite expensive but ideal for a caravan or trailer that has to be left in an insecure spot. They can also be used on a car.

Trackers

A tiny transmitter is fitted in your car. If the car is stolen the device is activated by the company that runs the scheme as soon as they are notified of the theft. The police have cars and helicopters fitted with detection equipment.

Car spark-plugs: SEE SPARK-PLUGS

DISABLING A VEHICLE

A car that has to be left for a long period of time can be disabled by removing a piece of the ignition system such as the distributor rotor arm, located under the distributor cap. Another trick is to swap the leads on the spark plugs, which will either disable the car completely or make it run so badly that if it is stolen the thieves may well abandon it.

Car tyre

Checking tyre condition   Time: $\frac{1}{2}$ hour or less

By checking your car's tyres regularly you may be able to cut down the number of punctures your car gets.

Pull on the handbrake firmly, then check each tyre for bulges, cuts and embedded objects such as nails. Pay special attention to the tyre walls, and don't forget to check the inner side. On the front, you can turn the wheels to either side to get at the inner side. To check the rear wheels make sure the handbrake is on, put the car in gear, chock the wheels and then inspect the tyres.

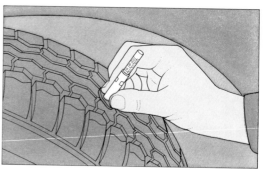

The tyres must have 1.6 mm of tread covering the central three-quarters of their width, over the whole circumference. Special gauges for measuring tread depth can be bought cheaply from car accessory shops.

If you do not have a gauge, use a coin to help you judge the depth of tread. On a 10p coin the top of the letters in the word pence are 2 mm from the edge.

Tyre pressure gauge

The simplest model of tyre pressure gauge available is about the size and shape of a pen.

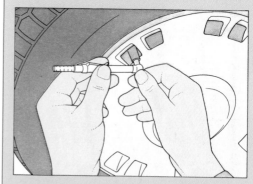

As the gauge is pressed briefly onto the tyre valve, the pressure inside is shown on a scale. The scale may show pounds per square inch (as used in the UK) and bars (used in the rest of Europe).

Checking tyre pressure Time: ½ hour or less

Keep tyres at the correct pressure to avoid damaging them and to maintain safe handling of the car.

Check your owner's handbook or the chart often displayed near the air line on garage forecourts to find out the correct front and back tyre pressures for your car.

Measure tyre pressure when the tyres are cold. You can check it with the air line at a garage, but if you buy your own pressure gauge you can check the tyres wherever and whenever you want and the results will probably be more accurate than they are with a garage pressure gauge.

What your car tyres can tell you

- More tread in the centre of the tyre than on the outside edge means the tyre is under-inflated.
- Excessive wear in the centre of a tyre suggests that it may be over-inflated.
- Excessive wear on the outside or inside of the tread on front tyres means incorrect front wheel alignment.
- Excessive wear in the tread of one front tyre could mean worn suspension or steering parts. Take the car to a garage to have suspension and steering checked.

Car upholstery

Cleaning car upholstery

Clean both vinyl and cloth upholstery with the soft brush attachment on your vacuum cleaner.

Wipe vinyl upholstery with a damp cloth, wrung out in soapflake solution. Then rinse the cloth and wipe off the soap. Alternatively, use an aerosol cleaner for vinyl car seats, available from a car accessory shop. If it is in particularly bad condition, you can use a liquid vinyl restorer.

The marks left by a ball-point pen on vinyl can be quite difficult to remove. Treat the mark as quickly as possible with soapflake solution on a nail brush.

Felt tip on vinyl is easier to get off: just rub the mark with a household cleaner, such as Jif or Ajax, on a cloth.

Treat any stains on cloth upholstery according to what has been spilled (see *Stains*). Use an upholstery shampoo or a car valeting spray foam occasionally.

Repairing upholstery

VINYL SEATS It is possible to repair splits with vinyl repair patches, which are available from car accessory shops in most standard colours. Although the repair won't be invisible, it will prevent the split spreading. If possible, insert a piece of vinyl behind the split to stop the repair patch sticking to the padding underneath it.

Clean and roughen the surface area round the edge of the split with fine abrasive paper wrapped round a flat scrap of wood. Wipe off all dust and then apply PVC adhesive (see *Glues*).

Stick on the patch and wipe off any excess adhesive. Hold it in place with masking tape while it sets. Leave the tape in place for as short a time as possible and clean off any residue that it leaves behind with white spirit.

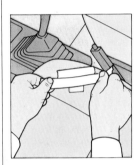

CLOTH SEATS Use a fabric adhesive (see *Glues*) to stick on a patch, cut from similar material to the seat cover.

To make the repair even neater, hold the patch in place with strips of masking tape while the adhesive dries. Then remove the tape.

To make a more lasting repair, stitch the edges of the tear together with a sturdy, curved needle and strong, matching thread.

Apply an antifray spray, then use a close whipping stitch (see *Stitches*), starting and finishing securely.

Car windows

Clearing iced-up windows Time: a few minutes

If conditions are icy and your windows have frosted over, start the engine and turn on the heater (as high as it will go) and windscreen demister to prevent new ice forming on the windows as you clean off the old.

Scrape the ice off the screen with a special plastic scraper or a credit card. Alternatively, use a can of spray-on deicer. Do not use hot water as it can crack the screen.

Keeping windows ice-free

You can stop all but the heaviest of frosts from icing up your windscreen by laying sheets of newspaper on the windscreen overnight. Hold the paper in place with the windscreen wipers.

REMOVING MUD
Always let mud on carpets or upholstery dry out completely before you attempt to vacuum or brush it out.

Carpet beetles

CLEANING A WINDSCREEN

Methylated spirit dissolves grease and removes dead insects. Apply it with a cloth. It is also useful for removing the sticky residue left on the inside of the screen by 'pay-and-display' parking tickets.

REPAIRING A CHIPPED WINDSCREEN

Small chips in windscreens can be repaired by windscreen glass specialists, or you can do it yourself. Use a filler, available from car parts shops. It comes with its own applicator to inject it into the chip. The kit is designed to be used once then thrown away.

Replacing windscreen-wiper blades Time: 1 hour or less

If the rubber blades on the windscreen wipers wear, you can replace them. Make sure that you buy the right size.

> YOU WILL NEED New rubber strips or windscreen-wiper blades. Possibly; a small screwdriver.

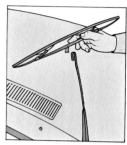

You must remove the whole blade from the windscreen-wiper arm even if you are only replacing the rubber strip. To do this, pull the arm right away from the windscreen into its normal cleaning position (left).

The windscreen-wiper blades may be attached to the arms in one of several different ways. Replacements come with full fitting instructions, but the method may differ from the ones they are replacing. Some have several clips to suit all types of arms.

Replacing a windscreen-wiper arm Time: ½ hour or less

If a wiper arm gets bent accidentally or the blade does not sit flush on the windscreen any more, it needs replacing.

> YOU WILL NEED Felt-tip pen or china-marker pencil, new wiper arm. Possibly: screwdriver, spanner.

Make sure the arm is in the parked position and mark its exact place on the screen with a china-marker pencil or a felt-tip pen. Pull the arm away from the screen until it clicks into the cleaning position.

If you can see a nut holding it in place, undo and remove the nut, then pull off the wiper arm. Push the new one on, making sure it is in exactly the same position as the old one, by lining it up with the mark you drew on the windscreen. Then screw the new arm in place.

If there is no visible nut, there will probably be a hinged cover over the end of the arm, where it is fixed to the car. Prise up this cover with a screwdriver, taking care not to let it slip and damage the car's paintwork.

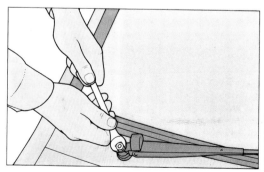

Prising up the cover may release the arm or there will be a nut or screw underneath. Remove it to release the arm.

In all cases, push the new wiper arm on, making sure it is in exactly the same position as the old one, by matching it to the mark you made on the windscreen.

Then refit the screw or nut if necessary and push the cover back into place. Check that it functions properly.

Windscreen washer maintenance Time: ½ hour or less

The most common problem with washers apart from running out of water is that the jets get blocked or spray water in the wrong place. Unblock jets with a pin.

On most cars you can also alter the direction of the water jets with a pin. You will see that the jet consists of a small ball with a hole in it. Use the pin to move the ball around to redirect the water jet.

On some older cars the jet is adjusted with a small screwdriver through a slot on the side of the jet.

Carpet beetles

If small, round holes appear in your woollen carpet, or along the seams of furnishings and clothes, you are probably the victim of carpet beetle infestation.

It is the larva (also known as a 'woolly bear'), not the adult carpet beetle that causes the damage.

The adult looks like a miniature brown, grey and cream ladybird and is only about 3 mm ($\frac{1}{8}$ in) long.

The woolly bear is fluffy and brown with golden hairs on each side. When it is disturbed, it rolls up and fans out these hairs to give the appearance of a golden ball.

Adult

Woolly bear

To get rid of carpet beetles, search the loft, especially along the eaves, for dead birds and old nests, as the larvae feed off feathers, bird droppings and dead fledglings. Throw away any pieces of old carpet from the loft.

Remove all fluff and debris from cupboards (including the airing cupboard) and cracks between floorboards, using the crevice attachment of a vacuum cleaner. Then go over carpets, curtains and upholstery with the appropriate attachments. Where possible, roll up carpets and rugs and clean the underlay and the floor.

Treat all affected areas with a spray or powder insecticide labelled for carpet beetle or moth control. Wear a protective mask if working in a confined space. Make sure that the insecticide gets right into cracks and crevices. Persevere, as immediate success is seldom achieved — sprays or powders may need to be applied several times.

If infestation continues, have fitted carpets and underlay cleaned professionally or call in a pest control company.

Carpet laying

When you are buying new carpet there is no point in laying it yourself. The laying charge is small compared with the total cost, and many carpet shops include free fitting.

However, if you have some secondhand carpet that is in good condition, the job may be worth doing. Don't consider undertaking this unless the carpet is large enough to cover the room in one piece.

Foam-backed carpet is easier to lay than carpet that requires a separate underlay, but watch out for deterioration in the foam. If it is in bad condition it is better to use a new underlay.

Start by clearing the room of furniture and removing any doors that swing into the room. Make sure the floor is clean and dry, and remove old tacks or staples.

Lay building paper over the floor to prevent dust blowing up between gaps in the boards. Fix the building paper to the floor with either double-sided adhesive tape, a hammer tacker or a staple gun.

If a wooden floor is in poor condition, cover it with hardboard, smooth side up (see *Floorboards*).

Laying carpet on a concrete floor

To fix gripper strips to a concrete floor, make sure the surface is dry and dust-free, then spread epoxy-resin glue on the gripper strips and press them onto the floor. Allow the setting time suggested on the pack. For the underlay, use an adhesive recommended by the underlay manufacturer.

Instead of nailing the carpet temporarily to the floor to begin the laying, hook it onto the gripper strips along one wall.

Laying unbacked carpet Time: about a day

YOU WILL NEED Steel tape measure, trimming knife or heavy-duty scissors, carpet gripper strips, hammer, hammer tacker or staple gun, carpet tacks, knee kicker (from a hire shop), bolster (see *Chisels*), mallet, carpet edging strip, screws, screwdriver.

PREPARING A TIMBER FLOOR Measure the room and cut the carpet roughly to size, allowing at least 3.8 cm ($1\frac{1}{2}$ in) of spare on all sides, to ensure adequate coverage.

Place the gripper strips around the room, about 1 cm ($\frac{3}{8}$ in) away from the walls with the spikes slanting towards the wall. Fix them to the floor with the nails that are already fitted to them. (For solid floors, see margin.)

Cut the underlay so that it sits inside the area bounded by the gripper strips, and fix it to the floor with a hammer tacker or with a staple gun.

Lay the carpet down on top of the underlay, with the excess carpet riding up the skirting boards.

LAYING THE CARPET Measure about 15 cm (6 in) in from one wall and fix the carpet to the floor with a few tacks. Starting from the centre of the opposite wall, stretch the carpet as much as possible and lock it on the spikes.

Move to the opposite wall and remove the tacks. Starting from the centre, use your knees and a knee kicker to hold the tension, leaving your hands free to lock the carpet onto the gripper spikes. Make sure the carpet is taut and free from wrinkles.

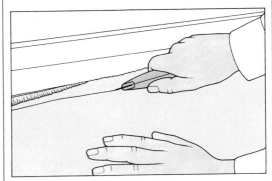

Trim off most of the surplus carpet, allowing about 1 cm ($\frac{3}{8}$ in) to fill the space between gripper and wall.

Then use a bolster and mallet to tap the surplus carpet into the space. If the skirting board is fixed slightly above floor level, tap the carpet into the gap.

Repeat the process for the other two walls and replace the door. If it sits too tightly on the carpet, remove a thin strip from the bottom (see *Door*).

Laying a foam-backed carpet Time: about a day

YOU WILL NEED Building paper, hammer tacker or staple gun, steel straightedge, trimming knife, carpet tacks, hammer, broom, dustpan, carpet tape, edging strip, screws, screwdriver.

COVERING THE FLOOR WITH PAPER Cover the floor with building paper fixed to the boards with a hammer tacker, staple gun or double-sided adhesive tape. Cut the paper short by the width of the carpet tape all round, leaving a strip for sticking the carpet to the floor later. The paper will prevent the foam backing from sticking to the floor.

Measure the room, and cut the carpet roughly to size, leaving at least 2.5 cm (1 in) surplus on all sides. Lay the carpet, allowing the surplus to ride up the skirting board.

Use a steel straightedge and trimming knife to trim the carpet carefully along one wall. Then temporarily tack the carpet in place along that wall so that it can't move. On a concrete floor, put down a few strips of double-sided tape.

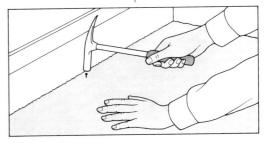

AVOIDING DAMAGE TO TILES OR PARQUET

It is possible to lay carpet on a decorative floor, such as tiles or parquet, without damaging the surface with glue or screws. Use liftable double-sided carpet tape which can later be peeled away leaving the floor unmarked. It can be used in any situation where you want to lay a temporary floor covering.

Knee kicker

A carpet stretcher (or knee kicker) has a spiked plate at one end to grip the carpet as you 'kick' the other end with your knee to stretch the carpet.

Move to the opposite wall, smooth the carpet as much as possible, then trim, leaving a 2.5 cm (1 in) surplus. Repeat the process for the remaining walls.

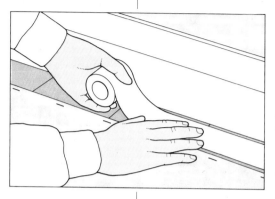

FIXING THE CARPET TO THE FLOOR Remove the tacks and lift the carpet, making sure you know which way it has to be laid. Make sure the floor is dry, clean and free of dust, then run strips of double-sided carpet tape around the edge of the room, bonding it firmly to the floor. Remove the backing paper.

Run more strips across the papered floor to form a chessboard pattern, removing the backing paper as you go. Carefully position the carpet, smooth out any wrinkles, then press down firmly to bond the carpet to the tape.

Stop carpet tiles from slipping

If carpet tiles are laid over an existing floor covering, such as sheet vinyl, you may find that they will slip under day-to-day pressure. You can prevent this from happening by putting down strips of double-sided carpet tape at regular intervals as you lay the tiles.

Carpet tiles for easy laying Time: about a day

If you have a small area or an awkward shape, carpet tiles are easier to lay. Types vary, but the usual method of laying is loose-fitting – butting the tiles against one another. Take the floor measurements to the carpet shop and get enough tiles to fill the space, with a few spares left.

If a wooden floor is in poor condition, put down sheets of hardboard first, smooth side up (see *Floorboards*). Nail them in place or use panel adhesive to secure them.

YOU WILL NEED Tape measure, chalked string, hammer, tacks, carpet tape, steel straightedge, coloured pencil, trimming knife.

FINDING THE STARTING POINT For the best results, always start laying the tiles from the centre of the room.

To establish the starting point, rub a length of string with coloured chalk. Tap in a tack at the centre points of two facing walls, tie the string taut from tack to tack, across the room, and snap a line to make a mark. Then do the same between the other two walls.

DEALING WITH A DOORWAY

In a doorway, fit an edging strip to cover the edge of the carpet and any other floor covering that meets it. Both single and double-edge strips are sold, for both plain and foam-backed carpets. The strip is nailed or screwed to the floor, then the covering section is tapped down to lock the carpet edge in place.

Having found the centre point, lay out rows of tiles along the chalked lines to find the ideal position for the central tile. You should ensure that the four sides of the room are edged with partial tiles of the maximum size. Try to avoid narrow strips of tile against a wall.

Use a strip of double-sided carpet tape to anchor the central tile in place. This will allow you to press adjoining tiles against it, without pushing it out of position. The adjoining tiles must be butted up tightly against it.

DEALING WITH THE EDGE OF THE ROOM When most of the tiles have been laid there will be a narrow strip of bare floor around the room. Lay a tile over one of the last-laid tiles. Lay another on top and slide it to the wall.

With a pencil of a contrasting colour, mark the edge of the top tile across the under tile. Then cut along the line, with a board underneath, using a steel straightedge and trimming knife. The cut piece will fit into the gap between wall and the last-laid tile.

All the last tiles to be laid should be anchored with strips of double-sided tape to keep them securely in place.

Carpet maintenance

(SEE ALSO STAINS)

Patching a damaged carpet Time: 2 hours or less

YOU WILL NEED Sharp trimming knife, adhesive carpet tape. Possibly: steel straightedge.

If a small area of carpet is severely damaged by, say, a burn or some spilt paint, the only solution may be to patch it. So whenever a new carpet is laid, keep a few offcuts in a polythene bag. If you have not kept any spare pieces of the carpet that needs patching, you will have to cut a patch from under a large piece of furniture.

Choose a matching piece of carpet, a little larger than the area to be repaired. Make sure the pile runs in the same direction by brushing it with your hand. Then lay the piece over the damaged spot, matching any pattern.

Hold the patch firmly in position and cut a rectangle through both the patch and the carpet beneath.

If the carpet has an underlay, be careful not to cut through it as well.

If the carpet is the type that has no raised pile, you can use a steel straightedge as a cutting guide. With others, you will have to cut freehand.

Remove the waste pieces. Take four pieces of double-sided carpet tape, and stick them to the floor or the underlay. Try to get the tape under the edge of the carpet so that both the carpet and the patch will be stuck down.

Put the patch into the hole and press it down firmly. Tease up the pile of the patch and the carpet around the join so that they blend together as well as possible.

Dealing with a dirty carpet

CLEANING SMALL PATCHES Use just enough carpet shampoo to moisten but not soak the area. (Some makes recommend using the foam only.) Lightly rub the shampoo over the surface, working inwards towards the centre of the patch. Wipe the area with a dry, clean cloth, removing as much moisture as possible.

CLEANING LARGE AREAS If you do not own a carpet shampooer or steam-cleaner, hire one from a dry-cleaner or hire shop. Many also sell cleaning fluids.

Leave the carpet to dry, preferably overnight, before walking on it or replacing furniture.

PROFESSIONAL ADVICE If you have any questions about the care or cleaning of carpets, contact the National Carpet Cleaners' Association, 126 New Walk, De Montfort Street, Leicester LE1 7JA (Tel. 01533 554352). They also offer a complaints and arbitration service.

Lifting a dent in a carpet Time: 1 hour or less

YOU WILL NEED Kitchen knife, clean cloth, iron.

When furniture is moved, it can leave dents in the carpet which may not rise naturally. They can be lifted with steam. But don't try putting a steam iron directly onto the carpet; it could melt artificial fibres.

Loosen the flattened pile with the tip of a knife, then cover it with layers of damp cloth. Apply a hot iron to produce steam, which will raise the pile. Allow the carpet to dry, then fluff it up with your fingers.

Avoiding wear on stair carpet Time: a day

Stair carpet gets heavy wear at the front of each tread, while the rest of the carpet is hardly touched. So it pays to move the carpet every year or so by about 7.5 cm (3 in) to spread the wear evenly.

YOU WILL NEED Tack lifter, hammer, carpet tacks, strip of hardboard, wooden spatula.

LIFTING THE CARPET Starting at the top of the stairs, look carefully to see how the stair carpet meets the landing carpet. If the stair carpet continues across the landing there's no problem.

Release the carpet from any edging strip, and use a tack lifter to remove tacks holding the end.

Roll the carpet down from the top, releasing it from the gripper teeth on each step as you go. Ease the teeth out – don't just pull – or you may damage the backing.

If the carpet is held by tacks, remove them with the tack lifter; if it is held by carpet rods, just remove them.

When you reach the bottom, you will probably find that the first step has a double layer of carpet – the bottom layer with the pile downwards. Remove the tacks and move the end away from the riser by about 7.5 cm (3 in) and tack it down again (wrong side upwards).

RELAYING THE CARPET You now have a small gap between the riser and the start of the carpet which can be filled with a strip of underfelt or folded newspaper.

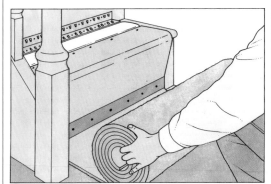

Take the carpet down to the base of the first riser and tack it in place through a strip of hardboard. Bring it back up and press it into the first gripper strip with a wooden spatula.

Work up the stairs, pushing the carpet onto the teeth, and making sure it is kept straight.

At the top of the stairs follow the original method of laying, folding over the surplus and tacking it down.

Replace any trim that you removed at the start.

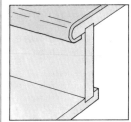

SAFETY FIRST WITH ELECTRICITY

Before starting any work on an electrical fitting or appliance, make sure to cut off the electricity supply – either by switching off at the main fuse box, or by unplugging the appliance.

TEST BEFORE YOU CLEAN

Before attempting to clean a carpet, test it for colour fastness by rubbing a small area with a light-coloured cloth moistened with the cleaning liquid. If the colour comes off onto the cloth, do not use the shampooer but call in a carpet-cleaning company (see page 69).

HOW TO AVOID FREQUENT HEAD-CLEANING

Always use a good make of tape in your cassette recorder. Do not be tempted by cheap tapes, which are often of poor quality. They can leave a deposit on the cassette heads, which will have to be cleaned frequently.

Carpet shampooer

A carpet shampooer is usually a 'wet-and-dry' vacuum cleaner with fittings that allow you to shampoo carpets. They are often called '3 in 1' cleaners.

How to avoid foaming

Use only the cleaning liquid recommended for your shampooer. Other solutions may create too much foam and take much longer to dry. If the carpet has been cleaned before with a foaming solution, use the shampooer-manufacturer's recommended defoaming agent with the correct cleaning liquid. It will reduce excessive foaming caused by the residue of old solution in the carpet.

Faultfinder guide: Carpet shampooer

If your machine goes wrong make the following checks before taking it to a repair shop.

Machine won't start

POSSIBLE CAUSE Loose connection or blown fuse.
ACTION Switch off the power at the wall socket and pull out the plug.

A modern moulded plug cannot be opened. Open an old-style plug and check that the wire connections are tight. Check the old fuse with a fuse tester (see *Fuse box*) or replace the fuse with a new one of the correct amp rating (see the rating plate).

Reassemble the plug, and plug in and test the carpet shampooer.

Machine runs but won't suck up water

POSSIBLE CAUSE Blocked suction pipe or inlet.
ACTION Switch off at the wall socket and pull out the plug. Remove the hose and nozzle from the shampooer and clear any obstruction from each section.

Check the inlet where the hose joins the body and clear any obstruction.

If the hose and nozzle sections are hard to separate, try holding them under a hot tap. Before refixing, spray the joints with neutral shoe polish or furniture wax. They will come apart easily next time.

Reassemble the hose and nozzle and switch on to see if the machine now works.

POSSIBLE CAUSE Full water tanks.
ACTION Switch off at the wall socket and pull out the plug. Check if the dirty-water tank is full. If it is, empty it, but handle it carefully because it can weigh as much as 18 kg (40 lb) when full.

Check the reservoir that holds the cleaning liquid solution. It may be empty. If it is, refill it.

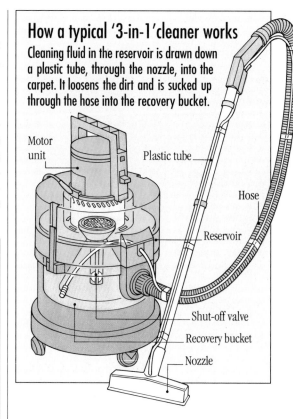

How a typical '3-in-1' cleaner works

Cleaning fluid in the reservoir is drawn down a plastic tube, through the nozzle, into the carpet. It loosens the dirt and is sucked up through the hose into the recovery bucket.

Motor unit

Plastic tube

Hose

Reservoir

Shut-off valve

Recovery bucket

Nozzle

Cassette recorder

Cleaning the casing and head Time: 1 hour or less

Cassette players need little cleaning if they are treated carefully and if good-quality cassettes are used. Apart from the compartment that is exposed when the tape door is open, do not try to clean the inside.

Switch off and unplug mains-operated recorders before starting. If the cassette unit is an integral part of a hi-fi system, unplug the whole system. With battery-operated recorders, remove the batteries to prevent the mechanism from operating while the head is being cleaned.

YOU WILL NEED Clean soft cloth, household spray cleaner, cotton bud and cleaning fluid, or head-cleaning tape.

THE CASING Before using any cleaning liquid, test it on a small area that is not normally visible, to ensure that it will not mark the finish.

Never use a cleaner that contains bleach or ammonia. Don't spray the cleaner directly onto the cassette recorder, and don't let the cleaner enter switches or controls. Spray the cleaner onto a cloth and avoid over-wetting.

Clean the cassette recorder case with the dampened cloth, and then polish off with a dry cloth.

THE HEADS AND PINCH ROLLER If the sound is muffled, the cause is probably a dirty recording head or playback head.

On some models you can reach the heads by opening the cassette compartment and operating the play mechanism without a tape being loaded.

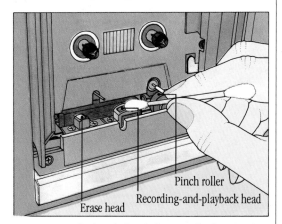

Erase head

Pinch roller

Recording-and-playback head

Coat a cotton bud with head-cleaning fluid and rub it across the head. Keep using fresh buds until no more dirt comes off. Using the same method, clean the pinch roller – the rubber wheel close to the heads.

Do not smoke or expose the cleaner fluid to a naked flame, as many head-cleaning fluids are flammable. Cleaning kits can be bought at hi-fi shops.

USING A HEAD-CLEANING TAPE If you can't get to the head, or are cleaning a car cassette player, buy a head-cleaning tape for cassette recorders and follow the instructions.

Freeing a jammed tape Time: 1 hour or less

Tapes can jam in a cassette player because of dirt on the pinch roller or because of condensation on the tape – which can occur when a tape is brought in from the cold.

> **YOU WILL NEED** Cleaning kit. Possibly: tape-splicing kit.

If a tape gets jammed, switch off and unplug the cassette recorder. Eject and remove the cassette, and then carefully pull the remaining tape free from the cassette player. In extreme cases, you may need to unwind the tape from the pinch roller or even cut the tape to extract it.

Once the tape is free of the cassette player, clean away any remaining particles of tape from the unit and then carefully rewind any loose tape back into the cassette case.

A pencil or ball-point pen makes a useful tool when rewinding tapes. Insert the pencil and turn it slowly, making sure that the tape rewinds without twisting. If it twists, pull it out slightly, straighten it and continue winding. Take care not to overwind it.

Faultfinder guide: Cassette recorders

Mains-powered recorder won't come on

- Make sure that the cassette recorder is plugged in and that both the mains socket and the recorder are switched on.
- If the power light still doesn't come on, check the mains socket by plugging in a table lamp, or some other appliance, and switching on. If it doesn't work, see *Electric sockets*. If the table lamp lights up, change the fuse in the recorder plug.
- If the recorder still doesn't work, take it to an electrical shop and ask if it is worth repairing.

Battery-powered recorder won't come on

- If the recorder has a lead, try using mains power.
- If it still won't work, the recorder is probably faulty and may be cheaper to replace than repair.
- If the recorder does operate on mains power, the fault lies with the batteries. Put in new batteries or recharge the rechargeable ones (see margin).
- If the fault persists, make sure that the battery connections are clean and are touching the batteries. Clean them with abrasive paper – an emery board used for filing fingernails is ideal. If the connections don't touch the batteries, remove the batteries and adjust them by bending them.
- If the recorder still fails to operate, the battery-powered mechanism is probably faulty. Either use it on the mains lead or return it for repair.

The tape fails to record

- Hold the cassette with the back edge facing you. At each end, there is a hole that should be covered by a plastic tab.
- If the tabs are missing, cover the holes with a small piece of sticky tape. Prerecorded cassettes have the tabs removed to stop you from recording over them unintentionally.
- If the cassette recorder still won't work, take it to a repair shop or replace it.

Tape plays at inconsistent speed

- Check that no tape is caught around the pinch roller. Then make sure the pinch roller is clean.

If the tape has been cut or broken, you can repair it with a tape-splicing kit which can be bought from a hi-fi shop. Follow the instructions that come with the kit.

It may be necessary to remove and discard a section of tape that has become badly creased or crinkled.

'BATTERY MEMORY EFFECT'

Do not top up rechargeable batteries after every use. Let them run right down first or they will not recharge fully. For example, if a cassette recorder has a rechargeable battery that lasts for an hour, and you recharge it every time you use it for a quarter of an hour, eventually the battery will only last for a quarter of an hour. This is because the battery 'remembers' how much it was recharged and works for only this period of time – 'battery memory effect'.

STORING CASSETTES SAFELY

Cassette tapes are coated with a magnetic layer that is affected by magnets, so they should not be stored near any magnetic source such as a loudspeaker or TV set. Keep cassettes in their cases and away from moisture. Never leave cassettes in direct sunlight in a car. They could become warped and unplayable.

Castors

Fitting a new plate castor Time: 1 hour or less

> YOU WILL NEED Bradawl, power or hand drill and a fine twist drill, screwdriver.

To put plate castors on a piece of furniture, first turn the furniture upside-down and support it, if necessary.

Position the castor plate centrally on the bottom of the leg and use a bradawl to mark the position of one of the screw holes. Make sure that the plate will be centrally sited when all the screws are in place.

Drill a fine pilot-hole for the screw. This stage is very important because it guards against splitting the wood at its weakest point when the screw is inserted.

Screw home the first screw and check that the castor plate is still in the correct position.

Then mark and drill pilot-holes for the three remaining screws through the plate, and screw them home.

Protect your carpet

Castor cups spread the load of the furniture over a much wider area than that of the castors alone.

This prevents indents from forming in a rug or carpet where a large, heavy object, such as a sofa or sideboard, stands in one place for a long time. Castor cups are available cheaply from most hardware stores.

Tightening loose screws on plate castors
Time: $\frac{1}{2}$ a day or less

Screws holding a castor to a furniture leg often work loose. It is possible to tighten them up yourself.

> YOU WILL NEED Screwdriver, scrap wood, chisel, mallet, trimming knife, bradawl, PVA wood glue, power or hand drill, fine twist drill.

Remove the castor by unscrewing the screws. Then use a sharp chisel or a trimming knife to make small, tapered pegs from scraps of softwood. Shape them to fit tightly into the screw holes in the leg of the furniture.

Apply a liberal coating of wood glue to the pegs and then gently tap them into the screw holes with a mallet. Drive them in as far as they will go.

Allow the glue to set thoroughly, and then carefully trim off any surplus wood with a trimming knife.

Put the castor plate against the leg base, positioning it centrally and use a bradawl to mark the position of one of the screw holes. Then drill a fine start-hole for the screw. This stage is essential – it reduces the danger of splitting the wood where it is weakest.

Screw home the first screw and check the position of the castor plate. Then mark and drill for the remaining screws and insert them too.

Replacing or fitting a peg-and-socket castor
Time: 2 hours or less

A peg-and-socket castor may need replacing, or you might want to fit castors to heavy furniture.

> YOU WILL NEED Power or hand drill and twist drill, mallet, tape measure or ruler.

Turn the piece of furniture upside-down. Use an old chisel to lever out any castors already in place. You may be able to use the existing holes for the new sockets. If castors have never been fitted, make new holes in each leg.

Draw two pencil lines on the bottom of each leg, diagonally from corner to corner, to form a cross and give you the exact centre of the furniture leg.

Drill a hole of the width and depth recommended in the castor instructions, where the lines intersect. Make sure that your drill is straight (see *Drill*).

Use a mallet to tap a socket into the hole. The serrated rim should sink into the furniture leg.

Apply a little petroleum jelly or grease to each castor peg then press them into the sockets. Tap each peg with the mallet until it clicks home.

Wheel castors can be fitted in any order, but if you are fitting ball castors, there are left and right castors. Fit the left-hand castors on diagonally opposite corners. Then put the right-hand castors on the remaining corners.

Fixing a split furniture leg Time: 1 hour

> YOU WILL NEED Screwdriver, chisel, wood glue, G-cramp, scraps of cardboard or hardboard, sandpaper, varnish, stain, mallet.

If the castor has a plate fitting, remove the holding screws. If it is a peg-and-socket fitting, lever out the socket with an old chisel.

Then open up the split with the tip of a chisel, apply a liberal coating of wood glue, press the parts together and hold them in place with a G-cramp.

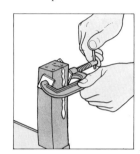

Use scraps of hardboard or card between the jaws of the cramp and the wood to make sure the furniture is not marked. Wipe away any surplus glue with a damp rag.

When the glue is set, smooth over the join with fine sandpaper to remove any rough areas. Then touch up with stain and varnish, and replace the castor.

If it is a peg-and-socket castor, separate the two parts so that you can tap the socket home with a mallet. Then firmly press the peg home into the socket.

Cats

Stop cats from soiling and scratching up seedbeds, by laying a cover of horticultural fleece, such as Agralan Envirofleece, secured with the pegs supplied or with bricks.

Delay planting seedlings until they are as robust as possible and protect them by barricading them with twigs or peasticks, or with frames made from wire hoops, draped with netting or clear plastic.

Bare, dug ground is especially attractive to cats, so keep flowerbeds and borders well-covered in foliage.

Chemical cat deterrents are expensive and of doubtful use. Some people say that you can keep cats out of your garden by leaving a sealed, clear plastic or glass bottle lying on the ground, half-full of water. It seems to be effective, but no one understands quite how it works.

Alternatively, try laying Catscat mats on open soil. The mats are anchored in the soil and have flexible plastic spikes that point upwards and discourage any cat that tries to dig a hole in the bed. The mats can be reused where necessary.

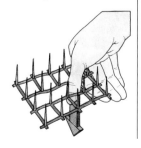

You are within the law to discourage cats by shouting or spraying water at them, and to make your garden and flowerbeds as unattractive as possible to them, but do not go beyond this and attempt to injure or kill them.

CD player: SEE HI-FI

Ceiling

One of the commonest ceiling problems is the appearance of cracks in the ceilings of first-floor bedrooms. They are often caused by heavy loads in the loft above. When you store heavy things in the loft, such as boxes of books, put them near supporting walls. Remember that loft joists are not as strong as floor joists, so don't overload them.

Fine hairline cracks Time: a day

> YOU WILL NEED Cotton dustsheet, stepladder, filling knife or paint scraper, fine surface filler, fine abrasive paper, sanding block, flexible ceiling paint, paintbrush or roller and tray, clean rags, safety spectacles.

Start by spreading a cotton dustsheet over the floor beneath the ceiling cracks.

Stand on a stepladder and remove any flaking material from the cracks with the filling knife. Then fill any larger cracks with fine surface filler.

Leave the filler to dry for a few hours, then lightly smooth rough areas with fine abrasive paper wrapped round a sanding block. Wipe over with lint-free rag, such as a piece of old sheet.

Coat the ceiling with flexible ceiling paint, following the instructions on the can. Ceiling paint remains elastic when dry, so it will hide fine cracks.

Larger ceiling cracks Time: parts of 2 days

> YOU WILL NEED Cotton dustsheet, safety spectacles, hat, stepladder, small trowel, old paintbrush, acrylic-based filler, fine abrasive paper, sanding block, emulsion paint, paintbrush or roller and tray.

Lay a cotton dustsheet on the floor beneath the cracks, cover your head and wear safety spectacles.

Standing on a stepladder, rake out the cracks with the point of a small trowel. Slightly undercut the plaster surrounding the crack, to give the filler something to grip, when it is applied.

Use an old paintbrush to remove dust, then fill the cracks with acrylic filler, which is more flexible than cellulose types.

Allow to dry overnight, then smooth with fine sandpaper wrapped round a sanding block. Repaint with emulsion.

Stains on the ceiling Time: a day or less

Most ceiling stains are caused by a fault in the plumbing system in the loft, or a leak in the roof. Before redecorating make sure that any leaks have been dealt with and that the stain has dried out.

> YOU WILL NEED Cotton dustsheet, stepladder, household cleaner, stain-blocking primer, matching emulsion paint, paintbrush.

Lay a dustsheet on the floor beneath the stain. Make sure that the ceiling is clean. If in doubt, wipe it over with a lint-free rag wrung out in water and either detergent or cleaning powder, such as Flash.

Coat the stained area with stain-blocking primer. It is available in cans or as an aerosol spray.

Allow the primer to dry, following the advice on the container, then repaint with emulsion paint.

Flaking paint Time: depends on the area

Flaking paint is usually found in older houses where distemper was once used on the ceilings. Distemper was a water-based paint, like whitewash. It makes a poor base for emulsion and often causes the new paint to flake off.

> YOU WILL NEED Cotton dustsheet, stepladder, safety spectacles, paint scraper, fine abrasive paper, sanding block, stabilising solution, paintbrush or roller and tray, coarse rags.

Spread a dustsheet over the floor. Standing on a stepladder, use a scraper to remove all the loose paint. Rub your hand on the ceiling and if a chalky deposit comes off, wipe it away with a coarse rag and plenty of warm water.

The chalky deposit is distemper, and if you feel you cannot remove every trace of it with the rag and water, rub the whole area smooth with fine abrasive paper wrapped round a sanding block.

Then coat the ceiling with stabilising solution, which will bond any remaining distemper to the ceiling.

Leave it to dry overnight, then redecorate the ceiling.

A bulge in the ceiling Time: parts of 2 days

A ceiling bulge is most likely to occur in an older house with lath-and-plaster ceilings. Over the years the plaster may lose its grip on the wooden laths. To do this job you will need to gain access from above.

If the ceiling is beneath the loft, it may be visible between joists. Otherwise, floorboards will have to be lifted in the room above (see *Floorboards*).

> YOU WILL NEED Stepladder, long piece of stout timber, a square piece of chipboard or thick plywood, vacuum cleaner, bonding plaster, bucket.

Get a helper to hold a square of board beneath the bulge while you wedge the length of timber tightly under it, pushing the ceiling back in place.

Remove the dirt from the upper surface of the ceiling, using a vacuum cleaner and attachment. Then pour a fairly runny mix of bonding plaster over the damaged area. It will anchor the damaged section in place.

Leave the timber prop in place for at least 24 hours until the plaster has set.

Removing old ceiling tiles Time: a day

Tiles made of expanded polystyrene may be fixed to ceilings to provide insulation or to create a decorative pattern. However, when you come to redecorate a room you may decide you no longer want them.

It is possible to remove them, but it is a tedious job and bits will fly about everywhere, so remember to protect your eyes with safety spectacles.

> YOU WILL NEED Cotton dustsheet, stepladder, paint scraper, safety spectacles, cotton gloves, hot-air gun.

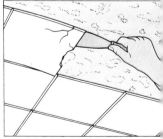

Slide a paint scraper under a tile and lift away as much of it as possible from the ceiling. Blobs or streaks of tile adhesive will probably be left behind on the ceiling.

Use a hot-air gun to warm the adhesive which should soften enough to be scraped off with a paint scraper. If the adhesive doesn't soften, chip it off with the paint scraper, but take care not to dig into the surface of the ceiling.

CRACKS THAT KEEP COMING BACK

You may find that some ceiling cracks are seasonal, caused by expansion and contraction of the fabric of the house or the foundations. These cracks are practically impossible to repair, as the force involved will crease or tear the toughest repair materials.

One possible solution is to fix expanded polystyrene or acoustic tiles to the ceiling. Or, if the cracks appear around the edge of the room, you could apply coving (see *Cornice & coving*). It will hide the cracks while still allowing them to move.

Papering after removing ceiling tiles

A fairly rough surface may be left after ceiling tiles have been removed. If so, the ceiling will have to be covered with textured paper — either Anaglypta or blown vinyl. Papering a ceiling is not easy, and you might decide to call in a professional to do the job.

Removing Artex-type coatings

If you want to convert a textured ceiling or wall back to a flat surface, you can use Artex Skimcoat which will give a smooth coating ready for redecorating.

It is possible to remove a textured coating completely, but the operation is very messy, so be sure to use plenty of dustsheets to protect the floor and furniture.

Never rub down a coating when it is dry. Older materials contained asbestos fibre, and the dust could be a danger to health. So always work with the surface wet.

YOU WILL NEED Dustsheets, steam wallpaper stripper, paint scraper, safety spectacles, cotton gloves, head covering. Possibly: coarse wet-and-dry abrasive paper, sanding block, rags.

Buy a steam wallpaper stripper or hire one from a tool-hire shop and use the steam it generates to soften the textured coating.

Then lift it away with a paint scraper. Protect your eyes and hands, and wear some form of head covering.

When most of the coating has been removed, you may need to smooth the surface with coarse wet-and-dry abrasive paper used wet and wrapped round a sanding block.

Keep the surface damp and wipe away the residue with a damp rag. When it has dried, redecorate it.

Central heating

(SEE ALSO BALL VALVE; HOT-WATER CYLINDER)

Understanding the system

BOILER Water is heated as it flows through the boiler. From there it travels to the radiators to heat the house. They may stand under a worktop, be fitted into the back of a fireplace or hang on a wall. Many boilers also produce hot water for domestic use (see *Hot-water cylinder*).

RADIATORS Most central-heating systems circulate hot water through radiators to warm the house. Two valves control the flow of hot water through each radiator – the hand valve which is used to turn the radiator off and on, and the lockshield valve, that needs pliers or an adjustable spanner to turn it, sets the flow of water to the radiator (see *Central-heating radiators*: 'Rebalancing the system').

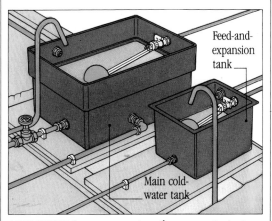

Feed-and-expansion tank

Main cold-water tank

OPEN SYSTEM In an open system, the same water is circulated constantly, but in case of any leaks and evaporation there is a top-up tank called the feed-and-expansion tank. This tank also accommodates the expansion of the water in the system as it is heated.

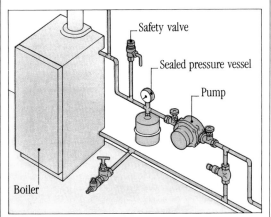

Safety valve

Sealed pressure vessel

Pump

Boiler

SEALED SYSTEM In a sealed system, the radiators and pipes are filled with water when the system is first installed. Any expansion of water in the system is accommodated by a sealed pressure vessel, partly filled with air.

An open-ended pipe, called the vent pipe, provides an escape route for air bubbles, steam and excess pressure in an open system. Sealed systems have a special preset safety valve to relieve any build-up of pressure.

PUMP In most systems, water is circulated by an electric pump which can be adjusted to work at different speeds. Setting the pump speed is a job for a heating engineer. All pumps should have isolating valves for easy replacement.

REMOVING TEXTURED PAINT

To find out if you have Artex or textured paint drop a flake of the coating into a cup of hot water. Artex will dissolve, textured paint will remain intact. Remove textured paint with proprietary textured paint remover.

PROTECTING THE CENTRAL-HEATING SYSTEM FROM FROST

If you do not have a frost thermostat and the house is left unoccupied for more than a few days during cold weather, the water in the heating and plumbing systems may freeze. An automatic central-heating system can help to lower the risk. Before you go away, set the timer so that it turns on during the coldest hours, for example, from 6 pm to 10 am. Turn down the thermostat so that heating is maintained at about 10°C (50°F). Open the hand valve at the end of each radiator. Make sure that the tanks and pipes in the loft are well-covered with insulation. There should be no insulation under the pipes or tanks, so as to allow heat up into the loft from the house.

TIME SWITCH The boiler and pump are turned on at pre-determined times by a time switch. Some models allow different settings on different days, to suit your needs.

What type of thermostat?

ROOM THERMOSTAT The thermostat senses the temperature of the air around it. It is set to the desired temperature then, when the air gets colder than this, the thermostat sends an electrical signal to switch the heating on. When the room temperature exceeds the preset level, the thermostat switches off the heating. The thermostat should be located on an inside wall in a room which will not be influenced by any heat source other than a radiator.

THERMOSTATIC RADIATOR VALVE The valve regulates the flow of water through a radiator. It is set to the desired room temperature and if the air is colder than this, the valve opens to allow a full flow of hot water through the radiator. Conversely, when the room is hot, the valve reduces the flow of water.

FROST THERMOSTAT It is usually used in addition to a normal room thermostat to try to prevent the whole system freezing up when the house is left empty.
    The central heating is under the control of the frost thermostat rather than the room thermostat. The heating is turned on when the temperature falls to a preset level, for example 3°C (37°F).

Faults in open-vented systems

A problem in open-vented systems is 'pumping over', where water is pumped out of the expansion pipe into the feed-and-expansion tank. It is a good idea to check for this problem whenever you are in the loft. Pumping over introduces oxygen into the system, and will cause corrosion.

Air can also be pulled into the system by the pump when it starts up, if it has been badly located. You can recognise this problem if there is a rush of air through the expansion pipe when the pump is started.

If you suspect that you have either of these common problems, don't try to fix them yourself; call a central-heating engineer (see margin) as soon as possible, otherwise you could end up making expensive repairs.

FINDING A HEATING ENGINEER

The engineer who installed a system is often the best one to service it. Alternatively, call your local gas company.

Otherwise, the Heating and Ventilating Contractors' Association will supply the names of reputable heating engineers in your area. They can be contacted at Esca House, 34 Palace Court, London W2 4JG (Tel. 0171 229 2488). Only installers registered with CORGI (Council for Registered Gas Installers) may carry out work on gas boilers.

Central-heating boiler

Stopping a leaking boiler Time: 3 hours or less

YOU WILL NEED Torch, strong stick, garden hose.

Turn off the boiler and the central-heating system. If you have gas central heating, turn out the pilot light. Turn off the water at the main stopcock (usually located under the kitchen sink or in the cellar).

Go into the loft. Turn off the water supply to the cold-water tank or the smaller feed-and-expansion tank, if there is one. Either turn off the service valve to the tank or tie up the float arm of the ball valve (see *Ball valve*). Then empty the tank by opening the cold taps in the bathroom.

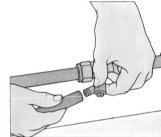

Connect one end of a hose to the drain cock, next to the boiler. Run the other end of the hose outside or into a toilet.

Open up the drain cock and drain off the water. You can now turn the main stopcock on again in order to restore the cold-water supply to the kitchen tap.
    Call a central-heating engineer (see margin, left).

Central-heating noise

The boiler, pump and circulating water in a central-heating system will make a certain amount of noise.

Quietening a noisy boiler

Some noise from the boiler is inevitable. If scale and corrosion debris collect in the boiler and restrict the water flow, the boiler may make a noise called 'kettling'. Using a chemical cleaner and then a corrosion-proofer in the system may reduce the noise (see *Central-heating radiators*).

Dealing with a noisy pump

If the pump is humming or making a rushing noise, turn off the central heating and call a heating engineer.

Quietening noisy pipes

AIR NOISE IN PIPES AND RADIATORS Air noises, like the sound of rushing water in pipes or radiators is usually due to air trapped in the system. Try bleeding the radiators with the pump turned off (see *Central-heating radiators*). If this does not solve the problem, call a qualified central-heating engineer; there could be a major fault.

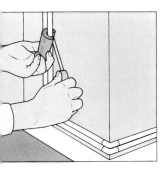

CREAKING PIPES As pipes expand and contract they creak and groan, especially where they touch the floor joists and walls. Pad these areas with foam plastic to reduce the amount of noise the pipes make.

HUMMING PIPES Humming in pipes is usually caused by vibration, which may be cured by the addition of extra support brackets along the pipes, where possible.

The noise may be the result of water moving too quickly through the system, either because the pipes are too small or they are carrying too much water. Call a central-heating engineer to adjust the system.

Central-heating radiators

Bleeding a radiator Time: a few minutes

A radiator that is cold at the top probably has air in it. Turn the central-heating pump off to give the air time to settle, then 'bleed' it out of the radiators.

> YOU WILL NEED Radiator key, piece of rag.

At the top of one end of the radiator you will find a square-ended valve – this is the air vent.

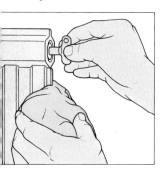

Push the radiator key over the valve-end; hold a rag underneath it with one hand to catch any drips of water, then twist the key half a turn anticlockwise.

Do not turn the radiator key too far, or the valve will drop out and be difficult to replace.

The escaping air will hiss. When the hissing stops and water starts to escape, quickly close the air vent by turning the key firmly clockwise. The radiator should become hot again in minutes as circulation is restored.

If, when you try to bleed the radiator, nothing comes out, the small bleed hole behind the screw in the vent may be blocked. Turn off both radiator valves (see 'Closing the valves', overleaf), remove the screw and unblock the hole with a needle. Replace the screw, open the valves and bleed the radiator, as described above.

Ball valve jammed closed Time: 1 hour or less

When top-floor radiators run cold and neither air nor water comes out when you try to bleed them, it is probably because the water level in the system has dropped, due to evaporation or a leak, and the feed-and-expansion tank has failed to refill it. The ball valve supplying the feed-and-expansion tank may have jammed closed.

Examine the central-heating system for evidence of a leak. Pay particular attention to radiator valves and the carpet below them. Once any leaks have been dealt with, unjam the ball valve of the feed-and-expansion tank.

> YOU WILL NEED Torch, WD40.

Go into the loft and find the feed-and-expansion tank of your central-heating system. It is smaller than the main cold-water tank, and it will probably be empty.

Move the ball float downwards, and water will flow into the tank. Spray WD40 onto the moving parts of the ball valve to prevent them from sticking again.

Once the ball valve is working you will probably need to bleed the upstairs radiators in order to get them working properly again (see 'Bleeding a radiator', left).

If the problem recurs, call a central-heating engineer to check for leaks in the system.

KEEPING A BALL VALVE WORKING

Whenever you have to go up into the roof space jog the ball valve on the feed-and-expansion tank to make sure that it is working.

Faultfinder guide: Central-heating radiators

Radiator cold on top, hot at bottom

CAUSE Air trapped.
SOLUTION Bleed radiator (see left).

Radiators at the top of the house cold

CAUSE The ball valve in the feed-and-expansion tank has jammed.
SOLUTION Free the ball valve in the feed-and-expansion tank (see above).

CAUSE Leak in system.
SOLUTION Repair leak. Refill system.

Patches of cold on a radiator

CAUSE Corrosion.
SOLUTION Flush out the radiator (see overleaf).

Some rooms hot but others cold

CAUSE Unbalanced system.
SOLUTION Rebalance the system (see page 79).

A fine jet of water spraying out of the radiator

CAUSE Pinhole leak due to corrosion.
SOLUTION Fill the hole (see overleaf).

Central-heating radiators (cont.)

UNSCREWING A RADIATOR UNION NUT

The union nut on a radiator is joined to the radiator, not the valve. To remove or loosen it, turn it in an anticlockwise direction, looking from the radiator to the valve.
The nut may require some force to shift it.
To avoid bending the pipe below the valve, hold it with a Footprint wrench while turning the union nut with an adjustable spanner.

Flushing out a blocked radiator Time: ½ a day or less

If a radiator needs bleeding often and has cold patches on its surface, it may be corroded inside. Corrosion produces hydrogen gas, which causes air locks, and ferric oxide, which blocks the radiator.

> YOU WILL NEED Adjustable spanner, Footprint wrench, pliers, radiator key, two bowls, bucket, garden hose, jointing paste.

Turn off both the valves on the radiator (see below).

REMOVING THE RADIATOR The radiator is full of dirty water. Protect the carpet under the radiator valves and on a route to the nearest outside door.

Use a radiator key to open the air vent (see 'Bleeding a radiator', previous page). Place a bowl under one of the valves and undo the union nut (see margin, left). Water will flow out of the valve and into the bowl. Swap the bowl for an empty one and pour the water into a bucket. Pull the valve away from the radiator.

Repeat the process with the other valve. The radiator should now be more or less empty. Lift it off its supports and carry it outside. You may need help to carry it.

FLUSHING OUT THE RADIATOR Use a hose to flush water through the radiator to remove any debris.

REPLACING THE RADIATOR Smear a little jointing paste on the thread of the valves and connect them up. Fully open the hand valve and use pliers to open the lockshield valve by the same number of turns that it took to close it. Do not close the air vent until water starts to run out.

Closing the valves

To close the hand valve on a radiator turn it clockwise. This stops the water flow through the radiator.
To close the lockshield valve, first take out the screw and remove the plastic cap. Then use pliers to turn the spindle of the valve clockwise until it will not turn any further. Count the number of turns it takes to do so. To open the valves reverse the process.

Repairing a pinhole leak Time: 1 hour or less

If a radiator becomes corroded, it can develop a pinhole leak and a fine jet of water will spurt out.

> YOU WILL NEED Pliers, abrasive paper, two-part epoxy repair paste, rubber gloves, matching radiator enamel, paintbrush.

Close both valves (see box, below left). Keep count of the number of turns it takes to close the lockshield valve, as you will need to open it the same amount, later.

Drain the water from the radiator to below the level of the leak (see 'Removing the radiator', left) to reduce pressure in the radiator enough to allow the repair to be made.

Use abrasive paper to rub off the paint for about 1.3 cm (½ in) round the pinhole leak, until you see bare metal.

Cut off equal quantities from two sticks of epoxy paste. Then, wearing rubber gloves, knead the pieces of paste to an even colour with your fingers.

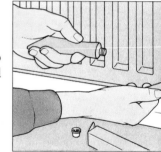

Apply the epoxy paste to the leak. It will set hard within minutes.

Restore pressure to the radiator by opening the valves, turning the lockshield valve anticlockwise as many turns as it took to close (see box, below left).

Finally, touch up the paint on the radiator.

Fixing a leaking radiator nut Time: 1 hour or less

> YOU WILL NEED Adjustable spanner, Footprint wrench, Fernox LS-X leak sealer, PVC tape, abrasive paper, matching radiator enamel, paintbrush.

If a radiator is leaking at a nut, try tightening the nut. Take care not to buckle the pipe (see margin, left).

If the leak persists press Fernox LS-X leak sealer around the area of the leak, pushing it into the joints. Bind the repair with PVC tape and leave it for 2 hours to set.

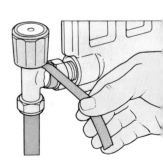

Remove the tape and smooth down the repair with abrasive paper. Then paint it to match the radiator.

Rebalancing the system Time: 1 day or less

If some radiators consistently remain cooler than others or take longer to heat up, try to rebalance the system. A system may also need rebalancing if a radiator is added.

When a central-heating system is installed it is balanced to make sure that each radiator gets the right flow of water. Because water flows most readily round the radiators nearest to the pump, lockshield valves are fitted to even out the water flow through the system. The valves restrict flow through the radiators at the beginning of the circuit and are open more fully on subsequent radiators.

> **YOU WILL NEED** Small adjustable spanner, screwdriver, pipe thermometer.

Put the central-heating timer switch to an 'on' phase and turn up the thermostat to full heat. Then open both valves on each radiator by turning them anticlockwise.

Work through the radiators in the house, starting at the radiator nearest to the boiler and moving in sequence around the circuit away from the boiler. Turn down the lockshield valve on each radiator so that the temperature difference between the flow and return pipes is roughly 11 °C (52°F). On the last radiator the lockshield valve should be almost fully open.

If a room is still too cold when the radiator is fully on you may need additional heating in the room.

Draining a central-heating system Time: ½ a day

Central-heating systems should be drained only when absolutely necessary. Because if air is frequently allowed to come into contact with wet internal surfaces, serious internal corrosion can result.

> **YOU WILL NEED** Spanner, pliers, radiator key.

DRAINING THE SYSTEM Switch off the boiler at the timer switch and either pull out the plug that provides electricity to the system, or take out the fuse at the house's main fuse box (see *Fuse box*).

Turn off the fuel, either at the isolating cock near the boiler or next to the meter. If you have a solid-fuel boiler, make sure the fire is out and the boiler is cold.

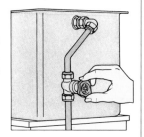

Stop the water supply to the feed-and-expansion tank. There should be a separate gate valve to control this.

If there is no gate valve, you can stop the water flow into the tank by tying the ball valve to a piece of wood which you have laid across the top of the tank.

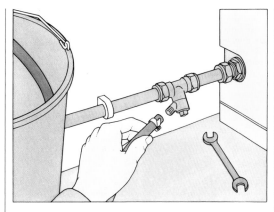

Find the drain cock, which may be near the bottom of the boiler, or low down on the heating system. Connect one end of a garden hose to it, using a clip if necessary, and take the other end outside or down a toilet.

Open up the drain cock with a spanner or pliers. Start opening the air vents on the radiators at the top of the house. This will gradually speed up the rate of water flow through the hosepipe. As the rate falls again open up the air vents on the lower radiators.

When all the water has drained away close all vents in case the water is accidentally turned back on.

REFILLING THE SYSTEM Close all the drain cocks and all the air vents in the central-heating system. Check that all work on the system has been finished.

Open the gate valve to the feed-and-expansion tank, or untie the ball valve, to let water in.

Open one of the air vents on the lowest radiator, until water starts to flow out, then close it. Repeat this with the air vents on all the radiators on the lowest floor, until the bottom of the system is full of water. Then do the upper radiators and check the system for leaks.

Make sure that the ball valve to the feed-and-expansion tank has closed itself off and that the water level in the cistern is just enough to float the ball. The remainder of the tank space is to allow for the expansion of the water in the system as it heats.

If the level is too high, close off the mains water to the tank. Open the drain cock and let some water out. Adjust the arm on the ball valve so that it closes the valve at the correct level (see *Ball valve*).

Remove the hose from the drain cock. Make sure that the drain cock is watertight. If it is leaking, you will have to drain the system again and call an engineer.

Switch on the electricity and turn on the gas. Relight the pilot light in a gas boiler, and the fire in a solid fuel or oil burning boiler. Turn on the system at the timer switch.

As the system heats up more venting will be necessary to get rid of air driven off from the water. Minor venting may be required for several days.

PREVENTING INTERNAL CORROSION

The iron oxide produced by internal corrosion in a central-heating system causes leaks and uneven heating, and is frequently the cause of early pump failure. You can avoid these problems by having a corrosion proofer added to the central-heating system.
A welcome side effect may be a quieter boiler.
It is essential that the correct corrosion proofer is used for the system, so consult a reputable heating engineer.

Ceramic tiles

Replacing a damaged tile Time: 2 hours or less

If a tile gets damaged, it is possible to replace it even when it is surrounded by others.

> **YOU WILL NEED** Safety spectacles, protective gloves, hand or power drill, masonry bit, 12 mm ($\frac{1}{2}$ in) cold chisel, club hammer, new tile, tile adhesive, notched spreader, X-spacers, grout, piece of sponge, damp rag, newspaper.

Wearing safety spectacles and gloves, drill holes in the damaged tile to give a starting point for the cold chisel.

Use the chisel and club hammer to cut away the old tile, working from the centre outwards. Take care not to chip the surrounding tiles. Chip off any remaining adhesive and grouting.

Check that your new tile fits the space, then butter the back of it with tile adhesive, using the notched spreader.

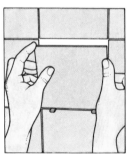

Press the tile into place, making sure there is even spacing all round. A few pieces of cardboard or even uncooked spaghetti can be used as spacers if there are no X-spacers handy.

RENEWING THE GROUT Mix a small amount of grout and press it into the gap with a piece of sponge. Smooth it with a finger and remove any surplus with a damp rag. A mixture of tile adhesive and grout is extremely hard to remove once it has dried, so clean the wall well while it is wet.

Wait two or three hours for the grout to harden, then polish the tiles with a ball of screwed-up newspaper.

How to cut tiles

When replacing damaged part-tiles, you will have to cut the new ones to fit. Cut the tiles with a straightedge and a hand-held cutter or, if tiles are tough, buy or hire a platform tile cutter. A small wheel cutter or stylus cutter may still be needed to remove strips narrower than about 5 mm ($\frac{3}{16}$ in). Protect your eyes with safety spectacles.

> **YOU WILL NEED** Metal straightedge, safety spectacles, tile cutter, china-marker pencil, tile file. Possibly: pliers, tile saw, G-cramp.

To cut a tile by hand, work on the glazed side. Hold a metal straightedge along the cutting line and stroke the tile cutter along it in one smooth stroke, cutting through the glaze only. Then place a pencil under the score line. Press down lightly on both edges of the tile to snap it.

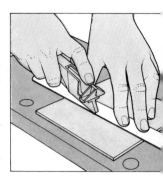

Should you have to remove a narrow section at the edge of the tile, snap off the waste with pincers or pliers.

To use a platform cutter, place the tile on the platform and align it with the cutter, using the measuring rule. Hold the tile in place, and run the cutting wheel away from you. Make sure you hear it 'whisper' as the wheel scores the tile glaze. After scoring, press down lightly on the arm, and the tile will snap along the scored line.

Clean up the cut line with a tile file, working with down-strokes while holding the glazed side upwards.

CUTTING OUT A CURVE Mark the line of cut with a china-marker pencil, then lay the tile flat on a bench with the part which is to be cut overhanging the edge.

Use a tile saw to remove the unwanted section. The tungsten-coated blade of the saw is circular so it cuts in any direction.

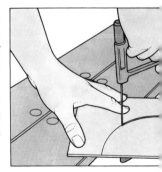

If necessary, clamp the tile to the work surface while you are cutting, but be careful not to damage it.

CUTTING OUT A RECTANGLE If you want to remove the corner of a tile, use a saw to cut one line, then score the second line on the glazed face with a tile cutter.

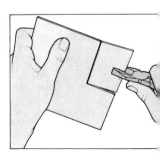

Snap off the unwanted piece with pliers (right).

Drilling holes in tiles

When drilling into tiles, always make a hole in the body of the tile. Drilling into the joints can chip the tile edges.

> **YOU WILL NEED** China-marker pencil, clear adhesive tape, hand drill or power drill, sharp masonry bit.

Mark the position of the first hole with china-marker pencil, then place a cross of clear adhesive tape over it.

Choose a masonry bit of the correct size for the wall plug and screw that will be used.

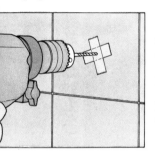

Put the drill tip on the mark and gently press until a dimple is formed in the glaze. As you start to drill, the tape will hold the bit in place and prevent it from skating over the glaze.

With a power drill, start on the lowest speed then speed up as the drill bites into the tile. Drill deep enough to allow the wall plug to sink below the tile; otherwise the tile may split when the plug expands as the screw is driven in.

Regrouting tiles Time: a day or less

If the grout in a tiled wall breaks up and falls out, a whole area may have to be regrouted.

> **YOU WILL NEED** Old penknife, old paintbrush, grout (use waterproof grout around a bath or shower), piece of sponge or rubber squeegee, clean rag, newspaper.

Dig out crumbling or discoloured grout with the blade of a penknife and brush out debris with an old paintbrush.

Use a piece of sponge or a rubber squeegee to apply the new grout. Wipe away the surplus grout with a damp rag, then use your finger or the cap of a ball-point pen to round off the grouting lines.

Leave it to dry for a few hours, then polish thoroughly with a ball of screwed-up newspaper.

Sealing between bath and wall Time: parts of 2 days

The gap where a wall meets a bath, basin or shower tray can be sealed with flexible sealing strips or silicone-rubber sealant. For details on how to use them, see *Sealants*.

Matching ceramic quadrant pieces are also available to give a neat finish to many sorts of tiles.

> **YOU WILL NEED** Ceramic quadrant moulding, tile adhesive, white silicone-rubber sealant, waterproof grout, clean rag.

Make sure you buy enough quadrant pieces to go the full length of the area to be sealed. Thoroughly clean the surfaces which will receive the quadrant pieces.

Spread tile adhesive on the backs of the quadrants, covering only the part that meets the wall. Press them firmly into place, matching the joins to the spacing between the tiles.

Allow the adhesive to set overnight, then seal the lower edge where the quadrant meets the bath or basin with white silicone-rubber sealant. The sealant stays slightly flexible to allow for the movement between surfaces which is common with baths and shower trays.

Finish by grouting between sections of quadrant to match the rest of the tiling. Wipe off excess grout.

Fitting a new soap dish Time: parts of 2 days

> **YOU WILL NEED** New soap dish, tile adhesive, clear adhesive tape, waterproof grout, duster. Plus tools for replacing a damaged tile (facing page) and tools for regrouting (left).

Remove a tile where you want to put the soap dish (see 'Replacing a damaged tile', facing page).

Clean out any remaining adhesive, then butter the back of the new soap dish with tile adhesive. Press the dish firmly in place, ensuring that the spacing is correct.

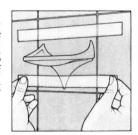

Then secure it to the surrounding tiles with strips of adhesive tape or masking tape, to prevent the weight of the soap dish from pulling it away from the wall.

Allow the adhesive to set overnight, then remove the tape and grout around the dish (see 'Regrouting tiles').

> ## Avoiding problems with ceramic tiles
> When buying ceramic tiles, always get a few spares and store them away in case they are needed later. It is often impossible to buy odd matching tiles, and they certainly won't be from the same batch, so the colours will be slightly different.
>
> Never mark the reverse side of a tile with a felt-tip pen. The unglazed part is porous, and the ink can sink through to the underside of the glaze. It will then be visible on the tile face and it can't be removed. Always make any marks on the glazed face, using a china-marker pencil which is easily wiped off.

Chair (SEE ALSO UPHOLSTERY)

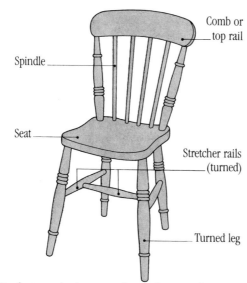

Comb or
top rail

Spindle

Seat

Stretcher rails
(turned)

Turned leg

Replacing a broken stretcher rail or spindle
Time: ½ a day or less

Some chairs have stretcher rails and spindles which have been turned on a lathe, and others have straight ones. It is unlikely that a replacement for a broken turned rail can be bought, so it will need repairing (see *Baluster*) before you fit it back into the chair.

However, if the broken rail is straight, you may be able to replace it with a piece of dowel. Take a piece of the broken rail with you when you buy its replacement and match it as closely as possible in colour, weight and shape.

> YOU WILL NEED Mallet or rubber hammer, bradawl, dowel or replacement rail, saw, sandpaper or rasp, PVA wood glue, cloth.

Tap the broken rail gently with a mallet or rubber hammer to get it out of its sockets in the chair legs. If it does not come out cleanly, use the bradawl to clear out any old bits of glue and wood.

Cut the replacement rail to the correct length, allowing for the sections that will fit into the sockets. With sandpaper or a rasp, shape the ends to fit into the holes snugly.

Cover both ends of the replacement rail – or the repaired rail – with wood glue and fit them into position. There should be enough flexibility in the legs to allow you to do this. Press the chair legs towards each other to apply pressure to the joint. The legs may need clamping, to keep a constant pressure on them while the glue dries. Use the tourniquet method (see margin, left).

Because floors are not always level, this part of the task should be done with the chair on a level surface such as a table. It will ensure that the legs set at the correct angle and the chair doesn't wobble later, when it is used.

Wipe off any excess glue with a damp cloth while it is still wet. Allow it to dry thoroughly before using the chair.

TOURNIQUET METHOD OF CLAMPING

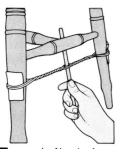

Tie a couple of lengths of string round the legs and protect the wood with wads of paper. Insert a stick or pencil between the strings and wind it round and round, twisting the string until the joint has been pulled tight. Catch the stick under a convenient rail to prevent it from unwinding.

Tightening loose legs and joints Time: ½ a day or less

> YOU WILL NEED Mallet or rubber hammer, sandpaper, wood glue, string, small stick, screwdriver and screws.

RAIL OR LEG JOINT Carefully knock the joint apart with a mallet or rubber hammer. Using sandpaper, take off all old, hard glue, right back to the wood surface.

SEAT JOINT Where a seat joint has come loose, check the reinforcing blocks in the corners below the seat. If they are fixed by screws, take out the screws and remove the blocks.

Clean the blocks with sandpaper and glue them back into place. Secure them in place with new, slightly larger-gauge screws driven into the existing holes.

Adjusting the length of a leg Time: ½ a day or less

> YOU WILL NEED Sandpaper, scraps of hardboard or plywood, trimming knife, wood glue. Possibly: wood stain or varnish.

Chairs will wobble if one leg is too long or too short.

If a chair leg is too long, it is probably only by a small amount. The easiest way to fix it is to use sandpaper to carefully rub away some of the leg end. Keep testing it on a smooth, hard, level surface until it stops wobbling.

If the chair leg is too short, experiment with thin slivers of hardboard or plywood. Build them up one by one until the chair stops wobbling. Test it on a hard, smooth, level surface.

Glue the slivers to the leg end and to each other and allow them to dry. When they are dry, trim off the excess wood with a trimming knife and smooth the end with sandpaper. Stain or varnish the added wood if necessary.

Chewing gum

Chewing gum stuck to a carpet or clothing can be removed with purpose-made products sold in some chemists and hardware shops. Follow the maker's instructions and test the product on a small, unseen area first.

Alternatively, leave the garment in a plastic bag in a freezer overnight, or hold a plastic bag of ice cubes over it for a while to harden the gum. With your fingernails or a blunt knife, pick the gum off the surface.

Then use a liquid stain remover on any remaining marks, and launder or sponge the area with warm water.

Chimney breast
Curing a damp patch

The most common cause of damp on a chimney breast is an unused and unventilated chimney. Rain or damp air collects in the flue and penetrates into the room.

First, have the chimney pot capped. This may be a job for a builder because it involves climbing on the roof. Then, if the fireplace has been sealed off, fit a ventilator.

> YOU WILL NEED Small plastic 'hit-and-miss' ventilator, pencil, padsaw or jigsaw, hand or power drill, twist bits. Possibly: screws and screwdriver or contact adhesive.

Mark the outline of the ventilator on the panel covering the fireplace, making it slightly smaller than the ventilating area of the ventilator. Drill holes in the four corners to accommodate the saw blade and cut out the opening.

Fit the ventilator over the hole with screws, or – if the panel is thin – stick it on with contact adhesive, following the instructions on the container.

Close the ventilator to prevent draughts when it's cold.

Chimney fire

! As soon as you realise that the chimney is on fire, telephone 999 and ask for the Fire Brigade.

Pull all movable carpets, rugs and furniture well back from the hearth. Then damp down the fire in the hearth, preferably using a watering can with some washing-up liquid added to the water. Sprinkled water is less likely to cause steam and smoke to blow into the room, and the detergent helps the water to 'stick' to the burning fuel.

Place a spark guard in front of the fireplace to prevent the fire spreading from the fireplace into the room. Then close all the windows and leave the room, closing the door behind you to restrict the air supply to the fire.

China & porcelain

No matter how careful you are, china and porcelain does get damaged. If the piece is part of a set or has sentimental value, it is worth trying to mend it.

Repairing a broken handle Time: 1 hour or less

> YOU WILL NEED Acetone, bowl containing sugar, rice or sand, epoxy-resin glue, masking tape, craft knife.

Handles tend to break at the point where they join the body of the cup, mug or jug. If the break is clean, it can be glued. Anything that holds hot liquid needs a heatproof join so use a heatproof epoxy-resin glue.

Clean the broken edges with acetone. Then place the cup or mug in a bowl of sugar, rice or sand so that the fragments of the broken handle are facing upward.

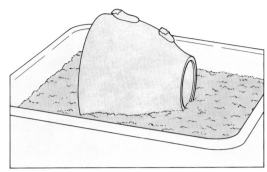

Following the manufacturer's instructions, apply glue to both faces of each break and press them together firmly. Feel the join with a fingernail to make sure of a perfect fit.

Use a strip of masking tape to hold the join while it is drying. The tape will come off easily afterwards. At normal room temperatures, the glue will set in 10 minutes. Once it is dry, remove any excess glue with the tip of a craft knife.

Until it has hardened, epoxy resin can be washed off hands and other surfaces with warm soapy water.

Repairing a chipped surface Time: ½ a day or less

When repairing a chip, buy a coloured epoxy putty that matches the colour of the china as closely as possible.

> YOU WILL NEED Very fine wet-and-dry abrasive paper, epoxy putty, craft knife. Possibly: matching enamel paint, clear lacquer and brushes.

Clean the damaged area of the china with very fine wet-and-dry paper, used dry, to make sure that there is no grease or soap left on it. Then prepare the epoxy putty, following the manufacturer's instructions.

Smooth some of the epoxy putty into the damaged patch of china so that it stands slightly proud of the surrounding area and leave the putty to dry for about half an hour.

Moisten a piece of fine wet-and-dry abrasive paper with water and rub the patched area until it is smooth and flush with the surrounding china.

If the colour of the putty does not match the china, touch it up with an appropriate enamel paint and then apply a coat of clear lacquer to the patch.

Stacking fine china

Sometimes the footing on a china plate is unglazed and may scratch the surface of the plate beneath it. Put paper towel between plates to protect them.

HAVING A CHIMNEY SWEPT

Chimney fires are often the result of neglect. Have a used flue swept once a year, especially if coal or wood is burned. Look in *Yellow Pages* under 'Chimney sweeps' for members of the National Association of Chimney Sweeps.

EXPERT HELP

You may not feel confident enough to mend a particularly precious piece of china. Help is available through the Conservation Register of the Museums and Galleries Commission, 16 Queen Anne's Gate, London SW1H 9AA. Call them on 0171 233 3683 and, for a small fee, they will send you the names of five repairers in your area.

Chip-pan fire

If a chip pan or frying pan catches fire, turn off the heat on the cooker immediately. Do not move the pan; flames could blow back, forcing you to drop it.

Cover the pan with a large pan lid, or with a fire blanket or damp towel to smother the flames. Do not throw water on it.

Leave a chip pan that contains a large amount of oil to cool for half an hour before removing the covering.

Chisels

The angle of the blade

A chisel blade has a main angle of 25 degrees, but the cutting edge is honed to 30 degrees. When buying a chisel, make sure the 30 degrees angle has already been honed.

How to sharpen a chisel

Blunt chisels do a poor cutting job. They are also dangerous because they can slip on wood, rather than cutting it, not only damaging the wood you are working on, but also possibly injuring you. So keep them sharp. You can either do it by hand, using an oilstone with a honing guide, or use a sharpening attachment fitted to a power drill.

BY HAND Buy an oilstone with medium grit on one side and fine on the other. The medium side will remove metal quickly, and the fine will give a final keen edge. Lightly oil the stone. Secure the chisel in the honing guide at an angle of 30 degrees, following the maker's instructions.

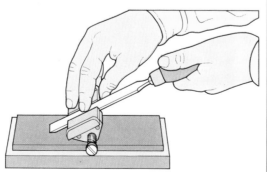

Roll the edge of the chisel back and forth over the stone, spreading the wear over all parts of the stone's surface. A slight burr will form, which you can feel with your nail.

Turn the blade over and rub the flat side lightly on the stone. Continue rubbing both sides until the burr breaks off. You will then have a keen edge to work with.

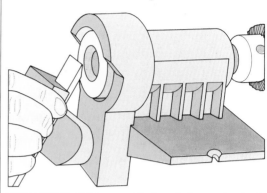

WITH A POWER ATTACHMENT Fit the spindle into the chuck of a power drill. Then put the chisel on the guide, following the maker's instructions. Sharpen lightly; the blade must not overheat while you are sharpening it.

How to use a chisel

Anchor the wood firmly to a workbench with G-cramps so that both hands are free. Use a mallet with a wood-handled chisel; hammers can only be used on plastic handles.

MORTISE CHISEL Start a mortise joint by using a drill to make a line of holes slightly smaller than the final width.

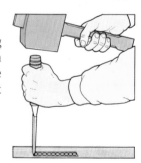

Cut away the remaining wood, holding the chisel in one hand and tapping the handle with a wood mallet held in the other.

BEVEL-EDGE CHISEL To make a halving joint or any other recess in wood, use a tenon saw to cut guidelines at each end of the area of wood which is to be removed.

Hold the chisel in one hand and guide the blade with the other to slice away the unwanted wood.

STORING CHISELS Never leave a chisel where it can fall; the blade is sharp enough to injure. Don't allow chisel blades to knock against each other – they damage easily.

CHISELS

Four types of chisel are used for DIY work around the house. Both the bevel-edge and mortise chisel are used for work with wood. The bevel-edge chisel is driven by hand, and the mortise chisel is used with a wooden mallet.
A cold chisel is used with a hammer to cut metal and a brick bolster is used with a club hammer for cutting bricks (see *Hammers*). Always protect your hands when working with a hammer and cold chisel or bolster.

PLASTIC BLADE GUARD New chisels are sold with plastic guards for the blades. Always protect the chisel with the guard when it is not being used, both to prevent damage to the cutting edge and to avoid injuring yourself.

BEVEL-EDGE CHISELS Designed for paring away wood, as in a halving joint. It is thinner than a mortise chisel, and is held in one hand and guided with the other. The bevel allows under-cutting, as when making dovetail joints.

MORTISE CHISEL Designed for making holes, such as the mortise in a mortise-and-tenon joint. Its sturdy body withstands heavy blows from a mallet.

COLD CHISEL (ALSO KNOWN AS A FLAT CHISEL) The cold chisel is made entirely of steel and is used with a hammer for cutting metal.

BRICK BOLSTER This spade-shaped chisel is used with a club hammer for cutting bricks.

SAFETY FIRST WITH ELECTRICITY

Before starting any work on an electrical fitting or appliance, make sure to cut off the electricity supply — either by switching off at the main fuse box, or by unplugging the appliance.

Bulb testers

It is possible to buy an inexpensive tester for Christmas-tree lights, which will make the identification of problem bulbs quick and easy.

BEING PREPARED FOR CHRISTMAS

Keep the original box containing any lights you buy so that you will know what replacement bulbs you need in the future. When you buy a string of Christmas-tree lights buy some spares at the same time. When you buy replacement bulbs make sure that they are for the right kind of bulb string and that they have the right type of caps (screw or push-in).

Christmas-tree lights

Testing a string of lights   Time: 1 hour or less

Always test the lights before putting them on the tree. If the string does not light when it is plugged in, one or more of the bulbs is loose or faulty.

> YOU WILL NEED   Spare light bulbs, bulb tester.

To test the lights unplug the string and lay it on the floor, freeing it of tangles. Make sure all the bulbs are intact and firmly in their holders. Check that the plug at the end of the flex is wired correctly (see *Electric plug*) and has a 3 amp fuse. Plug it in and switch it on.

If the lights do not come on, unplug them and change the fuse bulb, which is usually opaque. If the lights still don't work, unplug the string and test each bulb in turn with a bulb tester (see margin, left).

If you do not have a tester, keep replacing the bulbs one at a time with spares until the string lights up. If you get to the end and it still has not lit, buy a new set of lights.

Safety with Christmas-tree lights

- Buy a set with the BSI Kitemark. This means the maker has complied with safety requirements and the product is continually tested.
- If you want to use Christmas-tree lights outdoors, buy a set specifically designed for outdoor use.
- Make sure that the plug has a 3 amp fuse.
- Do not use a bayonet connector to plug a bulb string into a light socket; this does not offer the protection of a cartridge fuse.
- Never use lights in Britain that are made for use in countries with a different voltage from that in the UK.

Cigarette burns

Burns on a carpet   Time: a few minutes

Where the pile of a carpet has been singed, use sharp embroidery scissors to trim away the burnt area, back to its original colour.

Alternatively, shave the singed area lightly with a disposable razor.

Where the carpet has been burned right through, you can either cover it with a small rug or patch it (see *Carpet maintenance*: 'Patching a damaged carpet').

Burns on clothes

Some dry-cleaners will mend burns by fine darning or patching with a piece from a seam or pocket interior. You can do this yourself (see *Darning*; *Patching clothes*).

Burns on wood   Time: depends on area

Burns on antique furniture require specialist attention, but you can repair an inexpensive piece yourself.

A LIGHT BURN Where furniture is merely discoloured rather than burned, start with a cream metal polish.

Wrap your index finger in Cling Film, to protect it. Then cover it with a soft, grit-free rag. Put a little cream metal polish on the tip, so that you can concentrate on the damaged area. Rub the burn mark in the direction of the grain.

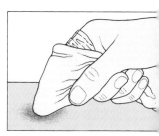

Rub it in well, and then use furniture polish as usual.

A MORE SERIOUS BURN Use a sharp craft knife to scrape the burned area until it is clean and flat. Work with the knife blade held horizontal to the surface.

Fold up a piece of white blotting paper into a compact chunk and saturate it with warm water.

Place it over the burn and hold it in place with Cling Film. Leave it for several hours to let the wood swell. Then remove the blotting paper and leave the wood to dry naturally. Sand gently along the wood grain with fine abrasive paper, then varnish or polish as required.

A DEEP BURN Use a blunt knife to scrape out the burned wood. Fill the hollow with a matching wood filler and use the knife blade to smooth it level with the surface. Let it dry, then touch it up with a fine paintbrush and a matching artist's oil (from an art supplier) to recreate the grain.

Burns on plastic laminates

You can treat light burns on plastic laminates by sanding them off with fine abrasive paper, but this will leave a roughened surface.

More serious burns require patching the surface, or you may prefer to replace an entire length of the laminate (see *Worktop*: 'Replacing a laminate worktop').

Burns on veneered furniture Time: parts of 2 days

YOU WILL NEED Veneer, craft knife, wood chisel, wood glue, screwdriver, brown paper, fine abrasive paper, shoe polish.

Buy a new piece of veneer with the same finish as the original from a large DIY shop or timber merchant.

Using a craft knife, cut a neat, oval shape round the burn. Make the cut as close to the burn as possible.

Dampen the section with a wet cloth, to soften the glue, then use a wood chisel to remove it. Remove all traces of glue left in the hole with the chisel.

Use the damaged piece as a template to cut a new piece of veneer. Check that the grain matches. Dampen the new piece to make it flexible, then stick it in position with wood glue. Wipe off surplus glue with a damp cloth and use a screwdriver handle to press the new veneer into place. Cover it with a piece of brown paper and lay a weight over the top then leave it to dry thoroughly.

Use fine abrasive paper to smooth off any rough edges and fill in any missing colour with shoe polish or artist's oil applied on a cotton bud. Repolish the veneer.

Circuit breaker: SEE RCD

Clay soil

Improving the structure of clay soil Time: depends on area

If you can roll a small handful of your garden soil into a sticky ball, it is clay. Clay soils are sticky in winter and brick-hard in summer, but with care they improve rapidly.

All clay soils become easier to work if you add organic material. Garden compost is best, but soil conditioners, such as seaweed, farmyard manure or bagged manure products such as Cow Pact are also available and will help to improve the quality of the soil. Spread the soil conditioner over the soil, then use a garden fork to turn it in.

Use about a barrow of compost or manure to 3 m² (3 sq yd) of soil – roughly an 8 cm (3 in) thick covering.

Dried seaweed meal also improves the structure of the soil. Apply 100-200 g per m² (3-6 oz per sq yd). Follow the instructions carefully when applying proprietary products; they could do harm if applied too thickly.

Choosing the right flowering plants for clay soil

If you choose your plants with care, a garden on clay soil can flourish. The plants in the drawing will grow well in clay soil, but flower at different times of the year.

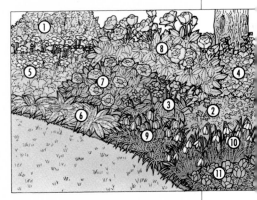

PLANTS THAT DO WELL ON CLAY SOIL

1 Flowering currants (*Ribes sanguineum*)
2 Hardy geraniums (*Geranium sanguineum*; also *G. pratense*; *G. macrorrhizum*; *G. endressii*)
3 Hellebores (*Helleborus atrorubens*)
4 Ivies (*Hedera spp*)
5 Japanese anemones (cultivars of *Anemone hupehensis* or *A. x hybrida*)
6 Lungworts (*Pulmonaria saccharata*)
7 Paeonies
8 Roses
9 Snake's head fritillaries (*Fritillaria meleagris*)
10 Snowdrops (*Galanthus nivalis*)
11 Winter aconites (*Eranthis hyemalis*)

PLANTS THAT WILL NOT THRIVE ON CLAY SOILS
● Bulbs – avoid the smaller, delicate ones which need light, warm soils.
● Alpine species which are usually grown in rockeries.

● Lilies – except the Madonna lily *Lilium candidum* and *L. pyrenaicum*. *Lilium regale* could also be grown if the soil is cultivated and well drained.
● Rock roses (*Helianthemum spp*).
● Sea hollies (*Eryngium maritimum*) and other eryngiums which grow naturally in sandy soils.
● Irises – especially the smaller ones. But *Iris foetidissima* grows well on clay.

Clothes line

Putting up a rotary clothes line

A rotary clothes line spins round a central pole. It is supplied with a socket which is hammered into the ground. The central pole then fits into the socket.

YOU WILL NEED Rotary clothes line, scrap wood, club hammer. Possibly: concrete.

Hold the socket at a right angle to the ground and hammer it in. Protect the end with a piece of scrap wood.

In soft soil, dig a hole and set the socket in concrete (see *Fencing*: 'Replacing a rotten post'). Plug the socket temporarily while you pour concrete into the hole.

A high-level clothes line

If a line is needed where you can't reach it from the ground, across a courtyard for example, fix a loop of line between two pulleys. You can then wind the line in and out as you hang out and take in washing.

KEEPING POCKETS IN SHAPE

Don't carry heavy objects around in your pockets. The weight will soon distort the shape of a garment, and will eventually make a hole. Use a handbag or briefcase instead.

MENDING FRAYED CUFFS

Leather reinforcements can be used to edge frayed cuffs, using the same method as for attaching elbow patches.

MAKING ELBOW PATCHES

Cut your own patches from a suitable thickness of leather. To make the perforations, run an unthreaded sewing machine around the edge, making sure that you use a needle suitable for thick fabrics.

Putting up a straight clothes line Time: 1 hour or less

A straight clothes line must be attached to two solid objects, such as the house wall and a garden post. The line is attached to a hook at one end, and passes through a pulley at the other, allowing it to be lowered and raised.

Use a metal anchor bolt to fix the hook or the pulley to the house. A standard wall plug won't grip firmly enough to hold the weight of a line of wet washing.

> YOU WILL NEED Metal anchor bolt with built-in galvanised hook, electric drill, masonry bits, pulley, cleat, wall plugs, screws, screwdriver.

The following technique assumes that one end of the clothes line is being anchored to a post, garage or tree and that the pulley is attached to the house wall.

Decide on a place on the wall for the pulley to be fitted. It should be above head height so that the clothes line can be pulled up out of the way when not in use.

Drill a hole in the wall large enough for the anchor bolt. Drill in the centre of a brick, not at a mortar joint.

Insert the bolt and turn the hook. A metal wedge will lock the wings of the bolt into the hole.

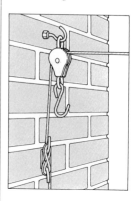

Attach a pulley to the hook. Drill holes in the wall below the pulley to take wall plugs and then use galvanised screws to screw a cleat to the wall. Use the cleat to wrap the washing line around.

Clothes moths

Clothes and house moths can ruin clothes and bedding. However, it is not the adult moths that damage wool, fur, feathers and hair, but the larvae – white caterpillars with brown heads – which feed on them.

Regular cleaning should prevent moths damaging textiles, but if an item is to be stored for any period of time it is best to take extra precautions.

Store clothes in sealed plastic, paper or cotton bags containing a disc of moth repellent and hang a moth repellent in each wardrobe. Also, spray clothes and blankets that are to be stored with an aerosol moth proofer.

Spray carpets and gaps in floorboards or shelves where dust and fluff collect with moth proofer. Upholstery should also be sprayed, but avoid spraying rubberised underfelt or carpet backing, as the spray could damage it.

Coats & jackets

Removing the shine on a jacket Time: a few minutes

Where parts of a jacket have become shiny through wear, take a hot steam iron and hold it over the shiny area without actually touching the fabric. An iron which delivers a controlled shot of steam is particularly good for this.

Replacing a pocket Time: 1 hour or less

The pockets in a coat or jacket often wear out long before the garment does, but it is possible to put in new pockets.

> YOU WILL NEED Scissors, paper or thin card, fabric, pins, sewing machine, steam iron, needle and thread.

Pull the damaged pocket lining through to the outside of the jacket. Then leave about 5 cm (2 in) attached to the garment and cut off the damaged area.

Lay the cut-off pocket on a piece of paper or thin card and draw round it, adding a seam allowance of 2.5 cm (1 in) all round. Cut out the shape to form a paper pattern.

Take a piece of suitable fabric (it won't show, so it needn't be a very close match) large enough to give two pocket shapes. Double the fabric and pin the paper pattern to it, making sure that the grain of the fabric runs the same way as it did on the original pocket.

Cut out two identical shapes. With the wrong sides facing each other, machine stitch round the curved edge, leaving the straight end open. The stitch line should be about 1.6 cm ($\frac{5}{8}$ in) in from the edge of the fabric.

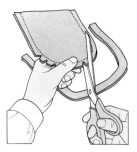

Trim the excess fabric off, as close to the stitching line as possible and cut out triangular pieces all round the outer edge of the curved section, to reduce the bulk when the pocket is turned inside-out.

Turn the right sides together and press with a steam iron. Stitch around the curved section again, so that the original seam is enclosed and no raw edges show.

STITCHING ON THE NEW POCKET With the remains of the old pocket protruding on the outside of the garment, pin the new pocket to it, matching the seams. Stitch into place.

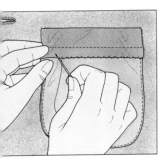

Taking care to keep the pocket sides separated, roll a small hem and whipstitch the raw edges where the old pocket joins the new, so that they lie flat (see *Stitches*). (You may need to unpick the lining of the garment just enough to allow you to put your other hand inside.)

Press the seam with a steam iron and push the pocket back inside the garment. Restitch the lining if necessary.

It is possible to buy a ready-made replacement pocket, and some have an iron-on facility, but do make sure that it will fit the remains of the existing pocket, before buying it.

Covering worn elbows Time: 1 hour or less

Leather patches are useful for covering worn elbows. Patches are sold, cut to size and perforated for sewing.

> YOU WILL NEED Leather patches, pins, needle and thread.

Ideally, the patches should be fixed to the outer fabric only. This involves unpicking the sleeve lining seam, working on the patch and then restitching the seam.

If you are not prepared to go to so much trouble, pin the patches over the worn elbows. Make sure that the sleeve lining is also pinned in the correct position and won't pull when the jacket is put on.

Try to pin through the perforations in order not to spoil the look of the patches. Tack the patches securely in place removing the pins in the process. Use a contrasting colour thread that will be easy to identify when it is removed.

Put on the jacket and check that the patches are in the right place and are not making the sleeves look puckered.

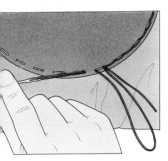

Use a strong needle and thread to stitch the patch into position through its perforations. Use a backstitch or a double layer of running stitches (see *Stitches*).

Finally, remove the contrasting tacking thread.

Cockroaches

Cockroaches are a serious problem because they can carry a variety of illnesses, including food poisoning.

The common or oriental cockroach is around 2 cm ($\frac{3}{4}$ in) long with a black, flat, oval body and long, whip-like antennae. The small German cockroach is a similar shape, brown and about 1 cm ($\frac{3}{8}$ in) long.

Cockroaches thrive in warm and humid boiler rooms, kitchens and heating ducts in buildings. They eat what they can find and contaminate food, containers and surfaces with which they come into contact.

Treat them with aerosol insecticide, which can be sprayed into nooks and crannies, or cockroach powder. If both methods fail, call the local authority Environmental Health Department or a pest control company.

Coffee maker

Noisy or slow filtering are sure signs of scale build-up in a coffee maker. Regular descaling is essential to prevent it.

Descale the coffee maker every six months if you live in a soft-water area, every three months in fairly hard-water areas and monthly in hard-water areas. Use a descaler that is intended for coffee machines and that does not contain acetic, hydrochloric or sulphuric acid.

Descaling a filter machine Time: a few minutes

> YOU WILL NEED Descaler. Possibly: filter paper.

Remove the nylon or gold filter. Although not essential, it is more hygienic to replace it with a paper filter.

Mix up the descaling solution with cold water, following the manufacturer's instructions. Do not use hot water because hot descaling liquid will cause damage.

Fill the coffee maker's water tank almost to the top with descaling solution, and make sure that the jug is in place. Switch on the machine and run about two cups of descaling solution through the coffee machine.

Switch off the coffee maker and leave it to stand for an hour. Switch on the machine and allow the remainder of the solution to run through.

After descaling and before making coffee, it is essential to run the machine through its operation cycle three or four times, using clean water each time.

HARD-WATER AREAS In areas with particularly hard water, run the descaling solution through the machine twice. Allow the solution to cool in between. The second descaling can be carried out without the one-hour delay.

HOW TO SERVE YOUR COFFEE HOT

Some machines, especially older ones and a few models from Continental Europe, produce coffee that is cooler than you might like. Older machines operate at between 70°C (158°F) and 80°C (176°F) to ensure that the optimum coffee-making temperature of 80-90°C (176°-194°F) is not exceeded.

New coffee makers operate at 90°C (194°F) to compensate for the British preference for adding cold milk. But if your machine produces lukewarm coffee, heat the cups with hot water first, and use warm milk or coffee whitener.

Descaling an espresso machine Time: ½ an hour or less

> **YOU WILL NEED** White vinegar.

An espresso/cappuccino machine may be fitted with a descaling indicator which is usually a warning light. When it comes on you must descale the machine.

Pass 570 ml (1 pint) of pure white vinegar through the machine twice, waiting about 10 minutes between each application to allow the machine to cool down.

Faultfinder guide: Espresso machines

PROBLEM	POSSIBLE CAUSE	REMEDY
Too many grounds in cup.	Dirty filter holder.	Clean the filter holder.
	Grains too fine.	Use a coarser coffee.
Filter holder won't come off.	Machine is switched off.	Switch on.
Noisy pump.	No water.	Refill.
Coffee flow is slow but the descaling light is not on.	Grounds too compressed, greasy or fine.	Don't compress the grounds. Or use a coarser coffee.

Cold-water tank

Water dripping through a ceiling

If water starts dripping through a ceiling in the house, check for an overflow in the bathroom.

If the water is coming from the loft, turn on every tap in the house, to empty the cold-water tank. Turn off the main stopcock to prevent more water entering the tank.

The stopcock is probably under the kitchen sink or in the cellar. If you can't find it, tie up the ball valve in the cold-water tank, using string and a piece of wood (see *Ball valve*: 'Stopping a constantly dripping overflow').

When the tank is empty turn off the taps.

Fixing a leaking tank Time: depends on cause

> **YOU WILL NEED** Torch, coarse abrasive paper, Fernox external leak sealer or Sylglas Plumberfix, rubber gloves.

If a steel cold-water tank rusts and springs a leak, it is possible to do a short-term repair. First, strip off the insulation and find the leak. Then empty the tank (see above).

FIXING A SMALL LEAK A pinhole leak can be most easily sealed using external leak sealer such as Fernox LS-X.

First rub down the area of the tank around the leak with coarse abrasive paper to remove any rust. Then sponge off any debris and dirt with clean water.

Dry the area then squeeze a small blob of leak sealer onto the hole and leave it to cure for about 2 hours. This type of leak sealer never sets absolutely hard.

Then refill the tank.

BLOCKING A LARGE LEAK Larger leaks are best tackled from inside the cold-water tank with a two-colour mix-and-knead sealer such as Sylglas Plumberfix.

First use coarse abrasive paper to remove any rust from the inside of the tank around the leak. This will probably enlarge the hole slightly.

Plumberfix consists of two sticks of material. Cut an equal amount from each stick and, wearing rubber or plastic gloves, knead them together to a uniform colour.

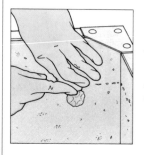

Cover the hole and an area about 2.5 cm (1 in) wide all around it with a layer of sealer about 6 mm (¼ in) thick. Force the sealer into the hole.

The sealer sets under water, so refill the tank immediately by opening the main stopcock.

A steel tank that has leaked once will almost certainly leak again. Having repaired a leak, get a plumber to replace the tank with a new plastic one.

Fixing an overflowing tank Time: depends on cause

A cold-water tank may overflow if the ball valve is not working properly or if the tank overflow is blocked.

> **YOU WILL NEED** Torch, piece of wire or stick. Possibly: hair dryer or filled rubber hot-water bottle.

Use wire or a stick to clear any blockage in the overflow. If it is blocked by ice, use an electric hair dryer or a hot-water bottle applied to the pipe to melt it. Probe the overflow again before refilling the tank.

Repair the ball valve if it is faulty (see *Ball valve*).

> ## A loft ladder and light for emergencies
> Install a folding loft ladder and an electric light point in the loft before anything goes wrong. This will make it easier to deal with any problems, such as a leaking cold-water tank, that may occur.

Collars & cuffs

A new collar can change the style of a garment, and the life of a piece of clothing can be extended by mending its collar or cuffs. Though it is possible to stitch by hand, the finish will be better if you use a sewing machine.

Fitting a Peter Pan collar Time: 2 hours or less

YOU WILL NEED Paper pattern, scissors, interfacing, fabric, sewing machine.

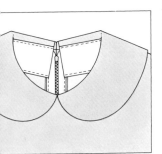

A Peter Pan collar is one of the easiest collars to fit to a bodice. Each half consists of two pieces of fabric with an interfacing between.

PREPARING THE COLLAR Buy a paper pattern and cut out the fabric and interfacing as directed in the instructions.

Pin the interfacing to the wrong side of the top section of the collar and tack it into position. Alternatively, use an iron-on interfacing which is fused to the fabric by heat.

Bring together the right sides of the two fabric collar pieces. Pin and tack the outside edge, ending off the stitching securely. Leave the neckline edge open.

Machine stitch where you have tacked, using a shorter stitch on the curved sections to give greater strength.

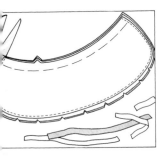

Trim away the excess interfacing very close to the stitching (it does not fray), and then trim the underside of the collar to about 3 mm ($\frac{1}{8}$ in) and the top layer to about 6 mm ($\frac{1}{4}$ in).

Make several snips along the curve, almost to the stitch line. Press well and turn right side out. Ease the seam with your fingers so that it lies flat. Press carefully so that the thickness of the seam allowance does not show through.

FITTING THE COLLAR TO THE SHIRT Remove the old collar by unpicking it. Press the garment around the neck area.

Place the right side of the new collar against the wrong side of the shirt neck. Pin, tack and stitch into position. Trim and clip the seam allowance. Put the collar into the finished position and hand stitch the wrong side to the neckline. Make sure that no stitches show through.

How to make tailor's tacks

Tailor's tacks are used to make temporary marks on fabric to indicate where they may be joined later.

Use an unknotted, double thread and stitch very loosely, several times, through both layers of fabric. Part the layers slightly and cut the threads that are stretched between them.

Each layer should now have a number of threads marking the points to be joined later.

Turning collars and cuffs Time: 2 hours or less

YOU WILL NEED Contrasting colour thread, needle, fine scissors or seam ripper, pins, sewing machine, matching thread.

A worn or discoloured collar or cuff can be disguised by turning it to put the underside on show.

COLLAR Mark the centre of the collar and the neckband with a tailor's tack (above) in a contrasting colour thread.

Carefully remove the collar from the neckband, using sharp embroidery scissors or a seam ripper.

Turn the collar and pin it back into the neckband, matching the tailor's tacks. Then tack it into position and machine-stitch along the original stitching line.

CUFFS Mark the centre of each cuff and its sleeve with a tailor's tack (as above), and then remove the cuffs.

Reverse one cuff and pin the end of the sleeve into it, matching the tailor's tacks. Tack it in position and then machine along the original line of stitching. Repeat with the second cuff.

If the cuffs have only one buttonhole, remember to put the left cuff onto the right sleeve and vice versa, when you turn them, so that the buttonhole is in the right place.

READY-MADE COLLARS

An alternative to making or reversing a collar is to buy one ready-made from a haberdashery department.

Compost

Garden compost is the best soil conditioner and it is vital for successful gardening.

A new compost heap should produce usable compost within four months if it is started in the summer. To maintain a constant supply of compost many gardeners keep two or three heaps, at different stages.

For rapid and effective decomposition combine bulky, vegetable waste, soft twiggy matter, dried grass or straw materials with natural activators, which are high in nitrogen and aid the rotting process, such as animal wastes, grass mowings, nettles, seaweed and comfrey leaves.

Commercial activators are available, but a well-layered, covered compost heap should need little extra help.

Getting rid of twigs and roots Time: 2 hours or less

> YOU WILL NEED Coarse garden sieve, spade, hammer or mallet. Possibly: shredder.

If twigs and roots have not decomposed in otherwise good compost, prop up a coarse garden sieve and throw the compost, by the spadeful, onto the sieve.

Once you have removed all the roots and twigs, use a hammer or mallet to break them down or run them through a shredder, then add them to your newest compost heap for further decomposition (see also *Shredder*).

Mature, ready-to-use garden compost should be moist, loose, dark brown and of uniform consistency. It should smell like rich leaf mould.

Moistening a dry heap Time: 1 hour or less

A compost heap that is too dry does not provide the right environment for bacteria to break down organic matter.

Interleave dry materials with grass cuttings, kitchen waste such as vegetable peelings and tea leaves – in fact, anything organic apart from meat or bread which will encourage rats. Avoid fallen leaves which may compact too much and not allow oxygen to circulate.

Alternatively, wet the compost, but take care not to flood it, especially if it is in a sealed container.

Drying out a wet and slimy heap Time: about 1 hour

Compost that is too wet becomes solid and slimy. It cannot break down because it contains insufficient oxygen.

> YOU WILL NEED Twigs, hedge clippings, prunings, straw, garden fork, newspaper strips.

Start a new heap, alternating layers of the wet compost with layers of dryer, looser material, such as newspaper torn into shreds, twigs, hedge clippings or straw.

Straw that has been used as bedding for domestic animals, such as rabbits, hens or horses, is ideal because it is rich in ammonia, which helps the breaking-down process. Finish with a layer of soil, about 5 cm (2 in) deep.

Try to site the new compost heap in a warm and sunny part of the garden. Heat is an important part of the rotting process. It should build up within a few days, reaching a peak of 65-70°C (149-158°F) before starting to cool after about a month. By this time the heap will have shrunk to about one-third of its original size.

Speed up the rotting process by turning the outer, less decomposed layers to the inside a couple of times.

If you do not want to turn the compost by hand, try a compost maker with a tumbler action. Most are barrel-shaped and mounted on a frame for rotating.

Comfrey for the compost heap

Comfrey is one of the best compost ingredients because it contains nitrogen and potassium. Grow a row of comfrey, cut it down two or three times a year and add the leaves to your compost. The Henry Doubleday Research Association recommends the strain Bocking 14. Buy it at the National Centre for Organic Gardening at Ryton Organic Gardens, Ryton-on-Dunsmore, Coventry CV8 3LG (Tel. 01203 303517) or from The Organic Gardening Catalogue, Coombelands House, Addlestone, Surrey KT15 1HY.

Computer cleaning

Routine cleaning Time: 1 hour or less

Static electricity attracts dust to computer screens, and keyboards collect airborne dirt. Clean all the computer parts when they start to look dirty.

> YOU WILL NEED Screen and keyboard wipes from computer shops. Or cotton buds, lint-free cloths, household spray cleaner, glass cleaner. Paintbrush.

Unplug the computer and remove any floppy disks or CDs from the disk drives before starting to clean.

TAKING THE TEMPERATURE

In winter you can tell if your compost heap is working by the steam that rises when you uncover it. You can thrust your hand in to test the temperature, but a cleaner method is to use a compost thermometer such as those made by Diplex Ltd, PO Box 172, Watford, Herts WD1 1BX (Tel. 01923 231784).

COVERING UP

You can buy covers for the computer, the screen and the keyboard at computer shops. They prevent dirt and dust accumulating while the computer is not being used.

Flexible sheaths are also available from computer shops to cover the keyboard. They stay in place as you type, but prevent dirt or liquid entering the unit.

Test any household cleaner on a small area that is not normally visible to ensure that it will not cause marks. Never use bleach or ammonia-based cleaners. When using specialist wipes, pads or cleaners follow the manufacturer's instructions. Do not spray or pour the cleaner directly onto the computer screen or keyboard; transfer it onto a cloth – avoiding over-wetting – then wipe the computer. Polish the cleaner off with a dry cloth.

Make sure that no liquid enters any switches, controls, disk drives or cooling grills; it could cause damage.

THE KEYBOARD Start by turning it upside-down and giving it a good shake to encourage small particles to fall out.

Turn it up the right way, and use a paintbrush to clean between the keys, and a cotton bud dipped in household cleaner to clean the tops and sides of the keys.

For the keyboard casing, transfer the cleaner onto a cloth and wipe it on. Polish off with a clean dry cloth.

THE SCREEN Some screens should only be cleaned with the cloth supplied – check in the manual. Use antistatic glass cleaner, or screen wipes on other types.

Liquid spilt on the keyboard Time: $\frac{1}{2}$ a day or less

If liquid enters any part of the computer, switch it off immediately, pull out the mains plug and contact your supplier or manufacturer. Alternatively, you could contact a computer repair specialist (see below, right).

If the spill is limited to the keyboard, you may be able to clean it yourself. However, if the keyboard is an old one – such as an IBM XT – do not try to repair it yourself because reassembly will be too difficult. You can buy a replacement keyboard fairly cheaply.

> YOU WILL NEED Kitchen paper towel or ordinary towel, lint-free cloth, hair dryer, WD40.

Before you start work, make sure that the computer is unplugged at the mains socket.

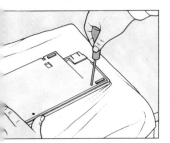

If you have a newer keyboard, turn it upside-down onto paper towel or an ordinary towel. Remove the retaining screws and carefully take off the back.

Be careful not to move or shake the keyboard unit because the key tops may fall out and be lost.

You can now remove the main board which will be either a flexible membrane or a printed circuit board. Dry it with a lint-free cloth and then a hair dryer.

If the spilled liquid has left a sticky residue, carefully rub the area with a cloth damped with WD40. Then dry it with a clean lint-free cloth.

! Do not use the hair dryer to dry the keyboard as the cleaning fluid is highly flammable.

Computer disks

Storing floppy disks

The most popular disk sizes are 3.5 in and 5.25 in. The 3.5 in is a flexible (or 'floppy') disk inside a rigid case. The 5.25 in is also a 'floppy', but is far more delicate because it is cased only in a flexible jacket.

If disks are kept too close to loudspeakers, a television, the computer screen or a printer, the magnetic field can damage them, so store them at least 1 m (3 ft) away. Keep the disks in a dry, dust-free place away from extreme temperatures, and in a disk box with a lid. Never leave disks where they could be damaged by dirt or spilled liquids.

> ### An index for each disk
> At the DOS prompt `c:\>` use the command `dir #a:>prn` to print a list of the contents of the disk. Store the list with the disk.
> From Windows, go to DOS via the DOS prompt `c:\>`, which is often found in the 'main' or 'tools' program group. At the DOS prompt `c:\>` use the command `dir a:>prn` to print a list of the contents of the disk. Type `exit` to return to Windows.

Getting specialist computer help

HELP WITH DISKS If your computer refuses to read the information on a disk, and you feel confident enough to try, you could use specialist software such as Norton Utilities or PC Tools which can be bought at computer stores. These tools are available for both DOS and Windows, and instructions come with the software.

Computer disks (cont.)

If you don't want to do this and the disk contains valuable information, contact a disk specialist such as Vogon (Tel. 0800 581263) which provides a 24-hour emergency data recovery service.

HELP WITH HARDWARE When your computer needs to be repaired, first contact the supplier or the manufacturer for help. If this is not possible – perhaps because they have closed down or they are not represented in this country – you can contact a repair specialist such as PC Service (Tel. 01159 711000).

SOFTWARE PROBLEMS If you have problems with software, you may be able to get help from the software manufacturer. Most will provide a telephone helpline, but you may have to pay for the service. Ask when you buy the product.

Alternatively, you could try PC Plus (Tel. 0839 517517). It is a telephone help line for any make of PC, which will try to answer questions about software problems such as: 'Why won't Word run on my PC?'.

The calls are charged at the premium rate and the service is available between 8 am and 8 pm on weekdays, 9 am and 6 pm on Saturdays and 10 am and 5 pm on Sundays.

Formatting floppy disks

Most disks purchased today are already formatted, but if you do purchase unformatted disks they will need to be formatted so that your computer can recognise and read them. On PCs running windows this is quite simple.

FORMATTING DISKS UNDER WINDOWS Locate 'File Manager' which can often be found in the 'Main Program' group, and click on it. Put a disk in the drive and move the arrow so that it covers either the A or B disk-drive icon, then click on it. If the disk is new, Windows will prompt:

The disk in A (or B) is not formatted. Do you want to format it now?

Click on 'Yes', then select FILE. From the menu bar select FORMAT DISK. Select the format required and then click OK.

Windows will then format the disk.

FORMATTING A 3.5 IN DISK FROM WINDOWS 95 Select MY COMPUTER. Select DISK and then FORMAT.

How to format a used floppy disk

If the disk that you want to format is not new, insert it then go to 'File Manager' and select 'Disk' from the 'Format' option. Then follow the procedure above.

Formatting will erase all of the information that is held on a disk, so never format a disk which contains information that you may need at a later date.

Formatting disks on older models of computer

If you are still using an older model of personal computer, disks may come in various sizes and are formatted in a variety of ways.

FORMATTING A 360 K DSDD (LOW-DENSITY) 5.25 IN DISK UNDER DOS Get to the DOS prompt **C:\\>**, and change to the directory where DOS is stored.

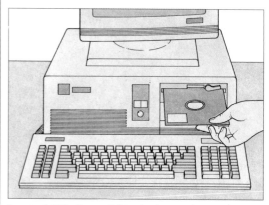

Insert a 5.25 in floppy disk in the drive and enter:

format a:/f:360

If your computer has two floppy drives and your 5.25 in drive is designated as **B:**, substitute **b:** for **a:** in the **format** command.

FORMATTING A 1.2 MB DSHD (HIGH-DENSITY) 5.25 IN DISK UNDER DOS Get to the DOS prompt **C:\\>**, and change to the directory where DOS is stored.

Put a 5.25 in floppy disk in the drive and enter:

format a:/f:1.2

If your computer has two floppy drives and your 5.25 in drive is designated as **B:**, substitute **b:** for **a:** in the **format** command.

FORMATTING A 720 K DSDD (LOW-DENSITY) 3.5 IN DISK UNDER DOS Get to the DOS prompt **C:\\>**, and change to the directory where DOS is stored.

Insert a 3.5 in floppy disk and enter the command:

format a:/f:720

If you have two floppy drives and your 3.5 in drive is designated as **B:**, substitute **b:** for **a:** in the **format** command.

FORMATTING A 1.44 MB DSHD (HIGH-DENSITY) 3.5 IN DISK UNDER DOS Get to the DOS prompt **C:\\>**, and change to the directory where DOS is stored.

Put a 3.5 in floppy disk into the drive and enter:

format a:/f:1.44

If you have two floppy drives and the 3.5 in disk drive is designated as **B:**, substitute **b:** for **a:** in the **format** command.

Computer error messages

Most PC users now run a Windows system. Windows is a method of communicating with the computer which allows the user to click a mouse pointer onto a picture on the screen called an icon, rather than having to type words and symbols. Windows is more user-friendly than the older MS-DOS operating system. It generally shows errors by displaying a 'dialog' box. For example, if you attempt to access the 'A' drive on your computer, but you have not placed a disk in the drive, Windows will display a dialog box which tells you that there is no disk in drive A, instructs you to insert a disk, then waits for you to respond by pressing either the Retry or Cancel buttons.

Error messages in DOS operating systems

The following information relates to IBM-compatible computers running PC-DOS or MS-DOS. The advice is especially intended for home users of personal computers with a 286 processor or a processor used in the early Amstrad PC range. The error messages given here are the most common of many that could appear on your screen.

'General failure reading C'

A computer with an internal hard disk will display, the error message:

`General failure reading drive C`
`Abort, Retry, Fail?`

The internal hard disk might have been damaged, but it may be possible to recover the situation. Restart the computer (see right). If the error message is repeated, switch off. Place the original computer master disk – marked MS-DOS Startup (normally Disk 1) – into the disk drive. If you don't have a startup disk, ask your supplier or the manufacturer to provide you with one. Switch on and you will see the prompt:

`Starting MS-DOS`
`Current date is Mon 11-01-95`
`Enter new date (mm-dd-yy)`

There is no need to change the date. Just press 'Enter' and then the screen will display:

`Current time is Mon 14:94:04.57`
`Enter new time`

There is no need to change the time. Just press 'Enter' and then the screen displays something like:

`Microsoft (R) MS-DOS (R) Version 6`
`(C) Copyright Microsoft Corp 1981-1993`

followed by `A:\>`.

Replace the MS-DOS Startup disk with the disk labelled MS-DOS Operating system. Then type `CHKDSK C: /f`.

The computer will check the internal hard disk and attempt to fix any errors. For further details about CHKDSK, look up 'CHKDSK' in your DOS manual.

Several lines of information will appear on the screen. They may report errors such as:

`Allocation error - size adjusted 64 lost`
`allocation units found in 1 chain`
`Convert lost chains to files y/n`

In this case reply 'Y', then when the information stops appearing remove all floppy disks from the disk drives and restart the computer (see above, right).

If the computer will not restart, reload the operating system onto the hard disk. The DOS manual gives instructions under 'Installing DOS'.

If the computer is still not working, and you are anxious to recover the data, you will need to get some expert help with the disk (see *Computer disks*: 'Getting specialist computer help').

If the fault occurs again, either now or later, you could try formatting the internal hard disk, but if the fault persists the disk may be damaged and need replacing. Contact the supplier or manufacturer of your computer, or a computer repair specialist (see *Computer disks*: 'Getting specialist computer help').

'General failure writing C'

A computer with an internal hard disk displays:

`General failure writing drive C`
`Abort, Retry, Fail?`

The internal hard disk might have been damaged, but it may be possible to correct it. Press R.

If it is still not working, press F and insert a formatted floppy disk in the floppy disk drive (see *Computer disks*: 'Formatting a floppy disk').

Instead of saving the information to the hard disk, save it to the floppy disk by changing the drive letter from `C` (or whatever letter designates the hard drive) to `A` in the Save statement, for example: `Save A: Document`.

Restart the computer (see above) and repeat the same actions that led to the error message. If it is still not working there may be a bad sector on the hard disk. Use the utility CHKDSK (see 'General failure reading C').

If this does not solve the problem and you are anxious to recover the data, you will need help with the disk (see *Computer disks*: 'Getting specialist computer help').

If the fault occurs again, either now or later, you could try formatting the internal hard disk, but if the fault persists the disk may be damaged and need replacing. Contact the supplier or manufacturer of the computer, or a computer repair specialist (see *Computer disks*: 'Getting specialist computer help').

'General failure reading A'

When starting a computer with a floppy disk the screen displays the following error message:

`General failure reading drive A`
`Abort, Retry, Fail?`

RESTARTING YOUR COMPUTER

A computer can be restarted in three ways:
• Switch it off and on again using the power switch.
• Use the 'Reset' button if one is fitted.
• Hold down CTRL and ALT keys, and press DEL.

KEEPING OUT OF TROUBLE

You can avoid expensive repairs to some extent by investing in relatively inexpensive software utilities such as Norton Utilities or PC Tools. Monthly testing using the software should help to guard against virus infection and it will also retrieve and repair corrupted information on the hard disk.

Computer error messages (cont.)

Switch off the computer and restart it (see previous page) to see if the error message appears again.

If it does, switch off the computer, place either the computer master disk marked 'MS-DOS Startup' or a copy – whichever disk you have not been using – into the disk drive and switch on.

If, when you respond as normal, the prompt `A:\>` appears, make a replacement MS-DOS Startup disk as described in your computer manual under 'Format', using a new formatted disk. Then continue with your work.

If the screen does not display the prompt `A:\>`, the disk is probably damaged (see *Computer disks*: 'Getting specialist computer help').

'General failure reading A'

A computer that is started up with a floppy disk displays the following message while you are working:

```
General failure reading drive A
Abort, Retry, Fail?
```

You are probably trying to read or write to a disk that is not formatted, or has been incorrectly formatted (see *Computer disks*: 'Formatting a floppy disk'). The disk may have a format unknown to your computer, or it may be incompatible – for example, a 1.2 MB disk in a 360 k drive.

If you are using an old computer, you may be trying to read a high density disk on a low density disk drive.

Find a computer with a high density drive and copy the information onto a low density disk.

If the message still appears, check that the floppy drive on the computer is working (see box, right).

'General failure writing A'

While you are working, the computer screen displays the error message:

```
General failure writing drive A
Abort, Retry, Fail?
```

The floppy disk may be damaged. Alternatively, it may be write protected – if the little window in the side of the disk is open, flick the tab down to close it.

Press R. No success? Press F, put a formatted disk in the external disk drive and save your data to it. Use CHKDSK as described under 'Data error reading (writing) A' (right) to verify that the original disk is usable.

If the disk is damaged, discard it. But if it contains valuable data, you will need help to retrieve it (see *Computer disks*: 'Getting specialist computer help').

Still no success? Check that the floppy drive is working.

'Data error reading C'

A computer with a hard disk displays the message:

```
Data error reading drive C
Abort, Retry, Fail?
```

Restart the computer (see previous page). If the fault persists see 'General failure reading C' (previous page).

'Data error writing C'

A computer with a hard disk displays the message:

```
Data error writing drive C
Abort, Retry, Fail?
```

The internal hard disk may have become damaged. Press R. If the error message is repeated, press F and restart the computer (see previous page).

Repeat the instruction that caused the error message and if it appears again, follow the procedure described under 'General failure writing C'.

How to check the floppy drive

If you suspect that your floppy drive is not reading or writing to a disk, make sure by trying to format a new disk. If it is successful, the drive is functioning properly. If not, it may be faulty. In this case contact the manufacturers or suppliers to get it fixed.

'Data error reading (writing) A'

These are the checks you should make if a computer with a hard disk displays the following message when saving information to the floppy disk:

```
Data error reading (writing) drive A
Abort, Retry, Fail?
```

The floppy disk might have become damaged. Press 'R'. If the message is repeated, restart the computer (see previous page) to see if the fault persists. If the message comes up again, the floppy disk is probably damaged.

Change to the directory where the operating system is located. This is often `C:\>DOS`.

Then type `CHKDSK A:` (space)`/f`. The computer will check the floppy disk and attempt to fix any errors.

Several lines of information will appear, after which the disk might be accessible. If you still have no success the floppy disk is probably faulty. Try a new one.

For more information about the CHKDSK facility, refer to the DOS manual under the section headed 'CHKDSK'.

'Data error writing A'

The computer displays the message:

```
Data error writing drive A
Abort, Retry, Fail?
```

The floppy disk might have become damaged. Press R. If the message is repeated follow the steps described under 'General failure writing A' (left).

'Not ready reading C'

A computer with an internal hard disk displays:

```
Not ready reading drive C
Abort, Retry, Fail?
```

Restart the computer (see previous page) to see if the

fault persists. If the message is repeated, there is a fault with the hard disk or the controller. Contact your supplier, manufacturer, or a computer repair specialist (see *Computer disks*: 'Getting specialist computer help').

'Not ready reading A/B'

A computer with a 3.5 in floppy disk drive displays the error message:

Not ready reading drive A
Abort, Retry, Fail?

Make sure the disk is pushed right into the drive and that the eject button is protruding from the front.

Try ejecting the disk and reloading it. Then check that the read/write light is illuminated on the drive. If it isn't, check the floppy drive (see facing page).

If the message is repeated there could be a fault with the floppy disk or the controller. Try restarting the computer to see if the fault persists (see page 95).

If the message is repeated contact your supplier, the manufacturer or a computer repair specialist (see *Computer disks*: 'Getting specialist computer help').

'Not ready reading A/B'

There are several checks you can make if a computer with a 5.25 in floppy drive displays the message:

Not ready reading drive A
Abort, Retry, Fail?

Make sure that the disk is in the drive the right way round. Usually the label should face the eject lever.

Also check that the disk is pushed right into the drive and that the eject lever is closed over the disk or the disk eject button is depressed (depending on the model).

Try ejecting the disk and reloading. Then check that the read/write light illuminates on the drive. If it doesn't, check the floppy drive (see facing page).

If the message is repeated it may indicate that there is a fault with the floppy disk or the controller.

Try restarting the computer to see if the fault persists (see page 95). If the message is repeated contact your supplier, manufacturer, or a computer repair specialist (see *Computer disks*: 'Getting specialist computer help').

'Non-System disk error'

The computer displays the message:

Non-System disk or disk error
Replace and strike any key when ready

This message usually means that the disk with which you are trying to start the computer is not a system start-up disk. Find your MS-DOS Startup disk, place it in the floppy drive and try again.

If the message is repeated the MS-DOS Startup disk is probably damaged. Use your copy of this disk and start the computer, then make a replacement system disk as described in your DOS manual under 'Formatting a disk'.

If this error message occurs when starting from a hard drive, the hard disk may be damaged.

Follow the steps described under 'General failure reading C'. If this is successful, you will probably need to rebuild the operating system on the hard drive. Refer to your DOS manual under 'Installing DOS' for further information on the procedure.

If it is unsuccessful, seek specialist help (see *Computer disks*: 'Getting specialist computer help').

Computer faults

How to clean a dirty mouse

The mouse is driven by a small ball that rolls across the mouse mat to direct the movement of the pointer. If the ball gets dirty your control of the screen pointer will deteriorate and the pointer will behave erratically.

> **YOU WILL NEED** Cotton bud, WD40 lubricant, lint-free cloth.

Switch off the computer and remove the mains plug, then unplug the mouse lead from the computer.

Then turn the mouse over to reveal the ball and its socket. The socket cover will probably have an arrow showing which way to turn it in order to detach it.

Undo the cover and remove it.

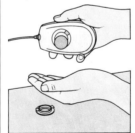

Then turn the mouse the right way up and catch the ball as it falls out.

Inside the mouse you should see three rollers; one small and two large ones. The larger two convert the movement of the ball in the mouse into signals to the computer. The rollers tend to collect dirt, causing the ball to slip and produce erratic results.

Dip a cotton bud in WD40 and clean the rollers, wiping the cotton bud along their length. Then clean the ball with WD40 on a cloth and wipe it dry. Reassemble the mouse.

Computer faults (cont.)

Faultfinder guide: Computers

Burning smell

- Switch off the computer and unplug it.
- Check that nothing is covering the cooling grille at the back of the computer or the display screen.
- If there is nothing obvious, have the computer checked by the shop where you bought it or by the manufacturer. Alternatively, contact a computer repair specialist (see *Computer disks*: 'Getting specialist computer help').

Power light won't come on

- Make sure that the computer is plugged in and that the mains socket and the computer are both switched on. Some computers have a switch on the processor box and one on the screen; check both.

    Still no power?
- Plug a table lamp or appliance into the mains socket and switch it on to make sure that the socket is supplying electricity. If not, get the faulty socket repaired (see *Electric socket* and *Fuse box*).

    Still no power?
- Check the fuse in the plug (see *Electric plug*).

    Still no power?
- The power lead could be faulty.

    If both the computer and printer have removable power leads you can check the computer power lead by using the printer lead instead.

    Still no power?
- Contact the supplier, the manufacturer or a computer repair specialist (see *Computer disks*: 'Getting specialist computer help').

Computer responds erratically to mouse

- If your computer has an infrared mouse, move on two steps to 'Try restarting the computer'.

    No better?
- Check that the plug at the end of the mouse cable is pushed into its socket in the computer firmly. If it is held in place with screws, make sure that they are tight.

    No better?
- Try restarting the computer (see page 95).

    No better?
- If you are using a mouse on a slippery surface such as a table top, try using a mouse mat.
- The cause may be a build-up of dirt inside the mouse preventing it from working properly. See 'How to clean a dirty mouse', previous page.

    Still no better?
- Contact the supplier or manufacturer, or buy a new mouse. They are not expensive.

Computer does not respond to mouse

- Check that the mouse lead is plugged firmly into the socket at the back of the machine.
- If the mouse lead appears to be connected properly, unplug it and examine inside the plug to see if any of the thin pins that hold it in position has broken or bent. Replace the mouse and lead if necessary.
- Check that you have the correct software installed on the machine to drive the mouse.
- Contact the supplier or manufacturer, or buy a new mouse. They are not expensive.

Computer doesn't respond to keyboard

The computer appears to be working but fails to respond to the keyboard.

- If you have an infrared keyboard, try restarting the computer (see page 95).
- If your computer has a 'Keylock' light, make sure that it is not on. Some computers have a 'Keylock' switch which locks the keyboard so that it will not respond when the keys are pressed. Press the 'Keylock' switch again to see if the computer responds.

    Still not working?

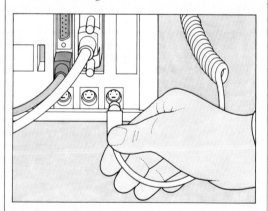

- Make sure that the plug at the end of the keyboard cable is plugged securely into the keyboard socket at the front or back of the computer. If it is held with screws, make sure that they are tight. Still not working?

- If there is a plug at the back of the keyboard, check that it is pushed into its socket securely.

    Still not working?
- Try restarting the computer (see page 95).

    Still not working?
- Contact the supplier, the manufacturer or a computer repair specialist (see *Computer disks*: 'Getting specialist computer help').

Computer printer

Cleaning the outside of a computer printer

Time: 1 hour or less

> YOU WILL NEED Printer wipes, or lint-free cloth and household spray cleaner or antistatic cleaner.

First, switch off the printer and unplug it from the mains.

Before starting to clean the printer, test the cleaning fluid on a small area that is not normally visible to make sure that it won't mark the finish.

Never use a cleaner that contains bleach or ammonia. The most suitable are general household spray cleaners or an antistatic cleaner, available from a computer shop.

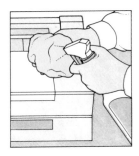

Don't spray the cleaner directly onto the printer. Transfer it onto a cloth and use the cloth to clean the unit. Make sure that no liquid enters any switches, controls or cooling grilles.

Rub off the polish with a clean, dry cloth.

Setting up a new application

If you have just bought a new application for your computer, such as word processor, database or spreadsheet, and the printer does not work properly, refer to the program's instructions and make sure that you have followed the set-up procedure correctly.

Check that you have correctly identified your printer model. Just transposing a number may cause a problem. If you cannot find your printer model on the program's printer list, refer to your printer manual. Printers often emulate other printer types, or the manual may suggest another model that can be used instead.

If you have no success, contact the supplier or a telephone helpline for advice (see below).

Getting specialist help for your printer

If your printer is not working properly, contact the manufacturer. Many have a telephone helpline, though you will probably have to pay for any help that you receive.

If the printer needs repairing, try to contact the supplier or the manufacturer first.

Alternatively, if you cannot get in touch with the supplier, contact a repair specialist such as PC Service (Tel. 01159 711000).

What model of printer?

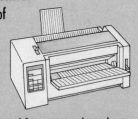

DOT MATRIX A 'matrix' of pins strikes the ribbon inside the printer in a sequence to form each character. Print quality is reasonable, but the printer is quite noisy.

It can change fonts and font size easily and print graphics. Inside the printer there is a print-ribbon cartridge which must be changed when it is empty.

DAISY WHEEL One of the earliest types of printer. It is generally used in offices. The printing wheel is the shape of a daisy, each 'petal' containing a single character.

Inside, there is a print-ribbon cartridge. Although print quality is very good, the printer is noisy and it cannot produce graphics or change fonts or font sizes without a change of daisy wheel.

INK JET There are three types of ink-jet printer, one of which is called a bubble jet. Ink jets and bubble jets squirt ink onto the paper to form each character. A bubble-jet printer uses air bubbles to force the ink onto the page.

A print cartridge inside contains the ink. Print quality is good and the printer is relatively quiet. It can change fonts and font size and is also able to produce graphics. Expensive models can equal the quality of some laser printers.

LASER PRINTER The paper is charged with static electricity which attracts the toner ink to create the image. The cartridge which contains the toner has to be changed when empty.

A laser printer produces prints of excellent quality and it operates quietly. It can produce graphics and is also able to change both fonts and font sizes.

Although laser printers can be expensive to buy the cost per printed copy is relatively low.

PROTECTING A PRINTER AGAINST DUST

To prevent dust accumulating on a printer when it's not being used, buy a printer cover from a specialist computer shop.

SAFETY FIRST WITH ELECTRICITY

Before starting any work on an electrical fitting or appliance, make sure to cut off the electricity supply — either by switching off at the main fuse box, or by unplugging the appliance.

Computer printer (cont.)

MONEY SAVERS FOR A LASER PRINTER

● When the toner cartridge runs out, remove it and rock it from side to side several times, then refit. This redistributes any unused toner and often gives another 20 copies. Make sure that you will not invalidate the printer's guarantee before following this advice.

● Buy a refill kit from a specialist computer shop and refill your toner cartridge. It costs about a quarter as much as a replacement cartridge.

MONEY SAVERS FOR AN INK-JET PRINTER

● Before following this advice check the terms of the printer's guarantee to make sure that you will not invalidate it.

Buy a refill from a specialist computer shop and refill the print head. It costs about a quarter the price of a replacement print head.

● Set your printer to 'draft' quality and only change back to print out the final copy.

Cleaning the inside of a laser printer
Time: 1 hour or less

Clean the inside of the printer each time you replace the ribbon, print head or cartridge.

> YOU WILL NEED Printer wipes or lint-free cloth, small clean paintbrush, cotton bud.

CLEANING THE LASER ASSEMBLY Switch on the printer.

Most laser printers produce a 'cleaning paper'. The paper contains a thick black strip, which you run through the printer to remove any build-up of toner on the laser and the toner assembly.

Do not use any other cleaning material.

Many printers produce the cleaning paper as part of the 'Test Print' procedure. If your printer does not, look at the manual under 'Cleaning the printer'.

When using the cleaning paper, make sure to feed it into the printer the correct way up. If you are not sure which is the right way, refer to the manual.

Discard the sheet after cleaning.

INSIDE THE CASING Now switch off and unplug the printer.

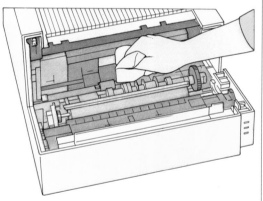

Open the printer and remove the cartridge. Then use either a printer-wipe or a dry lint-free cloth to wipe away any toner or dirt inside the printer.

Make sure that the casing of the toner cartridge is clean. Use a clean paintbrush to get into any awkward areas inside the printer, brushing outwards.

For small difficult-to-reach areas, use a cotton bud.

Cleaning the inside of an ink-jet printer
Time: 1 hour or less

> YOU WILL NEED Dry lint-free cloth, small clean paintbrush, cotton buds, WD40, methylated spirit.

CLEANING THE PRINT HEAD If your printer has a 'Cleaning' switch, start by using it to clean the print cartridge.

If there is no 'Cleaning' switch and you are having problems with the print quality, change the print head.

INSIDE THE CASING Switch off and unplug the printer.

Open the printer and remove the print cartridge. Take care not to touch the contacts or nozzles.

If the printer is a small one, start by turning it upside-down so that any large bits of dirt fall out.

Use a dry lint-free cloth carefully to clean any ink residue, paper dust and dirt inside the printer. To get into awkward places, use a clean paintbrush or a cotton bud, brushing outwards wherever possible.

THE PRINT ROLLER If the roller is accessible, carry out a small test first by putting some methylated spirit on a lint-free cloth and applying it to a small area at one end of the roller to ensure that it does not harm the roller material. If there is any sign of marking, do not continue, but wipe away the methylated spirit.

If all is well, wipe the cloth across the length of the roller, turning it as you go until all the roller is clean.

In ink-jet printers the print roller is often hidden. If this is the case and dirt is getting onto your pages, try coating an A4 sheet of paper with WD40 and feeding it, coated side against the roller, through the printer several times to remove as much of the ink residue as possible.

Use a cotton bud dipped in methylated spirit to clean the bail-bar rollers.

Finally, refit the print head.

Cleaning the inside of a daisy-wheel printer
Time: 1 hour or less

> YOU WILL NEED Lint-free cloth, small clean paintbrush, cotton buds, WD40, methylated spirit.

INSIDE THE CASING Switch off and unplug the printer. Then open it and remove the print-ribbon cartridge.

If the printer is a small model, you can start by carefully turning it upside-down so that any dust particles and large pieces of dirt fall out.

Use a dry lint-free cloth to clean out any ink residue, dust and dirt that has accumulated inside the printer.

To get into any awkward places in the printer use a clean paintbrush brushing outwards, and for difficult areas use a cotton bud.

THE DAISY WHEEL If the daisy wheel itself becomes contaminated with dirt and ink it can also be cleaned.

First, remove the daisy wheel. If you are not sure how to do this, consult your printer manual.

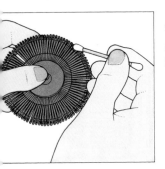

Dip a cotton bud in WD40 and clean each character on the daisy wheel in turn. Replace the wheel.

PRINT ROLLER First, put some methylated spirit on a lint-free cloth and apply it to a very small spot at one end of the print roller in order to make sure that it does not damage the material that the print roller is made from.

If there is any sign of marking, do not continue but wipe away all the methylated spirit. If all is well, continue to wipe the cloth along the length of the roller, turning it as you complete each length until the entire roller is clean.

To clean the bail-bar rollers, it may be easier to use cotton buds dipped in methylated spirit.

Finally, clean any ribbon guides in the printer with a cotton bud. Then replace the cartridge.

Cleaning the inside of a dot-matrix printer
Time: 1 hour or less

> YOU WILL NEED Lint-free cloth, small clean paintbrush, cotton bud, sheet of A4 paper, WD40, methylated spirit.

INSIDE THE CASING Switch off and unplug the printer.

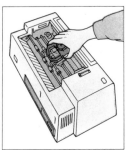

Open up the printer and then take out the print-ribbon cartridge.

If the printer is small, turn it upside-down so that larger particles of dirt fall out.

Then, use a dry lint-free cloth to wipe away any ink residue, paper dust and dirt.

To get into awkward areas, use a clean paintbrush, brushing outwards and clean any small, inaccessible areas with a cotton bud.

Do not replace the print-ribbon cartridge yet.

THE PRINT HEAD Spray a sheet of A4 paper with a good coating of WD40. Feed it into the printer so that the coated side ends up facing you and is the side to be printed on.

Plug in the printer and switch it on. Now type all the characters on your keyboard into the computer, and print them out onto the prepared paper.

Print them several times to ensure that the pins in the print head are well lubricated. This cleans all the individual print pins of any ink residue. As the cartridge is not in the printer, no characters will appear on the paper.

THE PRINT ROLLER Remove the coated paper, switch off the printer and pull out the mains plug.

Dampen some lint-free cloth with methylated spirit and carefully apply it to a small area at one end of the print roller to ensure that it does not harm the roller material.

If there is any sign of marking do not continue, but wipe away all the methylated spirit.

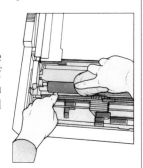

If all is well, wipe the cloth along the length of the roller, turning it as you complete each length until the entire roller is clean.

If the print roller is inaccessible, and dirt is getting onto your pages, coat an A4 sheet of paper with WD40 and feed it, coated side against the roller, through the printer several times to remove any ink residue.

Clean any visible bail-bar rollers with a cotton bud dipped in methylated spirit. Turn the rollers as you wipe them. Use cotton buds to clean any ribbon guides inside the printer. Refit the ribbon cartridge.

Plug the printer in, switch on and test it to make sure that all the characters are printing out. If not, see 'Faultfinder guide: Computer printer', next page.

Marking the roller for cleaning
When cleaning the roller, use a light coloured highlighter or wax crayon to make a mark at the starting point. Clean and turn the roller until the mark appears again. Clean it off with methylated spirit.

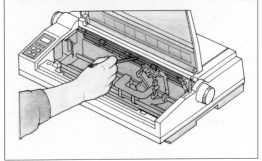

- A small lump of Blu-Tack under a print-ribbon cartridge moves the ribbon up slightly, using a different part of the ribbon and extending its life. This method will not work – and must not be attempted – on ink-jet or laser printers.
- Refill the print-ribbon cartridge yourself. It costs much less than a replacement cartridge. Check the terms of the printer's guarantee to make sure that you will not invalidate it by following this advice.
- If a cartridge is not the endless-loop type, you may be able to get more life out of it by winding the ribbon back into the empty spool.

Computer printer (cont.)

Faultfinder guide: Computer printer

All models

PROBLEM Power light doesn't come on.
- Make sure the printer is plugged in and that the mains socket, the computer and the printer are switched on.
- Check the mains socket by plugging in a table lamp or other appliance to see if it works. If it doesn't, see *Electric socket*. If it does, replace the fuse in the printer's plug.
- If the printer still won't work, the power lead may be faulty. Try using your computer lead. (If the printer then works, buy a new lead.)
- If it still fails to operate, contact the supplier, manufacturer or a computer repair specialist.
- Switch off the printer and unplug the computer and the printer from the mains.

PROBLEM Burning smell.

- If any cooling grilles are obstructed, clear them and switch on again. If there was no obstruction, take the printer to the supplier, manufacturer or a computer specialist.

PROBLEM Printer won't print.
- Is the printer plugged in and switched on?
- If so, make the following checks:
1 The printer is 'on-line' or 'ready'.
2 The data cable is securely plugged into both the computer and the printer.
3 The printer cartridge has ink, or toner, and is correctly installed.
4 The printer contains paper of the right size.
- If the printer still won't print, check if it will produce a test print (see the manual).
- If not, it is probably faulty. Contact the supplier or a computer repair specialist.
- If it does, enter **DIR>PRN** (in Windows, exit to DOS first). Has anything printed out?

- If it has, the fault probably lies with the application you are using. Look at the manual under 'Printers: Installation and Setting up'.
- If it hasn't, the computer is failing to communicate with the printer. Check that the data cable is firmly plugged into the printer and the computer and that the printer is 'on line' or 'ready', with paper available.
- If it still fails to work contact your retailer, the manufacturer or a computer repair specialist.

Dot-matrix or daisy-wheel printer

PROBLEM The print is faint.
- Is the print ribbon old? Try a new one.
- Is the ribbon damaged? Replace it.
- If there is a print-density control adjust it.
- Are you using different paper from usual? Try good-quality 80 gsm.
- Make sure the print-ribbon cartridge is correctly installed and seated.
- The print ribbon may be jammed. Free the mechanism or replace the cartridge.

PROBLEM Printing out incomplete or misshapen characters.
- DAISY WHEEL Check the daisy wheel itself for missing or damaged characters, and bent or broken arms. Replace the wheel if necessary.
- DOT MATRIX Pins may be jammed. See 'Cleaning inside a dot-matrix printer', page 101.

PROBLEM Operates but doesn't print.
- Is the print-ribbon cartridge installed? If not, install one.
- Print-ribbon cartridge not correctly installed or badly seated? Fit it properly.
- Print-ribbon cartridge at end of ribbon? Replace ribbon.
- Print-ribbon cartridge jammed? Free the mechanism or replace the ribbon.

Daisy-wheel printers only

PROBLEM Daisy wheel not installed or incorrectly installed? Install correctly.
- Daisy wheel damaged? Replace it.

PROBLEM Smudged print.
- Is the printer ribbon rubbing against the paper? If so, adjust it.

- Print-ribbon cartridge incorrectly fitted or seated? Refit.
- Have you recently reinked the ribbon? You may have overfilled it. Try a new one.
- Is the print-density control (if fitted) turned up too high? Adjust it.
- Have you changed to a heavier paper? Try 80 gsm paper.
- Is the inside of the printer dirty?
     If so, see 'Cleaning the inside of a daisy-wheel printer', page 100.

Ink-jet (bubble-jet) printer

PROBLEM Faint print.
- Is the print cartridge old? Either refill it or fit a new one.
- If there is a print-density control, adjust it.
- Are you using a different or low-quality type of printer paper?
     Try using good-quality 80 gsm paper.

PROBLEM Printing out incomplete or misshapen characters.
- Is the print head old? Install a new one.
- Make sure that the print head is correctly installed and seated.
- Printer or computer may be set up incorrectly. See 'Setting up a new application', page 99.

PROBLEM Printer operates but doesn't print.
- Ensure the print cartridge is fitted correctly.

- If the print cartridge is old or heavily used, it may be empty. Try a new one.

- The print-density control (if fitted) could be turned down to low. Increase it.
- If the printer or computer are new, they may not be set up correctly. See 'Setting up a new application', page 99.

PROBLEM Smudged print.

• Make sure the print cartridge is installed correctly.

• If you have refilled the cartridge yourself, you may have overfilled it. Try a new one.

• The print-density control (if fitted) might be turned up to high. Turn it down.

• Are you using a heavier printer paper than usual? Try using good-quality 80 gsm paper.

• Is the inside of the printer dirty? See 'Cleaning the inside of an ink-jet printer', page 100.

Laser printer

PROBLEM Faint print.

• Is the toner cartridge old? Try a new one.

• If a print-density control is fitted, try adjusting it.

• Some paper produces a fainter image. Try using good-quality 80 gsm paper.

• Make sure that the toner cartridge is correctly installed and seated.

PROBLEM Incomplete or misshapen characters.

• Is the toner cartridge old or heavily used? Try installing a new one.

• Make sure that the toner cartridge is correctly installed and seated.

• If the printer or computer is new, it may not have been set up correctly.

See 'Setting up a new application', page 99.

PROBLEM Operates but won't print.

• Make sure that the toner cartridge is correctly installed and seated.

• If the toner cartridge is old or heavily used, try fitting a new one.

• If a print-density control is fitted it might be turned down too low. Adjust it.

• If the printer or computer is new, it may not have been set up correctly.

See 'Setting up a new application', page 99.

PROBLEM Smudged print.

• If you have refilled the toner cartridge yourself, you might have overfilled it. Try using an old one.

• The print-density control (if fitted) might be turned up too high. Adjust it.

• If the printer has been moved, the toner cartridge might have been shaken. Try another cartridge.

• Is the inside of the printer dirty? See 'Cleaning the inside of a laser printer', page 100.

Computer virus

A computer virus is a program that has been written with the sole intention of infecting computers. Most viruses are harmful and damage information which is already stored on the computer.

Some lie dormant until a particular date, and are known as 'time bombs'. Others affect the computer system immediately they reach it.

These programs spread like biological viruses. A virus can reach a computer on a floppy disk that has been given to you; it can arrive through the Internet; it can come from a computer bulletin board or library; or it can be transmitted from another computer on a network or modem.

RECOGNISING A VIRUS The number of computer viruses in existence probably amounts to thousands and new ones are appearing all the time.

If your computer shows any of the following symptoms, it has probably been infected by one of them.

• Unfamiliar graphics – such as balls, faces or Pac Men – appear on the screen.

• Music, voices or strange sounds come from the speakers.

• Strange messages appear, such as:

April 1st HA HA HA You have a virus

• Characters disappear, or fall to the bottom of the screen.

• Files increase in size or change name.

• Files have strange messages in them, such as:

OOPS! Hope 1

• Details on the screen turn upside-down.

• The computer stops responding to the keyboard.

• The printer prints out whatever is displayed on the screen without warning.

• The computer appears to be running slowly.

• The hard disk access light is illuminated for no apparent reason.

• Extra characters may be added when you enter text; for example, test could become tttttttteeesst.

• The screen shows unusual error messages, such as:

Internal error 02CH. Please contact your hardware manufacturer immediately! Do not forget to report the error code!

CURING A VIRUS Antivirus programs, such as Norton's and Dr Solomon's, can be bought at computer shops.

Many antivirus suppliers offer regular upgrades that detect new viruses as they are discovered.

Some operating systems include an antivirus program, but it must be upgraded regularly to detect new viruses.

An antivirus program will scan all the files on the disks looking for viruses. If a virus is detected, the program will name it and offer to disinfect the system disk.

If a virus is found, all floppy disks that you own must be scanned and disinfected in case they are the source.

PREVENTING VIRUS INFECTION
• Where possible, use only new disks.
• Use an antivirus program to test any floppy disks that are lent, or sent, to you before using them.
• Treat all software downloaded from the Internet, World Wide Web, bulletin boards or software libraries in the same way as floppy disks.

Concrete floor

Resurfacing a damaged floor Time: $\frac{1}{2}$ a day or less

If the surface of a concrete floor has broken up, you can repair the holes with ready-mixed mortar which can be bought dry in bags from DIY outlets.

YOU WILL NEED Safety spectacles, heavy gloves, cold chisel, club hammer, dustpan and stiff brush, ready-mixed dry mortar, PVA building adhesive, bucket, board for mixing, old coarse paintbrush, small trowel or steel plasterer's float.

Protect your eyes with safety spectacles or goggles and wear gloves to protect your hands. (Mortar can burn your skin.) Using a cold chisel and a club hammer, chip away all the loose concrete.

Remove the dust and debris with a stiff brush.
To make up the mortar, add one part of PVA building adhesive to five parts of water, then add just enough of the liquid to the dry mortar to produce a dryish consistency, similar to that of a sand pie. Work on an old board.

Coat the damaged areas with neat PVA adhesive. Then press the mortar well into the damaged patches with a small trowel. For larger areas, use a steel plasterer's float (shown in the picture, left).

Do not over-use the float — you will weaken the surface of the concrete if you do; neat cement will be drawn to the surface and turn dusty when it dries.

Levelling a floor Time: 1 day or less

If a concrete floor is uneven, level it with a self-levelling, or screeding, compound. It comes ready-mixed in a tub.

YOU WILL NEED Self-levelling compound, small trowel, stiff broom, steel plasterer's float.

Take the compound straight from the tub with a small trowel and fill minor damage to a depth of 1.9 cm ($\frac{3}{4}$ in).

For the final surface, add water to the compound to form a more liquid consistency.

Sweep the floor with a stiff broom, then pour the contents of the tub onto the floor and spread it out evenly with a steel plasterer's float to form a layer between 1 mm and 3 mm (up to about $\frac{1}{8}$ in) thick.

It will dry sufficiently overnight to allow foot traffic, but let it dry thoroughly, for at least 24 hours, before applying any decorative covering.

Sealing a dusty floor Time: $\frac{1}{2}$ a day or less

Any untreated concrete floor will eventually develop a dusty surface. It is possible to seal it.

YOU WILL NEED Possibly: broom, dustpan, vacuum cleaner, PVA building adhesive, bucket, floor paint, large paintbrush.

Sweep up all loose dust or vacuum the whole area.
Mix one part of PVA building adhesive to four parts of water and, using a large paintbrush, liberally coat the floor with it — working from the farthest wall towards any door.

Alternatively, use floor paint, or garage-floor paint — which can withstand tyre marks and resist oil and grease.

Concrete path

Repairing cracks

Treat cracks in a concrete path with PVA building adhesive and ready-mixed mortar, as described in *Concrete floor*: 'Resurfacing a damaged floor'.

Removing algae and moss Time: parts of 2 days

Algae and moss growing on a path should not be ignored. When wet, they can be dangerously slippery.

> YOU WILL NEED Fungicide, watering can with rose, broom.

Apply fungicide with a watering can. After several days, the algae on the path should turn brown.

Sweep the path vigorously with a stiff broom to remove dead algae and treat it again with fungicide to inhibit any further algae growth.

Sweep the path again, a few days later.

Preventing slabs rocking Time: depends on the area

Most problems with concrete slab paths or patios can be traced to poor foundations. Rainwater often undermines the foundations of the path or patio, causing the slabs to rock. It is possible to restabilise them.

> YOU WILL NEED Garden gloves, spade, small trowel, heavy piece of timber, dry mortar, mixing board, watering can, batten, club hammer. Possibly: rubble.

Carefully lift the rocking slabs with a spade, move them away slightly and clean their undersides.

Consolidate the exposed ground, working rubble into any soft spots and tamping it down with a heavy piece of timber to just below ground level.

Make a dry mortar mix using bagged mortar and just enough water to dampen it, but no more. Apply five blobs of mortar to the gap, allowing it to heap up, then carefully lower the slab back into position.

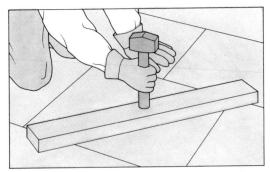

Place a batten right across the replaced slab so that it overlaps the surrounding slabs. Tap the batten with the handle of a club hammer until each replaced slab is level with the surrounding slabs. Allow the mortar to set for at least 24 hours before walking on the repaired area.

Resurfacing a concrete path Time: about a day

When the surface of a concrete path becomes rough, it can be resurfaced with a thin layer of concrete.

> YOU WILL NEED Broom, large coarse paintbrush, timber battens, wooden pegs, PVA building adhesive, bucket, shovel, fine concrete dry-mix, mixing board, safety spectacles, heavy-duty gloves, trowel or steel plasterer's float.

Sweep the path thoroughly, then paint it with PVA building adhesive diluted with an equal amount of water.

GETTING THE SURFACE LEVEL If you think you may have difficulty getting the surface level, use wooden pegs to fix timber battens on each side of the path so that the battens protrude 6 mm ($\frac{1}{4}$ in) above the old path level. They will contain the concrete and give you a level to work to.

TO MIX THE CONCRETE Use one part of PVA building adhesive to five parts of water and add them to a fine concrete dry-mix, to make up a dryish mix of concrete – about the consistency of a sand pie.

Mix the concrete on a board and protect your eyes with safety spectacles and your hands with heavy-duty gloves.

APPLYING THE CONCRETE Use a shovel and make sure that the concrete fills right up to the side battens. Tamp it down firmly with a length of timber held edge-on, to compact it. Aim for a thickness of about 6 mm ($\frac{1}{4}$ in) of concrete.

DRYING THE NEW CONCRETE In warm, dry weather, cover the newly concreted area with wet sacking or polythene sheeting to prevent it drying out too fast. Don't let anyone walk on it for at least 24 hours.

Avoiding cracks in a path

Cracks in a concrete path are often caused by long stretches of concrete being laid without any breaks.

When laying a path, insert a rough-sawn timber batten, about 10 mm ($\frac{3}{8}$ in) wide, across the path every 3 m (10 ft). The battens may be left in place after the concrete has set.

DEALING WITH ICY PATHS

If snow is forecast, spread sharp sand on the path to keep ice from bonding to the concrete. Clear snow with a spade, then spread more sand over the path.

Laying new concrete the easy way

Wet and Roll is an alternative to traditional concrete. Because it is laid dry, it takes a lot of the work out of concreting. Wet and Roll also gives a hard, crack-resistant surface.

Prepare the ground well, levelling it and filling soft spots with rubble. Then pour the dry-mix direct from the bag onto the area to be concreted.

Even out the dry-mix to about 5 cm (2 in) thick all over with a garden broom. Then use a steel plasterer's float to give as smooth a finish as possible.

Then sprinkle the concrete with water, using a watering can, in the quantity recommended.

To compact the surface, use a special light roller, available from the outlet that supplied the Wet and Roll. After 2 hours, sprinkle on more water. The new path will then be hard enough to walk on.

A STEAMLESS BATHROOM

To reduce steam in the bathroom, run some cold water into the bath first. Then feed hot water below the surface of the cold water through a short length of hose.

Mending a broken slab   Time: 1 hour or less

If a slab has broken in two, it can be glued together. But if it is badly damaged, discard it and get a new one.

YOU WILL NEED Garden gloves, stiff brush, PVA building adhesive. Possibly: sash cramps, wooden pegs and hammer.

Lift the slab, brush dirt off the broken surfaces. Apply PVA building adhesive liberally to both faces of the break. If you own or can borrow a pair of sash cramps, use them to force the pieces together and leave them for 24 hours.

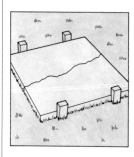

Alternatively, lay the slab on a flat area of earth or mown grass. Fit the pieces together and then hammer in pegs on both sides. Apply as much pressure as possible to push the pieces together.

Lay the slab back in place on a bed of new mortar, as it is important to ensure the repair is fully supported.

Repointing slabs   Time: depends on area

When the mortar pointing between the slabs of a path or patio is rendered crumbly by frost, it should be replaced.

YOU WILL NEED Small trowel, stiff brush and dustpan, dry mortar mix, board for mixing, watering can, old paintbrush, bucket.

Clean out any old pointing with the tip of a trowel and brush out dust and debris with a small, stiff brush.

Make up a very dry mix of mortar. Add just enough water to bind the mortar without obviously over-wetting.

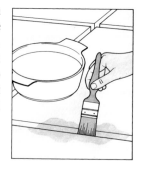

Dip an old paintbrush in clean water and dampen the cracks to be filled (right). Allow surplus water to drain off. Brush the mortar into the cracks, press it down and level it with the trowel, and then brush up any surplus.

Concrete mixing: SEE MORTAR

Condensation

Condensation increases as houses are made warmer and less draughty. Warm air holds more moisture vapour than cold, so steam from kitchens and bathrooms is rarely visible in a heated house. But when the moist air touches a cool surface, it condenses as droplets of water.

SOURCES OF MOISTURE The causes of condensation are easily traced — cooking, washing, drying, bathing and even breathing in an unventilated room.

Often the moist air can be isolated by shutting kitchen and bathroom doors, but this may not always be possible.

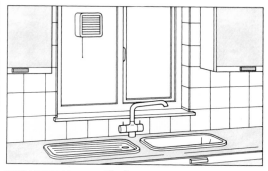

EXTRACTING THE AIR The best way to prevent condensation is air extraction. Fit an extractor fan in the kitchen, bathroom, above a shower cubicle and in a laundry room.

Ensure that a tumble drier is vented to the outside. And, when possible, sleep with a window open at night.

Useful reminder

Double glazing, cavity wall insulation and extra warmth will not necessarily solve the problems of condensation. They often merely move it on to other areas, such as cooler rooms, carpets and even into built-in wardrobes (see *Damp; Mildew & mould*).

A cooker hood which only recirculates air is no help at all. And a hood which is vented to the outside is not an efficient extractor of room air. It deals only with the immediate cooker area. Another extractor fan is needed to pull damp air down from the ceiling.

Extractor fans which incorporate a humidistat are switched on automatically when the moisture in the air reaches an unacceptable level. They are especially useful in kitchens and bathrooms.

VENTILATORS AND AIR BRICKS Ventilators and air bricks are not always effective because if the wind blows against them, cold air is pushed into the room and moisture-laden air will be moved to other parts of the house.

AIR EXCHANGERS Severe condensation can be solved by an air exchanger which extracts damp air and feeds in fresh air. It contains a heat exchanger that warms up the fresh air as it comes into the room so, unlike an extractor fan, it doesn't cool the room at the same time.

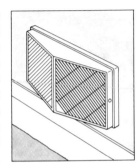

Cooker

Cleaning a self-cleaning oven Time: 1 hour or less

Special coatings on the back and side liners of catalytic and pyrolytic ovens – both gas and electric – allow you to burn off the grease which has accumulated through use.

YOU WILL NEED Cloth or soft brush, washing-up liquid.

Set the oven to above 240°C (475°F, gas mark 9) and leave it for about an hour to remove most of the grease.

Clean off any stubborn spots by using a cloth or soft brush and warm water with a little washing-up liquid. Never use oven cleaners or abrasive cleaners on catalytic or pyrolytic liners; they will damage the coating.

An oven that stays cold

If your oven won't come on, make these three checks before spending money on a service call.

- Make sure the automatic control is set to manual.
- On an electric cooker, make sure that the control unit on the wall beside the cooker is switched on.
- On an electric cooker, check to see if the cooker fuse has blown in the main fuse box (see *Fuse box*).

Protecting the oven floor

To lessen the drudgery of oven-cleaning, keep a spillage (or baking) tray permanently at the bottom of the oven to catch drips. But in an electric oven, first check that it doesn't cover any bottom heating elements. Remove the tray occasionally and clean it.

An alternative is to use wide aluminium foil and throw it away when it becomes greasy.

Cleaning an enamel-lined oven Time: 1 hour or less

Ovens that do not have the special coatings required for self-cleaning usually have an enamel lining, which may have to be cleaned with a chemical oven cleaner.

YOU WILL NEED Cloth or soft brush, cream kitchen cleaner, biological detergent. Possibly: oven cleaner, rubber gloves, goggles.

❗ Switch off an electric cooker at the control unit set into the wall beside the cooker before starting to clean it.

If a gas oven is supplied with mains electricity, switch it off at the wall socket and pull out the plug.

Remove all racks and trays – and the oven liners if they are detachable – and soak them in the bath in a solution of biological detergent which will 'eat' the grease. Use the right water temperature to suit the detergent. Protect the bottom of the bath with a shower mat or old towel.

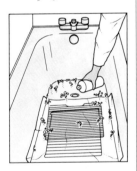

Use a cream cleaner on a damp cloth or soft brush to clean the inside of the oven. Do not use a scouring pad; it will scratch the enamel and attract more dirt in future.

For stubborn dirt, use a chemical oven cleaner. Read the instructions on the container carefully. Some cleaners work best in a cold oven, others at 50°C (122°F) (barely warm in a gas oven) and there are some that require as much as 200°C (400°F, gas mark 6) to work properly.

When using oven cleaners, which usually contain caustic soda, it is advisable to protect your hands with rubber gloves and your eyes with safety spectacles.

TREATING A COLD WALL

If condensation occurs on cold walls – perhaps in a bedroom next to a bathroom – it is often possible to reduce the risk by covering the affected walls with expanded polystyrene sheeting. It is sold especially as a wall covering, and provides a warm surface. Hang wallpaper over the expanded polystyrene. Cork tiles and wooden cladding also help to reduce condensation.

CLEANING A GLASS DOOR A glass inner door or a glass panel in the door itself can be cleaned with a cream cleaner on a nylon scouring pad, provided it is used gently.

Never use abrasive cleaners or wire pads; they may remove the heat-reflecting layer on the inside of the door, causing it to overheat and burn anyone who touches it.

How to clean gas burners

Take off the pan support and the cap over the burner when they are cool, and clean them with a cream cleaner and a stiff brush or an impregnated soap pad.

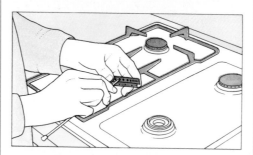

A matchstick or the tip of a plastic knitting needle may be used to clear the holes in the burners. Never use wire; it can distort the holes, the size of which is critical to the performance of the cooker.

Replace the parts and light the burners briefly to dry them out and prevent them from rusting up.

Cooker hood

Cooker hoods can be used over both gas and electric hobs to remove steam and cooking odours at source, and to protect the ceiling, cupboards and working surfaces from heat, steam and grease.

Do not fit a cooker hood above a cooker which has an eye-level grill, and never flambé a dish under a cooker hood as it is not designed to cope with very high temperatures at close range.

When to replace a filter

Some cooker hoods have an indicator to tell you when to change the grease filters. A build-up of grease on a filter is a fire hazard, so regular changing or cleaning is essential.

If your cooker hood does not have an indicator, the following recommendation, which is based on a family with two children eating two cooked meals a day, is a guide:

- Paper filters should be changed every three months.
- Metal and fibrous felt filters should be cleaned every three months. They can be reused after being washed.
- Charcoal filters should be changed every six months.

SAFETY FIRST WITH ELECTRICITY

Before starting any work on an electrical fitting or appliance, make sure to cut off the electricity supply – either by switching off at the main fuse box, or by unplugging the appliance.

What model of cooker hood?

There are two main types of cooker hood:

RECIRCULATING HOOD A charcoal filter removes most odours before recirculating the air into the room. Grease is captured by either a disposable paper filter or a washable filter made of metal mesh or fibrous felt.

EXTRACTING HOOD Before being vented to the outside, the air passes through a washable metal-mesh grease filter or a disposable filter. If the hood can be used in recirculating mode as well, it will also have a charcoal filter to capture and contain odours.

Changing or washing a filter   Time: 1 hour or less

YOU WILL NEED Screwdriver, rubber gloves. Possibly: new filter, washing-up liquid or liquid biological detergent.

REMOVING THE FILTER Disconnect the hood by pulling the plug out of the wall socket or switching off the power at the main fuse box. Then clear the hob of any obstruction.

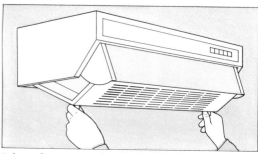

Release the screws or clips that hold the base of the cooker hood to the body. They are usually sited on each side of the underside of the hood. Take care when releasing the last screw, as some bases will drop under their own weight.

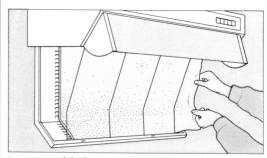

In most models the grease filter is held in place by metal retaining bars. Ease the filter out from behind the bars.

CHARCOAL OR PAPER FILTER Dispose of the grease-laden filter carefully – remember that it is a fire hazard and it may also attract vermin. Replace it with a new filter.

FIBROUS FELT FILTER Pull out the filter and wash it by hand. Do not wring it, as it will become distorted and impossible to refit. Lay the filter flat and press water out by hand, then allow it to dry naturally.

METAL FILTER Remove the metal filter. Many of them can be cleaned in a dishwasher, but if you do not have one, put it into a bath or basin of hot water and biological detergent. Protect the bottom of the bath with an old towel.

Let the filter soak for an hour or two and then use a stiff brush to remove any clinging grease. Rinse it in warm, clean water.

REPLACING THE FILTER In all cases, reverse the release procedure to replace the filter and the hood.

When a cooker hood will not work

If your cooker hood won't work, the problem might be a loose wire or a blown fuse. Take the plug out of the wall socket and check the fuse (see *Electric plug*). If you don't have a fuse tester, put in a new fuse. A cooker hood plug should have a 3 amp fuse. Restore the power. If the hood still does not work, turn off the power at the main fuse box and check the wall socket (see *Electric socket*) for loose connections

If the cooker hood is connected by a fused connection unit, test the fuse and replace it if necessary. If it still doesn't work, turn off the power at the main fuse box, remove the cover plate of the fused connection unit and make sure all connections are tight. Replace the cover plate and restore the power.

If it still does not work, call in an electrician.

Copper

Copper tarnishes quickly so clean it regularly. Use a brass and copper cleaner – the long-term type puts a tarnish-reducing film on the metal to keep it shining longer.

Coating copper with a clear lacquer makes the shine last, but it will eventually discolour beneath the lacquer.

The lacquer will then have to be removed with cellulose thinners or nail-varnish remover. Clean the copper very thoroughly before you lacquer it once more.

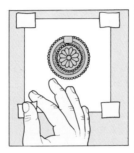

To polish copper that is part of wooden furniture, such as on drawer handles, make a rough template out of thin card to protect the wood. Stick it to the wood with masking tape and then polish the protruding copper.

Badly tarnished copper can be treated with a cleaning paste made from salt and lemon juice or vinegar.

If the copper is encrusted with dried metal polish, use a solution of 3 teaspoons of salt, 3 teaspoons of vinegar and 250 ml (9 fl oz) of hot distilled water. Use an old, soft toothbrush or cotton bud to clean intricate areas.

Verdigris (green stains) can be removed by wiping with neat ammonia. Rinse and dry immediately afterwards.

COOKING PANS Copper cooking pans are lined with tin or nickel to stop copper tainting the food. The exterior should be cleaned with a solution of vinegar and salt, then rinsed and dried. Have pans relined when the interior is worn.

Cork floor

Cleaning the floor Time: 1 hour or less

> YOU WILL NEED Broom or vacuum cleaner, bucket, floor mop, household floor cleaner.

Sweep the floor to remove loose dirt. You may need to clean the edges and corners with a vacuum cleaner.

Dissolve floor cleaner in water and dip the mop in the solution. Wring it out, because too much water may soak between the tiles and cause them to lift, then wipe the floor.

Reviving a 'tired' cork floor Time: parts of 2 days

Cork floors have a protective coating that can wear away.

> YOU WILL NEED Broom, household floor cleaner, lint-free rags, sturdy gloves, polyurethane varnish, large paintbrush.

Wash the floor thoroughly, using extra floor cleaner in the water. Allow it to dry thoroughly before proceeding.

Wearing sturdy gloves, use a lint-free rag to rub in a coat of flooring-grade polyurethane varnish. Work with the window open and remember to work towards a door.

Allow the varnish to dry overnight, then use a large paintbrush to apply a second coat of varnish. When it is dry, it should need no further treatment, apart from an occasional coat of emulsion polish.

Replacing a damaged tile Time: 1 hour or less

YOU WILL NEED Flexible filling knife, paint scraper, hot-air stripping gun or chemical paint stripper and brush, new tile, cork-tile adhesive and notched spreader.

Cut into the centre of the damaged tile with a filling knife. Slide the knife underneath the tile to lift it. Work towards the edges to loosen the whole tile and then remove it.

Soften any residual glue with a hot-air gun, and then scrape it off with a paint scraper (right).

If the heat doesn't soften the glue sufficiently, brush it with a chemical paint stripper, and follow the maker's instructions for removing it.

When the floor surface is clean and smooth, coat the back of the replacement tile with adhesive, using a notched spreader. Press the tile firmly into place and wipe off any surplus glue with a damp cloth.

Laying a cork floor

Cork tiles have different finishes. Some are coated with a tough vinyl film which is hard-wearing; some are sealed with polyurethane varnish; others are untreated. For the laying technique, see *Vinyl floor covering*.

If you buy untreated tiles, seal the undersides with flooring-grade polyurethane varnish before laying them, to reduce the risk of water penetration. Allow the varnish to dry thoroughly before laying the tiles.

Take great care not to let the tiles get dirty, and as soon as you have completed the floor, seal it with at least two coats of flooring-grade polyurethane varnish. If unsealed cork gets dirty, it is almost impossible to clean properly.

Cornice & coving

Plaster cornices, found in many older houses, can be renovated when a room is redecorated. Coving can be used in modern houses to hide cracks between walls and ceilings, as well as to add a decorative feature.

Restoring an old cornice Time: depends on area

YOU WILL NEED Garden spray, fine steel wool, penknife or narrow sculptor's spatula, plaster of paris. Possibly: chemical paint stripper, fine sandpaper, stepladder, cotton dustsheets.

CLEANING OFF DISTEMPER Layers of old decoration may obscure the detailed moulding of a cornice. If the coating leaves a chalky mark on your hand when you rub it, it has probably been distempered (a form of water-soluble whitewash), so it can be washed off with water. If the distemper has been painted over with another type of paint use a chemical paint stripper before trying to remove it.

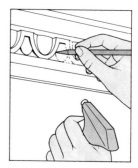

Use a garden spray to dampen only a small area of coving at a time. Allow the water to soak in then use a penknife or sculpting tool to pick out the build-up of distemper.

Take care not to apply leverage which could damage the moulding. On flat areas, use fine steel wool which can be bought from decorating shops.

REPAIRING DAMAGE It may be possible to build up damaged areas with plaster of paris and then reshape. Mix only a little plaster of paris at a time because it sets quickly. Build up the moulding layer on layer, then shape it with a knife blade and fine sandpaper.

Fitting new coving Time: depends on area

Three types of coving are available at DIY stores and builders' merchants. Expanded polystyrene and rigid foam plastic are lightweight and are sold in easily managed sections, so fixing is simple. Gypsum plaster coving is available in longer lengths up to 3 m (10 ft) and is heavier, so putting it in place needs two people.

YOU WILL NEED Coving, stepladder (two if you have a helper), steel tape measure. Possibly: chalked line, wallpaper scraper, suitable adhesive, masonry nails and hammer.

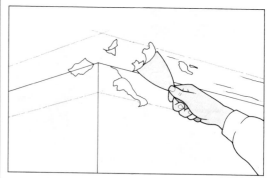

Scrape off any wallpaper or ceiling paper so that the new coving will be glued to bare plaster.

If the ceiling is uneven, use a chalked string to snap a straight line on the wall, marking the lower edge of the coving. Any gaps at ceiling level can be filled later.

PLASTIC COVING Some plastic coving systems come with ready-made corner pieces, so no mitre cutting is necessary.

Be sure to use an adhesive that is appropriate to the type of coving you are working with.

Starting from a corner, spread adhesive onto back of each section of coving and press it into position so that it fits snugly into the angle between wall and ceiling.

Remove any surplus adhesive while it is still wet.

If the wall or ceiling is uneven, don't force the coving to follow the surface; allow it to bridge the hollows. You can fill in the gaps with adhesive later.

Use only emulsion paint for decorating expanded polystyrene and rigid foam coving; gloss paint causes damage.

GYPSUM PLASTER Plaster coving has to be mitred at the corners so that the pieces fit snugly together.

A simple template, with cutting instructions, is usually supplied to help you cut the mitres, but experiment with the template on a small piece of coving before cutting a full length because it is easy to make a mistake.

The special adhesive supplied with the coving will usually hold plaster coving in place without extra support. But for a long, heavy piece, tap masonry nails into the wall under the bottom edge and just above the top edge of the coving to support it until the adhesive dries.

Fill any gaps between the sections of coving, or along the wall or ceiling, with adhesive.

Then prime the paper surface of the coving with plaster primer or general-purpose primer, and decorate with emulsion paint to match the colour scheme in the room.

What's the difference?

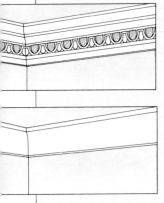

CORNICE An ornate decorative moulding made of either plaster or polystyrene, fitted to the top of a wall.

COVING A very plain, curved strip that fits into the angle formed by the meeting of the wall and ceiling, and links these two surfaces together.

Making your own mouldings

You can reproduce your own small sections of decorative plasterwork to patch a damaged area. All the materials you need can be bought at craft shops.

Use a rubber moulding compound to take a mould from an undamaged, matching section. Pour plaster of paris into the mould and allow it to set thoroughly (about an hour).

Cut out the damaged piece of cornice or coving to make way for the replacement. Cut the new piece to the right length, then stick it into place with PVA wood adhesive or special plaster-coving adhesive.

Crazy paving

One of the cheapest ways to make a path or patio is to fit together pieces of broken paving slabs.

Your local authority may sell off broken slabs which have been discarded during pavement resurfacing work. Alternatively, you can buy broken paving from a builders' merchant or a garden centre.

Paving is usually sold by the ton, and you will find that 1 ton covers approximately 8 m² (10 sq yd).

Laying a path   Time: about a week

YOU WILL NEED String, pegs, shovel, builder's rubble, cement, sharp sand, paving pieces, heavy piece of timber, straight timber plank, brick bolster, club hammer, builder's trowel, stiff brush.

PREPARING A FOUNDATION Decide on the width and route of the path, and mark out the area with string and pegs.

Clear topsoil to a depth of 10 cm (4 in), and ram in rubble with a heavy piece of timber to provide a firm surface.

You can get rubble from a demolition site or a contractor, or break up brick and stone to make your own.

Build a slight slope into the path, in order to help it to shed rainwater (see *Levelling*; 'Creating a sloping patio or path'). If the path runs along beside a house or another

REPLACING A LARGE PIECE OF PLASTERWORK
If a large area of cornice has been damaged, or if you wish to match existing cornice in another room, contact one of the specialist companies that make traditional fibrous plasterwork, using many of the original Victorian moulds. They are listed in *Yellow Pages* under 'Plastering & screeding'.

building, it should slope gently away from the wall. Make sure that the surface of the path is at least 15 cm (6 in) below the damp-proof course so that rain cannot splash off the path onto the wall above the damp-proofing.

LAYING THE PAVING The edges of the path must have solid support. You should either excavate below the level of the lawn and use the lawn edges as walls (right), or lay kerbing.

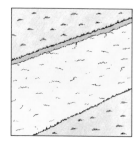

Pick out the pieces of paving with the straightest sides to line the outer edges of the path. Lay out the stones first in the shape of the path to make sure that they will all fit together. Then put them to one side in order.

Make up a dryish mortar mix of 1 part cement to 4 parts sharp sand. Only lay enough mortar to take two or three stones at once, or it will dry out before all the paving stones are in place.

Spread the mortar about 2.5 cm (1 in) thick. Roughen the surface with the point of a trowel and place the stones directly in position. Do not slide them.

Bed down the pieces of paving to form the path edges, leaving a gap of just over 1.3 cm ($\frac{1}{2}$ in) between the pieces. Then tap them in place with the handle of a club hammer.

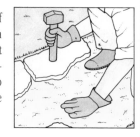

As you work check across the path for slope and use a straight timber plank or spirit level to make sure that the surface is even and none of the stones are tilted.

Fill in the middle of the path. Trim any pieces that do not fit with a brick bolster and club hammer, using the same technique as for cutting a brick (see page 168).

Some pieces of paving may be thicker than others and will need bedding more deeply into the mortar.

APPLYING MORTAR Make up a very dry mortar mix using 1 part cement to 2 parts sand by volume, and an absolute minimum of water – and brush it between the paving. Compact it with the tip of a trowel, then brush off any surplus. The dry mix will not stain or mark the paving stones.

CARING FOR YOUR BAT

To prevent damage, such as cracks, to a bat with a natural wood finish oil it properly. Use a clean rag to coat the bat with linseed oil.
If you play regularly, oil your bat at the start and end of every season and also once mid season, but do not over-oil. If a bat has not been used for a long time, it will need a good coating.
Bats with a synthetic covering, such as vellum, do not need oiling.

Cricket bat

Replacing a worn rubber grip

The rubber grip that covers the handle of a bat may wear out several times during the lifetime of the bat. You can buy a new rubber grip from any sports shop, but they are not easy to fit.

Grips are usually rolled onto the handle using a bat cone. Unless you can borrow a cone it is usually best to ask the sports shop to fit the grip for you.

Preparing a new bat

All new cricket bats need to be 'knocked-in', which involves hitting them with a bat mallet or an old ball in a sock. This prepares the surface for the battering it will take at the crease.

When you buy a new bat, ask if it has been pre-sealed. If it has not, oil it with linseed oil. Then knock-in the bat all over and for as long as possible, paying particular attention to the bottom and sides.

A cricket bat can suffer small gashes and splits. For a small split, try taping the bat with white binding tape, obtainable at sports shops. Wrap the tape all the way round the bat.
If a larger split appears you should take it to a sports shop or cricket specialist who can 'peg' it.

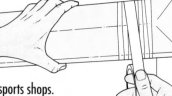

Repairing a broken stump Time: parts of 2 days

If a cricket stump snaps with a long, tapering break you can glue it together with wood glue. But if the stump snaps straight across, you will have to replace it.

YOU WILL NEED Wood glue, adhesive tape, fine sandpaper.

Apply an even coating of glue to the surfaces of the break then press them together tightly. Make sure it is straight, or the bails will not sit on top of the stumps.

Wipe away any surplus glue with a damp cloth. Then bind the break firmly with adhesive tape.

When the glue has set, peel off the tape and clean up all round the repair with some fine sandpaper.

Crystal: SEE GLASSWARE

Cupboards & wardrobes

Adjusting hinges   Time: 5 minutes per hinge

Most hinges on modern cupboards are usually concealed and have at least four screws, which can be used to adjust the position of the doors – both in relation to the cupboard and to doors on adjoining cupboards.

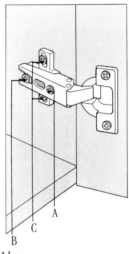

● To move a door closer to its neighbour, or to ensure that doors are parallel, turn screw A on each hinge.
● To move a door closer to or farther from the cupboard, loosen screw B and slide the hinge in or out. Tighten screw B.
● To move the door up or down in relation to the cupboard. Loosen screws C by one turn and move the hinge either up or down. Then tighten screws C.

Hanging a cupboard   Time: 1 hour

The exact method used for fixing a cupboard to a wall will depend on the type of wall. Different types of wall – for example, brick or plasterboard – will require different wall fixings (see *Wall fixings*).

> YOU WILL NEED Spirit level, pencil, power drill, masonry bit or twist bits, wall plugs, round-headed screws, screwdriver.
> Possibly: batten the length of the cabinet.

HANGING FROM FIXED HOLES Some cupboards have metal plates, with holes set in the corners at the back. These are the most difficult to hang as no adjustment is possible.

Prop the cupboard in place, for example on a table with piles of books, or ask a helper to hold the cupboard against the wall, so you have both hands free. Check with a spirit level and mark through the metal plates onto the wall with a pencil.

Take down the cupboard, drill the wall and plug it if necessary (see *Wall fixings*). Then fix the cupboard in place with round-headed screws.

SUPPORT WITH A BATTEN If the cupboard may need extra support to hold a heavy load, fit a batten to the wall immediately below where the base of the cupboard will be.

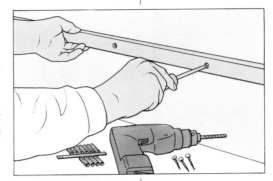

Drill holes in the batten, where the screws will go. Mark the position of the screws on the wall through the holes in the batten. Drill holes in the wall and insert wall plugs then screw the batten in place.

Lift the cupboard onto the batten and ask a helper to hold it in place while you mark through the fixing plates. Drill holes, fit wall plugs and screw the cupboard in place.

USING ADJUSTABLE HANGERS Some cabinets come with adjustable cabinet hangers which allow for adjustment once the cupboard is in place. But you still need to take care to get the cupboard as accurately placed as possible.

Alternatively, fit adjustable hangers yourself.

Strengthening a tubular clothes rail   Time: ½ an hour

To provide extra support and prevent a tubular clothes rail sagging in the middle, fit a centre support bracket.

> YOU WILL NEED Screwdriver, centre support bracket, pencil or bradawl, hand or power drill, twist bits, steel tape measure.

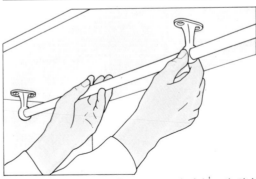

Remove the support bracket at one end of the rail. Slide the centre bracket onto the rail and position it centrally.

Hold the centre bracket in place and mark the screw holes on the underside of the shelf above. Remove the rail and drill the holes. Reposition the rail, and screw the support and centre brackets in place.

SPACE SAVER

Make better use of wardrobe space by fitting an extending wardrobe rail from front to back instead of side to side. As it slides forwards all clothes are easily accessible.

FIT A STRONGER CLOTHES RAIL

Replace a circular rail with an oval-shaped one which can support more weight.

Curtain poles & tracks

Fixing curtain track in place Time: ½ a day or less

Curtain track comes in a variety of designs and is made of either plastic or metal. For bay windows, plastic track will curve around the window and metal track may be available already curved by the supplier.

> YOU WILL NEED Steel tape measure, mini-hacksaw, bradawl, power drill and masonry bit or twist bit, screwdriver.

The curtain track needs to be wider than the window so that the curtains can be pulled right back out of the way. Measure the space that the track is to occupy and cut the track to length with a mini-hacksaw.

MAKING THE FIXING HOLES The curtain track will have to be fixed either to the top of the wooden architrave or else directly into the wall above the window opening.

First, put the wall brackets on the track at the spacing recommended by the manufacturers, on the packaging.

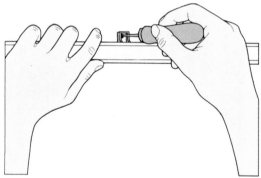

Hold the track in position against the wall and push a bradawl through the holes in the brackets to mark where the screw holes will have to be made. You will need to ask someone to help you if the track is a long one.

If the screws are to go into wood, make a narrow pilot hole with a fine twist bit. If they are to go into the wall, use a masonry bit large enough to take a wall plug. Put the holes at least 5 cm (2 in) above the window opening, otherwise the masonry may break away.

A wall that proves extremely hard probably contains a concrete lintel. Try using a power drill set on hammer action. If the concrete is too hard, fix a piece of wood across the top of the window, nailing it to the wall where it extends beyond the ends of the lintel. Screw the track to the wood.

If the plaster starts to break away from the wall, abandon the curtain track and use a curtain pole instead. A pole will only need to be supported at each end, rather than all the way along. Probe the wall above the window with a bradawl until you find the ends of the lintel and then drill and plug for the pole brackets.

PUTTING UP THE TRACK Screw the support brackets into the prepared holes in the wall. Then line up the curtain track so that it is positioned centrally over the window.

Undo the holding screws on the brackets to allow you to slide the track along until it is in the correct position, then tighten the screws. Put the hooks on the track and fit the end stops.

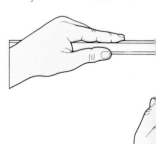

Choosing a curtain pole or track

Curtain poles are more decorative than tracks but they can only be used on straight walls. Curtain tracks can be bent to follow the shape of curved window alcoves.

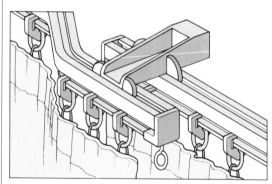

CURTAIN TRACK Can be fitted in two halves overlapping, so that the curtains will close properly when drawn. The least expensive type of track can be used if a valance will hide it.

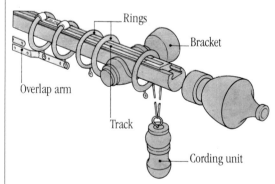

Rings

Bracket

Overlap arm

Track

Cording unit

CURTAIN POLES Available in two styles: either with loose rings around a plain pole, or with rings attached to gliders on a track (above). Loose rings can leave a gap where the curtains meet, but the glider type will allow the curtains to overlap in the centre, to cut down draughts.

ELECTRIC CURTAIN TRACKS Consider installing electric curtain tracks with a timeswitch to deter burglars. The curtains will be drawn automatically, at a time chosen by you, giving the impression that someone is at home.

Fixing brackets to the ceiling

If there is no space above the window, curtain-track brackets can be fixed to the ceiling. But ceiling plaster alone is unable to take the weight, so screws must go into the timber joists above.

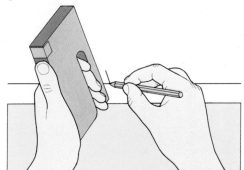

Locate the timber joists with a joist-and-stud detector which can be bought at DIY stores, and mark them.

Draw a pencil line on the ceiling where the track is to go, then mark where the joists cross the line and mark the drilling points.

If the joists are spaced awkwardly, or at right angles to the track, it may be easier to use a curtain pole which only needs to be fixed at each end.

Curtains

Keep curtains dust-free by cleaning them with the soft dusting-brush attachment of a vacuum cleaner.

Expensive curtains should always be cleaned by a firm of experts who will come to your home and measure the curtains, remove them for cleaning, and then rehang them.

WASHING CURTAINS Washing is suitable for unlined curtains made from washable fabric. If curtains are lined, have them dry-cleaned, since one fabric may shrink more than the other, making them hang badly. Some curtains have detachable linings, which can be washed separately.

DRY-CLEANING CURTAINS Use a coin-operated machine at a launderette for dry-cleaning, but first check that the cleaning solution is changed frequently, otherwise your curtains may come out with an unpleasant smell.

Whether they are dry-cleaned professionally or in a coin-operated machine, air curtains well, as the cleaning solution can produce toxic fumes.

If you transport them by car, keep the windows open and don't smoke, and if you rehang them immediately, leave the windows open for a few hours, particularly in bedrooms.

Lengthening curtains   Time: 2 hours or less

Curtains can be lengthened if you move to a house with large windows, or decide to move them to a taller window.

YOU WILL NEED Two pairs of matching short curtains or new fabric, scissors, pins, seam ripper, needle, thread.

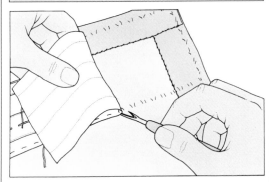

First, let down the hem and brush out any debris trapped in it, then release the heading tape. Wash or dry-clean the curtains. If there is enough fabric, turn up a smaller hem.

INSERTING EXTRA FABRIC If there is not enough fabric in the old hem to turn up a new one, insert one or more widths of new fabric – perhaps a pattern into plain curtains, or a plain colour into patterned ones.

Measure how long the new curtains need to be. Decide how many horizontal bands you plan to insert (two or three narrow bands will look better than one large stripe).

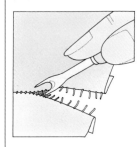

If the curtain has been lined, remove the lining by unpicking the side seams with a seam ripper (left) or a pair of sharp embroidery scissors. Be careful not to cut the fabric accidentally.

Cut the new fabric to size, leaving a 2.5 cm (1 in) seam allowance at the top and bottom, taking into account that you will also need to take the same seam allowance out of the existing curtain fabric.

Decide where you want the bands to run and mark the cutting lines on the curtains with a pin on each side.

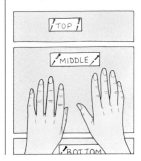

Cut along the lines on the curtain, making sure that you will be able put it all together again in the correct order – it may help if you mark the pieces top, middle and bottom.

Pin, tack and stitch the new bands of fabric into the original curtain fabric, finishing off each seam securely, then lengthen the lining by the same amount.

With wrong sides facing, stitch the lining to the curtains at the side seams (left) and press the seams. Turn the curtain the right way out, press all the seams and reattach the header tape.

LETTING THE CURTAINS SETTLE Hang the curtains in place for a few days so that the fabric can settle, before you hem them. If they are made from heavy fabric or are lined and interlined, hang them for a week before hemming them.

Recycling old curtains

Even the oldest curtains can have their uses.
• Cotton curtains make good dust sheets to protect furniture when you are decorating, or something to kneel on when you are working on the car.
• If the fabric is in good condition it can be used to make dressing-up clothes, cushion covers, peg bags, laundry bags or aprons.
• As a last resort, cut up the curtains for use as cleaning rags or as bedding for your pets.
• Whatever use you put old curtains to, give them a good laundering first to remove any dust.

Shortening curtains Time: 1 hour or less

YOU WILL NEED Scissors, pins, needle, thread. Possibly: unpicker.

Remove the curtains from the track. If you are going to take this opportunity to wash or dry-clean them, remove the hooks, release the header tape and undo the gathers.

Measure the new length, allowing 5 cm (2 in) or more for the hem, depending on the length of the curtain – the longer the curtains, the deeper the hem should be.

Cut off the unwanted fabric at the bottom. (It may be worth keeping the excess fabric in case you decide to lengthen them again some time in the future.)

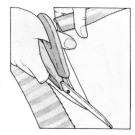

Hang up the curtains, fold up the seam allowance and then pin, tack and hand stitch the new hem into position. Make sure that both curtains are the same length.

Altering lined or interlined curtains

Whether you are lengthening or shortening curtains which are lined or interlined, remove the lining or interlining and adjust it before stitching it back in place.

If you are lengthening curtains, simply add new lining or interlining to the bottom of the old lining. It will not be visible, so it does not need to match.

Cutlery (SEE ALSO SILVER, STAINLESS STEEL)

Straightening a bent knife blade Time: a few minutes

YOU WILL NEED Wooden chopping board, thick card or blotting paper, hammer, metal polish, cloth.

The blade of a knife can become bent if too much pressure is exerted on the tip. It is possible to straighten it. Place the blade flat on a solid surface, such as a wooden chopping board, and allow the handle to lie off the edge.

Protect the blade with a piece of thin card or a wad of blotting paper, then hammer it firmly but gently until the tip flattens out.

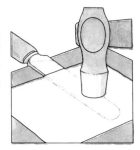

Polish the blade with a metal cleaner that is appropriate to the material from which the blade has been made.

Straightening a buckled knife blade Time: about a day

If a knife blade has developed a bend in the middle – for example, if it has been used for prising apart something that has stuck – it is possible to bend it back into shape.

YOU WILL NEED Clamp or vice, two blocks of hardwood. Possibly: wooden chopping board, thick card or blotting paper, hammer, metal polish, cloth.

Clamp the blade of the knife between two blocks of hardwood and leave it there for several hours, tightening the clamp occasionally. (If the wood is not very smooth, protect the blade with a wad of blotting paper.)

Alternatively, use the hammering procedure for bent blades (see 'Straightening a bent knife blade', above) repeating it at intervals until the blade is straight.

Reshaping a bent fork prong Time: 1 hour or less

> **YOU WILL NEED** Wooden ruler, clamp or vice.

If the prongs on a fork have become bent together, use a ruler to separate them one at a time.

For the best results, you may need to leave the ruler in position between each pair of prongs for an hour or so.

If all the prongs are bent upwards, protect them with a cloth, put them into a vice, and tighten the vice until all the prongs have reached the correct position.

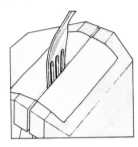

Fixing a loose handle Time: parts of two days

Wood, bone and plastic handles on cutlery can work loose with time, particularly if they are washed repeatedly in very hot water, or washed in a dishwasher against the manufacturer's recommendation.

> **YOU WILL NEED** Old screwdriver, abrasive paper, epoxy-resin adhesive, masking tape. Possibly: pliers or Mole grips, skewer.

Remove the loose handle. If you need to use pliers or Mole grips, protect the knife or fork with a cloth.

Prise out all the old adhesive inside the handle with the blade of a screwdriver. You may need to finish off with a thin kitchen skewer.

Rub the tang (the pointed metal end that fits into the handle) with abrasive paper to remove any old adhesive.

Mix up the epoxy-resin adhesive and fill the hole in the handle two-thirds full with it, using the screwdriver blade to press it right in. Push the tang firmly into the handle, until it is in the correct position. Wipe off any surplus adhesive with a damp cloth, and wipe the screwdriver blade.

Leave the adhesive to harden for the length of time recommended on the pack. Finally, remove the masking tape, and clean up the join with a damp cloth.

Reshaping a spoon Time: a few minutes

> **YOU WILL NEED** Dome-headed hammer, sturdy curved surface such as a darning egg, cloth.

Where the bowl of a spoon has curved inwards, wrap the head of a dome-headed hammer in a cloth and use it to tap the spoon gently back into shape.

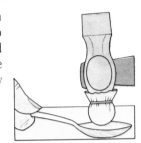

If the bowl of the spoon is distorted outwards, place it over a firm, curved surface (first protected with a cloth) and hammer it back into shape.

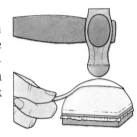

Caring for special surfaces

CARBON-STEEL KNIFE BLADES New carbon-steel knife blades are very much like stainless steel, but discolour easily and eventually look patchy.

Always wash and dry them immediately after use. Rub stains with a nylon scouring pad or an abrasive cleaning powder. Wipe carbon-steel blades with a few drops of cooking oil on paper towel before putting them away.

BONE AND IVORY HANDLES Wash only the blades, and keep the handles dry at all times. If you can't wash up immediately after a meal, soak the metal part of the cutlery in a jug of warm water and washing-up liquid.

Bone and ivory handles usually have silver blades. Store silver cutlery, when not in use, in acid-free tissue paper, available from jewellers and department stores.

MOTHER-OF-PEARL HANDLES Keep mother-of-pearl handles out of water, because they are porous and absorb grease easily. Wash blades in warm soapy water in which no other item has been washed, so that no grease gets onto the handles. Occasionally rub a small amount of white cream furniture polish over the handles.

BRONZE CUTLERY If it is looked after carefully, bronze will acquire a deep, glowing patina. However, as it stains very easily, it should be washed by hand immediately after use. Do not put it into a dishwasher.

Clean the pieces occasionally with metal polish, but wash them well afterwards. Rinse and dry them thoroughly with a soft cloth before using them.

Damp

Once you have identified the type of damp causing a problem, you can decide on the best treatment for it.

As a general rule, damp patches on mild, rainy days are almost certainly structural damp, whereas patches on cold, dry days are probably due to condensation in which case, see *Condensation*.

This section deals specifically with structural damp.

Finding the cause of damp ceilings

Damp patches on top-floor ceilings may indicate damage to the roof or chimney pots. Venture onto the roof to inspect it only if you feel confident. Always use a roof ladder which hooks over the ridge of the roof (see *Ladders*).

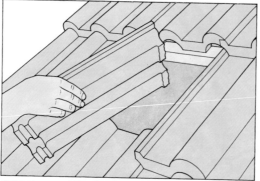

SLIPPED TILES Tiles should have small projections or nibs to hook over battens, but if the nibs have broken off treat the tiles in the same way as slipped slates (see also *Roof*).

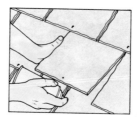

SLIPPED SLATES Lift a loose slate enough to remove any debris. Push it back into place, then inject a little expanding foam filler under the centre of the slate. Press it down (see also *Roof*).

LOOSE FLASHING When existing flashing round chimneys and dormer windows is sound but loose, use a bitumen rubber sealant as an adhesive to stick it back in place.

If it has become cracked or perished, clean away any crumbly mortar and coat it with flashing primer. Let the primer dry, and cover it with two overlapping layers of flashing tape, pressed firmly against the wall.

CRACKS BETWEEN FLAT ROOF AND HOUSE WALL Clean debris from existing flashing, then prime with flashing primer and cover with self-adhesive flashing tape, as above.

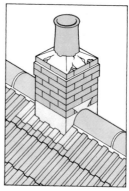

DAMAGED CHIMNEY Call in a builder to repair damage to any chimney pots or the flanching that surrounds the base of the pot.

LOOSE RIDGE TILES Take off loose tiles, remove debris, apply fresh mortar and bed the tiles into it. Fill spaces between tiles with mortar.

Damp walls

When damp appears on interior walls, there is a temptation to apply a material to seal it out. This is inadvisable, as damp often simply spreads beyond treated areas and causes further problems.

Always cure the source of the problem first. An anti-damp paint may then be used before decorating the walls.

GUTTERS AND DOWNPIPES Leaking gutters and downpipes can cause damp patches on the wall inside the house (see *Gutters & downpipes*).

WINDOWS AND DOOR FRAMES Gaps round windows and door frames are entry points for damp. During storms and high winds rain can be forced through even the smallest gaps, causing frame rot.

Start by scraping out the existing filler. This could be mortar or putty (both of which are far less suitable than a flexible material). Clean away any loose material and make sure that the gap is clean and dry.

Fill all round the frame with exterior grade sealant, forcing it right down into the cracks. Start at the top and then work downwards. The nozzle on the tube of sealant is angled to make this easy to do.

Smooth down the sealant with a wet finger or piece of damp lint-free rag. The sealant will remain flexible and allow slight movement of the frames.

POROUS POINTING The pointing between the bricks on the outside of a wall can become porous, causing damp on the inside. Faulty pointing should be repaired as soon as possible (see *Brickwork*).

OVER-POROUS BRICKWORK Porous brickwork can have a cooling effect on walls, which encourages condensation inside the house. Treat the walls with waterproofing liquid, such as Thompson's Waterseal or Cuprinol Clear Water Seal which keep out rain yet allow the wall to 'breathe'.

FAULTY DAMP-PROOF COURSE Damp patches indoors, at skirting-board level, can often be traced to faults in the damp-proof course. If you suspect problems, call in a reputable damp specialist company. Use a member of the British Wood Preserving and Damp-proofing Association. Look in *Yellow Pages* under 'Damp-proofing & control'.

To do the job yourself, borrow equipment from hire shops to inject a damp-proof course into walls. Make sure the equipment comes with full instructions.

Apart from faults in the damp-proof course, anything that bridges the course can cause problems, so keep flower borders, rockeries and stored building materials away from walls. Ensure that paths and patios are at least 15 cm (6 in) below the level of the damp-proof course.

Damp floors and basements

CONCRETE FLOORS A properly constructed concrete floor should have a built-in horizontal damp-proof course to prevent moisture rising up from the ground. But this may not be the case in older houses. If there are signs of damp rising through the concrete, treat the bare concrete with a bitumen-rubber waterproofing compound. If the damp persists, get professional advice.

BASEMENTS Ask for professional help from a surveyor or a local building control officer.

Darning

Darning can be done by hand or by machine, but hand darning is usually neater, especially on delicate fabrics.

Darning by hand Time: 1 hour or less

> YOU WILL NEED Darning needle, matching thread or wool, darning mushroom, scissors.

DARNING A HOLE Place a darning mushroom or the smooth base of a cup or jar under the hole, taking care not to stretch the fabric. Work on the right side, so that you can see the finished effect as you sew.

Use a darning needle and matching thread or wool. Start by running a neat frame of stitches round the hole in the fabric to strengthen it and stop it spreading as you darn.

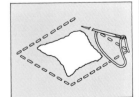

Lay a warp of threads running across the hole in one direction. Then weave a series of weft threads at right angles across them, taking a small anchoring stitch at each side. Fasten off securely, out of sight.

DARNING A TEAR Use a fine, sharp darning needle. If you can pull out a thread from the seam allowance use it as the darning thread. Do not use a very long thread.

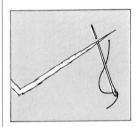

Tie a small knot in the end of the thread, or fasten it by taking a couple of small stitches on the inside of the fabric, then pull the thread through from the wrong side of the fabric to the right side.

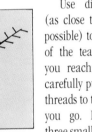

Use diagonal stitches (as close to each other as possible) to hold both sides of the tear together until you reach the other end, carefully pushing any loose threads to the wrong side as you go. Finish off with three small stitches.

If the tear is likely to have pressure put on it while being worn, darn the area very neatly too (see above).

Deathwatch beetle

Deathwatch beetles live in old timber, but are becoming rarer as the number of old buildings diminishes and others are treated for infestation. The distinctive, hollow tapping – often noticeable at night – is the sound of a beetle striking its head against wood.

Adult deathwatch beetles are a mottled greyish-brown with yellow patches. They are about 6 mm ($\frac{1}{4}$ in) long, and the holes in the wood through which they emerge are 3 mm ($\frac{1}{8}$ in) wide. Holes half this size are more likely to have been caused by furniture beetles (see *Woodworm*).

Small outbreaks of deathwatch beetle can be eliminated by spraying surfaces and injecting woodworm fluid into the holes. If a large area is affected, get help from a reputable wood preservation company.

Decanter:

SEE BOTTLES, DECANTERS AND JARS

DAMP WARDROBES AND CUPBOARDS

In most cases the problem is caused by condensation (see *Condensation*). Damp on external walls, which may or may not be adjacent to the damp wardrobe or cupboard, can also be traced to porous brickwork, bridged wall ties or faults in the gutters and downpipes.

DARNING NEAR A SEAM

You should find it easier to darn near a seam if you unpick the stitches and lay the garment flat.

PREPARING WOOL FOR DARNING

When using leftover wool to darn a well-washed hand-knitted jumper, shrink it to match first. Hold the lengths of wool over a pan of boiling water or the spout of a boiling kettle (mind your fingers) for a minute or so. Dry it before darning.

Deckchair

Exposure to sun and rain will eventually damage a deckchair. The canvas may rot or become discoloured by mildew and the woodwork can split or crack.

Replacing the canvas Time: 1 hour or less

First measure the length of the canvas you need. Most big department stores sell replacement canvas for deckchairs. It comes in the correct width and a range of colours.

> YOU WILL NEED Long-nosed pliers or an old chisel, replacement canvas, scissors, large-headed tacks, hammer.

Release the canvas from the frame, either by pulling out the old tacks with pliers, or by levering them out with an old chisel.

Using the old canvas as a guide, cut the replacement canvas to length. Turn the canvas pattern-side down on a level surface, such as the lawn.

Fold the deckchair flat and lay it face down on top of the canvas. Fold a 2.5 cm (1 in) 'hem' at one end of the canvas and wrap it round the rail at the end of the seat section. Make sure that the canvas is straight and is evenly positioned between the side supports of the chair.

Placing the tacks so that they won't show when the chair is in use, tack the canvas to the frame at 5 cm (2 in) intervals.

Before attaching the canvas to the other end of the frame, assemble the deckchair and check that you have got the canvas in the right position.

Lay the chair flat again. Pull the canvas taut at the other end, but don't stretch it. Repeat the fixing process.

Tightening a loose joint Time: ½ a day or less

> YOU WILL NEED Craft knife, PVA wood glue, block of wood or metal, hammer, oil.

If a joint has come loose, pull it apart carefully and scrape away any old adhesive with a craft knife. Coat the joint with wood glue and reassemble. Apply pressure to the joint with a string tourniquet (see *Chair*) until it has dried.

To repair a loose rivet, place a block of wood or metal under the rivet head to support it and act like an anvil, and then gently tap the other end.

If the rivet acts as a pivot point, apply a little oil.

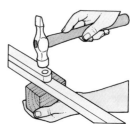

Decorators

When you are hiring a decorator stick to these simple rules to avoid wasting money on an unsatisfactory result.

They could also save you from becoming the victim of a 'cowboy' who might take your money and disappear.

- Whenever possible use someone recommended by a friend. Get as many recommendations as possible.
- Get several estimates for a job, then compare them closely for different specifications.
- Make sure that everyone working on your job is suitably qualified to do the work.
- Don't be misled by cheap quotes; they could mean sub-standard work. Time, approach to the job, and how much you like the people involved are all important too.
- Only hire a firm with insurance to cover any damage they may do to your property, or to themselves.
- Agree exactly what is to be done in advance – the cost, materials and time. Get a detailed quotation in writing.
- Don't change the job while it is being done by asking, for example, for extra work to be done, unless you agree the price of the changes beforehand.
- Never pay for all the materials or work in advance. On large contracts an interim payment is common.

The British Decorators Association is the main trade organisation that represents domestic decorating firms nationwide. Contact them (see margin, left) for details of members in your area and a code of practice leaflet. The BDA also has a complaints and arbitration procedure.

Members of the BDA must have current insurance and relevant qualifications such as the City and Guilds certificate at advanced craft level, National Vocational Certificates or time-served apprenticeships.

Deep-fat fryer

Deep-fat cooking is a safe method of cooking, but take care, because it combines electricity, high temperatures and flammable oil or fat. Improperly used, it can burn you and become a fire hazard.

Safety do's and don'ts

- Do use the handle to move the fryer basket.
- Do take great care when opening the fryer basket when it is in use, because escaping steam could scald your hands.
- Do keep the level of oil or fat between the minimum and maximum marks on the fryer.
- Do use the device fitted to most fryers to record the number of times the oil or fat is used.
- Do change the oil after 12 to 15 fryings (solid fat or lard should be used only once).
- Don't ever leave the fryer unattended when in use.
- Don't let the fryer sit on its electric cable.
- Don't use butter or olive oil – they will not get hot enough for deep frying.
- Don't put the fryer into water – just wipe it clean with kitchen paper and a damp, soapy cloth once it has cooled sufficiently to be handled.

Changing the oil or fat Time: 1 hour or less

YOU WILL NEED New cooking oil or fat, jug or container for used oil or fat, kitchen paper, soapy water, cloth.

Switch off and unplug the fryer, but do not proceed any further until both it and the contents are cold.

Fat or lard should be changed while they are still liquid, but not hot. They take about $1\frac{1}{2}$ hours to solidify.

Completely remove the lid of the deep-fat fryer.

Always use the handle to remove the basket from the body of the fryer, and then pour the oil carefully into a suitable container.

Wipe the inside of the fryer with kitchen paper to remove the last of the oil, and then wipe it thoroughly with a damp, soapy cloth to remove any particles of food. Then wipe the inside thoroughly with a clean cloth and dry well.

Some deep-fat fryers have renewable filters and others have permanent filters. Make a habit of changing or cleaning the filter every time you change the oil or fat.

Refill the fryer with new oil or fat to the correct level.

Faultfinder guide: Deep-fat fryers

Fryer smells

CAUSE Filter is blocked.
SOLUTION Replace filter.

CAUSE Oil is dirty.
SOLUTION Change oil every 12-15 fryings.

CAUSE Oil is unsuitable.
SOLUTION Replace oil with corn oil or vegetable oil.

Steam escapes from under lid

CAUSE Lid is not properly closed.
SOLUTION Close the lid.

CAUSE Sealing ring incorrectly assembled or faulty.
SOLUTION Fit ring correctly or replace ring.

Oil overflows

CAUSE Too much oil.
SOLUTION Let oil cool then pour off excess.

CAUSE Food lowered too quickly.
SOLUTION Lower food more slowly.

CAUSE Food is wet.
SOLUTION Dry the food before frying.

Food does not brown or crisp

CAUSE The pieces are too thick or too wet.
SOLUTION Cook for longer.

CAUSE Too much food.
SOLUTION Fry less food.

CAUSE Oil not hot enough.
SOLUTION Increase heat.

CAUSE Thermometer is faulty.
SOLUTION Take fryer to the supplier for repair.

Fryer makes spitting noises or bowl is getting pitted

CAUSE Water in the oil.
SOLUTION Change oil.

CAUSE Food is too wet.
SOLUTION Dry food before frying.

CAUSE Too much salt.
SOLUTION Reduce salt.

SAFETY FIRST WITH ELECTRICITY

Before starting any work on an electrical fitting or appliance, make sure to cut off the electricity supply – either by switching off at the main fuse box, or by unplugging the appliance

STORING A DEEP-FAT FRYER

A fryer can be stored with oil in it, if the oil is in good condition. If there is sediment, strain the oil though a clean J-cloth in a sieve before storing it. If it is not possible to remove fat or lard, store the fryer with the basket raised. Don't store solid fat for longer than two weeks. To reuse solid fat, cut it up into large chunks and heat it very slowly. Otherwise it could burn, or pressure might build up under the solid surface and cause a violent eruption.

Dishwasher

Dishwashers use both water and electricity, so take great care when dealing with any problems and make sure that the machine is disconnected from the electricity supply.

Basic emergency procedure Time: depends on emergency

In cases of leaking, flooding, alarming noises or blown fuses, the machine should not be allowed to continue with its cycle until the fault has been identified and fixed.

Follow this basic emergency procedure.

YOU WILL NEED Plastic bowl or bucket.

! Do not open the machine.

• Disconnect the dishwasher from the main power supply.

Switch off the machine, then the wall plug and then remove the plug from the wall socket.

Turn off the taps that supply hot and cold water to the dishwasher. This is in case a valve is jammed in the open position, and water is still flowing into the machine.

If the machine is leaking, siphon the water out of it into a bucket or large bowl. Lift the outlet hose from its usual position at the back of the machine, and lower it into a bucket or bowl, below the level of the water in the machine.

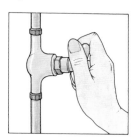

The water should drain out of the machine freely unless the problem is a blockage in the outlet hose.

If you need to stop the flow of water temporarily – while you empty the bowl, for instance – simply hold the open end of the hose up in the air. Repeat this as many times as necessary, until no more water flows from the hose.

At this stage it is safe to open the machine, but take care, as the contents may be very hot.

Once the machine is cool, it is safe to unload it and start working out what the problem is.

Clearing the inlet filter Time: ½ an hour or less

The inlet filter can become blocked and this will stop the dishwasher from working.

YOU WILL NEED Long-nosed pliers, nail brush.

 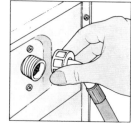

Turn off the water inlet stopcock. It is usually found on the pipe supplying water to the dishwasher.

Disconnect the hose at the inlet filter. If there is a rubber seal inside, remove it and the filter will be exposed.

Parts of a typical dishwasher

Although makes of dishwasher vary, their main features and functions are similar. If in doubt about your dishwasher, consult the manufacturer's handbook.

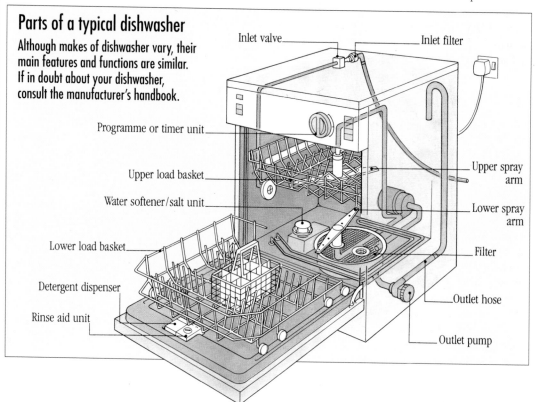

Inlet valve
Inlet filter
Programme or timer unit
Upper load basket
Water softener/salt unit
Lower load basket
Detergent dispenser
Rinse aid unit
Upper spray arm
Lower spray arm
Filter
Outlet hose
Outlet pump

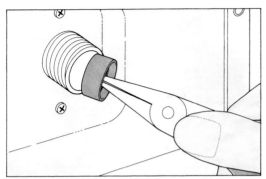

Remove the filter with long-nosed pliers and then clean it thoroughly with a nail brush. Replace it carefully, making sure it is sitting correctly, and is not skewed.

Replace the rubber seal and reconnect the inlet hose, making sure it is straight before tightening. Gently turn on the water supply at the stopcock. If the connection leaks, tighten it further.

Cleaning the outlet filters Time: $\frac{1}{2}$ an hour or less

YOU WILL NEED Rubber gloves, nail brush.

Because it deals with dishes covered with greasy food particles, a dishwasher has filters that prevent the dirt getting back onto the dishes during the recycling of the water. The filters can become clogged if not cleaned regularly.

Most dishwashers have two filters: a coarse one located in the centre of a larger, finer one, both set into the bottom of the cabinet. They should be cleaned regularly, especially after a big wash. Follow the manufacturer's instructions for releasing the filters.

At the same time, retrieve any small pieces of cutlery that have dropped into the bottom of the cabinet. Separate the filters, rinse them under running water and remove stubborn fragments with a nailbrush.

Cleaning the spray arms Time: $\frac{1}{2}$ an hour or less

The small holes in the spray arms can become blocked. They should be checked every six months.

YOU WILL NEED Rubber gloves. Possibly: old knitting needle.

Following the manufacturer's instructions, remove the spray arms and check the small holes. If they have become blocked with food particles, clean them out with an old knitting needle.

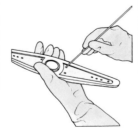

The spray arms should rotate freely. If they don't, dismantle and clean them. Most spray arms are held in place by a screw or nut that you can release by hand.

Faultfinder guide: Dishwasher

Dishwashers vary, so consult the maker's instructions first. If you are not confident about fixing it yourself go through the basic emergency procedure (shown on the previous page) then call a service engineer.

Machine won't work

CAUSE Power may not be switched on.
SOLUTION Turn on the power.

CAUSE A fuse may have blown.
SOLUTION Change the fuse.

Power on but machine won't work

CAUSE Door is open.
SOLUTION Close the door.

Machine won't move on from prerinse cycle

CAUSE Timer may be set for night use.
SOLUTION Alter the timer.

CAUSE Water supply may be turned off.
SOLUTION Turn on the water.

CAUSE Inlet filter may be clogged.
SOLUTION Clean the inlet filter (see facing page).

Water not pumping away

CAUSE There may be a kink in the outlet hose.
SOLUTION Straighten outlet hose.

CAUSE Outlet filter may be clogged.
SOLUTION Follow basic emergency procedure (see facing page) then clean the outlet filter.

Machine leaks clear water

CAUSE Clips on the hoses may be loose.
SOLUTION Follow basic emergency procedure (see facing page) then tighten any loose hoses.

Noise or vibration

CAUSE Floor may be uneven.
SOLUTION Stop machine. Level machine.

White deposits on dishes

CAUSE Wrong quantities of detergent, rinse aid and salt may have been added.
SOLUTION Adjust quantities.

CAUSE Lid of rinse aid unit open.
SOLUTION Close the lid of the rinse aid.

Doll (SEE ALSO TEDDY BEAR)

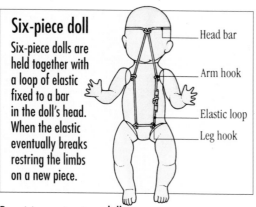

Six-piece doll

Six-piece dolls are held together with a loop of elastic fixed to a bar in the doll's head. When the elastic eventually breaks restring the limbs on a new piece.

Head bar
Arm hook
Elastic loop
Leg hook

Repairing a six-piece doll Time: ½ a day

If the elastic breaks the doll will fall to pieces, but you can restring it with a new piece of elastic.

> YOU WILL NEED Elastic, coat-hanger wire, long-nosed pliers, needle and thread.

Cut a piece of elastic that is twice as long as the doll's body and tie it in a loop. Stitch down the loose ends.

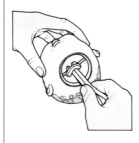

Push one end of the loop round the bar in the doll's head. Slip it through the other end of the loop.

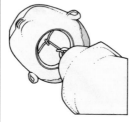

If the doll's head has a metal latch hanging from the bar, fit the elastic over the latch, not the bar.

Feed the elastic into the body through the neck hole.

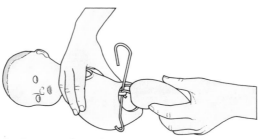

Bend a piece of coat-hanger wire into a hook. Use it to catch the elastic inside the doll's body and pull it out through a leg hole. Hook the leg onto the loop, and then attach all the other limbs in the same manner.

MENDING A DOLL

Rag dolls and soft calico dolls with vinyl heads can usually be repaired by hand with needle and thread.

Vinyl dolls have their heads and limbs attached to the body by push-on fittings. They are difficult to repair and may need professional care.

The Hastings Dolls' Hospital, 17 George Street, Hastings, East Sussex TN34 3EG (tel. 01424 444117), will give advice and repair some dolls. Antique dolls may be valuable, so do not attempt to repair one. Have it done by an expert.

Door (SEE ALSO GARAGE DOOR)

Easing a tight door Time: 2 hours or less

> YOU WILL NEED Screwdriver, carbon paper, candle stub. Possibly: drum or flap-wheel sander and power drill, small block plane, hammer, sprung draught strip.

Tightening all the hinge screws may be enough to free the door. If not, slip carbon paper between door and frame to check where the door is catching. Rub the stub of a candle on the sticking areas.

If the door is still sticking, use a drum sander or flap wheel with a power drill to abrade away the high spots.

Where jamming is severe – particularly if swelling occurs during damp winter months – remove the door from the frame and plane off about 3 mm ($\frac{1}{8}$ in). Then fit a sprung draught strip around the door frame (see *Draughtproofing*) to allow the door to expand and contract while maintaining a draughtproof seal round it.

Redecorate the door as soon as possible if the paint or varnish have been removed. Check that all door edges are sealed with paint or varnish to prevent damp entering.

Silencing a squeaking door Time: a few minutes

If there is rust on the hinges, apply easing oil first. Allow it to soak in for an hour, then wipe it away and apply household lubricating oil to the hinge joints. Work the door back and forth to get the oil into the joints. Wipe off the surplus.

Fixing a rattling door Time: 1 hour or less

> YOU WILL NEED Sprung draught strip, hammer. Possibly: pincers, old chisel and silicone rubber sealant.

A loose fit between door latch and striking plate often causes rattling. However, resiting the plate is difficult.

Instead, fit a nylon or phosphor bronze draught strip round the door frame. If the draught strip is correctly sprung (following the instructions) it will hold the door firmly in place.

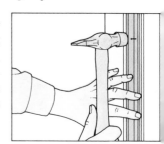

LOOSE GLASS PANEL If a glass panel rattles, remove the panel pins that hold the internal beading.

Then resite the beading closer to the glass, tapping in panel pins by sliding the hammer against the glass.

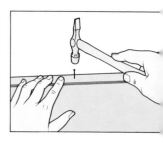

In some cases, removing the beading would damage the door. So use an old chisel to clean out the gap between the beading and the glass and insert a little clear silicone rubber sealant. Wipe away excess sealant while it is wet.

Stopping a slamming door Time: ½ a day or less

If a heavy door always closes with a bang, there are two ways in which you can try to quieten it.

> YOU WILL NEED Heavy-duty foam draught strip. Possibly: door restrainer/closer.

Buy a strip of the thickest self-adhesive foam draught strip available, long enough to run around the door frame.

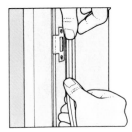

Bed the draught strip on the face of the door frame which the door hits when it bangs shut. This will absorb the force of the blow.

If this is not enough, fit a door restrainer/closer which will control the speed at which the door closes. Follow the fitting instructions that are supplied with it.

Tightening a sagging door Time: 2 hours or less

> YOU WILL NEED Screwdriver. Possibly: wood plugs, wood glue, hammer, chisel and mallet, trimming knife, bradawl.

The problem will probably lie with the hinge near the top of the door. Check the screws to see if they need tightening.

The screws may have pulled from their holes. If they have, remove them. With a chisel or trimming knife, make plugs of softwood that will fit into all the holes.

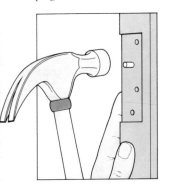

Apply wood glue to each plug and then hammer it in place. Trim off the surplus wood with a chisel and allow the glue to set.

Make start holes in each of the wooden plugs with a bradawl and then refit the hinge screws.

It may be that the top hinge is not recessed far enough. If the gap between the hinge edge of the door and the door frame is wider at the top than it is at the bottom, remove the hinge and slightly deepen the recess with chisel and mallet, then replace the hinge and check the door's angle.

Shortening a door Time: 2 hours or less

> YOU WILL NEED Steel straightedge and pencil, trimming knife, handsaw or power circular saw, sandpaper, screwdriver.

When carpet and underlay have been laid for the first time, or a replacement carpet with a thicker pile is used, you may find the door will not open properly.

Make a pencil mark at the bottom of the door to indicate the amount of door to be removed. Err on the cautious side. You can always sand a little more off, but you can't put wood back.

Remove the door and lay it flat on a work surface, then extend the mark you have made into a line that is parallel with the bottom of the door, running the full width of it.

Now score through the paint, along this line, with a trimming knife against a steel straightedge. This will prevent the paint becoming damaged and flaking off when you saw the strip of wood off the door.

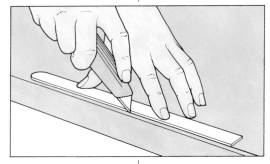

Saw along the lower edge of the scored line. Smooth the cut edge on both sides and replace the door.

Maintenance of door hinges

Hinges on interior doors should be oiled regularly and lightly. Wipe away excess oil with a clean cloth. On exterior doors, use grease instead, because oil evaporates rather quickly. Wipe off excess grease.

Replacing a rotten weatherboard Time: ½ a day or less

Many exterior doors have a piece of wood at the base called a weatherboard. It guides rainwater away from the gap under the door. Constant wetting can cause it to rot.

> YOU WILL NEED Screwdriver, claw hammer, replacement weatherboard, tenon saw, steel tape measure, sandpaper, clear wood preservative, paintbrush, power drill, twist and spade bits, bradawl, silicone rubber sealant, wood stopping, paint, varnish.

Weatherboards come in standard mouldings and are available in both hardwood and softwood.

REMOVING THE OLD BOARD Locate the holding screws. They may be hidden beneath paint and filler. Unscrew and prise off the weatherboard with a claw hammer.

It is a good idea to use the old weatherboard as a template to help you to cut the new one to the correct length.

PREPARING A NEW BOARD Smooth the new weatherboard with sandpaper, then apply a clear wood preservative.

Pay particular attention to the back of the weatherboard and the end grain because these areas are likely to allow moisture to soak in if not sealed completely.

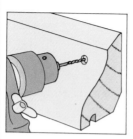

With a spade bit, bore holes the width of the screw heads approximately 6 mm ($\frac{1}{4}$ in) deep where the screws will be. From the centre of these holes drill through the wood, with a twist bit equal in diameter to the screw shank.

Drill pilot holes in the door. Apply a strip of silicone rubber sealant along the top edge of the weatherboard so that it will be between door and weatherboard.

Screw the weatherboard to the door, remove surplus sealant, then fill the holes with an exterior wood stopping (see *Fillers & stoppers*). Paint or varnish the weatherboard to match the rest of the door.

Straightening a warped door Time: 1 hour or less

If a door is badly warped, it may need replacing. But it is worth experimenting to see if the warp can be corrected.

YOU WILL NEED Timber batten, electric drill, masonry bit, wall plugs, screwdriver, block and wedge made from scrap wood.

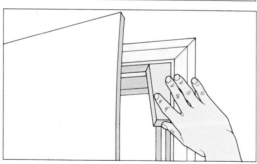

If the top of the door meets the frame first, insert a block of wood at the top, to force a gap of about 5 cm (2 in) between the door edge and the frame.

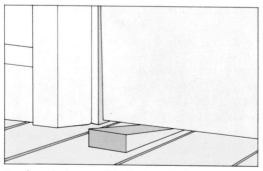

Now force the bottom of the door into the frame and wedge it in place. Leave it like that for at least 24 hours.

HOW TO CUT THROUGH A DOOR CLEANLY

When enlarging a hole in a door, always work from both sides of the door to the centre, to avoid damaging either face.

If the bottom of the door meets the frame first, wedge it open about 5 cm (2 in) at the base. Then drill and plug the wall above the closed door so that you can screw a batten across the corner. Use a block of wood to force the door closed.

If the bow in the door is central, wedge top and bottom open, and apply the batten to the centre of the door.

Maintaining sliding patio doors Time: 2 hours or less

YOU WILL NEED Old paintbrush, vacuum cleaner, dry lubricant or furniture polish, fine lubricating oil. Possibly: screwdriver, spanner.

If a door is difficult to open and close, clean debris from around the guide or track at the base. Use an old paintbrush or the small brush on a vacuum cleaner.

Apply a dry lubricant such as graphite or powdered PTFE, or rub the track with furniture polish and remove any surplus. Do not use oil or grease because they attract grit which will aggravate the problem.

Then use fine oil such as 3-in-1 to lubricate the upper wheels. Wipe all along the running area of the track with a clean rag to remove all dust and dirt.

Check that the doors are hung correctly. You can make small adjustments by tightening or loosening the nuts on the pendant bolts with a spanner.

Doorknobs
(SEE ALSO LOCKS AND LATCHES)

Tightening a doorknob

There are three main types of doorknob, each needing a slightly different treatment to correct any looseness.

YOU WILL NEED Screwdrivers, drill, twist bits, bradawl, scraps of wood, wood glue. Possibly: thin metal washers, hacksaw.

SPINDLE Older-pattern knobs fit onto a spindle, which may be threaded. Loosen the small grub screw in the knob, and if the knob turns on the spindle, it is a threaded one.

If the doorknob is loose, turn it until it feels comfortably tight, then tighten the grub screw until it grips the spindle firmly.

If an unthreaded type is loose, insert one or two thin metal washers between the knob and the plate.

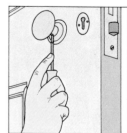

PLATE-MOUNTED KNOB On more modern patterns, a plate screwed to the face of the door holds the knob, which can rotate within the plate. A smooth spindle inserted through the door connects the two knobs.

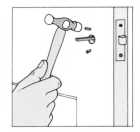

If the screws work loose, and won't tighten, remove them and fill the holes with small plugs cut from scrap softwood. Apply wood glue to the plugs before tapping them home.

Allow the glue time to set, then make a small pilot hole in each plug with a bradawl. Insert and tighten the screws. If the holes are too enlarged to be filled in this way, turn the plate the other way up on the door and make new pilot holes for the screws. Then screw it in place.

Where there seems to be too much space between the knob and the plate, loosen the grub screw and either push or screw the knob into place, depending on its type.

If it will not fit flush, the spindle is a bit too long. Use a hacksaw to shorten the spindle by the required amount.

DECORATIVE PULL-KNOB Many modern doors have a knob positioned so that it can be used to pull the door shut, but it is not designed to turn. If its screws work loose, tighten as described for a plate-mounted knob.

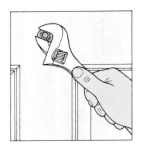

Some pull-knobs have a threaded spindle which passes through the door and is held with a nut on the inside. Tighten the nut if the knob is loose.

Double glazing
(SEE ALSO DRAUGHTPROOFING)

Condensation in sealed units

After about ten years, condensation can form between the glass panes of sealed double glazing units. This is because the dry gas between the panes becomes contaminated with moist outside air. Replacement is the only remedy.

Condensation in secondary units

If secondary double glazing units develop condensation, open them and wipe them with a chamois leather. Don't insert silica gel crystals to absorb moisture, because they release the moisture again when the sun warms them.

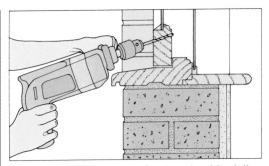

Persistent condensation can often be reduced by drilling three or four holes from the outside into the space between the panes. Use a power drill and a 3 mm ($\frac{1}{8}$ in) twist bit to make the holes in the face of the window frame (as above) or from the underside of the external sill. This admits cold air, which holds very little moisture.

Fitting DIY double glazing Time: depends on amount

Almost any house or flat can be given inexpensive DIY double glazing to reduce draughts and cut down noise.

> YOU WILL NEED Steel tape measure, mini-hacksaw, bradawl, screwdriver. Possibly: power drill, masonry bits, wall plugs.

USING A KIT Kits are available in aluminium or uPVC.

Some kits fit to the wall around the window; others are screwed to the wooden window frame. Some open on hinges; others slide open.

Although glass can be used with the double glazing kits, acrylic plastic is lighter and safer. A sheet 2 mm, 3 mm or 4 mm thick is usually recommended.

Measure the height and width of each window, and buy kits slightly larger than the window measurements. Cutting and fitting instructions, as well as advice on how to calculate the amount of acrylic you will need should be included with the kits.

The ideal gap between panes is 1.9 cm ($\frac{3}{4}$ in). Any more will allow air to circulate between the panes and reduce the insulating efficiency. A larger gap is recommended for soundproofing (see *Soundproofing*).

POLYTHENE SHEETING It is possible to insulate a window that is rarely opened or is hidden from view by sticking a sheet of polythene to the window frame with double-sided adhesive tape. However, do clean the window and frame thoroughly and dry them, before you start. Adhesive tape will not stick to dirty, damp or newly painted surfaces.

INSULATING FILM This usually comes in kit form with full instructions. Clear plastic film is attached to a window frame and then shrunk to fit with the gentle heat from a hair dryer to remove wrinkles.

You can extend the life of this type of double glazing by attaching the film to a timber batten frame and storing the frame, and attached film in warm weather.

HOW TO CUT ACRYLIC SHEET

For the best results, get acrylic sheet cut to size by a professional. If you try to cut it yourself, measure it exactly and leave the protective film in place while you work. Score the acrylic using a steel straightedge and a trimming knife fitted with a laminate-scoring blade. Position the sheet so that the scored line is near the edge of a table and snap the sheet. Alternatively, use a fine-toothed saw. Work slowly so that the heat caused by friction doesn't soften the plastic and bind the saw.

DOUBLE GLAZING AND FIRE SAFETY

If you are fitting secondary glazing that will be difficult to open quickly, consider the consequences of fire. Consider leaving an upstairs window unglazed, as an escape route, in case you get trapped by fire on the top floor.

REMOVING A MANHOLE COVER

Use a trowel to clear away any dirt or weeds from the cover. If the handholds have rusted away you'll need a helper. Push a garden spade between the cover and its frame and lever it upwards. Then get the helper to slip the end of a piece of wood between the cover and the frame. This will allow you to get hold of the cover to lift and remove it.

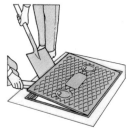

Manhole covers are heavy, so take care not to injure your back or fingers when lifting one clear.

PLASTIC CHANNELLING This comes in the form of a kit, with full instructions. Strips of plastic channelling are fitted around the edges of a sheet of glass or rigid plastic, and then fixed to the window frame with screws and fixing clips. Some systems have hinged channelling which allows the secondary glazing to be opened.

RIGID PLASTIC AND MAGNETIC STRIP Rigid plastic sheets can be fitted as secondary glazing using magnetic fixing strip and a self-adhesive metal ribbon. The system is designed for use with plastic up to 4 mm thick. Do not use glass, as it is too heavy for the system. Cover the metal strip with a thin coat of paint to match the window frame.

Downpipes:
SEE GUTTERS AND DOWNPIPES

Drains & gullies

Understanding the system

The drains of a house carry waste water, sewage and rainwater from the house to the public sewer. Rainwater and household waste may be carried separately.

Manholes are sited where branch drains from bathrooms and downpipes join the main drain. They give access to the system for maintenance and there are usually two or three manholes within a house's boundaries.

Gutters and downpipes collect rainwater from the roof and feed it to a gully in the ground next to the house. The gully may also collect water from the kitchen sink.

Unblocking an underground drain   Time: 2 hours or less

If a drain is blocked, the first sign may be an unpleasant smell from a manhole, water seeping from beneath the cover of a manhole, or an overflowing gully.

Another indicator of a blocked drain may be that a ground-floor lavatory fills with water when it is flushed, then the water slowly subsides.

> YOU WILL NEED Garden spade, piece of wood, small trowel, rubber gloves. Possibly: drain rods, pair of fire tongs.

LOCATING THE BLOCKAGE If a drain is blocked, at least one of the manholes will be flooded. To check how many are flooded, remove the manhole covers (see margin, left).

If one manhole is full of water and another is dry, the blockage lies somewhere between the two. If all the manholes are filled with water, the blockage lies either in the trap of the manhole nearest the street (see below), or somewhere in the drain between it and the public sewer.

ONE CHAMBER FLOODED If only one manhole is filled with water, you may have to hire a set of drain rods to unblock it (see 'Hiring drain rods' margin, facing page).

Screw together two or three of the ordinary drain rods, then fit the 'corkscrew' attachment to the end and then thrust this end into the flooded manhole.

Understanding the layout of the manhole nearest the street

The manhole on a property that is nearest to the street may be fitted with a trap to prevent unpleasant smells and rats coming up the pipe from the public sewer. A rodding arm – a straight pipe – above the trap gives access in order to clear any blockages which occur between the trap and the public sewer. The stopper which covers the rodding arm when it is not in use must be removed before use.

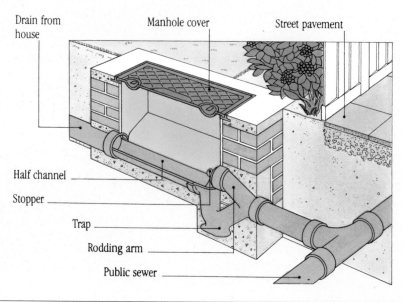

Drain from house

Manhole cover

Street pavement

Half channel

Stopper

Trap

Rodding arm

Public sewer

Feel for the half channel at the bottom of the manhole and push the corkscrew along it and into the drain. Never be tempted to twist drain rods anticlockwise as this will unscrew them and you will not be able to get them back.

However, twisting the rods clockwise may make it easier to push them along the drain and to withdraw them after the obstruction has been cleared.

Screw on more lengths of rod as necessary until you have found and cleared the obstruction.

The water level in the manhole will fall suddenly as the dammed-up sewage is released.

ALL CHAMBERS FLOODED You may opt to call a plumber in this case (see *Plumber*); but you could tackle it yourself.

The blockage will probably be in the intercepting trap of the manhole nearest the street (see 'Understanding the layout of the manhole nearest the street', facing page) and will have to be removed using drain rods.

Screw the 10 cm (4 in) drain plunger onto the end of two or three drain rods joined together. Lower this into the manhole and feel for the half channel at the bottom of the chamber.

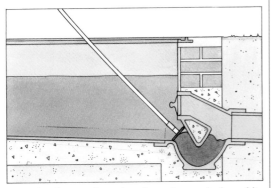

Move the plunger along this channel towards the public sewer until you can feel it entering the intercepting trap and coming up against the blockage.

Plunge down sharply into the trap three or four times. This should dislodge the blockage and the water should flow away, but if not, call a plumber.

Occasionally the length of drain between the public sewer and the intercepting trap may get blocked. This section of the drain is your responsibility even though much

of it may lie under the road. If the manhole has an intercepting trap you will have to get to the blocked drain via the rodding arm (see 'Understanding the layout of the manhole nearest the street', facing page).

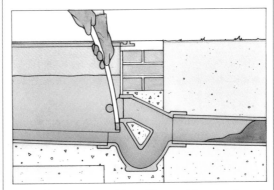

Knock the stopper out of the rodding arm by using the rods to lever behind the knob in the middle of the stopper. Then rod through that arm to the obstruction.

Sometimes the rodding-arm stopper can be forced out of position by back pressure from the public sewer. It is then washed into the intercepting trap and causes a partial blockage. If this happens, put on a pair of rubber gloves and retrieve and replace the cap by hand or use a pair of old fashioned fire tongs.

CLEANING UP AFTERWARDS After clearing a drain blockage, hose down the manhole. Then run the cold taps in the house for about 20 minutes to flush the drain. Clean the rods thoroughly in a bucket of soapy water after use.

Make working on drains easier

● Have a look at the drains when they are working properly so that you understand them in an emergency. Remove the manhole covers and note how branch drains connect to the main drain. Also note whether the manhole nearest the street has an intercepting trap and a rodding arm.
● If your drains are blocked, tell everyone in the house not to let any water out of baths, showers or toilets. Leave the system alone for an hour or so. This may give the water time to drain away a little, making any work much easier.
● Make sure that no one uses the system while you are working on it. Inform them when it is complete.

Unblocking a flooded gully Time: 1 hour or less

Water from the kitchen sink often discharges directly from an outlet pipe into a gully just outside the house. The gully has an intercepting trap as a barrier to smells from the sewerage system and it is usually protected by a grate.

BEWARE OF AN OPEN MANHOLE

After you have inspected a manhole replace the cover immediately. An open manhole is a danger to other people.

HIRING DRAIN RODS

A set of drain rods can be hired by the day quite cheaply. They can come with three main attachments — corkscrew head, rubber plunger and scraper.

Sound drainage systems, even those laid many years ago, only rarely become blocked. Recurring blockages suggest a structural defect. Possibly a drainpipe has broken or moved out of position. Tree roots can sometimes penetrate drains. If you have recurring problems get advice from the environmental health officer of your local district or borough council.

AVOIDING BLOCKED GULLIES

Building by-laws require that a waste pipe discharging into a gully should discharge above water level but below the level of the grid. This ensures that leaves cannot cause a blockage by settling on the grate and that the full force of the sink, bath or basin discharge is available to flush through the gully. It is possible to lengthen existing waste pipes and replace the grate with a slotted plastic version to accommodate the new pipe.

If the gully gets blocked, water will flood out of it and you may hear a bubbling noise when you pull out the kitchen plug as the waste pipe discharges underwater.

If the outlet pipe ends above the grate, the grate can become choked with leaves and kitchen debris, causing the water to overflow. If the pipe ends below the grid, the cause of the overflow may be a blocked trap.

> **YOU WILL NEED** Small garden fork, scrubbing brush, long rubber gloves, large sink-waste plunger, garden hose.

CLOGGED GRATE Push the end of a garden fork through the gully grate and lever it out of its seating. If the grate was blocked the water should run away.

Scrub the gully grate then replace it. If the grate is made of iron, you can clean it by putting it in an open fire for about half an hour, or by burning it with a blowtorch.

CLOGGED TRAP If the water does not subside when you remove the grate, the trap is probably blocked. Try plunging it with a large sink plunger, pressing down sharply several times.

If this doesn't work, put on long rubber gloves and reach into the gully and scoop out any rubbish by hand.

After clearing the blockage from the gully, give it a final clean by flushing it through with water from a hose.

Smells in upstairs bathrooms Time: ½ a day or less

Unpleasant smells in a bathroom may originate from the basin overflow (see *Baths & basins*).

If there is a hopper (like a funnel) on the downpipe outside the house to catch the waste from the bath and basin, the smells may originate from soapy water drying and decomposing inside the hopper head.

> **YOU WILL NEED** Bucket, washing soda, ladder, scrubbing brush.

Start by dissolving two or three handfuls of washing soda in a bucketful of hot water. Protect your hands.

Then, use a ladder to reach the hopper and scrub the hopper head clean very thoroughly with a scrubbing brush dipped in the washing-soda solution.

To flush out the hopper head, downpipe and gully, flush the remaining washing-soda solution around the hopper head and into the downpipe (right). Next, fill the bath with water and pull out the plug.

Removing a fresh-air inlet

A fresh-air inlet consists of a length of drainpipe which is connected to the final manhole on a property and taken up into the air beside it.

They are never installed now because they do not work well and can be a source of unpleasant smells. So if your outside drain has a fresh-air inlet, the metal box should be removed and the pipe sealed off with concrete. Call a plumber to do this for you.

Draughtproofing

Sealing draughty gaps around the house is a cost-effective way to save on heating bills (see also *Double glazing*).

Sealing a window against draughts Time: 1 hour or less

WOODEN CASEMENT WINDOW Clean the window frame and leave it to dry. Then apply the draught excluder of your choice round the frame (see facing page).

If you use self-adhesive foam strip, be sure to use a good quality make or it may last for only one season. Self-adhesive rubber strip will last longer than foam strip and is applied in the same way.

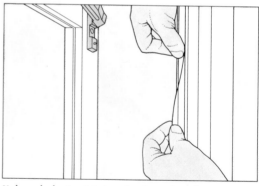

V-shaped plastic strip is a hard-wearing alternative. Cut the strip to length and stick it to the window so that the closing frame passes the folded edge first.

The strip has adhesive backing along one edge which holds it firmly, but if the window is opened and closed often, fix the strip in two or three places with small tacks.

METAL CASEMENT WINDOW To seal a metal casement window against draughts, use self-adhesive rubber or foam strip. Cut the strip to length and press it onto the window frame (not onto the window itself).

SEALING GAPS IN AN UNEVEN WINDOW FRAME Use silicone-rubber sealant to fill gaps on metal or wooden casement windows. It is particularly useful if the frame is warped.

Wash the frame and leave it to dry. Then use a sealant gun to apply a substantial strip of sealant to the frame.

Cover the closing edge of the window with soapy water, to stop the sealant sticking to the window. Then pull the window tight shut and reopen it immediately. Leave the sealant to set for about 2 hours (longer in cold weather).

SASH WINDOWS Use sprung metal strips or brush strips to seal the vertical surfaces on a sash window. Both types allow the window to slide over them easily. Cut the length required and nail or stick the strip in place.

Use self-adhesive brush strip where the horizontal rails meet. Stick it to the outside of the bottom sash so that it doesn't show inside when the window is open. Use strips of foam or rubber to seal the top and bottom of the window.

What model of draught excluder?

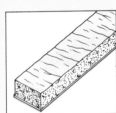

SELF-ADHESIVE RUBBER STRIP In P and E profiles. Used on interior doors and casement windows. Lasts longer than foam strip.

SELF-ADHESIVE FOAM STRIP Used on casement windows, the top and bottom of sash windows, and interior doors.

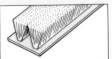

BRUSH STRIP Useful for moving parts, such as sash and casement windows and patio doors.

V-SHAPED PLASTIC STRIP For gaps on sash windows, wooden casement windows and doors.

Weatherproofing a door Time: depends on area

PROTECTING THE BOTTOM Door-strip draught excluders are made for either internal or external doors. Both come in standard lengths, so choose one at least as long as the width of the door then cut it to length if necessary.

On an internal door a rubber, plastic or brush seal attached to the base of the door with tacks or adhesive is usually sufficient.

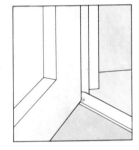

A sill excluder on an exterior door will help to keep draughts out. It is a bar of plastic or metal, fitted to the door sill.

On an exterior door, a two-part draught excluder, with one half fitted to the door and the other to the door sill, will keep out both wind and rain.

SEALING THE LETTERBOX The letterbox is a potential source of large draughts, especially if newspapers or letters keep it propped open. Fit a brush (left) or a flap excluder to the inside to keep out the cold air.

OVER THE KEYHOLE Fit a cover over the keyhole. Use a bradawl to mark for screw holes, then screw the keyhole plate to the outside of the door.

AROUND THE DOOR EDGE A sprung metal or nylon strip (see left) is the most durable way of sealing the edges of external doors. Cut the strip to size with tinsnips or multi-purpose scissors and pin it to the door frame. Alternatively,

TRACING DRAUGHTS

If the origin of draughts is not obvious, hold a lighted candle near to doors and windows. The flame will falter where there is a draught. Take care not to get the flame too near curtains.

you can choose from self-adhesive sprung plastic strips, brush strips or rubber strips, cut to size with scissors.

On internal doors, fit good quality self-adhesive foam strips, brush strips or rubber strips. Always attach draught excluders to the door frame rather than to the door.

Sealing gaps below skirting boards Time: depends on area

Skirting boards are often fitted leaving a gap between the bottom edge and the floor, which can let in draughts.

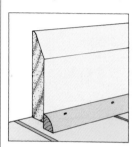

If carpet has not been pushed into the gap, use panel pins to fix quadrant beading to the base of the skirting board to seal it. Do not pin the beading to the floor because the boards will expand and contract when the weather changes.

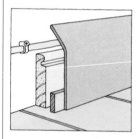

Alternatively, pin or glue a preformed skirting board, made of moulded plywood, over the original skirting. This seals the gap between the existing skirting board and the floor.

Preformed skirting board also offers space behind it to carry telephone extension cables, television aerials and electric cables – hiding them from sight.

Drawers

Easing a sticking wooden drawer Time: 1 hour or less

> YOU WILL NEED Possibly: kitchen spatula, hammer, wood glue, panel pins, chisel, fine sandpaper, tape measure, tenon saw, white candle stub or bar of soap.

FREEING A STUCK DRAWER If a drawer won't pull out, something inside is probably sticking out over the sides. If possible, remove the drawer above, then empty and repack the sticking drawer. If there is no drawer above, try inserting a kitchen spatula or another slim object to dislodge the obstruction. If all else fails a sharp jerk may dislodge it.

Once the drawer is out, check to see if a nail in the drawer frame is to blame. If there is a nail standing up too high, hammer it down into place.

REPAIRING THE RUNNERS Examine the strips of wood, called runners, that the drawer slides on. They may have come away from the side if the drawer has been overloaded. If so, glue and panel pin them back in position.

If the runners have become worn with age, prise them off with a chisel. If their undersides are still good, turn them over and refix them.

Or buy hardwood strips of the same dimensions as the old runners. Cut new runners to length and smooth them with fine sandpaper.

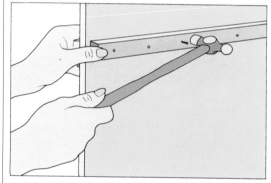

Drill fine pilot holes for panel pins in the hardwood, otherwise it will split. Then glue the new runners in place, and hammer in the panel pins, through the holes.

EASING THE DRAWER MOVEMENT Examine the base of the drawer or the grooves in the drawer sides and use sandpaper to smooth away any roughness in the wood.

Finally, rub meeting surfaces with the stub of a candle or a bar of soap to act as a lubricant and ease movement.

Repairing a split drawer base Time: 1 hour or less

Too much weight in a drawer can make the base sag or split or come away from its grooves.

> YOU WILL NEED Possibly: plywood or hardboard, tape measure, tenon saw, sandpaper, pincers, chisel, mallet, wood glue, household repair tape, sheet of polythene.

If the base is badly damaged, make a new one from plywood or hardboard of the same thickness. Use a saw to cut the wood to fit and smooth the edges with sandpaper.

If the base has split, you may be able to separate the pieces and then glue them together. Use pincers to pull out any nails holding the base to the back of the drawer.

Chip off the glue blocks on the bottom of the drawer with a chisel and a mallet. This will let you remove the drawer's base entirely.

Glue the edges of the split bottom and hold them in place with tape. Lay the bottom on a flat surface to dry.

Slide the base back into the drawer, nail it in place and reattach the glue blocks. Allow them to dry thoroughly.

Drills & drill bits

(SEE ALSO OVERLEAF)

Drilling to the right depth

If holes need to be drilled to an exact depth, such as when inserting wall plugs into a wall, use a depth gauge.

ADJUSTABLE ROD A metal rod is attached to the body of a power drill, or to a second handle. Set the rod behind the drill tip to the required hole depth. Drill until the rod comes into contact with the surface being drilled.

PLASTIC RINGS Fit a ready-made plastic gauge to a twist bit or masonry bit to guide you when drilling.

ADHESIVE TAPE Improvise a gauge. Mark the required depth by winding coloured tape around the bit.

How to drill a straight hole

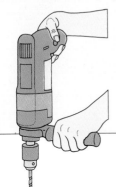

To make sure you are drilling straight, stand a try square on end beside the drill and ask someone to check that the drill lines up with it from the front and side.

Working safely with a power drill

- Always disconnect the drill from the power supply when you are changing attachments, or when you are going to leave the drill unattended.
- Use an RCD (residual current device) between the socket and the power tool.
- Never pull a plug from a socket by the cable.
- Never carry a drill by its cable.
- Check walls and floors with a battery-operated cable-and-pipe detector to locate cables and pipes before drilling holes (see page 158).
- When hammer-drilling, wear safety spectacles, ear defenders and a dust mask. For sanding and wire-brushing, wear safety spectacles and a dust mask.
- Clamp wood or other material to a bench so that you can hold the drill with both hands.
- Make sure that the plug is firmly gripping the cable and is correctly wired. Most drills are double-insulated which means no earth wire is needed.
- Never work in wet conditions, or near water, with a power drill. Use a cordless drill instead, if possible.
- Tie back long hair and avoid wearing ties or other loose clothes when drilling in case they get caught.

Sharpening tools and implements with a power drill

DRILL-BIT SHARPENER Both twist bits and masonry bits need to be sharpened if they are used often. They can be sharpened quite easily in a simple power-drill attachment that incorporates a grinding wheel.

Although it is not essential to bolt the sharpener to a bench, it is helpful because it leaves both hands free. Full instructions are supplied with the sharpener.

MULTIPURPOSE SHARPENER This attachment is suitable for sharpening not only drill bits, but also knives, scissors, garden shears, chisels and the cutting blades of rotary lawnmowers.

If you have a lot of tools and implements to sharpen, it may be worth the outlay. You will also need a bench or a garage shelf to work on, because the sharpener and the power drill have to be held down firmly.

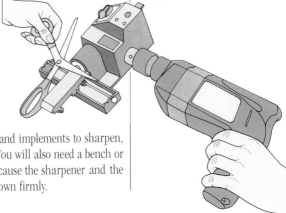

USE A FLAT BIT TO AVOID SPLITTING WOOD

Use a flat bit for holes that are between 6 mm and 38 mm ($\frac{1}{4}$ in and $1\frac{1}{2}$ in) in diameter. To avoid splitting the wood when drilling right through, drill from one side until the point of the bit just breaks through on the other. Move to the other side and complete the hole by drilling through the centre point.

LOOKING AFTER YOUR POWER DRILL

Keep your drill dry and remove dust from the chuck and vent holes. Get the drill serviced by the manufacturer if the motor runs erratically or sparks badly. Do not oil the motor.

DRILLS & BITS

Power drills and hand drills (also called wheel braces) make neat, straight holes. Each has adjustable chuck jaws that can hold various drill bits. A hand drill is used for work requiring fine control, such as furniture making, but a power drill is better for repetitive work and for tough materials such as metal and masonry.

Choosing a power drill

CHUCK SIZE The chuck adjusts the position of the jaws and is operated either automatically or by a chuck key. Power drills are specified by chuck size; the most common are 10 mm ($\frac{3}{8}$ in) and 12 mm ($\frac{1}{2}$ in).

HAMMER ACTION As well as rotating, the drill bit moves in and out, delivering up to 500 blows a second. This facility is designed for drilling concrete, stone or hard brick.

POWER A power drill should be at least 400 watts, but if heavy work is involved, such as drilling large holes in masonry, use a more powerful model. They are available up to 850 watts. The more powerful the drill, the less chance there is of overworking it.

REVERSIBLE ACTION For taking out screws.

GEARS Drills with two gears are more versatile. They have a greater twisting force at lower speeds, which makes them better for drilling large-diameter holes.

SPEED Choose a drill with variable speeds — either several fixed speeds or totally variable speed, or both. Most drills have a lock button, to keep the drill at a constant speed so that you can take your finger off the trigger while drilling.

COUNTERSINK BIT For making recesses to take the heads of countersunk screws.

DRILL AND COUNTERBORE BIT Designed to drill a hole for a screw, then counterbore so that the screw can be recessed into the hole. The hole is then filled or plugged. A special plug-cutting bit is available to produce plugs which fit the hole.

BULLET TWIST BIT Has a sharp starter point on the tip to hold the bit in place on smooth surfaces. Cutting spurs ensure a clean hole in metal.

HIGH-SPEED STEEL TWIST BIT Designed for drilling both metal and wood.

MASONRY BIT Designed to cut only masonry. It has tungsten carbide brazed into its tip. Tough versions are available for hammer-action drills. Must not be confused with twist bits.

GLASS DRILL Designed to make an easy start in glass. A glass drill has a smooth shank and a tungsten carbide tip shaped like a spear point.

CARBON STEEL TWIST BIT Only suitable for drilling wood.

BOSCH

CSB 550 RE
550 W · Beton Ø max. 15 mm · electronic

A hand drill for careful control

STANDARD HAND DRILL A hand drill gives fine control at low speed, which is useful when making pilot holes for screws.

A hand drill may have a smooth round handle at the top, or an open-grip handle. A side handle is sometimes useful to control the drill. Extra pressure can then be applied by pressing the top handle into the chest.

One or two small cogwheels transfer the drive from the large gear wheel to the chuck which holds the drill bit. The type with two cogwheels gives a smoother movement and is less likely to wear. The gears may be encased, protecting them from dust and grime.

Cordless drill for back-up

A cordless drill is a useful back-up to a standard power drill. Use it in damp or wet conditions, or where a trailing cable would be a hazard, or where no power is available. Power is indicated on cordless drills by voltage; 3.6 volt is enough for light work and simple screwdriving. For heavier work, cordless drills are available up to 12 volt. Recharging time varies from 1 to 12 hours. A special charger is available for drills with removable batteries. It can get a battery ready to work at full power in only 15 minutes.

FLAT BIT (ALSO KNOWN AS A SPADE BIT) Made of flat metal, with a centre point and cutting edges, it is designed for use at high speed and comes in sizes up to 38 mm ($1\frac{1}{2}$ in).

Some cordless drills have a battery in the handle which is recharged in a charger base (above). A second battery can be used in the meantime.

BLACK & DECKER

III TWISTLOK

7.2V   BD6050

BLACK&DECKER BD7221/BD6050 7.2V

Drought-stricken garden

Diverting rainwater into a butt Time: 1 hour or less

Rainwater is better for mature plants than water from a tap, so even in a wet year it is a good idea to collect rainwater. If you fit a diverter onto a downpipe from the roof you can store rainwater in a butt to use in the garden.

> YOU WILL NEED Hacksaw, diverter, tape measure, water butt.

Garden centres and hardware stores sell rainwater butts and diverters. The diverter redirects rainwater from a downpipe into a water butt. Then when the butt is full, the water is automatically directed back into the downpipe.

The water butt tap will need to be high enough off the ground to allow you to fit a watering can under it, so you may want to buy a butt with legs, or a separate leg section. Otherwise, you could raise the butt to the required height on a brick plinth (right).

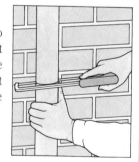

Place the butt next to the downpipe at the correct height and mark where the diverter will fit into it. Cut out the section of downpipe with a hacksaw.

Then fit the diverter according to the instructions supplied with it. You may have to use an adapter if you are fitting the diverter to a square downpipe.

What type of mulch?

Mulches stop moisture from evaporating at the soil surface and prevent the soil baking hard in the summer.

As a mulch slowly decomposes it improves the soil composition and gives it better water retention. The best soil improvers, such as composted bark or cocoa shells, decay quite quickly and need replenishing most often but their benefits to the soil probably outweigh the extra cost.

Apply a mulch over wet ground, ideally in late spring.

SHREDDINGS Shreddings make a good mulch, but are valuable as a soil improver only if they are composted first. Fresh shreddings take nitrogen from the soil, depriving plants and causing leaves to turn yellow. Note that fresh rhododendron shreddings are poisonous to dogs.

COMPOSTED BARK A good mulch, particularly pine bark, which has fewer oils than other conifers. Apply the bark about 5-7.5 cm (2-3 in) thick. A more economical alternative may be to cover the area with newspaper and to spread about 2.5 cm (1 in) of bark over it.

LAWN MOWINGS Grass makes a good mulch, especially under fruit bushes or ornamental shrubs. Keep the mulch from touching the stem. If weedkiller has been used on the lawn do not use the clippings from the next two cuttings.

COCOA SHELLS They suppress weeds effectively and conserve moisture well, though they are quite expensive. Lay the loose shells in a layer about 5 cm (2 in) thick, and pour on water. This will bond them together and make a mat which has a strong chocolate smell.

ARTIFICIAL MULCH Effective for retaining moisture, particularly useful when planting trees and shrubs. But can be unsightly. Specially designed perforated plastics such as Plantex, Agralan Permalay and Vitax Weedblock reduce evaporation while allowing water or liquid fertiliser to permeate. Improve its appearance by sprinkling bark on top.

Dry rot

Dry rot can cause serious damage and decay to a house, spreading from floor to roof in as little as six months. If you suspect your house has dry rot, call in a specialist as quickly as possible (see margin, left).

RECOGNISING DRY ROT A musty smell, and timbers that are soft and cracking across the grain are the first signs.

White tendrils spread out from airborne spores, seeking out new wood. They produce pancakelike fruiting-bodies (right) that shed more rust-red spores. When rot is advanced, it looks like a blanket of cotton wool, under the floorboards.

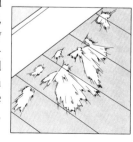

TAKING ACTION Get a specialist builder to cut out and burn all affected timber, for a metre (or a yard) beyond the last visible signs of rot. Soak all replacement timber and all the surrounding masonry in a proprietary dry rot fluid.

PREVENTING A RECURRENCE Dry rot takes hold easily in damp, unventilated areas, so eliminate any damp in the structure of your house as soon as possible (see *Damp*).

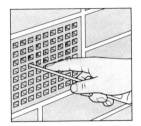

Start by improving the ventilation in damp parts of the house. Also, regularly check that the air bricks around the house are clear, and are allowing fresh air to circulate freely.

Dyeing

Don't dye a valuable item; get it done professionally.

Follow the manufacturer's instructions to the letter and make sure that the dye is suitable for the fabric. Polyesters and acrylic fabrics won't take a dye.

HOT-WATER DYES Also called multipurpose dyes. They are usually added to water with a measure of salt.

Wash the item to be dyed and leave it damp. Submerge it in the dye mixture and bring it to the boil. Then simmer – the length of time depends on the fabric.

Hot-water dyes can be used on nylon and natural fabrics such as cotton, linen, viscose, silk and wool. To avoid matting, bring wool to the boil slowly and allow it to cool afterwards, before rinsing in warm water.

COLD-WATER DYES Dissolve the powder in hottest tap water. Add colour fixative and salt. When dyeing wool omit the salt and fixative and add vinegar instead. Soak the damp fabric in the mixture for about an hour.

HAND DYES Mix the powder with hottest tap water, to give a bright, permanent colour to small items or when doing creative experiments such as tie-dye. For special effects hand dyes can be used in a microwave oven.

MACHINE DYES For bigger items, such as jeans, dyeing in a washing machine is ideal. Colours are permanent and evenly spread throughout by the action of the machine.

DYE REMOVERS Noncolourfast, natural fabrics can be returned to a neutral shade before dyeing. This product is for use by hand, not in a washing machine. To be safe, only use dye removers in a well-ventilated area.

Removing colour before dyeing Time: 1 hour or less

This method is suitable for all fabrics except wool and silk, which should not be boiled violently.

> YOU WILL NEED Rubber gloves, flame and rustproof container, dye remover, washing powder.

Remove any metal buckles or buttons on the garment, then weigh it while it is still dry. Soak the garment in warm water for a few minutes.

Dissolve dye remover in 570 ml (1 pint) of warm water, then fill a flame and rustproof container with very hot water and add the dye remover.

Completely submerge the damp fabric in the container. Boil the water, stirring constantly for 30 minutes or until the colour is removed, whichever is sooner. Simmer wool or silk for 20 minutes then allow it to cool.

Rinse it well, wash it by hand and then rinse it again. The article is now ready to be dyed.

Getting the right colour

The dye and original fabric colours determine the final result. Use a dye colour at least as strong as the fabric colour. White or cream will take most colours successfully.

Blue + yellow = green

Green + red = brown

Green + yellow = lime

Pink + pale blue = lilac

Red + blue = purple

Yellow + purple = brown

Dyeing (cont.)

Dyeing in a washing machine Time: 2 hours or less

Large items such as sheets, towels and jeans can be dyed easily in a washing machine. The machine's action ensures that the fabric is thoroughly agitated and that the colour is spread evenly. There is also less mess.

> YOU WILL NEED Rubber gloves, dye, salt, washing powder.

Wash the item to be dyed, even if it is new. Any sort of dressing will reduce the fabric's ability to absorb colour.

Empty the dye powder into the drum of the machine and tap it through the holes in the drum.

Add 1 kg (2 lb) salt in the same area, and tap through the holes. Put in the damp article, unfolded. Run a 60°C cotton cycle without prewash.

When the programme is finished, add washing powder and run through a complete cycle at the hottest temperature for the garment – preferably 95°C. This should also clear the machine of any colour residue, but to be really sure, it is advisable to run another complete cycle with nothing in the machine apart from soap powder.

Removing dye from a saucepan

Dye stains in an enamel saucepan can be removed by covering the stain with a solution of 1 teaspoon of bleach to 570 ml (1 pint) of water and leaving it to stand in the pan overnight.

A discoloured aluminium pan can be cleaned by filling it with water and adding a little lemon peel, rhubarb or tomato. Boil until the stains have gone.

Dyeing in a microwave oven Time: $\frac{1}{2}$ an hour or less

A microwave is excellent for special effects such as tie-dyeing. Use a hand dye and only natural fibres, such as cotton, lawn, cambric and calico. The method is not suitable for wool or any synthetic fabrics.

! Do not use this method with rayon or viscose as it could produce harmful fumes.

> YOU WILL NEED Rubber gloves, dye, microwave bowl, microwavable Cling Film, 570 ml (1 pint) water, detergent.

Remove any metal fastenings from the item to be dyed, and wash it. Prepare to create the special effect by tying or knotting the fabric in the desired pattern.

Put on rubber gloves and prepare the dye according to

the maker's recommendations in a large microwave-safe bowl. Make sure that the loaded bowl will not prevent the microwave turntable from operating.

Place the article in the bowl and work the dye solution into it very thoroughly. Cover the bowl with microwavable Cling Film and microwave on High for 4 minutes.

Remove the bowl and rinse the item in cold water, until the water runs clear. Then dry it naturally, away from direct heat and sunlight.

Wash the dyed fabric separately from other items for at least two or three washes.

Faultfinder guide: Dyeing

Bad results when dyeing can sometimes be reversed by using a dye remover and starting again. If not, the only solution is to learn from your mistakes.

Patchy result

CAUSE The fabric has not been stirred enough during the dyeing process.

CAUSE The container was not big enough to keep the fabric fully submerged and moving freely.

CAUSE The article was not saturated before dyeing.

CAUSE The fabric was not washed thoroughly so its finish prevented the dye from being absorbed evenly.

Reduced colour

CAUSE For a hot-water dye – the water did not reach boiling point or simmer for long enough.

CAUSE Too little dye was used.

CAUSE For a cold-water dye – not enough salt or fixative has been added.

Over-concentration of colour

CAUSE Too much dye was used.

Little or no colour penetration

CAUSE The fabric is unsuitable for dyeing.

CAUSE The wrong type of dye was used for the fabric.

Incorrect colour

CAUSE The original fabric was not light enough, stain free or clean.

CAUSE The original fabric colour has affected the result. See 'Getting the right colour', previous page.

BEWARE OF MARKS ON THE FABRIC

Dye will not cover up a stain on a garment, nor will it hide bleach marks or a pattern. Where possible, get rid of the stain (see *Stains*) or use a dye remover first.

Earrings

Cheap earrings frequently fall apart, but if they have become favourites it is worth trying to mend them. It is possible to buy replacement pieces, called findings or fixings, from jewellers and craft shops.

Replacing a glued fixing   Time: a few minutes

YOU WILL NEED Suitable glue. Possibly: piece of fine-grained foam rubber or a pencil rubber, pins.

Choosing the correct glue is important and depends on the material of which the earring is made (see *Glues*).

Clean the fixing and the decorative part of the earring at the point where they meet.

If the earring is for pierced ears, remove the butterfly and push the post into a piece of fine sponge or a pencil rubber, making sure it is vertical. Apply the adhesive according to the manufacturer's instructions and position the decorative part on the post. Allow it to dry.

For earrings that clip on, force the fixing into the sponge or rubber, holding it level with a few pins, if necessary. Apply the adhesive, add the decorative part and allow it to dry.

Repairing a wire fixing   Time: a few minutes

YOU WILL NEED Small long-nosed pliers or tweezers.

The wire hooks on handmade earrings can come adrift or get distorted. Depending on the type and style, use a very fine pair of pliers or tweezers – the type sold in craft shops – to gently reshape them to their original shape.

You may find you need to straighten out the wire a little, reattach the earring and bend the wire to secure it. Always treat wire gently when you are reshaping an earring; too much pressure may cause it to break.

Preventing sore ear lobes   Time: a few minutes

YOU WILL NEED Possibly: clear nail varnish, replacement fixings, self-adhesive foam pads or masking tape.

Many people make the painful discovery that their ears are allergic to some metals. Solve the problem by inserting a barrier between the metal and your ear.

POST-AND-BUTTERFLY EARRINGS Separate each post from its butterfly (the piece with the hole in it). Paint them both with clear nail varnish. Make sure they are both completely dry before using them again.

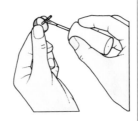

Alternatively, if you are fond of the earrings and only the posts and butterflies are made from the offending metal, buy new gold, silver or surgical steel posts and butterflies (which won't cause irritation) from a jeweller or a craft shop. Fix them with a suitable glue (see *Glues*).

CLIP-ON EARRINGS It is also possible to suffer an allergic reaction to clip-on earrings. Use very small pads of self-adhesive sponge to cover up the metal parts that will touch the ear. Replace the pads regularly.

Kits are available at the jewellery counters of department stores. Temporary shields can be made from small strips of masking tape, but make sure they don't show.

Repairing a broken earring   Time: a few minutes

When part of a favourite but not valuable earring breaks off, you may find that jewellers are unwilling to undertake the repair. Try to mend it yourself, as long as the break is clean and no parts are missing.

YOU WILL NEED Adhesive, Blu-Tack or Plasticine, pins.

Choose an adhesive that is suitable for the material from which the earring is made (see *Glues*).

Fix the main part of the earring into a piece of Blu-Tack or Plasticine, so that the force of gravity will help and not hinder the setting process. Use pins to support it.

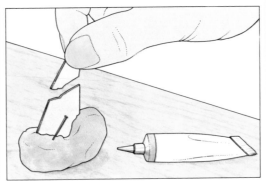

Clean the earring along the break. Following the maker's instructions, apply the adhesive and join the pieces. If necessary, support the smaller piece with more Blu-Tack or Plasticine, to ensure it dries in the correct position.

Earthing

To protect against electric shock, earth wires, known as protective conductors, run through the house. They provide a safe escape path for any electricity which leaks out of the system. They ensure that fuses or circuit breakers will cut off the supply in the event of a fault.

Starting at the main earthing terminal, which is usually in the consumer unit, protective conductors run in every cable to the earthing terminals of socket outlets, switches and fixed appliances. The earth wires in flexes continue the protection to portable appliances.

Bonding conductors run from the main earthing terminal to clamps fitted to metal water and gas pipes. There may be additional bonding conductors, usually in the bathroom. All give vital protection against electric shock and must never be disconnected.

Most modern homes have protective multiple earthing (PME), which means that the electrical system is earthed through the electricity company's neutral conductor which is connected to earth at several points.

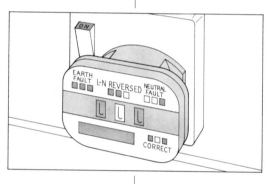

It is possible to check the earthing system in your house with a plug-in tester, following the maker's instructions. If it indicates a fault, consult a qualified electrician. Also, call a qualified electrician for any installation or alteration of the earthing system in your home (see *Electrician*).

Elastic

Replacing stretched or snapped elastic
Time: a few minutes

In some garments, elastic is contained in a fabric casing. With laundering and wear, it may become stretched, or even break. Stretched or snapped elastic is easily replaced.

YOU WILL NEED Embroidery scissors or stitch ripper, replacement elastic, safety pins, needle, matching thread.

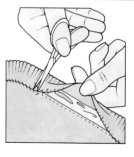

STRETCHED ELASTIC Using sharp embroidery scissors or a stitch ripper, unpick a small section of the stitching along the edge of the casing that encloses the elastic, and check the width of elastic used. Buy a card of elastic of the same width.

Cut a length of new elastic that will be comfortable for the wearer, who may have gained or lost weight recently.

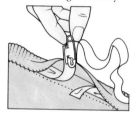

Pull a loop of the old elastic out through the casing. Cut the old elastic and keep hold of the cut ends. Use a safety pin to attach one end of the new piece to one end of the old.

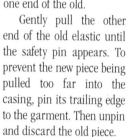

Gently pull the other end of the old elastic until the safety pin appears. To prevent the new piece being pulled too far into the casing, pin its trailing edge to the garment. Then unpin and discard the old piece.

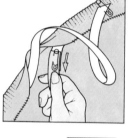

Overlap the ends of the new elastic by about 2.5 cm (1 in) and stitch them together firmly, using small hemming stitches along the edges and across the raw ends. Slip the joined section back into the casing and sew up the seam.

SNAPPED ELASTIC Where the elastic has snapped or come undone, open the casing as described above, and remove the old elastic completely.

Fasten a safety pin to the end of a suitable length of replacement elastic and work it through the casing with your fingers. Pin the trailing end of elastic to the garment so that it doesn't disappear into the seam (see above).

Sew the ends together and restitch the casing.

Knitting with shirring elastic

Most knitting yarns, especially those with very little 'give' in them, such as cotton, feel much firmer if ribbed waistbands and cuffs are knitted in conjunction with shirring elastic.

Shirring elastic is available in a number of colours; however, if it does not match the yarn and will be too noticeable, complete the garment without it. Then use a tapestry needle to weave the elastic along the inside of the ribbed sections. Best results are gained from running the shirring elastic behind every plain stitch in every second or third row.

This method can also be used to extend the life of knitted garments with cuffs and waistbands that are starting to stretch through wear and washing.

Electric blanket

Most low-voltage electric blankets and duvets have thermostatic heat controls and are safe to use all night. But to be sure, check the manufacturer's recommendations.

Cleaning methods

Electric over-blankets and duvets have detachable leads and can be washed by hand or in a washing machine. Wash on the 'wool' setting in a washing machine, and allow the blanket or duvet to dry naturally.

Electric under-blankets are not usually washable; they should be shaken out or wiped with a damp cloth.

Read the care instructions on the blanket or duvet.

Storing techniques

Do not fold an electric blanket or duvet or cause kinks in the electric wires that run through it – store it rolled up and do not place anything heavy on top of it.

If storage space is limited, leave an electric under-blanket in place, but disconnected, on the bed.

Servicing recommendations

Send an electric blanket back to its manufacturer for servicing every two or three years. They will check it and do any necessary repairs for a small fee.

Although electric duvets are no longer produced in Britain, they are still used and need servicing every two or three years, in the same way as electric blankets.

Electric fire

Replacing the heating element Time: a few minutes

If an electric heater is not giving out any heat, first check that it is firmly plugged in and switched on at the wall socket.

Then check that the heater is turned on as well as the 'fire effect'. On some models of heater it is possible to have only the 'fire effect' turned on, for decoration.

Then replace the fuse in the plug (see *Electric plug*). Check the wire connections and tighten any loose ones.

If the heater still doesn't work, an element probably needs to be replaced. You should be able to see which element is broken.

> **YOU WILL NEED** New heating element, screwdriver or spanner. Possibly: pliers.

The element is a spiral of conductive wire which is either wound round a heat-resistant core or runs inside a silicone glass tube. It is supported at each end by a heat-resistant bracket, and held in place by a knurled nut.

Unplug the fire from the wall socket.

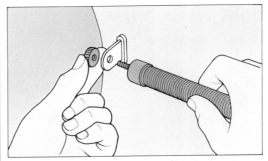

Loosen the nuts or screws at the end of the broken element and remove it. Fit the new element and tighten the nuts or screws. Plug in the fire to test the new element.

Electric fuses:

SEE ELECTRIC PLUG; FUSE BOX

Electrician

More than 3000 fires a year occur in the UK as a result of faulty or inadequate wiring. Choosing a competent electrician is a matter of safety as well as convenience.

Try to choose an electrician who is a member of the Electrical Contractors Association (ECA) or the National Inspection Council for Electrical Installation Contracting (NICEIC). Both organisations stipulate that their members should carry out a high standard of work and be adequately insured. Both have a complaints procedure.

Look for the organisations' logos in *Yellow Pages* under 'Electrician' or contact the ECA or the NICEIC for a list of their members (see margin). Regional Electricity Company showrooms, public libraries and Citizens Advice Bureaux also hold lists of NICEIC members.

Six tips for electrical work

When hiring a contractor follow these simple guidelines.

- Use an ECA or NICEIC contractor.
- Try to get a contractor recommended personally by a friend or relative.
- Get estimates from two or three companies.
- Always get a written quote specifying the job to be done, the time it will take and the materials to be used.
- Never pay for work in advance.
- Get a completion certificate when the work has been finished. This records that the work has been done to the appropriate British Standard.

FAN HEATER

The element in a fan heater is supported on heat-resistant brackets. A fan blows air across the element to be warmed, and out of a grille at the front of the heater. To get to the element take off the front of the fan.

USEFUL ADDRESSES

- National Inspection Council for Electrical Installation Contracting, Vintage House, 37 Albert Embankment, London SE1 7UJ Tel. 0171 582 7746
- Electrical Contractors Assoc., Esca House, 34 Palace Court, London W2 4HY Tel. 0171 229 1266
- SELECT (Scottish Electrical Contractors' Association) Bush House, Bush Estate, Midlothian EH2 0SB Tel. 0131 445 5577

SAFETY FIRST WITH ELECTRICITY

Before starting any work on an electrical fitting or appliance, make sure to cut off the electricity supply – either by switching off at the main fuse box, or by unplugging the appliance.

Electricity bill

Measuring electricity

The unit of electricity consumption as it appears on your bill is the kilowatt hour (abbreviated as kWh); this is the equivalent of 1000 watts, used for one hour. The price of each kWh is shown on your bill. Each appliance has a wattage marked on it. Divide the number into 1000 to give the number of hours you will get from the appliance for the cost of one unit of electricity. For example:

100 watt bulb	10 hours
15 watt mini fluorescent	50 hours
65 watt fluorescent	13 hours
Television (60 watts)	17 hours
Video recorder (27 watts)	37 hours
Refrigerator	24 hours
Iron	2 hours
Kettle	12 pints of water

Reading your meter

There are three types of domestic meter that record how many units of electricity the household is consuming.

To calculate the number of units you have used since the last time the meter was read, subtract the figure on your last electricity bill from the present reading.

DIGITAL METER Modern meters have a row of figures rolling over to register how much electricity has been used. Write down the figures exactly as they are, but ignore the one on the extreme right.

TWO-TARIFF METER Where you have an Economy 7 or White Meter, you can read and record both rows of figures exactly as they appear on the meter. Ignore the figure on the extreme right of each row.

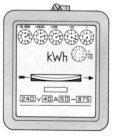

DIAL METER Old meters have a row of dials. Record the figures indicated on the dials, reading from left to right. Ignore the red dial. Read the last figure that a hand has passed, not the one it is nearest to.

Electric plug

Wiring a plug Time: 1 hour or less

All plugs for 13 amp sockets should have sleeves on both the current-carrying pins to prevent fingers from touching the live metal when the plug is partly out of the socket.

Replace plugs that do not have this safety feature.

YOU WILL NEED Screwdrivers, trimming knife, wire-and-cable cutters. Possibly: wire strippers.

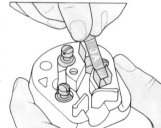

Unscrew the plug cover. Prise out one end of the fuse and pull out the other. Use a screwdriver to loosen the terminals so that they will take the wires. Then, if necessary, loosen the flex grip slightly to take the flex.

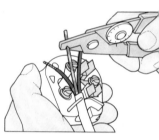

Cut the wires so that they are just long enough to reach the terminals. In some makes of plug, the wires need to be different lengths; in others, they are of equal length. Strip off the insulation to expose more wire if necessary.

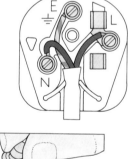

Connect the wires to the terminals in this order: fix the brown-coated wire to the terminal marked L, the blue-coated wire to the terminal marked N and the earth wire (which is green and yellow) to the terminal marked E or ⏚.

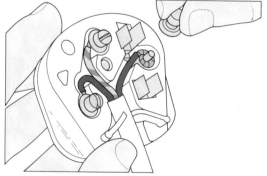

POST TERMINALS Some plugs have terminals that stick up. Wind each wire-tip clockwise around the correct terminal so that it doesn't loosen as you tighten the screw. A bad connection could cause sparking and overheating.

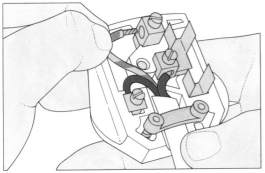

HOLE TERMINALS On plugs that have terminals with holes, push the wires into the holes until no bare wire is showing, then tighten the screws to make the connection.

DOUBLE-INSULATION Many appliances are double insulated, meaning that they need no earth connection.

They will have a two-core flex. Connect the wires to the L and N terminals. If the wires are both the same colour, it doesn't matter to which of the L and N terminals you connect them.

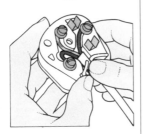

Secure the flex in the grip, making sure that it is held firmly in place by its outer sheath. Check that the fuse you have is correctly rated for this type of appliance, then replace it and screw on the cover.

Moulded-on plugs

Most appliances are sold with a moulded-together, one-piece plug and flex. Never try to use one that has been discarded. Throw it away so that a child is not tempted to push it into a live socket.

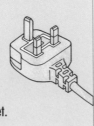

Selecting the correct cartridge fuse

A three-pin plug must have the correct cartridge fuse to protect the flexible cord of the appliance, to prevent it from being overloaded and then overheating. A fuse with too high a rating could cause a fire.

Find out the correct fuse for an appliance by looking at the wattage rating on its rating plate. The plate is normally at the rear of the appliance.

! Do not use fuses of amp ratings other than those that have been specified by the manufacturer.

3 AMP FUSE Should be used for appliances rated up to 700 watts, including:

- Electric blanket
- Clock
- Hair dryer
- Hi-fi system
- Lamp
- Radio
- Slow cooker
- Travel iron

13 AMP FUSE Used for appliances rated between 700 and 3000 watts, including:

- Deep-fat fryer
- Dishwasher
- Electric fire
- Freezer
- Iron (normal)
- Kettle
- Refrigerator
- Toaster

TELEVISION SETS Some TV sets need a 13 amp fuse despite being rated below 700 watts, partly because of the brief surge of current as they are switched on. Follow the recommendation on fuse size given in the maker's leaflet.

Stripping the end of a flex

Use a sharp trimming knife to remove a suitable portion of the outer sheath of the flex. Take great care not to cut the insulation on the wires inside. (If you do, cut off the damaged piece and start again.)

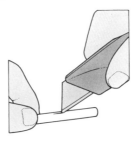

Cut each of the wires to the appropriate length with wire-and-cable cutters, and use the trimming knife to strip 1.6 cm ($\frac{5}{8}$ in) of the plastic coating from the tips of the wires. Take care not to cut the inner wires.

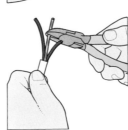

Repairing a sparking or hot plug Time: 1 hour or less

Switch off the electricity at the wall and remove the plug from the wall socket and open it with a screwdriver.

Check that the wires are tight in their terminals and that they are not damaged or blackened. If they are, rewire the plug (see 'Wiring a plug', facing page).

Overheating may also be the result of having a high wattage appliance (such as a 3 kW heater) switched on for a long time, or from a coiled or kinked flex. Switching off for a while and checking the flex should cure the problem.

Wire-and-cable cutters

Also called side cutting nippers, wire-and-cable cutters have jaws for cutting flex and cable, but cannot be used to strip the insulation.

Wire strippers

Wire strippers come in various designs. This type has jaws with sharpened tips. An adjustable stop ensures that only the insulation is removed and the copper wire is left undamaged.

A combined wire cutter and stripper has jaws that consist of plier tips, grooves to strip insulation from wires and a wire cutter.

CUTTING OFF POWER TO AN FCU

Before working on an electrical appliance which is connected to the power supply by a fused connection unit (FCU), switch off and remove the fuse. If there is no switch, simply remove the fuse.

CHECK THAT A CIRCUIT IS DEAD

Make sure that a circuit is dead before working on it, even when changing a broken light bulb. Turn off the circuit at the main fuse box. If you are not sure which switch isolates it, turn off the main switch. Always double-check before starting work. On a lighting circuit turn a switch on and off a few times to make sure the light doesn't come on. On a power circuit plug a lamp in and make sure it won't turn on. Finally, check that the lamp is not faulty by trying it in another socket which is working.

Electric socket

Replacing a damaged socket Time: 1 hour or less

A damaged socket can cause an electric shock or a fire. Replace it or call an electrician to do it for you.

YOU WILL NEED Screwdrivers, pliers.

Turn off the electricity at the main switch on the fuse box. Undo the two screws that hold the socket in place.

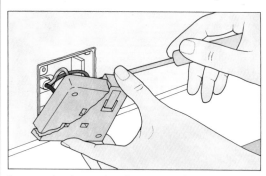

Ease out the damaged socket. Loosen the screws on the three terminals on the back. Draw a quick sketch of how many conductors are connected to each terminal, as the new socket must be connected in the same way.

Disconnect and remove the damaged socket and clean out any broken pieces of plastic from the mounting box. Use pliers to tidy up the ends of the wires by twisting them.

Reconnect the wires to the correct terminals in the new socket. The red wire goes to the terminal marked L. The black wire goes to the terminal marked N, and the yellow-and-green (or bare) wire to the terminal marked E or $\perp$. If the earth is bare, fit a piece of yellow-and-green sleeving.

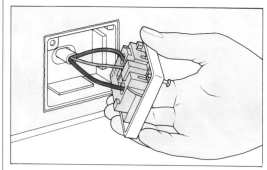

The wires must be in place before the screws are tightened. Tug the socket gently to check that they are firmly fixed.

Secure the socket on the mounting box with the two screws. There should not be a gap between the mounting box and the socket plate, but do not overtighten it or you may crack the plastic.

Switch on the mains, then plug in an appliance and switch on. If it still doesn't work, call in an electrician.

What model of socket?

STANDARD SOCKETS These outlets have rectangular slots to take three-pronged 13amp plugs. There are single, double and triple versions, with switches or without, and some have a light to show when they are on. Sockets can be either flush or surface-mounted.

FLOOR SOCKETS Some sockets are designed to fit into a timber floor to avoid trailing flexes from the wall in larger rooms. These have a spring-loaded cover to keep dust out of the slots.

MULTISOCKET UNIT For appliances that would otherwise take up more than one socket (hi-fi equipment, for example) it is possible to buy purpose-made mini-plugs designed to fit only into their own multisocket unit, which has its own fuse.

Multisockets can be either freestanding or wall-mounted, and are connected to standard 13amp sockets through 13amp plugs.

FUSED CONNECTION UNIT (FCU) A fused connection unit is sometimes used for appliances that need permanent connection to the power supply, such as freezers, electric cookers or a heated towel rail.

The flex can enter the socket through a hole in the faceplate or from behind. The fuse is behind a door in the faceplate. A light indicates that the power is on.

Embroidery & tapestry

Embroidery and tapestry are unlikely to be colourfast. Being handmade and handfinished, they can be damaged easily and, as a result, should be cleaned with great care.

Cleaning embroidery and tapestry

Tapestry chair covers, stool tops and cushions can be vacuumed very gently with an upholstery nozzle, if in good condition. Don't use water, stain remover or any type of upholstery shampoo on embroidery or tapestry.

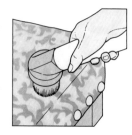

Hold the nozzle just above the item so that dust is removed but threads are not pulled. Sturdier tapestry, such as footstool covers, can be brushed gently with the nozzle.

Lift dust from antique or valuable pieces – or any that contain beads – using a baby's hairbrush. Do this once a week or when dust starts to build up. Do not use a vacuum cleaner nozzle as its suction is far too strong and may pull off beads or break fragile threads.

If embroidery or tapestry needs dry-cleaning or repair of any sort, get expert advice from The Royal School of Needlework, Apartment 12a, Hampton Court Palace, East Molesey, Surrey KT8 9AU (Tel. 0181 943 1432).

For the addresses of specialist dry-cleaners contact:
Dry Cleaning Information Bureau,
Textile Services Association,
7 Churchill Court,
58 Station Road,
North Harrow,
Middlesex HA2 7SA
(Tel. 0181 863 8658).

Behar Profex in St Alban's Place, Upper Street, London N1 0NX (Tel. 0171 226 0144) will clean and advise.

Repairs to tapestry or embroidery

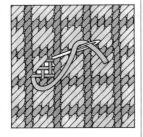

LOOSE THREADS Where a piece of tapestry or embroidery has loose threads or a little unravelling, use a tapestry needle (size 20 for wool, 22 for cotton thread) to gently pull and stitch the threads into place.

FRAYING If the base canvas or fabric is fraying, dab it with a little stick glue, such as Pritt, to prevent further fraying and secure it with careful stitching, using toning thread.

MOTH DAMAGE Seek professional help if there is moth damage and the piece is valuable. Otherwise, treat it with a moth repellent, although this may affect the colours.

Enamel

Most household appliances are finished in either stove enamel or vitreous enamel.

STOVE ENAMEL Washing machines, dishwashers and fridges are often coated with stove enamel.

Try to avoid knocking hard items against stove enamel as it chips easily. If this happens, use a product such as Joy Porcelainit to fill in chips and touch up scratches. Follow the instructions on the pack. Radiator paint, available from DIY shops, is a good alternative.

Clean stove enamel by wiping it with a cloth wrung out in a solution of washing-up liquid. Dry with kitchen paper. Greasy surfaces can be cleaned with neat washing-up liquid or concentrated liquid cleaner. Rinse thoroughly.

VITREOUS ENAMEL Baths, ovens and other appliances may be covered with vitreous enamel, although many modern baths are made of either glass fibre or acrylic.

Vitreous enamel is produced by fusing glass to metal, and is tougher and less likely to chip than stove enamel. Harsh abrasives will scratch it, so it should be cleaned by wiping with a cloth wrung out in a detergent solution.

If it is very dirty, use a cleaning product approved by the Vitreous Enamel Association. Look for their mark on the product's label and follow the maker's instructions.

VITREOUS ENAMEL DEVELOPMENT COUNCIL

Chips and scratches on vitreous enamel should be treated in the same way as described for stove enamel.

For more detailed advice on cleaning and looking after vitreous enamel, you can contact the Vitreous Enamel Association at 41 Snowdrop Drive, Attleborough, Norfolk, NR17 2PP, or call their helpline (Tel. 01953 454666).

ENAMELWARE Saucepans, teapots and mugs may have a vitreous enamel coating or simply a sprayed-on polyamide (plastic) finish. Be sure to dry them immediately after washing if you live in a hard-water area, or a white film may develop on the enamel.

Use a cleaner recommended by the Vitreous Enamel Association to remove more stubborn marks.

If a pan with an enamelled interior is heavily stained, fill it with a weak solution of liquid household bleach – about 5ml (1tsp) to 570ml (1 pint) cold water. Rinse it thoroughly before using.

Avoid cooking acid foods, such as rhubarb, in enamel pans as they can cause staining.

Enamel paint (see also *Paints*)

Finely ground pigments give enamel paint the high gloss which distinguishes it from other paints. It is nontoxic, making it suitable for children's toys. It can be used on wood or metal and can be brushed or sprayed onto wooden furniture. It lends itself to re-touching chipped or damaged areas. After use, clean your paintbrushes with white spirit.

Enamel-painted surfaces can be wiped clean with a damp cloth. Heavy soiling can be removed with a small amount of non-abrasive liquid household cleaner on a damp cloth.

FITTING A NEW PULL CORD

It is rare for the pull cord on an extractor fan to break, but they can become discoloured with use. Contact the manufacturer for a replacement kit or for the name of your nearest stockist. The replacement cord will contain simple instructions.

Extension lead:

SEE FLEXES & CABLES

Extractor fan

An extractor fan that has been installed in a kitchen or bathroom is usually connected to the power supply by a fused connection unit. Always switch off the power and remove the fuse before working on the fan.

Cleaning a window-mounted fan Time: 2 hours or less

> YOU WILL NEED Rubber gloves, screwdriver, clean paintbrush or old toothbrush, clean cloth, soapy water. Possibly: white spirit.

Working inside the room, undo the screws holding the front grille. Take care as you loosen them, because they may be holding the fan in the window.

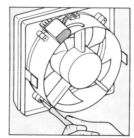

Press the release button, if the fan has one, and gently remove the front grille. On some models there may be a second cover to remove.

Disconnect and remove the fan's motor and the blade assembly. Place them on a kitchen table or worktop in order to clean them.

Wash the grille in warm, soapy water and dry it thoroughly with a clean cloth. If the fan has been used in a kitchen, it may be necessary to use a little white spirit or a concentrated liquid cleaner on a rag to remove the grease.

Don't use an abrasive cleaner on the plastic casing of an extractor fan — you might scratch its smooth finish and make it easier for dirt and grease to cling to the casing.

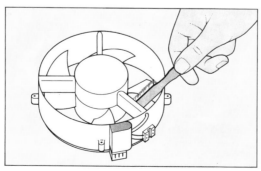

Brush the motor and blades with an old toothbrush or a clean paintbrush to remove all dirt and dust. Do not use water or allow them to get wet at all.

Use a clean cloth wrung out in soapy water to wipe the plastic housing and clamp plate which are still attached to the window-pane. Then dry them carefully with a soft, dry cloth.

Reassemble all the parts in reverse order, restore power and test that the fan works properly.

If an extractor fan stops working Time: ½ an hour or less

Extractor fans in kitchens and bathrooms are connected to the mains via a fused connection unit on a spur that runs off an existing circuit. The unit is normally located on a wall some distance from the fan and has a built-in switch.

> YOU WILL NEED Screwdriver. Possibly: fuse tester, new fuse.

Turn off the power at the main fuse box and remove the fuse from the fused connection unit.

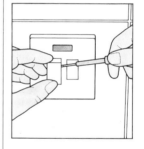

You may have to lever the fuse out of the unit with a screwdriver, but take care that you do not damage the connection box.

Test the fuse with a fuse tester, if you have one, and replace the fuse if it is faulty. Alternatively, insert a new fuse and test the fan. If the fault does not lie with the fuse, the wiring may be at fault and may be quite easy to repair.

! Remember to turn off the electricity at the mains again, before proceeding any further.

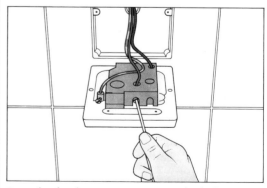

Open the fused connection unit to check the wiring. Tighten the screws and put a little pressure on each wire, to make sure it is connected properly.

Replace the fuse and the cover, restore the power and test the fan. If it still won't work, call an electrician.

Eyelets

There are two types of eyelets: embroidered and metal.

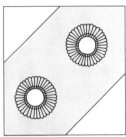 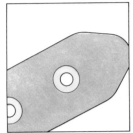

An embroidered eyelet is a hole which is usually edged with fine buttonhole stitch (see *Stitches*) in a soft fabric or a lightweight belt.

A metal eyelet is used to create a hole in any 'hard' fabric such as denim, or in a fabric-covered buckram belt or in a leather belt.

Making an embroidered eyelet   Time: ½ an hour or less

YOU WILL NEED Pencil or ball-point pen, fine needle, matching thread, embroidery scissors.

Decide where you want the eyelet to be made and mark the spot with a pencil or ball-point pen. Keep marks as small as possible.

To make sure that the eyelet will not fray or tear, make a ring of tiny, evenly spaced running stitches round the mark (see *Stitches*).

The size of the ring will determine the size of the finished eyelet. Cut away the centre of the hole with fine embroidery scissors, leaving a very small margin of fabric between the hole and the circle of stitches.

Use a tiny buttonhole stitch or neat oversewing to edge the entire hole. Keep the stitches as small and as close to one another as possible. End off by taking two or three very tiny stitches, one on top of the other, on the inside of the garment.

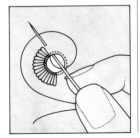

Inserting metal eyelets   Time: a few minutes

Metal eyelets are much stronger than embroidered eyelets. They are sometimes sold singly and can be inserted with a special pair of pliers. However, they are usually bought in a belt-making kit which contains a small metal tool that makes the hole and correctly shapes the eyelet.

It is a good idea to experiment on a scrap of material of the same weight before working on the belt or garment.

YOU WILL NEED Pencil or ball-point pen or tailor's chalk, metal eyelet kit, hammer.

Decide where you are going to insert the eyelets and mark the spots with a pen or pencil. Use tailor's chalk if the fabric is dark. On a belt, holes are usually made about 2.5 cm (1 in) apart to allow for changes in the waistline.

Work on a flat, hard surface that cannot be damaged.

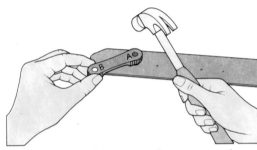

With the right side of the garment facing, position the cutting end of the metal tool over the first mark. One or two sharp blows with a hammer on the cutting end of the tool should remove a neat circle from the belt.

Push a metal eyelet into the hole with the smooth end showing on the right side of the belt.

Turn the belt over, and place the other end of the tool over the sharp end of the eyelet. Hammer it once or twice to fold the edges of the eyelet flat. Take care not to hammer too hard, or you may distort the 'right' side of the eyelet.

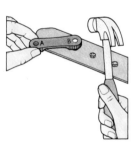

Decorative eyelets

Eyelets and eyelet Poppas (which are two-piece eyelets and come in kits with a special applicator) can be used for effect on jackets, jeans and accessories.

They are available in various colours and sizes and some styles can take a decorative 'cap' which snaps on to cover the outside fixing.

Where the style of a garment calls for lacing, facing rows of metal eyelets can be inserted.

Fencing
Choosing the right fence for your garden

When choosing a fence take the location into account. In windy areas an open fence is less likely to be blown down.

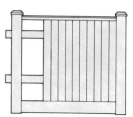

CLOSEBOARD Good as a screen. Pretreated timber will last a long time, but otherwise treat the fence regularly with preservative. A closeboard fence is costly and takes time to put up.

PANEL Ready-made panels are easy to put up and panel fencing is cheaper than closeboard. It makes a good screen and with regular preservative treatment it will last 5-8 years.

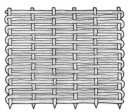

HURDLE OR WATTLE Makes a useful screen for growing plants. This is a cheap form of fencing, though it does not last very long. Treat it regularly with preservative. Suitable for windy areas.

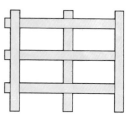

POST AND RAILS Relatively cheap. It makes an attractive decorative feature and is suitable for windy areas. If it is treated with preservative or paint regularly it will last a long time.

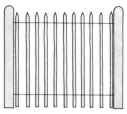

CHESTNUT PALING A good boundary. Paling is comprised of stakes joined by wires. It is easy to erect and will last for a long time if it is well cared for, so apply preservative regularly.

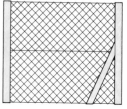

CHAIN-LINK FENCING Good security fencing. It is cheap and fairly easy to put up. Plastic-coated wire requires minimal maintenance and lasts longer than the bare metal version.

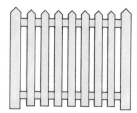

PICKET FENCING Decorative and good for marking boundaries. Picket is cheap and easy to erect. It will last a long time if well looked after. Coat it regularly with preservative or paint.

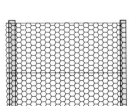

NETTING Ideal for animal pens. Netting is cheaper than chain link but not as durable. It is easy to put up but needs stretching. Once it is in place it needs little maintenance.

POST AND WIRE Galvanised wire is stretched between wood or concrete fence posts. Ideal for enclosing a large area. Post and wire is cheap and lasts a long time with little maintenance.

Replacing a rotten post Time: parts of 2 days

Wooden fence posts are vulnerable to rot because they are in constant contact with the damp soil.

> YOU WILL NEED Spare timber lengths, pincers or claw hammer, general-purpose saw, narrow spade or hole borer, steel tape measure, builder's line, spirit level, hardcore, coarse concrete, mixing board, replacement post, galvanised nails. Possibly: cold chisel, club hammer, safety spectacles, gardening gloves, brackets for replacing fence panels, screws and screwdriver.

DIGGING UP THE FENCE POST Support the panels on each side of the rotten post with lengths of timber. This should stop it falling when the panel is released from the fence post.

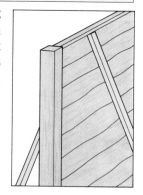

Use pincers or a claw hammer to prise out the nails holding the fence panels to the rotten post. On closeboard fencing you will have to cut through the arris rails where they enter the rotten post.

Saw off the post to about 30 cm (1 ft) above ground level, then dig out the stump. If the stump is set in a concrete base, it may be possible to lever it out (see margin, facing page). Otherwise, wear safety spectacles and heavy gloves and break up the concrete with a cold chisel and club hammer or an industrial hammer drill.

Square up the hole to 76 cm (2 ft 6 in) deep and add a 15 cm (6 in) layer of rubble for drainage. Mix a batch of coarse concrete to a stiffish consistency that holds a slope.

PUTTING IN THE NEW POST
Stand the new fence post in position in the hole. Attach a builder's line or string to neighbouring posts to align the new post with them.

Ram a layer of rubble and soil around the base with a piece of wood. Then add alternate layers of concrete and rubble. Check as you work that the post remains vertical.

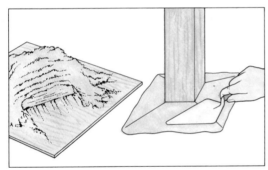

End with a layer of concrete just above ground level. Slope it away from the post so that it sheds water. Then support the post with lengths of timber for 24 hours.

On a panel fence fasten the panel to the post using either specially made fence clips and screws (right) or galvanised nails.

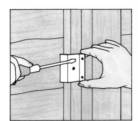

On a closeboard fence use an arris-rail bracket designed specially to fix the arris rail to the fence post (right). Brackets are also available for fixing rails to concrete posts.

Reinforcing a rotten fence post Time: ½ a day

If a fence post rots or breaks underground, but the rest of the post is sound, it can be supported with a ready-made concrete spur or a steel bracket.

If the rot extends above the gravel board you will have to free the fencing from the post on both sides before you can cut the rot out, so it may be simpler to replace the post.

> **YOU WILL NEED** Claw hammer, wood preservative, narrow spade or post-hole borer, spirit level, power drill, spade bit, adjustable spanner, hardcore, concrete, concrete support spur, coach bolts. Possibly: plumb line.

USING A CONCRETE SPUR Support the panels on each side of the rotten post with lengths of timber (see 'Replacing a rotten post'). Coat the whole post with wood preservative.

Using a hole borer or a spade, make a hole 51 cm (20 in) deep and at least 30 cm (12 in) square next to the damaged fence post.

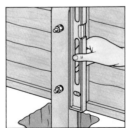

Hold the spur against the post. Put the bolts in the holes in the spur and strike them firmly with a hammer to mark their positions.

Use a drill with a spade bit to drill holes right through the post at the marks.

Push bolts through the post and spur so the threaded ends are on the spur side.

Slip washers and nuts onto the ends of the bolts and tighten with a spanner.

Use a spirit level or a plumb line to check that the post and spur are vertical.

REMOVING A FENCE-POST STUMP

If an old fence-post stump is set in concrete, drill a hole through the stump then thread some strong wire through the hole and twist the ends together with pliers to form a loop. Make a fulcrum with a pile of bricks or something similar. Put one end of a strong piece of timber such as a fence post through the loop and balance it on the fulcrum. Lever out the stump by pushing down on the other end of the timber.

CEMENTING SHORT CUTS

To cement a fence post quickly you can use Supamix Post Fix cement instead of rubble and cement. It is sold in 25 kg (55 lb) bags, each suitable for erecting one post.

PRESERVING FENCE POSTS

- Use pressure-impregnated fence posts if possible.
- Soak untreated wood in preservative (see *Wood preservative*).
- Paint preservative onto fences that are not pressure-impregnated about once a year.
- Do not use creosote to protect wooden fence posts near plants.

REPLACING A GRAVEL BOARD

Replace the gravel board, which runs along the bottom of the fence, as soon as possible if it starts to rot. Prise it off with a claw hammer, pincers or a screwdriver. Secure the new board with galvanised nails or rustless screws. If necessary lower the level of the soil so that it doesn't touch the fence.

Brace the fence post and concrete spur with lengths of spare timber (such as spare fence posts). If necessary, hammer a nail into each side of the fence post and wedge the timbers underneath the nails to hold the fence post firm. Then mix a batch of coarse concrete to such a consistency that it is stiff enough to hold its shape.

Ram hardcore into the bottom of the hole, then pour in the concrete. Allow it to set for 24 hours.

USING A READY-MADE BRACKET An alternative to securing a rotten post with concrete is to use a Postite bracket. These steel brackets are strong and easy to use. They can also be used to give extra support in windy areas.

The pointed stake on the bracket is hammered into the ground and the metal plate is screwed onto the fence post.

EXTRA SUPPORT If the fence is exposed to high winds you can give it extra support by adding timber support stays. Each stay should be about three-quarters of the length of the post. Use a spare fence post or a length of timber 75 mm (3 in) by 50 mm (2 in) and cut one end so that it rests at an angle of about 40 degrees to the fence post. Nail the stay to the post and sink the other end to about the same depth as the fence post. Put a large stone at the bottom of the hole to support the stay, and fill the hole.

Fence-post spikes

In firm soil and in sheltered spots you can use ready-made post spikes such as Metpost and Fencefast instead of digging out or boring holes. They consist of a spiked steel support which is hammered into the ground and a square cup on top that holds the post.

Fillers & stoppers

(SEE ALSO SEALANTS)

What kind of filler or stopper?

Fillers and stoppers are used for repairing cracks and gaps in wood, plaster or masonry. Some types can be bought ready to use; others need mixing. Be sure to choose the correct type for the job you are planning.

INTERIOR FILLER (ALSO CALLED CELLULOSE FILLER) Used indoors to patch cracks or small holes in plaster, wood or masonry. One example is Polyfilla. Available in powder or paste, it is workable for about an hour, sets hard after two hours, and can be drilled and screwed into once it is dry. It should not be used on damp surfaces. Interior filler can be painted when it has dried.

Interior fillers classed as fine are not affected by damp.

EXTERIOR FILLER Used to patch cracks or holes in outside masonry. Based on cement, it can be used for repairing the pointing on brickwork. It is workable for 45 minutes, becomes hard after 2 hours and is weather-resistant after 24 hours. It can be painted.

ALL-PURPOSE FILLER More expensive than interior or exterior fillers, but can be used inside or out in masonry, wood, plaster, glass or metal, and can be painted. Available in powder or paste, it sets within 2 hours and dries to a tough, slightly flexible finish that is largely weather-resistant but should not be exposed to long-term dampness.

PLASTIC WOOD FILLER Is available as an adhesive paste. Use it indoors or out to fill cracks or small holes in wood. It is available in various colours to match the wood, and sets after about 10 minutes.

WOOD STOPPING Available in both interior and exterior grades. It comes in a limited range of colours, but is much stronger and more adhesive than a plastic wood filling.

EPOXY-BASED WOOD FILLER The pack contains two ingredients that react chemically when mixed. It sets quickly and will be hard within 20 minutes. Mix only as much as you can use in 5 minutes. It can be used inside or out, and flexes naturally with wood as it expands or contracts. It makes a very strong repair. Some types produce a dense surface that is suitable for painting and others have a porous finish that will accept a stain.

FOAM FILLER A sticky, expanding foam applied under pressure. It is used for filling gaps in brickwork, inside or out, and can even be used as insulation or for holding slates and tiles in place. Apply it to a wet surface. It is workable for about 6 minutes and expands to 60 times its original volume. It forms a skin in 1-2 hours and, once dry, can be cut, sanded and painted. It is excellent for hard-to-reach places because it expands to fill the available space.

PUTTY A mixture of powdered chalk and linseed oil. It can be used as a general-purpose wood filler where wood is to be painted, but is quite difficult to handle. Unlike sealants, it will eventually harden and crack.

Filling gaps and cracks in interior walls
Time: depends on area

> YOU WILL NEED Small trowel, old paintbrush, flexible filling knife, interior filler, old plate, medium sandpaper.

Use either a ready-to-use interior filler or mix up a powdered one with water on an old plate.

Rake out any loose plaster with a small trowel and then dust the gap very thoroughly with an old paintbrush.

Use a flexible filling knife to apply the filler so that it is raised slightly proud of the surrounding surface.

After about 2 hours, check that it has set and then smooth it flush with the wall with medium sandpaper. Redecorate as necessary, but make sure that the surface is clean and dust-free before you do.

Filling gaps and cracks in wood Time: depends on area

Choose a filler or stopper that is suitable for the job. For instance, where wood is badly damaged and strength is required, use a hardener and an epoxy-resin wood filler.

If the wood is to be painted, an all-purpose filler may be sufficient. Wood that is to be left natural should be repaired with a coloured wood filler or stopping.

> YOU WILL NEED Old paintbrush, filler or stopping, flexible filling knife, medium sandpaper. Possibly: paint, paintbrush, cloth.

Clean out the gap or crack with an old paintbrush and then prepare the filler or stopping. Apply it with a flexible filling knife, allowing it to protrude slightly above the surface of the surrounding wood.

Allow it to set thoroughly and then smooth it back with medium sandpaper, working with the grain of the wood. If necessary, paint or stain it to match the surrounding area, but clean it first with a slightly damp cloth.

Filling holes in awkward places Time: less than an hour

Holes such as those through which waste pipes leave kitchens or bathrooms can be filled with an expanding foam filler that comes in a pressurised container and has an extended nozzle. Read the instructions carefully – full details appear on the container. Wear plastic gloves (often supplied with the product) and safety spectacles.

> YOU WILL NEED Old paintbrush, water, foam filler, serrated knife, plastic gloves, safety spectacles. Possibly: paint.

Using an old paintbrush, clean out the dust and loose plaster in the gap which is to be filled. Dampen the area.

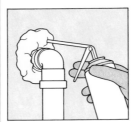

Spray the foam into the gap until it appears on both sides. Bear in mind that it will expand, filling all the hidden parts of the hole.

Leave it to set and, once it has dried, trim off the excess with a serrated knife. Then redecorate the surface if you think it is necessary.

Fireplace

No matter what solid fuel is used in a fire or stove, the flue should be swept at least once a year. Not only does this remove accumulated soot, but it also provides a regular report on the state of the flue. If the lining of the flue is crumbling, consult a reputable builder.

Curing a smoking chimney

Smoking is one of the commonest problems experienced with solid-fuel fires. It is often the result of efficient draughtproofing in a room, which starves the fire of the oxygen it requires. Consequently, increasing the ventilation in the room may cure the problem.

FLOOR VENTILATORS A pair of small ventilators, set into the floor on each side of the hearth as close to the fire as possible, will probably increase the airflow sufficiently to stop the problem.

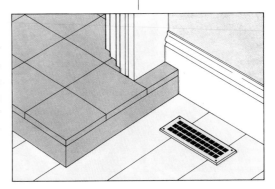

Fireplace (cont.)

FAST START FOR A FIRE

When a fire is slow to draw, plug in a hair dryer nearby and give the fire a fairly long blast with the dryer set on high. Hold the dryer at floor level and direct the air at the base of the fire, to encourage the flames to burn upwards. Do not direct the blast down onto the top of the fire or the room will fill with smoke.

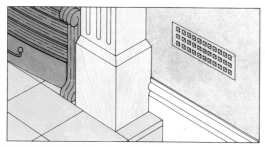

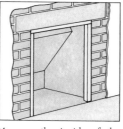

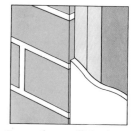

AIR BRICKS If the floor is made of concrete or is carpeted, small air bricks could be put into the wall on each side.

HIGH-LEVEL VENTILATION If low-level vents are impossible, cut a small amount off the top of the door to let air in.

Or fit a small hit-and-miss ventilator in the wall above the door. Cool air is drawn into the room at a high level. It mixes with, and is warmed by, the warm air already there and does not cause a cold draught.

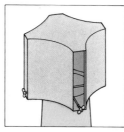

CHIMNEY COWL If you find extra ventilation does not help, call a specialist cowl company for advice. They may recommend a suitable cowl (left) or, in severe conditions, advise a chimney fan to force the air flow.

Repairing a cracked fireback   Time: 1 hour or less

If a fireback is badly cracked, it is probably better to have it replaced, but a small crack can be repaired.

> **YOU WILL NEED** Wire brush, old paintbrush, water, fire cement, small trowel.

Use a wire brush to clean the area. Then brush out any fine dirt with an old paintbrush. Wet the crack with water.

Following the maker's instructions, apply fire cement to the crack and smooth it with a small trowel. Leave it to harden for at least two days before lighting a fire.

Sealing a disused fireplace   Time: about a day

> **YOU WILL NEED** 3 lengths of 25 mm x 25 mm (1 in x 1 in) softwood, steel tape measure, set square, tenon saw, panel adhesive, power drill, masonry bits, wall plugs, 50 mm (2 in) No.8 screws, fire-resistant Masterboard, panel saw, twist bit, padsaw, hit-and-miss ventilator with fixing screws, paint.

It is possible to have an unwanted fireplace bricked up, but if there is a chance that it may be wanted again one day, it is better to make the seal temporary.

Measure the inside of the fireplace and cut the softwood into battens to form a simple three-sided frame to be fixed inside the fireplace.

Recess them sufficiently to ensure that the Masterboard will be flush with the surrounding wall once it has been added.

FIXING BATTENS TO A SMOOTH SURFACE Where the inside wall of the fireplace is smooth, coat one face of each wooden batten with panel adhesive and press it to the wall. Allow the glue to dry thoroughly before proceeding.

FIXING BATTENS TO AN UNEVEN SURFACE If the inside wall of the fireplace has a rough or uneven surface, it will be necessary to screw the battens to the wall.

Drill screw holes through the battens first, then hold the battens against the wall and mark the position of the nails on the wall through the holes with a pencil or a nail.

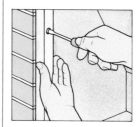

Use a masonry bit to drill holes for wall plugs. Put in the plugs and screw the battens to the wall.

Using the steel tape measure, set square and panel saw, cut the piece of Masterboard to fit into the gap snugly.

Near the base of the Masterboard, mark where a hit-and-miss ventilator will be inserted. Drill a hole at each corner of the rectangle and then use a padsaw to cut the hole (see *Saws*).

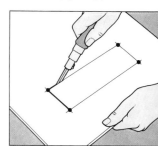

Fix the hit-and-miss ventilator to the Masterboard using the screws that are supplied with it.

Then apply a coat of panel adhesive to the front face of the batten frame and press the Masterboard firmly against it, ensuring that it makes good contact all round.

Decorate the Masterboard to match or contrast with the surrounding wall, and as soon as possible after completing the task, get a builder to cap the chimney pot to prevent rain from entering.

Fishing reels

- Bail-arm wire
- Bail-arm bracket
- Saddle
- Drum
- Body
- Drag knob
- Bail-arm screw
- Roller
- Reel foot
- Latch cover
- Reel drum

There are two main types of fishing reel – the fixed-spool reel and the fly reel. Most manufacturers will carry out minor repairs, but you can do some repairs yourself, with parts from fishing tackle shops or the reel manufacturer.

Fitting a new bail-arm wire on a fixed-spool reel

Time: ½ an hour or less

If the bail-arm wire breaks, you can replace it yourself. You will need to work under a good light.

> YOU WILL NEED Screwdriver with 6 mm (¼ in) blade, mini hacksaw, new bail-arm wire.

Some models require a slotted screwdriver. To make one; take an old screwdriver with a blade 6 mm (¼ in) across and use a mini hacksaw to cut a slot 3 mm (⅛ in) wide and 3 mm (⅛ in) deep in the tip of the blade.

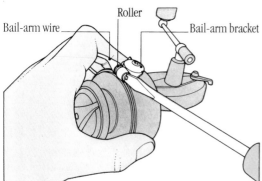

- Bail-arm wire
- Roller
- Bail-arm bracket

Use the slotted screwdriver to remove the screw which secures the old bail-arm wire to the reel. Retain the old roller to use again if it is undamaged.

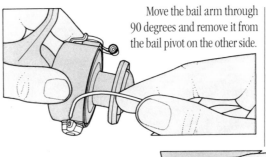

Move the bail arm through 90 degrees and remove it from the bail pivot on the other side.

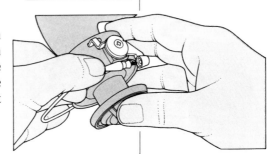

Secure the new bail-arm wire to the pivot, then push the threaded end, with the roller attached, through the retaining bracket. Secure it with the slotted screw.

Replacing a bail-arm spring on a fixed-spool reel

Time: ½ an hour or less

The bail arm on a fixed-spool reel winds the line onto the reel. If the spring breaks, the arm loses its tension and cannot be adjusted. It will need to be replaced.

The spring housing may vary slightly from one type of reel to another. If necessary consult the manufacturer's instructions to identify the type of reel being used.

> YOU WILL NEED Suitable screwdriver, new spring.

Depending on the reel, you may need a plain, cross-slot or slotted screwdriver (see left) to undo the slotted screw which holds the bail-arm wire to the bail-arm bracket.

Then remove the screw that secures the bail-arm bracket to the reel body.

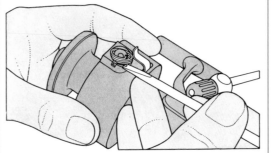

Remove the old spring. Replace with a new spring, noting that the horizontal tail is fitted into a slot on the body of the reel and the vertical tail is fitted to a hole in the bracket.

OVERHAULING A FIXED-SPOOL REEL

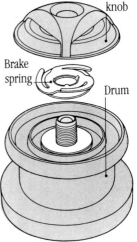

- Drag knob
- Brake spring
- Drum

Every six months, remove the drum and oil the brake spring. If the reel has a screw-hole lubrication point at the end of the body, apply a few drops of thin oil every three months. If the line wears a groove in the roller, fit a new roller. If it is not renewed, it can break the line.

Replacing a fly-reel spring and pawl Time: 1 hour or less

If the reel will not 'hold' the fishing line, either a spring or a pawl may be broken. They can both be replaced.

YOU WILL NEED Cross-slot screwdriver, new pawl or spring, pliers.

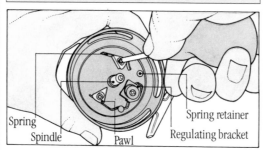

Spring · Spindle · Pawl · Spring retainer · Regulating bracket

Lift off the reel drum and remove the screw and washer that secure the damaged pawl to the base of the reel.

There is an indentation in one side of the spring to fit the spring retainer. Remove the old pawl and the broken spring.

Using fine pliers, fit a new spring into the regulating bracket, then round the retainer and the stud on which the pawl will be fixed. Replace the pawl and screw it in place. Then replace the reel drum and test the reel.

Fishing rod

Rebinding a ring Time: 1 hour or less

If the rings that carry the line are loose, rebind them. The binding technique is the same for all rod types.

YOU WILL NEED Whipping thread, craft knife, clear adhesive tape, dope, small brush, varnish.

Set aside a 7.5 cm (3 in) piece of thread for a loop.

Tape one foot of the ring to the rod and start binding the other. Work from the centre of the ring outwards, binding over the end of the thread to hold it securely.

Bind without letting the threads overlap. Make the new binding tight and neat by holding the reel of thread in one hand and twisting the rod with the other, keeping tension on the thread.

As you near the end, double the 7.5 cm (3 in) piece of thread and lay it across the binding at the side. Bind six times over the loop, leaving the eye of the loop free.

Cut loose the whipping thread from the reel, leaving only a short length, and push it through the eye of the loop. Keep pressure on it, to prevent it unwinding.

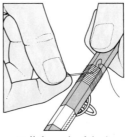

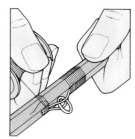

Pull the ends of the loop so that they drag the thread end under the new binding.

Trim off the protruding thread and bind the other ring foot in the same way.

Dope the thread and varnish it when it is dry.

Fitting an end ring Time: 1 day or less

When the end ring at the tip of a rod is pulled off or lost you can glue on a replacement. Large sea-fishing rods may require some binding, too.

YOU WILL NEED Epoxy-resin glue, new end ring, methylated spirit, fine file.

Use a matchstick to dab some epoxy-resin glue on the end of the rod. Trickle glue into the ring tube and then fit the tube over the end of the rod.

Line up the end ring with the other rings on the rod and wipe off any surplus glue with a cloth dipped in methylated spirit. Leave it to dry for several hours.

When the glue is dry, if it is a deep-sea rod, use a fine file to smooth the end of the new ring to allow the binding to lie flat, then bind the ring in place (see above).

Flashing

Flashing is the seal applied where two surfaces meet on the outside of a house – such as a dormer window and a roof, or an extension and a main wall. Unless properly sealed against rain, these are potential weak spots on a building and should be checked regularly. The first internal signs of flashing failure are damp patches on walls.

Many older houses have metal flashings which have been set into the brickwork. With time, the mortar holding them in place begins to crumble and will need to be replaced.

However, some newer buildings may have self-adhesive flashings that are easier to replace (see bottom of page).

Many flashings are at high levels, and while it is possible to inspect them from the ground through binoculars, repair work should be undertaken by a builder with the correct equipment.

However, there are some lower-level repairs which can be done – such as patching, repairing or replacing flashings above a porch, garage or shed.

Renewing flashing mortar   Time: depends on amount

Where lead flashing has been fixed into the horizontal mortar joint, weathering or settling of the wall can damage the mortar and make it crumble.

> **YOU WILL NEED** Ladder, hammer and cold chisel, old paintbrush, bucket, small trowel, bagged mortar. Possibly: all-weather sealant.

If the flashing seems in good enough condition to be reused, chip away the crumbling mortar with a hammer and cold chisel to a depth of about 1.3 cm ($\frac{1}{2}$ in). Then brush the entire area clean with an old paintbrush.

Dampen the area round the exposed joint with clean water and push in the old flashing. Wedge it firmly in place with scraps of folded lead, if they are available, or small wooden wedges.

Repoint with the mortar, matching the pointing to the rest of the wall (see *Brickwork*). Once the mortar has dried, pull out wooden wedges and fill the holes with more mortar. Lead wedges can be left in place.

Reshape the lower edge of the flashing to fit snugly against the roof.

It may be necessary to secure it with a bitumen-based all-weather sealant.

Applying self-adhesive flashing   Time: depends on amount

When lead or zinc flashing shows signs of severe deterioration, remove it entirely and replace it with self-adhesive flashing. If, however, the flashing is damaged only in certain places, cover it with self-adhesive flashing.

> **YOU WILL NEED** Ladder, hammer and cold chisel, mortar, wire brush, flashing primer, old paintbrush, self-adhesive flashing, craft knife, wallpaper seam roller.

REPLACING FLASHING With a hammer and a cold chisel, chip out any old mortar that is holding the flashing in place and remove the flashing entirely.

Clean the joint thoroughly with a wire brush and repoint the joint with mortar. Allow it to dry overnight.

Next day, clean the area again. Paint a coat of flashing primer along the joint to be covered. Allow it to dry for 30 minutes to an hour, depending on the manufacturer's instructions.

Cut two strips of flashing the length of the area to be covered. Working along the joint, peel off the backing paper from one strip and position it to cover both roof and wall equally.

At internal corners, snip the lower edge of the flashing, and overlap the cut edges to form a neat corner.

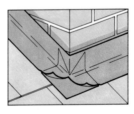

Fit an extra square piece of flashing to cover an external corner. Then attach the main strip. Snip the lower half of the flashing and splay the edges to fit the corner snugly.

Trim off any excess flashing and then use the seam roller to smooth down the entire length of flashing.

Peel the backing off the second length of flashing and position it about 5 cm (2 in) above the first strip.

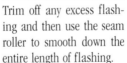

Smooth down the second layer with the seam roller.

COVERING OLD FLASHING Clean the damaged areas thoroughly and apply flashing primer. Then apply lengths of new self-adhesive flashing as shown above.

WHAT SIZE OF FLEX OR CABLE?

Both flexes and cables come in a range of sizes.

FLEX:
- 0.5 mm² for small lamps and lights (up to 3 amps)
- 0.75 mm² for lamps and small appliances (up to 6 amps)
- 1 mm² for appliances up to 2300 watts (2.3 kW) (up to 10 amps)
- 1.25 mm² for appliances up to 3000 watts (3 kW) (up to 13 amps)
- 1.5 mm² for appliances up to 3600 watts (3.6 kW) (up to 16 amps)

CABLE:
- 1 mm² for lighting circuits
- 2.5 mm² for the power circuits
- 6 mm² for circuits to cookers and showers
- 10 mm² for large cookers

Repairing cracks or small holes Time: depends on area

YOU WILL NEED Wire brush, bitumen-based sealant. Possibly: flashing primer, self-adhesive flashing, trimming knife, wallpaper seam roller.

FINE CRACKS To repair a fine crack in the flashing, first scrub the area clean with a wire brush then apply bitumen-based sealant.

SMALL HOLES If the holes are small or scattered, patch them with self-adhesive flashing.

Clean the surrounding area and coat with flashing primer. When it is dry, cut small lengths of flashing, position them and press them down well with a seam roller.

Fleas on pets

Fleas lay their eggs in soft, warm places such as pet fur, clothing, bedding and feathers. They are most active in the warmer months of August and September.

Treating an infested pet

Violent scratching every few minutes indicates that a pet may have fleas. Pets may also develop a skin allergy.

Flea collars repel fleas rather than kill them. But if the house is infested, they offer little protection to the pet. Look out for any signs of irritation after fitting a collar which may indicate an allergic reaction.

YOU WILL NEED Flea aerosol, shampoo or powder.

Comb your pet's fur over paper to remove any dead fleas, droppings and pupae. If the pet is badly infested, live fleas will also be obvious.

Apply a veterinary flea aerosol, flea powder or special dog shampoo. They are available from your vet, who will advise on the right product for your pet. Many are unsuitable for pets under a certain age.

Treat your pet outdoors and follow the instructions.

SPRAYING A CAT Cats can become upset when sprayed, so work quickly and calmly when applying a spray.

If possible, have someone hold the cat while you spray, but if you are working alone, have the spray can open and ready to use before you start treating the animal.

Put the cat on a smooth, steady surface, such as a garden table. Take it gently by the scruff of the neck and lift it so that only its hind feet are on the table.

Spray once down the cat's front, once on each side of its body and once along its back. Spray behind its ears, but not its face. The process should take only a few seconds and should be over before the cat begins to struggle.

Start spraying cats when they are quite young, so that they become used to the process.

TREATING A DOG Dogs are not generally upset by being sprayed and seldom struggle. They can also be treated with a flea-killing shampoo.

Treating infested houses

YOU WILL NEED Flea spray or powder, vacuum cleaner.

Vacuum throughout the house; but before you start spray the inside of the vacuum-cleaner bag with flea spray to kill any fleas that are sucked up. Respray each time the cleaner bag is emptied. After vacuuming, spray right through the house, particularly under sofas and beds.

Burn infested animal bedding. Thoroughly wash infested human bedding at the highest temperature that the fabric can take. Vacuuming a mattress helps, but remember to spray insecticide inside the bag before starting.

Spray or puff flea insecticide into the cracks between floorboards and skirting boards.

Birds can be infested with fleas, so remove any birds' nests from the eaves or loft of the house.

If none of these methods succeeds in curing the infestation, contact your local authority environmental health officer or a pest control company.

Flexes & cables

Flex (short for flexible cord) is used to connect appliances and lights to the mains supply. All flex contains insulated wires called cores within a plastic sheath. The fixed wiring that carries electricity round the house, behind walls and under floors, is called cable.

THREE-CORE FLEX Brown is live (called line or phase by electricians), blue is neutral and green/yellow is earth.

TWO-CORE FLEX Two-core flex, without an earth, is used for non-metallic light fittings and double-insulated appliances such as hair dryers and power tools.

TWO-CORE-AND-EARTH CABLE Two wires are insulated – red is live (also called line or phase), and black is neutral. The third, bare wire, is the earth.

THREE-CORE-AND-EARTH CABLE The cable contains four wires – a bare earth wire; a red live wire, and one yellow and one blue wire for linking two-way light switches.

Lengthening a flex with a connector Time: ½ an hour

When extending a flex on an appliance, never connect two lengths of flex by twisting the wires together and binding them with insulating tape. This could cause a fire. Either fit a new flex of the correct length or use a flex connector. The new flex must be the same size and type as the original.

> YOU WILL NEED Screwdriver, flex connector (one or two piece), extension flex, wire cutters, craft knife.

ONE-PART FLEX CONNECTOR Remove the plug from the flex of the appliance. Then open the flex connector and loosen the flex grips. Lay the flexes to be joined over the open connector and bare the coloured wires so that each reaches the correct terminal in the connector (see *Electric plug*: 'Stripping the end of a flex').

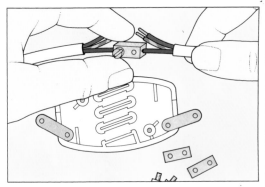

Take the brass strip connectors out of the casing and connect wire to like-coloured-wire. In some flexes both wires will be the same colour so it will not matter. Screw the wires tightly into the connectors.

Replace the strip connectors in the casing. Secure each flex in its cord grip and fit the cover. Cut the new flex to length then connect a plug (see *Electric plug*) and test.

TWO-PART CONNECTORS Two-part connectors are often used on electric tools used outdoors. They are damp-proof and shatterproof. Buy a connector of a suitable amperage for the appliance. To fit, first cut the plug from the appliance's flex. Then separate the two parts of the connector.

The flex from the power source must be attached to the part of the connector with the holes. Otherwise the connector pins will be live when the power is on and could be touched if the connector is pulled apart.

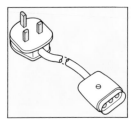

Put the connector covers on the flexes. Strip off a section of the flex's plastic outer sheath (see *Electric plug*: 'Stripping the end of a flex') and pass the coloured wires through the cord grips on each part of the connector.

Then screw them into the terminal holes. In three-pin plugs do the earth connection first. Then tighten the flex grips and slide the covers down the flex so each terminal block is secured inside its cover. Screw the covers tight.

Check that the two parts join firmly. Then fit a plug to the end of the new flex and test.

Replacing a flex Time: ½ an hour or less

For details on how to replace worn flexes on a domestic iron, see *Iron*: 'Replacing a worn cord'.

> YOU WILL NEED Screwdrivers (possibly cross-point of different sizes), a new flex, wire cutters, craft knife.

Unplug the appliance. Make sure that access to the terminals is possible through the casing. If the cover is not a simple one, held in place with screws, it is best not to attempt this job; have it done at an electrical repair shop.

Remove the screws from the casing, taking note of where each one goes. Open the casing carefully, so as not to disturb any internal components it holds in place.

Find the terminal block for the flex, then loosen the screws and remove the flex. Prepare the end of the new flex so that it matches the old one (see *Electric plug*: 'Stripping the end of a flex') and insert it through a flex grip, if there is one.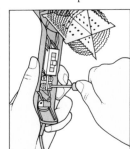

Connect each wire to the correct terminal and close the casing. Then fit a plug to the flex, switch on and test.

Flies: SEE BLUEBOTTLES

Floorboards

Take great care when working on boarded floors. There may be cables or pipes below which could be damaged. Use a pipe-and-cable detector to pinpoint hazards, and mark the positions on the boards with a pen or pencil.

Curing squeaking boards

> YOU WILL NEED Talc or graphite powder. Possibly: screwdriver, screw with thread right up to the head.

Squeaking is caused by floorboards rubbing against each other. It can often be cured by locating the source and puffing talc or graphite powder between the boards.

If this fails, locate the nearest joist and screw the boards tightly to it. The positions of the joists are indicated by lines of nails in the floor.

Or you can drive a fully threaded screw (the thread goes right up to the head) between two floorboards that squeak. It will prevent them from moving and rubbing against each other.

Securing a loose board   Time: 1 hour or less

YOU WILL NEED Screwdriver, screws. Possibly: pipe-and-cable detector, hammer, oval wire nails, pieces of batten.

Lift the board and check that there are no cables or pipes underneath. Alternatively, use a pipe-and-cable detector if the board is not completely loose.

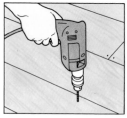

Screw loose floorboards to the nearest joists. Make a clearance hole for the screw shank, and be sure to countersink the screw heads.

If a board has been cut and there is no support below, nail a batten to the side of the joist. Rest the board on the batten and screw it down.

Replacing a damaged board

Take a piece of damaged floorboard to a timber merchant to ensure that you get the same thickness and width. For old houses, boards may have to be machined to size.

YOU WILL NEED Claw hammer, steel bolster (wide-blade cold chisel), batten, oval wire nails. Possibly: pipe-and-cable detector, nail punch, general-purpose saw, new board.

If the boards are butted together (without tongue and grooving), start at one end of the damaged board. Tap a bolster into the gap between the ends, and lever up the damaged board.

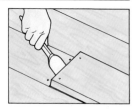

As the nails are gradually pulled loose and begin to rise, press the board down. This should expose the nails which can then be eased out with the claw of a hammer.

If the nails won't move, drive them down into the joist with a nail punch. In an older house, do not do too much heavy hammering in case you damage any plaster ceilings below.

As the board is lifted, slip scraps of batten into the gap to hold the board up while you continue to lever out any other nails.

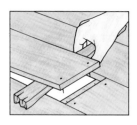

If the board is only worn, you may be able to turn it over and refit it with the unmarked side upwards, but if it is badly damaged, cut a new board and nail it in place.

Replacing a tongue-and-groove board

If the floorboards are tongued and grooved, first use a pipe-and-cable detector to check the area below.

Then use a general-purpose saw to cut through a tongue for the complete length of the floorboard.

Lever the board up from the cut side, not from the short end. Ease the other side away from the adjacent floorboard.

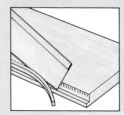

Cut a replacement floorboard to the same length, and check that it is the correct way up. Then cut away the lower section of the groove with a tenon saw.

Turn the board over again and insert the new board's tongue into the neighbouring groove. Lower the cut side of the new board onto the adjacent tongue. Nail or screw it in place.

Surfacing boards with hardboard

YOU WILL NEED Oil-tempered hardboard sheets, hammer and deep-drive panel pins or panel adhesive, fine-tooth hand saw.

If a floor shows signs of wear, or boards are ill-fitting and let in draughts, you can fit hardboard sheets to give a smooth surface for a new floor covering. The sheets do not affect underfloor ventilation, which is vital for healthy timbers.

Multiply the length of the room by the width to get the area in square metres or square feet. Buy the right amount of oil-tempered hardboard in the largest size you can transport, or have full-size sheets delivered.

Fix it to the floor, smooth side up, either with deep-drive panel pins or with panel adhesive. If you use panel pins, hammer them in all round the edges of each board 12.5 cm (5 in) apart and 1 cm ($\frac{3}{8}$ in) in from the edge.

Leave fitting odd spaces and awkward shapes until last. You may be able to use offcuts from larger boards.

If you use panel adhesive, spread it on the back of the boards in strips about 30 cm (12 in) apart, and around the edges of each board. Do not use adhesive if there is a chance you will want to lift the flooring at some time in the future.

Panel adhesive is sold in cartridges for use in a simple trigger-operated gun. For more details about panel adhesives and how to use them, see *Glues*.

Sanding and varnishing a floor   Time: parts of 2 days

Plain, varnished floorboards are an attractive surface if they are well cleaned and properly prepared.

Hire an industrial floor sanding machine and edging sander from a tool-hire shop, and make sure you are given full instructions for using them.

> YOU WILL NEED Floor sander, edging sander, masking tape, tack rag (see *Painting tools*), lint-free rag, floor varnish, wide paintbrush. Possibly: pincers, nail punch, hammer.

Remove tacks and staples from the floor with pincers. Drive in any projecting floorboard nails with a nail punch.

Seal the doors to the rest of the house with masking tape, even though the machine will have a dust-collecting bag. Then put on a face mask and safety goggles and proceed to sand the floor, following the instructions.

Vacuum the floor, and then wipe it with a tack rag to make sure you have removed all the dust.

Apply a coat of floor varnish with a lint-free rag, working the varnish into the wood. Leave it overnight, then apply two further coats of floor varnish using a brush. Do not walk on the floor for at least 24 hours.

Flowers, cut

Pick flowers from the garden in the morning or at dusk, but not in the hottest part of the day.

It is often possible to prolong the life of most cut flowers by recutting the stems at an angle while holding them under water. This freshly exposes the water-conducting cells in the stem and ensures that they work efficiently.

Cut flowers should be plunged into tepid water, almost up to the blooms, then left to soak for several hours. Then when arranging the flowers, remove any leaves which will be below the water line in the vase. They will rot and speed up the pollution of the water if they are left on the stem.

Try to keep arranged flowers out of draughts and direct sunlight – they will last longer in cool rooms.

Treating different types of stem

WOODY STEMS Cut lilac, honeysuckle and hydrangea with a sharp knife. Stand them in boiling water for 30 seconds, then up to the neck in tepid water for 6-8 hours.

FLESHY STEMS Before arranging spring flowers, such as lily of the valley, narcissus, anemone, grape hyacinth or scilla, leave them overnight in cold water to let their milky sap drain out. Cut off any white parts on the lower stem.

FIBROUS STEMS Split the stems of daisies, marguerites and chrysanthemums and stand for 3 hours in tepid water.

HOLLOW STEMS Dahlia, delphinium and lupin stems should be cut straight across, then turned upside-down and filled with water. Plug each stem with wet cotton wool.

MILKY STEMS Poppies, euphorbias and zinnias exude milky sap which fouls the water. Seal stems by placing them in 5 cm (2 in) of boiling water for about 10 seconds. Protect the flower heads by wrapping them in plastic bags. Then let the flowers stand in cool water for a while.

FOLIAGE Ornamental foliage, such as coloured kales and cabbages, vines and ivies, should be completely immersed in cold water for about 4 hours before being arranged. Do not soak grey foliage because it will lose its colour.

> ## Keeping heads held high
>
> Before arranging flowers such as tulips, which are inclined to droop, pierce each stem right through with a pin, just below the flower head. They should hold their heads up for a much longer period.

Fluorescent tube
(SEE ALSO LIGHT FITTINGS)

A fluorescent tube has no filament to burn out. It is made of glass and coated inside with powder. When the power is switched on, the powder inside the tube emits light.

Replacing a worn-out fluorescent tube
Time: a few minutes

If the light does not come on and there is blackening at each end, the tube probably needs replacing. Before doing so, turn off the electricity at the switch.

> ### TRANSPORT CUT FLOWERS SUCCESSFULLY
>
> Cut flowers need protection when being transported. In warm weather, soak the flowers in cool water in a cool, dark room before the journey. Then lay them in a box surrounded by damp paper. In cold weather, insulate them with bubble plastic or newspaper, and keep them out of the wind while loading them into the car. To transport a posy of flowers, wrap the stems in damp kitchen roll or cotton wool, then put them into a plastic bag and seal it with a rubber band.

> ### KEEPING WATER FRESH
>
> Proprietary water conditioners are available to feed the flowers and combat the bacteria in a vase. Cheaper, homemade variations include small quantities of charcoal, lemonade or vinegar, which can all help to prevent the stems from becoming clogged up.

TIPS FOR PROCESSING FOOD

- Don't run a processor, liquidiser or blender for more than about 5 minutes without a break, because the motor may overheat. Consult the manufacturer's instructions for recommended running times.
- Always cut up any solid ingredients and feed them into the liquidiser while it is running. Do not put in all the dry or solid ingredients then switch on. They might stall the motor and damage it.
- Do not try to grind coffee beans in a liquidiser or attempt to convert granulated sugar into castor sugar, unless the instructions allow it.

SAFETY FIRST WITH ELECTRICITY

Before starting any work on an electrical fitting or appliance, make sure to cut off the electricity supply – either by switching off at the main fuse box, or by unplugging the appliance.

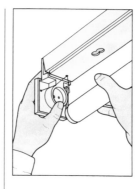

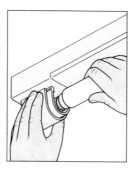

DOUBLE PIN FITTING The pins are held in sockets at each end. On one design you can ease out one of the sockets, which is hinged (left). Then lift the tube clear of the cap at the end.

On another design, you turn the tube 90 degrees and then pull it out.

BAYONET FITTING To take out a fluorescent tube with a less common bayonet fitting, first slide back the socket covers. Then press the tube against the spring-loaded holder and twist.

Repeat at the other end to release the tube.

Fitting a new starter Time: a few minutes

If the tube is flickering, or lights up for only a few seconds the problem may be the starter, which is much cheaper to replace than the tube. The starter is a small cylinder about 3.2 cm ($1\frac{1}{4}$ in) long, which is held in a clip.

Turn off the electricity at the mains. Remove the tube.

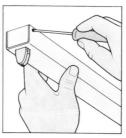

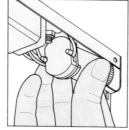

If the starter has a protective casing over it. Undo the screws holding the casing in place and remove it.

Remove the starter from the clip and detach it from its holder by pressing it and turning it anticlockwise.

Install a new starter, of the same size and wattage as the old one, by reversing the procedure. Test the light.

Food processor

Most blenders, mixers, grinders and juicers work on the same principle. They are powered by an electric motor which drives the implements that cut, grate and mix.

Cutter blades should be kept sharp. If they become blunt, they place a strain on the motor.

Sharpening cutter blades Time: $\frac{1}{2}$ an hour or less

The blades on a food processor are made of stainless steel. Some machines use disc-type cutters which are almost impossible to sharpen at home and should be taken to a dealer or returned to the manufacturer for sharpening.

Other blades, however, can be sharpened at home but should be handled extremely carefully because even a blade that needs sharpening could still cut your hand.

YOU WILL NEED Greenstone (available from tool shops and ironmongers), vice.

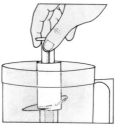

Remove the blade from the processor, handling it carefully. Even if it needs sharpening, it may still be sharp enough to cut you badly.

Grip the blade in a vice. Hold the greenstone firmly at a 15° angle to the blade, and stroke it away from you, along the edge of the blade.

Carefully turn the blade round, and repeat the process to sharpen the other face of the cutting edge. It may be necessary to repeat this a number of times, depending on how blunt the blade has become.

! Do not run your finger along the edge to test for sharpness. Instead, cut the edge of a piece of paper.

Faultfinder guide: Machine stops or won't start

If the food processor will not work or stops unexpectedly there are various checks you can make:

- Check that the plug is firmly in the wall socket and the connection to the machine has not worked loose.
- Make sure that the machine has not switched itself off because of extreme vibration, which can happen on a hard surface, such as a bench.

Some machines have a projection on the bowl that acts as a switch. Make sure the bowl has not turned slightly and switched the machine off.

- If there is still no power, open the plug to examine the fuse and check that the connections are firm.
- If the body of the machine is hot, it may have overheated. Let it cool before turning it on again. Some machines have a safety switch that will trip if the machine overheats. If it won't start once it has been allowed to cool, consult the dealer or repair service.

Freezer: SEE REFRIGERATOR AND FREEZER

French polish

Routine care of french-polished surfaces

Dust french-polished furniture infrequently, and only when the piece needs it. Use a grit-free duster, touching the surface of the wood very gently and moving with the grain. Do not use oiled or treated dusters.

Occasionally use a wax polish, applying it very thinly and buffing it up well. Once or twice a year is usually often enough to keep the surface in good condition.

Removing a ring on a french-polished surface
Time: ½ an hour or less

If a spill is left, it will leave a white mark on french polish. Severe damage should be dealt with by a professional french polisher, but small marks can be removed at home.

> YOU WILL NEED 60 ml (2 fl oz) olive oil, 150 g (5 oz) paraffin wax, furniture-grade wire wool (grade 00000), soft cloth.

Heat the olive oil and paraffin wax in a small saucepan until the wax has just melted. Stir to blend thoroughly. Dip a piece of wire wool into the warm mixture, and stroke it over the damaged area, following the grain.

Keep applying the mixture until the mark disappears. Leave it for 15 minutes and then buff it gently, with a very soft cloth, along the grain of the wood.

Frost protection: SEE INSULATION

Frozen pipes: SEE PIPES

Furniture moving

If you follow a few sensible guidelines, the moving of large pieces of furniture should be danger-free:

- Before starting to move an item, make sure that it will fit through any doors and round any corners on the route.
- Get help whenever possible if the furniture is heavy.
- Leave the moving of special items like pianos to experts.
- Remove all drawers and loose shelves. Empty those that cannot be removed, in order to lighten the load.
- Lift out sliding glass doors and lock hinged doors, or tape them shut with masking tape.
- Pad vulnerable corners with wads of cloth or paper, held in place with masking tape.
- Unplug, coil up and secure trailing cables and flexes.

Techniques for moving furniture

- Low-loading trolleys are designed to make moving heavy furniture as easy as possible. Hire shops supply numerous kinds of moving equipment, such as trolleys that can be used to move furniture upstairs (right).

- If you can't buy or hire a trolley, try improvising with cooker rollers (also known as Easy Riders).

- You may be able to drag furniture across the floor by easing it onto an offcut of carpet or an old curtain.
- Alternatively, roll the furniture on broomsticks or thick dowel rods, feeding them under from the front.
- If floor covering has to be fed under a piece of furniture that has legs, use a thick section of timber, such as a fence post, to help you to lever it off the ground.

Lay the covering up to the furniture. Then use a pile of bricks as a fulcrum to help you to lever the furniture clear of the ground. Ask someone else to steady the furniture as you raise it, and get a second helper to feed the new floor covering under the furniture.

Fuse box (SEE ALSO ELECTRIC PLUGS; RCD)

Emergency action – circuit failure   Time: 1 hour or less

If all the lights suddenly go out on one floor, or all the power sockets in one part of the house stop working, a fuse has probably blown at the main fuse box.

Although the fuse is easy to replace you should try to find out what caused it to blow, and then repair it.

> YOU WILL NEED Possibly: fuse wire, new cartridge fuse, torch, fuse tester, screwdriver.

Identify the circuit that failed, then turn off and check for damage any appliances or lights that were in use on the circuit when it failed. If you find one that has damaged flexes or switches, don't plug it back in but get it repaired.

REPAIRING A SCRATCH

If a french-polished surface is lightly scratched, hide the damage with a scratch remover liquid. It fills the scratch and because it is available in light, medium and dark, the scratch blends into the wood (see also *Wooden furniture*). Do not try to repair a large scratch on a valuable piece yourself. Instead, have it treated by a professional french polisher.

REACT FAST TO SPILLS

When a drink is spilt or a glass leaves a wet ring on a french-polished surface, mop it up immediately and rub your finger over the mark. There is sufficient oil in your skin to give the mark a fine coating. Follow up, as soon as possible, with a careful application of wax polish.

Fuse box (cont.)

If you don't find any signs of faults, then make sure you are not overloading the circuit. The load on a lighting circuit should total no more than 1200 watts, or approximately ten lights. A socket circuit cannot supply any more than 7200 watts. To calculate the total wattage of the appliances on a circuit look at the rating plate, usually found on the bottom of each appliance.

Once you have found the cause of the power failure you can replace the blown fuse (see below).

When the power has been restored, test the circuit by turning on the appliances or lights one by one. If the fuse blows again, call an electrician (see *Electrician*).

Resetting miniature circuit breakers (MCBs)

MCBs work like fuses to detect faults and guard against the overloading of a circuit. On a faulty circuit, the lever will be in the 'trip' position or the button will have popped out.

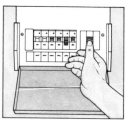 

Switch off the power at the main switch, which is on the fuse box or on a box installed near the meter.

Switch the tripped circuit breaker back into the 'on' position. Turn on the power again at the main switch.

If it switches off again immediately, check the circuit protected by the MCB for faulty appliances or light fittings and for overloading (see above).

Replacing a rewirable fuse

Turn off the main switch, which is on the fuse box or on a box installed near the meter. Find the blown circuit fuse by looking for scorch marks. If the fuse carriers have been marked to show which circuit they protect, you should be able to find the blown fuse easily. Otherwise examine each carrier in turn, replacing it before going on to the next.

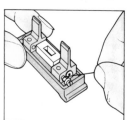 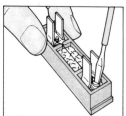

PROTECTED FUSE Replace the fuse wire by feeding it through the carrier's porcelain tunnel. Then secure it with a screw at each end.

BRIDGED FUSE Run the exposed fuse wire from one terminal to the other and secure it at each end with the vertical screws.

Use only fuse wire of the amperage that is marked on the carrier: 5 amp wire for a lighting circuit, 15 amp for single appliance circuits, 30 amp for socket circuits. Don't rely on the fuse wire in place as a guide – it may be wrong. It is dangerous to use thicker wire than the correct one.

Changing a cartridge fuse

Switch off the power at the main switch on the fuse box. Identify the blown fuse. If the fuse carriers have not been marked to show which circuits they protect, look out for signs of burning or charring on the cartridge fuse or test each fuse with a purpose-made fuse tester (see margin).

Replace the faulty cartridge fuse with one marked with the rating shown on the carrier. Don't rely on the fuses in place as a guide – they may be wrong. Keep spares handy.

Never use a larger cartridge than the correct one, or you will have dangerously insufficient protection.

Replace the fuse carrier, close the fuse box and turn the power back on at the main switch.

The power centre of the house

Electricity enters the house through the service cable. From here it passes into a sealed unit containing a fuse called a service cut-out. Do not tamper with either the service cable or the sealed unit.

Two cables (coloured red and black) go to the electricity meter and on to the fuse box (now more commonly known as the consumer unit).

The fuse box distributes electricity to all the circuits in the house and provides protection from electrical faults. It contains the main switch, the earthing terminal block for all the household circuits, and the fuses for all the circuits. To make finding blown fuses easier, label each circuit – 'upstairs lighting', 'ground-floor power', 'garage' etc.

Many modern consumer units incorporate safety devices such as a residual current device (RCD) and miniature circuit breakers (MCBs).

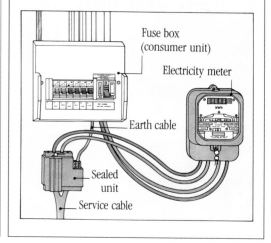

Fuse box (consumer unit)

Electricity meter

Earth cable

Sealed unit

Service cable

Garage

Making a folding workbench Time: about a day

> **YOU WILL NEED** Timber, tape measure, tenon saw, wood glue, $\frac{3}{4}$ in oval nails or panel pins, hammer, MDF (medium density fibreboard), hand saw, power drill and masonry bits, wall plugs, folding flap stays, screws and screwdriver.

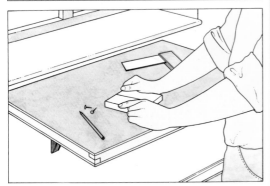

If there is not room in your garage for a permanent work-bench you can make a sturdy folding worktop.

Make a simple rectangular frame from 25 mm x 25 mm (1 in x 1 in) prepared timber of a size to fit the available space. The total depth of the shelf from front to back should not exceed 40 cm (16 in).

Use halving joints (see *Woodworking joints*) at the four corners, glued and nailed. Cover the frame on both sides with sheets of 6 mm ($\frac{1}{4}$ in) MDF (see above), nail-ing and gluing it in place.

Drill and plug the wall. Attach two heavy-duty folding flap stays. A pair of these stays will take a load of 130 kg (20 st). Fix the brackets so that the work surface will be at a comfortable height. Fix the shelf to the brackets.

Removing oil stains Time: depends on the area

> **YOU WILL NEED** Cat litter, stiff yard broom, old dustpan and brush, watering can or garden hose. Possibly: detergent or proprietary path cleaner.

Pour cat litter onto the stain to soak up the surface oil.

Where oil has had time to soak in, use a proprietary path and patio cleaner, or a strong solution of detergent and water. Work the solvent or detergent into the stains with a stiff broom until the oil is loosened and a soapy deposit is formed. Leave it for five to ten minutes, then wash it away with plenty of clean water. Repeat for stubborn stains, if necessary.

To prevent further staining on a newly cleaned floor, coat the floor with a purpose-made garage floor paint, that has been formulated to withstand oils and chemicals.

To save any further mess occurring, catch leaking oil in a drip tray until the car can be serviced.

Ideas for storage in the garage

STORING BICYCLES Make a cycle rack with dowels sticking out of a wooden frame, or buy a ready-made cycle hanger. Or fit a couple of metal wall hooks to hold a bicycle.

STORING TOOLS Perforated hardboard on a timber frame makes a good wall-mounted storage board for tools. Make hooks from coat-hanger wire, or buy them ready-made, to hold tools. Draw round each tool with a marker to help you to replace it correctly and to identify missing tools.

Alternatively, a wire trellis with S-shaped hooks fixed into it can provide a versatile hanging board for tools.

Another storage idea is to adapt a shelf by cutting out the appropriate shapes to hold individual garden tools.

NAILS AND SCREWS Keep small bits and pieces out of the way but visible and readily accessible by storing them in jars, and then screwing the lids to the underside of shelves.

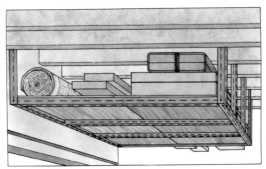

HIGH-LEVEL STORAGE Screw strip metal supports to the garage ceiling joists and hang a platform from them to store light items such as suitcases.

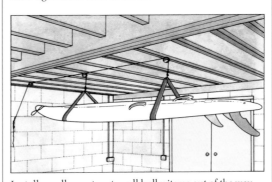

Install a pulley system to pull bulky items out of the way.

HANGING SHELVES Suspend shelves from rafters using chains attached to the rafters with screw eyes or S hooks. Drill holes through the shelves and hold them in place with bolts through the chain.

STORING GARDEN CANES Canes, fishing rods or garden umbrellas can be kept in a length of plastic drainpipe, mounted on the garage wall with drainpipe brackets.

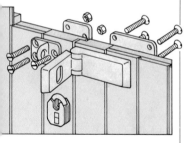
Garage door

Repairing a rotted door bottom Time: ½ a day

> **YOU WILL NEED** Power drill and twist bit, general-purpose saw, tape measure, PVA wood glue, replacement timber.

Drill a starting hole above the backing rail. Saw and prise out the rotten wood to make a hole with a regular shape.

Cut tongue-and-groove timber to size and glue the pieces together to fill the hole in the door. Then glue and screw the new wood to the backing rail.

Fixing a sagging door frame Time: ½ a day

A heavy timber garage door may sometimes pull the door frame away from its fixings in the wall.

> **YOU WILL NEED** Screwdriver. Possibly: power drill, claw hammer, adjustable spanner, anchor bolts, flat bit, masonry bit, twist bit, chisel and mallet, PVA wood glue, sandpaper, try square.

FRAME PULLED AWAY FROM BRICKWORK Remove the garage door by unscrewing the hinges. Then remove the existing fixings holding the frame to the wall and replace them with suitably sized anchor bolts. An anchor bolt expands as you turn it, to give a tight fit.

You may have to enlarge the holes in both the timber and brickwork to accommodate the new bolts, using a power drill and an appropriate bit (see *Drills & drill bits*).

Make sure the frame is square then tighten the bolts.

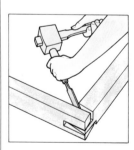

DOOR FRAME PULLED APART If one of the frame's joints is pulling apart, remove the door. It may be necessary to remove the frame as well. Lever apart the faulty joint with a chisel and mallet.

Clean off any remaining old adhesive from the joint with abrasive paper, then glue and screw the frame section back in place, drilling new holes for the screws if necessary. Use a try square to check that the joint is square.

Fixing a sagging door Time: about a day

The weight of a timber door can gradually pull it out of shape or out of position on its hinges.

> **YOU WILL NEED** Screwdriver, power drill and twist bit. Possibly: tape measure, tenon saw, sliding bevel.

DOOR NOT SITTING CORRECTLY ON ITS HINGES It may be possible to correct the door by adjusting the hinge.

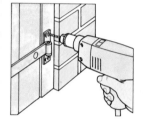

Unscrew the door at the problem hinge. Then position the door correctly and mark the hinge's new position. Reattach the hinge, drilling new screw holes in the frame if necessary.

THE DOOR SAGS Remove the sagging door by removing its hinges and check for loose joints. Pull apart the sagging joints if necessary.

Use a try square to realign the door so that the joints are square then reglue and screw them back together.

LOOSE DOOR BRACE The wooden planks that make up the door are held together by a diagonal brace. If the brace works loose, the door may no longer fit its frame.

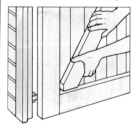

If the door brace comes loose, you can either screw it back into position with rustproof screws or replace it with new wood. Cut the timber to fit into the corners of the door and screw it in place from the front.

Improving garage security

TIMBER DOOR If you have alternative access to the garage you can bar the main garage door from the inside to give added security. Make four timber or metal brackets (see margin) and screw one onto each side of the door frame and one onto each door. Slot a stout timber into the brackets to hold the door shut.

METAL UP-AND-OVER DOOR Make two timber or metal brackets (see margin) and screw one on each side of the door frame, about 46 cm (18 in) below the top. Slot a stout timber into the brackets to prevent the door opening.

Maintaining an up-and-over door

- To keep the door opening smoothly keep the channels in which the wheels run free of dirt and debris.
- Oil wheels and pivots, but not springs.
- Springs may become tired with age, or the securing hooks may fail. Contact the door manufacturer for replacements. They must be identical in size and strength. Some are colour coded for identification.
- To realign the garage door in its frame, adjust the nuts on the bolts that hold the springs.

Garden furniture

(SEE ALSO DECK CHAIR)

Every spring and autumn, examine any garden furniture that stands outside all year round. Repairing minor damage as it occurs will extend the life of most garden furniture and keep it safe to use.

Tightening loose joints on wooden furniture

Time: depends on amount

> YOU WILL NEED Rubber hammer, chisel, waterproof wood glue. Possibly: G-cramps, string, pencil.

Using a rubber hammer, tap apart loose joints.

Chisel away any old adhesive. Then apply wood glue to the joints and reassemble the chair.

Tap the joints into place and clamp into place with G-cramps until they have set. Alternatively, apply pressure to the joints with a tourniquet made with string and a pencil or stick (see *Chair*).

Weatherproofing hardwood furniture

Time: depends on amount

> YOU WILL NEED Steel wool or fine sandpaper, damp cloth, teak oil, kitchen paper. Possibly: yacht varnish.

Garden furniture which has been made from hardwood such as teak needs to be oiled once a year.

Remove blemishes from the wood using steel wool or fine sandpaper (right). Wipe the surface well and apply a liberal coat of teak oil. Allow it to soak into the wood for half an hour, and then wipe off any excess with kitchen paper.

Alternatively, hardwood furniture can be weatherproofed with yacht varnish, which moves with the wood as it expands and contracts, and does not crack or peel.

Weatherproofing softwood furniture

Time: depends on amount

To prevent softwoods from rotting, a water-resistant wood stain treatment is needed. It allows the surface of the wood to 'breathe', but keeps out moisture, so preventing the wood from cracking, peeling or blistering.

> YOU WILL NEED Cloth, fine sandpaper, water-resistant wood stain. Possibly: hard bristle brush, matching wood stopper.

If the wood is in reasonable condition, wipe it with a cloth to remove any grit. Apply one or two coats of water-resistant wood stain, allowing it to dry between coats.

If the wood is slightly damaged, brush away any loose splinters. Then fill cracks or holes with a wood stopper that matches the surrounding area as closely as possible. Smooth it into the cracks or holes with your finger.

Leave it to dry, then sand it smooth. Wipe the wood with a cloth, then apply water-resistant wood stain.

Replacing a broken slat

If a teak slat in a garden table or chair is broken, you may not be able to find a replacement slat in a DIY store. It may be worth taking the old one to a timber merchant and asking for a new piece to be cut to the same size. It will be expensive, but it will save the table from having to be abandoned.

When fitting the new slat, drill fine pilot holes for the nails, as hardwood splits easily. To avoid rust stains, use nails or panel pins made of brass.

Caring for upholstery Time: depends on amount

> YOU WILL NEED Possibly: large needle, strong thread, sponge, upholstery shampoo, glycerine, hydrogen peroxide 6% BP (20 vol).

Before storing cushions in a dry place for the winter, check the fabric for tears. Repair them with matching thread.

If the fabric is grubby, shampoo it lightly with a sponge dipped in the foam of an upholstery shampoo, or with a cleaner specially formulated for garden furniture.

Grass stains can be removed by rubbing the area with glycerine. Remove mildew stains from upholstery with a half-and-half mixture of peroxide and water.

If storage space is limited, leave the furniture outdoors and cover it with fitted, weatherproof covers, available from garden centres and through mail-order catalogues.

TESTING WOOD FOR WATER RESISTANCE

To test whether wood that has been waterproofed with a water-resistant paint or wood stain will last another season, drip water onto the surface. If the finish is still in good condition, droplets will form on the surface. But if the water is absorbed, the furniture will need recoating.

REMOVING MOSS AND LICHEN

If wooden garden furniture has developed patches of moss and lichen, paint the affected area with a garden fungicide. When the growth has been killed, brush it away with an old paintbrush.

Caring for metal furniture Time: depends on amount

Check all metal furniture during summer, as well as after winter storage. Chips in paint can result in serious rust.

Make sure all moving parts are kept oiled, but wipe off excess oil to avoid staining your clothes.

> YOU WILL NEED Warm soapy water, cloth, fine glasspaper or wire wool, metal paint, wire brush, sugar soap, wet-and-dry abrasive paper, paintbrush, rust killer, primer and gloss paint.

REGULAR CARE Wash furniture that is in good condition with warm, soapy water and leave it to dry.

Use wire wool or fine glasspaper to rub down any areas where paint has chipped off. Then touch up the exposed areas with metal paint in a matching colour.

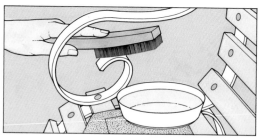

REPAIRING RUST DAMAGE Brush the furniture vigorously with a wire brush to remove any flaking paint or rust.

Scrub the area with a sugar soap solution and while the metal is still wet, rub it with wet-and-dry abrasive paper. When dry, treat the whole area with a rust killer, taking care to follow the manufacturer's instructions.

Paint the chair using a primer and gloss paint or else a metal paint, and leave it to dry thoroughly before using it.

SAFETY FIRST

Always wear safety goggles when removing paint and rust, and use a mask if spraying paint, even out of doors.

Spray painting ornate furniture

Spray painting gives a good finish to ornate metal garden furniture and is much quicker to apply than painting with a brush.

Work out of doors and place the chair or table on sheets of newspaper. Weight the paper all round to prevent it blowing up and sticking to wet surfaces.

Cleaning resin and plastic furniture
Time: depends on amount

> YOU WILL NEED Warm soapy water, non-abrasive liquid household cleaner, cloth.

A regular wash with warm, soapy water should be sufficient to keep resin and plastic furniture looking smart.

Stubborn marks can be removed with a non-abrasive, liquid household cleaner. Treat the surface gently, to avoid scratching or dulling it.

Gardening contractors

Before hiring a gardening contractor, consider carefully whether you really need one. You may be able to do most of the work yourself at a fraction of the cost – laying a new lawn by using roll-out lawn turfs, for example.

If the work requires a level of skill or special equipment that you do not have, you probably do need a contractor.

CHOOSING THE CONTRACTOR Following a few sensible guidelines can cut down the risk of later problems:

● Start by looking through *Yellow Pages* under 'Garden Services' and 'Landscapers' for gardening contractors. If specialist skills such as tree surgery are needed, make sure the contractor is qualified to do the work.
● Personal recommendations by friends or neighbours are valuable, so ask around.
● Shortlist two or three contractors and ask to be shown examples of their work – which is a good reason to use a locally based firm.
● Use a contractor who is a member of a professional association because this gives you access to an arbitration and conciliation service if things should go badly.

GETTING THE WORK DONE Once you have selected a contractor, follow these guidelines:

● Make sure that both you and the contractor have insurance that covers damage to life and property in your garden, as well as theft of or damage to equipment and any materials left there.
● Work out all the details of the job; most disputes are caused by misunderstandings about the job specifications.
● Many contractors are prepared to be flexible, performing the specialist jobs while you carry out unskilled work.
● Even if you hire a contractor to do the entire job, prepare to be involved. It is wise to keep an eye on the job, to make sure it is done the way you want – particularly where any error or misunderstanding could not easily be repaired, such as with tree surgery.
● Do not sign anything that states you are satisfied with the completed job if you are not satisfied or have not had time to inspect it thoroughly.
● A contractor is obliged by law to carry out the work agreed upon with reasonable skill and care, within a reasonable time, to make a fair charge and to use materials that are appropriate to the job.

If the work is not done to your satisfaction, ask the contractor to put it right within a specified time.

Should your contractor argue about your complaint, and refuse to cooperate with you, take the matter to the appropriate arbitration or conciliation service.

Advice and guidance for garden work

Many associations guarantee the standard of work carried out by their members and will help to resolve disputes that arise over work that has been done.

BALI (British Association of Landscape Industries) supplies names of qualified and recommended contractors. Members have to meet the standards set by the British Association of Landscape Industries and the training standards of the British Landscape Industry Training Organisation. Contact them at Landscape House, 9 Henry Street, Keighley, West Yorkshire BD21 3DR or telephone them on 01535 606139.

ARBORICULTURAL ASSOCIATION
Members will be either consultants or contractors. Consultant members are qualified to give you advice about trees.

Contractors, (also known as tree surgeons), are qualified to undertake work to a specification. A list of members can be obtained from the Secretariat, Arboricultural Association, Ampfield House, Ampfield, nr. Romsey, Hants SO51 9PA (Tel. 01794 368717).

Garden security

You can reduce the chances of theft from your garden, or of suffering financial loss if you are robbed.

● Make sure your insurance policy covers the contents of your shed and garage, in addition to your garden furniture, statuary and fountains.
● Keep a record of the serial numbers of garden machinery and equipment. Mark all movable property with your post code. It makes identifying items easier if they are recovered by the police. Thieves may also be deterred from taking things that carry identification marks that cannot be hidden or easily removed.
● Take photographs or videos of any valuable items in your garden, making sure distinguishing details are clearly visible. Where possible, include a ruler or some other object in the picture, to give an indication of size.
● Do not leave machinery such as hedge trimmers, mowers or trimmers unattended in the garden while you have a break, particularly if they are visible to passers-by.

● Ride-on tractor mowers can be thief-proofed when not in use. A clamp is bolted to the floor of the shed or garage and when the mower is in position over it, security flaps on all sides are padlocked together, to enclose the mower. The padlock is covered, to protect it from bolt cutters.

● Install security lights that are triggered by movement, and also consider extending your house alarm system to the shed or garage. Battery-powered alarm systems are available, and they are suitable for DIY installation.

● Secure gates, sheds and garages with good quality locks, such as a strong padlock, a mortise deadlock or other high-security lock. Your insurance company may be able to offer precise specifications.
● Join a Neighbourhood Watch – or start one. It is useful to have observant neighbours keeping an eye on your property while you are away. Keep them informed of any expected repairs, deliveries or removals – many burglars masquerade as workmen or delivery services.
● Put away all tools and equipment after use. Apart from their monetary value, ladders, spades and forks can help a burglar to break into your house.
● Use a heavy-duty chain and padlock to secure large valuable objects to a concrete slab which has been set into the ground, or buy an earth anchor (see margin).

● Even quite large objects can be stolen when owners are away or asleep. Make it more difficult for thieves by winding a length of heavy-duty chain through several items such as a barbecue and garden furniture when they are not in use. Then secure the ends of the chain with a strong padlock.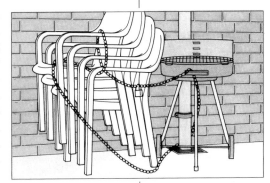

● Don't place trees or shrubs growing in tubs where they can be seen easily and taken by opportunist thieves. Pot plants or hanging baskets are at risk in front gardens in high-crime areas, too.
● To prevent a plastic dustbin lid from being blown away in high winds or taken by vandals, attach it to the bin with a length of chain. Fasten the ends of the chain with a padlock or a length of sturdy wire.
● Position a valuable statue in the centre of a cultivated area, so that thieves leave prints of their shoes or car tyres.

Continued overleaf

PROTECT PROPERTY WITH AN EARTH ANCHOR

Large, valuable items need to be secured firmly to the ground when they are not in use, whether they are kept indoors or out. Consider using a metal earth anchor which is driven into the ground and then locked, making it almost impossible to pull out. It is attached to a heavy-duty chain which is threaded through or wound round the object and then padlocked.

- Prickly hedges and plants, including blackthorn, holly, pyracantha, berberis, and thorny varieties of rose should be positioned where they will deter intruders.

Garden wall (SEE ALSO BRICKWORK)

Crumbling top course Time: depends on area

Damp and frost can rot the top course of a garden wall and result in it crumbling. It is possible to remove the damaged layer and replace it with new bricks.

Contact local demolition contractors and suppliers of rescued building materials for matching bricks.

> YOU WILL NEED Safety spectacles, gardening gloves, steel bolster, club hammer, cold chisel, wire brush, builder's line and line spirit level, bag of mortar mix, trowel, old paintbrush, brick waterproofer, long spirit level.

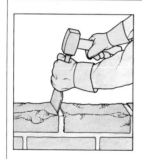

Wearing safety spectacles to protect your eyes and gardening gloves to protect your hands, use a steel bolster (a wide bricklayer's chisel) and a club hammer to remove all the damaged bricks.

Use a cold chisel to chip away all the remaining mortar. Then rub the exposed bricks clean with a wire brush.

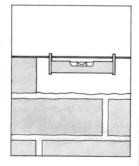

If possible, set up a horizontal builder's line to show the height of the new brick layer. Use a line spirit level to make sure that the builder's line is level.

Make up a dryish mortar mix about the consistency of a sand pie. Then damp the top row of bricks, and apply a bed of mortar about 2 cm ($\frac{3}{4}$ in) thick.

Hollow the mortar layer down the centre with the trowel point and place the first brick hollow-side down on the mortar so that its end is not in line with the end of the brick below. Then tap it into place with the handle of the trowel.

Cover the end of the next brick with a layer of mortar about 1.9 cm ($\frac{3}{4}$ in) thick and smooth it at the four edges. Tap the brick in place. Repeat to the end of the row. As you work, check with a long spirit level that the top of the bricks are level. When the new brickwork is complete point it to match the rest of the wall (see *Brickwork*).

When the mortar is set, treat the whole wall with a clear waterproofing liquid to protect it from future damage.

Cutting a brick

Place the brick, hollow-side down, on a bed of sand. Use a bolster and club hammer to lightly score the brick at the point where it is to be cut.

Then place the bolster in position and give one sharp blow with the club hammer. The brick should split cleanly along the line of the bolster.

Gas appliance

Using gas appliances safely

- Ensure that there is adequate ventilation when using any gas appliance, particularly those using LPG (bottled gas) which do not have a flue – open a window or turn on an extractor fan.
- Gas central-heating boilers, water heaters and gas fires need to draw in air from outside and also need a flue to get rid of burnt gases. Most modern boilers and water heaters have room-sealed (or balanced) flues which draw in air and expel burnt gases through the same flues.

Others have conventional flue pipes to remove burnt gases, either feeding up through the chimney or running up the outside of the building, and they require a free flow of air through ventilators or air bricks in the walls of the room in order to burn safely.

These vents and flues should never be blocked, as they can send poisonous fumes back into the room. Do not attempt to alter or close them off under any circumstances. An obstructed flue can kill.

If, for any reason, you suspect that the flue of the appliance is blocked, turn off the appliance immediately and call a CORGI-registered gas engineer or Transco.

Gas bill

Working out what your gas has cost so far

A ROUGH GUIDE Whenever you wish, you can work out the rough cost of the gas you have used since the last bill.

First find out how many units of gas you have used: read the meter and subtract the reading on your last bill from the new reading. To work out a rough price per unit, divide the total charge for gas (excluding VAT and the standing charge) on your last bill by the number of units on the bill. Multiply the units used since the last bill by the unit price to get the total cost of the units used since then.

THE EXACT CALCULATION To make an exact calculation, subtract the number of units shown on the last bill from the present reading on your meter. Multiply the units you have used by 2.83 to find out the amount of gas supplied to your home, measured in cubic metres. If you have a new meter which already measures gas in cubic meters, you do not have to do this calculation.

Then calculate how much energy the gas has provided, measured in kilowatt hours (kWh). This depends on its volume, and its calorific value which varies slightly according to its origin. Multiply the number of cubic metres by the Volume Conversion Factor and then by the calorific value, both of which are given on the front of the bill. Divide the result by 3.6 to give the number of kWh provided.

The price per kWh is shown on the bill. Multiply this by the number of kWh used, and add VAT and the standing charge.

Reading your meter

DIAL METER Older meters have a series of small dials with pointers. Read only the figures on the four black dials.

Record the reading on each dial, starting with the one on the left. If the pointer is between figures, write down the lower number, but if it lies between 9 and 0 write down 9.

DIGITAL METER A modern meter has a digital display. On this type of meter you need to read only the first four figures.

Gas fire

Fitting a new radiant   Time: $\frac{1}{2}$ hour or less

Traditional style gas fires are fitted with fire-clay bars that glow when they are hot. These are called radiants and they come in two types: box radiants and bar radiants. Replacements for both types are usually available from British Gas shops or gas appliance dealers.

> YOU WILL NEED New radiants.

Used radiants are fragile, so remove the broken radiant before going to buy its replacement, in case you break a good radiant while removing the faulty one.

BAR RADIANTS They are usually found on older gas fires, supported in slots at each end of the fire.

To reach the broken bar, you must remove all the bars above it. Detach each bar by lifting one end up and out of its slot.

BOX RADIANTS Most gas fires have a metal grille sprung into slots at each side of the fire. Once the grille has been removed, box radiants can be lifted up and tilted, then pulled out, bottom first.

Servicing gas fires

A gas fire should be serviced regularly (about once a year) by a CORGI-registered gas engineer, who will clean it, test it and repair any faults. It is best to have it done in the autumn, so that it is ready for winter.

Gas lamp

If your camping gas lamp suddenly goes out or starts to sputter, first check that you have not run out of fuel. If not, the mantle may need replacing. Always keep a spare.

Replacing the mantle   Time: a few minutes

> YOU WILL NEED New mantle.

Remove the glass shade and any bits of the old mantle. Mantles vary in size according to the type of lantern. If in doubt, take the lantern with you to buy new mantles.

MAINTAINING GAS BOILERS

To ensure that your gas boiler or heater is well maintained and safe, take out an annual contract with a CORGI-registered gas engineer or your gas supplier.

DETECTING CARBON MONOXIDE

Faulty gas fires, boilers and water heaters will give off carbon monoxide at dangerous levels. Because it is silent, invisible, odourless and tasteless, carbon monoxide is difficult to detect without a special carbon monoxide detector.

Some detectors have card indicators that change colour if the gas is present in the air, and are useful for detecting low levels of carbon monoxide. Others are mains or battery-powered and have audible and visible alarms. Detectors should be fitted near and slightly above gas fires, water heaters and boilers, and must be checked regularly. However, a detector is no substitute for the regular servicing of all gas appliances.

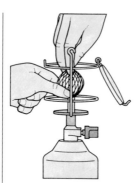

Fix on the new mantle by stretching the larger opening in the mantle over the rim of the burner head so that it rests in the groove of the burner body.

Next, stretch the mantle's smaller opening to fit into the groove on the spigot.

Arrange the mantle fabric evenly. Then use a match to set fire to it. This will 'burn off' the mantle so that it assumes the correct shape. It is essential that the mantle is burnt off before using the lamp, otherwise it will disintegrate with the first rush of gas when it is lit.

Replacing the glass shade Time: a few minutes

To replace a broken gas-lamp shade, unclip the top of the lamp, remove any remaining pieces of the old shade and slot the new one into place. Replace the top of the lamp.

Gas leak

If you smell gas

● Extinguish all naked flames.
● Do not turn electrical switches either on or off, and make sure no one operates the doorbell. Either of these actions can create a spark sufficient to ignite gas.
● Open windows and doors to let out any gas and get in as much fresh air as possible.
● Check that gas rings, fires and pilot lights have not blown out. If they have, turn them off and wait for a few minutes before relighting (see 'Pilot light problems' page 168).

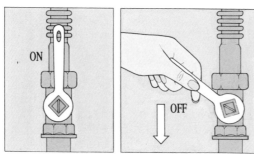

● If the smell persists, turn off the gas supply at the main tap next to your meter. When the lever is parallel with the pipe the gas is ON, when it is at right angles to the pipe the gas is OFF. (Do not turn on a light or strike a match.)

● Then telephone Transco, the company responsible for attending to all gas leaks, on 0800 111 999.

GAS DETECTOR

Your sense of smell is the best detector of gas. However, if you have difficulty smelling gas fit a gas detector in your home.

Make sure that any gas detector you fit complies with the British Standard BS7348.

Gate (SEE ALSO FENCING)

Hanging a garden gate Time: ½ a day or less

YOU WILL NEED Power or hand drill, twist bit, rustless screws, two T-hinges, five or six wood wedges, hammer or mallet.

Place the gate between the two uprights. Tap small wedges around the gate to hold it in place. There should be a gap of about 6 mm ($\frac{1}{4}$ in) between the upright posts and the gate. Choose whatever size gap you need at the bottom of the gate, making sure there is adequate clearance all the way through the swing as the gate is fully opened.

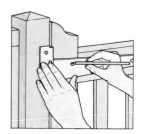

Hold the T-hinge in place so that it centres on its cross rail and then mark where the screw holes will go.

Then drill pilot holes to get the screws started. Fix the hinges in place with rustless screws, then fit the latch.

Tightening loose hinges on a wooden gate
Time: 2 hours or less

YOU WILL NEED Screwdriver, power drill, twist bit, bradawl.

If the screws are loose in their holes, replace them with thicker ones. But if the new screws won't fit through the holes in the hinges, you will have to plug the screw holes.

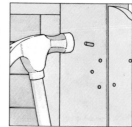

Cut some wooden plugs from a piece of scrap softwood, dip them in PVA wood glue and hammer them into the holes.

Trim off any surplus wood and make a pilot hole for the screws with a bradawl. Screw the hinge back into place.

Alternatively, if the screw holes are badly worn or rotted, move the hinges up or down and drill new screw holes.

Fixing a sagging gate Time: ½ a day or less

YOU WILL NEED Screwdriver, mallet or rubber hammer, sandpaper, mortise chisel, try square, waterproof PVA wood glue.

Unscrew the gate from the post and check all the joints. If the joints are loose, tap them apart with a mallet or rubber hammer. Clean off old adhesive with sandpaper or a chisel. Apply waterproof PVA wood glue and remake the joint.

Check the corners of the gate with a try square before the adhesive sets, and realign the joint if necessary. Leave to set for about 24 hours before putting it back on the post.

FIXING A CROSSBRACE If one of the crossbraces on a gate has come loose or has rotted, you can tighten up the screws (see 'Tightening loose hinges on a wooden gate', facing page) or else replace the brace with a new piece of wood.

To provide the necessary support, the brace must run from the bottom hinge to the latch side.

Securing a broken latch Time: 1 hour or less

> YOU WILL NEED Screwdriver, power drill, twist bit.

Remove the broken latch and buy one that matches it as closely as possible. Secure the bolt section to the gate, using the same holes if possible.

If you have to make new screw holes, shut the gate and hold the latch part in the correct closed position to mark for screw holes. Drill start holes with a twist bit.

Cleaning rust off a metal gate Time: ½ a day or less

> YOU WILL NEED Wire brush, safety spectacles, paintbrush, rust-inhibiting primer, emery paper, gloss or enamel paint, special gloss or enamel brush cleaner.

Put on safety spectacles and use a wire brush to remove all loose and flaking rust.

Treat bare areas with rust-inhibiting primer, then rub the metal with emery paper before painting. Or use a rust-inhibiting enamel which needs no primer or undercoat. Prepare the surface beforehand with emery paper.

Fitting a self-closing device Time: ½ hour or less

Adding a gate spring to the hinge side of a gate will force it to shut automatically. This can be useful for keeping small children or animals from straying.

> YOU WILL NEED Hand or power drill, twist bit, screwdriver, non-rust screws, gate spring, steel tape measure.

Close the gate and position the gate spring diagonally between the gate and the post, following the instructions. Drill start holes for screws and screw the spring in place.

Glass (SEE ALSO GLASSWARE; WINDOWS)

Getting rid of glass

It is dangerous to put broken glass in the dustbin. Instead, take it to the nearest bottle bank or, if there isn't a bottle bank nearby, to the local tip. There will be a place allocated for glass. Store the broken glass in a strong box, clearly labelled, until you have time to dispose of it.

Sticking glass to glass

Use an anaerobic adhesive called Glass Bond for sticking glass to glass, such as when you repair a glass vase.

The adhesive will set in daylight to give an invisible, watertight join. Make the join at your leisure in artificial light, then move the item into daylight to set.

Cutting glass

If you are going to cut it yourself, always try to work with new glass because as glass ages it becomes more difficult to cut. Take old glass which needs cutting to a glazier.

> YOU WILL NEED Newspaper, chinagraph pencil, white spirit, wheeled glass-cutter, steel straightedge or ruler, steel tape measure, safety spectacles, heavy gloves.

Lay newspaper on a table and place the glass on top, using the lines of print to help you get a straight line. Mark a cutting line with a chinagraph pencil.

Use a steel straightedge to position the glass-cutter correctly. Lubricate the glass-cutter's wheel with white spirit.

Hold the cutter with your index finger in the hollow on the handle and place it on the cutting line, as far from you as possible. Press down and draw the cutter along the line towards you.

Lift the glass and tap lightly along the underside of the scored line with the ball-shaped end of the cutter.

Put on safety spectacles and heavy gloves then place the glass so that the scored line is immediately above the edge of the straightedge.

Press down firmly on either side of the scored line, and the glass should break cleanly along the score.

CUTTING CIRCULAR HOLES IN GLASS

It is best to ask a glazier to do any complex work such as cutting large circular holes.

CUTTING A THIN STRIP If you are only removing a thin strip of glass, place the strip over the edge of the table so that the score lines up with the edge. Then, wearing heavy gloves and safety spectacles, grip the edge between thumb and forefinger, apply pressure firmly and snap the glass.

If the strip is too narrow to grip with your fingers, use pincers, or one of the rectangular recesses in the nose of the glass-cutter.

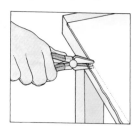

Drilling glass

Use a variable-speed power drill and a special glass drill bit, which has a smooth shank and a tungsten carbide tip, shaped like a spear point. It is designed to make an easy start to drilling through a sheet of glass.

Decide where you want to position the hole and mark a cross on the glass with a chinagraph pencil.

Then stick a ring of putty or Blu-Tack onto the glass, round the mark, and pour in enough white spirit to form a small pool inside the ring.

Put the tip of the drill bit onto the mark and start it turning slowly. Continue drilling until the tip penetrates the glass. Then remove the ring of putty, turn the glass over and complete the hole from the other side.

Glasses: SEE SPECTACLES

Glassware

Cleaning cut glass, crystal and lead crystal
Time: a few minutes

Always wash cut glass, crystal and lead crystal by hand and not in a dishwasher. Using a dishwasher will eventually cause white, cloudy marks, known as etching — and they are impossible to remove.

> YOU WILL NEED Plastic washing-up bowl, hot water, washing-up liquid, soft cloth, lint-free tea towels. Possibly: soft-bristled brush, ammonia.

Before starting, take off any rings with hard stones in case they scratch the glass. If you are wearing rubber gloves, keep a firm grip on each piece as you wash it.

To avoid knocking pieces of glass against hard surfaces or against each other, wash them one at a time in a plastic washing-up bowl.

Use a soft-bristled brush to clean any crevices in cut glass. Badly stained cut glass should be filled with a mixture of water and washing-up liquid with a few drops of ammonia added, and left to stand overnight.

When washing a wine glass, hold it by the bowl, not by the stem in case it breaks off. Rinse it in clean, hot water.

Drain each glass, upside-down on a folded tea towel. Dry them all while they are still warm, with a lint-free tea towel. Store glasses the right way up, to prevent damaging their rims, and do not stack them one inside another.

Separating two glasses Time: a few minutes

If glasses are stacked one inside the other, two glasses may get stuck together. You can separate them by taking advantage of the fact that glass reacts fast to changes in temperature, by expanding and contracting.

> YOU WILL NEED Ice cubes and cold water, bowl of warm water, jug of hot water.

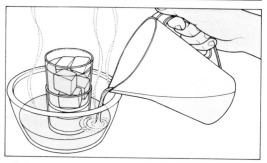

Fill the inner glass with ice cubes and cold water. Stand the glasses in warm water. Add hot water (not boiling) until the outer glass expands and the inner glass contracts sufficiently to allow them to be separated.

Rewiring crystal drops on a chandelier

The wires that hold the crystal drops on a chandelier can be replaced if they wear out. Use matching flexible wire such as fuse wire, and form it into loops, to allow the drops to turn freely.

Specialist repairers can supply replacement drops and repair significant damage to chandeliers. Look in *Yellow Pages* under 'Lighting Goods Retailers'.

Repairing the broken stem of a wine glass
Time: 1 hour or less

This method creates a clear, waterproof join but it relies on sunlight penetrating the entire join to trigger the setting action of the glue. It will not work on coloured glass or glass with a high lead content, such as crystal – use a two-part acrylic adhesive for these.

> **YOU WILL NEED** Warm soapy water, lint-free cloth, Glass Bond, sticks of modelling clay, craft knife.

Carefully clean the raw edges of the broken glass by washing them in warm, soapy water. Then rinse the pieces in clear, hot water and dry them with a soft, lint-free cloth.

Work indoors and do not expose the adhesive to sunlight until you are ready for it to start setting. Cover one surface of the break with a thin layer of Glass Bond.

Put the two surfaces together and run a fingernail across the join to check that it is perfect.

Leave the repaired glass in a sunny place (such as on a windowsill) to set.

If necessary, support the glued join with modelling clay, but make sure that it doesn't block the sunlight.

The entire join should be exposed to sunlight to make sure that the chemical process takes place correctly; it will not be triggered by electric light.

Setting is rapid: on a sunny day it takes as little as 10 seconds; but on a dull day allow 1 or 2 hours. The strength of the bond will continue to increase during the next 24 hours, so do not handle the item for a while. Once the join is strong, any excess adhesive can be removed with the blade of a craft knife.

Restoring scratched glass   Time: depends on area

Glass tables, mirrors and watch faces, as well as drinking glasses and glass bowls can be marred by a scratch. Many scratches can be removed.

> **YOU WILL NEED** Possibly: chamois leather, metal cleaner such as Brasso, soft cloth.

A very shallow scratch on a glass surface may be removed eventually by rubbing it with a clean chamois leather, but it will take some time – up to an hour.

However, if the scratch is deeper and time is limited, use a soft cloth dipped in Brasso or jeweller's polishing paste. Polish the scratched area gently. To avoid over-rubbing, keep checking to see if the mark has gone.

Cleaning glass light fittings and chandeliers
Time: depends on amount

To be really effective, glass light fittings and chandeliers must sparkle and reflect light. They should be dusted regularly and washed, in place about every three months.

> **YOU WILL NEED** Old bed sheet or cotton dustsheet, stepladder, bowl, methylated spirit, household ammonia, soft cloths.

! Before working on a light fitting, turn off the power at the main fuse box. Make sure that the light bulbs are cool.

Mix up a solution of one part methylated spirit, one part household ammonia and two parts of water.

Protect the floor directly under the light by spreading out an old bed sheet or a cotton dustsheet. Then set up a sturdy stepladder which has a flat surface on which to rest the bowl of cleaning solution and the cloths.

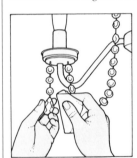

Using a soft, clean cloth, dip it into the solution and wipe each piece of glass gently. Dry with a lint-free cloth, if necessary.

Repairing a damaged glass, bowl or vase
Time: depends on amount

If the damage is severe or the glassware valuable, have the repairs done professionally. If the piece is not valuable enough to warrant professional care, it may be worth attempting to repair it yourself.

> **YOU WILL NEED** Possibly: crystal engraving kit, Glass Bond, metal cleaner, fine wet-and-dry abrasive paper, pencil.

REPAIRING CHIPS Very small chips out of the rim or base of a favourite glass or vase can be smoothed away with an electric crystal engraver, available in some craft shops.

If necessary, you can fill in larger chips with Glass Bond. Apply a series of tiny drops of Glass Bond to the chipped area, letting them cure in sunlight, until the chip has been filled.

> ### Crystal engraver
> The crystal engraver has a grinding tip, and its high-speed action smooths away rough surfaces. It handles like a pen and can also be used with a diamond tip to personalise and security-mark valuable items.

Leave for 24 hours, and use a sharp craft knife to trim the dried glue so that it is flush with the rest of the glass. Polish the area with metal cleaner, then wash and dry.

REGRINDING A RIM Numerous tiny chips in the rim of a glass may make it necessary to regrind the entire rim.

Lay a sheet of fine wet-and-dry abrasive paper on a flat surface. Wet the glass and turn it rim-down onto the paper. Using a circular movement, gently rub the glass all over the paper. Keep dipping the glass in water to keep it cool and to aid the grinding process.

Once the chips have been removed, round off the edge with a piece of wet-and-dry paper wrapped round a pencil.

Finally, polish the rim with Brasso or other metal cleaner on a soft cloth. Wash and dry the glass.

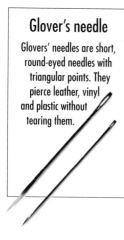

Glover's needle

Glovers' needles are short, round-eyed needles with triangular points. They pierce leather, vinyl and plastic without tearing them.

Gloves

The care label inside the gloves will show if they can be washed or if they should be dry cleaned. Don't allow gloves to become badly soiled before cleaning them.

Washing leather gloves Time: 1 hour or less

YOU WILL NEED Warm water, soap flakes or glove shampoo, towel, clothes pegs, wire coat hanger.

Unless the leather is very fine, wear the gloves to wash them. Very fine leather gloves should be washed 'empty'.

Dissolve soap flakes in warm water or dilute 1-2 tablespoons of glove shampoo in 1.15 litres (2 pints) of warm water. Gently work the bubbles into the leather. Avoid wringing or twisting the leather. Badly marked parts can be cleaned with a sponge dipped in neat glove shampoo.

Rinse thoroughly in clear water, then remove the gloves carefully and rinse the insides as well.

Lay them on a towel, and 'blot' them to remove excess water. Blow gently into each glove to open it. Using clothes pegs and a wire coat hanger, hang the gloves to dry, out of direct sunlight. If they are delicate, lay them on a dry towel and allow them to dry naturally. When the gloves are nearly dry, put them on to restore their shape, and rub them gently to soften the leather.

Light-coloured gloves can be sprinkled with talcum powder once they are absolutely dry and then rubbed with a soft cloth to soften and shine the leather. This is most easily done while wearing the gloves.

Repairing woollen gloves Time: 1 hour or less

YOU WILL NEED Darning needle, matching wool.

To keep the work taut, wear the glove, right side out, while you are darning it. If you are right-handed, wear the damaged glove on your left hand, and vice versa.

SPOT-CLEANING SUEDE AND LEATHER GLOVES

Spots can be removed from suede and leather gloves by rubbing them with a piece of stale bread. For better control, wear the gloves while doing it.

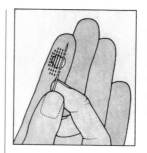

Starting well beyond the damaged area, weave your needle through the stitches, following the lengthways grain of the knitting. Turn at the end and run another row, parallel to the first.

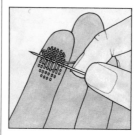

Cover the damaged area in this fashion, then turn and work parallel rows at a right angle across the first group, weaving them under and over alternate rows (see also *Darning*).

Don't work too tightly or the glove will pucker and pull. Finish off securely, inside the glove.

Repairing leather gloves Time: 1 hour or less

YOU WILL NEED Glover's needle, matching silk thread.

SPLITS BETWEEN FINGERS With a fine blanket stitch, sew along both edges of the split. Then use a whipstitch to join the rows of blanket stitch (see *Stitches*).

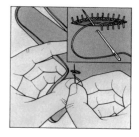

WORN FINGER TIP With one finger inside the worn tip, edge the hole with a fine blanket stitch. Then work a second circle, based on the first. Continue to work in a decreasing circle until the hole is neatly filled.

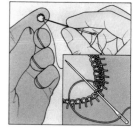

Glues

If the chart (right) does not specify the task you have in mind, try to find a similar task. It will give you an indication of the type of glue you will need. Further information about that type, together with some brand names, is listed overleaf to help you to select the right glue. If you are still unsure, consult the manufacturer. Most manufacturers have technical advisers who will give advice on the phone.

Some plastics, including polythene, cannot be glued; but hard polystyrene and PVC (vinyl), can.

The right glue for the job

Ceilings

TASK Replacing an expanded-polystyrene ceiling tile or a ceiling rose.
GLUE TYPE Expanded-polystyrene adhesive.

TASK Fixing plaster coving to ceiling or wall.
GLUE TYPE Panel or coving adhesive.

Walls

TASK Replacing ceramic wall tile.
GLUE TYPE Purpose-made ceramic tile adhesive or panel adhesive.

TASK Applying cork tiles to plastered wall.
GLUE TYPE Expanded-polystyrene adhesive or purpose-made cork adhesive.

TASK Fixing wood panelling or a dado panel to an interior wall.
GLUE TYPE Panel adhesive.

Floors

TASK Resticking vinyl floor tiles.
GLUE TYPE Contact or flooring adhesive.

TASK Fixing loose wooden flooring block.
GLUE TYPE Wood glue or bitumen/rubber flooring adhesive.

Furniture

TASK Fixing wood to wood (repairs to wooden furniture or picture frame).
GLUE TYPE Wood glue.

TASK Fixing fabric or carpet to wood.
GLUE TYPE Fabric adhesive.

TASK Fixing sheet laminate to wooden surface (re-covering kitchen cupboard).
GLUE TYPE Contact adhesive.

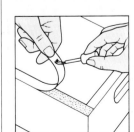

TASK Fixing plastic strip to wood (e.g. trim on white furniture).
GLUE TYPE Two-part acrylic.

TASK Metal to sheet laminate (such as fixing the trim onto a kitchen cupboard).
GLUE TYPE Epoxy resin.

Ornaments, toys and household crockery

TASK Mending a toy or piece of kitchenware made of rigid plastic.
GLUE TYPE Superglue, two-part acrylic or hard-plastic glue.

TASK Mending a broken china ornament.
GLUE TYPE Superglue or epoxy resin.

TASK Mending a snapped wine glass stem (but not coloured glass or lead crystal).
GLUE TYPE UV-active acrylic adhesive (anaerobic adhesive – hardens in daylight).

TASK Fixing glass to metal (reattaching metal beak to crystal duck ornament).
GLUE TYPE Superglue.

TASK Fixing a broken plate.
GLUE TYPE Epoxy resin.

TASK Reattaching loose stone to metal base of earring or pendant.
GLUE TYPE Superglue or epoxy resin.

TASK Making or mending a model car or aeroplane (plastic).
GLUE TYPE Hard-plastic adhesive.

TASK Making a model plane from balsa wood.
GLUE TYPE Wood glue or clear glue.

Soft materials, fabrics and clothing

TASK Patching a plastic raincoat or mending a child's blow-up toy.
GLUE TYPE PVC adhesive.

TASK Fixing a leather sole to a shoe.
GLUE TYPE Purpose-made leather adhesive.

TASK Fixing felt to base of vase or ornament.
GLUE TYPE PVA glue, clear glue or fabric glue.

TASK Fixing rubber sole to shoe.
GLUE TYPE Clear glue or special adhesive supplied with sole.

TASK Repairing a book (see *Book*).
GLUE TYPE Wood glue or clear resin.

TASK Fixing fabric to card or paper (e.g. trimming a lampshade).
GLUE TYPE Fabric adhesive, PVA glue or clear adhesive.

Outdoors

TASK Fixing metal to wood (e.g. metal trim on wooden handle of small garden fork).
GLUE TYPE Two-part acrylic or epoxy resin.

TASK Fixing joint in outdoor wooden furniture.
GLUE TYPE Waterproof wood adhesive.

TASK Mending a broken terracotta pot.
GLUE TYPE Epoxy resin, waterproof PVA or terracotta epoxy putty (see *Terracotta pots*).

TASK Fixing ceramic plaque to wall.
GLUE TYPE Waterproof PVA tile adhesive or panel adhesive.

TASK Repairs to canvas, caravan roofs, wellington boots.
GLUE TYPE Rubber-based fabric adhesive.

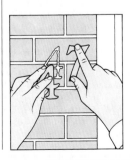

TASK Fixing metal to a brick or rendered wall.
GLUE TYPE Heavy-duty epoxy resin or panel adhesive.

Glues (cont.)

Glue guns

Hot-melt glue guns are loaded with a stick of solid glue which melts as the gun heats it. Glue is applied when the trigger is squeezed or the stick pushed. Bonding and setting is quite quick, taking from 20 to 90 seconds.

A glue gun offers a quick and accurate way of making repairs to items that will not come into contact with heat – such as shoe soles, decorative mouldings and loose tiles.

What kind of glue?

There is no glue which sticks everything, so check the manufacturer's recommendations carefully before you select the glue for a job. Take into account the nature of the two surfaces you wish to stick together, the area to be glued, and the use to which the object will be put.

Before you start working make sure you have the recommended solvent or cleaner, to remove surplus glue.

Superglues

Also called cyanoacrylates, these fast-acting glues bond in seconds. They are too thin to fill gaps, so surfaces must meet perfectly. They can be used on metals and ornaments, but not on domestic china which is washed, because the bond can fail when wet – use an epoxy resin instead.

SOME BRAND NAMES Bostik Super Glue 4, Devcon Super Glue, Evo-Stik Super Glue, Loctite Supergluematic, Permabond C, Uhu Superglue Gel.

CLEANERS Some have their own solvent, others react to acetone. Read instructions carefully. If skin becomes bonded, soak it in warm, soapy water and the glue will eventually come away, doing no harm to the skin.

Epoxy resin

A very strong adhesive, suited to most rigid materials. It is supplied in two parts which react chemically as they are mixed. Fast and slow-drying types and a gap-filling paste are available, as well as heavy-duty types. They produce a water-resistant bond that resists moderate heat and corrosion. However, they are not suitable for gluing clear glass to clear glass, as the bond will be visible; use a UV-active glue.

SOME BRAND NAMES Araldite Standard and Rapid, Bostik Epoxy, Humbrol Superfast Epoxy, Loctite Tough Bond, Permabond E, Plastic Padding, Super Epoxy Glue.

CLEANER White spirit.

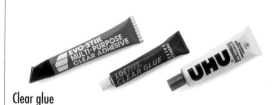

Wood adhesive

There are many woodworking glues suitable for bonding wood, wood veneer, laminated plastic and chipboard. Waterproof types are available for outdoor uses.

SOME BRAND NAMES Unibond PVA Wood, Bison Wood Glue, Bostik Wood, Loctite Wood Bond Rapid, Unibond Woodworker, Evo-Stik Wood Resin W, Humbrol Carpenters' Wood Glue, Humbrol Cascamite Powdered Resin Wood Glue, Brummer Wood Adhesive, Evo-Stik Wood Adhesive Waterproof, Unibond Waterproof Woodworker.

CLEANER Clean with a damp cloth while glue is still wet.

Clear glue

A clear, general household adhesive that is usually solvent-based and gives a water resistant, flexible bond.

SOME BRAND NAMES Loctite Clear, Uhu All Purpose, Bostik All Purpose, Dunlop Clear, Evo-Stik Multi-purpose Clear.

CLEANER Acetone (nail polish remover).

Purpose-made adhesives

There are many glues available for specific tasks, such as gluing soles onto shoes, fixing ceramic tiles to walls, fixing flooring tiles, doing plumbing repairs and mending items that will be exposed to extreme heat. In addition, many sealants are highly adhesive (see also *Sealants*).

SOME BRAND NAMES Evo-Stik's Leather, Fabric and Paper

Adhesives, Evo-Stik Floor Tile Fix & Grout, Loctite Vinyl Bond, Cemfix Tile Adhesive, Sylglas Plumberfix, Evo-Bond Building Adhesive, Tetra Fix 'n Grout, Denso Plumberfix.
CLEANERS Various. Read instructions on pack.

Paper-and-card adhesives

There are a wide range of adhesives, pastes and glue sticks available for light household and craft uses.
SOME BRAND NAMES *Pastes*: Clam Standard Paste, Evo-Stik Paper Adhesive, Gloy Gum, Uhu Gluepen. *Rubber solution*: Cow Gum. *Stick glue*: Pritt Stick, Uhu Stic. *Children's glue*: Bostik Gluetime, Copydex, Gloy Patch, Pritt Childsplay. *Reusable adhesives*: Bostik Blu-Tack, Pritt Tak, Uhu Tac.
CLEANERS Most respond to a damp cloth. Peel off rubber solution or use lighter fuel (highly flammable). Lift off reusable adhesive with a clean piece of the same adhesive.

UV-active acrylic

Activated by exposure to ultraviolet light. Used to repair glassware or stick glass to metal, but not for lead crystal, coloured glass or items exposed to high temperatures. Repairs the item at leisure in artificial light – bonding is delayed until the repair is exposed to the ultraviolet rays in natural daylight. Once set, the bond is water-resistant.
SOME BRAND NAMES Loctite Glass Bond, Dunlop SAS 700.
CLEANER Remove any excess adhesive with a damp cloth before exposing the repair to natural light.

Fabric adhesive

Used for sticking carpets and fabrics. Latex-based, it is white when wet, but dries clear. Rubber-based waterproof types of fabric adhesive can be used for repairing canvas.
SOME BRAND NAMES Copydex, Evo-Stik Fabric. *Rubber-based*: Bostik Weatherproof, Hi-Gear Tent Adhesive.
CLEANERS Wipe with a damp cloth while it is still wet. *Rubber-based*: Lighter fuel (highly flammable).

Expanded-polystyrene adhesive

Suitable for sticking expanded-polystyrene ceiling tiles, coving and veneer to walls or ceilings.
SOME BRAND NAMES Unibond Polystyrene and Plaster Cove, Evo-Stik Ceiling Tile.
CLEANER Soapy water, while the adhesive is still wet.

Contact adhesive

Used for bonding sheet materials. Adhesive is applied to both surfaces, which are pressed together when touch-dry. Some stick tightly as soon as the surfaces touch, but others allow a little time in which to adjust the positioning of the surfaces before final bonding takes place. Some panel adhesives can be used as contact adhesives. Clear contact adhesives are good for general household repairs. Some are water-based, but many are solvent-based.

PLAN REPAIRS CAREFULLY

When mending an item with a number of breaks, it is worthwhile having a 'dry run' first. Pieces may need to be replaced in a certain order. Note the order and position in which they should be reattached, in order to achieve a perfect fit.

HOLDING PIECES IN PLACE

Rubber bands or clear adhesive tape are useful for holding pieces in place while glues are setting.

Glues (cont.)

SAFETY WITH SOLVENTS

Take care when working with solvent-based adhesives — ensure good ventilation and keep naked flames and cigarettes away.

SOME BRAND NAMES *Solvent-based*: Bostik Contact, Clam 3, Evo-Stik Impact. *Solvent-based with 'slip' period*: Bison-Tix, Dunlop Thixofix, Evo-Stik Timebond. *Water-based*: Evo-Stik Impact 2. *Clear adhesive*: Evode.
CLEANERS *Solvent-based*: Acetone (nail polish remover), Evo-Stik Adhesive Cleaner(191). *Water-based*: damp cloth.

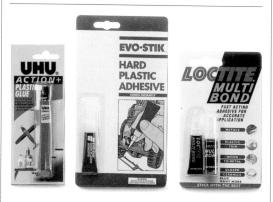

Hard-plastic cement

Widely used for making plastic models and for mending toys and household items made of rigid plastic. Some types soften the plastic as they bond, so care must be taken not to contaminate surface finishes.
SOME BRAND NAMES Evo-Stik Hard Plastic Adhesive, Humbrol Polystyrene Cement, Uhu Action + Plastic Glue, Loctite Multi Bond.
CLEANERS Evo-Stik Cleaner, Loctite Detach, acetone. For cleaning advice from Humbrol, telephone 01482 701191.

PVA and synthetic resin adhesives

Supplied in small quantities for gluing wood and for use in craftwork (see 'Wood adhesive'). In larger quantities, it can be added to concrete mixes to improve adhesion, to seal dusty concrete floors and other porous materials such as stone. Waterproof types are used outdoors. PVA tile adhesives will fix ceramic tiles to brickwork, concrete and plaster.
SOME BRAND NAMES Unibond Original PVA Adhesive & Sealer, Evo-Stik Flooring Adhesive, Rapide, Clam 7, Dunlop Fast Bond Wood Glue, Evo-bond Building Adhesive, Dunlop PVA Wall Tile Adhesive. *Heat and water-resistant*: Aerolite 306, Borden Cascophen, Humbrol Cascorez.
CLEANERS Usually a damp cloth, but read the instructions.

KEEP IT CLEAN

Grease from fingers will affect a bond, so keep items to be repaired clean until the repair work starts. If any time is likely to elapse, store the pieces in a polythene bag until they are needed.

Panel-and-flooring adhesive

A paste used for fixing decorative panelling, insulating panels, architraves, skirting boards, plasterboard and floor panels to walls and floors. Panel adhesives are also available in cartridges that can be used in a sealant gun.
SOME BRAND NAMES Evo-Stik Wall Panel Adhesive, Dow Corning Panel & Coving Adhesive, Vallance Liquid Nails Gripfast, Bostik Panel and Coving, Unibond Unilast Construction and Panel.
CLEANER Water soluble, while still wet.

PVC adhesive

Softens plastic surfaces and makes a very good bond. It is ideal for flexible PVC or vinyl, such as plastic raincoats and beach balls. Polythene and nylon cannot be glued.
SOME BRAND NAMES Bisonyl Vinyl, Loctite Vinyl Bond, Evo-Stik Leather Adhesive.
CLEANER Acetone (nail polish remover), but used sparingly to avoid damage to the surface.

Two-part acrylic adhesives

Used for fixing metal, glass, ceramic or plastic surfaces to each other. The two parts are applied, one to each surface, and remain dormant until the surfaces come in contact with each other, when a chemical reaction takes place. Like most glues, this adhesive will not stick plastics with a slightly oily or waxy feel (polypropylene or polythene). In addition, it should not be used on containers that will be used to hold hot liquids.
SOME BRAND NAMES M890, Loctite Multi-Bond, Bostik Hyperbond.
CLEANER Wipe with cloth or tissue. When dry, any excess adhesive can be cut away with a trimming knife.

Graffiti & scribbles

The best way to get rid of graffiti outside the house and children's scribbles inside, is to paint over the marks. Where papered walls are concerned, it may be possible to cover them with spare wallpaper.

Where painting is not possible (on brickwork or car bodywork, for example) the only option is to try to remove the mark without damaging the surface any further.

Drawing on walls

Encourage children to scribble on very large drawing pads or in colouring books instead of on walls.

An improvised blackboard provides children with an alternative surface to draw on. Stick a piece of hardboard to the wall with panel adhesive (see *Glues*), with the smooth side out. Paint it with black or green blackboard paint, and make a ledge at the base to hold the chalk and collect any falling dust.

Always remove graffiti and drawings as soon as you can, to give ink, paint or wax less chance of becoming permanent. Test the solvents or chemicals you intend to use on a small patch first, preferably one which will not show (see 'Using flammable materials', below, right). Work lightly to avoid damaging the original surface.

AEROSOL PAINT ON CERAMIC TILES AND MELAMINE Apply cellulose thinners, such as an acetone-based nail varnish remover, on a clean rag, and work lightly in small, circular movements. Alternatively, use a nail-polish remover pad, such as Quickies, which is a circle of lint-free fabric, impregnated with nail-polish remover.

If the mark is a particularly stubborn one, use Belco Finishing Compound, available from car accessory shops. Alternatively, use a graffiti remover, designed to get rid of spray paint, which is available from DIY stores.

AEROSOL PAINT ON BRICKWORK Paint enters the pores of brickwork, breezeblock and cement, and is extremely difficult to remove. Do not use a chemical paint stripper, as it makes a mess that is impossible to remove.

Instead, look for a spare brick of the same colour, and rub it over the surface of the marked brickwork (see *Brickwork*: 'Unwanted paint on brickwork').

On breezeblock and cement, paint over the marks.

FIBRE-TIP PEN MARKS ON HARD SURFACES First apply undiluted washing-up liquid, or methylated spirit.

If this does not work, use a household cream cleaner such as Jif. For especially stubborn marks, use Belco Finishing Compound, available from car accessory shops.

An aerosol spray designed to remove marker pen and other types of ink graffiti can be bought at most DIY stores. Alternatively, use methylated spirit on a soft cloth.

INK MARKS ON STANDARD WALLPAPERS Ink usually soaks into wallpaper and cannot be removed. It must be patched.

First, conceal the ink mark as effectively as possible, by spraying or painting over it with a stain-blocking primer. This will cut down the chance of it showing through the wallpaper patch you are going to apply.

Tear a piece of matching wallpaper so that its decorative surface is undercut and has a feathered edge. Then carefully paste it over the stained area, matching the pattern neatly.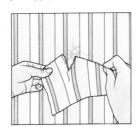

INK MARKS ON WASHABLE WALLPAPER AND VINYL Ball-point pen marks on vinyl or other washable wall coverings can be treated with methylated spirit on a cotton-wool bud. You can remove marks made by marker pens that contain spirit-based or indelible ink, in the same way.

Marks made by a water-based felt-tip pen ink should respond to undiluted washing-up liquid on a damp rag.

BUYING PENS AND INK REMOVERS

When you buy felt-tip pens or Magic Markers, buy also the appropriate Stain Devil stain remover. If clothes or carpets become marked, you can act quickly.

Using flammable materials

Some of the chemicals used to remove graffiti, such as acetone-based solvents, are flammable. Follow these simple safety rules when using solvents.

Always read the label before starting work, ensure your work area is well ventilated, and do not smoke. Wear safety spectacles if using a scrubbing brush. Store the container well out of children's reach.

WAX CRAYON ON WALLPAPER Ask a helper to hold two sheets of paper towel over the crayon mark. Apply heat from an iron. The paper will absorb the melted wax.

Remove any remaining traces of colour by dabbing the area with methylated spirit on a cotton bud. If the stain persists, consider patching the area (see previous page).

PAINTED OUTSIDE WALLS OR TIMBER Use a graffiti remover or a cream cleaner such as Ajax or Jif to get rid of unwanted spray paint from painted outside walls or timber.

If the mark won't budge, use a stain-blocking primer such as Polycell Stain-Block, then paint over it.

Gravel path

Repairing gaps in a gravel path

Gravel is inclined to shift and form bumps and troughs, especially when cars drive over it, so paths and drives need to be raked quite regularly to keep the spread even. If a deep cavity appears, it is probable that the ground has subsided.

Do not simply fill up the cavity with more gravel; it is better to remove all the gravel from the depression and then ram in rubble to improve the foundations of the path. Finally, rake the gravel back over the gap.

Edging a path

Gravel paths need an edge to prevent the gravel from spreading onto the garden. Use bricks or concrete edging blocks set on edge in mortar. Make a slope of mortar on the garden side of the bricks to help them to resist the outward pressure of the gravel.

KEEPING WEEDS AT BAY

Use an old watering can to sprinkle weedkiller onto the gravel about once a year. Do not do this job on a windy day when the weedkiller could contaminate other areas of the garden.

BUYING NEW GRAVEL

New gravel can be bought by the bag from builders' merchants and garden centres.

Greenhouse

A greenhouse lengthens the growing season and protects plants through the winter, but even a simple, unheated one can cause problems unless it is properly maintained.

Routine maintenance for a greenhouse

Regular maintenance of a greenhouse means that it will last longer and the plants grown in it will be healthier. If a greenhouse has to be positioned alongside a wall, make sure there will be enough space between the wall and the greenhouse to allow for easy cleaning and repair.

There are three main types of greenhouse, and a wide variety of plastic to use instead of glass in the panes.

UNPAINTED WOOD Wooden greenhouses which have not been painted should be protected against rot every two or three years with a wood-preservative treatment.

PAINTED WOOD Painted wooden greenhouses should be inspected regularly and repainted as often as necessary.

ALUMINIUM Not only are they virtually trouble-free, but they have the advantage that replacement glass can be clipped into place in a few minutes. Cleaning and disinfecting them is also fairly quick and easy.

GREENHOUSE GLASS If your greenhouse is positioned so that it is vulnerable to vandalism, or if you have children, consider installing toughened glass, for safety.

Alternatively, use plastic, although it scratches more easily than glass and it suffers more from condensation.

Antifog plastics are available. They have been treated to prevent the formation of large droplets of condensation. Standard plastic can be sprayed with a product which makes condensation form in a fine film, rather than in droplets which run down the surface.

Polycarbonate is an alternative to ordinary plastic or Perspex. It is most commonly used in public greenhouses because it is so tough.

GUTTERS AND DOWNPIPES Clear out leaves regularly and seal small leaks with a commercial sealant (see *Sealants*). Replace them if they are cracked or broken.

CLEANING Remove dead leaves and diseased material as soon as they occur. Clean the entire greenhouse thoroughly at least once a year, using a garden disinfectant and paying particular attention to brickwork, glazing bars and glass or plastic. Give a final rinse with clean water.

Grout

Replacing crumbling grout Time: depends on area

> YOU WILL NEED Raking tool or penknife blade, old paintbrush, piece of sponge.

Dig out loose and crumbling grout. Dust thoroughly, then apply new grout. It may come ready-mixed in a tub or as a powder to mix with water. Add the powder to the water to avoid lumps. Don't pour the water onto the powder.

Press the grout well into the cracks with a sponge.

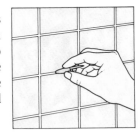

Wipe away any excess grout with a damp rag, then use something like the cap from a ball-point pen (the pointed end) to smooth the joints and create a rounded finish to the grout.

Leave the grout overnight to set, then polish the tiles with a ball of newspaper to remove any grout dust.

Killing mould and brightening grout on tiles
Time: depends on area

> YOU WILL NEED Fungicide, old toothbrush, soapy water. Possibly: proprietary grout whitener or emulsion paint, fine paintbrush.

Discoloration of the grout between tiles is usually caused by mould growing on the damp surface.

First, kill the mould with a proprietary fungicide. The mould may have discoloured the grout; if so, scrub it thoroughly with an old toothbrush and soapy water.

Then use a proprietary grout-whitener with a sponge applicator over the discoloured grout. Alternatively, use an exterior grade emulsion paint, applied with a fine paintbrush. Finally, wipe away the excess with a damp cloth.

Guitar

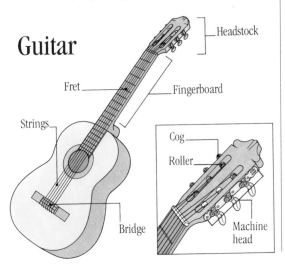

Headstock

Fret

Fingerboard

Strings

Cog

Roller

Bridge

Machine head

Replacing a broken string Time: $\frac{1}{2}$ hour or less

> YOU WILL NEED New string.

Start by removing the ends of the broken guitar string from the bridge and the machine head. Then thread the new string through the hole in the bridge and secure it in the same way as the other strings have been secured.

Feed the other end of the guitar string through the hole in the roller and then turn the key clockwise until the string has wound round the roller four or five times.

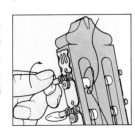

Caring for your guitar

To keep a guitar in good condition rest it on a soft surface and wipe it every month with a soft cloth moistened in a little corn oil. Wipe the fingerboard under the strings with a clean, dry rag every time the instrument has been played.

Lubricate the cog mechanisms with a light, easing oil such as WD40. If a cog sticks, use a graphite-based penetrating fluid to free it.

Replacing a broken roller Time: 1 hour or less

The machine head is the metal band holding the cogs and the tuning rollers on the headstock. Some guitars have one metal band running down each side of the headstock and others have a plate for each cog.

If a roller breaks, free all the strings and unscrew the machine head. Buy an identical machine head from a music shop and replace the damaged roller (see 'Spares for a machine head', right).

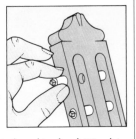

If you cannot buy an identical machine head, it is advisable to replace all the instrument's machine heads.

SPARES FOR A MACHINE HEAD

The tuning roller and cog mechanism in the machine head of a guitar can be obtained only as a unit; the rollers and cogs are not available separately. So if you change a machine head it is a good idea to keep the old one for spare parts.

NEW STRINGS

Guitar strings are not interchangeable between different models of guitar, so the appropriate type of string must be used on each sort of guitar.

CLEANING OFF RUST

Always wear safety spectacles to protect your eyes from flying particles when you clean off rust. Do not try to make the metal shine as new.

Drain clearer

This tool can be hired or bought, and consists of a flexible wire spiral which is inserted into the blocked downpipe. When its handle is connected and turned, the wire rotates, clearing the blocked pipe.

NETTING OVER GUTTERS

Sections of gutter netting are available to keep leaves and debris out of gutters. Check that wet leaves do not coat the netting and cause water to flow over the gutter rather than into it.

Gully: SEE DRAINS AND GULLIES

Gutters & downpipes

Understanding the system

Rainwater drains off the roof into the gutters running round its edge. The gutters slope down to an outlet where the water runs through a downpipe down the wall of the house, and away through the drains.

Gutters and downpipes can be made of aluminium, cast iron or plastic. If gutters and downpipes do not function efficiently, damp can affect the structure of the house.

Clearing gutters

Clear your guttering and downpipes on a fine day each spring and late autumn, and check for damage.

> YOU WILL NEED Extension ladder, ladder stand-off (see *Ladders & scaffolding*), protective gloves, old dustpan brush, garden trowel, bucket with S-hook. Possibly: wire brush, hose.

To clear out guttering made from cast iron, scoop out any silt, grit or other debris with a garden trowel.

If the gutter is plastic use a dustpan brush or a piece of wood to sweep or scoop out any debris.

Do not push the debris down the downpipe because it could cause a blockage which would be difficult to remove.

If a downpipe does get blocked, examine the top end for debris. Use a length of wire, bent to a hook at the end, to pull up anything blocking the pipe.

If the blockage is out of reach or won't move, hire a sink or drain clearer (see margin). Wind the probe into the downpipe until it pushes through and attaches itself to the obstruction, then ease it up and out.

Once the pipe is clear, use a garden hose to wash out the gutter and downpipe, and to dislodge any remaining debris. The water should be able to flow quickly and freely to the downpipe, leaving the gutter empty.

However, if a pool of water remains, the gutter needs realigning so that it slopes evenly down to the downpipe.

Safety first with ladders

● Always secure the ladder at both its top and bottom. Its feet must be on a firm, level surface and its top must rest against something solid.
● Never lean a ladder on guttering or a windowsill. Use a stand-off (see *Ladders & scaffolding*).
● Don't be tempted to overreach while you are working — you could fall. Move the ladder instead.
● Wear shoes with a good grip to prevent slipping.

Treating a rusted cast-iron gutter Time: depends on area

> YOU WILL NEED Emery cloth, wire brush, rust killer, paintbrush. Possibly: roof-and-gutter sealant, glass-fibre filler (the type used for car-body repairs), black bitumen paint or gloss paint.

Rub off small rust spots with emery cloth and clean off larger patches of rust with a wire brush. Then apply a coat of rust-neutralising primer to the cleaned parts.

Fill any small cracks or leaking joints with a roof-and-gutter sealant and plug any large holes with glass-fibre filler (available from car repair shops). Smooth the filling so that it does not obstruct the flow of water.

Finally, to protect against any future rust attack, apply two coats of black bitumen paint or gloss paint.

Repairing leaking cast-iron guttering
Time: depends on area

Fill small cracks or leaking joints with roof-and-gutter sealant. Alternatively, you will have to remove the leaking section to make the repair. Cast-iron guttering is heavy, so get help when lifting it.

> YOU WILL NEED Two ladders with stand-offs, wire brush, penetrating oil, adjustable spanner, epoxy repair paste, glass-fibre bandage, paintbrush, black bitumen paint or gloss. Possibly: mini-hacksaw, paint scraper, new bolts.

With a wire brush, scrub off rust around the bolts holding the leaking gutter in place. Then apply penetrating oil.

Undo the nuts with an adjustable spanner. If they won't move, cut through the bolt with a mini-hacksaw.

Use a paint scraper to clean off any paint from the area to be repaired. Use an epoxy repair paste and glass-fibre bandage to bond the broken gutter.

Apply the paste then press a glass-fibre bandage on top, working it into the paste. Finish off with another layer of repair paste.

Try to do most of the repair outside the gutter and make sure that any repair inside the gutter is smooth, so that debris does not catch on it.

Once the repair has set, replace the gutter section on a bed of roof-and-gutter sealant. Then set new bolts in the roof-and-gutter sealant to seal any gap between the bolt and the hole. Fit and tighten the nuts. Use a mini-hacksaw to cut off any surplus length of bolt.

Paint over the repaired area with black bitumen paint or gloss paint that matches the rest of the guttering.

Connecting gutter systems

Check whether your neighbour's system will be compatible when you buy new guttering. Gutter sections for linking different systems are available from DIY stores or builders' merchants.

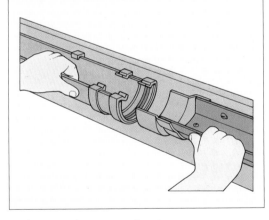

Replacing a plastic gutter bracket Time: ½ hour or less

If a bracket has broken, drive a long, strong nail into the fascia board under the gutter to support it. Then unscrew and remove the damaged bracket.

Take the old bracket to a DIY store and buy an identical replacement. It helps to know the make of rainwater system, which is probably embossed on the pipes.

Brackets at the joints of plastic systems may incorporate a neoprene foam gasket to ensure a good seal. This will need to be of the same make as the rest of the system if the gutter sections are to lock in place correctly.

Fixing a sagging plastic gutter Time: 1 hour or less

If a screw holding a gutter support bracket in place comes loose the gutter can sag and water may run down the wall.

> YOU WILL NEED Ladder and stand-off, screwdriver, drill with a twist bit, zinc-plated No 8 or No 10 screws.

Remove the sagging section of the gutter then remove the loose screw and try fitting a larger one.

If this does not work, move the bracket. Mark the position of the new screw hole and hold the gutter in place to check that water flows freely to the downpipe.

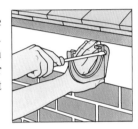

Drill new holes in the fascia board for the screws. Screw the bracket firmly in place and replace the gutter section. Check again that water flows freely.

Sealing a broken downpipe Time: 1 hour or less

Use a length of self-adhesive flashing tape (see *Tape*) to bind over small cracks. If a piece of downpipe breaks off, fix it back in place with epoxy repair paste and glass-fibre bandage (see 'Repairing leaking cast-iron guttering').

Securing a loose downpipe Time: ½ hour or less

Downpipes are held to the wall by pipe nails or screws and wall plugs. If the fixing comes loose and the downpipe vibrates, it could break or its joints could come apart.

CAST-IRON PIPE Remove the loose section of downpipe, starting from the bottom section, and working upwards.

Prise out the pipe nails with a claw hammer, using a piece of wood as a pivot, to prevent damage to the brickwork of the wall.

Hammer wooden plugs into the holes left in the wall. Trim off any surplus wood, then refix the downpipe, hammering new nails back into the filled holes.

PLASTIC PIPE Remove the screws holding the loose section of downpipe. Renew the wall plugs if necessary.

It may be easier to move the clip up or down the pipe and drill new holes to get a firm fixing. But do not move a clip positioned at a joint in a downpipe system, as it is needed to strengthen the joint. Fit an extra clip instead. Then fill any old holes with mortar or exterior filler.

JOINTS IN DOWNPIPES

Leave the joints in cast-iron downpipes unsealed because they can indicate where an obstruction is located in a blocked pipe — water will pour from the joint immediately above the blockage. If a plastic downpipe or offset bend becomes unjoined, seal the parts back together with pipe solvent adhesive (available from a plumbers' merchant or a pipe supplier) or reseat the ring seals.

Hair dryer

Cleaning an overheating hair dryer   Time: a few minutes

If the hair dryer cuts out while you are using it, or it won't start at all, the problem may simply be dirt caught in it.

A fan inside the hair dryer sucks in air through a vent at the back. The air is heated up as it travels across an electric element and then is blown out through the front.

The air being sucked in also carries loose hairs, hairspray, fluff from towels and dust, all of which will gradually accumulate in the vent.

If the build-up of debris at the back restricts the flow of air through the hair dryer, it causes the electric element to overheat and the hair dryer cuts out automatically.

Unplug the hair dryer and use tweezers to remove the accumulated grime from the grille over the vent at the back. Then clean the front and the back with a vacuum cleaner, using the soft brush attachment. To prevent the dirt from building up again, clean the hair dryer regularly.

Tightening a loose connection   Time: ½ an hour or less

If the dryer doesn't work at all, first check that it was plugged in properly. Next, unplug it from the socket and check for loose connections at both ends of the flex.

LOOSE CONNECTION AT THE PLUG If the flex is not tightly connected to the plug, rewire the plug (see *Electric plug*). Plug the dryer into the socket and test it.

If this doesn't solve the problem, put a new fuse into the plug (see *Electric plug*) and then test it again.

LOOSE CONNECTION AT THE DRYER If the hair dryer is still under guarantee, take it back to the supplier, because any attempt to repair it will invalidate the guarantee. If the guarantee has expired, however, you can try to tighten up the connections yourself.

Unplug the hair dryer and remove the screws holding the casing together. These are often inset and may be tamper-proof screws, but with a little patience you should be able to undo them. Gently prise apart the casing and inspect the wiring inside. Tighten any loose connections.

Reassemble the hair dryer, plug it in and test it.

Hammers   (SEE ALSO OPPOSITE)

Using a hammer

When using a hammer, hold the handle near the end and keep your eye on the nail. Start the nail by tapping it gently into the wood. Then swing the hammer with a firm stroke, pivoting your arm from the elbow so that the handle is at right angles to the nail, at the moment of impact.

HAMMERING SMALL NAILS Start the nail by tapping with the cross pein of a Warrington hammer (also known as a pin hammer). When the pin stands by itself, turn the hammer over and use the flat face to drive the nail home.

Support a small nail in a piece of cardboard and drive it in with a hammer until it is just above the surface of the wood. Then rip the card off. Or use a comb or piece of Blu-Tack to hold the nail in place.

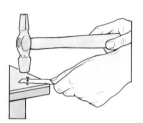

Handbag

Repairing a tear   Time: ½ an hour or less

Some leather handbags are sold with a small piece of matching leather attached to the swing tag. This can be used to patch a tear in the leather. Alternatively, look for a similar colour and weight of leather in a craft shop.

If you are unable to match the leather, and the tear is a neat one, patch it with strong webbing or a similar fabric.

> YOU WILL NEED Replacement leather or patch fabric, scissors, contact adhesive or purpose-made leather glue, appropriate solvent. Possibly: needle, thread to match lining of bag.

Cut the patching material so that it is large enough to cover the tear. Apply a thin layer of adhesive to the right side of the patch and to the inside of the damaged area. If the bag is lined, unpick the seam of the lining near the damaged area to allow easier access to the area.

Allow both surfaces to become touch-dry. Position the patch inside the torn area, ensuring that it will cover the complete length of the tear. Bring the glued surfaces together, applying gentle pressure round the edges of the tear, making as neat a patch as possible.

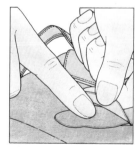

Wipe away any excess adhesive with the appropriate solvent and, if necessary, restitch the lining of the bag.

Tightening a catch on a snap-shut handbag
Time: a few minutes

> YOU WILL NEED Long-nosed pliers. Possibly: a small hammer.

The snap-shut catch on a handbag may feel loose if the two opposing pieces do not meet with sufficient pressure. This can usually be fixed with a pair of long-nosed pliers.

Continued on page 186

HAMMERS

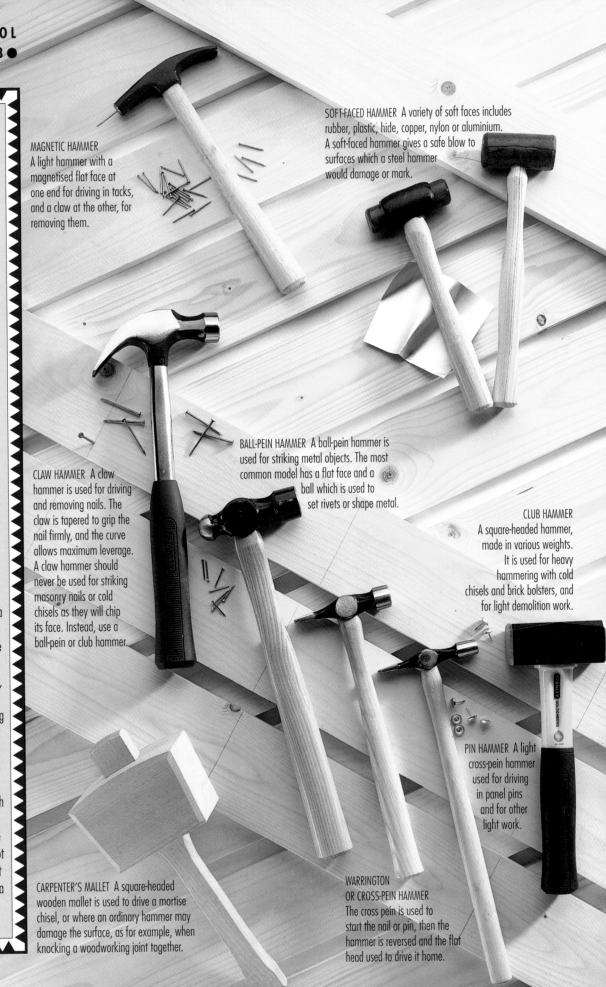

Different types of hammer are used for a wide range of DIY applications. There are hammers designed to tap fine tacks in place, drive in large nails, assemble woodworking joints and lever out nails. Mallets and hammers are used to drive chisels for fine woodwork or for rough masonry jobs. Some hammers have soft faces, and will not damage surfaces that would be marked by a metal hammer.

MAGNETIC HAMMER A light hammer with a magnetised flat face at one end for driving in tacks, and a claw at the other, for removing them.

SOFT-FACED HAMMER A variety of soft faces includes rubber, plastic, hide, copper, nylon or aluminium. A soft-faced hammer gives a safe blow to surfaces which a steel hammer would damage or mark.

CLAW HAMMER A claw hammer is used for driving and removing nails. The claw is tapered to grip the nail firmly, and the curve allows maximum leverage. A claw hammer should never be used for striking masonry nails or cold chisels as they will chip its face. Instead, use a ball-pein or club hammer.

BALL-PEIN HAMMER A ball-pein hammer is used for striking metal objects. The most common model has a flat face and a ball which is used to set rivets or shape metal.

CLUB HAMMER A square-headed hammer, made in various weights. It is used for heavy hammering with cold chisels and brick bolsters, and for light demolition work.

PIN HAMMER A light cross-pein hammer used for driving in panel pins and for other light work.

CARPENTER'S MALLET A square-headed wooden mallet is used to drive a mortise chisel, or where an ordinary hammer may damage the surface, as for example, when knocking a woodworking joint together.

WARRINGTON OR CROSS-PEIN HAMMER The cross pein is used to start the nail or pin, then the hammer is reversed and the flat head used to drive it home.

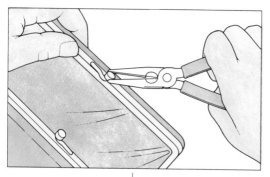

Use the pliers to adjust one or both sides of the catch, twisting them so that you increase the pressure under which they meet one another. Keep on adjusting until the catch closes firmly and reopens easily under moderate pressure.

You may find that the catch has loosened because the handbag's side hinges have come loose. In this case, open the bag and place the outside of the hinge on a hard, flat surface, so that the pin that holds the hinge is exposed.

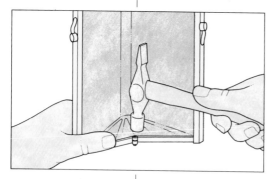

Working inside the open bag, use a small hammer to lightly tap the head of the pin. Keep on tapping the pin head and testing the hinge until it feels tighter.

Heater:

SEE ELECTRIC FIRE; GAS HEATER

DISGUISING AN OLD HEMLINE

When lengthening a child's skirt or trousers, you can cover the old hemline with braid, rickrack, ribbon or lace.

Hems

A hem provides a neat finish to a piece of fabric. It may be as part of a garment, such as a skirt, or on soft furnishings, such as curtains or loose covers for furniture.

To make hems as unnoticeable as possible, use matching thread and keep the stitches very small and regular (see *Stitches*), catching up the minimum fabric in each.

On skirts and trousers, do not leave long gaps between stitches as they could allow a heel to catch in a gap and rip down a whole section of the hem.

Making a rolled hem   Time: depends on length

Rolled hems are very narrow and should never be pressed. They are often used on fine fabrics such as silk and chiffon, where a conventional hem would look unsightly.

YOU WILL NEED Fine needle, matching thread.

Trim the edge to be hemmed to a clean, straight line. Remove any frayed threads. Do not pin the fabric at all, but roll the edge of the fabric until the raw edge is concealed. For the best results, use a fine needle and matching thread.

EMERGENCY HEM REPAIR

When there is no time to restitch a hem that has come down partially, a length of double-sided adhesive tape will provide a short-term repair.

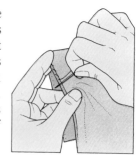

Keeping tension on the rolled edge, so that it does not unroll, take the smallest possible hemming stitches (see *Stitches*). Work a small part of the hem at a time, keeping the rolled hem as narrow as possible. End off neatly and securely.

Rolled hems can be made by machine, using a special foot that rolls the fabric and holds it in place while it is stitched. They are not as neat and inconspicuous as hand-stitched rolled hems, and are more suitable for hemming flared skirts and the bottoms of blouses or shirts.

Making a false hem   Time: depends on length

A false hem is a good way to lengthen trousers and skirts, but calls for matching fabric or one that is similar in colour and weight. Wide bias binding of a matching colour, available in haberdashery departments, is often used.

YOU WILL NEED Sharp pointed scissors or an unpicking tool, extra fabric or binding, pins, matching thread, needle.

Unpick the existing hem and remove any debris that may have collected inside it. Clean the garment and press it well to remove all traces of the original hemline.

Cut a piece of matching fabric of the required depth and length. Wherever pieces will join, add a seam allowance of 1.9 cm ($\frac{3}{4}$ in). For a better result, cut the fabric on the cross – that is, diagonally across the fabric's grain.

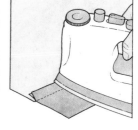

With right sides facing, stitch the new fabric to the end of the garment.

Then turn the garment inside out and press the hem seam allowance upwards, to lie flat (right).

Fold the new hem up inside the garment and press along the new hemline. Make sure the false hem is not visible from the outside. Stitch the new hem in place with small, neat hemming stitches (see *Stitches*).

If you are using wide bias, open the larger hem of the binding and pin it, along its fold line to the right side of the old hem. Stitch it by hand or with a sewing machine.

Turn it to the inside of the garment, press it so that it is invisible from the front, and stitch it neatly in place.

Hemming a leather garment Time: depends on length

Leather is usually too bulky to be hemmed in the normal way. It should be either top-stitched or glued in place.

> YOU WILL NEED Chalk, paperclips, scissors. Possibly: wedge-point machine needle, matching thread, contact adhesive or purpose-made leather glue, mallet.

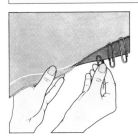

Leather can be damaged by pins, so mark the hem with chalk and fold it up with paperclips.

TOP-STITCHED HEM To reduce bulkiness, trim away any excess leather so that a hem of only 1.6 cm ($\frac{5}{8}$ in) is left.

Using a wedge-point needle, machine-stitch along the right side of the garment, 1.3 cm ($\frac{1}{2}$ in) from the edge. The stitch-length setting should be 3-4 mm (6-8 per in).

If necessary, add a second row of top-stitching, 3 mm ($\frac{1}{8}$ in) below the first. Press with the iron at a low setting, using a press-cloth to protect the leather.

GLUED HEM With a pencil or piece of chalk, mark the position of the hem on the right side of the garment and trim off any excess, allowing a 5 cm (2 in) turn up.

Spread glue on the inside of the hem and the area it will cover when it is turned up. Make sure you are using a glue that allows you to move the glued surfaces for a short while after contact. Special glues for leather are available.

Fold up the hem along the marked line and, working upwards from the fold, finger-press the surfaces together. To make sure that no glue gets onto the right side of the garment, keep cleaning your fingers as you work.

To ease the fullness on a hem that curves, cut small wedges out of the raw edge and force the edges together, making sure that the finished curve is smooth and has no 'corners' on it.

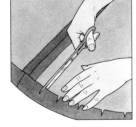

When you have pressed the entire hem into place, beat it gently on the inside with a wooden mallet.

Make sure that the hem is completely dry before you wear the garment.

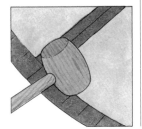

Hi-fi (SEE ALSO CASSETTE RECORDER)

Most hi-fi units consist of a turntable for records, a radio tuner, a CD player, a single or double cassette unit, an amplifier and two loudspeakers.

Rack systems are usually made up of separate units and are often mounted in a cabinet. Midi systems are similar to full-sized rack systems but are smaller. Mini and micro systems are even smaller and do not include a record turntable.

Hi-fi units will usually need little cleaning or maintenance if they are properly used and cared for.

Cleaning a hi-fi unit Time: a few minutes

Always unplug the hi-fi unit and remove any cassettes, records or CDs before starting to clean it.

> YOU WILL NEED Lint-free cloth, aerosol household cleaner.

Before using a cleaning liquid, test it on a small area of the hi-fi that is not usually visible to make quite sure that it doesn't mark the finish. Never use a cleaner that contains bleach or ammonia.

Spray the cleaner onto a cloth, without over-wetting, and wipe the unit thoroughly. Never spray or pour the cleaner directly onto the hi-fi and don't let any liquid get inside the components. Polish with a clean, dry cloth.

What to do if the power light fails to come on
Time: a few minutes

First, make sure that the hi-fi is plugged in and that both the mains socket and the hi-fi are switched on. If the light still does not work, make the following checks.

> YOU WILL NEED Possibly: screwdriver, new fuse, table lamp.

Check the mains socket by plugging in a table lamp or some household appliance and making sure that it works. If it doesn't, see *Electric socket*.

If the lamp does work, replace the fuse in the hi-fi plug. The hi-fi may be plugged into a four-way adapter, in which case you will need a 13 amp fuse in the adapter plug and an appropriate fuse in each of the hi-fi plugs. Refer to the hi-fi manuals for fuse ratings.

If the hi-fi still does not operate, contact the supplier, the manufacturer or a hi-fi repair shop. To find a hi-fi repairer, look in *Yellow Pages* under 'Hi-fi'.

What to do if a turntable gives poor-quality sound
Time: depends on extent of the job

> YOU WILL NEED Cotton bud, record-cleaning fluid, antistatic cloth (all from hi-fi shops). Possibly: new stylus or cartridge.

If you are getting poor quality or muffled sound when you play a record, it is most probably being caused by a build-up of dirt on the pick-up stylus (or needle).

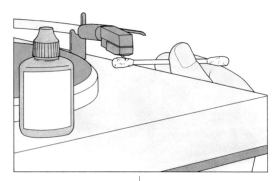

Dip a cotton bud into record-cleaning fluid and carefully wipe it against the stylus with a back-to-front movement. Take great care, as any rough treatment will damage the stylus, leading to complete failure.

Inspect the record for any dust, hairs or dirt and carefully wipe it clean with an antistatic cloth. If the sound quality is still poor, the stylus may need replacing.

Following the instructions in the hi-fi manual, remove the stylus (possibly together with the pick-up cartridge). Obtain a replacement from a hi-fi shop or the manufacturer, and fit it into the pick-up arm.

Poor reception on the tuner

Should the tuner produce a bad sound, make sure that the FM and AM aerials are plugged in and that you are tuned to a known station. Newspapers list the frequencies.

Check if you are in a poor reception area. A better aerial will make an improvement (see *Radio aerial*).

If the problem persists, it suggests a fault with the tuner. Return it to the supplier or the manufacturer, or take it to a hi-fi repair shop. Look in *Yellow Pages* under 'Hi-fi'.

The CD player jumps or sticks Time: 1 hour or less

> YOU WILL NEED Antistatic cloth, CD repair-and-cleaning kit, small clean paintbrush, cotton bud.

If a CD jumps, gets stuck or does not play correctly, remove the disc and look for any hairs, marks, greasy fingerprints or scratches. Wipe it carefully with an antistatic cloth.

You can probably fix it with a repair kit, if it has been scratched. The three-stage process involves cleaning, filling and protecting the disc. Instructions come with the kit.

If the fault persists, debris may have become stuck inside the player. Remove the CD, then switch off the unit at the mains. If your model has a lid that opens to give access to the mechanism, inspect the inside for any hairs or dust. Use a small, clean paintbrush very carefully and remove any particles. A cotton bud can also be used to remove particles from hard-to-reach corners.

The player may not allow access to the mechanism (as in the drawer-loading types) in which case, use a high-pressure aerosol containing only air, which can be bought at some camera shops. Make sure that it is an air-only type, then put the end as far inside as you can and give several blasts of air. This may clear out the debris.

If the fault persists, check the laser lens for any dirt, fluff or greasy finger marks. They will need cleaning off.

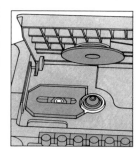

The lens is small and circular, looking rather like a fish eye, and is usually found on the bottom of the unit, towards the centre.

If it is a drawer-loading model, you may be able to dislodge dust, which could be causing the problem, by using an air-only aerosol spray. These are available from camera shops.

Finally, if the CD player is still malfunctioning, return it to your supplier, the manufacturer or a hi-fi repair shop (look in *Yellow Pages* under 'Hi-fi').

Sound comes from one speaker only

> YOU WILL NEED Set of headphones. Possibly: second set of speakers.

Plug a set of headphones into the headphone socket on the hi-fi amplifier to discover if the fault lies with the speaker or the hi-fi. If only one of the headphones works, the fault lies with the hi-fi and you should take it to the supplier, the manufacturer or a hi-fi repair shop. If the system consists of separate units, and all of the parts play through one speaker you only need to take back the amplifier.

If both headphones work, check that the speaker leads are plugged in correctly, both at the hi-fi and speaker ends. If the fault persists, swap the leads between speakers. If the fault then occurs on the other speaker, the lead is faulty and needs replacing.

If the original fault persists, borrow a second pair of speakers and try using them. If the fault still continues, the cause lies in the hi-fi amplifier. If the fault is cured, the speaker is faulty.

Whatever the result, contact the supplier, manufacturer or a hi-fi repair shop to get an estimate for repairs. Look in *Yellow Pages* under 'Hi-fi' for repair specialists.

No sound comes from either speaker

> YOU WILL NEED Set of headphones. Possibly: second set of speakers.

Plug a set of headphones into the headphone socket on the hi-fi amplifier. If the headphones do not work, the fault lies with the hi-fi. Take the hi-fi unit back to the supplier or the manufacturer or to a hi-fi repairer.

If both the headphones work, check that the speaker leads are properly connected to the hi-fi and the speakers.

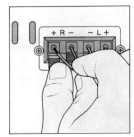

If the fault persists, borrow another pair of speakers and plug them into the hi-fi. If the fault still persists, it lies with the hi-fi unit. If it is cured, your speakers are faulty. Contact the supplier, the manufacturer or a hi-fi repairer for a repair estimate. Look in *Yellow Pages* under 'Hi-fi'.

Hiring equipment

The correct tools will make a job quicker and easier. Most tools can now be hired. Tell the hire company what job you are doing and they will recommend the best tools.

Check on the deposit, as well as delivery and collection charges, and the accessories and safety gear available in advance. Get a demonstration of any unfamiliar or dangerous equipment and written safety instructions.

Do not accept any electrical equipment with patched or damaged cable or with the internal insulation showing where the cable enters the tool or plug, and always use a residual current device (see *RCD*) with 230 volt equipment.

Hire shops usually require two documents (such as a bill, driving licence or passport), and a deposit to cover any damage. Some offer a damage waiver of about 10 per cent of the hire charge which is paid in advance, and saves you the cost of replacing accidentally damaged equipment.

Equipment can be hired for a day, a weekend, a week or longer. If you need the tools for longer than agreed, call the hire shop and advise them.

To find a reputable equipment-hiring company contact Hire Association Europe, 722 College Road, Birmingham B44 OAJ (Tel. 0121 377 7707) who will put you in touch with local HAE members.

Or else look in *Yellow Pages* under 'Hire Services – Tool and equipment'.

SKIP HIRE Companies offering skips for hire are listed in *Yellow Pages* under 'Skip hire'. Get a number of quotes first, including one from your local authority which may offer better rates than commercial operators.

If the skip is to stand on a public road, you will need a council permit. Check that lamps are supplied to hang on the skip at night. Wherever the skip is positioned, it must not cause an obstruction or pose a risk to pedestrians.

Home security

Even simple precautions will deter an opportunist intruder. To guard against a break-in, keep ladders and garden spades locked away, never leave windows open when you go out, do not leave keys under the mat or hanging inside the letterbox, and fit the best locks you can afford – or which your insurance company recommends.

FRONT DOOR A simple cylinder nightlatch does not offer adequate protection against a determined intruder.

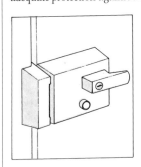

Replace it with a deadlocking cylinder nightlatch. This type of latch cannot be moved without the key once the key has been turned. This means that even if a panel of glass beside the latch is broken by an intruder, the latch cannot be turned by hand to open the door.

For extra security, add a mortise deadlock lower down the door. The five lever model is the most secure. Make sure the mortise deadlock you buy conforms to BS3621.

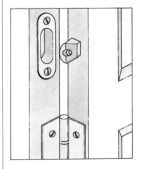

Hinge bolts add extra protection, particularly to outward opening doors. These bolts are fixed on the hinge side of the door and, when the door is closed, prevent it from being levered from its hinges.

A peephole viewer allows you to inspect callers without opening the door. The lens gives a wide-angle view of the doorway, without the caller being able to see in. Ideally, link the viewer with a porch light so that you can see who is calling at night, before opening the door.

A door restraint or door chain allows you to speak to callers without fully opening the door. Choose one which fixes securely to the door and frame.

BACK DOOR A back door is more vulnerable because it is usually hidden from the road. Have rack bolts fitted at the top and bottom of the door for extra security.

REDUCING TOOL-HIRE COSTS

Plan the job thoroughly, then prepare the location and do as much work as possible before hiring the equipment. This should save time and keep hire costs to a minimum. Avoid delivery costs by arranging to collect and return small items yourself.

BUYING HIRE EQUIPMENT

Hiring a piece of equipment may help you decide whether it is worth purchasing your own. Some hire shops arrange the sale of equipment you would like to keep, and it may be more economical to buy if work is to be extended over a long period.

MAKE SURE YOU ARE COVERED

Before deciding which measures to take to protect your home, check your insurance policy. Many policies spell out what security measures they expect to be taken. You must comply with the measures to ensure that a claim is met.

If you are in any doubt, talk to the crime prevention officer at your local police station.

A rack bolt is housed in the edge of the door and is operated from the inside by a serrated key. There are no visible signs of the rack bolt's existence on the outside of the door to alert a potential intruder.

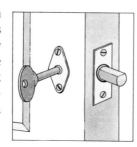

Replace any glass that could be at risk with laminated glass, which contains a tough layer of clear plastic, sandwiched between two panes of glass. Though the glazing may be cracked, it is almost impossible to break.

CASEMENT WINDOWS Various devices are available to prevent the window being opened even if the glass is broken. The lock may prevent the handle moving; it may anchor the casement stay, or it may lock the frames together. A version of the rack bolt, commonly used on doors, is available with a shorter bolt, for windows. Fixing instructions are supplied with each type of window lock.

SASH WINDOWS Fit bolts that lock the two sashes together. Some can be fixed so that the window can be opened for ventilation without affecting security.

LOUVRE WINDOWS To stop the glass in older windows from being prised from the frames, use an epoxy-resin adhesive or silicone-rubber sealant to seal it into the frames.

BURGLAR ALARMS Get expert help in choosing a burglar alarm system by contacting the crime prevention officer through your local police station. He or she can advise you which type of alarm is best suited to your needs, and recommend a reputable installer. The advice is free.

Types range from a simple independent battery operated unit, sensitive to movement or body heat, to systems involving micro switches on windows, doors and under carpets. Be sure to choose a reliable system. In many areas alarm systems must be registered with the police, who need to be notified of at least two keyholders. There must be a 20 minute cut-out period for audible alarms.

LIGHTING UP THE HOUSE A dark house advertises that there is no one home. Lights and electrical equipment can be turned off and on when you are out, using time switches and lights operated by a photoelectric cell.

Outdoor security lights which detect heat or movement are also available. Make sure that they are high enough not to be tampered with. (See also *Security lights*.)

HOME SAFE Small safes are available to hold valuables such as jewellery. Some are installed under a floor, others in a wall while others are disguised as power sockets.

MARKING YOUR VALUABLES

To make it easier to recover your valuables if they are stolen, engrave your initials and postcode onto them with an electric engraving kit (see margin, p.173). Or use a special marker, which becomes visible only under ultraviolet light.

HOOKS AND EYES ARE NOT FOR EVERYONE

Don't use hooks and eyes on children's clothes or on dolls' clothes. They are difficult for children to do up. Velcro touch-and-close tape and press studs or snap fasteners are much easier for children to use. People who have difficulty using their hands will also manage press studs more easily than hooks and eyes.

Security inside the house

Unless internal doors lead to passageways or other flats, leave them free of locks. Once an intruder is in the premises he may cause considerable damage breaking them open. The same applies to drawers and cupboards: keep valuables in a safe instead.

Alternatively clean out a food can with a lid and use this to store small valuable items, hidden among the other cans in the food cupboard.

Hooks & eyes

Use hooks and eyes to close an opening in a garment when you want the edges to meet without overlapping, or to overlap by only the smallest amount. They are usually sewn on by hand and are not very strong, so they should not be used where any pressure will be exerted on the closure.

Making a new eye Time: a few minutes

If an eye has come off, make a new eye with matching thread, to avoid having to replace the hook and eye set.

Remove any pieces of thread remaining from the lost eye. The new eye will go in the same position on the garment, unless the garment was previously too loose or too tight.

Secure the thread on the inside of the garment and bring the needle up through one of the fixing marks and down through the other to create a loop the size of the original eye.

Take two or three more stitches through the same spots and secure the thread at the back, but do not cut it off. This part of it creates the basis of the new straight eye.

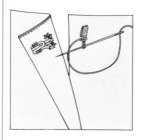

Bring the thread to the front again and cover the stitches of the new eye with fine blanket stitches (see *Stitches*).

When the entire eye has been covered in this way, take the thread through to the back and fasten off securely.

Hose

Repairing a leaking hose Time: 1 hour or less

Should you accidentally pierce your hose with a garden fork, or discover that it has split, repairing it is quite easy. Hose repair connectors are available in garden centres, hardware shops and DIY centres. Make sure that you buy a connector that has the same diameter as your hose – it will probably be 12 mm ($\frac{1}{2}$ in).

YOU WILL NEED Trimming knife, screw-on hose connector.

Disconnect the hose from the water supply and cut away the damaged section of the hose, making sure you leave a clean edge. Then fit the hose connector according to the manufacturer's instructions.

With a three-piece connector, take the connector apart and fit each of the two outer sections into a cut end of the hose.

Attach the centre piece to one section and screw the other onto it. The tighter they are screwed together, the more effective the connection will be.

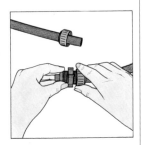

Adding a double-check valve to an outdoor tap
Time: $\frac{1}{2}$ an hour or less

Outdoor taps are required by law to be fitted with a double-check valve which prevents fertiliser or pesticide being siphoned from a hose-end feeder back up through the tap. This could happen if there were a sudden demand for water – by the fire brigade, for example.

Most garden taps have a threaded spout, and the double-check valve screws straight onto it.

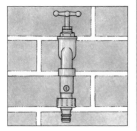

If, however, your garden tap has a smooth spout, there are two options: either get a plumber to fit a new tap that incorporates a double-check valve, or buy a pair of hose connectors that convert a smooth spout to a threaded one.

What kind of hose connector?
Various fittings make it possible to connect hoses to taps and to a range of accessories, such as sprinklers.

HOSE-END CONNECTOR
Used at both ends of a hose to connect it to a tap connector and accessories such as sprinklers.

DOUBLE MALE CONNECTOR Snap fits to two hose-end connectors to temporarily join two lengths of hose.

Y CONNECTOR A three-way connector that joins a hose to two others, to allow watering in two places at once.

ROUND-TAP CONNECTOR
Connects a hose to a standard, round or oval-spouted garden tap, which has no thread.

THREADED-TAP CONNECTOR Screws onto garden taps with a threaded spout, to be used with a hose-end connector.

MULTI-TAP CONNECTOR
Fits a wide variety of square, round and mixer taps.

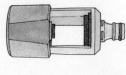

DUAL-TAP CONNECTOR
Allows two hoses to be connected to the same tap. They can then be used together or singly.

Choosing a hose

Hose can be bought in lengths that range from 15 m (49 ft) to 50 m (164 ft). If you need a longer hose, buy two lengths and join them with a connector. Choose a multi-purpose hose with a braided reinforcement – most are guaranteed for about ten years.

A hose will last longer if it is stored on a reel. Most reels come complete with a length of hose attached. Choose one that has a smooth unwinding action when pulled from any direction.

Cassettes of fabric hose are compact and, because water is squeezed out as the hose is wound back into the cassette, are lighter to carry about. However, the whole hose has to be unwound before it can be used.

WINTER STORAGE FOR HOSES

Few hoses are designed to remain outdoors in winter; water trapped inside the hose may freeze and expand, causing the hose to split. Unless the hose can be stored in a very sheltered spot outdoors, it is best to take it into a shed or garage.

KEEPING A HOSE OFF THE PLANTS

Plants often get damaged when a hose is dragged across a flowerbed by mistake. Prevent this by hammering small stakes into the ground at appropriate points before starting to water. They will prevent the hose 'cutting corners' and breaking young plants.

Hot-water cylinder

Leaking hot-water cylinder – emergency action

A LARGE LEAK Stop water entering the hot-water cylinder. There are three possible ways to do this. Either close the gate valve on the cold-supply pipe from the cold-water tank to the hot-water cylinder (this is usually the pipe going through the ceiling above the hot-water cylinder). Or tie up the ball float in the cold-water tank (see *Ball valve*). Or, if it is supplied direct from the mains, turn off the main stopcock (usually under the kitchen sink or in the cellar).

Turn on the hot taps in the bathroom to drain the pipes and switch off the central heating and any immersion heater. Then drain the hot-water cylinder.

Drain a thermal storage unit, a combination boiler or the internal coil of an indirect cylinder at the boiler (see below and *Central-heating boiler*).

Drain an immersion heater, a direct cylinder and an indirect cylinder at the drain cock, which is found on the pipe supplying cold water at the base of the cylinder. To do this, connect a hose to the drain cock, run it to an external drain or a toilet, then open the drain cock.

If you cannot open the drain cock, you will have to siphon out the contents of the hot-water cylinder once the water has stopped flowing from the bathroom taps.

Start by removing the hot-water outlet pipe from the top of the cylinder, or from the immersion heater.

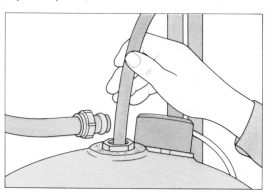

Insert a hosepipe and take the other end to an outside drain or a toilet. Suck the end of the pipe until the flow of water begins, then leave the water to drain out.

Once the system is drained and the leak has stopped, call a plumber or heating engineer (see *Plumber*).

DO NOT TOUCH

Do not try to repair a modern, high-pressure hot-water cylinder yourself. Instead, call a heating engineer (see *Plumber*).
A high-pressure hot-water cylinder has the following distinguishing characteristics:
- There will be some written indication on the cylinder.
- The cylinder has a safety valve.
- There is no cold-water tank.

Understanding the hot-water system

IMMERSION HEATER Cold water is piped into a hot-water cylinder. It is heated by one or two electric heating elements inserted through the cylinder wall. An immersion heater may be used in conjunction with other types of hot-water cylinders to supplement the hot-water supply in a house.

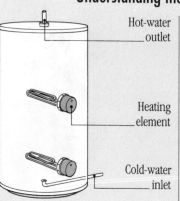

Hot-water outlet

Heating element

Cold-water inlet

CYLINDER AND BOILER Domestic hot water is heated directly or indirectly by a boiler and stored in a cylinder.
In an indirect system (right), the boiler heats water which runs through a coil in the cylinder to heat cold water piped from the cold-water tank. In a direct system, water is heated by a back boiler then piped to a cylinder to be stored.

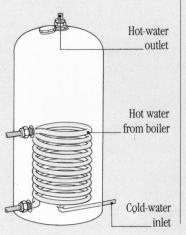

Hot-water outlet

Hot water from boiler

Cold-water inlet

COMBINATION BOILER Mains cold water is heated as it passes through the boiler on its way to the taps. The boiler also heats water for the radiators. This system has no cold-water tank or hot-water storage cylinder and is most suitable if the amount of hot water required is quite small – for example, in a flat or a small semi-detached house.

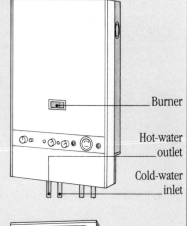

Burner

Hot-water outlet

Cold-water inlet

THERMAL STORAGE UNIT The boiler heats water which is stored in a cylinder. Mains pressure cold water runs through a coil in the centre of the cylinder where it is heated very quickly by the hot water surrounding it. This system provides hot water at mains water pressure.

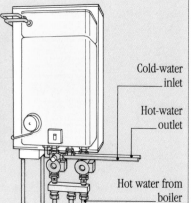

Cold-water inlet

Hot-water outlet

Hot water from boiler

A SMALL LEAK Damp linen in the airing cupboard could indicate that there is a small leak in a hot-water cylinder.

If the cylinder has a coat of foam insulation do not try to repair it. Drain it (see facing page) and call a plumber or heating engineer. If the cylinder has a removable insulating jacket or no jacket, you can try to repair it.

For a tiny leak, using Fernox LS-X or Plastic Padding to stop the hole is the simplest temporary solution. Take off the insulating jacket and clean the area, first with medium and then fine sandpaper.

Squeeze a small amount of leak sealant onto the hole. Place a lightly oiled coin over it, and hold it in place with a strip of porous adhesive tape (medical tape will do). Once it has stopped, call a plumber to investigate the cause of the leak and repair it.

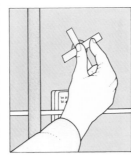

Preventing frost damage to the system

CYLINDER COLLAPSE In cold weather, ice may block the pipes to and from the hot-water cylinder, sealing the system. As a result a partial vacuum can form inside the cylinder, causing the walls to collapse.

To avoid this, insulate the pipes in the loft (see *Insulation*) and in cold weather keep the central heating on overnight, but turn down the room thermostat.

IF YOU GO AWAY IN THE WINTER On an indirect system, alter the timer and room thermostat so that the heating comes on at a low level in the coldest hours.

If you have a direct cylinder hot-water system heated by an independent boiler, a back boiler or an electric immersion heater, drain the system.

Attach a hose to the drain cock (usually located beside the boiler or on the cold-water pipe supplying it). Take the other end to an outside drain. Then close the main stopcock and open the drain cock.

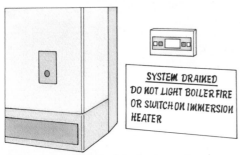

SYSTEM DRAINED
DO NOT LIGHT BOILER FIRE
OR SWITCH ON IMMERSION
HEATER

Make a warning sign and display it prominently next to the switch for the boiler and/or immersion heater.

House-dust mites

House-dust mites do not bite, but their faeces contain a protein believed to trigger asthma attacks and wheezing. They are barely visible and live in carpets, soft furnishings and bedding, feeding on scales shed from human skin.

Reducing levels of house-dust mites

It is impossible to eradicate house-dust mites entirely, but there are ways to reduce the levels in your home.

VACUUM-CLEAN EVERY WEEK Vacuum mattresses and pillows at least once a week using the upholstery tool. Use the machine's crevice tool on foam mattresses.

Set the vacuum cleaner to 'low', if possible, in order not to pull off buttons.

If anyone in your home is allergic to house-dust mites, it may be worth buying a vacuum cleaner designed to retain house-dust mites in its dust-collecting bag or container. The makers claim this reduces allergic reactions.

REGULAR CLEANING Wash or dry-clean pillows at least every six months, and wash or dry-clean blankets, underblankets and duvets at least once a year. Follow the care instructions supplied with each item.

CONTROL HUMIDITY You can keep house-dust mites at bay by keeping down the level of humidity in your house.

Beds make a humid refuge and breeding ground for house-dust mites because each year an average human loses 204 litres (45 gallons) of sweat in bed.

You can significantly decrease the level of humidity in a bedroom by sleeping with a window open, and airing the room and beds as often as possible. A dehumidifier in the room may also help. Also, do not damp-dust the furniture, avoid hanging washing over radiators to dry, and do not keep pot plants or glasses of water in a bedroom.

Houseplants

Houseplants live in an environment that is not natural to them, so they are susceptible to various disorders. If they are treated promptly and correctly, however, they may be saved from severe debilitation or even death.

The most common causes of death in houseplants are underwatering or overwatering. Consult a good gardening guide to find out how often to water indoor plants.

REPLACING A CYLINDER

When you ask a plumber or heating installer to supply and install a new hot-water storage cylinder it will save time if you can give the dimensions of the existing cylinder and say what type it is (see facing page).

MITEPROOF BED LINEN

Miteproof mattress covers act as a barrier against the mites' faeces, but they are only effective when used with new or clean bedding.

GETTING MEDICAL HELP

Ask your doctor for help in dealing with an allergy to house-dust mites. He or she may also be able to advise on appropriate products to combat the mites.

Faultfinder guide: Houseplants

Brown spots or blotches on leaves

CAUSE They could be the result of too much strong sunlight through water droplets on the foliage. Or they could be fungal leaf spots.
REMEDY Move plant out of direct sunlight. Treat fungal spots regularly with a systemic fungicide.

Sudden fall of leaves

CAUSE If there has been no previous sign of distress, this could be due to shock, caused by extreme heat or cold, or the severe drying out of the roots.
REMEDY Identify the source of shock and remove the plant from its influence. Move it to a more suitable position and try to keep it properly watered.

Yellowing leaves

CAUSE Some plants, such as azaleas, prefer acid conditions. Most tap water is alkaline or 'hard'.
REMEDY Water only with treated water such as distilled water, rainwater (which tends to be acid) or filtered water (which has had most of the lime removed). Do not use water that has passed through a water-softener, because it contains salts that are harmful to plants.

Spindly, pale leaf growth

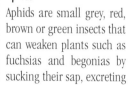

CAUSE This is probably the result of too little sun and too much water or fertiliser.
REMEDY Move the plant to a brighter position but don't let it get too hot, and do not overwater, especially during winter.

Leaves falling from a new or recently repotted plant

CAUSE The problem could be the caused by the trauma of being moved from one site to another, or into a much larger container.
REMEDY Try to minimise shock to a plant by acclimatising it slowly to changes in environment, such as the journey from a warm garden centre to a cold car, without some form of protection such as a bag or plastic cover; or from a bright conservatory to a dark corner indoors.

When repotting, avoid transferring the plant into a considerably larger pot, even if you expect it to grow very big eventually. Take it up in gradual stages, each pot a little larger than the one before.

Damaged leaves

CAUSE Some plants have very sensitive and brittle leaves which can be damaged if people brush past them regularly. Alternatively, the plant may be in a position that causes the leaves to press against a wall. If there are holes in the leaves, it may be that insect pests of some sort are attacking it.
REMEDY Move the plant to a safer or more spacious position. Check for signs of insects and treat accordingly (see 'Identifying pests and diseases').

Flowers drop off at bud stage, or do not form at all

CAUSE Could be the result of a succession of shocks, such as irregular watering, being moved to a draughty position or very dry air in a centrally heated room.
REMEDY Stand the plant on a bed of pebbles in a tray of water and spray it with water regularly. Check the soil for moisture, often.

CARING FOR PLANTS IN A CENTRALLY HEATED HOME

Centrally heated homes present plants with much drier environments than they would experience in natural conditions. In order to keep them healthy and growing well, make sure they get the right amount of humidity.
Plants bought in garden centres and nurseries usually have care instructions. Alternatively, consult a gardening book.
Some houseplants respond well to a regular, gentle spray of water. Others need to stand on pebbles kept moist in a tray. Grouping plants together so that they create a microclimate of their own, works well too.

Identifying pests and diseases
Aphids

Aphids are small grey, red, brown or green insects that can weaken plants such as fuchsias and begonias by sucking their sap, excreting sticky honeydew and also transmitting viruses. In addition, they may cause sooty mould.
TREATMENT Aphids are fairly susceptible to insecticides and can be treated with soft soaps or derris dust, both of which are acceptable to organic gardeners.

Chemical pesticides such as permethrin and malathion are also suitable for the treatment of aphids.

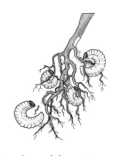

Vine weevils

The signs are badly stunted and wilting new growth. The adults are seldom seen, as they attack leaves at night, but when the plant is lifted out of the pot, small cream-coloured grubs, about 2.5 cm (1 in) long will be seen in the compost and round the roots.

TREATMENT This once-rare pest has become common. If the plant is in really bad condition, throw it away, but treat the rest of your houseplants which are very likely to have become infected with vine weevils, too.

The only really effective treatment is a biopesticide containing specially selected, naturally occurring nematodes – small, predatory organisms that quickly dispose of the pests. Most garden centres stock details of both the Nature's Friend and the Defenders' nematode treatments.

Sooty mould

Seen as black mould growing on the honeydew from sap-sucking pests. It clogs the leaf pores and reduces the plant's ability to absorb light. It is often seen on citrus plants because they are prone to aphids.

TREATMENT Remove the sooty mould with a cloth soaked in a solution of washing-up liquid, and then eliminate the insects that caused the honeydew – they are very likely to be aphids, whitefly or scale insects (see details for the treatment of these pests elsewhere in this section).

Red spider mite

These mites are so tiny that they are extremely hard to see. The signs of their presence on houseplants include yellow speckling or black spots on leaves. In addition, there may be premature leaf-fall and sometimes a white web between stem and leaf.

Red spider mite will attack a variety of plants but are particularly damaging to busy lizzies (*Impatiens*).

TREATMENT Bio controls are most effective if you have a severe infestation. Both Nature's Friend and Defenders have a treatment for red spider mite.

Treatments such as derris dust, malathion and systemic insecticides can also be used, but it appears that many red spider mites are resistant to insecticides.

Whitefly

An infestation of whitefly will show up as large numbers of white larvae, up to 3 mm ($\frac{1}{8}$ in) long, on the undersides of leaves, especially on the leaves of pelargoniums and tomato plants.

The larvae suck sap and produce sticky honeydew that encourages sooty mould. Adults look like minute moths.

TREATMENT Spray with permethrin or pyrethrum or an insecticidal soap such as Safer's for Houseplants until all signs of infestation have disappeared. Do not repeat too often – whitefly quickly develop resistance to pesticides.

Mealy bug

These pests look like small bits of white fluff and are found under leaves and clustered on the stems of a plant.

TREATMENT Treat at once, wiping the bugs off with a damp cloth. For very severe infestation, spray the plant with a systemic insecticide.

Grey mould (botrytis)

Seen as fluffy grey mould covering stems and leaves and spreading to buds and flowers. In cool, moist, still conditions, begonias, cyclamen and gloxinias seem to be particularly susceptible.

TREATMENT Cut away the affected part of the plant, improve ventilation, reduce misting and watering. Move the plant to a warmer position and, if necessary, use benomyl to discourage further infection.

Scale insects

Protected by a waxy cover, they excrete a sticky honeydew on ferns and plants of the citrus family. Inspect the underside of leaves for numerous tiny brown or transparent discs stuck along the veins.

TREATMENT Remove the scale by hand, gently prising it off with a finger nail. Alternatively, wipe the leaves with a cotton-wool swab dampened with methylated spirit. Very few sprays will prove really effective against scale.

Houseplants (cont.)

Trouble-free houseplants to enliven a home

Philodendron scandens

One of the easiest house-plants to grow, it is also known as heartleaf philo-dendron as its glossy leaves are heart-shaped. They go deep green as they mature. It is a climbing plant but can be made to bush by pinching out some of the growing tips.

Spathiphyllum wallisii Known as a peace lily or sail plant, it will tolerate shade and the high temperatures of modern houses as long as it is kept in moist soil. Placing the pot

on damp gravel in a saucer or planter helps to maintain the moisture.

This plant is grown for its fountain of glossy, dark green leaves and its white, sail-like flower heads, which appear in spring and late summer and last for a long time. It grows to a height of about 30 cm (12 in).

Tradescantia fluminensis Popular and very accommodating, this small-leaved, trailing plant is better known as

Wandering Jew. Its pointed leaves have deep purple un-dersides. Not only is it very easy to grow indoors, but it is quite easily propagated by planting stem-tip cuttings in the compost.

An attractive variation, Quicksilver, has variegated, white-striped leaves and grows robustly indoors.

Aspidistra elatior This most favourite of Victorian house-plants is also called the cast-iron plant because it tolerates shade, pollution and a much greater degree of neglect than most house-plants. Still grown for its long, dark, upright, glossy leaves, it should be kept out of the sun.

Nephrolepsis exaltata Commonly known as Boston fern, it likes warm, humid places, such as a bathroom, and does well in shade. It is easy to maintain, long-lived, and will continue to grow all year long when kept moist and out of draughts.

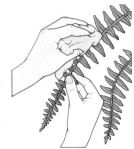

It is usually pest-free, but if it gets scale or mealy bug, wipe the fronds with a soft cloth dipped in methy-lated spirit. Do not use leaf-shine treatments or any type of insecticide on it.

Repotting a plant Time: ½ an hour or less

When a plant grows too large for its original container, repot it into a slightly larger one. The plant may not thrive if the new container is too big for it, so choose a pot that is about two sizes up.

> YOU WILL NEED Larger container with drip tray, potting mixture. Possibly: small pebbles or gravel.

If you are using a clay pot, place a curved piece of a broken pot over the drainage hole, to prevent soil falling through, and to assist drainage. Plastic pots do not need drainage material. However, if the pot is to stand in a saucer, put a layer of small pebbles in the base of the pot, to prevent the plant becoming accidentally waterlogged.

Place moist, new potting mixture in the base of the pot and tap it gently on a hard surface to settle it. Always use purpose-made potting soil – not soil from the garden, as this may contain weeds, pests or diseases.

To remove the plant from the old container without damaging it, place one hand over the surface of the soil with the plant protruding between your fingers.

Then turn the pot upside-down and, if it is made of flexible plastic, squeeze the sides gently with your other hand. The plant in its soil will slip out into your hand.

If the plant is in a hard plastic or clay pot, hold it in the same way, but gently tap the sides and base of the pot with the handle of a garden trowel to loosen it.

Very gently shake off some of the old soil that clings to the roots. Untangle the roots and, holding the plant very carefully, spread them out over the surface of the fresh potting mixture in the new pot.

Position the plant so that the roots are splayed out and resting on the potting soil and the base of the plant is about 2.5 cm (1 in) below the rim of the pot.

Make sure the plant is in the middle of the pot and carefully add more potting compost all round it.

Do not press it down too hard, because this reduces the air in the soil and could cause the plant to become unhealthily waterlogged.

Tap the pot on the work surface to help the roots to anchor themselves. Add more potting compost until the surface is 2.5 cm (1 in) from the rim of the pot.

Water the plant, but do not overwater. It should be sufficient to fill the pot to the brim and allow it to drain.

Keeping houseplants healthy

• Plants that are well looked after should not get pests or diseases. Try to give them the amount of warmth, light and water that suits them.

Most of the houseplants sold in garden centres come with specific cultivation instructions. Make sure the plants you buy do have detailed instructions, or else consult a reliable book about houseplants as soon as possible after buying the plant.

• In centrally heated rooms, houseplants such as cyclamen will do much better if their pots rest on a base of pebbles or gravel which is always kept damp.

• Keep a plant's conditions stable: if it spends all day in a warm, centrally heated room, don't leave it on the windowsill, behind curtains, on cold nights. The sudden drop in temperature will harm it.

• Keep plants out of draughts. It is possible to check for draughts by lighting a candle and placing it beside the plant. If the flame flickers, it is in a draught.

Keeping plants watered when you're on holiday

Before going away on holiday, group your houseplants together, out of direct sunlight, and drench them with water. Choose a cool room in summer and a warmer one in winter. Most houseplants will last a week without being watered, but if you are going away for longer, there are various ways to make sure that they will not dry out.

WATER-CONDUCTING WICKS Most garden centres and DIY outlets sell packets of water-conducting wicks that allow a slow but consistent supply of water from a bowl or jar to reach the plants grouped round it.

HOMEMADE WICKS It is possible to make your own water-conducting wick from easy-to-find items in the house.

Fill a glass jar or plastic container with water and hang a strip cut from an old pair of tights or a laddered stocking in the water. Pierce the lid and thread one end of the strip through it, and then screw the lid in place.

Using a pencil, poke the other end of the strip into the base of a plant pot, finding a way round any pieces of drainage material. Stand the pot on top of the container.

INDIVIDUAL CLOCHE Place three or four sticks round the rim of the pot. Make sure they are taller than the plant. Pull a clear plastic bag over them, so that it does not touch the leaves and fasten it with string.

Stand the pot on its drip tray. This methods helps to retain the moisture in the soil by preventing evaporation.

BATH-TUB CONSERVATORY Line the bath with plastic sheeting and then place a thick layer of newspaper in the bottom of the bath. Place the plants, without their drip trays, on the newspaper and drench the plants and paper.

Cover the bath with a sheet of clear plastic, and then seal off the sides using masking tape. Don't let the plastic touch the plants — use canes stuck into the soil to hold it clear, if necessary. Leave the curtains open in the bathroom for the light.

This method is not suitable for keeping furry-leaved plants moist; use a water-conducting wick for them.

Ice skates

One of the most common problems with ice skates is blunted blades. You can tell when the blades need regrinding, by a lack of grip when you are skating. Regrinding is not a job you can do yourself, but the service is available from all ice rinks and most shops that stock skates.

Replacing screws in skates Time: a few minutes

A skate has up to 12 screws fastening the blade to the boot; eight in the sole and four in the heel. As the boot gets worn the screw holes can get bigger, until eventually the screws drop out. If you don't manage to retrieve the loose screw just use a half-inch No. 4 round-headed screw.

> **YOU WILL NEED** Screw, matchsticks or a strip of plastic wall plug, penknife, screwdriver.

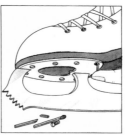

Cut some matchsticks or a piece of plastic wall plug to the same length as the depth of the hole and then use them to pack the hole. (The hole is usually about 1.3 cm ($\frac{1}{2}$ in) deep.) Then fit the screw and tighten it with a screwdriver.

Take care that the screw does not go right through into the boot. If it looks as though it will, use a shorter one.

Ice skates for hockey usually have their blade fittings riveted. If the blades come loose, they can be refitted at a specialist skate shop or at an ice rink. Alternatively, you may be able to rivet them yourself (see *Riveting*).

Insulation (SEE ALSO DOUBLE GLAZING)

Insulation can reduce the heat loss from a house by as much as 50 per cent, as well as protecting your home from the inconvenience and expense of frost damage.

Insulating the loft floor Time: about a day

Insulate the loft floor if the area is going to be used only for storage (the roof must be insulated, instead, if you intend using the loft as a study, bedroom or play room).

> **YOU WILL NEED** Possibly: building paper, scissors, mineral-fibre or glass-fibre blanket or pelleted mineral wool or expanded polystyrene beads, face mask, rubber gloves.

Moisture can percolate up through the plasterboard ceilings of a house, causing condensation in the loft. To prevent this you can lay a reflective foil building paper, foil side down, between the joists in the loft. Before you buy the paper, examine the plasterboard. There is no need to fit the paper if the plasterboard already has a foil facing.

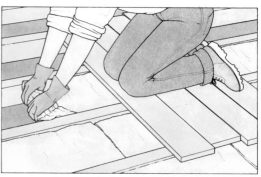

Protect your hands with gloves and wear a face mask if you intend to fill the gaps between the joists with glass fibre or mineral-wool blanket or pelleted mineral wool. Leave a gap of about 5 cm (2 in) at the eaves for ventilation.

The ideal depth of loft insulation is about 15 cm (6 in), so top up old insulation if necessary and possible. Take care not to compress the insulation as this will reduce its effectiveness (see 'How much to buy?', margin, right).

If you use expanded polystyrene beads, level them with a piece of scrap wood that fits snugly between the joists.

Insulating the loft roof Time: about a day

If the loft is to be used for storing valuables that could be affected by extremes of temperature, it is better to insulate the roof, rather than the floor. Also, if the loft is used as a room, or you plan to convert it, insulate the roof.

> **YOU WILL NEED** Possibly: rubber gloves and face mask, expanding-foam filler, building paper, scissors, drawing pins, mineral-fibre or glass-fibre blanket, string, waterproof tape.

If there is no felting under the roof tiles, seal large gaps between tiles with expanding-foam filler. Then cut a roll of building paper into strips so that the paper fits between the rafters with a turn-up on each side.

Press the paper close to the tiles and fix it to the rafters with drawing pins. Where the paper reaches the bottom of the roof, push it as far into the eaves as you can reach. This should make sure that any water that runs down the paper drips into the gutter outside.

If the lengths of paper are not long enough and you have to overlap them, start at the top and allow a good 7.5 cm (3 in) overlap. Seal the join with waterproof tape.

Hammer tacks or drawing pins into the rafters at about 15 cm (6 in) intervals, allowing them to protrude slightly.

Then fill the space between the rafters with either mineral-fibre or glass-fibre blanket and hold it in place by winding string back and forth between the tacks.

Insulating exterior walls

Cavity-wall insulation is the best way of cutting down heat loss through external walls for all but timber-framed houses. If you insulate a timber-framed house, use the same techniques as for a house with solid walls.

For solid walls, you can have an external insulating coating applied. Or apply plasterboard backed with expanded polystyrene direct to the internal faces of walls.

All wall insulation should be carried out by a specialist company. For a list of reputable local insulation companies contact the National Cavity Insulation Association, PO Box 12, Haslemere, Surrey GU27 3AH (Tel. 01428 654011).

Protecting a cold-water tank from frost

> YOU WILL NEED Steel tape measure, mineral-fibre or glass-fibre insulating blanket, scissors, string, rubber gloves, face mask, adhesive tape, brown paper.

Measure the height of the tank and the distance all the way round it. Wearing rubber gloves and a face mask, cut enough mineral-fibre or glass-fibre blanket to wrap right round the tank. One piece of the blanket will probably reach about three-quarters of the way up the tank walls so you will need to use two lengths. Trim them to size.

Fit the blanket round the tank, holding it in place with string, tied at about 20 cm (8 in) intervals. Make sure you do not tie the blanket too tightly as the string may compress the blanket and cut down its ability to insulate.

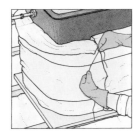

For extra insulation, particularly if you used two pieces of blanket, cover the blanket with a large piece of brown paper, held in place with adhesive tape and more string.

Do not insulate the tank bottom or the floor space below the tank, as heat rising through the floor will help to protect the tank from frost.

Fitting a cold-water tank lid   Time: $\frac{1}{2}$ a day

A cold-water tank must have a lid to keep out dirt and to protect it from frost. You can buy plastic covers for round tanks and you can make one for a rectangular tank.

> YOU WILL NEED Steel tape measure, 12 mm ($\frac{1}{2}$ in) thick medium density fibreboard (MDF), 75 mm (3 in) thick expanded polystyrene sheet, double-sided carpet tape. Possibly: power drill with a hole-saw, plastic funnel.

Make a lid from MDF cut to about 2.5 cm (1 in) larger all round than the tank top. Your local DIY store or timber merchant may do the cutting for you. Cut a sheet of expanded polystyrene to fit exactly into the top of the tank,

and tape it centrally to the blockboard with double-sided carpet tape. On the lid, mark a point immediately below the outlet of the vent pipe from the hot-water system.

Use a power drill with a hole-saw to cut a hole in the lid. The hole must be large enough to accommodate the bottom of a plastic funnel. Insert the funnel into the lid so that it will catch water dripping from the vent.

Insulating a rectangular cold-water tank
Time: $\frac{1}{2}$ a day or less

> YOU WILL NEED 4 sheets 75 mm (3 in) expanded polystyrene, bread knife, adhesive tape, 8 wooden meat skewers.

With a bread knife, cut four sheets of 75 mm (3 in) thick expanded polystyrene to cover the sides of the tank, each overlapping the edges by about 2.5 cm (1 in) all round.

Cut holes in the sheets to accommodate pipes protruding from the tank. Place the sheets around the tank and hold them in place with adhesive tape at first, then with eight wooden meat skewers, two at each corner — one at the top and one at the bottom.

Insulating a hot-water cylinder   Time: $\frac{1}{2}$ a day or less

Uninsulated hot-water cylinders will lose heat and waste energy. By fitting your hot-water cylinder with a lagging jacket it is possible to cut energy waste by nine-tenths.

Measure the height and the distance round the middle of your hot-water cylinder. Buy a 75 mm (3 in) thick segmented insulating jacket of the appropriate size.

Remove any items stored in the airing cupboard and also take out any shelving that might get in the way.

Thread all the loops of the jacket segments onto the collar or piece of cord that is provided. Then tie the cord round the pipe at the top of the cylinder.

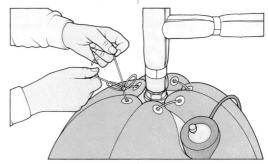

Smooth the segments down the sides of the cylinder so that they overlap slightly and cover the entire surface. Fit the first belt, not too tightly, near the top. Then fit a second near the bottom. Space the belts in between at equal intervals. Do not allow the jacket's segments to cover the thermostatic control of an immersion heater.

HOW MUCH TO BUY?

Before buying loft-insulating material, measure the depth of your ceiling joists. Ideally, insulating material should be between 10 cm (4 in) and 15 cm (6 in) thick — anything deeper will produce less savings per pound spent. However, if your joists are less than 10 cm (4 in) thick and you intend laying some sort of flooring on top, do not lay insulation deeper than the joists. Compacting it will decrease its effectiveness and will be a waste of money.

CUTTING COSTS

Reduce costs by buying insulation materials in the summer, when they are less in demand. Also, contact your Citizens Advice Bureau or your local council — you may be eligible for a grant to help with insulating your house.

Before starting any work on an electrical fitting or appliance, make sure to cut off the electricity supply — either by switching off at the main fuse box, or by unplugging the appliance.

INSULATING A ROOM OVER A GARAGE

The concrete floor of a room over a garage can be cold. Coat the concrete with bitumen-rubber waterproofing compound. Then lay a reflective foil-faced building paper, foil side up. Follow this with a good quality carpet underlay before laying the carpet.

Insulating pipes   Time: depends on amount

Water pipes can freeze unless they are lagged effectively. The easiest method is to use snap-on foam insulation.

> YOU WILL NEED Snap-on foam insulation, clear adhesive tape, rubber gloves, glass-fibre pipewrap.

Snap the plastic foam insulation over the straight runs of pipe, pressing each length firmly up against the next.

Where the pipe turns a corner, cut the insulation at an appropriate angle, fit it snugly round the bend, and bind the join with a clear adhesive tape.

Make sure you put lagging behind pipework that is against external walls, because cold transmitted through the wall could freeze the water in the pipe.

Remember to lag the vent pipe of the hot-water system, which usually hangs over the cold-water tank, and the central heating system vent (if there is one), which hangs over the feed-and-expansion tank in the loft (see *Central heating*: 'Understanding the system').

Wearing rubber gloves, use glass-fibre pipewrap to protect vulnerable points that the foam plastic will not cover, such as sharp changes of direction and points where pipes are secured by pipe clips. Push pipewrap under the pipe on one side of every pipe clip and over the pipe on the other side. Leave only the handles of gate valves exposed.

Sealing an overflow pipe from icy air

Cold air coming up the cold-water tank's overflow pipe can freeze the water in the tank. Avoid this by extending the overflow inside the tank with a piece of plastic tube, roughly the same width as the overflow pipe. Heat the end of the tube in boiling water and stretch it over the end of the overflow pipe where it enters the tank. The free end of the tube should be submerged in the water to prevent cold air entering the tank through the pipe.

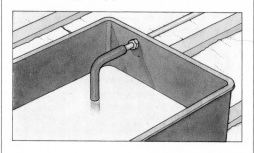

Iron

Most irons are made with both steam and non-steam functions. Some have additional features such as 'shot of steam'. If your steam iron develops a fault, it is better to return it to the dealer, as it is complicated to repair.

Irons with no steam function at all, known as dry irons, are usually sold as travel irons. It is possible to replace the element in a dry iron.

Replacing the heating element in a dry iron
Time: 2 hours or less

Find out first if replacement elements are available for the model you have. In some irons, the element is incorporated in the soleplate and, as it is not possible to repair a faulty element, the whole unit must be replaced.

Elements vary, so take the old element with you to buy a new one, to be sure of getting the correct replacement.

> YOU WILL NEED Screwdriver, new element.

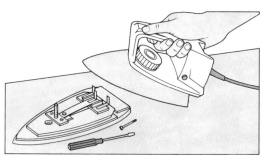

A dry iron consists of a soleplate, an element, a thermostat, a body and a handle, all held together by screws. Remove the screws to separate the body and handle.

On most models, this will expose the thermostat which is fixed to a pressure plate. Beneath that is a sheet of heat-reflecting material, and beneath that, sandwiched between two layers of heat-resistant material, is the element.

Loosen the screws to expose the element, disconnect the wires and screws holding it in place and remove it. Then put the new element in place and connect it up. Finally, reassemble the iron, plug it in and test it.

Caring for the soleplate

Soleplates may be coated with chrome, porcelain enamel, stainless steel or nonstick Silverstone. These make the iron heavier than standard aluminium, but they allow it to move more swiftly over the fabric, and speed up the job.

CLEANING Check the manufacturer's cleaning instructions, as some makes recommend specific treatments. If no recommendations are made, use a mild household cleaner on a damp cloth. Never use a scouring powder or a metal pad; these could scratch the surface.

In the case of a synthetic fabric that has burnt onto the soleplate, use a damp cloth dipped in bicarbonate of soda, or a proprietary soleplate cleaner such as Vilene Iron Cleaner or the cleaner recommended by the manufacturer.

STARCHING If you use starch on your clothes, spray it on the inside of the garment and iron on the outside. Clean the soleplate regularly while the iron is still warm.

If the soleplate picks up a lot of starch, set the iron on warm and rub it over a damp, coarsely woven cloth or a towel, held taut over the edge of the ironing board.

AVOIDING LIMESCALE Most steam irons are designed to use tap water, but they may clog up with limescale if used with hard water. Some irons have replaceable cartridges to soften the water; others use distilled or deionised water. Some have a removable plate that collects scale. Clean it with a proprietary descaler or by soaking it in vinegar.

If you have a tumble drier with a condenser, the water from the collection tank is ideal for use in a steam iron. Alternatively, buy a demineralising bottle which contains crystals which remove the lime from tap water.

AVOIDING DAMAGE Don't iron over zips, buttons, press studs or hooks and eyes. They could damage the soleplate.

STORAGE Always empty a steam iron before storing it and stand it in an upright position to prevent drops of water remaining on the soleplate and staining it.

Replacing a worn cord Time: 1 hour or less

When the fabric covering of an iron's cord becomes worn, don't put off replacing it until the coloured plastic-covered wires are showing – replace it it straight away.

YOU WILL NEED Screwdriver, trimming knife, replacement cord. Possibly: new plug.

The replacement cord you buy should have a braided cover and be able to withstand continuous twisting.

Make sure the iron is disconnected from the mains.

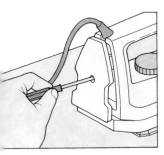

Remove the plate at the back of the iron that covers the entrance of the cord.

This should expose the terminals; but if it does not, you may also have to remove the soleplate.

Disconnect the wires, noting how they were connected. Then use a trimming knife to remove the outer casing of the new cord, taking care not to cut too deep. Connect the exposed coloured wires to the appropriate terminals. The brown wire goes to the terminal marked L, the blue to N, and green and yellow to the terminal marked E.

Fit a new plug to the other end of the new cord. You can take the plug off the old cord and use that as long as it is not a moulded-on type (see *Electric plug*). Test the iron.

Ivory (SEE ALSO JEWELLERY; PIANO)

Keeping ivory white

Ivory varies in colour from white to dull yellow. You can control its colour to some extent by where you keep it.

Regular daylight will keep the ivory a creamy colour. Regular exposure to direct sunlight will bleach it almost white – but too much sunlight can cause cracking.

Ivory that is rarely exposed to daylight will turn yellow. To prevent piano keys from yellowing, leave the lid open as much as possible during daylight hours.

Cleaning ivory

YOU WILL NEED Soft cloth or chamois leather. Possibly: soft toothbrush or baby's hairbrush, almond oil, cotton wool, methylated spirit.

Dust ivory regularly with a soft cloth. If it has been intricately carved, use an old toothbrush or a baby's hairbrush to get the dust out of any small crevices.

Maintain the shine with an occasional, light application of almond oil on cotton wool.

Clean ivory carefully with methylated spirit on cotton wool – but not if the ivory is valuable or antique.

Do not let ivory get wet: it is semiporous and will absorb water which leaves marks when it dries.

Washing ivory-backed hairbrushes
Time: a few minutes

YOU WILL NEED Soapflakes, towel.

When washing ivory-backed brushes, keep the ivory out of the water. Never soak this type of brush.

Swish the brush bristles around in a solution of soapflakes and warm water. Keep the ivory clear.

Rinse the bristles in warm, clear water to get rid of the soap. Then rinse again in cold water to help to stiffen the bristles.

Place the brush, bristle-side down, on a towel and allow it to dry naturally. This could take a couple of days.

Do not try to speed up the drying process artificially, as too much heat could cause the ivory to crack.

Jacking a car: SEE CAR TYRES

Jar: SEE BOTTLES, DECANTERS & JARS

Jewellery

Cleaning jewellery

Most jewellery, apart from pearls and coral, can be washed in a mild washing-up liquid solution. Always wash your jewellery in a plastic bowl with an old facecloth in the bottom to protect the jewellery and to keep it safe.

Before tipping out the water, lift out the facecloth carefully, making sure all the jewellery is on it. Let the water strain through the cloth. Then rinse each item in a little clean water and dry it carefully with a clean linen cloth.

Never wash jewellery under a running tap in a sink or basin with the plug out – the risk of loss is too high.

GOLD AND PLATINUM Rub gently with a piece of chamois leather. Avoid ordinary cloth, as it may harbour grit. Gold chains can be cleaned with a soft toothbrush and a warm, well-dissolved solution of pure soapflakes and water. Allow them to dry before rubbing gently with a chamois leather.

SILVER JEWELLERY SET WITH PRECIOUS STONES Clean with a special silver polish or a mild washing-up liquid solution. Do not use very hot water as stones could fall out if the metal settings expand.

Add a little ammonia to the water to help loosen any dirt, and use a soft toothbrush to clean intricate jewellery.

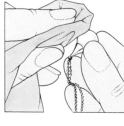

PEARLS AND CORAL Treat both pearls and coral alike, rubbing them very gently with a clean chamois leather. Their surfaces are so easily scratched or chipped that they must be handled with great care.

Never wash a string of pearls, as the water will eventually rot the thread. Have valuable pearls restrung regularly to avoid having the thread break unexpectedly.

Pearls should be worn frequently because they respond to the natural oils in the skin. Never apply hairspray or perfume after putting on pearls as the chemicals in these cosmetics can affect the pearls adversely.

DIAMOND RINGS AND NECKLACES Loosen any dirt at the back of the setting using an old toothbrush and then wash the ring or necklace in warm water and washing-up liquid in a small plastic bowl.

Rinse each piece well and dry it with a soft linen cloth.

IVORY Whiten yellow ivory by rubbing it with a cloth dipped in 6% BP (20 vol) hydrogen peroxide. It will stay white for longer if stored in the light and not hidden away.

Do not wash ivory, as it is semiporous and, in time, getting wet will cause it to develop hairline cracks. Rub it with a soft cloth dipped in almond oil to give it a protective coating because it is liable to become stained by make-up. If it is badly stained, have it cleaned professionally.

WOOD Wipe wooden jewellery with a slightly damp cloth and finish it with a little wax polish or olive oil. Do not wet wooden jewellery as it may warp or crack when it dries.

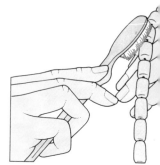

BEADS AND STONES Clean bead and stone necklaces with a soft toothbrush that has been dipped into a bowl of dry baking soda. Brush the beads gently and then rub them with a soft cloth.

AMBER As a regular cleaning treatment, wipe amber with a cloth dipped in warm, soapy water, and dry immediately. Water makes amber cloudy, so don't leave it in for any length of time. Buff with a chamois leather. Do not use alcohol or any form of solvent as it will remove the shine.

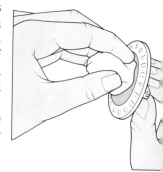

To remove greasy marks from amber, wipe it with a clean cloth (right) on which you have put a small drop of almond oil, or dab it with a ball formed from a thick slice of fresh, white bread. This will lift off much of the grease without doing any harm to the amber.

OPALS Dry-wash opals by putting them into a small jar of powdered magnesia, which is available from chemists. Swirl them round gently and then leave them overnight. Remove the powder with a soft, clean brush.

Opals are brittle and can break easily, so do not subject them to extremes of temperature. They also scratch very easily, so should always be handled gently.

ACRYLIC JEWELLERY Sponge with a weak solution of washing-up liquid and warm water. Rinse off soapy solution and wipe the piece with a clean, damp cloth.

Scratches can be made less noticeable by polishing gently with a metal polish and wiping clean.

CAMEO Use a soft brush dipped in a weak solution of washing-up liquid and warm water with a drop of ammonia in it. Do not immerse a cameo in water.

Straightening a brooch pin or hook Time: a few minutes

> YOU WILL NEED Smooth-jawed jewellery pliers. Possibly: small piece of scrap wood with shallow saw cut; round-nosed jewellery pliers, fine file.

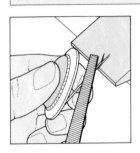

If the pin on a brooch gets bent, you can straighten it with smooth-jawed pliers. If the tip of the pin has been badly bent, cut a shallow groove in a piece of scrap wood, rest the pin in it and file the bent tip until it is smooth and straight (left).

Check that, in straightening the tip of the pin, you have not affected the way in which it fits into or under the hook. If you find that the pin touches the brooch when it is done up, you may have to adjust the hook by bending it.

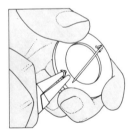

Hold the hook with a pair of round-nosed pliers just above its root. Gently bend the unconnected side upwards, to open up the curve of the hook.

Then, with round-nosed pliers, reshape the hook so that it will hold the pin correctly. If the hook breaks off while you are attempting to do this, solder it back into position (see *Soldering*) or take it to a jeweller.

Restringing a bead necklace Time: 1 hour or less

> YOU WILL NEED Polyester thread, very fine beading needle, long-nosed pliers, embroidery scissors.

Thread the beading needle with a length of polyester thread that matches or tones with the beads and is about three times the length of the finished necklace. Attach one half of the clasp to the end of the thread, fastening it securely. Then make a knot close to the clasp.

Feed the first bead onto the needle and slide it up to the knot. Make a loop and pass the needle and thread through it. Do not tighten the loop yet.

Push the tip of the needle into the loop beside the bead, pressing the bead hard against the first knot. Slowly pull on the thread to tighten the loop. Keep the needle in place.

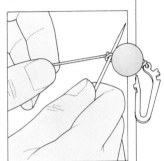

Using the needle, guide the knot tightly against the bead, all the while pulling on the thread and pressing the bead firmly up against the starting knot.

Then finish off the knot by using long-nosed pliers to push the knot as close to the bead as possible. Restring the remaining beads in the same way. Finally stitch the second half of the clasp onto the string of beads.

To secure the end of the thread, take it back through the last two beads, knot it and cut it off with fine scissors.

> ## Safe storage techniques
> Because pearls and opals are fragile and very easily scratched or damaged, they should be stored in individual boxes or in soft, lined bags, to prevent them from being knocked against other, harder pieces.
>
> Diamonds should also be stored separately; they are so hard that they can damage other jewellery.

Tightening a V-spring Time: 1 hour or less

> YOU WILL NEED Narrow-bladed knife.

Bracelets and necklaces often have clasps with a V-shaped spring which fits into a flat sheath. If the spring is broken, take it to a jeweller for repair. If it becomes loose, you can tighten it by opening it slightly with the blade of a knife.

Insert the knife blade between the leaves of the V-spring and turn it, to force them slightly wider apart.

Check how well the V-spring grips its sheath. Continue forcing the spring open until it engages in the sheath with a clicking sound and holds firmly in place.

Jump-starting a car:
SEE CAR EMERGENCIES

Kettle

Electric kettles have a heating element shaped to fit the inside of the kettle. If the kettle is allowed to boil dry or overheat, the element may fail and have to be replaced.

If you are at all unsure about your ability to replace an element, have it done by an appliance repair company.

Replacing an element Time: 2 hours or less

It is fairly easy to fit a new element to a non-automatic kettle, or change the washers, if leaks occur. An automatic kettle is more complicated; when replacing the element, take care not to tamper with the thermostat.

Elements vary, so take the old one with you when you buy a replacement so that you can match it.

> YOU WILL NEED New element. Possibly: pipe wrench, cloth, limescale remover, old toothbrush, screwdriver, long-nosed pliers.

Switch off and unplug the kettle from the wall socket. Empty it and remove the connecting cord from the back.

TRADITIONAL-SHAPED, NON-AUTOMATIC KETTLES Metal and plastic kettles of this style have elements that are fixed in place by the screw-threaded, tubular retaining nut which also houses the connecting cord .

In a metal kettle, the retaining nut will be chrome-plated metal. In a plastic kettle, it is usually plastic.

Unscrew the retaining nut. It may be possible to do this by hand. If not, wrap a cloth round the nut to avoid damage, and then use a pipe wrench.

Removing the nut should reveal a fibre sealing washer. Throw it away, because the new element should have been supplied with replacement washers.

The element and a rubber sealing washer can now be removed from inside the kettle. Discard them, too.

If limescale has formed round the opening, clean it off with a limescale remover and an old toothbrush. Dry well.

Slip a new rubber washer over the new element and fit them into the kettle.

Then fit a new fibre washer onto the part of the element that is outside the kettle.

Refit the retaining nut. Then fill the kettle to make sure that the join is watertight, and test the new element.

TRADITIONAL-SHAPED AUTO-MATIC KETTLE Some of the traditional-shaped kettles have their switch and their connecting cord housed in a plastic section that forms part of the handle.

As makes and models of kettle vary, you may have to adapt this information to suit the kettle you have.

Remove the connecting cord to expose the earth pin. It has a slotted nut which can be loosened with a fine but wide-tipped screwdriver. This will release the switch-housing from the body of the kettle.

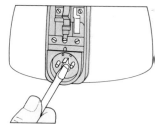

In some models, it may also be necessary to remove the water level indicator inside the kettle, in order to release the switch housing.

Ease away the switch housing, and two securing bolts will be exposed. They hold the element in place. Remove the nuts and carefully take out the element and washers from the inside of the kettle. Abandon the old washers.

Refit the new element and new washers and reassemble the kettle. Test for leaks before switching it on.

JUG KETTLE (AUTOMATIC AND NON-AUTOMATIC) A plastic housing covers the point where the connecting cord plugs into the body of the kettle. Unscrewing the two screws (left) will reveal the retaining nut that holds the element in place.

The kettle will probably be made of plastic, and so will the nut that holds the element in position.

There should be a washer between the metal element and the plastic body of the jug, but it is unlikely that there will be one where the outer body of the jug and the plastic housing of the connector cord meet each other.

Remove the failed element. A metal guard is fixed beneath the element, to prevent it burning the bottom of the kettle. It may be attached to the element fixing; if it should come loose, replace it with the new element.

Insert the new element and washer, and reassemble the parts. Test for leaks before using the kettle.

CORDLESS KETTLE A cordless kettle has an element fitted in the base of the kettle body. It connects to the power via a socket which is built into the separate base.

Replace the element in the same way as for a jug kettle, but take care to get a watertight fit.

A leak into the base, which is live when the kettle is switched on, could result in water running onto the work-top and acting as a conductor which could transmit an electric current and give an electric shock.

Faultfinder guide: Kettles

Kettle leaks

! Do not use.
• Disconnect kettle at once.

POSSIBLE CAUSE The retaining nut may be loose or the element washers may have deteriorated.
SOLUTION Tighten the retaining nut. Refill and check for leaks. If it still leaks, replace element washers or fit a new element with new washers.

Kettle will not heat

POSSIBLE CAUSE Kettle cord connector is not properly pushed into the wall socket or the kettle.
SOLUTION Push in firmly at both ends.

POSSIBLE CAUSE Faulty plug, wall socket, or cord connector.
SOLUTION Check that fuse has not blown. Check electrical connections in the plug and cord connector, if it is not a moulded unit (see *Electric plug*) and in the socket (see *Electric socket*).

POSSIBLE CAUSE Safety device activated.
SOLUTION Reset device (see margin).

POSSIBLE CAUSE Blown element.
SOLUTION Replace element.

Kettle will not switch off automatically

POSSIBLE CAUSE Lid not properly closed.
SOLUTION Close lid firmly.

POSSIBLE CAUSE Too much water in kettle.
SOLUTION Turn off by hand. Do not overfill in future.

Kettle will not heat a second time after having boiled

POSSIBLE CAUSE Some kettles take longer to recover and restart their boiling cycle.
SOLUTION Check kettle's instruction book. Allow extra time if necessary.

Safety tips for electric kettles

Kettles bring electricity, water and heat together, so there is a high potential for injury.

OUT OF REACH If there are children in the house, keep the kettle well out of their reach and never let the flex dangle over the edge of a work surface.

LET IT COOL Never pour water into a kettle immediately after it has boiled dry; the cloud of steam that will result could scald your face and hands.

SWITCH OFF Do not pour water from a non-automatic kettle while it is switched on. You may expose the element and cause it to overheat. Or you may forget to switch off the kettle when you put it down, and it will boil dry and could be a fire hazard.

Key: SEE LOCKS AND LATCHES

Knitwear

(SEE ALSO BUTTONHOLES; DARNING; ELASTIC)

Preventing holes in elbows

Elbows are usually the first places to go on jumpers and cardigans, and should be patched (see *Patching clothes*) or darned (see *Darning*) as soon as signs of wear appear.

The patching or darning should cover more than just the worn area on the garment. It should extend about 2.5 cm (1 in) beyond the damage, all round, so that it is attached to firm knitting which won't give way when the garment is worn again.

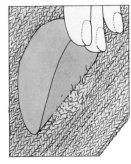

Cleaning knitwear

DRY-CLEANING Expensive items of knitwear should always be dry-cleaned rather than washed, especially if they are trimmed with braid or gilt thread.

Knitwear with appliquéd motifs should be dry-cleaned too, unless the care instructions say otherwise, because the appliqué may be made of a fabric that shrinks at a different rate from the garment itself.

Although dry-cleaning is expensive, it will prolong the life of a garment and keep it looking good.

WHEN A KETTLE IS SLOW TO BOIL

If your kettle takes longer to come to the boil than it did when it was new, examine it for limescale. Limescale can build up quickly if you live in a hard-water area. Remove it with a proprietary descaler.

SAFETY FIRST WITH ELECTRICITY

Before starting any work on an electrical fitting or appliance, make sure to cut off the electricity supply – either by switching off at the main fuse box, or by unplugging the appliance.

RESETTING A SAFETY DEVICE

Some older models of non-automatic kettle have a mechanical safety device. A pin ejects the mains lead from its socket at the back of the kettle if it overheats or boils dry. To reset the kettle, push the pin back into place with a pencil or the end of a wooden spoon. Some models cannot be reset, and will need a new element.

WASHING KNITWEAR Many less expensive items can be washed, even if the labels say dry-cleaning is preferable. Test a small, less noticeable area first such as the inner part of the sleeve, above the elbow.

If the colour runs or the look of the knitwear appears to change, it is better to have it dry-cleaned.

Wool should always be hand-washed unless the label states that it is machine-washable. Hand-washing is gentler, and special attention can also be paid to collars and cuffs which get more soiled than the rest of the garment.

If the garment is knitted from man-made fibres and the care instructions indicate that it can tolerate machine-washing, use the setting shown on the care label and add a fabric softener to the wash.

Fluffy garments should be washed on their own in case they shed fibres on the rest of the load.

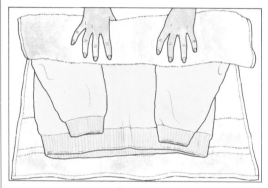

DRYING KNITWEAR A quick way to get rid of excess water in hand-washed knitwear is to lay it flat on an old towel and smooth it out, then roll them both up, swiss-roll fashion.

Lay the roll in the bath, and tread gently along the roll with bare feet. This speeds up the towel's absorption of the water and cuts the drying time considerably.

Lay the knitwear flat to finish drying. It is a good idea to buy a special net drying-rack which lets air circulate round the garment, speeding up the drying process.

Using a drying-rack allows you to reshape and smooth the garment, and prevents the stretching and peg marks which occur when a garment is hung on a line.

Recycling hand-knitted garments

If you are particularly fond of the wool used in a hand-knitted garment that does not fit any more, it may be worth unpicking it carefully and using it again.

Wind it into skeins as you unpick it, and then wash it gently, to allow most of the kinks to fall out. Do not stretch the wool while it is wet – it cannot be reknitted satisfactorily if it has been stretched.

When it is thoroughly dry, roll it up into balls, applying just enough tension to get rid of the last of the kinks.

Wool recycled in this way is quite good enough for use in children's garments, dolls' clothes and knitted toys.

Dealing with stretching and shrinking

SHRUNKEN GARMENTS Knitwear containing natural wool becomes matted if washed in hot water, and very little can be done to restore it. However, it may be worth wetting the garment again and stretching it on a flat surface.

STRETCHED GARMENTS Do not try to shrink a stretched garment in a very hot wash because its texture may be damaged. If it is not severely stretched, wash it according to the care instructions on the label. Afterwards pull it into shape, tightening and reshaping cuffs, waistbands and necklines. Then lay it flat and allow it to dry naturally.

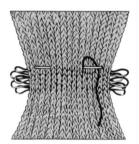

You may need to thread some shirring elastic of a suitable colour through the garment's cuffs and waistband to restore the fit (see *Elastic*). Make sure that the elastic does not show on the outside of the garment.

Donate your unwanted wool

If you decide not to use your recycled wool – or have balls of wool or yarn left over from a hand-knitted garment – you may like to donate it to one of the many charities whose volunteer workers knit and crochet blankets and clothes for the needy.

Keeping knitwear looking new

It is worth spending a few minutes 'tidying' a knitted garment every time it is washed or cleaned.

REMOVING 'PILLS' Pills are the small fluffy balls of wool that appear on a knitted garment wherever there is any friction – such as where sleeves rub against sides.

Because they are not loose threads or stitches, they can be removed without damaging the garment. Pull them off by hand, one at a time if there are not many.

A large crop of pills can be removed with fine, sharp scissors, but take care not to cut the garment.

The safest way to get rid of them is to use a battery-powered gadget rather like an electric razor, to shave the pills off the garment. However, this can be rather time-consuming.

REMOVING FLUFF Dark-coloured, machine-made knitwear can look old if fluff and threads attach themselves to it. Use a fluff-removing roller to improve the look of it.

Alternatively, try wrapping several strips of sticky tape round the palm of your hand, with the sticky side out, and pat and drag it all over the garment. You may need to renew the tape two or three times if there is a lot of fluff to be removed from the garment.

PULLED THREADS An individual thread may get stretched and hang out of the garment. Unless the thread is broken, it is often possible to ease it back into place.

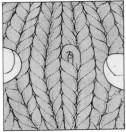 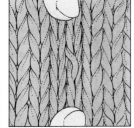

Stretch the area gently, first widthways then lengthways. | Keep stretching it until the loop has disappeared.

If a loop will not respond to being stretched back into place, poke it through to the inside of the garment and either leave it loose or, if it is long enough, work it into the back of the stitches with a tapestry needle.

If the loop has broken, thread each end, in turn, into a needle with a big eye, such as a tapestry or darning needle, and take it through to the inside of the garment. Work each thread into the backs of the adjacent stitches.

Knives

Sharpening a knife Time: a minute or less

Some knives with 'laser' blades never need sharpening, but most knives will become blunt at some time.

To keep a knife in the best possible condition, make a point of sharpening it regularly. Use a wood or polypropylene chopping board, which will not blunt the blade. Store knives in a knife block or in a magnetic knife rack.

TRIMMING KNIFE A sturdy knife with a blade that can be replaced by unscrewing the handle and putting in a new blade (right). Hooked blades are used for cutting vinyl and linoleum; and both straight and hooked blades can be used for trimming.

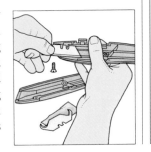

CRAFT KNIFE Some have blades that can be snapped off to expose a new cutting surface as soon as one becomes blunt (right). Others have disposable blades that are sold in packs. The blade is held in place at the end of a handle which is shaped and held like a pencil.

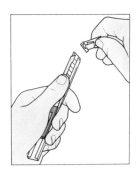

POCKET KNIFE Stroke both sides of the knife blade with an oilstone, using a circular movement. Keep sharpening until the blade will slice easily through a sheet of paper.

When the blade is sharp, strop it on a leather strap or old belt smeared with polishing compound (see margin).

DOMESTIC KNIVES Use a simple wheel sharpener on kitchen knives and cutlery. Draw the blade through the vee formed by two sets of hardened blades (right).

Alternatively, use a steel or an electric sharpener.

Using a craft knife or trimming knife

Use a non-slip cutting board such as a sheet of hardboard or rubber. Wherever possible, anchor the work so that both hands are free. Always cut away from you.

Using a steel

Hold the steel, pointing away from you. Place the widest part of the knife blade at the top of the steel and hold it at an angle of about 15°.

Draw the knife along the top of the steel, sliding the blade across, so that the knife tip is against the steel at the end of the stroke.

Draw the other side of the blade up the underside of the steel at an angle of 15°. Slide the blade across the steel as above.

Repeat both steps, working away from, then towards, the handle of the steel until the knife is sharp.

SAFETY FIRST WHEN USING KNIVES

Never use a blunt blade – it will do a poor job and is more likely to slip than a sharp blade.

STROPPING A BLADE

Improvise a leather strap with an old leather belt and spread polishing compound on it. (The compound is available from ironmongers, hire shops and engineers' merchants.) Then stroke the blade up and down the strap, leading up and down with the blunt side.

At the end of each stroke, reverse the direction of the knife by rolling it over the blunt edge, not the sharp edge.

Lace

Machine-made lace can usually be washed, and comes with a care label. Follow the instructions closely.

If washing by hand is recommended, use a mild detergent such as Lux flakes or Stergene in warm (not hot) water. If washing by machine is allowed, put the lace into a pillow case first, to prevent it catching on other items.

If machine-made lace is discoloured, use a proprietary net curtain whitener to restore it.

Do not try to clean valuable lace at home. It should be cleaned professionally. Get the name of your nearest specialist cleaner from The Dry Cleaning Information Bureau. Contact the bureau at The Textile Services Association, 7 Churchill Court, 58 Station Road, North Harrow, Middlesex HA2 7SA, telephone 0181 863 8658.

Washing discoloured handmade lace

Time: ½ a day or less

If you intend washing a large piece of lace, protect your clothing with a waterproof apron and cover the floor with old towels or newspaper before starting.

> **YOU WILL NEED** Distilled, softened or purified water, old towel, plastic bowl, sheet of plastic.

Washable handmade lace that is discoloured should be soaked in cold, distilled water for several hours. It is important to use distilled, softened or purified water, as these will not leave mineral deposits in the lace.

Place an old towel in the bottom of a plastic bowl and lay the lace on top of it, before covering it with distilled water to a depth of about 5 cm (2 in). The towel supports the lace when you lift it out of the water, so that it is not distorted by the weight of the water it contains.

After a while, the dirt will start to float to the surface.

To change the water, lift the narrow end of the towel slightly and roll it over carefully so that the lace is covered totally. Make sure you work below the surface of the water, to stop the lace from picking up the dirt floating on the surface.

Lift out the rolled towel carefully, discard the water and then add more distilled water. You may have to repeat this several times, until there appears to be no more dirt.

Lift out the lace for the last time, peel it off the towel and lay it on a smooth surface, such as a sheet of plastic or a kitchen working surface.

Gently pat and pull it into shape, then use a clean white towel to blot as much moisture from it as possible. Allow the lace to dry naturally, away from direct sunlight.

Restoring the shape of washed lace Time: a few minutes

> **YOU WILL NEED** Pencil, paper, scissors, plastic sheet, cork mat or ceiling tile, rustless pins. Possibly: gum arabic.

If the lace is an unusual shape, or has to fit a specific shape once it is dry – such as an overlay on the collar of a dress – make a paper template of its size and shape before washing it. Lay the lace on a sheet of clean white paper and trace round its outline. Cut out the template and lay it on a piece of cork or an expanded polystyrene ceiling tile.

Wash the lace and place it on a sheet of clear plastic.

Lay the lace and plastic over the paper template and gently manipulate the lace into shape, using the template to guide you. Hold the lace in the desired shape by pinning it all round with rustless pins.

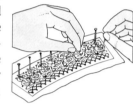

Allow the lace to dry naturally, out of direct sunlight.

STIFFENING LACE If the lace needs stiffening, dissolve 30 g (1 oz) of gum arabic – obtainable from most chemists – in 285 ml (½ pint) of warm water and submerge the lace in it briefly after it has been washed.

Lay it out, reshape it and let it dry, as described above.

How to clean and store lace safely

Although lace is delicate, it should last well if it is stored, handled and laundered carefully.

- Wash or dry-clean lace frequently, as a build-up of ingrained dirt is difficult to remove.
- Store it in a cool, dry place with a sachet of silica gel obtained from a florist or camera shop to help to maintain the dryness. Sachets of silica gel are often found in the packaging of cameras and camcorders.
- Wrap the lace in acid-free tissue paper (obtainable from good jewellers and cutlery shops) to prevent it being stained by wooden drawers or cardboard boxes. Do not use ordinary tissue paper.
- Large pieces of lace can be rolled round a cardboard tube, such as those inside a kitchen-foil roll. Cover the cardboard tube with acid-free tissue paper first, and then wrap another layer over the lace.
- Treat rust stains on lace with neat lemon juice and salt or a proprietary rust-stain remover. Put a few drops on a clean white cloth and dab gently.
- Don't use fabric conditioner when washing lace: the additives in it may soften it too much or damage it.
- Never spin, wring or tumble-dry washable lace.

Lacquer

Lacquer is a popular finish for furniture. It dries rapidly to form a hard, glossy, water-resistant surface.

Hiding deep scratches in lacquer Time: depends on area

> YOU WILL NEED Scalpel or craft knife, matching wood stain, artist's paintbrush, clear lacquer, fine pumice powder, linseed oil.

Clean away any debris from the scratch with a scalpel or craft knife, and a clean, dry paintbrush.

Apply a matching stain with a fine, artist's paintbrush. Then pour a little clear glossy lacquer into an old saucer and apply layers to the scratch with a clean brush until it is level with the surface, allowing each layer to dry thoroughly.

When the lacquer is dry, mix fine pumice powder with linseed oil and rub it over the surface with a cloth.

Repairing fine scratches in lacquer Time: depends on area

> YOU WILL NEED Rottenstone, felt, linseed oil.

Sprinkle rottenstone over the affected area, then rub gently to just beyond the scratches with felt soaked in linseed oil.

Wipe the area once the scratches have disappeared. Rub over the whole surface with rottenstone, until the repair blends in with the rest of the lacquer.

Ladders & scaffolding

Get the right ladder for the job

Always use the right ladders or scaffold towers for the task. Most of them can be borrowed from your local hire shop.

LADDER Ladders are made of timber or aluminium, in a range of lengths from 2 m (7 ft) to 16 m (52 ft). The longer ones come in two or three parts to make moving and storing them easier.

Some have trays for tools and materials and holders for paint cans, leaving your hands free to work. Stand-offs hold the ladder away from fragile guttering to give you a better working position and to prevent slipping.

STEPLADDER For all interior decorating and most work around a bungalow, a stepladder is usually adequate. Timber stepladders are heavier but more stable than aluminium ones. The flat platform or tray is designed to hold tools and materials as you work, never as a place to stand.

LOFT LADDER An ordinary ladder will not give you enough of the stability necessary for climbing into and out of the loft, so fit a permanent loft ladder, if at all possible.

Make sure that whatever design of ladder you choose, it does not restrict the entrance too much. Bear in mind that you will probably need to lift things in and out of the loft.

ROOF LADDER Working on a roof is difficult and dangerous and best left to the experts. If you do venture onto the roof it is vital to use a roof ladder. It comes with wheels so you can move it in position while standing on a second ladder.

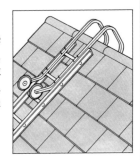

When it is almost in the correct position on the roof, turn it over so that the hook catches over the roof ridge, holding the ladder firmly in the right place.

Ladder safety

- Anchor the base of the ladder with a sandbag or with a rope attached to a stake set into the ground.
- Always have at least three rungs clear above the guttering for a handhold at the top of the ladder.
- Prevent the ladder from sliding as you work on guttering by screwing a large zinc-plated screw eye into the fascia board and then lashing the ladder to it.
- Do not lean across to out-of-reach areas; always move the ladder along instead.
- Remove tools and other materials from a tools tray before moving your ladder on to a new position.
- Don't ever stand on the top platform of a stepladder.

- Always use a stand-off to keep the ladder away from the guttering and to prevent it from slipping.

CLEANING A LACQUERED SURFACE

Never overdo the cleaning. Use about 570 ml (1 pint) of hot water and $1\frac{1}{2}$ tablespoons of boiled linseed oil, available from hardware or DIY stores. Try to keep the mixture hot while you are using it. Apply the mixture, with a soft, lint-free cloth and rub lightly. When the furniture is dry, finish off with furniture polish. If the surface is very dirty you may need to use steel wool or pumice powder mixed with linseed oil to make a paste.

HOW TO STORE A LADDER

Store a ladder in a locked workshop or garage, if possible. If it must be left outside, buy special lockable security brackets which hold the ladder horizontally against a wall.

DOMESTIC SCAFFOLD TOWERS Scaffolding will provide an excellent working platform, particularly for exterior decorating or work on guttering. Narrow versions of the scaffolding tower are available for use on stairways.

Make sure that the scaffolding is erected on a solid base. The maximum height of a freestanding scaffolding tower is 3.7 m (12 ft). If the tower is any taller, secure it to a building. Hire scaffolding from your local hire shop and advice on safety and erection should be supplied with it.

Putting up a ladder

Whenever possible get help to move or put up a ladder. If you have to put it up on your own, use the method below.

Lay the ladder down at right angles to the wall, with the climbing face down and the bottom against the wall.

Hold the top of the ladder, lift it above your head and 'walk' your hands up the rungs towards the wall.

When the ladder is vertical, lift the base away from the wall. The foot of the ladder should be 1 m out for every 4 m of its height (1 ft out for every 4 ft).

Lamp: SEE LIGHT FITTINGS

Lampshades

Parts of a wire-framed lampshade

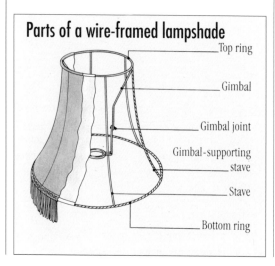

Top ring

Gimbal

Gimbal joint

Gimbal-supporting stave

Stave

Bottom ring

Re-covering a cardboard lampshade Time: ½ a day or less

Stiff cardboard lampshades have only a top ring, a bottom ring and a gimbal. The cardboard keeps the rings apart.

This design of lampshade is not easy to clean, but provided it is not heavily patterned, it is possible to re-cover it with curtain fabric or left-over wallpaper.

First strip off any old trim and wipe the shade clean.

> YOU WILL NEED Fabric or paper, measuring tape, pencil, ruler, scissors, paper-and-card adhesive. Possibly: needle, thread, braid.

CYLINDRICAL LAMPSHADE Measure the lampshade's height and its diameter. Mark the outline of the shape on the wrong side of the paper or fabric to be used to cover it.

Add 2.5 cm (1 in) to the length and, if you are using fabric, allow a similar margin on the height. This extra fabric, top and bottom, should be folded over and ironed, to make a neat edge.

SLOPE-SIDED LAMPSHADE First make a paper pattern (see 'Re-covering a wire-framed lampshade', facing page).

Cut the new cover allowing for an overlap at each seam.

If you are using fabric to cover the shade, allow a small margin at the top and bottom, and press or stitch it down. Snip round the edge to ease the fold if necessary.

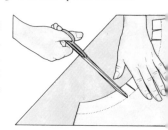

ATTACHING THE NEW COVER Apply about 2.5 cm (1 in) of paper-and-card adhesive round the top and bottom of the old shade, and along the seam that runs from top to bottom.

Starting at the side seam, wrap the fabric or paper carefully round the shade, smoothing out any bubbles.

Apply more glue along the surface of the starting point of the new cover, and firmly press the other end onto it.

Cleaning a lampshade Time: ½ an hour or less

Lampshades should be dusted regularly. Glass and glass-fibre lampshades need only a wipe down with a damp cloth, but those made from linen, crepe, chiffon or plastic can usually be washed.

First test that the fabric is colourfast by rubbing a damp, clean, white cloth over the surface. If colour is transferred onto the cloth, it is better to avoid wetting the fabric at all.

> YOU WILL NEED Washing-up liquid, soft cloth, towel.

Remove the lampshade and dust it. Then make up a mild solution of warm water and washing-up liquid. Clean the shade with a cloth dipped in the solution.

Rinse the shade under cold, running water and pat it dry carefully with a clean towel and leave it to dry naturally.

Inspect the shade when it is almost dry. If the fabric appears to have sagged or stretched slightly, rotate it near a source of gentle heat, such as a naked light bulb, to tighten it.

Replace the shade, making sure it is not tilted at an angle which could bring it into contact with the light bulb.

Re-covering a wire-framed lampshade
Time: ½ a day or less

It is possible to make a new cover for a wire-framed lampshade if it gets damaged, or you change a colour scheme.

> YOU WILL NEED Scissors, insulating tape, cotton tape, pencil, ruler, lining fabric, covering fabric, pins, needle, thread. Possibly: brown paper, braid or ribbon.

Remove the original fabric from the frame and, if it is in reasonable condition, save it to use as a pattern to help you to cut the new fabric to the correct size and shape.

If it is not usable, you can make a paper pattern.

MAKING A PAPER PATTERN Use a piece of brown paper that is long enough to reach a little more than half way round the widest part of the lampshade frame.

Wrap the paper tightly round the frame, creasing it along both the staves that support the gimbal. Crease along the upper and lower rings as well.

Lay the paper flat, draw along the folds and cut out the shape. Check that it is accurate, against the frame.

PREPARING THE FRAME Wipe the frame clean and then, with the exception of the two staves that support the gimbal, wind insulating tape round the staves.

Bandage the two gimbal-supporting staves with 1.9 cm (¾ in) wide cotton tape that matches the colour of the new shade. Bandage over the starting point and finish off at the other end with a neat knot. Trim off any excess tape.

Then bind the top and bottom rings with cotton tape, covering the start and finish points of all the covered staves.

CUTTING THE FABRIC Fold the lining fabric in half and lay the paper pattern on top of it. Cut round the pattern, allowing a 2.5 cm (1 in) margin for seams and hems, all round.

This will give you two identical halves of the lining.

Take one half and pin it to the frame, along both fabric-covered staves, so that it fits snugly. With a pencil, mark where the staves lie under the fabric. These will be the seam lines.

Unpin the lining from the frame then cut out and mark two pieces of cover fabric, in exactly the same way.

FITTING THE LINING Put the two pieces of lining together and stitch 6 mm (¼ in) inside each drawn seam line. This is because the lining is smaller in diameter than the cover. Use a small running stitch or a backstitch (see *Stitches*).

Place the lining inside the frame, with the wrong side facing outwards. Line up the side seams with the cotton-covered staves and keep them in place with a pin at each stave. Then, starting at the bottom ring, fold the lining up over the ring and pin it to itself.

Snip open a small amount at the end of both side seams and fold the flaps over the points where the cotton-covered staves join the top ring, pulling the lining taut.

Pin the lining securely round the ring and then, still pulling the lining taut as you work, fold the rest of the lining over the top ring and pin it in place.

Stitch the side seams to the cotton-covered staves and then stitch round the top and bottom rings, keeping all visible stitching on the outside. (Eventually, it will be concealed by the covering fabric.) Trim off any excess lining.

FITTING THE COVERING FABRIC Lay the two pieces of covering fabric face to face, and stitch along the seam lines. Turn the fabric right side out and place it over the lined frame, matching the seams with the seams on the lining.

Starting with the top ring, pin the covering to the cotton-covered staves and both rings so that it is taut. Then unpin the rings a little at a time and fold the excess fabric to the inside, out of sight. Stitch the cover into place, round both top and bottom rings, keeping the stitches small and regular.

OPTIONAL FINISHES Stitch braid or ribbon to the outside of the shade at the top and bottom, for a finishing touch.

Lavatory (SEE ALSO BALL VALVE)

Understanding the system

The toilet is made up of a pan and a cistern. These two may be joined directly together or linked by length of pipe.

HIGH LEVEL This type is still found in older houses, but it is noisy and obsolete. Pulling the chain lifts an iron bell above a standpipe in the cistern. When the chain is released the bell falls, forcing water down the standpipe.

LOW LEVEL Low-level suites are quieter than high-level ones. The cistern is fitted to the wall behind the lavatory pan. It is connected to the lavatory pan by a short pipe which is called a 'flush pipe' or 'flush bend'.

Depressing the flush lever pulls a perforated disc up through the dome of the inverted U-bend. A plastic flap called a siphon diaphragm closes the holes in the disc as it is raised so that water is pushed over the top of the U-bend and down the flush pipe. But it opens the holes to allow the water to flow through the disc as it is lowered.

The flow of water continues until the cistern has emptied.

CLOSE-COUPLED The cistern rests on the back of the pan to form a single unit.

The flush mechanism works in the same way as that of a low-level suite. Close-coupled suites can have one or two traps.

Double trap siphonic suites are both quiet and efficient. A pressure-reducing device projects from the space between the traps into the channel, through which the flushing water passes. As water flows to the bowl it creates a partial vacuum, which has the effect of pulling out the contents of the bowl even before the flush begins.

Straightening a lavatory pan

If the lavatory pan is not level, the flush may not work properly. Use a spirit level to check that the rim of the toilet pan is level from side to side and front to back.

If not, loosen the screws which hold it to the floor and use slivers of wood, strips of vinyl tiles, or any other packing underneath the pan to level it. Then screw it down again.

Fixing a noisy lavatory Time: depends on cause

> YOU WILL NEED Possibly: new diaphragm ball valve, large adjustable spanner.

Diaphragm-pattern ball valves have a quieter refilling action than Portsmouth ball valves, which are prone to water hammer, so substitute one for the other to cut down on noise if necessary (see *Ball valve*).

If a diaphragm-pattern valve is noisy, check if it has an underneath outlet. If it does, replace it with a more modern version – one with an overhead outlet.

For quieter refilling, choose a ball valve that has a sprinkler-bar outlet and direct it so that the water sprinkles onto the wall of the cistern instead of splashing directly into the water in the cistern.

Alternatively, turn the outlet so that it discharges water over the body and float arm of the valve.

Clearing a blockage in the outlet pipe
Time: 1 hour or less

If the water rises up the lavatory pan when the flush is operated, there is probably a blockage in the outlet pipe.

First check under the manhole covers outside the house to see if the outside drain is blocked. If one or more manholes are flooded, see *Drains*. If not, tackle the blockage from inside the bathroom.

> YOU WILL NEED A large sink plunger or a couple of drain rods and a 10 cm (4 in) drain plunging disc. Possibly: drain auger, domestic mop.

Use a large sink plunger which has a rubber hemisphere with a diameter of about 10 cm (4 in).

Alternatively, you could use two drain rods and a 10 cm (4 in) plunging disc.

You can also use a mop on a broom handle as a plunger to clear the blockage. Throw the mop away afterwards.

Plunge firmly into the outlet of the pan with whatever implement you decide to use. The water should then run out. However, if plunging does not solve the problem, feed a drain auger through the lavatory and out into the outlet pipe or drain, to dislodge any blockage that may be there.

Squaring-off an uneven outlet joint

If the joint between the pan outlet and the outlet pipe is not squarely connected, the water will probably rise up the pan before draining away. If the joint is made of non-setting mastic, or there is a plastic connector between the lavatory pan and the pipe socket, you can unscrew the pan from its base and realign it. If it is a ground-floor lavatory, with a cement joint between pan and drain, call a plumber.

Faultfinder guide: Lavatory

Water rises up pan

PROBLEM Blocked outlet pipe.
SOLUTION Unblock pipe (see facing page).

No resistance or flush when handle pulled

PROBLEM Broken link.
SOLUTION Fit a new link (see right).

Flushes but doesn't clear the pan

PROBLEM Cistern not refilling to proper level.
SOLUTION Raise the water level (see *Ball valve*).

PROBLEM Pan rim obstructed by scale or rust.
SOLUTION Clean with descaling product.

PROBLEM Pan not level on its base.
SOLUTION Straighten pan (see facing page).

PROBLEM Blockage between flush pipe and pan rim.
SOLUTION Clean the cone connector on the flush pipe (see 'Replacing a rag-and-putty joint', overleaf).

PROBLEM Putty from rag-and-putty joint between the flush pipe and the pan has blocked the flow.
SOLUTION Replace with a rubber cone connector (see 'Replacing a rag-and-putty joint', overleaf).

PROBLEM Flush pipe not connected squarely.
SOLUTION Square off connection (see 'Replacing a rag-and-putty joint', overleaf).

PROBLEM Pan outlet isn't connected squarely.
SOLUTION Square off (see above) or call a plumber.

Lavatory does not flush at all

PROBLEM Cistern not refilling to the correct level.
SOLUTION Raise the water level (see *Ball valve*).

PROBLEM Siphon diaphragm failed.
SOLUTION Renew siphon diaphragm (see right).

Fixing a broken link Time: 1 hour or less

YOU WILL NEED New link, wire cutters.

Take the lid off the cistern and flush the lavatory by sharply pulling up the rod protruding from the dome of the siphon (right).

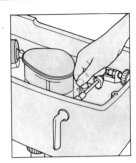

If the rod is not visible, feel under the rim of the siphon for the disc to which the rod is attached. Push the disc up and the end of the rod will emerge from the siphon dome.

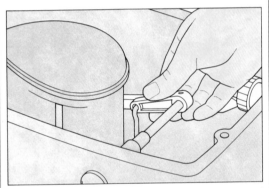

Fit a new link, or make a temporary repair with a piece of coat-hanger wire, slotting one end through the rod and the other through the pivot connected to the flush handle.

Renewing a siphon diaphragm Time: ½ a day or less

If the lavatory will not flush, or the flush action is sporadic, then the siphon diaphragm may need replacing.
You may need someone to help you with this job.

YOU WILL NEED Replacement siphon diaphragm, adjustable spanner, string and batten, bowl, scissors.

LOW-LEVEL CISTERN First, turn off the water supply to the cistern (see *Ball valve*: 'Stopping an overflow').

Flush the toilet, either with the handle or by pulling up the flush rod – or bail the water out of the cistern.

Unscrew the lower nut, connecting the outlet of the flush pipe to the cistern, and pull the flush pipe to one side.

Next, remove the large retaining nut immediately below the cistern. Make sure you have a large bowl handy to catch the water that will flow from the cistern.

An easy-change siphon

Some manufacturers have developed a siphon that can be taken apart easily. An easy-change siphon makes it possible to change the siphon diaphragm without cutting off the water supply. It is probably a good idea to fit a removable siphon when you change a siphon diaphragm, to save time in the future.

Lavatory (cont.)

Unhook the flushing arm and siphon rod. Remove the inverted U-bend and push out the rod. The disc at the end of the rod will carry the remains of the siphon diaphragm.

Fit the new diaphragm, cutting it to size if necessary, and reassemble the mechanism.

CLOSE-COUPLED SUITE Shut off the water supply to the cistern by turning off a servicing valve, or by draining the cold-water tank (see *Cold-water tank*).

Empty the cistern either by flushing or by bailing it out.

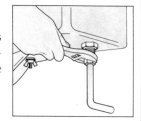

Disconnect the cistern's water supply pipe and overflow pipe, by undoing the nuts below the cistern.

Unscrew the nuts securing the cistern to the lavatory pan and the nuts holding it to the wall. Lift the cistern off the pan and empty out any remaining water.

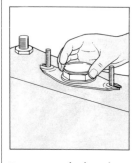

Turn the cistern over and unscrew the large nut holding the siphon in position. Remove the siphon and exchange the worn siphon diaphragm for a new one.

Repairing a leaking lavatory-pan outlet
Time: ½ a day or less

A leak in the junction between a lavatory pan and the outlet pipe, is most likely to be found in a toilet which has a joint made of putty, which may dry out and crack.

> YOU WILL NEED Large screwdriver or old chisel, waterproof building tape such as Sylglas tape, non-setting mastic filler such as Plumbers Mait.

Rake out the existing putty-and-rag jointing material with a screwdriver or an old chisel.

Leave the space between the outlet of the lavatory pan and the outlet-pipe socket clear.

Wrap two or three turns of waterproof building tape round the outlet of the lavatory pan. Push the tape down hard into the socket of the outlet pipe.

Fill the space between the outlet pipe and its socket with mastic filler such as Plumbers Mait. Then wrap two or three more turns of waterproofing tape round the completed joint.

Alternatively, you can replace the joint with a modern push-fit plastic drain connector. Unscrew the pan from the floor and disconnect the flush pipe. Pull the pan forward and fit the new connector. The cupped end goes over the pan outlet and the narrow end inside the outlet pipe. Refit the flush pipe and the pan.

Replacing a rag-and-putty joint Time: about 2 hours

The flush pipe may be joined to the pan with a joint made from rag-and-putty. A putty joint is unhygienic and stray pieces of putty can block the flush pipe, so replace it.

> YOU WILL NEED Old chisel, sharp knife, rubber cone connector.

Chip away the rag-and-putty joint with an old chisel.

Fit the small end of a rubber cone connector to the flush-pipe outlet. Then fold back the large end of the connector and slip it over the pan inlet.

Curing continuous siphoning

Continuous siphoning is only associated with high-level toilet suites. Water continues to flow down the flush pipe and the cistern does not refill. Pulling the chain again breaks the siphon and the cistern refills.

The heavy iron bell, which is pulled up when the toilet is flushed, has three studs on its rim that hold it above the bottom of the well in the base of the cistern. The siphon breaks when air passes under the rim.

Over time grit, hard-water scale and rust will form a sludge at the bottom of the cistern. When the studs on the base of the bell sink into this, air is prevented from passing under the rim of the bell. Water flowing into the cistern passes straight under the rim, through the dirt and then down the flush pipe.

To clean the cistern, start by cutting off the water supply to the lavatory cistern. Outside lavatories usually have a stopcock on the water supply pipe inside the lavatory compartment. Flush the toilet to empty the cistern.

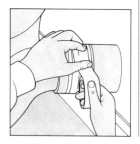

Take off the cistern lid and remove the heavy iron bell and the lever on which it is suspended.

PREVENTING CONDENSATION ON A CISTERN

When the warm, moist air in a bathroom comes into contact with the cold sides of a lavatory cistern it condenses. This can become a serious problem if the water drips onto the floor.

Reduce the problem by running a couple of inches of cold water into the bath before turning on the hot tap when running a bath and do not drip-dry washing over the bath.

Fit an extractor fan so that dry air from the rest of the house flows through the room.

Scoop the accumulated debris out of the cistern with your hand. Replace the bell and the operating lever. Only half-open the stopcock when restoring the water supply, because refilling quickly can also contribute to siphoning.

Replacing a lavatory seat Time: 1 hour or less

Seats and covers are usually plastic and form one hinged unit. If the seat or cover cracks or breaks, replace the set.

The toilet seat or cover can be broken if someone stands on it to replace a light bulb or to open a window.

> YOU WILL NEED Matching seat and cover.

The seat and cover are hinged at the back, and fixed to the lavatory pan by bolts passing through holes at the back of the pan, onto which butterfly nuts are screwed. Undo the butterfly nuts and remove them and their washers. Lift the old seat and cover off the pan.

Remove the butterfly nuts from the fixing bolts. Put the new seat and cover unit on the pan and push the bolts through the holes. Slip washers over the bolts protruding through the back of the pan, then screw on the butterfly nuts and tighten by hand. Do not use a wrench of any kind to tighten the butterfly nuts or you may crack the pan.

Lawn

Most lawns suffer from weeds at some time. Gardeners are becoming more tolerant of the less rampant types, but there are ways of keeping unwanted weeds to a minimum.

MOW THE LAWN REGULARLY Constantly cutting back the weeds' foliage slows their rate of growth.

MAINTAIN THE LENGTH OF THE GRASS Keep the grass about 2-4 cm (1-1½ in) long, to allow it to grow healthily and prevent bare patches that are quickly colonised by weeds.

DON'T ALLOW WEEDS TO SEED If dandelions and buttercups are carrying seed heads, pick them off, collect them in a plastic bag and dispose of them so that they cannot germinate.

KEEP THE LAWN HEALTHY Leave fine clippings on the lawn after mowing as a mulch to feed the lawn. There are many makes of spring and autumn fertiliser. Follow the manufacturer's instructions carefully, and do not use an autumn fertiliser in spring or vice versa.

Alternatively, apply a diluted mixture of liquid seaweed. Use it in a hose-end feeder, at the rate of half a millilitre to a litre of water. (It is used on golf greens and race tracks.)

Another way to give your lawn a tonic is to mix equal amounts of sieved sharp sand and sieved garden soil as a top dressing. Apply 1.5 kg per m² (3 lb per sq yd), working it into the lawn with a stiff garden broom.

What weeds can tell you about a lawn

Sometimes weeds are a useful signal that your lawn maintenance is inadequate. Here's what they mean.

YARROW An increase in this feathery-leafed weed means that the lawn is dry and probably under-nourished. Feed and water it more regularly.

PARSLEY PIERT The grass is under-nourished and has been cut too short. Feed regularly and raise the blades on your mower.

WHITE CLOVER Another sign of undernourishment or lack of water. Rake the clover to loosen it before mowing, mow often and regularly, and feed the lawn with a fertiliser high in nitrogen.

SELFHEAL Indicates bad drainage. Spike the area with a garden fork, moving it about to open up the holes. Remove by hand as much of the selfheal as you can. Treat large areas with a selective weedkiller.

Getting rid of weeds Time: depends on area

> YOU WILL NEED Possibly: lawnmower, suitable weeding trowel, chemical weedkiller.

THISTLES AND MEADOW BUTTERCUPS Regular mowing will severely weaken them to the point that most will die.

DANDELIONS, DOCKS AND CREEPING BUTTERCUPS Though mowing can weaken them, most will need to be treated with a spot weedkiller or removed by hand.

A strong, narrow weeding trowel is the best implement for hand-weeding. Choose a trowel that is appropriate to the soil type: working in heavy clay will bend most tools, so choose a sturdy one; in sandy ground, use a long, double-toothed garden fork to loosen the weed's roots.

REMOVING WORM CASTS

Worm casts can spoil the look of a well-kept lawn, but most gardeners value the fact that worms aerate the lawn. They collect the casts and use them for potting soil. In clay soil, the casts should be allowed to dry before being swept up with a light, lifting movement of a broom or besom, to avoid smearing them across the lawn.

ALTERNATIVES TO GRASS

If you cannot reduce the shade over an area of lawn that is plagued with moss, consider an alternative covering. Daisy lawns, chamomile lawns and even thyme can create attractive ground cover in areas that are not heavily used. Alternatively, put the area under paving stones and decorate it with plants in containers. As a last resort, if you cannot get rid of the moss, get rid of the grass instead, and enjoy the mossy area.

Lawn (cont.)

Scarifying tools

Scarifying involves using a garden rake with considerable downward pressure. It digs into the turf and drags out dead, matted grass.

A spring tine rake is more flexible and does not sink as far into the turf. It is used for removing surface debris from a lawn.

PLANTAINS AND DAISIES Because these weeds lie flat in the lawn, they are unaffected by mowing. Try to remove them all by hand or, alternatively, use a chemical weedkiller.

CLOVER AND SLENDER SPEEDWELL These weeds should be treated at an early stage with a chemical weedkiller.

Long-term treatment of moss Time: depends on area

In order to avoid bare patches and patchy regrowth, remove the cause of the moss, rather than attacking it direct.

Feather-like, trailing fronds of moss indicate that there is too much shade on the lawn or that its drainage is poor.

> YOU WILL NEED Garden rake, garden fork, lawn fertiliser, compost, soil, sand, garden brush or broom. Possibly: lime, moss killer, lawn seed.

Scarify the lawn by raking away all the dead thatch, loose moss and surface matting on the lawn.

Aerate the lawn by spiking it with a garden fork or a long-handled, hollow-tined fork. Move the fork backwards and forwards, in the ground, to open it up.

Feed the lawn regularly during spring and autumn. Apply the fertiliser as directed by the manufacturer, when the lawn is dry but the soil beneath is damp. If there is no rain within the next two days, water it in thoroughly.

Give the lawn a top dressing of fine, completely rotted compost, good-quality soil or loam and sand (increase the amount of sand for heavy soils). This will stimulate growth of new shoots, fill small hollows and improve the lawn's drainage and water-holding capacity.

Whichever top dressing you choose, use about 1.5 kg per square metre (3 lb per square yard) and brush it evenly over the lawn with a sturdy garden broom.

If you suspect the soil is acid and dry, test its pH (see *Soil testing*: 'Treating acid soils'). If the pH is lower than 5.5, give a dressing of ground, dolomite lime (which is slow-acting), applying about 50g per square metre (2 oz per square yard). Apply it in either autumn or spring.

If all else fails, try using a lawn sand that contains a mosskiller, and then rake out the dead moss. Loosen the soil in the bare patches that result, and sow lawn seed or lay turf (see 'Repairing a bald patch', facing page).

RECYCLING UNWANTED TURF

Turfs cut from a waterlogged lawn will probably not be good enough to replace after the lawn has been drained, but they will make excellent potting material — either on their own or mixed with a proprietary compost. Stack the unwanted turfs in an out-of-the-way part of the garden, preferably in a black plastic bag, and leave them for a year or so. The resulting loam will be crumbly, rich and fertile.

Treating brown patches

IRREGULAR OR CIRCULAR PATCHES Could be burn marks, from spills of oil or petrol from a motor mower. Make a habit of refuelling the mower away from the lawn.

If the patches are caused by a dog urinating on the lawn, reseed the damaged areas and protect them with barriers of sticks while the lawn grows again. In future, water the spot immediately after the dog has urinated.

Compaction of the soil, or debris buried beneath the lawn, can also produce brown patches. Aerate the ground, remove any debris, level the area and reseed or returf it.

PATCHINESS WHICH SPREADS RAPIDLY If the affected area is interesting to birds, it is likely to be infested with the grubs of crane flies, known as leatherjackets, which eat grass roots. This occurs in badly drained soil, and aerating the soil to improve drainage will help to cut down attacks.

If the birds do not keep the grubs under control, try watering the patch last thing at night and covering it with a sheet of black plastic. In the morning, the grubs will be on the surface of the lawn. Collect and kill them yourself or leave them there for the birds to eat.

PATCHINESS AND OVERALL DRYNESS Drought is a major cause of patchiness, especially on sandy soil. Long-term improvement can be achieved by top dressing and feeding. Water the lawn before it dries out, if possible, and set your lawnmower blades to give not quite such a short cut — the grass will feed more efficiently if it is slightly longer.

For a quick fix, spike the ground, then water it well.

FAIRY RINGS Various fungal infections, which are often known collectively as fairy rings, can be a problem.

The most common type, a fusarium patch, occurs in spring and autumn and is recognisable by a white or pale pink cotton wool-like mould at the outer edge of a yellow-brown patch.

Spiking the turf and refraining from using nitrogenous fertilisers will help to reduce the likelihood of infection.

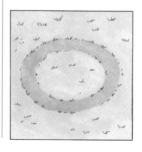

Rings caused by other fungi, such as puffballs and shaggy caps, often show up as single green circles on an underfed lawn.

The fungi decompose dead organic material in the lawn, which releases nitrogen. The grass is fed by the nitrogen and grows faster than the surrounding area. Feed the rest of the lawn to help it catch up with the green rings.

The true fairy ring is caused by a fungus called *Marasmius oreades*, and shows as double dark green rings with a brownish area between them.

Remove the affected area, to a depth of about 30 cm (12 in). Replace with fresh soil and reseed or returf the lawn.

Getting rid of thatch Time: depends on area

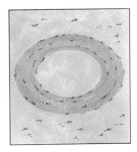

Thatch often occurs on well-established, but rather neglected lawns. It is recognisable as a layer of fibrous material – bits of dead moss, grass and other debris – just below the surface of the lawn.

A thin layer of thatch does no harm, but when it gets to a depth of 2.5 cm (1 in) it acts as a barrier to water, and is likely to inhibit essential aeration of the soil.

> YOU WILL NEED Rake, garden brush. Possibly: sharp sand, garden soil, sieve, garden fork, scarifying tool.

Remove the thatch by raking and brushing the lawn. Then, if the soil is of poor quality, top dress the lawn with a mixture of sieved sharp sand and garden soil. Apply about 1.5 kg per m² (3 lb per sq yd).

In the autumn, aerate the soil with a garden fork or a hollow-tined fork. Then follow up by scarifying the area with a rake or scarifying tool (see facing page, margin).

Repairing a bald patch Time: depends on area

Bald patches can be caused by the removal of large clumps of tough grass or weeds, by spills of oil, by dog urine, or even by heavy use. It is possible to repair most patches.

> YOU WILL NEED Half-moon edger. Possibly: turf, fork, grass seed, fine netting or garden fleece.

With the half-moon edger, cut a neat square round the bald area and lift out the damaged turf. Replace it with healthy turf of the correct size. Firm it down, fill any cracks round the edges with sifted, loamy soil, and then water it.

If the damaged area is too small to warrant turf, clear it of all traces of weeds and fork it over lightly. Make a fine, level, firm tilth and resow with grass seed.

To protect the patch from birds while the new lawn is developing, cover the area with fine netting or garden fleece. Water it regularly if there is no rain.

Levelling a bump or hollow Time: 1 hour or less

Bumps in a lawn can get 'scalped' by the lawnmower, and become bare, giving weeds a chance to colonise the area.

Hollows tend to drain more slowly than the rest of the lawn, so the grass will be much greener and lusher and, as a result, the risk of disease is increased.

Small hollows can be filled gradually by sprinkling thin layers of loamy soil over the area but this process needs to be repeated regularly and takes a long time.

Do not roll bumps flat – this will compact the earth and make it more difficult to cover with grass. Minor surgery is the best solution for noticeable bumps and hollows. It is best undertaken in autumn or spring.

> YOU WILL NEED Half-moon edger, spade, rake. Possibly: topsoil.

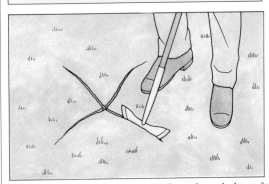

Using a half-moon edger, cut an X shape through the turf above the bump or hollow, extending the cuts a little way beyond the affected area in each direction.

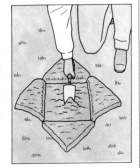

Fold back the four sections of turf, taking care not to pull on them and make them crack or tear apart. Then use a trowel or small spade to add or remove as much soil as necessary.

Rake the new surface level and then gently replace the four sections of turf and lightly firm the repaired area by hand. Look at it from a slight distance to make sure that you have added or removed enough to make the lawn level.

If it is not, or you have over-compensated, repeat the process until you are satisfied with the result. Finally, firm the whole area, top dress it lightly and water well.

MOLES IN YOUR GARDEN

Molehills are unsightly in a lawn, but the crumbly soil that is thrown up makes an excellent top dressing for the lawn or compost for potting. If you are determined to rid your lawn of moles, try mothballs or creosoted rags, stuffed down the run. Or sink a bottle, half-filled with water, into a run – as the wind blows across the exposed neck, it makes a noise that moles dislike. Chemical repellents are considered more successful than sonic mole scarers, but nothing is totally effective. If you are determined to get rid of your mole, contact an extermination service through your local council.

Half-moon edger

A sharp-edged tool that gives a neat, clean cut. It is used for edging lawns and flowerbeds at the start of the season and for remedial work on lawns (see 'Levelling a bump or hollow', left). Choose one with a stainless steel cutting edge if you have a heavy, clay soil.

Good edges are the product of regular care rather than an emergency blitz. Tackling problems promptly gives the best results.

- Edge regularly; almost as often as you mow.
- Avoid walking on the edges of the lawn.
- After edging a lawn, sweep grass roots out of flowerbeds, to prevent them from regrowing.
- Make sure the blades of your edging shears are kept sharp, to avoid tearing or wrenching the grass.
- Prevent low plants from growing over the edge of the lawn.

HOW LONG
SHOULD THE
GRASS BE?

A good height for a family lawn during the summer is between 2-4 cm (1-1½ in). It will look neat and the grass will grow healthily. Cutting the grass any shorter will make it vulnerable to disease and drought, because there will not be enough 'green' to maintain good health.

When to water a lawn

An established lawn which is mown often, with the clippings left as natural fertiliser, should not need watering. However, sometimes it may need a little extra care, especially during long, dry periods.

LONG GRASS TURNS BROWN WHEN CUT When a lawn has been allowed to grow rather long, it will turn brown after its first short cut.

Water the lawn thoroughly in the morning or evening — and not during the heat of the day.

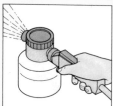

To help it to regain its original colour, give it a feed of liquid seaweed, applied with a hose-end feeder. Dilute it at the rate of 1 ml seaweed to 1 litre of water.

DROUGHT THREATENS A NEW LAWN If a period of drought is forecast soon after you have sown a new lawn, spray it with water very lightly, just as you would seedlings, morning and evening, and feed the whole area with liquid seaweed as described above.

Repairing the damaged edge of a lawn
Time: depends on area

The look of a lawn can be spoiled by a worn or damaged edge. It may have been caused by being trodden down, or overhanging plants may have caused dieback. However, it is possible to restore the lawn's edge.

YOU WILL NEED Half-moon edger, spade, replacement turf or grass seed. Possibly: small sticks or wire mesh.

Using a half-moon edger, cut a neat square through the turf around the damaged section of lawn edge. With a spade, cut carefully underneath the square and then lift it clear of the surrounding lawn.

Turn the square back to front and set it in place again. This restores a sharp edge to the lawn, but will leave a ragged hole a little way in from the edge.

Level this hole by filling it with a little sandy loam, and sprinkle some grass seed over it. Water it well and protect it with sticks or wire mesh, until the grass has regrown.

Lawnmower

Keeping blades sharp on a cylinder mower
Time: a few minutes

YOU WILL NEED Possibly: carborundum paste, proprietary blade-sharpener.

There are two ways to sharpen the blades of a cylinder mower: either by rubbing them with an abrasive paste or by using a purpose-made blade sharpener.

SHARPENING WITH A PASTE Spread the paste (which is available from most hardware stores) along the edge of the blades and then run the machine for a short while — or push it back and forth, if it is a push mower.

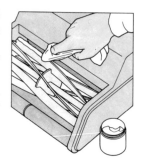

This will produce a light grinding action against the cutter bar and will sharpen the edges of the turning blades.

BLADE SHARPENER A clip-on abrasive blade sharpener is available from garden centres. Fit it to the cutter bar of the mower.

Turn on the power and run the motor for a minute. Allow it to cool for 15 seconds. Repeat a couple of times.

With a push mower, push the machine backwards and forwards to sharpen the blades.

If the blades have become very blunt, you may need to use a second sharpener to get them sharp enough.

Replacing a rotary-mower blade

If a blade has been damaged by hitting a stone and the damage cannot be repaired by filing, the blade will need to be replaced.

Similarly, if a blade is bent, don't waste your time trying to hammer it straight because the hammering will probably cause more damage. Replace it with the manufacturer's recommended blade.

Because blades vary from model to model, take the damaged one with you when you buy a new one.

Replacing or sharpening a blade on a hover mower
Time: 1 hour or less

Blades on a hover mower differ with the model. Some smaller models have easily replaced plastic blades that clip on to a revolving disc. Larger models have solid, rotating bars.

> YOU WILL NEED Spanner provided by the manufacturer.
> Possibly: new blade, new washer, vice, file, penetrating oil.

Work on a firm surface. You will need to tilt the mower, but if it is petrol-driven, do not tilt it more than 45 degrees.

If the mower is electric, disconnect it and tilt it to reveal the cutting bar. Undo the securing bolt, using the spanner provided by the manufacturer. You may need to loosen it with penetrating oil if it is stiff or rusted.

Remove the washer, if there is one, and the bar. But unless you wish to change the cutting height of the mower, try not to disturb the distance washers which are positioned above the blade. They determine the height of the cut – the more washers that are installed, the shorter the cut the lawnmower will give.

To sharpen the blade, place it in a vice and file the cutting edges, following the original angle carefully, or use a blade sharpener (see 'Rotary blade sharpener', page 221).

When refitting the blade, whether it is new or recently sharpened, make sure that it is positioned correctly. The cutting edges must be facing forward when the blade is turned clockwise.

Screw in the securing bolt by hand, then tighten it with the spanner.

SAFETY FIRST WITH ELECTRICITY

Before starting any work on an electrical fitting or appliance, make sure to cut off the electricity supply – either by switching off at the main fuse box, or by unplugging the appliance.

Choosing your next lawnmower

A mower can have a spiral-shaped cylinder blade or a flat, rotating blade. It can be electrically operated, petrol-powered, battery-operated or pushed by hand. A mower can be supported by wheels or float on a cushion of air. Various combinations are available and they all have advantages and disadvantages.

CYLINDER MOWER Cuts with a scissor action. Spiral-shaped blades roll across a fixed cutting blade. It may be hand-powered, electric or petrol-driven (pushed or self-propelled). Ride-on models exist, too.

ADVANTAGES: A sharp, precise cut.

DISADVANTAGES: Generally more expensive. Blades must be set precisely and kept sharp. Not good on long grass, unless the front roller is removed.

ROTARY MOWER Has a horizontally fixed blade which cuts by rotating at high speed. It has wheels and may be electric, petrol-powered (self-propelled or pushed), battery-operated, or tractor-powered.

ADVANTAGES: A good, rapid cut. It can be set to mow closely or through fairly long grass. Usually reasonably priced.

DISADVANTAGES: Can be fairly noisy and small ones may not have a grass-box.

HOVER MOWER Cuts with a blade moving horizontally at high speed, like a rotary, under a metal or plastic canopy. This creates a cushion of air, on which the mower floats, so it has no need of wheels. Usually electrically powered, but some models are petrol-driven.

ADVANTAGES: Light and easy to use, with a gliding action. Copes well with uneven ground and banks. Easy to maintain. Reasonably priced.

DISADVANTAGES: Small models do not have a grass-collecting box. Fairly noisy, and an even cut is quite difficult to achieve. It cannot safely be used on wet grass.

MULCH MOWER Similar to a rotary mower, but has a mechanism that cuts the grass clippings very finely and blows them back onto the lawn as a mulch. There is a wheeled, petrol-powered type (pushed or self-propelled) and some models have a key-start. An electric hover version catches large clippings in a grass-box and blows smaller ones back onto the lawn, to feed it.

ADVANTAGES: Eliminates the need to collect long grass clippings, and feeds the lawn at the same time. Works well on uneven ground.

DISADVANTAGES: They are generally only available in larger sizes and can be fairly expensive. They do not give a perfect, close cut.

Repairing bar blades on a rotary mower
Time: 1 hour or less

Some rotary mowers have a single bar blade with integral cutting edges; others have a bar with detachable cutting blades fixed at each end.

> **YOU WILL NEED** Spanner supplied by manufacturer. Possibly: vice, file, pencil or screwdriver, replacement blade or blades, small stiff brush, replacement nuts and bolts.

INTEGRAL BLADE Use the spanner supplied by the manufacturer to undo the bolt that holds the bar blade in place. Remove the blade carefully; it may still be quite sharp.

Fix the blade in a vice and file both cutting edges. Take care that you follow the original angle of the cutting edge.

To make sure that the sharpening process has not unbalanced the blade, take it out of the vice and clamp a pencil or screwdriver into the vice. Slip the blade onto the pencil or screwdriver.

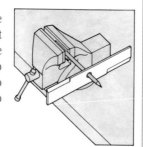

If one end of the blade hangs lower than the other, it is too heavy. Keep filing the blunt side of the bar until it balances perfectly. Refit the blade to the mower.

If the old blade is damaged beyond repair, fit a new one.

DETACHABLE BLADE ENDS It is not easy to resharpen blade ends — it is better to replace them completely when they become either worn or damaged.

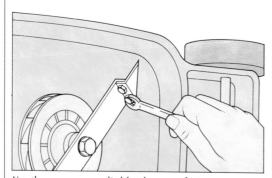

Use the spanner supplied by the manufacturer to remove the blade ends from the main bar. There is no need to loosen the bar when replacing the blade ends.

Brush the bar clean and attach the new blade ends. Make sure that the cutting (or slanted) edges of the blades are leading when you spin the bar clockwise, looking at the bar from beneath the mower.

Always replace detachable blade ends in pairs, and fit new nuts and bolts, in order to keep the bar balanced.

ADJUSTING A LAWNMOWER'S CUTTING HEIGHT

Smaller rotary mowers usually have plastic spacers or metal discs which can be added or removed to lower or raise the blade. With larger models and with cylinder mowers, the cutting height is adjusted by raising or lowering the wheels in relation to the blades.

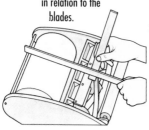

If you have an old cylinder mower and are not sure what cutting height has been set, turn it upside-down on the lawn and rest a straightedge from the front roller to the back roller. With a ruler, measure the distance between the bottom of the straightedge and the cutting blade. Any height adjustment can be made by raising or lowering the front roller.

> ## A weekly mower maintenance routine
> Regular maintenance, after each mowing, will reduce the possibility of problems occurring.
>
> • After use, disconnect the mower from the power supply or turn off the motor. Clean the blades and undercarriage with a stiff brush and an oily rag.
> • During cleaning, make sure the blades are still sharp and are undamaged. If there is damage, you may need to fit new blades or a new cutter bar. Blunted blades can be sharpened.
> • Put the battery of a battery-powered mower back on charge as soon as you have finished using it.
> • Store the lawnmower in a dry, secure place.

Renewing disc blades on a rotary mower
Time: 1 hour or less

Some rotary mowers have a central, rotating disc with either circular or rectangular blades fixed to it. The blades cannot be sharpened, but circular ones can be turned in order to present a new cutting edge.

Rectangular blades must be replaced completely.

> **YOU WILL NEED** Spanner supplied by manufacturer. Possibly: screwdriver, old knife, replacement blades, replacement nuts, bolts and washers.

CIRCULAR BLADES Be careful when working with these blades — they are very sharp, particularly when new.

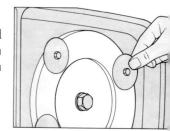

Loosen the nuts that hold the blades in place. Turn each blade so that a fresh cutting edge faces outwards.

Tighten the nuts. Once the blades have been used all round, remove them and replace them with new ones.

RECTANGULAR BLADES There are usually four rectangular blades attached to the central disc: two above and two below.

The two attached to the upper side of the disc are blower blades that disperse the grass, and the lower two blades cut the grass. Replace all four at the same time.

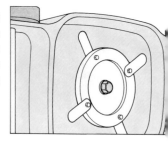

Use the spanner provided by the manufacturer to remove the whole disc assembly from the machine while you work on it. Clamp it into a vice on a stable working surface.

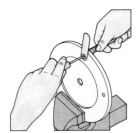

With a screwdriver and the spanner, loosen the nuts and bolts that hold all four blades to the disc.

Scrape away any dirt, so that the new blades fit snugly. Use new nuts, bolts and washers when fitting the new blades. Do not over-tighten them. Each blade should be able to move freely on its bolt.

Extending the cable on an electric mower
Time: ½ an hour or less

If you need an extension to your cable, buy the right length and weight of cable and a sturdy, waterproof connector of the type made specially for gardens. To fit the connector, see *Flexes & cables*: 'Lengthening a flex with a connector'.

SAFETY POINTERS Remember to unplug the mower before attempting any work on it.

Keep a constant check on all the cables on an electric mower and replace them as soon as you see signs of wear.

Be particularly careful about the handlebar switch control cable: on some models, it may be possible to replace it yourself. On others, the manufacturer might recommend that you take the machine to an approved agent.

Rotary blade sharpener

It is possible to buy a rotary blade sharpener which fits on the end of any make of electric drill. It can resharpen a blade to the correct angle within a few minutes, and there is no need to remove the blade from the lawnmower.

The sharpener can also be used to put a sharp edge onto spades, hoes and lawn edgers.

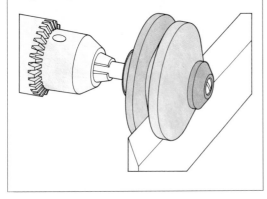

Getting a lawnmower serviced
Have major servicing or repairs done by a company that specialises in your make of mower. Get an estimate from about three companies before choosing one.

Ask the service company to return any parts that they replace, so that you can check that they have done everything they have charged you for.

If you are not satisfied with the service, put your cause for complaint in writing and send it to the company, and if the problem is still not resolved, contact the manufacturer. If the service company is a member of the GMA (Garden Machinery Association) you can also write to The Administration Manager, British Agricultural and Garden Machinery Association, 14-16 Church Street, Rickmansworth, Hertfordshire WD3 1RQ. He will offer an arbitration service if a disagreement reaches stalemate.

What to do if the mower won't start

! Turn off (and unplug it, if the mower is electric) and put it on a firm surface while you make the following checks.
● Check that the blades are not jammed. Remove any debris. Some mowers have an automatic cut-out to protect the motor. Try the mower again.
● Check that all the leads are connected and that the cables are not frayed. Tighten leads and replace cables, if necessary.
● On an electric lawnmower, check the fuses and the circuit breaker. Make sure the mains socket is live by trying another appliance, such as a lamp, in it.
● On a petrol mower, check that there is enough petrol and oil in the machine and just how long it has been in there. Replace any petrol that has been in the machine for more than a month, as it can deteriorate significantly.

Because petrol changes slightly to suit the temperature of the season, summer-bought petrol may not ignite in autumn or winter temperatures, and vice versa. This can make the lawnmower run unevenly, or not work at all.
● Check that the air filter is clean. If not, clean it, following the manufacturer's instructions carefully.

● Take out the spark-plug and clean it thoroughly with a wire brush or replace it if necessary (see *Spark-plugs*).

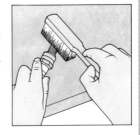

● If the mower is fitted with a drive belt, inspect it – it may have snapped or become worn. Replace it if necessary.
● If the mower still won't start, take it to a service centre.

LAWNMOWER HELPLINES

Call any of these numbers for help and advice about products, spares and servicing:
Atco Qualcast: 01449 742130,
Black and Decker: 01753 574277,
Flymo: 01325 300303.

CHANGING THE OIL IN A MOTOR MOWER
● Always follow the instructions in the user's manual.
● Check that the petrol tap is in the 'off' position.
● Check whether the fuel should be drained off.
● Run the machine for a few minutes before changing the oil: warm oil flows more freely.
● Make sure that you have a disposable container that is large enough to hold the dirty oil.
● Take the dirty oil to a petrol station or rubbish tip with an oil disposal or recycling unit.
● Do not pour oil or petrol down a drain, and avoid spilling either on the lawn — they will both kill the grass.

Storing a lawnmower in winter

CLEAN THOROUGHLY Brush off mud or grass. Remove rust marks with a rust treatment, and oil or repaint the damaged area, if necessary. Grease or oil the bearings, rub metal parts with an oily rag and spray them with WD40.

NUTS AND BOLTS Tighten any nuts that have worked loose during the mowing season. Do not over-tighten.

SERVICE If the mower has been operating badly, take it to a reputable service agent (see 'Getting a lawn-mower serviced', previous page). Do not attempt to make intricate repairs on a fairly new mower, as you may invalidate the manufacturer's guarantee.

PETROL MOWER Drain the mower of petrol and oil, as they will deteriorate. Clean and adjust the spark plug.

ELECTRIC MOWER Check the cable for wear. If a section is damaged, cut it out and join the ends with a water-proof connector. Or replace it entirely, if necessary.

BATTERY-POWERED MOWER Remove the battery and recharge it fully. Store it in a warm, dry place.

Leaded lights

Fixing leaking joints Time: depends on the area

When rainwater seeps in through very small gaps between the lead and the glass, the gaps can be sealed with exterior-grade polyurethane varnish. Brush the varnish into the joints with an artist's paintbrush. Fill larger gaps between the lead and glass with clear silicone rubber sealant.

> YOU WILL NEED Penknife, clear silicone rubber sealant, smoothing tool such as half a clothespeg.

Use a penknife to clean any dirt from the joints between the glass pieces and the lead holding them in place.

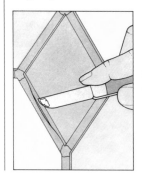

Slightly ease the lead away from the glass and smear in a little clear silicone rubber sealant on the tip of a penknife blade.

It will act both as a seal and an adhesive.

MAKING YOUR OWN 'LEADED LIGHTS'

If you want to match an existing leaded panel, or make your own, you can buy self-adhesive lead strip and stick it to both sides of a single sheet of clear glass. It gives a realistic impression of a leaded light. Transparent liquid stains are also available to colour glass. The materials, together with instructions, can be obtained from North Western Lead Co (Tel. 0161 368 4491).

Press the lead firmly back in place with a smoothing tool such as half a wooden clothespeg or the handle of an old knife. Wipe away surplus sealant while it is still wet.

Flattening a bulging window panel Time: 2 hours or less

A panel of leaded glass is flexible because it is made from several small pieces of glass. A panel may be pushed out of shape if someone knocks or leans against it.

> YOU WILL NEED Chisel, metal casement putty, smoothing tool such as half a wooden clothespeg, clear silicone rubber sealant. Possibly: clear rigid plastic sheet, glass.

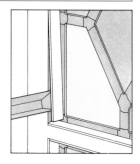

Use a chisel to prise off the wooden beading which holds the whole leaded-light panel in place.

Carefully remove the panel and lay it on a flat surface. Seal any gaps between the lead and the glass as described under 'Fixing leaking joints' below, left.

Pressing down the lead 'cames' should flatten the panel, but if a bulge remains it may be possible to add a sheet of 2 mm clear rigid polystyrene or acrylic sheet, or 3 mm glass, when replacing the beading.

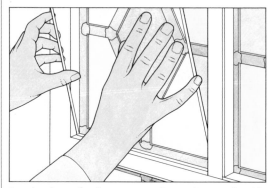

Put the sheet of polystyrene, acrylic or glass on the side where the panel is bulging out, to press it back in place.

If the rebate in the frame is deep enough, use the polystyrene, acrylic or glass on both sides of the leaded light. Apart from flattening the bulge in the panel even more effectively, it will also make the panel weatherproof and will greatly improve the security of a door.

REPLACING THE PANEL Put metal-casement putty in the rebate of the frame and replace the panel (see *Window*: 'Replacing a broken windowpane'). Hold it in place with the old beading, fixed with clear silicone rubber sealant.

Leather

(SEE ALSO GLOVES; SHOES & BOOTS)

Caring for leather jackets and coats

The care label on a leather garment will tell you whether it can be washed or should be dry-cleaned.

If the article is washable, treat it with a solution of one part mild detergent to five parts water. Test for colour fastness first on a small, little-seen area of the leather. If the colour comes out, weaken the solution. Use a soft cloth to wipe the solution over the garment until it is moist, but not saturated. Leave the solution for a few minutes, then wipe it off again with a clean, moist cloth. Then wipe dry.

Marks made by a ball-point pen will come out if treated immediately with a little milk or white spirit on a clean cloth. Rinse off the milk or white spirit, making sure you do not leave milk in the seams, or it will begin to smell after a while.

! If you are in any doubt about how to treat the leather take it to a dry-cleaner or contact the manufacturer.

Renewing the top of a leather desk Time: ½ a day or less

YOU WILL NEED Replacement leather, tape measure, scissors, cloth and soapy water, wallpaper paste and brush, soft cloth, metal ruler and trimming knife.

Cut off the damaged sheet of leather. Measure the area and add on about 1.3 cm (½ in) all round. Order the new leather from an upholsterer's supplier.

Clean the top of the desk with warm, soapy water. It must be completely clean because dirt will show through the leather once it is in place. Allow the surface to dry.

Make up the wallpaper paste according to the manufacturer's instructions. Coat the top of the desk and the wrong side of the leather with paste. Place the leather onto the desk and press it carefully into place. Smooth it with the soft cloth to remove any creases or air bubbles, then allow to dry for about an hour. Using a metal ruler and craft knife, cut off the excess leather from around the edges, taking care not to damage the wood.

Looking after leather upholstery

Vacuum or dust leather upholstery regularly, but do not use chemical polishes or soaps on it.

Clean it only when absolutely necessary, using a strong solution made with water and a non-alkaline soap, such as Dove, or soapflakes. Dip a cloth in the suds and use it to clean the leather with a light, circular motion.

Rinse off the soap with a clean cloth wrung out in clean, cold water. To avoid saturating the sofa, use as little water as possible, particularly if you have an aniline-treated sofa. If you are unsure about how to clean or look after the leather contact the manufacturer.

LEATHER DESK Regularly rub hide food into a leather desk top using a soft cloth. Avoid getting hide food on the surrounding wood of the desk or on any embossed gilding.

Clean dirty marks off the leather with a damp cloth, squeezed out in suds made from pure soap and water.

Ball-point pen marks can often be removed with milk or a little white spirit, but be careful not to remove the colour of the leather (see 'Caring for leather jackets and coats').

Fountain-pen marks may be removed by sponging off with water, as long as the ink is not permanent.

Levelling

Creating a sloping patio or path

Always lay a patio or path on a slight slope, to shed rainwater. Slope the path away from buildings to avoid water soaking into the bricks and causing structural damage.

Tap in a wooden peg on the higher side of the path. The top represents the finished level of the path. It must be at least 15 cm (6 in) below the level of the damp-proof course if the path is next to a house.

Decide the amount of the required fall. On a path 1 m (3 ft) wide the depth of fall should be about 1.3 cm (½ in). On a path 3 m (10 ft) wide the depth of fall should be about 2.5 cm (1 in).

Tap in a second peg on the lower side of the path. Then take a block of wood the same thickness as the required fall and put it on top of the second peg.

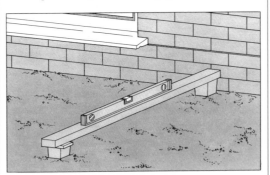

Lay a straight length of timber across the pegs and rest a spirit level on it. Tap the peg with the block on top into the ground until the spirit level shows that the timber is level.

Remove the spirit level, the timber and the block, and repeat the process about every 1 m (3 ft) along the path. Then lay the concrete so that it reaches the tops of the pegs.

Light fittings

PUTTING UP A LEVEL SHELF

An easy way to put up a level shelf is to fix one bracket to the wall, then put the shelf in place with a spirit level resting on it while you mark the position for the next bracket.

WHAT TYPE OF FLEX?

Pendant light fittings can have either two-core or three-core flex. Three-core flex must be used when a fitting has accessible metal parts; two-core flex is used when a fitting is plastic or double-insulated.

Some flexes, already fitted to a pendant lamp, may not be colour-coded or have an earth. Read the maker's instructions, but usually either wire can be connected to either the live or neutral terminals.

What model of spirit level?

The success of many jobs – from fitting shelves to building walls – depends on achieving a true level. Various models of spirit level are available.

LINE LEVEL A small spirit level with hooked ends is hung from a tight cord to fix a horizontal line for large projects like walls.

TORPEDO LEVEL A short spirit level, about 25 cm (10 in) long, is adequate for jobs such as shelf-levelling.

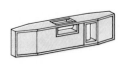

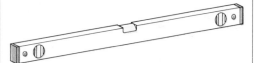

FULL-SIZE LEVEL For building work, a spirit level that is at least 61 cm (24 in) long is needed. It contains two or more vials (a clear tube containing a bubble) for checking both horizontals and verticals.

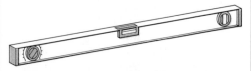

ADJUSTABLE VIAL Some models of level have a vial which can be revolved and set at any required angle.

Finding a long-distance level

A transparent hose can be used to fix a level when there is a long distance between two pegs or where you need to check levels around a corner. Fill the hose with water, making sure there are no trapped air bubbles. Tip out a little water so there is an empty section at each end.

Align one end of the hose against a height mark, holding the end vertically. Get a helper to hold the other end where you want to mark the second height mark.

The height of the water at one end of the hose will match the height of the water at the other end, giving your helper the position for the second mark.

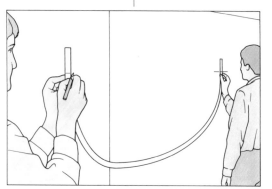

Light fittings

Removing a broken bulb Time: a few minutes

Sometimes, as you try to replace a bulb, the glass breaks. The metal edge is very sharp and there is a danger of electrocution, so don't try to remove it with your fingers.

! Turn the power off at the fuse box, not just at the switch. (See *Fuse box*: 'The power centre of the house'.)

If the bulb has the common bayonet type cap, use a pair of pliers to grip the filament base in the centre. Push the filament base firmly inwards and rotate it anticlockwise to free the lugs from the bulb-holder. Alternatively, try using a cork to push the filament base in, and then turn it to release it from the bulb-holder.

With Edison screw bulbs you need only to turn the filament base anticlockwise with pliers. Don't use pliers on the cap itself or you risk damaging the bulb-holder.

Put in the new bulb, restore the power and test the light.

Replacing or reconnecting a bulb-holder
Time: a few minutes

The flex from the ceiling rose ends in a bulb-holder. Plastic bulb-holders can become brittle or discoloured with age and may need replacing.

If the bulb-holder comes loose, it may need refitting. Bulb-holders with metal parts must be used in conjunction with a three-wire, earthed flex, connected to the earth terminal in the light fitting. Metal lampshades must always be used in conjunction with metal bulb-holders.

YOU WILL NEED New bulb-holder, screwdriver, sharp knife.

Switch off the power at the main fuse box before starting. Remove the light bulb and unscrew the ring that holds up the lampshade. Remove the lampshade.

What type of end cap?

When you buy a light bulb make sure that it is the correct wattage and has the correct end cap.

BAYONET CAP Two contact points and two pins. To fit, push in and twist. There are two sizes of bayonet cap. Make sure you buy the right one.

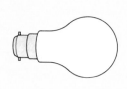

EDISON SCREW One end contact and a wide screw thread. To fit, turn the bulb clockwise two or three times.

Unscrew the upper cover from the bulb-holder and slide it up to reveal the flex connections. Prise the wires out of the grooves and remove the wires from their terminals. Cut off a short piece of flex and strip the end (see *Electric plug*: 'Stripping a flex') so that enough wire is exposed to reach the terminals of the new bulb-holder. Thread the new upper cover onto the flex.

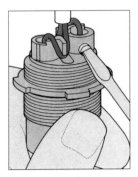

Screw the brown and blue wires into the terminals. If the bulb-holder has a switch, the terminals should be marked L and N. If there is no switch, the wires can go to either terminal. Each goes through a groove on the central pillar and under a retaining lug.

If a three-core flex is being fitted to a metal bulb-holder, connect the green-and-yellow wire to the earth terminal on the cover.

Screw down the upper cover, making sure that the wires are undisturbed. Also make sure that only the outer sheath of the flex can be seen.

Fit the shade on the body of the holder and secure it in place with the retaining ring. Do not overtighten or you may have difficulty removing it in the future.

Insert a light bulb, no stronger than the recommended maximum wattage marked on the shade. Restore the electricity supply and switch it on.

Rewiring a pendant light Time: 1 hour or less

The bulb-holder hangs from a flex connected to a ceiling rose. Terminals on the rose connect incoming wires from the circuit cable to the flex that leads to the bulb.

A heavy light fitting, such as a chandelier, hangs from a chain fixed to the ceiling joists. It will probably have to be removed before you can get at the rose.

The circuit cable in a ceiling rose should be left alone, but the pendant flex can be changed if it becomes damaged, or if you want a longer or shorter flex.

YOU WILL NEED Stepladder, screwdrivers, wire-and-cable cutters, sharp knife, flex.

! Switch off the power at the main fuse box (see *Fuse box*: 'The power centre of the house').

Remove the light bulb and the shade. Unscrew the cover of the ceiling rose and slide it down the flex.

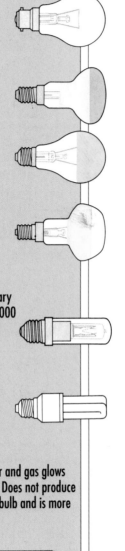

What model of light bulb ?

ORDINARY BULB A tungsten element glows white-hot, giving out light in all directions.

REFLECTOR LAMP The silvered inside throws most of the light forward. Used if a beam of light is required.

CROWN SILVERED BULB Light is thrown back by a layer of silver to give a well-defined spotlight beam.

PARABOLIC ALUMINISED REFLECTOR The shape of the reflector determines the size of beam. Often used outdoors because it can withstand sudden temperature changes.

TUNGSTEN HALOGEN LAMP Like an ordinary bulb but with twice the life – about 2000 hours. It gives 25 per cent more (and crisper) light for the same wattage.

ENERGY-SAVING LIGHT BULB It runs four times longer on one unit of electricity than a normal bulb, and lasts seven times longer. Works like a scaled-down version of a fluorescent tube.

FLUORESCENT TUBE A mixture of powder and gas glows when current flows through the tube. Does not produce as much heat as a conventional light bulb and is more cost effective. Needs special fittings.

Check the position of the wires from the flex into the rose. On most fittings, there will be a row of terminals, with the brown and blue wires from the flex connected to the terminals, one at each end of the row.

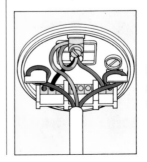

If the flex has an earth, it will be coloured yellow and green and connected to a separate earth terminal.

WHAT TO DO IF A HOLDER RING STICKS

If you are replacing an old holder, the ring that holds up the shade may stick. Petroleum jelly rubbed onto the holder and ring may release it. If not, break the ring carefully using pliers. It is usually possible to buy replacement rings if you don't want to renew the entire holder.

FITTING A DIMMER SWITCH

You can fit a dimmer switch to control the amount of light in a room. Dimmers can't be used with fluorescent lights, and most are not suitable for lighting circuits that can be switched on from two points. To fit a dimmer switch see 'Replacing or repairing a switch'.

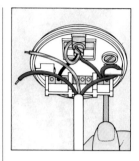

Loosen the two or three terminals that hold the flex wires. Remove the wires, taking care not to disturb any of the wires entering the rose from the circuit cable.

Slide the ceiling rose cover off the old flex.

Prepare both ends of the new flex (see *Electric plug*: 'Stripping a flex'), using the old flex as a guide. Fit a new bulb-holder (see page 224) to one end and thread the other end of the new flex through the ceiling-rose cover.

Connect the wires at the other end of the new flex to the terminals in the same way as the old flex was connected. Tighten the terminals. If there are little notches above the terminals, fit the wires into them.

Slide the ceiling cover up the flex and screw it back onto the rose, making sure that only the outer sheath can be seen. Then replace the light shade and the light bulb. Switch on the power again at the main switch and test it.

Light switch

Replacing or repairing a switch   Time: 1 hour or less

A switch plate that has been damaged or cracked should be replaced. Identify the type – one-way or two-way – and buy one of the same kind. A light controlled from only one position has a one-way switch. A light controlled from two places, for example on a staircase, needs a two-way switch.

You may want to replace an ordinary switch with a dimmer switch, which lets you vary the amount of light.

If a switch plate hisses or sparks, there may be a loose terminal behind it, which will need to be repaired.

YOU WILL NEED   Screwdrivers. Possibly: masking tape, replacement switch, stepladder.

! Switch off the power at the main fuse box (see *Fuse box*: 'The power centre of the house') before starting this job.
Unscrew the switch plate from the mounting box.

With a touch-switch, the switch portion can be eased gently from the plate with a screwdriver to expose the screws. Ease the switch plate from its mounting.

If the problem is merely loose wires and there is no need to replace the switch, check each terminal for signs of damage and clean the tips of the wires. Screw the wires firmly back in their respective terminals.

If the switch needs replacing, note the position of the wires and also whether it is a one-way or two-way switch.

ONE-WAY SWITCH A single two-core and earth cable enters the back of the mounting box. It does not matter which of the terminals the red and black wires go to on the back of the switch.

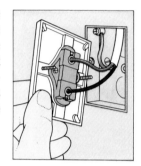

TWO-WAY SWITCH Two cables enter the mounting box. One is a two-core and earth cable with a red wire, a black wire and an earth (bare or green-and-yellow) wire.

The other is a three-core-and-earth cable with yellow, blue, red, and earth (bare or green-and-yellow) wires.

A two-way switch has three terminals that are usually marked L1 and L2 (or 1 and 2) and com (or common). Occasionally the common is marked A and the other two terminals A1 and A2. Use masking tape to mark which wire goes to which terminal in the switch.

WIRING THE NEW PLATE Loosen all the wires from their terminals, but do not interfere with the green-and-yellow (or bare) earth wire that is normally found connected to the metal mounting box (except in older systems).

Reconnect each wire to the correct terminal on the new switch plate and make sure they are screwed in firmly. Remove any tape labels and press the switch plate onto the mounting box. Make sure that none of the wires has become trapped between the plate and the mounting box.

Screw the plate in place with no gap between it and the mounting box, but do not overtighten it or it may crack.

Replacing a pull-cord switch   Time: 1 hour or less

YOU WILL NEED   Stepladder, new pull-cord switch, screwdriver.

In a bathroom, extra precautions must be taken because of the risk of electrocution if water and electricity meet. So any electrical appliance (such as a heater or a light) must be controlled by a pull-cord switch to avoid wet hands touching the switch. Pull-cord switches may also be used in other rooms to make a light switch easier to reach. They have the same wiring as wall-mounted light switches.

❗ Before you start, turn off the electricity at the main fuse box (see *Fuse box*: 'The power centre of the house').

Remove the screws holding the cover plate in place. (If no screws are visible, the whole plate probably twists off.) This may reveal the wires in their terminals, but if not, unscrew the mounting box. Then release the wires and remove the remains of the mounting box.

Thread the cable through the centre hole in the new mounting box and screw the box in place.

Connect the red and black wires to their terminals. It does not matter which goes to which. If there is an earth wire, screw the tip into the earth terminal, marked E or ⏚ .

Press the faceplate gently over the mounting box and screw it in place until there is no gap between the two. Then turn the power back on and test the switch.

What model of pull-cord switch?

OLD STYLE PULL-CORD SWITCH The cord is connected to a lever fixed to the mounting box. When replacing the cord, remove the cover plate and tie a new cord in place (see below).

NEW STYLE PULL-CORD SWITCH The cover plate is attached to the cable, so does not come off easily. Do not attempt to replace the cord yourself – if it breaks, call an electrician.

Changing the cord on an old style pull-cord switch

❗ Switch off the power at the main fuse box (see *Fuse box*: 'The power centre of the house').

Undo the cover plate (if there are no screws visible, it probably twists off) and remove any remains of the old cord, noting how it is tied inside the switch. Tie the end of the new cord to the lever in the switch. Then thread the cord through the hole in the cover plate and replace the cover. Remove the toggle from the old cord and tie it on the new one. Restore the power and test the switch.

If the cord on a new style switch breaks above the cord connector (see margin) call in an electrician to repair it.

Limescale & hard water

Rainwater which has absorbed calcium bicarbonate (a form of lime) from the ground is known as 'hard water' when it comes out of the tap.

When hard water is heated to more than 70°C (158°F), the lime is deposited on kettle elements and hot-water pipes, forming a rock-like coating called limescale.

Evaporating hard water also leaves a grey deposit of limescale on sinks, baths and basins. Thick encrustations of limescale can form around the outlets of taps and can also block up the holes in shower sprinklers.

Removing limescale

Limescale can restrict the flow of water through taps and shower heads as well as being unsightly.

> YOU WILL NEED Possibly: chemical limescale remover, washing-up liquid, vinegar, scourer, cloth, rubber or plastic gloves.

❗ Do not use proprietary limescale removers on an enamel bath because they are acid-based and may damage it.

Clean an enamel bath by scrubbing with a round nylon scouring pad soaked in a strong solution of washing-up liquid and water. You can shift stubborn tidemarks by rubbing them with paraffin, turpentine or white spirit.

Read the instructions carefully before using limescale removers and protect your hands with plastic gloves.

To remove the limescale from round the spout of a tap, submerge it in a small container of white vinegar or limescale remover. Hold the container in place with a small towel, draped round the tap.

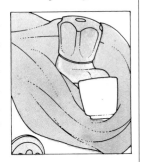

BLOCKED SHOWER HEAD If the shower head is blocked by limescale, unscrew it and soak the pieces in vinegar.

Brush out any sediment or slime inside the head with an old toothbrush before you reassemble it (right).

Alternatively, you can use a proprietary shower cleaner. Follow the instructions carefully and keep it well away from children.

If the problem persists, install the Hard Water Handset from the Mira Showers range, which fits most other models. Pressing the perforated plate on the handset pushes metal pins through the holes in the shower head, and clears any limescale. Do this regularly for good results.

Pull-cord connector

You can fit a cord connector on a pull-cord switch so that if the cord breaks or becomes frayed you can replace it easily. Simply unscrew the connector, fit a new cord to the bottom section, then reattach the connector.

227

HARD-WATER BENEFITS

Statistics suggest that in areas with hard water, heart and circulation diseases are less common than average.

MOVING AN APPLIANCE OVER LINOLEUM

When moving an appliance that stands on lino, in order to clean behind it, place a piece of hardboard in front of the appliance and ease the load on to the board. Slide it over the board, which will remain still. This should prevent scuff marks and indentations on the linoleum.

LOOKING AFTER LINOLEUM

Sweep linoleum regularly and wipe it over with a damp mop. Use a solvent-based polish to enhance the sheen. Rub away scuff marks with fine steel wool, dipped in white spirit.

Softening hard water

INSTALLING A MAINS WATER SOFTENER All hard-water problems are solved by a mains water softener. As hard water passes through the softener a chemical reaction changes the calcium bicarbonate in the water to sodium bicarbonate, which does not form limescale.

Plumbing bylaws state that mains water softeners must be plumbed into the rising main after the branch that takes cold water to the kitchen sink, so that unsoftened water is still used for cooking and drinking.

This type of softener is best installed by a plumber.

SOFTENING SMALL AMOUNTS OF WATER Washing hair or hand-washing clothing can be easier in softened water. Calgon (chemical name: sodium hexametasulphate) is sold by supermarkets, pharmacies and hardware stores for softening small quantities of hard water. Just add two or three tablespoons to the water.

Preventing boiler scale without softening water

There are three methods of preventing the build-up of water scale in boilers, kettles, hot-water pipes and on immersion heater elements. However, limescale will still build up on taps, bathroom surfaces and ball valves.

MICROMET CRYSTALS Hang a plastic mesh of Micromet crystals (sodium and calcium phosphates) in the cold-water tank. The crystals prevent the chemicals in the water forming scale when the water is heated.

ELECTROLYTIC WATER CONDITIONING Water flows through a stainless-steel tube with a zinc lining. The tube is in contact with the copper rising main and acts like a simple battery, creating a tiny electric current. As the current passes through the water it changes the nature of the scale-forming chemicals in the water, causing them to remain in suspension in a fine slurry that is washed through the pipes. Have it installed by a plumber.

MAGNETIC WATER CONDITIONING A powerful magnetic field changes the scale-forming chemicals into a suspended slurry that is washed through the pipes. Some magnetic conditioners consist of two powerful magnets shaped to fit the rising main, and installation of this type is a simple DIY job.

Other models must be plugged into the electrical system to create an electromagnet, and may need to be installed by an expert. However, if there is a convenient power point, you may be able to do it yourself.

Linoleum

(SEE ALSO VINYL FLOOR COVERING)

Repairing damaged linoleum Time: depends on area

> YOU WILL NEED Steel straightedge, trimming knife, double-sided carpet tape. Possibly: broad cold chisel, acetone.

Cut a spare piece of linoleum (lino) larger than the damaged area, or cut a piece from a hidden area on the floor.

Position the new lino over the damaged area, so that the pattern matches, and cut a rectangle which covers the damaged area. Cut through both the new and old lino.

Remove the waste piece. If the linoleum is glued to the floor, lift it with a broad cold chisel, then clean off the rest of the adhesive from the floor with acetone (nail polish remover) on an old cloth. Line the hole with double-sided carpet tape and press the patch firmly in place.

Lloyd Loom furniture

Lloyd Loom furniture is a type of wicker furniture made from coils of paper wrapped round steel wire. The furniture is moulded when the paper (wicker) is soft, then baked, painted and baked again to make it rigid.

Clean Lloyd Loom furniture with a soft cloth and soapy water, but do not get it too wet. Rub stubborn marks with household detergent such as washing-up liquid or Jif Micro Liquid on a soft cloth, but do not saturate the wicker. Leave it to dry naturally, away from direct heat sources.

Use cans of spray paint to recolour Lloyd Loom furniture, as hand painting will clog the small spaces between the strips of wicker and spoil the look of it. For the best results, hold the spray can about 15-23 cm (6-9 in) from the furniture.

Paint over the existing finish. Do not try to strip off the old paint because the process will ruin the furniture.

Locks & latches

If you lose your door keys, or if you move house and want to feel more secure, you may want to change a door lock. It is often cheaper to replace the working part of a lock than to buy a whole new lock.

Changing a cylinder-nightlatch mechanism
Time: 2 hours or less

> YOU WILL NEED Screwdriver, pliers, self-grip wrench. Possibly: mini-hacksaw.

REMOVING THE OLD LOCK Working from inside the house, unscrew the lock cover to expose the screws which hold the lock mechanism in place in the door.

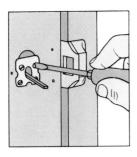

Loosen the screws until the cylinder becomes free and can be taken away from the outside face of the door. A flat connecting bar will also come away.

Take the old mechanism to a locksmith and buy a matching unit, which is supplied with its own keys.

FITTING THE NEW LOCK Hold the connecting bar in a self-grip wrench, and snap it off with pliers at one of the V grooves or cut it off with a mini-hacksaw so that the bar matches the old one in length. Reassemble the lock.

Changing a mortise-lock mechanism
Time: 2 hours or less

> YOU WILL NEED Screwdriver, pencil, scrap of wood, hammer.

REMOVING THE OLD LOCK Undo the screws that hold the lock in place. Then use a screwdriver, pivoting on a pencil or scrap of wood, to lever the lock out of the door edge.

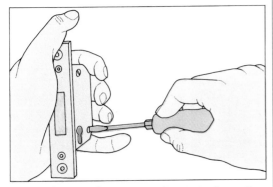

Unscrew the cover plate to expose the existing levers. Note their position and make a simple sketch of them.

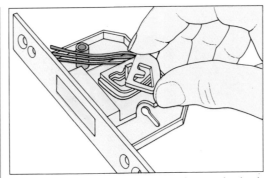

Now ease the levers off the pin and take them, or the sketch you made of their details, to a locksmith to buy a matching replacement set and some new keys.

FITTING THE NEW MECHANISM Place the new levers in the lock in the order in which they were supplied by the locksmith. It is important not to separate the levers until you are ready to insert them into the lock.

Replace the cover plate and screw it in place. Then gently tap the lock back into the recess in the door and replace the screws. Check that the keys work. If they don't, check that you have the levers in the right order.

Freeing a stiff lock Time: 1 hour or less

> YOU WILL NEED Screwdriver, file. Possibly: lubricating oil, car grease or petroleum jelly, graphite or PTFE powder lubricant.

If the key is hard to turn, it is possible that the door may have sagged slightly, causing the bolt of the lock to jam against the striker plate. You may be able to make small adjustments to the relationship between the bolt and plate.

Use a file to deepen the opening in the striker plate. Keep on filing away small amounts until you feel the bolt move freely when the key is turned.

In cases where the key will not turn at all, it may be necessary to remove and reposition the striker plate.

A mortise lock on an external door may become hard to operate because the lubricant has dried out or parts have corroded. Remove the screws holding the lock in the door frame, prise out the lock and carefully open the casing by removing the screw (see left). Add car grease or Vaseline to all working parts and to bolts and latches. Close the case and replace the lock.

Cylinder nightlatches should be lubricated by puffing a dry lubricant such as graphite or PTFE powder into the key hole. Don't use oil; it attracts dust, and will clog up.

REMOVING A BROKEN KEY FROM A LOCK

Never force a key in a lock. Cylinder-nightlatch keys in particular can break quite easily if sufficient pressure is applied. If a key breaks, try to extract it with a pair of needle-nosed pliers or a piece of stiff wire.

Alternatively, insert a piece of fretsaw blade into the lock to dislodge the key. If this fails, remove the whole cylinder and take it to a locksmith.

EASING A FRONT-DOOR LATCH

If the latch on a front door does not slide in easily when you close the door, lubricate it by rubbing it with the end of a candle.

STORING LUGGAGE

Wrap individual cases and bags in polythene to prevent them from becoming dirty. You may like to keep a lavender bag or perfumed sachet in each to prevent them smelling musty when it is time to use them. To save space, keep smaller bags or cases inside larger ones.

EASY-TO-REMOVE SCREWS AND BOLTS

Wipe the threads of screws and bolts with Vaseline before screwing them into position. It will make them far easier to remove in the future.

PREVENTING SNOW FROM STICKING

Rub the end of a candle over spades and shovels to discourage soil and snow from sticking.

Loft (SEE ALSO INSULATION)

Traditionally constructed pitched roofs contain a large amount of space which can be adapted to make a useful storage area or extra living space.

STORAGE SPACE If the loft is to be used for storage only, no planning permission is necessary.

First top up whatever insulation you have between the joists (see *Insulation*). Then lay down a platform made of sheets of flooring-grade chipboard and nail it to the joists.

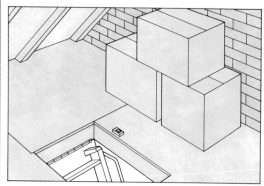

Store heavy items next to supporting walls and get an electrician to install a light with a switch by the loft hatch.

Safety is essential if you intend to make use of the loft space. Fit a proper loft ladder (see *Ladders & scaffolding*) rather than using a stepladder, which will be unstable.

AN EXTRA ROOM If the loft is to be used for living space, building regulations must be considered. Planning permission is not usually necessary unless you enlarge the roof or change its appearance, or interfere with the privacy of your neighbours by overlooking their windows or garden. Check with the planning department of your local council before starting work, to make certain.

Lubrication

Lubrication reduces friction between surfaces and makes their movement against each other smoother and easier. There are many different lubricants which can be used, depending on the types of surfaces involved.

CANDLE WAX Useful for lubricating sliding surfaces, such as the runners on drawers and sledges, and door latches.

GREASE Used on machinery where lubrication is required to last, or is exposed to air where oil would evaporate.

ENGINE OIL Used in different grades for general lubrication of moving parts – from car engines to lawnmowers.

HOUSEHOLD OIL Designed to loosen seized-up parts, as well as to lubricate moving parts and to discourage metal corrosion by sealing out air and water.

PENETRATING OIL Designed to ease jammed and rusted moving parts; a seized stopcock, for example.

FINE GRADE OIL For lubricating the parts of very delicate machinery such as sewing machines and clocks.

AEROSOL OILS Often referred to as maintenance sprays, the finely dispersed droplets penetrate, lubricate and displace any moisture. (See also *Bicycle lubrication*.)

Aerosol oils also guard against rust, but they can evaporate quickly in exposed locations.

DRY LUBRICANTS These include talc, graphite powder, and finely ground PTFE – the material used to coat nonstick saucepans. Dry lubricants are useful for timber surfaces, in locks where oil could attract dust, and curtain tracks, where oil might damage the curtain fabric.

Luggage (SEE ALSO HANDBAG)

Leather cases should be treated with a leather dressing, available from saddlery shops, to keep them supple and prevent cracking. Follow the instructions on the container.

Wash plastic fabrics with a mild water and detergent solution, then dry them with a soft cloth.

Repairing a tear in a case Time: 1 hour or less

YOU WILL NEED Embroidery or craft scissors, leather or vinyl patch, PVC glue or leather glue or Superglue, staple gun.

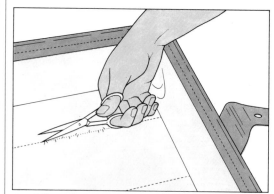

Carefully undo the interior lining in the area of the tear. Use small embroidery or craft scissors to help you unpick the stitching. Take care not to cut the lining fabric.

Glue the patch in place, following the instructions on the glue pack, and press the edges of the tear towards each other. Then replace the interior lining, using a staple gun.

Marble

Marble may look and feel tough, but it is actually quite easily damaged and should be cleaned carefully. Valuable marble should be cleaned professionally – look in *Yellow Pages* under 'Marble Services' for a specialist company.

There are two types of marble. One is fine and close-grained; it is usually white, and is used for making statues and also for ornamental carving.

The other has a variegated, salami-like appearance, which is caused by mineral impurities, and is used in large sections, on floors, walls, columns and tabletops.

Variegated marble may be damaged by powerful stain removers, so always test the method you are about to use on an inconspicuous spot, before tackling the task.

General maintenance of marble

POLISHED MARBLE Objects should be dusted or wiped with a soft, damp cloth, as necessary.

MARBLE FLOORS Wash with a solution of water and a mild household liquid cleaner, such as Jif Bathroom, on a soft mop or cloth, and wipe dry.

MARBLE WORKTOPS Wipe regularly with a cloth wrung out in a solution of soapflakes or washing-up liquid.

Alternatively, wipe the worktop with lemon juice or white vinegar – but do it quickly, to avoid letting the acid damage the marble surface.

Marble is porous, so don't allow water or any other liquid remain on it for any length of time. Make a point of wiping up fat spills immediately.

MARBLE FIREPLACES Sponge the area with a solution of soapflakes, then rinse and dry with a soft cloth.

Then, on coloured marble only, apply a thin coat of microcrystalline wax furniture polish such as Renaissance, which is obtainable by mail order from Picreator Enterprises Ltd (Tel. 0181 202 8972).

Do not use polish on white marble, however, as there is a danger that this may turn it yellow.

If you have difficulty finding cleaning, polishing and touch-up preparations for marble, contact A. Bell & Co (Tel. 01604 712505) who supply products for the care of marble, by mail order.

Washing a piece of marble Time: ½ an hour or less

YOU WILL NEED Soapflakes, white cloths or white paper towel.

If the piece of marble has a base or support made of wood, separate them before you start to clean the marble, in order not to wet or damage the wood.

Gently sponge the piece of marble with a soapflakes solution, rinse it off and dry it well with a white cloth or white paper towel. Do not soak the marble. On large pieces, work on one area at a time; complete the entire cleaning process for each area, as you work.

Do not use coloured cloths or patterned kitchen paper, in case the dye in them comes off on the marble.

Masonry drills: SEE WALL FIXINGS

Mattress

Caring for a mattress

A mattress should give at least ten years of good service, if it is cared for correctly.

DAILY Remove the bedding and air the mattress for about 30 minutes, so that the moisture that bodies have secreted overnight can evaporate. This will reduce the level of house-dust mites in the mattress (see *House-dust mites*).

WEEKLY Turn the mattress over, from side to side or from head to toe, to prevent it from taking on the shape of the sleeper. Foam mattresses do not need turning so often.

Putting a child in a full-sized bed

Put a child into a full-sized bed with a new mattress when he outgrows his cot. His back can be damaged by sleeping on an old 'hand-me-down' mattress.

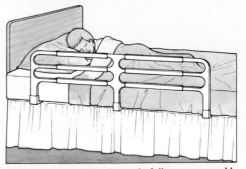

If you are worried that he might fall out, it is possible to fit side-bars which can be removed later. However, if he complains that the bed feels too long, make it up 'apple-pie' fashion, to keep him feeling secure.

Mattress (cont.)

THREE-MONTHLY Vacuum clean the mattress gently, taking care not to dislodge buttons or tufts on the mattress. Then turn it over and vacuum clean the other side.

MATTRESS COVERS Covering a mattress will keep it clean for longer, particularly mattresses used by children and invalids. A plastic sheet placed under the mattress cover will prevent staining, but in a centrally heated bedroom, it can make the sleeper too hot.

GETTING THE LENGTH RIGHT

A mattress should be 15 cm (6 in) longer than the tallest person sleeping on it.

NEW MATTRESS, NEW BASE

When buying a new mattress, buy a new base too, unless the existing base is solid or slatted. A new mattress on an old, misshapen base will take on the indentations of the base and not benefit the sleeper.

What kind of mattress?

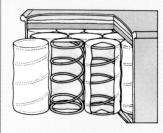

POCKET SPRUNG The most expensive type. Each spring has its own cloth cover, and is unaffected by the depression of neighbouring springs. Gives excellent support, especially in a double bed where the sleepers are of different weights. Some makes allow a choice of support to suit each person.

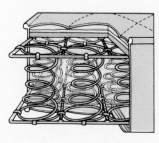

OPEN SPRUNG Wide range of quality and price. Because springs are linked, they are affected by the depression of the springs surrounding them.

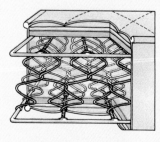

CONTINUOUS SPRUNG A slightly cheaper mattress. Springs are formed in a continuous web, but as there are more of them, quality is good.

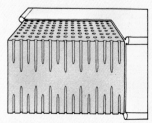

LATEX FOAM Usually reasonably cheap to buy, although a good quality foam mattress can cost more than a cheap sprung one. The mattress may be made of a number of layers of foam. It may often (but not always) be lighter and easier to turn than a sprung mattress and it does not collect as much dust.

Removing urine stains from a mattress
Time: 1 hour or less

> YOU WILL NEED Diluted biological laundry detergent, sponge. Possibly: 6% BP (20 vol) hydrogen peroxide.

Turn the mattress on its side to prevent water soaking in, and sponge the affected area with cold water. Sponge it again with a diluted mixture of a biological detergent. Then sponge the stain once more with clean water.

To remove the stain on pale-coloured ticking, mix 1 part of 6% BP (20 vol) hydrogen peroxide with 6 parts of water and dab it onto the stain. Then dry it off with a hair dryer, once the mark has disappeared.

If the stain is on a detachable mattress cover, soak it in clean water, then launder it normally in a biological detergent. Then bleach the stain in the same way.

Air the mattress thoroughly before making up the bed.

Removing bloodstains from a mattress
Time: 1 hour or less

If a mattress becomes bloodstained, treat it immediately.

> YOU WILL NEED Bicarbonate of soda, water, cooking salt.

Prop the mattress on its side to prevent water sinking right in and making it too wet, and then apply a thick paste of bicarbonate of soda and water to the stain. Allow the paste to dry thoroughly, and then brush it off.

If the stain is still very noticeable, apply more of the paste and repeat the whole process until the mark is less noticeable. Sponge the area with cold, salty water and speed up the drying process with a hair dryer.

Air the mattress thoroughly before remaking the bed.

Removing vomit from a mattress Time: 1 hour or less

> YOU WILL NEED Soda syphon or bottled soda water, upholstery shampoo, sponge, antiseptic.

Remove as much solid matter as possible and then prop the mattress on its side to prevent moisture soaking in.

Squirt the stained area with a soda syphon if you have one, or blot it with bottled soda water and paper towel.

Dilute a little upholstery shampoo and work it into a lather with a sponge. Pick up some foam with the sponge and dab it over the stained area, trying not to saturate it.

Finally, pour a few drops of antiseptic into warm water and dab the solution over the area, to disinfect it.

Use a hair dryer to get the mattress thoroughly dry.

Metal furniture

When buying metal furniture, ask how to clean it. Some parts may have been coated with a non-tarnish lacquer finish, which needs no more than a wipe with a cloth wrung out in a mild washing-up liquid solution. Any stronger method of cleaning could damage the lacquer.

Cleaning iron furniture Time: depends on amount

YOU WILL NEED Rubber gloves, old newspapers. Possibly: scouring pad, household cream cleaner, steel wool, paraffin, rust remover, hard bristle brush or wire brush, cotton-wool balls, white spirit, metal paint, clear lacquer, clear varnish.

This could be a messy job, so protect your hands with rubber gloves and cover the floor with old newspapers.

Remove any spots of rust by rubbing them with a scouring pad and a household cream cleaner.

Alternatively, try using a pad of steel wool soaked in paraffin or in a proprietary rust remover.

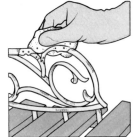

Rust on large pieces of furniture can be cleaned off with a hard bristle brush or a wire brush and then wiped clean with cotton-wool balls dipped in white spirit. Do not use water to clean it, as this will promote more rust.

To cut down on future maintenance, consider painting the furniture with a metal paint or with a clear lacquer or varnish suitable for metal surfaces.

Renovating a tubular chair Time: about a day

It is possible to restore a rusted folding garden chair.

YOU WILL NEED Screwdriver, medium-grade glasspaper or wire wool, soft cloth, rust preventer, narrow paintbrush, gloss paint, replacement canvas, scissors. Possibly: needle and strong thread, metal washers, heavy-duty riveter.

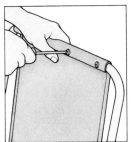

Take off the old canvas by unscrewing the nuts and bolts which hold it and the support bars in place.

If it was stitched or riveted in place, unpick or cut it away. Retain the old canvas to use as a cutting pattern.

REPAIRING THE FRAME Smooth down any rust patches on the frame and support bars, using glasspaper or wire wool. Wipe the frame and dry it thoroughly with a soft cloth.

Coat the frame and support bars with rust preventer and allow this to dry completely.

Apply two coats of gloss paint, making sure the first coat is dry before applying the second. To prevent the paint from running, use a narrow paintbrush and do not overload it with paint. Obviously, for the best finish, do not handle the frame until the paint is completely dry.

REPLACING THE CANVAS Using the old canvas as a pattern, cut out a new seat and back support.

Starting with the seat, wrap the canvas round the support bar and attach it to the frame by reusing the original nuts and bolts. You may need to make holes in the canvas with the points of a pair of scissors.

Repeat this on the other side, and then replace the back in the same way. Tidy up any raw edges of canvas by stitching them into place.

It is possible to rivet the canvas into position. Prepare the canvas, making small holes for the rivets.

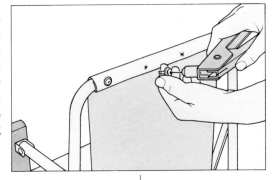

It is advisable to place a metal washer between the rivet and the canvas, on both sides, to stop the fabric tearing when in use. Make two or three practice attempts on scraps of canvas before doing the riveting (see also *Riveting*).

Mice

Even if you cannot see any mice, you will know they are in your house from their small, dark, oval droppings, or the holes they leave when they nibble through food packets.

They also nibble through electric cables, piping and timber to sharpen their teeth, and they can climb well. They carry several diseases and illnesses, including food poisoning, which can be transmitted to humans.

Getting rid of mice

YOU WILL NEED Bait, mousetrap. Possibly: mouse-killer.

SETTING TRAPS Get rid of mice by setting traps baited with dried fruit, nuts, fruit-and-nut chocolate or cooked bacon (cheese is less attractive to mice). Conventional mouse-traps kill mice by snapping down on the spine or neck of the victim, but can only kill one mouse at a time.

'Humane' traps work by enclosing mice in a small cage. You can then empty the cage in open space or woodland some distance from your house.

OTHER METHODS If you don't like traps, use a mouse poison, available from hardware shops. Some brands send mice to sleep before they die. Follow the instructions on the pack, and store it well out of children's reach.

If you have serious mouse infestation, call in your local authority environmental health department or a pest control company, which may use stronger preparations than those that are available over the counter.

Blocking mouseholes

YOU WILL NEED Wire wool, quick-setting cement. Possibly: expanding foam filler, trimming knife, paint or wood stain.

Gaps round pipes can let mice into your home. They also come in through broken air bricks (see *Air brick*).

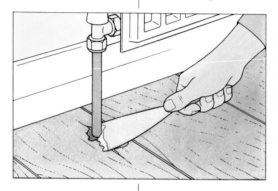

Keep mice at bay by blocking holes round pipes with wire wool, and then covering the wire wool with quick-setting cement. Once it has dried, sand it to a smooth finish and, if necessary, redecorate.

Alternatively, spray a foam filler into the hole. The foam will expand to fill the available space, blocking up even the smallest holes, before setting hard.

When it has set, any excess can be cut off with a trimming knife and the surface redecorated.

Microwave oven

Microwave ovens use electromagnetic waves to vibrate the molecules of fat, sugar and water in food. The vibrations are so rapid – about 2450 million per second – that they create friction and, in turn, heat.

There are no liquid molecules in a food container, so it is not affected by the microwaves. It feels warm, but not hot, to the touch because some heat is conducted through the food into the container. Because microwaving times are so short, the container does not usually have time to absorb a great deal of heat from the food.

A microwave oven is perfectly safe to use, provided the oven casing is not tampered with. Microwave ovens have an automatic cut-out which turns off the microwaves as soon as the oven door is opened.

SAFETY FIRST WITH ELECTRICITY

Before starting any work on an electrical fitting or appliance, make sure to cut off the electricity supply – either by switching off at the main fuse box, or by unplugging the appliance.

Cleaning a microwave oven

AFTER EACH USE Wipe the inside of the cabinet with a damp cloth, paying special attention to the door and its seal. Greasy splashes can be removed with a soapy cloth or a proprietary microwave cleaner. Do not use abrasive pads.

If the turntable is removable, wash it after each use and dry it thoroughly. Take care not to chip it.

Some models have an air filter or splash guard in the roof of the oven. Clean it thoroughly, following the maker's instructions.

Wipe the outer cabinet with a damp cloth, and remove grease with a liquid cleaner. Do not pour water into or onto the oven. Dry all surfaces with paper towel.

BETWEEN DISHES When cooking strong-smelling foods, one after the other, wipe the condensation from the cabinet and door, between dishes, to avoid tainting the food.

STUBBORN SMELLS Strong-smelling foods such as fish or curry can leave a bad smell in a microwave, especially if it is impossible for you to clean it immediately after cooking.

Make up a mixture of three parts water and one part lemon juice. Place it in a microwave-safe jug or bowl and microwave it on the 'high' setting for 5-10 minutes. Then wipe and dry the inside of the oven with paper towel.

YEARLY SERVICE A microwave oven should be checked for microwave leakage by a service engineer once a year. Many companies offer a free leakage test. Look in *Yellow Pages* under 'Microwave ovens – food'.

Safety tips

● Even when the container feels only slightly warm to the touch, the food inside it can be extremely hot. Take care when eating food taken straight from the microwave.
● Do not line the oven with foil or wrap food in large pieces of foil for cooking. And do not use metal containers or containers with metallic decoration. Also, avoid using metal bag ties or metal meat skewers. They will cause sparks, known as 'arcing', and may damage the oven.

However, small pieces of tin foil, used to cover parts of the food that might otherwise become overcooked (such as the tail of a fish, or the exposed bone tip of a chicken drumstick), will do the oven no harm.

● It is essential that the door should close tightly, so do not shut it with anything between it and the cabinet. Do not hang tea towels on the door, or lean on it.

● Do not heat oil or fat in a microwave – it may overheat and burst into flames because the temperature cannot be controlled with accuracy.

● If food makes popping noises while it is being microwaved, it is overheating. Stop the cooking programme and test the centre of the food to see if it has heated through. If it has, remove the food. If it is still cool in the centre, cook it for the rest of the time at a lower setting.

● Do not attempt to dry clothing in a microwave.

● Use only microwave-safe Cling Film, and do not use newspaper or recycled paper in a microwave. Impurities in it may cause arcing which, in turn, could cause a fire.

● If fire breaks out inside the oven, do not open the door. If possible, switch off at the wall and remove the plug, unless it is one of those which open automatically when switched off. If you can't switch off, just let the fire burn itself out.

● Do not operate the microwave when it is empty.

Faultfinder guide: Microwave oven

Oven won't work

POSSIBLE CAUSE Not plugged in.
ACTION Plug in and switch on.

POSSIBLE CAUSE Set on 'Auto Start'.
ACTION Set on 'Manual'.

POSSIBLE CAUSE Door is open.
ACTION Close door.

POSSIBLE CAUSE Clock not set correctly or cooking programme not correctly selected.
ACTION Reset.

POSSIBLE CAUSE Loose wire or blown fuse in plug.
ACTION Check wiring. Replace fuse if necessary.

Arcing, sparking or burning inside cabinet

POSSIBLE CAUSE Unsuitable cookware being used.
ACTION Switch off. Then remove any metal objects and pieces of kitchen foil that may be causing it.

Mildew & mould

Mildew is a fungus which thrives in warm, damp conditions. It grows and breeds, so get rid of it as soon as the characteristic black or brown spots appear. Avoid leaving damp clothes in a dirty linen basket or in a washing machine for longer than necessary.

SHOWER CURTAINS Damp shower curtains tend to breed mildew. If the fungus has just appeared, sponge it with a weak solution of household bleach or antiseptic liquid. Treat bad cases of mildew with a fungicide mixed according to the manufacturer's instructions.

WASHABLE FABRICS To remove mildew wash normally, following the instructions on the care label. If this does not work, soak the garment for a maximum of 10 minutes in a solution of hydrogen peroxide (1 part 6% BP (20 vol) hydrogen peroxide to 6 parts cold water).

Alternatively, try soaking white linens and cottons in a solution of household bleach – about one tablespoonful of bleach to 570 ml (1 pint) of water – then wash as normal.

Rub the affected area of coloured fabrics that are stained with mildew or mould with a bar of hard household soap.

Then leave the fabric in the sun for a few hours to kill the spores. Take care to check the garment regularly as the sun could bleach the fabric. Then wash as normal.

NON-WASHABLE FABRIC Brush the item vigorously with a clothes brush. Do this outdoors to prevent the spores from infecting other fabrics. Then spray the fabric with antimildew solution.

LEATHER Leather is particularly prone to mildew, though regular applications of hide food should provide some protection. If mildew appears, sponge the leather with a weak disinfectant solution. Use 5 ml (1 teaspoon) of disinfectant to 570 ml (1 pint) of water. Allow the leather to dry naturally, away from artificial heat sources, then wipe it over with neat mouthwash and buff dry with a duster.

CLEANING VALUABLE FABRICS

Seek advice about cleaning valuable fabrics from the Textile Services Association, 7 Churchill Court, 58 Station Road, North Harrow, Middlesex HA2 7SA (Tel. 0181 863 775 5).

Mirror

DON'T GET STEAMED UP

A steamed-up mirror is inconvenient when you come to shave or put on make-up after taking a bath or shower. Heated pads, which connect to the bathroom lighting, are available to fit behind the bathroom mirror to prevent condensation.

Heated mirrors with built-in demisters are also available from the Heated Mirror Company (Tel. 01666 840003). Mirrors to be used in steamy conditions should have a special protective backing to stop moisture from damaging the silver backing.

PUTTING UP MIRROR TILES

Mirror tiles and small mirrors may be fixed to the wall with double-sided, self-adhesive pads. They must be fixed to a clean, dry, flat surface. Painted, emulsioned or tiled walls are fine, but do not stick mirrored tiles to wallpaper.

Killing mildew on interior walls Time: depends on area

Condensation and structural damp both encourage mildew growth, so take steps to cure or prevent them, see *Damp*; *Condensation*.

> YOU WILL NEED Proprietary fungicide, small heater. Possibly: wide paintbrush, safety spectacles, rubber gloves.

PAINTWORK Apply fungicide to the paintwork, with a brush. Leave for 24 hours before rinsing it off with clean water. Wipe the area clean with washing-up liquid and warm water. Then apply another coating of fungicide to prevent the spores growing again. Be sure to protect your eyes and hands from splashes of fungicide by wearing safety spectacles and rubber gloves.

WALLPAPER Do not apply fungicide over wallpaper; strip off the affected paper back to the bare plaster. Apply fungicide to the plaster. Leave the fungicide for 24 hours then rinse it off with clean water.

When putting up new wallpaper use a paste which contains fungicide, to deter mildew growth.

Preventing mould in wardrobes

FITTED WARDROBES Fitted wardrobes, particularly those on exterior walls, may suffer from damp or condensation. This can make clothes smell or may even cause them to rot. There are some precautions you can take.

Fit a small ventilator above and below each wardrobe door to encourage the flow of air. If there is no space, it may be possible to fit the ventilators into the doors.

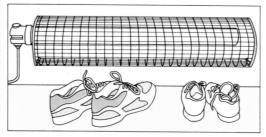

Get an electrician to fit a small tubular heater or airing-cupboard heater at the base of the wall.

This type of heater uses no more electricity than a light bulb so it shouldn't cost too much to run, but it will prevent mould by keeping the chill off the wardrobe and encouraging air circulation.

Fit a small protective shelf above the heater to prevent clothes from falling onto it (see *Shelves*).

FREE-STANDING WARDROBE Keep large items of furniture such as free-standing wardrobes pulled slightly away from the walls. This will allow a circulation of air behind and discourage damp and mildew.

Mirror

Cleaning mirrors Time: a few minutes

ROUTINE CLEANING Dry the surface of the mirror with paper towel or a clean, dry cloth. Apply window-cleaning fluid, then wipe off with a clean duster and polish.

Alternatively, make up a solution of 1 tablespoon of white vinegar diluted with 2.3 litres (4 pints) of water. Apply the solution with a chamois leather.

HAIRSPRAY MARKS Wipe the mirror with neat methylated spirit to get rid of hairspray deposits.

SPOTS ON THE MIRROR If black spots have formed behind the glass, this is a sign of deterioration of the silver backing. You can patch minor blemishes of this kind.

Turn the mirror over and carefully scrape away the damaged area until only bare glass is showing.

Spread a little clear glue onto a piece of metallic foil of a suitable size, and press it over the bare patch.

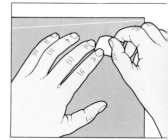

A coat of ordinary gloss paint applied to the back of the mirror will protect the silvering from further damage.

BADLY DAMAGED SILVERING You can make minor repairs to silvering (see above), but it is not possible to resilver a mirror completely, yourself. So if the mirror is valuable take it to a glass merchant to be resilvered.

Screwing a mirror directly to the wall Time: 1 hour

> YOU WILL NEED Mirror, pencil, power drill, masonry bit, wall plugs, mirror screws with decorative domes, 8 plastic washers.

The mirror may come with a hole already drilled at each corner. If not, you need a hand drill and a glass drill bit which will produce holes a few millimetres larger than the thickness of the screws.

Start drilling from the front of the mirror (see *Glass*). Holes should be at least 2.5 cm (1 in) from the edge. As soon as the tip penetrates the silvered side of the glass, turn to the back of the mirror to complete drilling. This will prevent the silvering from chipping off.

Hold the mirror in position and mark through the holes with a pencil. Drill holes in the wall to take wall plugs and insert the plugs. Slip a plastic cup washer onto each mirror screw and push it through each mirror hole.

Slip a washer onto each of the screw tips and then screw the mirror to the wall. Screw the decorative domes into the screw heads until they are finger tight.

Hanging a mirror with mirror clips   Time: 1 hour

Mirror clips screw to the wall and hook over the mirror to hold it in place. The number of clips used depends upon the size of the mirror you are going to hang.

Fixed clips hold the base of the mirror and support its weight, and sliding clips can be adjusted to hold the mirror snugly around the sides and top.

> YOU WILL NEED Mirror clips, metal and plastic washers, large piece of card, pencil, scissors, bradawl, power drill, masonry bit, wall plugs, screwdriver, spirit level.

Cut a piece of card the same size as the back of the mirror and lay it in position. Put the clips round the mirror, with the two fixed clips at the bottom, and mark their position on the card with a pencil.

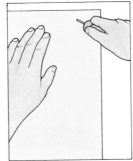

On the fixed clips, mark the position of the holes and on the sliding clips mark the centres of the slots.

Use the card as a template, and make small marks on the wall with a bradawl, to position the clips exactly.

Check with a spirit level that the marks you have made are level with one another. When you are satisfied that they are, drill the wall and insert wall plugs in all four holes.

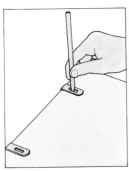

Fit countersunk washers to the screws and fix the two base clips to the wall. Insert plain metal washers between the clip and the wall, then tighten them until the clips are held firmly, and the screw heads are recessed in the countersunk washers.

Fix the sliding clips in position and tighten the screws until the clips are tight, but are still able to slide. Then slide them out as far as they will go.

Stand the base of the mirror on the two fixed clips and then press the mirror against the wall. Push in the sliding clips until they hold the mirror firmly in place.

Replacing a damaged framed mirror

> YOU WILL NEED Masking tape, screwdriver, old chisel, gloves.

If the glass is broken, lay strips of masking tape over it to keep it in place while you are working on it. If the frame is worth keeping, turn the mirror on its front, remove the hanging cord and unscrew the hanging rings.

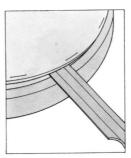 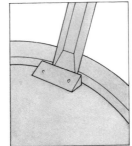

Strip off any sealing paper and ease out the backing board with an old chisel.

Then prise off the wooden blocks that hold the mirror securely in the frame.

Wearing strong gloves, remove the broken glass and dispose of it carefully (see *Glass*: 'Getting rid of glass'). Take the frame to a glazier to have a new mirror fitted.

Moles: SEE LAWN

Moped fuse

A blown fuse may be the cause of a sudden electrical failure with a moped, such as the lights not working.

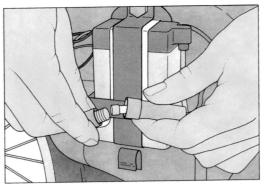

Most mopeds have a single fuse, located in a plastic holder which is attached to the positive cable from the battery. Open the holder and take out the fuse.

Examine the fuse to see if it has blown. If it is the type which has a plastic body, examine the metal strip that runs along the side of the body. You will know that the fuse has blown if the metal strip has melted.

Fuses with a glass body have a fine wire inside. If the fuse has blown, the wire will have melted. If it has blown, replace it with another of the same amp rating.

If a new fuse blows again immediately, there is a short circuit somewhere in the moped's electrical system. Unless the fault is obvious, such as a loose connection or a damaged cable, get it traced by a mechanic.

Moped lights

Changing a bulb Time: ½ an hour or less

> YOU WILL NEED Screwdriver, new bulb, rag. Possibly: penetrating oil, emery paper.

STOP LIGHT, TAIL LIGHT OR INDICATOR Remove the plastic lens, which will be held in place by one or two screws.

Then remove the blown bulb. If it is rusted into its holder because of moisture inside the light unit, squirt some penetrating oil into the part where it is stuck and leave it for about 30 minutes before trying again.

When the bulb is out, look inside the holder to see if it is rusted. Sand off light rust with emery paper.

Clean away any sanding dust and oil with a rag, then push the new light bulb into position. Finally replace the plastic lens and screw it in place. Check that it works.

HEADLAMP BULB The headlamp reflector unit is usually held in position by one or two small screws, either on the sides or the top and bottom of the headlamp shell. Remove the screws and pull the reflector unit out of the shell. The bulb will be fixed onto the rear of the reflector by a holder. Usually it is removed by pushing and twisting or by pushing back two spring clips. Put the new bulb into the reflector unit and refit the holder. Then replace the reflector unit in the headlamp shell and screw it back in place.

Moped maintenance

A care and maintenance routine will help to ensure that your moped is as safe to ride as possible and that it gives you trouble-free service. Decrease the recommended time between checks if you cover a lot of miles on your moped, because parts will get worn out more quickly.

Daily maintenance Time: a few minutes

LIGHTS Before setting off, make sure that all the lights and switches are working properly. On many models the engine has to be running for all the lights to work.

They should not flicker when tapped, or be affected when other lights are turned on. If they do, it usually indicates a loose or dirty connection in either the wiring or the bulb. Check the bulb first and if it is loose, tighten it. If the connector is dirty or corroded, clean it with emery paper. If the bulb is in good condition, check the wiring.

Lenses should not be dirty, damaged or missing and indicators should flash between 60 and 120 times a minute. You must have a rear reflector, and the stop light (if your model has one) must come on when the brakes are applied and go off when they are released.

ENGINE OIL Check the engine oil every time you use the moped. On most models with two-stroke engines there is an inspection window in the oil tank.

Fill up the tank to the upper-level mark with two-stroke oil.

On some old machines the oil is mixed with the fuel to a recommended ratio.

TYRES AND WHEELS The best way to check the tyres is to place the moped on its centre stand. Raise each wheel off the ground in turn and rotate it slowly by hand.

Check each tyre for cuts, tears, bulges or exposed ply or cord in the tread or wall. Also, check that the tyre is seated correctly on the wheel rim and that the valve stem is not damaged in any way, or out of alignment.

Check the tread depth, too. If the moped has a lower engine capacity than 50 cc, the base of any groove in the original tread must still be visible.

Machines with larger engines must have tread of at least 1 mm, forming a continuous band on at least three-quarters of the breadth of the tread all the way round.

If the tyre has arrows on the sidewall they must point in the direction that the wheel rotates.

Ensure that there is no sideways movement between wheel and frame and that both wheels are well secured.

Weekly maintenance

BATTERY Check the electrolyte level every week. Most mopeds use a battery with a transparent body so that you can easily see the level. If it is below the minimum level mark, top it up with distilled water.

TRANSMISSION The chain or transmission arrangement on mopeds varies a great deal from model to model. Some are completely enclosed in a transmission housing part-filled with oil, and maintenance consists of no more than changing the oil once a year.

Other models use an exposed chain like the chain on a bicycle. Oil this type lightly. If it is protected by a chain guard there will be a plug in the guard that pulls out to allow access to the chain for oiling.

Chain tension on many models is automatically maintained by a spring device. Some models need to have the tension manually adjusted by moving the rear wheel backwards. On this type of moped, inspect the tension weekly and adjust it if necessary. The exact method varies, so consult the owner's handbook.

Monthly checks

BRAKES As the brake shoes wear, the amount of play in the brake lever will increase. Ideally the lever should move about 10-15 mm ($\frac{1}{2}$ in) before the brake begins to work.

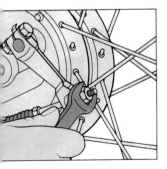

Take up any excess by turning the cable-adjuster nut at the wheel-end of the cable. An ordinary spanner fits the nut in most cases.

If there is a knurled nut at the wheel-end of the cable, it can usually be turned by hand. There are some models of moped that also have a knurled adjuster at the lever-end of the cable for making minor adjustments.

Some models have a wear indicator, in the form of a mark or arrow on the hub, which shows the limit that the brake operating arm, pulled by the cable, can travel before the shoes have worn too thin and will need replacing.

STEERING Put the moped on its centre stand so that the front wheel is clear of the ground. Then turn the handlebars as far round to the left as they will go, and then all the way to the right.

Only slight pressure should be needed to turn them and there should be no grating noises or uneven feeling when turning the handlebars. Check that no other part of the machine restricts the free movement of the steering and that the handgrips and any clamps are not loose.

Take the moped off its stand and apply the front brake. Rock it back and forth to check for any forward or backward movement in the steering bearings – there should be none.

SPARK PLUGS Clean and gap a spark plug once a month (see *Spark plug*: 'Cleaning and gapping a spark plug').

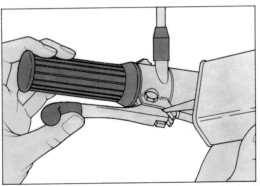

OILING THE CABLES Once a month, oil the exposed ends of the brake cables (and the clutch cable if one is fitted).

SUSPENSION To check the damping action of the front suspension, straddle the moped and apply the front brake. Push down on the handlebars so that the forks depress and make sure that they move freely without grating. If they don't, or if there seems to be a lack of damping, get the machine checked and fixed by a mechanic.

Hold the front wheel between your knees. Try to move the handlebars from side to side to check for freeplay in the front suspension. If the handlebars can be moved while the wheel stays still, there may be wear in the suspension. Get it checked professionally.

Now check the rear wheel by sitting on the saddle and depressing the rear suspension a few times, again checking the damping action and freedom of movement.

Put the moped on its centre stand and check for sideways play by trying to move the rear wheel sideways.

Six-monthly checks

SERVICING THE CABLES Disconnect the handlebar end of each cable and trickle light oil down inside the casing. The best way to do this is to form a cup of Plasticine around the outer casing at the end of the cable.

Then suspend the cable in an upright position and very carefully trickle light oil into the Plasticine cup.

Leave it in this position overnight so that the oil has time to trickle down the full length of the cable.

FILTERS Oil filters and air filters need cleaning or changing every six months. They differ considerably from model to model, so consult the owner's manual.

TUNING It is best to get a qualified mechanic to check every six months that the moped's carburation and ignition systems are set up for maximum efficiency.

Yearly maintenance

The transmission, brakes, steering, suspension and tyres need a thorough check once a year. This is probably best left to a garage, though you could check the tyres yourself.

If the brakes have visible wear indicators, you will be able to tell at a glance if they need attention at the garage. Otherwise they will need dismantling, so that you can check for wear in the brake shoes.

Some mopeds need partial dismantling of steering and the suspension for greasing, which is best left to a garage.

Transmission systems can vary a great deal. For some models the only maintenance that is needed is to change the oil, which you can do yourself quite easily.

Moped security

Almost all mopeds include a steering lock, either as part of the ignition switch or as a separate key-operated lock on the forks. However, on its own, a steering lock will provide very little protection against determined thieves.

WHEEL LOCK For increased security you can use a good quality chain and padlock or a rigid U-lock to help to prevent your machine from being wheeled away.

A rigid U-lock is stronger than most security chains, but it will usually pass through the wheel only. For better security, try to get it to pass around part of the frame too.

A security chain has the advantage of being able to pass through a wheel and the frame, so that the wheel cannot be removed easily. It can also be used to tether the machine to a fixed object such as railings.

However, do remember that a moped is a motor vehicle so it should not be parked on the pavement. You risk being given a parking ticket if you do.

IMMOBILISERS Alarms and immobilisers similar to those used on cars are increasingly popular for large motorbikes, and some types are suitable for mopeds.

However, immobilisation will only stop the machine from being ridden away; it will do nothing to prevent it from being lifted up and carried away.

METAL STAMPING Major parts can be stamped with the registration number to deter the thieves who strip down mopeds for parts. This is a less expensive version of the 'Datatag' system used on large, expensive motorbikes.

Mortar

Making a mortar mix Time: depends on amount

Mortar is made by mixing Portland cement, sand and water – and, sometimes, hydrated lime. Mortar's main uses are for bricklaying, for pointing between bricks, and for repairing concrete surfaces.

It is possible to buy all the ingredients that you will need, ready-mixed or separately, from most DIY centres.

Making mortar 'buttery' and gluey

You can make mortar more 'buttery' and much easier to work, by adding a squirt of washing-up liquid to the mixing water.

To give a better grip when doing repair work, add 1 part of PVA building adhesive to 10 parts of water (by volume). The area being repaired can also be painted with neat PVA before the mortar is applied.

The most convenient form of mortar is a dry mix which is sold in paper sacks ranging in size from 5 kg (11 lb) to 40 kg (88 lb). You only need to add clean water.

If you want to make up your own mortar, always use fresh cement powder. Once opened, bags of cement are difficult to store without hardening. Buy builders' (soft) sand to add to the cement.

YOU WILL NEED Mixing board, trowel, watering can, bucket.

BAGGED MIX Empty some of the dry mix onto a mixing board. Make a hollow in the centre of the pile and add a little water. Use a trowel to work the water into the mix.

Mix it well until it is an even consistency and fairly dry – like a beach sand pie. If it is wetter, the mortar will not hold its shape and will also cause stains. When it is ready, carry the mortar in a bucket to where it's needed.

SEPARATE INGREDIENTS If you are going to need larger quantities of mortar, it will be cheaper to buy the ingredients separately and mix them together yourself.

Use a shovel instead of a trowel, or consider hiring a concrete mixer from your local hire shop.

Mortar and concrete for different uses

Mortar and concrete are variations of the same basic recipe. Different mixes, measured by volume not weight, are made for different uses.

MIXING MORTAR For general repairs and laying bricks in the garden use a mixture of 1 part cement and 3 or 4 parts washed builders' sand.

If you are going to point a brick wall, make up a mixture of 1 part cement, 2 parts hydrated lime and 8 parts washed builders' sand.

MIXING CONCRETE For shed foundations, garage floors and drives use a mixture of 1 part cement, $2\frac{1}{2}$ parts sharp sand and 4 parts coarse aggregate.

For paths, steps, and pools use 1 part cement, 2 parts sharp sand and 3 parts coarse aggregate.

Mosaic tiles

Regrouting existing tiles Time: depends on area

YOU WILL NEED Old penknife or small kitchen knife, rubber squeegee or sponge, old paintbrush, grouting compound, rag.

If the grout has become discoloured or soft, use the blade of an old knife to scrape it out. Dust the gaps with an old paintbrush, then apply new grout.

Spread the fresh grout into the gaps with a rubber squeegee or a piece of sponge and wipe away any surplus with a damp rag. When the grout is dry, polish the tiles with a ball of screwed up newspaper.

Repairing a damaged tile Time: 1 hour

If a tile has been chipped, perhaps through drilling to take a fitting, the most difficult task is to find a replacement.

If you are unsuccessful, it may be possible to use a tile that you have removed from a hidden area.

YOU WILL NEED Power drill and masonry bit, old chisel, hammer, safety spectacles, tile adhesive, grouting compound.

Drill holes in the damaged tile and insert an old chisel. Lever out the damaged pieces, working from the centre outwards. Take care not to damage the surrounding tiles.

Apply tile adhesive to the new tile and press it in place.

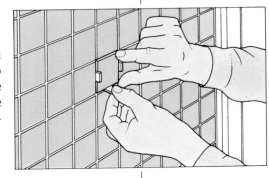

Centre the new tile with strips of cardboard to stop it from slipping, until the adhesive sets. Remove the strips and finish off by regrouting the repair.

Mosquitoes

Keeping mosquitoes at bay

Although, in hot countries, mosquitoes can cause serious illnesses such as malaria and yellow fever, in cooler climates they do little more than irritate. A mosquito bite that is scratched, however, can become infected. To avoid being bitten by mosquitoes try one of these remedies.

CITRONELLA CANDLES Available from DIY centres, bigger supermarkets and wherever barbecue equipment is sold. Suitable for outside use, they shed light and give off a pleasant smell which repels mosquitoes.

SLOW-BURNING COILS Sold in camping shops. When lit, they give off an odourless smoke which will kill mosquitoes. They are effective indoors and will last almost all night.

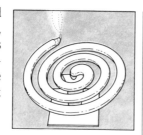

ELECTRIC-PLUG REPELLENT Available in chemist shops. The plug is fitted into a wall socket, and as it warms up, mosquito-repellent pellets inside it begin to melt. It is suitable for all-night use.

ELECTRIC MOSQUITO TRAP Emits ultraviolet light which attracts mosquitoes. They fly into the trap and are electrocuted. Wall-mounted, it can be used both indoors and out.

WRIST AND ANKLE BANDS Available from chemists. Bands are impregnated with a mosquito repellent and keep mosquitoes away from wrists and ankles.

CREAMS, GELS AND SPRAYS A single application of any of these will keep mosquitoes away for about three hours.

INSECTICIDAL SPRAY Spray bedrooms thoroughly with an insecticidal spray. It is even more effective if the spray is used after the light has been put out, as some mosquitoes will stay hidden until it is dark.

FLY SWATTER The most rudimentary way to kill mosquitoes. Remember that a mosquito may be full of blood if it has recently had a feed, and swatting it will make a mess.

No more mosquitoes in your garden

In Britain, mosquitoes are most active between March and October, when the females need to feed on blood in order to lay their eggs.

Mosquito larvae develop in still or stagnant water, so getting rid of potential breeding places will stop mosquitoes breeding and developing in your garden.

- Clean out water butts and birdbaths regularly. Refill the birdbath with clean water.
- Get rid of all unwanted containers in the garden and turn wanted ones upside-down, so that rainwater cannot collect in them.
- Remove damp debris from gutters and drains.

MOT test: SEE CAR MOT TEST

Mouldings (SEE ALSO OVERLEAF)

Mouldings are lengths of shaped wood, MDF, plaster, expanded polystyrene or polyurethane, which are used to cover up gaps or add decoration. Mouldings can be used at the tops and bottoms of walls, round doors, windows and light fittings, on wall panelling and on furniture.

Most small wood mouldings are made from ramin, a light-coloured, fine-grained hardwood that tends to split easily, so drill fine holes before driving pins through it.

Repairing a damaged plaster moulding

If a plaster moulding has been damaged, you may be able to repair it yourself, or even make a replacement section (see *Cornice & coving*: 'Making your own mouldings').

Replacing a damaged wooden moulding
Time: depends on amount

YOU WILL NEED Dovetail saw or fine-tooth tenon saw, claw hammer or old chisel, pincers, wood glue, pin hammer, nail punch, fine oval nails or panel pins, template former, fine sandpaper, wood filler. Possibly: interior filler.

Make a template of the good moulding using a template former and then take it to your local timber merchant where you may be able to find a moulding to match it.

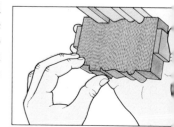

If there is nothing that matches, most companies will produce profiles to match yours, but they will be expensive.

With a dovetail saw or a fine-tooth tenon saw make shallow angled cuts at both ends of the damaged area, cutting towards the piece to be removed. This will make for a neater joint later.

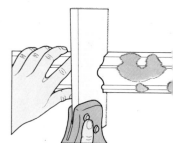

For large mouldings, lever out the damaged piece with a claw hammer. For smaller mouldings use an old chisel. Remove any nails or pins with pincers. Make good any damage to the plaster below with interior filler.

With a tenon saw, cut a piece of the new moulding that is slightly longer than the piece that is to be replaced.

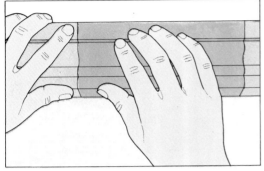

Carefully mark and repeat the shallow angle at each end, using the removed pieces as a template. Apply wood glue to the ends and press the moulding in place.

If the moulding is being fitted to wood, secure it with fine oval nails or panel pins. Sink the heads with a nail punch and fill the indents with matching wood filler. Apply wood filler to the joints if necessary. Allow it to set thoroughly, then lightly sand it down.

If the moulding is to be fixed directly on to a plastered wall, as with a door architrave, spread panel adhesive on the back of the replacement piece and stick it to the wall.

Fitting a picture rail

> YOU WILL NEED Pencil, steel straightedge, spirit level, 6 cm (2½ in) cut nails or 4.4 cm (1¾ in) no.8 gauge countersunk screws, wall plugs, hammer, nail punch, screwdriver, wood filler.

Mark a pencil line along the walls at the required height, with a straightedge and spirit level. Lengths of rail can usually be nailed direct to the walls with 6 cm (2½ in) cut nails. On a hard wall, use 4.4 cm (1¾ in) no.8 gauge countersunk screws and wall plugs. On a partition wall nail the rail to the timber studs. Use screws with plasterboard fixings. Cover screw and nail heads with wood filler.

Putting up a decorative ceiling rose   Time: 1 hour or less

Decorative roses may be made from expanded polystyrene, foamed rigid polyurethane or plaster. Most ceiling roses come with a recessed back to accommodate an existing small plastic ceiling fitting, so check that you can fit your new rose over the fitting. If you are replacing an old decorative rose you will need to unscrew it or prise it off first.

> YOU WILL NEED Replacement rose, stepladder. Possibly: bradawl, screwdriver, appropriate adhesive, screws, pencil, cordless drill.

Turn off the power supply at the main fuse box. Then remove the lampshade, bulb and bulb-holder.

EXPANDED-POLYSTYRENE CEILING ROSE Pierce the centre of the ceiling rose, then spread expanded-polystyrene tile adhesive all over its back. Feed the light flex through the hole, push the rose up the flex and press it into place.

PLASTER CEILING ROSE If you have removed an old decorative rose from the ceiling, the joist may be visible.

If the joist is not visible, use a joist-and-stud detector to establish where it runs (see *Curtain poles & tracks*: 'Fixing brackets to the ceiling'), and then make a faint pencil mark on the ceiling along the line of the joist.

To avoid over-handling the new plaster rose, cut an accurate template of it out of the back of the box it came in. Mark the centre of the template and pierce it. Draw a pencil line through the centre, right across the template.

Feed the end of the light flex through the hole and hold the template against the ceiling, aligning the pencil line with the line on the ceiling. With a bradawl, pierce the template and the ceiling at two points along the line.

Transfer the marks from the template onto the rose and drill through the centre of the rose and the screw holes.

Put matchsticks in the screw holes to keep them clear, while you spread ready-mixed cove adhesive onto the back of the rose. Feed the light flex through the rose, line up the screw holes, and press the rose against the ceiling. Feed the screws into the holes and screw them into place.

Musty smells

Damp conditions encourage the growth of mould spores which emit a dank, musty smell. Curtains, upholstery, carpets and clothes can all be affected. Find the source of the damp and eliminate it (see *Damp*; *Mildew & mould*).

Getting rid of musty smells in a washing machine
Time: 2 hours or less

Musty smells coming from inside a washing machine can be caused by a clogged filter. Clean the filter thoroughly (see *Washing machine*) and the smell should go.

In machines that do not have filters, the smell can be caused by an accumulation of limescale in the outlet hose. Pour a cup of household bleach or descaling liquid into the machine and set the machine to the shortest cycle. You may need to repeat the treatment until the smell has gone.

Before using it again, run a complete cycle with the machine empty, to make sure all traces of bleach or descaler have been washed away. Allow the machine to dry out and air for a while after each wash.

Timber mouldings

MOULDINGS

Mouldings are available in various designs and materials – from highly ornate carved wood to plain plaster and lightweight expanded polystyrene. They can be used to hold glass or carpets in place, to disguise cracks and rough edges, or simply to decorate a room or a piece of furniture.

STAFF AND PARTING BEADS
Both used in wooden sash windows to hold the sashes in place.

CORNER MOULDING To cover a corner where two boards join. Hides screw fixings.

GLASS BEAD Used to hold glass in door and window frames.

TRIANGLE For finishing internal corners. It can be used as stair rods and, consequently, is also known as stair-rod moulding.

QUADRANT MOULDING Used for covering gaps between floor and skirting, and between wooden windows and the window sill.

ARCHITRAVE Hides the join between a door frame and wall.

SKIRTING
Hides the join between a floor and a wall.

WEATHER MOULDING
Fits on the bottom of an exterior door to keep out rain.

SQUARE OR RECTANGULAR MOULDING Used for finishing the edges of shelves made of blockboard, chipboard or plywood.

PICTURE RAIL A large moulding running round a room, high up on the walls. Pictures are hung from it.

DADO RAIL A moulding which separates the upper and lower section of a wall, often with different decoration above and below.

Plaster and plastic mouldings

CORNICE An ornate decorative moulding fitted to the top of a wall.

WOODEN ORNAMENTS Many designs of wooden ornaments are available for decorating doors, walls and furniture.

CORBEL A decorative bracket which projects from the wall. Usually used to support a cornice or an arch.

COVING A curved strip that fits in the angle between wall and ceiling.

CEILING ROSE A circular or oval decorative moulding which sits in the centre of a ceiling, often round the light fitting.

Nail punch

A nail punch is used to drive nails below the surface of the wood. The resulting little hole is then plugged with filler.

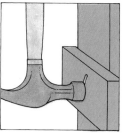

AVOID BENT NAILS

When nails bend while you are driving them home it is usually because the hammer is slipping from the nail head. Reduce the risk of this happening by roughing the hammer's striking face with coarse emery paper.

SHORTENING A BOLT

If you want to shorten a bolt, screw on the nut first and then cut the bolt with a hacksaw. Unscrew the nut to correct any slight distortion of the thread caused by cutting.

Nails & nailing

Nails still have a part to play in construction work, though super-strong adhesives now replace them in many jobs.

Essential nailing techniques

● Always nail the thinner piece of wood to the thicker.
● Hammer the tip of a round nail to flatten it so that it does not split the wood as it is driven in.
● Avoid splitting by drilling start holes for nails in hardwoods or brittle wood such as pine.
● When using a line of nails, try to avoid running them along the same grain line; the wood will probably split.

● To give extra strength to a timber joint, use longer nails and then clench (bend over) the protruding part.

● It is possible to improve the holding power of a joint by hammering the nails in at an angle (skew nailing).

● Use annular (or ring) nails for nailing into end grain, but try to avoid end grain if possible as it gives a weak join.

Nuts & bolts

(SEE ALSO SPANNERS & WRENCHES)

When you buy nuts and bolts separately make sure they have the same type of thread. Four types of thread are commonly sold – Metric, Unified Fine (UNF), Unified Coarse (UNC) and ISO Inch.

If you want to replace a missing bolt in an old appliance or machine, even more types of thread are possible: British Standard Whitworth (BSW), British Standard Fine (BSF) and British Association (BA). The only way you can be sure of buying the right type is to take a matching bolt to a specialist hardware shop and ask for the same sort.

Alternatively, contact the appliance manufacturer.

HEADS, NUTS AND WASHERS Most bolts have hexagonal heads. But a coach bolt has a domed head with a square collar, which bites into the wood as the nut is turned.

A machine screw is a bolt which has a slotted head which must be tightened with a screwdriver.

Nuts are usually hexagonal, but they may be square. Wing nuts are shaped to be tightened by hand.

A washer is put onto a bolt before a nut is screwed on.

Preventing a nut from coming loose

If a nut and bolt are subjected to vibration, as in a car, you can prevent them working loose by first tightening them and then applying a little silicone rubber sealant to the thread closest to the nut.

Alternatively, screw on a second nut and tighten it against the first, while holding the first nut with a second spanner. Or use a spring or toothed washer behind the nut.

Six ways to remove a jammed bolt

● Apply penetrating oil to the nut and leave it to soak in. Then use a spanner long enough to give good leverage, and work in short, sharp jerks rather than a steady pull.

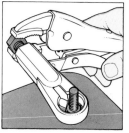

● Place a nut splitter over the nut and tighten it. It cuts through the nut and leaves the bolt undamaged.

● Cut off the nut or bolt head with a mini-hacksaw and remove the other end with a pair of pliers.

● Drill off the head of the jammed bolt with an HSS twist bit of the same diameter as the bolt's shank. Then use a self-grip wrench to pull out the bolt from the nut end.

● If the bolt has snapped, use a screw extractor. Drill into the end of the bolt with an HSS twist bit, and screw in the extractor in the reverse direction from normal.

As soon as it seizes, use a self-grip wrench or spanner to turn it.

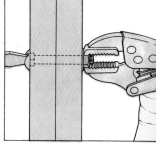

● If you have to remove a round-headed bolt which has seized up, first cut a slot in the head of the bolt with a hacksaw. Use a screwdriver in the slot to hold the head of the bolt still and loosen the nut with a self-grip wrench or spanner.

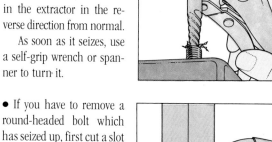

Overflow pipe: SEE BALL VALVE

Paint (SEE ALSO OVERLEAF)

Painting a room or the outside of a house involves two different surfaces: walls, on which a non-gloss paint is used, and woodwork, which is usually given a gloss finish.

Walls are usually painted with one or two coats of interior or exterior grade emulsion paint.

Woodwork has traditionally been painted with three different paints – primer on the bare surfaces, oil-based undercoat to hide the old colour and oil-based gloss to give the final shiny finish (see also *Enamel*).

A modern alternative for woodwork is a type of gloss paint which doesn't need an undercoat. Apply two coats for extra toughness or to cover a previous dark colour.

Primers, sealers and undercoats

KNOTTING Applied to wood knots before the primer coat, to prevent resin from oozing out of the knot and then seeping through to discolour subsequent layers of paint.

PRIMER Applied to new or exposed wood, plaster or metal to seal pores and form a key for other paint to grip. Stain-blocking primer is also available, which is sprayed or painted onto old stains to stop them bleeding through the new decoration. Always select a primer that is appropriate to the surface being painted – for example, choose a wood primer for a wooden surface.

PRIMER SEALER For use on stained walls and plaster, old bituminous coating and areas treated with preservative. Scales of aluminium form a barrier to seal the surface.

COLD GALVANISING PAINT Applied to damaged, galvanised metal and new iron and steel. It gives a zinc-rich coat which acts like a primer and prevents rust.

STABILISING SOLUTION Mainly used on external walls to bind a chalky or crumbly surface together and to provide a firm support for applying paint. Do not apply it as a precaution, but only when it is necessary.

FLOOR SEALER Used to seal porous or powdery concrete, stone or brick floors before painting. Used indoors and out.

UNDERCOAT Applied over primer, usually on wood, to hide the old paint colour – unless it is the same colour as the new coat. Use as many coats as necessary. An undercoat is not necessary with a one-coat gloss paint.

Top coats for the inside of the house

VINYL MATT EMULSION Gives a matt finish that disguises some surface flaws. Do not use it on heated surfaces or on areas that are subjected to heavy condensation, such as bathrooms or shower rooms. No undercoat is necessary.

VINYL SILK EMULSION Gives a smooth, tough finish with a soft sheen, on walls and ceilings. It will not resist condensation. No undercoat is necessary.

EGGSHELL For walls where exceptional resistance to wear, dirt and steam is necessary. No undercoat is needed.

GLOSS A tough, shiny wood finish. Usually used with an undercoat, but some types do not require an undercoat.

ANTI-CONDENSATION PAINT Insulates the wall, reducing the risk of condensation. Doesn't require an undercoat.

TEXTURED PAINT Ideal for hiding irregular surfaces, but textured paints, such as Artex, can be difficult to remove.

RADIATOR ENAMEL Quick drying and keeps its whiteness. Available as a spray. Use primer, but not undercoat.

FLEXIBLE CEILING PAINT Takes only one coat to cover minor blemishes such as fine cracks. Needs no undercoat.

ANTI-DAMP PAINT Protects new decoration in areas that were affected by damp. Use only once the damp source has been dealt with. No undercoat needed.

ALUMINIUM PAINT For use on pipework and storage tanks. Aluminium paint reflects sunlight, so it keeps down the temperature of the surface it covers. It does not require an undercoat unless it is used on wood.

MATT BLACK PAINT Recommended for wooden beams and panelling, and wrought-iron work. Useful in darkrooms. No undercoat is necessary on primed surfaces.

ENAMEL PAINT AND LACQUER Produces a high gloss. Use a primer and an undercoat for the best effect. Also available as an aerosol spray. Ideal for painting white woodware.

Top coats for the outside of the house

MASONRY PAINT Most brands contain silica or nylon fibre (for strength) and a fungicide. Most are unsuitable for use in temperatures below about 5°C (41°F). Do not use an undercoat. If the surface of the wall is chalky or crumbly, apply a stabilising solution before painting.

GLOSS Two coats of traditional oil-based gloss are used on woodwork over coats of knotting, primer and undercoat. Some glosses are flexible so that they will not crack when the wood expands and contracts.

Modern microporous gloss allows the wood to 'breathe', so that water in the wood can escape without blistering the paint. It needs neither a primer nor an undercoat.

Continued on page 250

PAINT

Primers are used to seal bare wood, plaster and metal; undercoats are used to obliterate other colours, and topcoats protect the surface. A topcoat used inside a house must be suitable for the surface being painted and also for the nature of the room — for example, a bathroom wall must be able to withstand steam. Paint for the outside of a house must resist summer heat and winter cold — and rain all year round. There is a paint for every surface and situation; descriptions are given on the previous page.

COLD GALVANISING PAINT

ANTI-BURGLAR PAINT

ANTI-CONDENSATION PAINT

ENAMEL PAINT AND LACQUER

FLOOR SEALER

PRIMER SEALER

GLOSS (INDOORS)

TILE AND BRICK RED

STABILISING SOLUTION

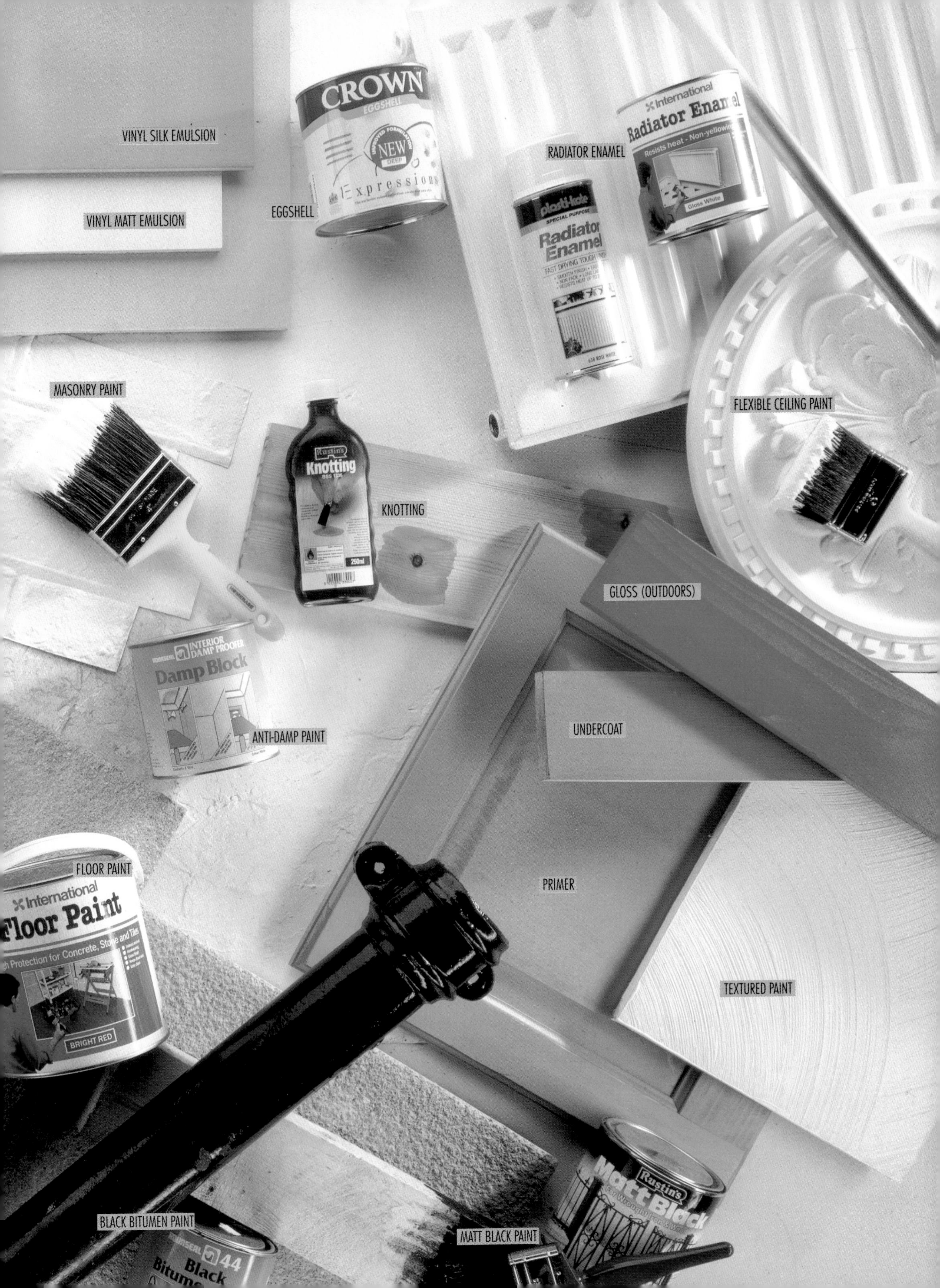

VINYL SILK EMULSION

VINYL MATT EMULSION

EGGSHELL

CROWN
EGGSHELL

NEW
DEEP

Expressions

RADIATOR ENAMEL

International
Radiator Enamel
Resists heat - Non-yellowing

Gloss White

plasti-kote
SPECIAL PURPOSE
Radiator
Enamel
FAST DRYING TOUGH

MASONRY PAINT

FLEXIBLE CEILING PAINT

Rustins
Knotting

KNOTTING

GLOSS (OUTDOORS)

INTERIOR
DAMP PROOFER
Damp Block

ANTI-DAMP PAINT

UNDERCOAT

PRIMER

FLOOR PAINT

International
Floor Paint
h Protection for Concrete, Stone and Tiles

BRIGHT RED

TEXTURED PAINT

BLACK BITUMEN PAINT

MATT BLACK PAINT

Rustins
Matt Black

Black
44
Bitume

WATER-BASED PAINT

An alternative to traditional oil-based paint is water-based paint. It is fast drying and smells less than oil-based paint. Water-based paint is non-flammable and can be washed out of brushes with soap or detergent and water.

YACHT ENAMEL Developed specifically for boats, yacht enamel gives wood a tough, mirror-like gloss finish which provides maximum protection against scuffs. It needs both a primer and an undercoat for the best effect.

FLOOR PAINT Includes garage floor paint and doorstep paint. Anti-slip safety floor paints and quick-dry versions are available. The floor may need to be sealed first.

BRICK AND TILE RED Provides a waterproof matt finish on outdoor brick surfaces such as windowsills and walls. Apply a primer if the brick is new or has been repointed.

ANTI-BURGLAR PAINT Non-drying paint for use on railings and drainpipes as a deterrent to intruders. The painted surfaces must be well above normal reach to avoid staining the clothing of innocent passers-by. Porous surfaces must be sealed before painting. No undercoat is required.

BLACK BITUMEN PAINT For exterior surfaces where waterproofing is required, such as on gutters and downpipes.

Painting indoors

The secret of good painting is good preparation and using the right tools for the job, and good quality materials.

Preparing the room

Move out as much of the furniture as possible. Take down curtains and remove loose carpets and rugs. Preferably lift a fitted carpet, but if this is impractical, protect it very well with polythene under cotton dustsheets.

Coping with problem ceilings

PEELING PAINT Peeling probably occurs because there is untreated distemper beneath the paint. If the peeling is only in small patches, remove the loose paint with a scraper, then wash the exposed areas with clean water and a rough rag such as a piece of towelling. If the surface still feels chalky, treat it with a stabilising solution. If peeling is widespread, the whole ceiling must be stripped (see *Ceiling*: 'Flaking paint').

POLYSTYRENE TILES Paint with emulsion any number of times, but do not use gloss as the tiles will become a fire risk. If the ceiling is to be papered, remove the tiles first (see *Ceiling*: 'Removing old ceiling tiles').

TEXTURED SURFACE You may want to remove an Artex-type finish. This is a messy job, but it can be done (see *Ceiling*: 'Removing Artex-type coatings').

Painting a ceiling

PREPARING THE SURFACE Erect a scaffold using a scaffold board between two stepladders, so that you are working with your head about 7.5 cm (3 in) below the ceiling. Wash the paintwork with sugar soap dissolved in warm water.

 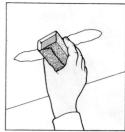

Press some interior filler into minor cracks with a filling knife and leave it to set.

When the filler has hardened, smooth it down with a piece of fine sandpaper.

On bare plaster, mix a solution of 1 part water to 1 part emulsion and use it as a priming coat before applying two undiluted emulsion topcoats.

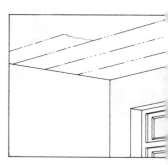

APPLYING PAINT If the ceiling has been painted before, use a paintbrush, a roller or a paint pad to apply at least two coats of emulsion. Work in regular strips, starting near a window.

To ensure that you get good coverage on all textured finishes, apply the second coat at right angles to the first.

Use an extension handle or broomstick fitted to the hollow handle of a roller or pad, to paint most of the ceiling. But paint the edges of the ceiling with a brush, at the end of the job, as the roller will not go right into the corners satisfactorily.

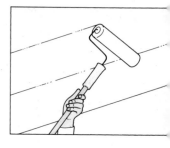

Painting a wall

Dissolve sugar soap in warm water and use it to wash down the wall. Start at the top and work down. Fill minor cracks with an interior filler, and larger cracks or areas missing plaster with ready-mixed plaster (see *Plaster*). When it has set, rub over with medium sandpaper on a sanding block.

Paint walls before woodwork and start at the top. If the wall is already painted, apply at least two coats of emulsion, perhaps more if the previous colour was very dark.

USING A ROLLER OR A BRUSH Stand on a board supported by two stepladders and work across the top of the wall in a horizontal band about 60 cm (2 ft) deep. Apply the paint in random, diagonal strokes. Move down and work the lower bands, carefully blending the edges of the bands.

USING A PAINT PAD Start near a corner and work in all directions within an area of about 60 cm (2 ft) square. Work across the top of the wall in this way, then move down and work the next band, blending the edges well. Apply the paint with a gentle scrubbing action.

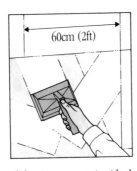

60cm (2ft)

Old wallpaper can be painted, but it may not give ideal results. Test an area first to make sure that the paper does not bubble or come away from the wall. If it does, then you must strip the wallpaper from the wall.

Use vinyl emulsion to paint over vinyl wall coverings. Do not attempt to paint over wallpaper with any sort of metallic pattern, as it will show through the paint.

Painting skirting boards

Ideally, lift carpets to prevent damaging them, but if you decide to leave the carpet in place, protect it well with cotton dustsheets over polythene sheets.

Prepare the surface of the skirting boards in the same way as you would for window frames (see overleaf).

Work along the skirting, protecting the brush with a piece of card to prevent it from picking up dirt. Use a wide paint-brush, always finishing in the direction of the wood grain.

Painting a concrete floor

PREPARING THE SURFACE Remove all surface dust from the floor with a vacuum cleaner. Clean dirty areas with a strong solution of detergent in warm water or with a proprietary engine-cleaning fluid such as Gunk.

If the surface is particularly crumbly or porous, use a proprietary concrete floor sealer. Alternatively, use a PVA building adhesive, diluted at the rate of about 1 part adhesive to 4 parts water, to seal the surface.

APPLYING THE PAINT Use a nylon roller or a wide paint-brush to apply floor paint (see *Paint*). Always start at the far wall and work towards the point of exit from the room.

Painting wooden furniture

PREPARING THE SURFACE Strip off any existing finish, right back to the bare wood (see *Paint stripping*).

APPLYING THE PAINT Prime and undercoat the wood, then apply the finishing coat in thin layers, to avoid runs. A spray paint may be the best way to finish highly textured surfaces such as those found on cane furniture (right).

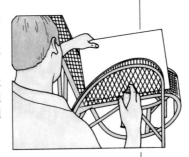

Painting doors

PREPARING THE SURFACE Wash down the existing paintwork with a strong solution of sugar soap in water, and clean the keyhole and the top of the door. Fill cracks with interior filler or wood filler and rub it smooth when set.

APPLYING THE PAINT Open the door before you paint it and leave the frame until last, so you will cover any splashes. As the brush empties, cross-brush to even out the paint.

PAINTING ORDER For the best results, paint the sections of a door in the right order.

Paint a flush door in squares from top to bottom (right).

If it is a panelled door, paint the panels first, then the framework (far right).

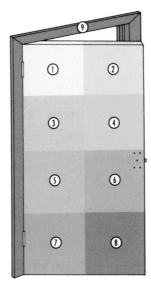

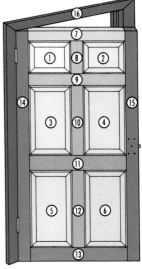

TOUCHING UP CHIPPED WOODWORK

Use Tipp-Ex to cover small chips in white paintwork such as skirting boards. The coats dry quickly to make an almost invisible instant repair. Take care not to drip it onto the carpet.

Painting window frames

As open windows present a security risk, paint windows and frames early in the day so that they are dry by nightfall. Apply thin coats to meeting surfaces to avoid sticking.

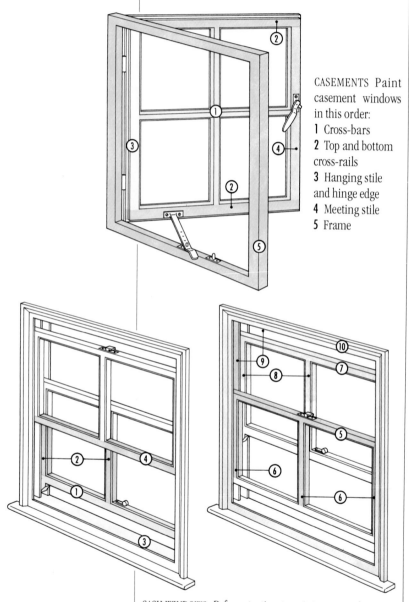

CASEMENTS Paint casement windows in this order:

1 Cross-bars
2 Top and bottom cross-rails
3 Hanging stile and hinge edge
4 Meeting stile
5 Frame

SASH WINDOWS Before starting to paint, open and reverse sash windows (above, left). Paint them in the following order: 1 Meeting rail; 2 Vertical bars as far as possible; 3 The area that the inner sash rests on and the lower runners; 4 Cross-rail and underside.

Reverse the sashes again (above, right), then paint in this order: 5 Cross-rail; 6 Vertical bars; 7 Cross-rail; 8 Rest of vertical bars; 9 Soffit (under the top of the window frame) and the top part of the runners behind the sash cords; 10 Frame. Take care not to get paint on the cords as they will harden and fail sooner than necessary.

PREPARING THE SURFACE If the paintwork is sound, rub it down with a strong solution of sugar soap in warm water. This will clean the surface and take off enough of the glaze to ensure that the new paint gets a good grip.

Remove scuff marks on wood with cleaning liquid, such as Jif, on a cloth. If the marks persist, try cleaning liquid on fine steel wool, rubbing lightly.

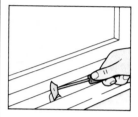

If the paintwork has been scratched, remove any loose paint with the tip of a shave hook (left) and paint the bare wood with primer.

When it is dry, follow with layers of undercoat, building the scratch up to the same level as the surrounding paint. If the scratch goes deep into the wood, use a wood filler.

Where all the paintwork is in poor condition, use either a chemical paint stripper or a hot-air gun to remove it.

On metal frames, wash down sound paint with sugar soap in warm water. Use a wire brush to remove flaking paint, then smooth rough areas with emery paper. Touch in the remaining areas with primer and undercoat.

If all the paint is in poor condition, strip it back to bare metal and apply primer and undercoat before painting.

APPLYING THE PAINT Stick masking tape to the glass, leaving about 2 mm ($\frac{1}{16}$ in) of glass exposed to ensure that the paint will seal any gap there may be between the glass and the frame.

Apply primer and undercoat to any bare wood or metal. When the undercoat is hard, rub lightly with fine sandpaper. Finish both wooden and metal frames with thin topcoats of gloss. Use a 2.5 cm (1 in) brush on the mouldings and a 5 cm (2 in) brush for the main frame sections.

Using an aerosol can

Aerosol is expensive for use over large areas, but useful on small surfaces. Follow the instructions on the can.

Mask off any areas you do not want to paint using masking tape and paper. If you are spraying a small item such as a piece of furniture, protect the surrounding area with a piece of cardboard or a sheet, or build a small spray booth with a cardboard box. Gradually build up thin coats of paint. You do not need to wait for each coat to dry completely before adding the next layer, but it should be dry enough not to run. Hold the can upright, at least 15 cm (6 in) away from the surface. Keep the aerosol moving.

Faultfinder guide: Painting

The paint is flaking and losing its grip

The surface may be too smooth (because of old gloss paint), or too chalky (as with untreated distemper). Rotting timber or rust may be pushing the paint off. Alternatively, a wood with an open grain, such as oak, allows air to escape, pushing the paint off the surface.
● Strip large areas and paint again from scratch.
● Rub down small areas, fill with a wood filler, apply primer and undercoat then repaint.

The paint blisters

Prick a blister.
● If water appears, damp is trapped under the paint. Strip the paint with a hot-air gun. Use the gun to dry the wood. Then prime the surface and apply undercoat and topcoat.
● If there is no water, the wood may have air trapped in open grain. Strip the area. Fill the grain with epoxy-based filler and repaint. If the grain is fine, omit the filler and use flexible or microporous gloss.

The paint cracks or 'crazes'

Incompatible paints have been used together.
● Strip the area completely and repaint it.

The paint has runs and 'tears'

Too much paint has been applied in a thick coat.
● If the paint is still wet, brush out runs.
● If it has started to dry, leave it to dry, then rub down the surface with fine sandpaper. Dust the surface then apply a new topcoat sparingly.

Stains and dark patches show through paint

● If a stain shows through the paint, apply a primer sealer or a stain-blocking primer, then repaint.
● Untreated knots in wood can ooze resin. Strip the affected area, then use sandpaper to expose the knot. Brush knotting (see *Paint*) over the area, leave it to dry then repaint it.

The painted surface is gritty

Dirt or dust in the paint is the cause.
● Once the paint is dry, rub it down until it is smooth, with damp wet-and-dry paper. Wipe it clean, then apply a new coat of paint.

The paint has wrinkled

A second coat was applied before the first had dried.
● Strip the surface and repaint it.

Painting outdoors

Some faces of a house need attention more often than others and for different reasons. North-facing walls can suffer from damp and mould. South-facing walls may peel from the drying effect of the sun.

If you are painting a house in cold autumn weather, condensation can be a problem. As you go along, dry off the area you are working on with a hot-air gun on a low setting.

Paint will dry more quickly in the summer, but the warm weather also brings flying insects which get stuck in the paint. Try to work in the shade, avoiding the sun as it moves round the house.

Never paint on a windy day because dust and insects will be blown about. The ideal type of weather for painting outdoors is dry, warm and slightly overcast.

Painting exterior walls

PREPARING THE SURFACE Remove any dust and grime from brickwork with warm water and a firm scrubbing brush. Do not use soap or detergent because they are likely to leave white stains on the bricks.

Remove stains that have been left by mortar on the bricks with a cement solvent such as Disclean or Brickie, both of which are available from builders' merchants.

Kill mould and algae on smooth, rendered walls with a proprietary fungicide, widely available in DIY shops.

Once the mould is dead brush it off vigorously with a stiff-bristled brush. Wear safety spectacles and a face mask to protect yourself.

Then wash down the walls with sugar soap in warm water. Start at the top, so that the dirty water runs down over the part of the wall that is still dirty.

Clean a textured surface such as pebbledash with a dustpan brush or with an old 10 cm (4 in) paintbrush, dipped into a solution of warm water and sugar soap. If any pebbles fall off, see *Pebbledash* for repairs.

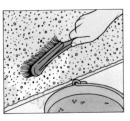

Then hose the wall down with clean water. However, do not use a high-pressure hose, because it can force water into very small gaps in the wood round the window and door frames and may encourage the development of wet rot.

PAINTING A CHAIR

Tap long tacks into the base of a chair's legs so that they stand well clear of the floor while you paint.

WORKING IN THE RIGHT ORDER

● Tackle meeting surfaces such as window frames first, so they have a chance to dry before they must be closed at nightfall.
● Try to avoid working on a particular wall of the house until the sun has passed over it.
● Paint the woodwork before you paint the walls, but do all the preparation of walls and woodwork first.

CHOOSING UNDERCOAT

An undercoat should be a close match with the colour of the final topcoat. The undercoat and topcoat should also be of the same brand.

APPLYING THE PAINT Avoid painting good facing brickwork – it is difficult to achieve a satisfactory finish. The paint cannot be successfully cleaned off later and rarely looks attractive. If, however, you find you have to paint facing brickwork, use an exterior grade emulsion applied with a rough-surface paintbrush. Apply at least two coats.

Apply masonry paint to rendered walls with a medium-bristle clean dustpan brush or a 10 cm (4 in) paintbrush or shaggy nylon paint roller. Use dustsheets to protect areas such as porch roofs and window sills and adjoining flowerbeds and paths.

Paint textured walls with a clean dustpan brush or a 10 cm (4 in) paintbrush, dabbing the paint into crevices. A textured wall will take about twice as much paint to cover as a smooth-surfaced wall.

Painting exterior woodwork

PREPARING THE WOODWORK Wash sound paintwork with a strong solution of sugar soap in warm water. This will take off enough of the glaze for the new paint to grip.

Remove scuff marks with cleaning paste such as Jif on a cloth. If the marks persist, try rubbing them lightly with cleaning paste on steel wool.

If the paintwork is scratched, remove any loose paint with the tip of a shave hook. Paint primer onto bare wood and when it is dry, follow with layers of undercoat, building the scratch up level with the surrounding paint. When the undercoat is dry, rub lightly with fine sandpaper.

Remove areas of damaged paint with a hot-air gun or use a chemical paint stripper. Fill cracks and gaps with an exterior-grade wood filler.

When it has set, smooth it with fine sandpaper, working along the grain of the wood. Remove all the dust with an old paintbrush.

Gaps round window or door frames should be filled with exterior-grade sealant. When it has hardened, paint the sealant to match. Prepare areas of bare wood with wood primer. Use undercoat on primed, bare wood and to cover old paintwork of a different colour. Topcoat alone will not disguise an old coat of paint. Once the undercoat is dry, lightly sand it with fine sandpaper and dust it off.

APPLYING THE TOPCOAT Apply two coats of gloss to exterior wood surfaces. Use a 2.5 cm (1 in) paintbrush for window frames, an angled paintbrush for 'cutting in' where surfaces meet and a 5 cm (2 in) paintbrush for wider areas.

The right sequence for painting a window

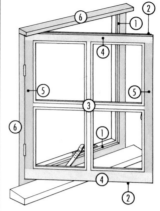

CASEMENT WINDOW
Paint the window in the order shown:
1 Rebate
2 Edge of window
3 Glazing bars and putty
4 Top and bottom rails
5 Vertical bars and hinge edge
6 Frame

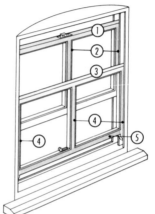

SASH WINDOW
Reverse the two sashes and follow the sequence shown:
1 Horizontal rail
2 Accessible surfaces of vertical bars
3 Horizontal rail
4 Vertical bars
5 Horizontal rail and underside

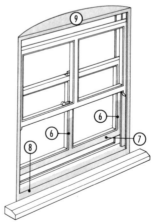

Then restore the sashes to their normal position, and complete in the following order:
6 Remainder of vertical bars
7 Horizontal rail
8 Wood beneath the window and up the outside runners
9 Frame

Painting tools (SEE OVERLEAF)

Caring for paintbrushes and rollers

STORING BRUSHES OVERNIGHT Suspend paintbrushes overnight in white spirit or water in a jam jar. Only the bristles should be submerged because the metal parts will rust and water will make the stock of the brush swell.

Never let a brush rest on its bristles; they will kink under the pressure. Instead, suspend it from a piece of stiff wire through a hole in the handle. Some brushes come with a hole, otherwise you can drill your own.

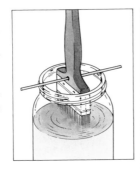

CLEANING BRUSHES, ROLLERS AND PADS Rinse water-based paint out of brushes and rollers with warm water, then wash them well in soapy water. Clean oil-based paint off brushes and rollers with white spirit or a proprietary brush cleaner. To clean a paint pad, rub it on paper to get rid of most of the paint, then rinse it in clean water. It is quicker if you use soap as well, but make sure you rinse it all out.

RESCUING A STIFF BRUSH Soak stiff brushes in paintbrush restorer and, wearing a rubber glove, work the bristles with your hand to ease out the trapped paint.

Using a spray gun

Follow the instructions given by the manufacturer. Dilute the paint if necessary and mask off surrounding areas. Wear a face mask. Hold the gun at right angles to the surface at a distance of about 30-46 cm (12-18 in). To avoid runs apply a number of thin coats rather than one thick one.

Do not hold the gun in one position for any length of time or the paint will build up and cause drips and runs. Never swing the gun in an arc; it will create an uneven surface of paint. Always clean out the spray gun after use. Never spray in windy conditions.

Paint stripping

Stripping paintwork with a scraper

The simplest way to remove old paint is to scrape it off. When scraping paint off woodwork pull the scraper in the same direction as the grain of the wood as far as possible.

A Skarsten scraper is a special hand-held tool with a sharp, replaceable blade. It will scrape off paint back to bare wood on flat and convex surfaces. A serrated blade can be used to break up thick layers of paint.

Using heat to strip old paint

Use either a hot-air gun or a blowtorch to soften the paintwork. A blowtorch can scorch the surface quite easily.

Do not leave either type of heat stripper on one area for too long or the paint will scorch. When the paint bubbles, use a shave hook or scraper to scrape it off.

! Never put newspaper on the floor when using any type of heat stripper, and keep a bucket of water close at hand. Drop smouldering paint into the bucket as you work.

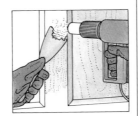

Wear gardening gloves (not plastic or rubber) when you are scraping off the softened paint, and try to angle the scraper so that hot paint does not fall on your hands.

Use a chemical stripper near windows, particularly in cold weather, since excessive heat can crack the glass.

Stripping paint with chemical products

Chemical paint strippers are available either as liquid or paste. Wear safety goggles and gloves when using either.

LIQUID PAINT STRIPPER Use a rag to liberally dab the liquid onto the surface and leave it to attack the paint film.

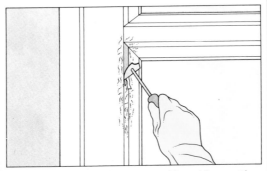

Give the paint plenty of time to wrinkle and loosen. Then lift it off with a shave hook or scraper. Clean the paint from awkward areas with fine steel wool.

PASTE PAINT STRIPPER Apply a thick coating of a paste paint stripper to the surface and leave it until a skin forms.

Using a narrow-bladed paint scraper, lift the paste away from the surface.

It will bring the paint away with it. This method is best for stripping intricately moulded surfaces such as fireplaces or cornices.

Always neutralise the remaining stripper, as directed on the can, before redecorating the exposed surface.

PAINTING TOOLS

An essential part of decorating any room is preparing all the surfaces correctly. So scrapers, a filling knife and a hot-air gun are as necessary as paintbrushes, rollers or painting pads.

PAINT ROLLERS Sleeves made of foam are suitable for smooth walls. Mohair is good for fine finishes, but is unsuitable for textured surfaces, and if used with gloss paint is difficult to clean.

PAINT TRAY Used to hold paint which is applied with a roller or pad.

Use a long-pile (shaggy) nylon or imitation lambs' wool for textured surfaces, and a special tough, shaggy nylon for external surfaces such as pebbledash.

ROLLER POLE Some rollers have a hollow handle to hold an aluminium pole or broomstick, so that you can paint a ceiling from the floor.

WINDOW-SCRAPER For scraping paint from glass. The best have blades slightly inset to leave a couple of millimetres of paint to seal the join between the glass and the frame.

RADIATOR ROLLER A small roller on a long wire handle is designed for reaching behind central-heating radiators and into other difficult areas.

SKARSTEN-TYPE SCRAPER Sharp, hooked blades remove dry paint. Protect your eyes with safety spectacles when using one. They are available in several different sizes.

SHAVE HOOKS For scraping off heat-softened paint from curved and flat surfaces.

PROTECTIVE STRIPS Used with a cotton dust-sheet to keep paint off a carpet. They tuck in under the skirting board.

PAINT KETTLE A small amount of paint can be poured into the paint kettle so that the rest of the paint does not get contaminated with grit. Especially useful for outdoor work.

MASKING TAPE Adhesive paper tape, used to mask off areas not to be touched by paint. It will peel off easily within a few hours, but after a number of days the adhesive hardens and the tape can be difficult to remove.

PAINTBRUSHES Use 12 mm ($\frac{1}{2}$ in), 25 mm (1 in) and 50 mm (2 in) flat brushes for most types of painting. A wider surface, like a flush (unpanelled) door, calls for a 75 mm (3 in) brush. A 6 mm ($\frac{1}{4}$ in) or 12 mm ($\frac{1}{2}$ in) angled tip is best for working around window frames, as it allows you to get close to the glass without painting it.

PAINTING PAD A foam pad is covered with mohair pile. It is a convenient alternative to a paint roller as it is far less likely to spatter. Unsuitable for rough surfaces such as Artex.

TACK RAG A tack rag is a duster impregnated with a resin, sticky enough to pick up fine dust. The rag is wiped over a surface just before paint is applied to make sure it is clean.

HOT-AIR GUN Resembles a large hair dryer. There is no flame, but it produces considerable heat which softens paint. The stripper can get very hot even though nothing is visible at the nozzle.

WIRE BRUSH For removing rust and other loose debris from metal or masonry. A circular brush is also available, for use with a power drill. Protect your eyes with safety spectacles.

NYLON BRUSH Gently removes traces of paint from detailed wooden surfaces, after a chemical paint stripper has been applied. Protect your eyes with safety spectacles.

PAINT SCRAPER Also called a stripping knife. Used to remove old paint from flat surfaces once the paint has been softened.

BLOWTORCH The flame will remove paint quickly but it will burn the surface beneath it in seconds if it is left on one spot for too long.

FILLING KNIFE Used to apply fillers to wood and walls. More flexible than a paint scraper.

Patching clothes

Patching is used where darning a hole or stitching up a tear in a garment would not give a sturdy enough repair. It is particularly useful when repairing a fabric that frays.

Making a sew-on patch   Time: $\frac{1}{2}$ an hour or less

YOU WILL NEED Scissors, pins, needle, thread, patching fabric. Possibly: sewing machine.

PREPARING THE HOLE Cut the hole so that it forms a square or rectangle and make a 6 mm ($\frac{1}{4}$ in) diagonal cut into each corner.

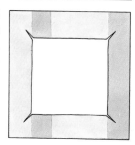

Turn up the edges of the hole, as far as the clipped point, onto the right side of the garment. Pin them in place and then slip-stitch the raw edges to the garment (see *Stitches*). If the fabric is likely to fray, stitch two or three times across the corners to strengthen them.

PREPARING THE PATCH Cut a patch about 5 cm (2 in) longer and wider than the hole. Ideally, the patch should be of the same fabric. Make sure to cut the patch with the grain running in the same direction as on the garment. Turn the edges over all round to the depth of about 1 cm ($\frac{1}{2}$ in) on the wrong side of the patch. Tack and press it.

APPLYING THE PATCH With both right sides facing the same way, pin and tack the patch over the hole, making sure that it covers the turned-back edges completely.

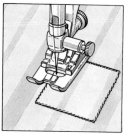

If possible, machine-stitch the patch onto the garment, sewing as close to the edge of the patch as possible.

Alternatively, sew the patch into place by hand, using a neat, small backstitch. Then remove tacking stitches.

Applying an iron-on patch   Time: a few minutes

Iron-on patches can be bought from most haberdashery departments. The heat from the iron melts the adhesive in the patch and bonds it to the garment. Follow the manufacturer's instructions when applying the patch.

QUICK FIX FOR WATERPROOFS

If a waterproof garment gets torn, use tent repair tape to patch it. Waterproof Elastoplast may also be used as a temporary patch.

Patching jeans   Time: depends on method

Because it is so thick, denim is rather difficult to sew by hand, so use either iron-on patches or leather patches (see *Coats & jackets*) for a quick repair.

To sew on a denim patch, use the method described in 'Making a sew-on patch'. Use a sewing machine unless the hole is in a position that makes it inaccessible.

If you have to sew the patch by hand, use a thimble, a sturdy needle and very strong thread.

When children's denim clothes need to be patched, you could use a contrasting piece of fabric or buy one of the embroidered motifs that are often sold in haberdashery departments.

Patio

Cleaning a patio   Time: 2 hours or less

A proprietary patio cleaner, available at a DIY store, will kill off algae as well as loosen grime. However, if algae and moss are particularly severe, kill them with a fungicide first, following the instructions on the container.

YOU WILL NEED Patio cleaner, watering can, stiff broom, garden hose. Possibly: fungicide, cat litter, concrete cleaner.

Following the manufacturer's instructions, dilute sufficient patio cleaner in clean water to clean the whole area.

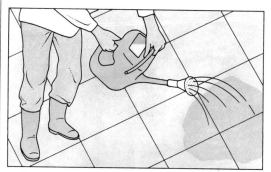

Apply it to the patio with a watering can fitted with a rose or sprinkler bar. Scrub it in well with a stiff broom, then wash it off with a hose and the broom.

USING A HIGH-PRESSURE JET A patio can also be cleaned with a high-pressure jet hose, which can be hired and then connected to your garden tap. However, be careful if there is mortar in the joins between the patio slabs — make sure that the jet of water does not dislodge any of it.

BARBECUE STAINS Cover new fat splashes with cat litter, ground to a powder beneath your heel. Sweep it up when it has absorbed the grease. Older marks can be removed with a concrete cleaner available in most car accessory shops.

Curing a rocking slab Time: 1 hour or less

Slabs can often become unstable as a result of having been laid on sand. Rain seeps between the slabs and disturbs the sand causing uneven bedding.

> YOU WILL NEED Garden spade, bagged dry mortar mix, mixing board, builder's trowel, watering can, club hammer.

Lift up the unstable slab with a spade, taking care not to chip its neighbours. Clean off any debris from the back of the slab and remove loose sand or soil from the hole.

Make up some mortar, using a minimum of water (see *Mortar*). With a trowel, put five heaps of mortar in the hole – one heap at each corner and one in the centre.

Dampen the underside of the slab with clean water. Drain off the surplus, and then lower the slab onto the mortar. Gently tap the slab with the handle of a club hammer until it lies flush with the other slabs. Do not tread on it for 24 hours.

Repointing slabs Time: depends on area

If frost breaks up the mortar between the stone slabs of a patio, it should be repointed with new mortar.

> YOU WILL NEED Builder's trowel, garden broom, bagged mortar mix, mixing board.

Dig out all loose mortar and debris with the point of the trowel, and brush the gaps clean. On a mixing board, make up some mortar using a minimum of water, to give a mix which will compact in gloved hands – rather like a beach sand pie, with no sign of moisture.

Dampen the joints about five minutes before you are ready to start pointing.

Apply mortar to the joints, pressing it home with the point of the trowel.

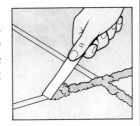

Smooth it down with a piece of stick, then brush up any surplus mortar. Because the mortar is dry, it will not stain the slabs.

Leave it to harden thoroughly before walking on it.

Pebbledash

Pebbledash is a decorative form of rendering produced by flinging (or dashing) pebbles at a wet coat of mortar.

The most common problem experienced with pebbledash is that sometimes the rendering comes away from the masonry in large bubbles, which are either immediately visible or make a hollow sound when tapped.

Repairing loose pebbledash Time: depends on area

> YOU WILL NEED Polythene sheet, club hammer, cold chisel, stiff brush, old paintbrush, mixing board, trowel, plastering sand, cement, hydrated lime, bucket, coal scoop, safety spectacles, working gloves, wooden float, ladder. Possibly: new pebbles.

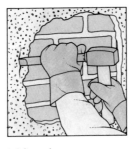

REMOVING LOOSE RENDERING Lay a polythene sheet along the base of the wall. Wearing safety spectacles and gloves, hack away the loose rendering with a club hammer and a cold chisel or steel bolster, until sound rendering is reached.

Brush away all loose material from the area.

APPLYING NEW RENDERING Dampen the exposed wall by splashing it with clean water, using an old paintbrush.

On a mixing board, make up a fairly dry mix of mortar using 6 parts plastering sand, 1 part cement and 1 part hydrated lime (measured by volume). It should keep its shape when squeezed. Apply it with a trowel, finishing about 1.3 cm ($\frac{1}{2}$ in) below the surface of the rest of the wall.

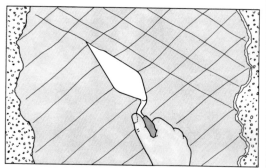

Allow the rendering to dry for about 20 minutes, then make criss-cross marks on it with the point of the trowel. This produces a key for the topcoat.

Now gather up the old pebbles and tip them into a bucket of water to wash off the dirt. Use as many of the old pebbles as possible, as they will be a similar colour to the rest of the wall. If you have to buy new pebbles from a builders' merchant, get about 5 kg per m² (11 lb per sq yd).

Make up a second batch of mortar, using 5 parts of plastering sand, 1 part cement and 1 part hydrated lime. This time make a slightly softer mix by using more water.

With a wooden float, apply the mortar to the patches, bringing it up so that it is flush with the surrounding wall surface.

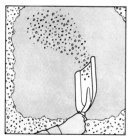

While it is still wet, remove the stones from the bucket of water, load them onto a coal scoop and fling them at the rendering.

Pick up any that fall off the wall, reload the scoop and continue until the patched areas match the rest of the wall.

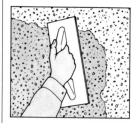

When a patch is complete, press the wooden float all over the pebbles to firm them into the surface.

DISGUISING NEW PEBBLES If the pebbles are new and the patches show up, the only way to hide them is for the whole wall to be coated with masonry paint, applied with an exterior-grade shaggy nylon paint roller. As well as decorating the house, the paint will fill cracks and crevices and help to bind the whole surface together.

Cleaning pebbledash   Time: depends on area

To remove mould and algae from pebbledash, apply fungicide with a garden spray. Wear safety spectacles.

You can buy the fungicide from hardware shops or DIY stores. Apply it according to the directions on the pack, allow plenty of time for the fungicide to work.

Spray the wall with a garden hose and brush it with a medium-bristle dustpan brush. Do not add soap or detergent to the water — they will leave white stains.

Be careful when cleaning old rendering as the pebbles may be loose. Treat areas that seem loose by brushing on a coating of waterproof PVA building adhesive diluted with equal amounts of clean water.

Personal stereo

A personal stereo is a miniature cassette recorder which sometimes includes a radio. For details of how to clean it and remove a jammed tape, and for a general faultfinder guide, see *Cassette recorder*.

Tape plays slowly   Time: a few minutes

YOU WILL NEED New batteries.

If a tape plays slowly, the batteries are probably going flat and need replacing — or recharging if they are of the rechargeable type. If the fault persists with rechargeable batteries, they may be suffering from 'battery memory effect' (see *Cassette recorder*).

Tape plays at varying speeds   Time: depends on cause

YOU WILL NEED Possibly: new batteries.

If the tape plays at varying speeds (known as 'wow and flutter'), first try putting in new batteries or recharge the existing ones if they are rechargeable.

If the fault continues, the pinch roller could be dirty or the tape could be caught around the roller (see *Cassette recorder*: 'Freeing a jammed tape').

Sound from one earpiece only   Time: $\frac{1}{2}$ an hour or less

If it is possible, borrow another set of headphones and plug them into the stereo to discover if the fault lies with your own headphones or with the unit.

PLUGGING A WALKMAN INTO HI-FI OR TV

An adapter kit can be bought for a personal stereo, enabling it to be plugged into a hi-fi unit, television, video or other sound source. By doing this, you can amplify your Walkman music, play a tape through a hi-fi system that has no cassette deck, record sound off the television or put music onto a video tape.

Alternatively, plug your headphones into the headphone socket of a hi-fi set or a radio. If the fault persists, the problem must be with the headphones. Faulty headphones are usually not worth repairing; new ones can be bought quite cheaply at a hi-fi shop.

If the headphones are not faulty, the problem lies with the unit. Return it to the supplier, the manufacturer or a hi-fi repair shop to get an estimate for repair.

Photographs & slides

In some cases, damaged photographs or slides can be repaired. If they are particularly precious take them to a professional photographer for advice and repair. It is worth having copies made of special photographs before they get damaged. If you no longer have the negative, you can still get copies made, working from the photograph, although they will not be of the same quality.

Separating stuck photographs and negatives
Time: ½ an hour or less

PHOTOGRAPHS The only safe way to separate photographs that have stuck together is with steam. It will take time, but don't try to rush the process and pull them apart in case you rip the surface from one of them.

Don't soak them as you may damage the paper backing.

NEGATIVES As they have no paper content, negatives can be separated by being immersed in tepid water. They will float free of each other quite quickly, without any harm being done.

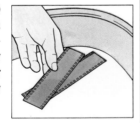

Dry them carefully by blotting them with a clean, lint-free cloth, and when they are completely dry, flatten them between the pages of a book, if necessary.

Storing 35 mm slides

Looking for a particular slide is easier if they are all kept in polyester viewing sheets, rather than the boxes they are supplied in. Polyester sheets last much longer than plastic ones, and won't crack. Sheets capable of holding 24 slides each are available in most photographic shops. The filled sheets can be stored in a folder or ring-bound file.

To protect particularly valuable slides, store them in sheets that have a dust cover attached, as well. If you have to store large numbers of slides in polyester sheets, hang them in suspension files in a cabinet. This allows you to group and identify sheets for easy access. Store your slides in a cool, dry, dark place – not in the attic or the cellar, where they can be affected by extremes of temperature. Heat, humidity and light can affect their colour dyes.

Piano

To remain in good condition a piano needs the right combination of humidity and temperature. It also needs to be positioned correctly, tuned regularly and played often.

Controlling humidity in the piano room

> YOU WILL NEED Hygrometer. Possibly: bowl of water, light fitting, 15 watt light bulb.

The humidity in the room should be between 50 and 55 per cent. It can be measured on a hygrometer which can be bought at a hardware shop.

TOO LITTLE HUMIDITY If the air in the room is too dry it will very likely cause the piano to go out of tune.

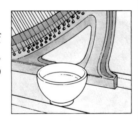

Place a small bowl of water inside the piano's case, at floor level. Position it so that it can't be knocked over.

Alternatively, consult a piano tuner about installing a humidifier in the room.

EXCESS HUMIDITY Too much humidity can cause rusted strings, hardened hammer felts and the distortion of component parts. Look for the cause and treat it (see *Damp*). If the humidity cannot be brought down, install a 15 watt light bulb in a holder inside the piano, fixed securely to the case. Leave it on permanently, checking the bulb regularly.

Keeping the temperature constant

The ideal temperature for a room which contains a piano is 17-21°C (63-70°F). It should not be allowed to exceed 22°C (72°F) because high temperatures can cause the wood to shrink and split.

Try to prevent rapid fluctuations of temperature and humidity in a room containing a piano – for example, do not open a window last thing at night.

Selecting the right position for a piano

Do not stand a piano against a damp wall, or beside a window that may let in damp air. Don't risk drying it out by placing it near a radiator, or in direct sunlight, either.

PEDAL PROBLEMS

When the pedals on an upright piano squeak, remove the bottom door of the piano and apply a few drops of light household oil to the pedal screws. If the pedals are loose, tighten the screws.
Keep the pedals shiny by polishing them occasionally with metal polish.

HOW TO TELL IF KEYS ARE IVORY

Ivory keys are made in two sections. The join is at the point where the black keys end, and may be almost indiscernible in a well-made piano. Plastic keys are made in one piece.

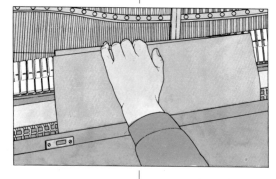

Cleaning a piano   Time: ½ an hour or less

> **YOU WILL NEED** Chamois leather, washing-up liquid. Possibly: cotton-wool balls, methylated spirit, metal polish, appropriate furniture polish or wax, vacuum cleaner.

KEYBOARD If plastic keys are looking dirty, lift them up, six at a time, and wipe them with a chamois leather wrung out in a weak solution of washing-up liquid.

If the keys are made of ivory, use a cotton-wool ball moistened with methylated spirit. Do not allow the meths to trickle between the keys or touch the polished wood.

Very dirty ivory keys can be cleaned with either Brasso or T-Cut, which is obtainable in car accessory shops.

WOODEN CASE On a modern piano with a natural finish, use a neutral-coloured paste polish such as Antiquax or Lord Sheraton Furniture Balsam. On an older piano, especially one with a french-polished surface, use furniture wax sparingly (see *French polish*). Do not polish it more than twice a year. A high-gloss polyester finish should be polished with an all-purpose cleaner polish such as Johnson's Wax Free Sparkle or Mr Sheen.

INSIDE Remove dust from the inside of the case with a vacuum cleaner. Even better results are obtained if the vacuum cleaner is capable of blowing the dust away.

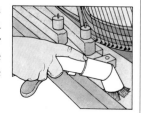

Keeping a rarely used piano in good condition

If a piano is unlikely to be used for any length of time, cover the working parts and keyboard with sheets of dry brown paper.

If the keys are made of ivory, they may go yellow if kept covered, so remember to expose them to daylight regularly in order to keep them white (see *Ivory*).

Put moth repellent on top of the paper, to deter moths, and sachets of silica-gel crystals on the paper to help to cut down the damaging effects of high humidity or dampness.

Protect a piano which is likely to be exposed to direct sunlight by covering it with a dustsheet during the day.

Freeing a stuck key   Time: ½ an hour or less

Sometimes the balance and guide pins under a key get stuck in the small holes in the underside of the key. The holes have a cloth lining, known as a bushing. Dampness can cause the bushings to swell and trap the pins.

Expose the hammers and keys by lifting off the front of the piano and the keyboard cover. Then remove the nameboard. Lift the stuck key gently, and also lift the hammer to take the pressure off the key. Ease the key out.

The guide pin fits into the hole at the front of the key. The balance pin fits into the hole halfway along the key.

Check the state of the felt bushing in each hole. If the felt has swollen, press it back into place with a screwdriver. If it has worn away, get a new felt bushing fitted. Then replace the key in the same way as you removed it from the keyboard.

Pictures

Repairing a picture frame   Time: depends on damage

As a general rule, don't attempt to clean or restore pictures and frames if you suspect that they may be valuable, in case you reduce their value. Seek professional help.

> **YOU WILL NEED** Trimming knife, pincers, wood adhesive, tack hammer, block of metal or hardwood with true right angles, gummed paper. Possibly: mini-hacksaw, small pieces of wood veneer, chisel, hand or power drill, twist bits, fine gauge dowel, panel pins, sprigs or tingles, glass cleaner, cloth.

Picture frames develop loose joints when the humidity in a home is reduced – such as when central heating is introduced. Where possible, remove the picture from the frame before attempting to repair it. Cut through the backing papers and adhesive tape with a trimming knife.

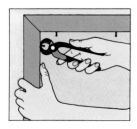

Remove the panel pins or picture tingles (the small, flat metal triangles that are fired into the edge of the frame to hold the backing) with pincers, and lift out the backing, picture and glass.

If the mitred corners are held by nails, ease them apart sufficiently to be able to insert wood glue into the gap.

Place the glued corner over a square block of wood, to make a right angle, and gently tap the nails back in place. Allow the glue to set.

FOR EXTRA STRENGTH Working on the back of the frame, use a mini-hacksaw to make a fine cut across the corner, about two-thirds the thickness of the frame.

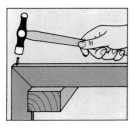

Apply wood glue to both sides of a small piece of veneer and slide it into the cut.

Allow the glue to set, then chisel off the excess veneer – or use a trimming knife.

LARGE PICTURES With large picture frames, drill across the angle, using a twist bit to match the diameter of a small dowel. Apply wood glue to a piece of dowel and tap it into the hole. Trim off surplus dowel. Before it sets, check the angle against a wooden or metal square.

REASSEMBLY Clean both sides of the glass and lay it in the frame. Replace any mount, the picture and backing card. Keep them in place by knocking in panel pins, sprigs or tingles, taking care to press the repaired corner against a firm surface, to avoid opening the joints again.

Finish it off by applying strips of adhesive tape or gummed paper along the join between backing and frame to keep out dust.

Inspect your pictures regularly

Look closely at your pictures to make sure that they are not being affected by damp, insect infestation or sunlight. Deal with these problems promptly.

Damp pictures should be moved to a drier, but not sunny, position. Do not hang them above a radiator. Let them dry naturally.

Insect infestation on valuable paintings should be dealt with immediately by a picture restorer. Non-valuable pictures can be opened (see left), the frame and glass cleaned thoroughly, and new backing card put in. If you are unable to open a picture, spray the back and frame with an insecticide.

Repairing the moulding Time: 2 hours or less

Most gilded or painted frames have a base of gesso, which is a white, plaster-like substance. If gesso mouldings fall off they can usually be glued back in place with wood glue. If small pieces are missing, it is possible to repair the damage yourself. However, if large pieces have gone, ask a picture restorer to repair the frame.

> YOU WILL NEED Rubber mould-making compound, car-body filler paste, sandpaper, wood glue, paint to match frame.

Create a mould of the missing piece by pressing some rubber mould-making compound (obtainable from craft shops) onto an undamaged section of the moulding.

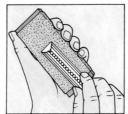

Remove the mould from the frame and then press some car-body filler paste into it. Allow it to set.

When it has dried, remove it from the mould, and sand the base carefully until it fits the damaged area.

Fix it in place with wood glue, making sure it matches the rest of the frame. When the glue has dried, decorate the patch to match the rest of the frame.

Carved wooden frames

If a carved wooden frame is damaged, take it to a picture restorer, rather than attempting to repair it yourself. Carved wooden frames can be valuable, and professional care is advisable.

FITTING HANGING RINGS TO A PICTURE FRAME

Pictures bought ready-framed will usually have hanging rings already attached. But sometimes it may be necessary to fit them yourself.

Screw eyes should be fitted about one-third of the way down from the top of the picture. Start off the holes with a fine awl, to prevent the wooden frame from splitting. Screw in the eyes tightly and thread picture wire or nylon thread through them. Knot it securely.

Do not use string to hang pictures – in time it will rot.

Making and using a positioning aid Time: a few minutes

Sometimes when you position pictures 'by eye', getting the hooks in the right place can be difficult. A homemade positioning aid can make it easier.

> YOU WILL NEED Possibly: pliers, wire coat hanger, piece of softwood, 3.2 cm (1¼ in) wood screw.

FOR A LIGHT PICTURE Cut a 25 cm (10 in) length of wire from an old coat hanger. Curl one end to form a handle and bend the other end to form a 90° angle.

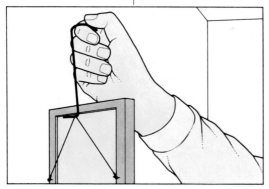

Hook the right-angled end of the wire under the hanging cord of the picture, with the sharp end pointing towards the wall.

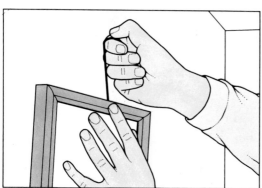

Position the picture on the wall while it is hanging from the wire. When you have decided where it will go, press the sharp end of the wire into the wall to mark the fixing point for the picture hook.

FOR A HEAVY PICTURE Cut a length of any type of softwood, about 15 mm (½ in) thick and 30 cm (12 in) long.

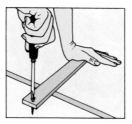

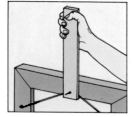

Near the bottom of the wood, drive in a 3.2 cm (1¼ in) screw, but leave the head of the screw protruding slightly.

To use the positioning aid, hang the picture from the screw head so that it is level and balances perfectly.

Lift it by its 'handle' and when the picture is in the right position, press the sharp end of the screw into the wall behind, to mark the spot where the hook will go.

PROTECTING THE WALL SURFACE

When hanging pictures, you may be unwilling to draw lines on the wall surface with a pencil. An alternative is to use cotton thread of a contrasting colour, held in place with small pieces of Blu-Tack.

Cleaning a picture

OIL PAINTINGS Use oil-painting cleaner from an art shop, but stop the treatment if paint colour is coming off. If the picture was varnished, apply two or three coats of aerosol varnish after cleaning it.

GLASS-COVERED PICTURES Clean with a little glass cleaner on a soft cloth. Do not spray cleaner onto the glass in case it seeps under the edge and onto the paper.

To clean between the glass and the picture, take the picture out of the frame (see 'Repairing a picture frame') and wash the glass in warm soapy water.

GILT PICTURE FRAMES If the frames discolour, clean them with a little turpentine or white spirit on a cotton bud. On a non-valuable frame treat damaged gilt with a wax gilt such as Treasure Gold available in art shops.

GOLD LEAF FRAMES Treat discoloration with a solution of 1 part ammonia to 12 parts water applied with a cotton bud. Rinse the area with clean water on a cotton bud. Pat dry with a soft, clean cloth.

WOODEN FRAMES Polish the wood with furniture cream and buff it with a soft, clean cloth.

Pipe lagging: SEE INSULATION

Pipes

What to do when a pipe bursts

The first sign of a burst or leaking pipe will probably be water dripping through a ceiling directly below the loft which contains the pipes and tanks.

Turn off the main stopcock immediately. It is usually found under the kitchen sink or in the cellar. If you can't find the indoor stopcock or it has jammed, close the water company's stopcock outside. It is located in a purpose-made hole near the boundary of the house, or set into the pavement outside (see *Stopcock*).

Turn on all the cold taps to drain the cold-water tank and pipes. Close them when the water stops flowing.

Find the burst pipe. If the leak is in one of the pipes leading out of the cold-water tank, you can restore the cold-water supply to the kitchen tap.

Turn off the gate valve on the pipe leading to the leak, or tie up the ball valve on the cold-water tank (see *Ball valve*). Then you can turn the stopcock back on. Call a plumber or repair the burst yourself (see page 266).

The plumbing in a typical house

There are several ways of distributing water in a house. A typical house with central heating and a cold-water tank is shown below, but in some houses there may be no cold-water tank and all cold taps, the lavatories and the hot-water cylinder may be supplied direct by the main.

For simplicity, no central-heating pipes are shown in the illustration. Water enters the house through the rising main, which branches off to supply water direct to the kitchen cold-water tap and a garden tap.

The rising main also supplies water to the cold-water storage tank in the loft (see *Cold-water tank*). The cold-water tank stores water and then supplies it to the bathroom cold taps, all the lavatories in the house and the hot-water cylinder, as it is required.

The water for the hot-water taps in the house is heated indirectly by hot water from the boiler which runs through a coil in the hot-water storage cylinder (see *Hot-water cylinder*: 'Understanding the hot-water system'), which is usually in one of the upstairs rooms.

The boiler may burn a variety of fuels and it is often located in the kitchen. Cold water is piped to it from the small feed-and-expansion tank in the loft which is fed by a branch from the rising main.

The boiler and the hot-water cylinder each have a safety-vent pipe to relieve any build-up of pressure. The safety-vent pipes discharge into the feed-and-expansion tank and the cold-water tank.

The water supply to the house can be cut off by closing a stopcock on the rising main by hand. There is usually one under the kitchen sink or in the cellar. A second stopcock, owned by the water company, is located near the boundary of the property (see *Stopcock*).

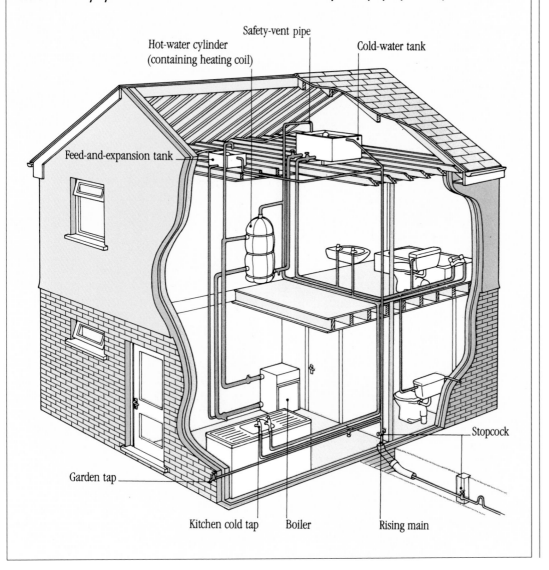

Safety-vent pipe

Hot-water cylinder
(containing heating coil)

Cold-water tank

Feed-and-expansion tank

Garden tap

Kitchen cold tap

Boiler

Rising main

Stopcock

Pipes (cont.)

EMERGENCY PIPE REPAIRS

Several products are available from a builders' merchants or DIY store that will help with emergency repairs of leaking pipes. These include:

● Mechanical clamps with rubber pads that can be screwed tightly onto the pipe.

● Leak-sealing tapes that can be bound over the leak to weld into a waterproof skin.

● Epoxy-resin fillers that can be used with a gauze bandage to seal off the leak.

● Short lengths of pipe with compression coupling ends that can be inserted into the pipe after the defective length is cut out.

Thawing out a frozen pipe

The first sign of a frozen pipe is an empty tap during cold weather or a lavatory cistern that will not refill. Take action immediately or the plug of ice will grow large enough to split the pipe. And as it grows larger the ice will become more difficult to thaw out.

First locate the ice plug. Pipes in the loft, against a cold wall or near the eaves, or with thin or missing lagging are particularly vulnerable to freezing.

If water flows from the kitchen cold tap, but none runs into the main cold-water tank, the rising main is blocked (see 'The plumbing in a typical house', previous page).

If the cold-water tank is filling normally, but the bathroom taps are not working and the lavatory cistern is not refilling, the blockage is in the distribution pipe from the cold-water tank to the bathroom.

If the hot-water taps are empty, the blockage lies somewhere in the distribution pipe from the cold-water tank to the hot-water cylinder or boiler.

When you have found the blockage, strip the pipe of its lagging and apply heat to melt the ice.

Use a hot-water bottle, a hair dryer or a cloth soaked in hot water. Copper piping conducts heat well, so the heat will travel along the pipe to melt the ice.

! Never use a blow torch to thaw out a frozen pipe in the loft. The dry roof timbers can be easily set on fire.

Repairing a burst compression joint Time: ½ a day or less

Pipes carrying water around the house are joined by either compression fittings, which the water pipes are screwed into, or soldered joints. If a compression joint is leaking, it may have been forced open by ice inside the pipe.

YOU WILL NEED Torch, adjustable spanners, leak sealer (such as Fernox LS-X).

First stop the flow of water and empty the leaking pipe (see 'What to do when a pipe bursts', page 264).

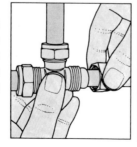

Hold the body of the compression joint with one adjustable spanner, unscrew the cap nut with another and pull it away from the body of the joint.

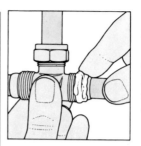

A copper ring or 'olive' sits around the pipe where the pipe end enters the body of the fitting. Smear Fernox LS-X around the olive and onto the screw thread on the compression joint.

Then screw the cap nut back onto the body of the compression fitting and screw it up hand tight.

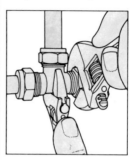

Hold the body of the joint with one spanner and use another spanner to tighten the cap nut another one and a quarter turns. Restore the water supply.

Repairing a split pipe or soldered joint
Time: 1 hour or less

YOU WILL NEED Rubber or plastic gloves, two-part epoxy putty leak sealer (such as Plumberfix), pipe-and-hose repair tape.

If a soldered joint has pulled apart or if the pipe has split, you can use two-part epoxy putty sealer such as Plumberfix, available from DIY shops and plumbers' merchants, to make a quick, permanent repair.

The epoxy putty comes in two different coloured pieces. Cut equal sized chunks from each and, wearing rubber or plastic gloves, knead them vigorously together until the two colours blend evenly.

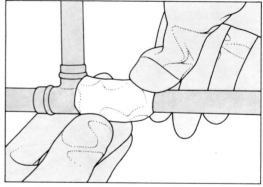

Force the putty into the split or round the leaking joints, covering an area about 2.5 cm (1 in) on each side of the leak to a thickness of about 6 mm ($\frac{1}{4}$ in).

Bind the repair with pipe-and-hose repair tape. Restore the water and leave the putty to set for 24 hours. Remove the tape and rub down the putty with abrasive paper.

Piping on upholstery

Piping is used as a decorative finish on the seams of cushions and fabric-covered furniture. It is made by wrapping fabric round cord and inserting it in a seam in the cover.

Repairing piping Time: depends on area

Where decorative piping has torn away from a seam, it is possible to stitch it back into place.

ON CUSHIONS AND LOOSE COVERS Take the cover off the cushion or piece of furniture and turn it inside-out.

Unpick the seam that held the piping for about 7.5 cm (3 in) on both sides of the damaged area. Stitch in the loose threads to prevent the seam opening any further. Reposition and pin the piping between the two pieces of fabric. Tack along the seam and remove the pins.

Fit the piping foot to your sewing machine (or a one-sided zip foot) and, using matching thread, stitch along the seam. Start stitching about 2.5 cm (1 in) before the opening you made in the seam and continue for the same distance past the end of the opening.

If there are loose threads, finish them off by hand-sewing a few backstitches with each one (see *Stitches*).

If you do not have a sewing machine, hand-sew the seam, using small backstitches.

ON NON-REMOVABLE COVERS If it is impossible to get at the inside of the seam, you will have to repair the loose piping by hand from the outside of the seam. Wear a thimble on a finger of each hand to protect your fingers.

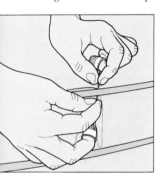

Make a knot in the end of the thread and conceal it in the seam. Catch up the fabric on both sides of the piping in tiny stitches, passing the needle from side to side (left). Keep the tension even, to prevent gaps and puckers. Fasten off firmly.

Cleaning piping on a chair or sofa

If piping on a chair or sofa is very dirty and the cover can't be removed for washing or dry-cleaning, make up a solution of soap flakes — or use an upholstery cleaner — and apply it with an old toothbrush.

Work at the dirty sections gently. To avoid over-wetting, use the foam only and wipe it off with a damp cloth. Keep the solution away from the rest of the cover in case it leaves a 'high-water mark'.

Planes

The wide variety of prepared timbers and wooden mouldings available in DIY stores means that for most DIY work a plane is not necessary. However, if you need to reduce a piece of wood, as when trimming a new door to size, use a smoothing plane about 25 cm (10 in) long. A model with a replaceable blade eliminates the need for sharpening.

How to adjust the blade of a plane

To adjust the depth of the cut, turn the knurled knob. Start with it set so that you can feel it just protruding from the base, but take care not to cut yourself.

If the cut seems too deep, turn the knurled knob to retract the blade slightly; if it is too shallow, set the blade to cut deeper.

Look along the bottom of the plane to check the blade. If it is not level, adjust it by moving the lever to left or right.

Plaster (SEE ALSO CORNICE & COVING)

Plastering a whole wall is a skilled job and is best left to a professional plasterer. But you can do repairs to plaster yourself, using either traditional plaster or a special DIY plaster. There are four main types of plaster.

UNDERCOAT PLASTER Quick-setting, pink or grey plaster, designed to be applied direct to bricks or building blocks.

FINISHING PLASTER A topcoat to be used over undercoat plaster. Layers should be about 2 mm ($\frac{1}{16}$ in) thick.

SKIM-COAT PLASTER A creamy-white topcoating that gives a particularly fine finish. It can be bought ready-to-use.

ONE-COAT PLASTER A relatively new generation of plasters intended for the amateur. One-coat plaster can be applied direct on bricks, building blocks or plasterboard, and can be used for both filling and finishing.

Most types can be applied to a depth of 5 cm (2 in) without slumping, as standard plasters do. Some are sold ready-mixed in tubs; others need water. They stay workable for at least an hour and will dry white or pink.

Plaster (cont.)

PATCHING A TEXTURED SURFACE

First repair any cracks and holes in the plaster. Then apply textured paint, mixed to a thick consistency, with the tip of a brush. Dab it on thickly. Then use a sponge to create the main pattern by dabbing, lifting or swirling. Or you can use a special textured roller.

MIXING YOUR OWN PLASTER

If you make your own plaster from dry powder, stir the ingredients in the packet with a stick in case they have separated. Then measure out the amount of water recommended on the packet into a bucket. Add powder to the water, stirring continuously until you have a pliable, uniform mix.

Filling cracks and holes Time: depends on area

> YOU WILL NEED Small trowel, old paintbrush. Depending on size of job: interior filler or plaster, old plate or bucket, filling knife or plasterer's trowel. Possibly: batten, plasterer's hawk.

Dig out all loose and crumbling material with the point of a trowel and remove dust with an old paintbrush.

CRACKS AND SMALL HOLES Wet cracks and holes with clean water on the paintbrush. Mix up some interior filler or finishing plaster (which is cheaper) on an old plate or saucer.

Using a narrow filling knife, smooth filler into any cracks and very small holes (left) in the wall.

For larger holes, use finishing plaster and apply it with a wide filling knife. Press the plaster well into the cracks and holes.

Pull the knife over the repaired area at an acute angle to smooth the plaster. Scrape away any surplus.

LARGE HOLES Wet any brickwork exposed by the damage. Then mix some undercoat plaster and load it onto a hawk.

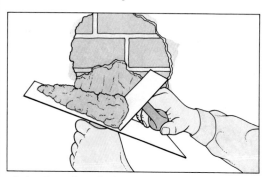

Lift the plaster from the hawk into the hole with a plasterer's trowel held at an angle of 45 degrees to the wall.

Fill the hole to within 3 mm ($\frac{1}{8}$ in) of the surface and, before it sets, lay a straight piece of wood over the hole and 'walk' it across to check that there are no high spots.

Allow the undercoat two hours to set. Then mix up a batch of finishing plaster. Heap it onto the hawk, lift it with the plastering trowel and spread it over the repair.

Smooth it out with the edge of the trowel. Allow about 20 minutes for it to set, then damp it with clean water applied with the old paintbrush. Use the trowel again, with a smoothing action, to make sure the surface is perfect.

Allow the repaired area to dry thoroughly and then redecorate it to match the surrounding wall.

Repairing a damaged corner Time: $\frac{1}{2}$ a day or less

A corner of a wall that protrudes into a room or passage may be damaged by furniture moving or children's games.

> YOU WILL NEED Small trowel, thin batten, power drill and fine drill bit, masonry nails, hammer, old paintbrush, one-coat plaster, plastering trowel, medium sandpaper and sanding block. Possibly: saw, corner trowel.

Chip away the damaged plaster with a small trowel. Cut a thin wooden batten about 38 mm ($1\frac{1}{2}$ in) wide and longer than the damaged area. Drill it top and bottom, close to one edge, to take small masonry nails.

Place the batten on the wall so that the undrilled edge is aligned with the surface of the adjoining wall. Tap the nails through the holes in the batten and into the wall plaster, leaving their heads protruding.

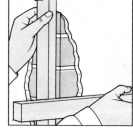

Dampen the corner with an old paintbrush. Then, with one-coat plaster and a plastering trowel, build up the damaged area on the adjoining wall, finishing it so that it is level with the edge of the batten.

When the plaster has dried remove the nails and slide the batten away from the corner. Then reposition it over the repair (right).

Realign the batten with the adjoining wall, then tap in the nails and complete the plastering.

PLASTERING TOOLS

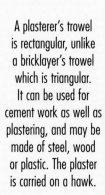

A plasterer's trowel is rectangular, unlike a bricklayer's trowel which is triangular. It can be used for cement work as well as plastering, and may be made of steel, wood or plastic. The plaster is carried on a hawk.

HAWK The mixed plaster is carried to the wall on a hawk, which may be made of aluminium, plastic or wood.

PLASTERING TROWEL The rectangular steel trowel has a handle fitted to the centre. Professional plasterers may use a laying-on trowel which has a thicker blade for applying the plaster, and a finishing trowel with a thinner, more flexible blade for final smoothing. But a laying-on trowel is sufficient for DIY work.

CORNER TROWEL The trowel can be used to finish an external corner by dipping it in water and running it down the damp plaster. Trowels are also made for internal corners.

POINTING TROWEL Normally used for brickwork, a pointing trowel is useful for cleaning out broken plaster in a damaged wall.

FLOAT A wooden trowel, called a float, is used to give the surface of plaster or concrete a fine finish. Floats may also be made of plastic.

Remove the batten, allow the plaster to set for about two hours, then lightly rub the corner with medium sandpaper wrapped around a sanding block. Slightly round-off the corner to make it less prone to damage.

Alternatively, if you have a corner trowel, you could smooth off the corner while the plaster is still damp.

Plasterboard

Plasterboard, nailed to a wooden framework, is widely used for making walls and ceilings in modern houses. You can identify a plasterboard wall by the hollow sound it makes when tapped. A wall that is made from bricks or building blocks sounds solid.

Plasterboard consists of aerated gypsum sandwiched between two layers of tough paper – one ivory-coloured for painting or wallpapering, and one grey for plastering.

It is more prone to damage than masonry and plaster.

Repairing dents and small holes

Carefully remove any loose material and if there is any loose paper, trim it off. Then treat it as a normal plastered wall (see *Plaster*: 'Filling cracks and holes').

Repairing a large hole Time: ½ a day

> YOU WILL NEED Trimming knife, fine-tooth hand saw, piece of plasterboard, length of string, drill and twist bit, small trowel, panel adhesive, one-coat plaster.

Use a trimming knife to cut the hole in the board to a rectangular shape. Remove all loose debris.

Cut a piece of scrap plasterboard large enough to overlap the hole by about 6 mm (¼ in) all round.

Drill a hole in the centre of the patch. Knot a length of string at one end and thread it through the patch – ivory-coloured face first.

Butter the edges of the grey side with panel adhesive, then insert the patch diagonally through the hole, with the grey side facing out.

Holding the string, pull the patch tightly up against the rear face of the plasterboard. Leave it for 20 minutes to allow the adhesive to take hold, then – holding the string again – fill the remaining recess with one-coat plaster.

When it is almost flush, cut off the string and finish plastering. Smooth with the edge of the trowel and allow a couple of hours to set. Then lightly sand the patch with medium sandpaper, taking care not to damage the adjoining paper layer.

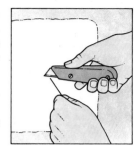

Pliers SEE ALSO FACING PAGE

Pliers are designed for gripping small objects. Don't use them instead of spanners to tighten a nut, because they will round off the nut's corners, making it impossible to turn. If the pliers are likely to cause damage to the object they are gripping, put a piece of rag between the jaws.

Using pliers for gripping

The broad jaws of engineer's pliers are designed to be used in two ways, and are useful in a variety of tasks.

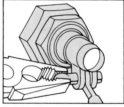 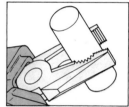

Small objects, such as the head of a split pin, can be held and twisted with the flat jaws at the tip.

Larger, round objects, such as the plug of a ball valve, can be held with the curved jaws while it is unscrewed.

Needle-nosed pliers have narrow jaws which can be used for tasks such as pulling plastic wall plugs out of a wall, and for holding a small nut while you get it started on a bolt.

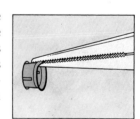

Bending metal with pliers

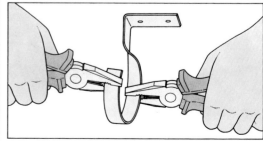

Two pairs of pliers, one in each hand, can be used to bend a piece of metal, such as this simple flowerpot holder.

PLIERS & PINCERS

Pliers are made in many designs — for general and specialist use — but engineer's pliers and long-nose pliers are most useful around the house.

FLAT-NOSE PLIERS Designed for lighter work than engineer's pliers. The flat nose is ideal for bending wire or metal.

LONG-NOSE PLIERS Useful for holding and positioning small objects such as nuts and washers. Side cutters can be used for cutting lightweight wire.

ENGINEER'S PLIERS
Tough serrated jaws are combined with curved jaws for gripping. A pair of sharp edges can be used to cut wire or electric flex, and side slots allow even greater pressure to be exerted on heavier-gauge wire.

ROUND-NOSE PLIERS
Used for forming small loops in wire and metal strips.

ELECTRICIAN'S PLIERS
Similar to engineer's pliers, but with handles insulated with plastic. However, they should never be used to work on live electrical appliances or wiring. Always disconnect the power at the mains first.

SLIP-JOINT PLIERS
The jaws can be adjusted to give two widths of opening — for gripping small objects and large ones.

CARPENTER'S PINCERS
Designed for pulling out nails. The jaws grip the nail, while a rolling action levers it out of the wood. Some models have a claw in one handle for removing tacks.

Working with wire

A pair of engineer's pliers is essential if you are working with wire in the garden — perhaps fixing a climbing plant to a wall. Cut the wire to length in the small jaws on the side of the pliers.

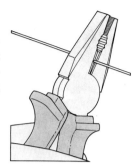

Don't try to cut stainless steel or sprung wire with them, because they are harder than the jaws of the cutters.

Plumber

Employing a 'cowboy' plumber in an emergency could be a costly mistake, so take the following precautions:

- Try to choose a plumber before problems arise.
- Whenever possible use a plumber who has been recommended by a friend or relation.
- Choose a plumber who is a member of the Institute of Plumbing (MIP). For more details, see page 17.
- For gas central heating find a plumber registered with the Council for Registered Gas Installers (see page 168).
- For small jobs such as renewing a tap, repairing a burst pipe or fixing a toilet, try to find a small, established plumber in your area.
- Try to give the plumber as much detail as possible about the job over the telephone, so that he comes prepared.
- For a major job get two or three estimates before you decide which firm to use, and get a written quote from the chosen firm before the work starts.

Pond

A fall in the level of the water in a pond can be caused by evaporation. But if it falls by more than about 1 cm ($\frac{1}{2}$ in) a week, it is possible that the pond is leaking.

Before you can mend a leak, it is necessary to remove plants and fish from the pond and store them safely.

Removing plants and fish from a pond
Time: depends on quantity

> YOU WILL NEED Plastic buckets and baths. Possibly: large sheet of polythene, lengths of timber, nails, hammer.

Store the fish in plastic (not metal) buckets and baths. Their surface area must make up no less than a quarter of the surface area of the pond, and the water in each of them should be no less than 30 cm (12 in) deep.

Store plants and fish separately, because disturbed oxygenating plants may foul the water and harm the fish. Cover the fish container with a net to protect the fish from cats and place it in a shady part of the garden.

When there are too many fish and plants to store in buckets and basins, you can hold them in temporary ponds made with doubled sheets of polythene.

If there are suitable holes in the garden, line them with the polythene and transfer fish and plants into them.

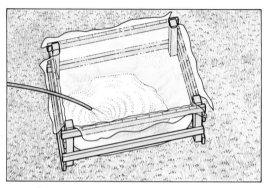

If there are no suitable holes, build rough wooden frames above ground and line them with polythene.

Mending a leak in a concrete pond Time: about a day

It is possible to buy fast-setting cements that set within 10 minutes and are hard and waterproof within 30 minutes. For small leaks you can use fast-setting cements that will set under water, which saves having to empty the pond before starting the repair.

> YOU WILL NEED Fast-setting cement, trowel. Possibly: large plastic sheet, PVA building adhesive or waterproofing powder.

Empty the pond sufficiently to expose the crack. Clean away any loose cement and slightly undercut the edges of the crack with a trowel to make a better repair.

Fill the crack with fast-setting cement, and spread it out beyond the crack in all directions, following the maker's instructions.

If you decide to use a normal cement mixture, add some waterproofing powder to the mix. It will take longer to dry than a fast-setting cement, so protect the patched area with a sheet of plastic. If you have not waterproofed the patch, brush the area with a PVA building adhesive.

Time must be allowed for the lime to leach out of a cement patch, so fill the pond and leave it for two or three days. Then empty it completely and refill it. Alternatively, treat it with Silglaze which seals in the free lime.

Mending a leak in a flexible pond liner

Time: 2 hours or less

Flexible pond liners can be made of butyl, polythene or PVC. Repairs to liners of this type are quite easy, but finding the leak may take some time.

> YOU WILL NEED Plastic buckets or hose, plastic funnel, dry sand, repair kit. Possibly: methylated spirit, bag of sand, rope.

Bale the water out with a bucket. Or, if the pond is raised, you can siphon the water out. Put one end of a hose into the pond then suck on the other end to start the flow of water. To avoid getting the area too wet, drain it into a bucket.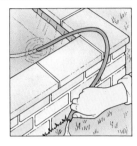

When you have emptied the pond, clean and dry the inside and search it for damage. Once you have located the hole, remove the cause of the damage.

Using a funnel and a little dry sand, replace any sand that may have been washed away from beneath the hole by the water as it leaked out.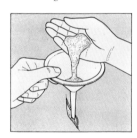

Use a repair kit appropriate to the liner material to patch the liner, following the manufacturer's instructions.

WORKING UNDER WATER When it is not possible to empty the pool, try to make the repair under water. First clear away any sand that may have gathered round the tear.

Cut a patch that is large enough to cover the tear and clean it with methylated spirit. Apply adhesive to the entire surface of the patch and press into place over the tear.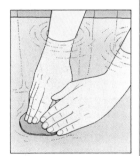

To make sure that the patch sticks well, it may be necessary to weigh it down with a bag of sand on the end of a rope.

Mending a leak in a rigid pond liner

Time: depends on treatment

A rigid pond liner is usually made of glass fibre. It is strong and resists ice and frost well. It rarely develops leaks but, if it does, it can be mended with a glass fibre repair kit, available in most motor accessory shops.

> YOU WILL NEED Plastic buckets or hose, glass fibre repair kit. Possibly: new rigid pond liner.

Empty the pond with a plastic bucket or a hose (see 'Mending a leak in a flexible pond liner'), and patch the leak, following the instructions on the repair kit.

If the mend is going to look conspicuous, or you are unable to disguise it sufficiently well with plants, you may prefer to replace the liner.

Faultfinder guide: Pond

Observing the colour of the water in the pond can help you to diagnose the problem.

Water is dark grey-blue

POSSIBLE CAUSE The level of oxygen is low. Decaying leaves and pond plants may be the cause.
ACTION Clean out the pond. Placé a net over the pond in autumn to catch falling leaves.

Water is blue-green

POSSIBLE CAUSE Rapid growth of algae.
ACTION Wash some wheat or barley straw, bind it into small sheaves and float them on the surface. As it begins to rot, it removes the nutrients that algae feed on. Use a handful of straw for every cubic metre (or cubic yard) of water. Remove the straw soon after it begins to rot to prevent it from polluting the water.

Water is bright green and cloudy

POSSIBLE CAUSE Blanket weed, a form of algae.
ACTION Catch strands of blanket weed on a strong stick. The cloudiness should go within a few hours.

An oily film on the surface

POSSIBLE CAUSE Oil or petrol, probably from a petrol mower that has been used close to the pond.
ACTION A thin layer will eventually disperse, but a thicker one can be lifted out by laying old cloths on the surface, then lifting them and wringing them out where the oil can do no harm.

POSSIBLE CAUSE It may be vegetable oil from rotting organic matter, such as leaves.
ACTION Remove dead leaves from the pond.

WHEN TO CLEAN A POND

Because a delicate balance of plant and animal life builds in a pond, avoid cleaning it out completely too often. A small pond should be cleaned out once every five years, and a large pond once every ten years – or when it looks necessary.

GETTING RID OF POND ODOURS

Rotting algae and organic matter cause unpleasant smells in a pond. A product called Aquaplancton is available to speed up the digestion of organic matter in muddy water and reduce the odour. For more information, contact Aquaplancton at Clavering Cote, Little London, Stowmarket, Suffolk IP14 2ES (Tel. 01449 774532).

273

Pond (cont.)

REMOVING PONDWEED

Pondweed has a central stem with leaves growing closely all round it. If the pondweed in your pond appears to be growing too profusely, remove some of it, but pick off any trapped creatures and return them to the water. Sometimes the removal of too much pondweed may upset the balance of the pool, because submerged weeds are necessary in moderate quantities to ensure healthy water.

Dealing with pests in a garden pond

Never spray insect pests in a pond. Pesticides can poison the water and affect fish and other pond-dwellers. Fish will eat a good number of pests, so consider stocking the pond with a few, if you have not already done so.

WATER LILY APHID Red-brown aphids that damage leaves and flowers. Spray them off the leaves with a hose. Fish in the pond will eat them. In autumn aphids lay eggs in trees of the Prunus family, so if you have one near your pond, give it a tar oil wash to break the cycle.

SNAILS Often imported on new pond plants. They do some good by eating algae, fish waste and decaying leaves, but in large numbers they will start eating new growth. Do not use slug pellets to kill them.

Instead, float a stump of lettuce on the pond overnight, then take it out in the morning, and kill only the snails with pointed shells that are clinging to it. The round, flat, ramshorn snails are not harmful.

POND INSECTS Nymphs and larvae of dragonflies, water boatmen, water scorpions, whirligig beetles and great diving beetles. They attack eggs, fry and small fish, but are themselves eaten by larger fish.

It is neither possible nor desirable to get rid of all pond insects, but if it is necessary you can reduce their numbers by trawling through the water with a pond net and disposing of any predators you find.

ANCHOR WORMS AND FISH LICE Parasites that attach themselves to fish. Catch the fish and dab a little paraffin on the parasite. When the parasite falls off the fish, treat the infected area with a fish antiseptic.

Alternatively, use a proprietary brand of parasite cure; many are available from garden centres and pet shops.

BIRDS Herons, and to a lesser degree, kingfishers and gulls. A heron stands in the pond and catches fish with a rapid thrust of the head. You can deter it by covering the pond with sturdy netting. To birdproof your pond less conspicuously, make the pond deep and steep-sided.

Do not try to guard the pond by surrounding it with fishing line tied to a series of small sticks — herons will step over it and small birds may fly into it and be injured.

Cleaning and restocking a pond Time: depends on size

Spring or early summer is the time to refresh a pond. There is no need to empty it, unless it is in bad condition.

FRESHEN WATER Use a garden hose to refresh the pond, but add a pool conditioner (available in DIY and garden centres) which neutralises the chlorine content of tap water.

Alternatively, run the water into a number of buckets and allow it to stand overnight before pouring it into the pool. This allows the chlorine to evaporate and the water to reach the same temperature as the water in the pool.

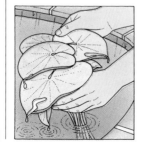

WATER LILIES Lift the plants out of the pond and remove all old foliage. Throw away the centre part and replant the strong side shoots in a fresh position.

Look at the other water plants and discard any that are not beginning to show signs of healthy growth.

FISH Goldfish and comets do well out of doors, but before you introduce new fish, calculate how many the pond can support. Allow approximately 5 cm (2 in) length of fish to every 30 cm² (5 sq in) of water surface.

Lower the plastic bag containing the new fish into the water, and leave it there for about an hour, to let the water in the bag adjust to the pond temperature. Then release the fish gently into the pond. Do not do this on a very hot day as the fish may suffocate in the bag.

Feed the fish small amounts of good quality food. Take care not to overfeed them. They should rise to the surface eagerly when you sprinkle the food onto the water and eat it straight away. Uneaten food will foul the water.

PROTECTING TODDLERS

If you have a toddler and are worried about your pond, clean it out and fill it with large, attractive pebbles. Leave the plants in position and place the pebbles carefully round them. Refill it with water and keep it topped up. It will look attractive and yet present no danger. Alternatively, anchor a pond net over the pond, but always supervise small children who may be fascinated by the fish in it.

Cleaning pond lights   Time: depends on number

> **YOU WILL NEED** Hose. Possibly: warm soapy water.

Pond lights are usually submerged, and submerged lights will collect algae and other debris. To clean them in the pond, just hose them gently. If you have to remove them from the pond, turn off the power supply at the mains first. Wash them in warm, soapy water, rinse and replace them.

Pottery: SEE CHINA AND PORCELAIN

Power failure

Emergency action

If all the lights suddenly go out on one floor, or all the power sockets in one part of the house stop working, a fuse has probably blown at the main fuse box (see *Fuse box*: 'Emergency action – circuit failure').

If the electricity goes off throughout the house, report it to your local electricity company's 24 hour emergency number, listed under 'Electricity' in *The Phone Book* (business and services section). They will be able to tell you if there is a fault in the power supply to your whole area, and when the power is likely to be restored. (See also *Refrigerator & freezer*: 'What to do in a power failure'.)

If your house is the only one affected, check your main supply switch. If your supply is protected by a residual current device (RCD) check to see if it is switched off. Reset it. If it will not reset, check the circuits (see *Fuse box*: 'Resetting miniature circuit breakers').

If you cannot find any other reason for the lack of power call the electricity company using the 24 hour emergency line. There may be a fault in the cable that supplies power to your house. There is no charge for repairs to the electricity company's cable and fuse.

NUISANCE TRIPPING   If you are suffering from 'nuisance tripping', where the RCD keeps switching itself off for no apparent reason, report it to the electricity company.

Prams & pushchairs

Cleaning a pram or pushchair   Time: a few minutes

> **YOU WILL NEED** Damp cloth, detergent, absorbent cloth.

Check the manufacturer's instructions to see if the seat is machine-washable. If not, sponge it with a cloth wrung out in mild detergent solution or upholstery shampoo. Wipe the frame with a soft, clean cloth.

Allow the pram or pushchair to dry completely before folding it up, to avoid the risk of mildew forming. If there is a plastic rain cover, always dry it thoroughly with a soft, absorbent cloth before folding it up.

Repairing split upholstery   Time: ½ an hour or less

Large tears in the upholstery should be dealt with professionally, but smaller ones can be mended at home.

> **YOU WILL NEED** Suitable patch, scissors, clear glue, tweezers. Possibly: small piece of scrap paper.

Cut a patch from a piece of strong fabric. Make it about 1 cm (½ in) larger all round than the tear itself.

On an absorbent fabric, apply a generous amount of clear adhesive to the surface of the patch only, and slip it into the tear, using tweezers to position it under the tear. Press down firmly on the damaged area.

If the surfaces are not absorbent, apply the glue to both the inside of the tear and the face of the patch.

Support the glued surface inside the tear with a little piece of crumpled paper, to hold it away from the padding.

Allow both glued surfaces to become tacky – which should take about 10 minutes – and then use tweezers to remove the crumpled paper and position the patch inside the tear. Then press down on the damaged area firmly.

Maintaining a pram or pushchair
Modern prams and pushchairs should give many years of trouble-free service.

- Get a yearly service done by the manufacturer or a reliable service agent.
- If the wheels squeak, spray the axle sparingly with WD40 – not with oil or grease.
- To keep the body of a telescopic model folding easily, spray the frame regularly with furniture polish.
- Check all rivets and fixing devices regularly, and tighten them as necessary.
- Inspect brakes, wheels and tyres regularly. Get them replaced or repaired as necessary.

BENEFITS OF A FIVE-POINT HARNESS

Many pushchairs are fitted with only a three-point harness, which has waist and crotch straps only. This may not be enough if the child is very active or you are walking over rough ground. It is possible for an energetic toddler to climb out of a three-point safety harness, especially if unattended. A five-point harness has shoulder, waist and crotch straps and gives more safety and control. It is possible to convert a three-point harness by buying one with shoulder straps and clipping it onto the D-rings of the pushchair at waist height.

PUSHCHAIR SAFETY

Never leave a small child unattended in a pushchair. Make sure that the child's fingers (and those of other children) are well clear of the wheels and any moving parts or folding joints.

Pressure cooker

Parts of a typical pressure cooker

The number of weights used on the control valve of a pressure cooker dictates the pressure and, therefore, the temperature at which the food inside cooks – all three weights giving maximum cooking temperature. The safety plug releases pressure if it gets too high.

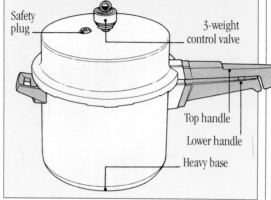

Safety plug

3-weight control valve

Top handle

Lower handle

Heavy base

Fitting a new sealing ring Time: $\frac{1}{2}$ an hour or less

If steam escapes from between the handles, or all round the lid, the sealing ring needs replacing.

> YOU WILL NEED Replacement sealing ring, washing-up liquid. Possibly: kebab stick or old kitchen knife.

The thick rubber sealing ring is located in a groove under the lid. The old seal should come away easily, but if it is difficult to loosen, use a wooden kebab stick or an old, blunt knife to ease it out. Try to avoid damaging the groove in the process.

Wash out the groove with a mild solution of washing-up liquid and then dry it very thoroughly.

Fit the new seal under the rim, taking care to get it under the aluminium lugs which help to lock the lid to the body of the cooker.

Resetting a safety plug Time: a few minutes

Many models of pressure cooker have a safety plug fitted in the lid that does not need to be replaced, every time it

comes into action. However, on most models of pressure cooker, this plug should be replaced at least once a year.

The safety plug consists of a shaped metal pin that fits into a hard rubber seating. It is activated when the pressure reaches the safety limit; the metal pin pops up and allows the excess pressure to escape.

To reset it, take the pressure cooker off the heat, wait until all the steam has escaped and remove the lid.

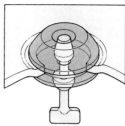

Turn it upside-down on a hard surface. Hold down the rubber seating around the pin with your thumbs, and press down on the pin with a finger. It should pop back into place.

Before replacing the lid, try to find out why the safety plug blew. Check that the water level is correct and that the steam escape hole under the control valve is not blocked.

If it blows again, the rubber seating may have perished and the whole safety plug will need replacing.

Replacing a safety plug Time: a few minutes

A new plug can be obtained from your dealer, but as plugs vary, take the old one with you. You may have to order a new one from the manufacturer.

> YOU WILL NEED Replacement safety plug. Possibly: pliers.

To remove the old plug, lay the lid right side up on a worktop, and press on the pin. It should push through.

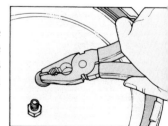

If it is difficult, pull the pin through from the inside using pliers, although this shouldn't be necessary. Then push out the rubber seating.

Push the new plug into place from inside the lid.

Puncture:

SEE AIR BED; BICYCLE TYRES; CAR TYRES

Push-starting: SEE CAR EMERGENCIES

Putty
Working with putty

Although modern sealants are widely available, putty is still the most common material for glazing. Linseed oil putty is used for timber frames and metal casement putty for metal frames. There is also a dual-purpose putty which can be used on either timber or metal.

Hold a ball of putty in your hand, with part of it between finger and thumb. Dispense a strip, pressing the putty into place with your thumb.

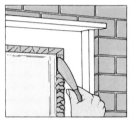 Use the flat side of a putty knife to press the strip into the shape you want it.

 Then draw the straight side of the knife along it, pressing down, to smooth the surface.

Surplus putty may ooze from either side of the blade. Leave it until you have finished, then lift it away with the putty knife. Rub off any small bits with your fingers. Let it harden for at least a fortnight before painting.

Problems with putty

PUTTY TOO HARD If putty gets cold, it goes hard. You can soften it by working it in the warmth of your hands for a few minutes. A drop of linseed oil can also help.

PUTTY TOO STICKY When putty is too sticky to handle easily, roll it in newspaper to absorb some of the excess oil. Repeat the action with clean paper. Dip your hands in water before working with the putty to prevent it sticking.

BIRDS EATING PUTTY Some birds, especially tits, like to eat the linseed oil in putty. Discourage them by mixing some black pepper with new putty before applying it.

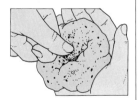

PUTTY WON'T STICK The surface may be greasy or dirty, so clean it thoroughly with white spirit, then apply a coat of primer. Allow it to dry, then apply the putty.

Quarry tiles
Replacing a damaged tile Time: parts of 2 days

YOU WILL NEED Safety spectacles, protective gloves, cold chisel, club hammer, new tile, notched spreader, tile adhesive, waterproof grout, piece of sponge, damp rag.

Wearing safety spectacles and protective gloves, use a cold chisel and club hammer to chip away the tile, starting at the centre and working outwards. Also, chip away any old adhesive that the tile leaves behind.

Spread adhesive on the back of the new tile, using a notched spreader. Lower the tile into place and check the gaps all round. Leave the adhesive to set for 24 hours.

Finish off by regrouting all round the tile (see *Grout*).

Cutting quarry tiles Time: a few minutes

If an edging tile has been broken, cut a new one to replace it. Measure it carefully, allowing space for the grout.

YOU WILL NEED Tile cutter or hammer and cold chisel, safety spectacles, cotton gloves, steel rule or straightedge, pencil. Possibly: brick, pincers, rasp or carborundum stone.

A heavy-duty platform tile cutter is capable of cutting tiles up to 11 mm ($\frac{7}{16}$ in) thick (see *Ceramic tiles*). Buy one, or hire it from a local tool-hire shop.

Alternatively, you can use a hammer and cold chisel.

 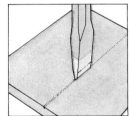

On the face of the tile, mark where you want to cut, then lay the tile, face up, on a hard, smooth surface.

Put on safety spectacles and gloves, and then tap a clear V line on the tile with a cold chisel and hammer.

Hold the tile in both hands and strike its back, along the scored line, against the edge of a brick. The tile should break cleanly along the scored line.

Use the hammer and chisel, or pincers, to snap off any thin sections of the tile which remain when it has been cut. If the newly exposed edge is too rough, use a rasp or carborundum stone to smooth it down.

CRACKING PUTTY

Putty around window frames can crack and pull away from the masonry, letting in damp. Dig out any hardened putty and replace it with an exterior grade flexible sealant (see *Windows*).

BRIGHTENING UP QUARRY TILES

Use a cream cleaner or a household cleaning powder dissolved in a little warm water to wash quarry tiles. Scuff marks can be removed by light rubbing with steel wool lubricated with white spirit.

If the old finish is worn or dull, clean it off with a strong detergent solution. You can then either use tile polish to spruce up the tiles, or paint them with brick and tile red, a specially formulated paint (see *Paint*).

Radiator:

SEE CAR COOLING SYSTEM; CENTRAL HEATING

Radio aerial

A radio tuner, which is usually used as part of a hi-fi system, may come with aerials that do not give adequate reception in your area. Separate aerials are needed for FM and AM (AM includes both long and medium waves).

Making an FM aerial Time: ½ a day or less

A simple homemade aerial mounted in the loft should improve reception in all but the worst reception areas. A cable must run from the aerial to the radio, avoiding metal objects such as pipes, so plan the route first. Then buy the right length of good coaxial cable.

> **YOU WILL NEED** Aluminium-alloy tubing, hacksaw, dowel to fit inside tubing, power drill, high-speed steel bit, 2 solder tags, 2 small nuts and bolts, spanner, coaxial plug, 75 ohm coaxial cable, trimming knife, solder, soldering iron, cord.

MAKING THE AERIAL Use a hacksaw to cut two pieces of alloy tube, each exactly 76 cm (30 in) long. Push the tubes over a piece of tight-fitting dowel, leaving a gap of no more than 2.5 cm (1 in) between them.

Drill a 3 mm (⅛ in) hole through the tube ends and the dowel and fit a solder tag to each with a nut and bolt.

MAKING THE LEAD Buy a coaxial plug and enough 75 ohm coaxial cable to reach from the aerial in the loft to the radio, wherever it is in the house, plus a little extra.

Use a trimming knife to cut off the outer insulation at one end of the cable for about 2.5 cm (1 in). Push back the copper braid and remove the insulation round the inner wire so that about 1 cm (⅜ in) of the inner wire is left insulated.

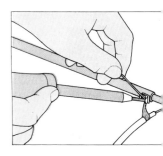

Solder the inner wire to one solder tag, then twist the bits of braid together and solder them to the other tag, making sure there is no chance of the two touching each other and shorting.

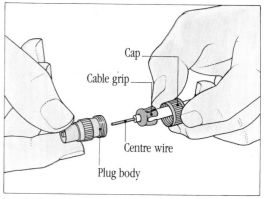

Cap

Cable grip

Centre wire

Plug body

Attach the other end of the cable to the coaxial plug, making sure that the braid is gripped firmly by the cable grip and the centre wire is central in the plug body.

RIGGING UP THE AERIAL Hang the aerial in the loft by cords attached to the rafters, keeping it well clear of metallic objects such as iron water tanks and pipes. Run the lead to the radio by the shortest possible route, avoiding pipes and electric cables, and plug it into the aerial socket.

Making an aerial for medium and long waves (AM)
Time: ½ an hour or less

> **YOU WILL NEED** Plastic-insulated single-core wire, wire strippers.

Using wire strippers, bare about 2 cm (¾ in) at one end of a length of plastic-coated single-core wire. Push the bared wire into the AM socket, which is usually located at the back of the radio set.

Bare the other end of the wire and take it to a picture rail or over a curtain rail. You will need to experiment for a while to find the position that gives the best reception.

EARTHING THE RADIO If the radio has an earth terminal, you may be able to reduce interference on both AM and FM by pushing one end of a second wire into the earth terminal and connecting the other end to an earthed metal pipe. All plumbing with metal pipes should be earthed.

A quick and easy FM aerial

You may need an FM aerial in a hurry, or there may be no easy way to run an aerial from the loft to a radio in the house. In either case, take a length of flat twin-core bell wire, or some two-core mains flex, and separate the wires at one end until there are two pieces 76 cm (30 in) long.

At the other end, fit a coaxial plug by soldering one wire to the cable grip and the other to the connector pin. Plug it into the aerial socket of the radio. Spread the two separated lengths apart and fix them under a bookshelf or along a picture rail. Experiment until you find a position that gives the best reception.

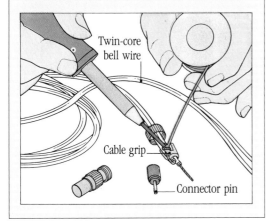

Twin-core bell wire

Cable grip

Connector pin

Rats

Rats must be eliminated as soon as possible, because they carry diseases, some of which are fatal, and do a lot of damage by fouling large areas and gnawing through woodwork, pipes and electric cables. They burrow underground or into soft material to make their nests in dirty places like sewers and rubbish dumps.

How to keep your property rat-free

CLEAR UP Do not encourage rats by leaving food out of doors. If you put bread out for birds, leave it on a feeder or in a hanging net rather than on the ground and put it out in the morning, because rats feed at night. For the same reason avoid leaving plastic bags filled with refuse outside overnight, and always close rubbish bins tightly and don't put cooked food or meat and bones on your compost heap.

CLOSE UP Eliminate any potential nesting sites. Close gaps under sheds, remove wood piles, cut down patches of weeds and undergrowth, and block holes in buildings.

RAT POISON Proprietary rat baits are usually sold in ready-to-use sachets. Leave the poison in 'rat runs' between nest and feeding places. They should be easily identifiable by the presence of droppings.

GET HELP If the infestation is too persistent or severe for you to deal with yourself, call a pest control company or your local Environmental Health Department. They will be able to use methods that are not available to the public.

RCD (RESIDUAL CURRENT DEVICE)

An RCD, which is also called a residual current circuit breaker (RCCB), is a safety device. It checks the balance between live and neutral currents on a circuit. If there is an imbalance, current may be flowing out through a faulty appliance or flex, so the RCD cuts off the electricity.

What model of RCD?

RCD-PROTECTED PLUG The plug is fitted to the flex of an appliance, specially one used outdoors, where the risk of electrocution is greater, such as a lawnmower or hedge trimmer.

ADAPTER RCD Fits between any 13 amp, three-pin socket and an appliance to act as a protected socket. It can be moved from socket to socket.

RCD-PROTECTED SOCKET An ordinary double socket outlet can be replaced by an RCD-protected socket outlet. It is best fitted by an electrician.

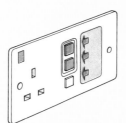

WHOLE-HOME RCD Must be installed by an electrician. It is fitted close to the meter and may replace the main switch. All or part of the wiring system in the house may be protected. See *Fuse box* for another type.

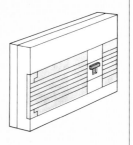

GETTING GOOD RECEPTION FROM AN FM AERIAL

An FM radio aerial should hang broadside on to your local FM transmitter. If you don't know the direction, move the aerial about – while someone inside listens to the radio – until you get the best reception. Or look along your street to see if any houses have FM aerials on the roof, and copy the direction in which they are pointing.

Records

Storing records

Records are made of vinyl which is easily scratched and damaged. Warping from exposure to heat and scratches from mishandling are two main types of damage.

Never store or leave records against a radiator, electric heater or other direct source of heat. They should not be left in direct sunlight on window shelves – and never on the dashboard or seats of a car.

Ideally you should store records upright in their cardboard sleeves, in a place where the temperature remains fairly constant, such as the living room.

Cleaning a vinyl record

YOU WILL NEED Antistatic cloth, record-cleaning fluid, record-cleaning cloth or pad.

INITIAL CLEANING If your records are very dirty, or have never been cleaned before, first use an antistatic cloth to remove static electricity, which can cause the sound to 'crack' and 'pop'. Then clean the records with record-cleaning fluid as directed by the maker.

THE STYLUS If reproduction quality seems poor, the record stylus may also need gentle and careful cleaning (see *Hi-fi*: 'What to do if a turntable gives poor-quality sound').

REGULAR CLEANING Clean records before each playing. Use an antistatic cloth to discharge any static that has been created in removing the record from its sleeve.

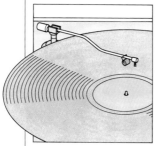

CLEANING ATTACHMENT A record-cleaning device that consists of a carbon-fibre brush and felt pad can be attached to the arm of your record player.

The device can be bought at most hi-fi retailers. It brushes debris out of the grooves and then wipes the record with the pad, as it plays. Some people prefer to use the brush when the record is not actually playing – to ensure optimum playing quality. To finish off, the record should be wiped with a record-cleaning cloth or pad to remove any remaining dust or debris.

Refrigerator & freezer

Defrosting a freezer or freezer compartment
Time: 2 hours or less

Choose a time when stocks in the freezer or the freezer compartment are low. Remove the contents and either wrap the food in layers of newspaper or load it into large dustbin bags and cover the bags with a duvet or blanket.

Turn off the appliance and remove the plug from the wall socket. Then place cloths or sheets of newspaper round the base of the fridge or freezer. If it has a drainer hole, place a bowl to catch the melting ice.

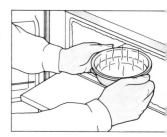

Place bowls of hot water inside the freezer compartment to speed up the thawing process and keep the door closed.

Keep refilling the bowls with hot water, as it cools very quickly. Do not chip away at the ice, as you may damage the lining of the freezer compartment.

To speed up the process and melt ice in awkward spots, use a hair dryer to blow hot air into the freezer, but do make sure that the hair dryer does not get wet.

When all the ice has melted, wash away any stains with a soft, clean cloth and a warm solution of bicarbonate of soda, and dry the inside of the compartment with a soft dry cloth. Restore power to the fridge or freezer. Close the door for half an hour, to let it cool, before replacing the food.

Fitting a new interior light bulb Time: a few minutes

! Switch off the refrigerator at the wall socket. It may be necessary to feel for the light socket when replacing the bulb. This means there is the risk of an electric shock.

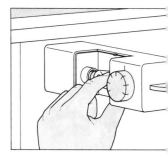

Remove the plastic light cover and unscrew or twist out the old light bulb. If the bulb should break, take great care when dealing with it (see *Light fittings*: 'Removing a broken bulb').

If the filament has broken, discard the light bulb. Fit a replacement bulb and replace the plastic cover. Then plug the refrigerator back in and switch it on. If the light does not come on, examine the light switch.

This is the little knob which is depressed when the door is closed. It should pop out when the door is opened. It is possible for it to become jammed in the 'off' position, or ice up so that it does not react to the opening of the fridge door.

Fitting a new refrigerator door seal   Time: 1 hour or less

A faulty door seal will allow warm air into the cabinet and should be replaced as soon as it is noticed. Some door seals are clipped into a recess in the door and others are bonded to the door. In either of these cases, call a service engineer to do the job. If the seal is held in place by screws, it should be possible to replace it yourself.

> **YOU WILL NEED** Screwdriver, soft cloth, replacement seal.

Replacement seals are usually obtainable through the manufacturer. Phone the customer services department with the model number of your refrigerator and they will

---

Faultfinder guide: Refrigerators and freezers

Most refrigerators have a compressor which circulates the gas that cools the interior of the cabinet.

However, some refrigerators do not have a compressor; instead they have an absorber tube in the form of a coil at the back of the appliance. Absorber-type refrigerators, which are less common, have the advantage of being silent in operation. They can run on gas or electricity and are most commonly used in caravans, boats and in hotel rooms – as mini-bars.

Appliance won't work

POSSIBLE CAUSE Fuse or wiring in plug is faulty.
ACTION Open plug and check fuse and wiring.

POSSIBLE CAUSE A build-up of ice in freezer compartment is affecting the power supply.
ACTION Defrost freezer.

POSSIBLE CAUSE Compressor may be broken.
ACTION Call an engineer.

Appliance operates but does not get cool

POSSIBLE CAUSE Faulty door seal.
ACTION Check door seal and replace if necessary.

POSSIBLE CAUSE Ventilation inadequate for absorption-type refrigerator.
ACTION Check air vents and remove winter covers if they have been left in place when season changes. Also check gas pressure regulator, if appropriate.

POSSIBLE CAUSE Light stays on when door is shut. (Bulb is warm to touch after door has been shut for hours.)
ACTION Call engineer to replace light switch.

POSSIBLE CAUSE Loss of refrigerant.
ACTION Call an engineer.

Cabinet too cold and icing up

POSSIBLE CAUSE Thermostat is set too high. The freezer may be set on 'Quick Freeze'.
ACTION Defrost and reset to lower temperature.

POSSIBLE CAUSE Thermostat is faulty.
ACTION Replace if possible, or call an engineer.

Fridge or freezer operates noisily

POSSIBLE CAUSE The floor is not level.
ACTION Adjust legs if possible or level with small wedge.

POSSIBLE CAUSE Fridge or freezer is touching other objects which may be amplifying its vibrations.
ACTION Make space all round.

POSSIBLE CAUSE Shelves, drawers or contents may be badly placed inside cabinet.
ACTION Position drawers and shelves correctly. Spread contents evenly, with bottles not touching.

Door sags or doesn't close properly

POSSIBLE CAUSE Hinge is loose or damaged, possibly as a result of pulling on handle when moving the appliance.
ACTION Check the hinge and tighten it if necessary. Make sure the adjustment hasn't affected the fit of the door seal. If the hinge is damaged, call an engineer.

Handle is loose

POSSIBLE CAUSE Wear and tear.
ACTION Tighten screws that hold the handle in place (sometimes positioned behind a removable panel).

Water in cabinet of auto-defrost fridge

POSSIBLE CAUSE Drainer tube is blocked.
ACTION Clear drainer tube (see overleaf).

PREVENTING SMELLS IN A REFRIGERATOR

Always store food in a container or wrapped in Cling Film to prevent it tainting other foods or being tainted by them.

Some fruits, including strawberries and pineapple, will taint milk or butter if not properly covered.

To get rid of smells in a refrigerator, fill an egg cup with bicarbonate of soda and place it on a shelf.

Plastic 'eggs' that contain a fridge deodoriser are available in many supermarkets.

MOVING A REFRIGERATOR OR FREEZER

Always empty a refrigerator or freezer before moving it. Don't pull on the door handle when moving it because you will probably damage the hinges.

Use a low-loading trolley (see *Furniture moving*). Alternatively, tilt the refrigerator back and slip an old rug or blanket under the front. Lower the refrigerator and pull it along on the blanket.

---

arrange for a replacement seal to be sent to you. Make sure that you have a replacement seal of the correct type and size before taking off the damaged one.

Take out all food and any removable sections in the door, such as egg racks or butter trays, before starting.

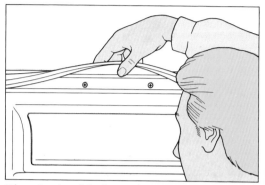

Lift up the edge of the door seal to expose the screws which hold it in place. Loosen the screws and check to see if this destabilises the moulded inside of the door.

On some models of refrigerator the screws hold both the seal and the moulded inside of the door in place.

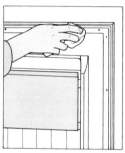

If it is stable, remove all the screws as well as the old seal. Clean the door frame with a soft, damp cloth then dry it.

Fit the new seal at the top and insert the screws. Adjust the seal to fit all round and then tighten the other screws.

However, if the inside of the door seems likely to come away, loosen the top and side screws only and ease out the old seal as far down the sides of the door as possible.

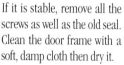

Fit the new seal to the top part of the door and tighten the top screws sufficiently to support the inner part of the door.

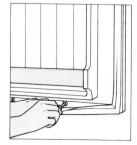

Then loosen the bottom screws and ease out the rest of the old seal.

Complete the fitting of the new seal and fully tighten all the screws round the new seal. Close the door and check that the new seal is being compressed evenly all round.

What to do in a power failure

• Do not open the door. Food in a refrigerator will keep cool for several hours, provided you keep the door closed. Food in an unopened freezer will take 24 hours to thaw, so it should be able to survive a power cut of up to 8 hours.

• Keep the room cool. Open doors and windows to get as much cool air into the room as possible.

• Insulate the appliance by throwing a blanket over it, but do not cover the condenser (the tubes at the back of the appliance).

• When the power is restored, take a quick look inside the appliance to make sure that frozen food has not thawed, and then do not open the door again for at least three hours. If only some frozen foods have thawed, remove them and cook them.

• If the power failure is prolonged and all the food thaws, take it out and cook as much of the raw food as possible once the power is restored. This can then be refrozen and eaten at a later date.

Precooked food that has thawed should be heated thoroughly and eaten. What cannot be eaten should be given or thrown away. Do not refreeze precooked frozen foods that have thawed.

• If you think you are in for a spate of power failures, run the stocks of frozen foods down as low as possible, and set the freezer to its maximum freezing temperature, in order to extend the time it will take for the remaining food to thaw.

• Make sure that your house insurance policy also covers the loss of food in a power failure.

Clearing a drainer tube Time: ½ an hour or less

If water collects in the bottom of a refrigerator that is supposed to defrost automatically, the problem may be that the drainer tube is blocked.

The ice on the evaporator unit is melted by the defrost heater which is controlled by the thermostat. The water runs into a channel at the back of the cabinet, and drains out through a tube into a tray situated on top of the compressor unit, where it evaporates. The tube can become blocked by particles of food or by the growth of mould.

> YOU WILL NEED Coat-hanger wire, scrap of cloth.

Empty the refrigerator and cover the food with newspaper or a blanket to keep it cool. Then unplug the appliance from the mains and pull it out to expose its back.

Crimp one end of a piece of coat-hanger wire round a scrap of cloth that is small enough to go through the drainer tube. Feed the other end of the wire into the tube and push it through, taking care not to puncture the tube.

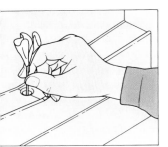

It will come out near the tray above the compressor. Pull the wire through carefully and the cloth should clear the drainer tube.

If necessary, do this a number of times, with clean scraps of cloth, until the drainer tube is clear.

Choose the coolest position

Refrigerators and freezers function by getting rid of heat, and if they are placed in a hot position, they have to work much harder to stay cold.

Don't put a fridge or freezer next to the oven, or in a position where it will be exposed to direct sunlight for most of the day.

Make sure that air can circulate all round it, even if it is tucked under a kitchen worktop.

Riveting

Riveting is a quick and easy means of joining two pieces of metal by piercing them and placing a metal rivet in the hole. The ends of the rivet are flattened to hold it in place.

Softer materials such as canvas, leather or plywood can be riveted, but may need a washer to strengthen the join.

Standard riveting is quite a skilled job, but a small hand tool, known as a blind riveter or pop riveter, is available fairly inexpensively and is quite easy to use.

Using washers with a rivet

When you intend pop riveting lightweight materials such as canvas, leather or plywood, use two metal washers, one on each side, to strengthen the join (see 'Riveting a leather handle on a sports bag', right). But if only one side of the join is accessible, use a single washer, slipping it over the end of the rivet before putting it into the hole.

How pop riveting works

To rivet two flat surfaces together, first drill a hole of a suitable size through both of them, to take the rivet.

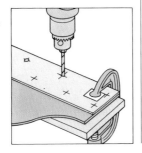

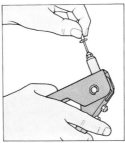

Insert the stem of the rivet (usually the thinner end) into the nozzle of the riveter. Put the other end of the rivet through the holes you have drilled.

Squeeze the handles of the riveter. This makes its jaws grip the central stem inside the rivet. As pressure is applied, the stem of the rivet is drawn backwards into the riveter, deforming the end of the rivet and flattening it.

Finally, the stem will break off and can be withdrawn.

Choosing the rivets

Rivets are usually made from aluminium, copper or stainless steel. They are available in short, medium and long, with diameters of 2.4 mm, 3.2 mm, 4.0 mm and 4.8 mm.

The length of the rivet being used depends on the total thickness or 'grip' of the materials that are being joined. Long rivets have a maximum grip of 1 cm ($\frac{3}{8}$ in), medium rivets have a grip of around 6 mm ($\frac{1}{4}$ in), and short ones have a maximum grip of 3 mm ($\frac{1}{8}$ in).

If the rivet is too long, it is difficult to set and makes an untidy join. If it is too short, the join may not be secure. So it is important to get both length and diameter right.

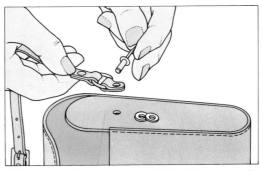

If the join is to bear any sort of load, make sure that the diameter of the rivet you use is no less than the thickness of the thickest material being joined.

Riveting a leather handle on a sports bag
Time: a few minutes

When the leather handle has come away from the main part of a bag, it can be riveted back on again. To prevent it from tearing, use washers with the rivets. Practise on scrap material of similar weight before starting the job.

REMOVING AN OLD RIVET

Chisel or grind off the head of a round-headed rivet. Then remove the shaft by hammering it through with a nail punch. Drill out the head of a countersunk rivet, using a high-speed electric drill. Hammer out the shaft with a nail punch.

YOU WILL NEED Awl, short rivets, steel washers, pop riveter.

Working on a firm surface, position the flat part of the handle on the bag and use an awl to make two or three holes through both handle and bag.

Push the stem of a short rivet into the nozzle of the riveter.

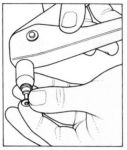 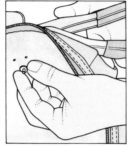

Slip a washer over the end of the rivet then push it through the holes.

Place another washer over the end of the rivet that is protruding into the bag.

Gently squeeze the handles of the riveter. As the rivet is flattened, it will grip both washers. Keep squeezing the handles until the stem of the rivet breaks off.

Release the riveter's handles, open them with a slight jerk, and the unwanted stem should drop out. Repeat as many times as necessary, until the handle is secure.

Rocking horse

Fixing a bedraggled mane   Time: ½ a day or less

If a rocking horse's mane starts to look tattered and thin it is possible to improve its appearance yourself.

YOU WILL NEED Chisel, strip of Rexine or soft leather, PVA wood glue, extra horsehair (available from rocking-horse makers), putty knife, damp cloth.

Using a chisel, clear the channel down the horse's neck of old hair, glue and any other debris.

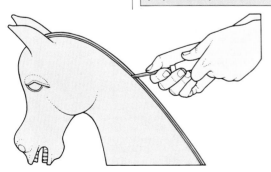

Cut two strips of Rexine or soft leather, 5 mm ($\frac{3}{16}$ in) wide and the length of the groove. Lay one of the strips on a flat surface and cover one side of it with PVA glue (see *Glues*). Arrange the hair evenly across the glued strip.

 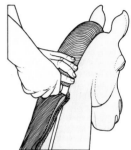

Run a line of glue over the hair above the first strip. Cover it with the other strip of Rexine and press it down firmly until the glue is set.

Squeeze a line of glue into the channel in the horse's neck. Then force the Rexine strips into the channel with a fine putty knife.

Remove any surplus glue with a damp cloth while it is wet, then leave the new mane to dry.

Roller skates

Traditional roller skates have two 'trucks', each holding two wheels. See *Skateboard* for repairs. A more modern design, called a roller blade, is like an ice skate with all the wheels in a line down the centre. See *Ice skates* for repairs.

Traditional skates have rubber stoppers at the front; roller blades have stoppers at the back. When a stopper starts to wear out, unscrew and replace it.

Roof

Working on a roof safely

Do not tackle roof work unless you feel comfortable working at heights – and even then, only when you have the correct equipment. You need an extension ladder higher than gutter level, and a roof ladder that is designed to hook over the roof ridge (see *Ladders & scaffolding*: 'Get the right ladder for the job' and 'Ladder safety').

Erect the extension ladder so that there are at least three rungs above gutter level to give you a handhold, and place a sandbag across the base to stop it from slipping.

Fit a stand-off to the ladder; the rubber feet will grip the wall. (Never lean a ladder against a plastic gutter because it can slip very easily.)

For added safety, insert a large screw eye in the fascia board just below the guttering. Tie one of the upper rungs of the ladder to the screw eye with a strong rope.

Wheel the roof ladder up the roof, then turn it over so that the hook passes over the ridge (see *Ladders & scaffolding*: 'Get the right ladder for the job').

Then climb from the extension ladder onto the roof ladder. On no account move off the roof ladder or overreach while you are working on it.

You can carry the small items you need in a holster and pouch on a leather belt. Stuff a cloth between the roof and a rung of the roof ladder to support larger tools and to prevent them from slipping down the roof.

Replacing a loose or damaged slate Time: 2 hours or less

A damp patch on an upstairs ceiling could be caused by a slipped or broken roof slate which is allowing rain through a gap between the other slates.

New slates can be bought from builders' merchants or specialist roofing suppliers (look in *Yellow Pages* under 'Roofing materials'). Try to match the colour.

> YOU WILL NEED Sheet of lead, zinc, copper or aluminium (from builders' merchant), tinsnips, hammer, 38 mm (1½ in) alloy nails. Possibly: slate ripper, new slate, expanding foam filler.

Take some time to prepare safe access to the roof, with an extension ladder and a roof ladder, as described in 'Working on a roof safely' (left and above).

Remove the damaged or loose slate. If it won't move, slide a slate ripper up under it and locate the nails holding it in place. Hook one side of the ripper around the nail and jerk sharply to cut it. Repeat with the second nail, if necessary, and clean off any debris.

Note where the slate will line up when it is replaced, then use tinsnips to cut a strip of lead, zinc, copper or aluminium, 2.5 cm (1 in) wide and long enough to nail to the batten, plus sufficient to turn up round the bottom of the slate.

Using alloy nails, fix the metal strip to a batten in the space between the two slates on either side.

Line up the new or loose slate with its neighbours, then bend up the metal strip to hold it firmly in place.

GLUING THE SLATE IN PLACE An alternative to nailing is to position the slate, lift it and squirt in a line of expanding foam filler. Press the slate onto the foam, which will act as a weatherproof adhesive. A further alternative is to use an exterior-grade panel adhesive to hold the slate in place.

Sealing a cracked tile or slate Time: 1 hour or less

> YOU WILL NEED Wire brush, safety spectacles, flashing tape, trimming knife, flashing primer. Possibly: floor or tile paint.

Clean the area round the crack with a wire brush, wearing safety spectacles to protect your eyes. Cut a strip of flashing tape large enough to cover the crack, and overlap it by at least 2.5 cm (1 in) on each side.

Brush flashing primer onto the tile or slate so that it covers an area equal to the size of the tape. Then apply the tape and press it down firmly. An old wallpaper seam roller is an ideal tool for this (right). On a coloured tile, the repair can be disguised with matching floor or tile paint.

REPAIRING BLISTERED ROOFING FELT

Clean the area round the blisters with a brush, then make a cross-shaped cut in each blister. Lift the four flaps and clean out any dirt. Fill with bituminous mastic crack filler and press the flaps back in place. Apply a light coating of filler over the repair.

Roof (cont.)

What sort of tile?

To buy replacement tiles, find a local supplier in *Yellow Pages* under 'Roofing materials'. If you need an unusual type, contact a demolition contractor.

PLAIN TILES Two nibs beneath the top edge of the tile hook over a roof batten to hold the tile in position. Every third or fourth row can be nailed in place through nail holes in the tiles.

SINGLE-LAP TILES Each tile interlocks with the tiles next to it on both sides. Some types hang from the battens on nibs, with alternate rows nailed to battens. Others are held with metal clips nailed to battens.

RIDGE TILES Curved or angled tiles used to cover the gaps at the ridge or hips of a tile or slate roof.

Replacing a damaged tile Time: 2 hours or less

> YOU WILL NEED Wood wedges, large trowel, slate ripper, chisel.

PLAIN TILE To remove a damaged plain tile, use small wooden wedges to support the two tiles from the row above, which overlap the damaged one.

Slip a large trowel under the damaged tile and lift it until the nibs on the tile are clear of the batten. Draw out the tile on the trowel holding it steady with your thumb.

If the tile is nailed in place, try wiggling to loosen it. If this fails, use a slate ripper to cut through the nails.

Lay the replacement tile on the trowel and reverse the process to fit it in place. Then remove the wedges.

SINGLE-LAP TILE If a tile has been broken, push up the tiles which overlap it. Then tilt the broken tile sideways to release it from its neighbours. You may need to experiment a little.

If there is resistance, it may be because the tile is held with a clip. In that case, lever it up with an old chisel to release it. If the clip stays in place, you can fit a new tile

into it. If the clip comes away with the tile, don't worry; a tile or two without a clip will be perfectly safe.

If the tile is held by nails, use a slate ripper to cut them. Hook one side of the ripper round the nail and jerk it sharply to cut it. Repeat with any further nails.

Slide the new or loose tile into place and readjust the surrounding tiles.

Refixing loose ridge tiles Time: depends on number

> YOU WILL NEED Extension ladder, roof ladder, safety spectacles, cold chisel, hammer, builder's trowel, dry mortar mix, mixing board, bucket, old paintbrush, PVA building adhesive, water.

Set up an extension ladder and a roof ladder as described in 'Working on a roof safely'. Take some time doing this, to make sure that your access to the roof is safe.

Remove the loose ridge tiles and chip away all loose mortar with a cold chisel and hammer. Protect your eyes with safety spectacles while doing this part of the job.

On a mixing board, make up a dryish mix of bagged mortar, adding 1 part of building adhesive to about 10 parts of clean water (see *Mortar*).

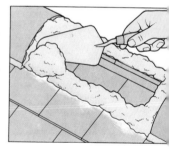

Use an old paintbrush to dust the area to be repaired, then coat it with neat PVA building adhesive. Then apply a bed of mortar to both sides of the ridge.

Damp the ridge tiles in water and press them firmly in place, tapping them lightly with the trowel handle.

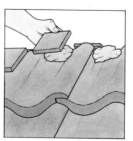

With single-lap tiles, bed strips of tile in the hollows with mortar before adding the ridge tiles.

Finally, use the trowel to repoint the gaps between the ridge tiles by filling them with mortar.

REFLECTING BACK THE SUN'S RAYS

The dark colour of a bitumen coating on a flat roof absorbs the sun's rays, making the room below hot in summer and causing the roof covering to deteriorate. Reduce heat absorption by coating the roof with a reflective roof paint that can be bought at DIY stores.

Coating a flat roof with bitumen compound
Time: ½ a day

Years of life can be added to a felt covering on a flat roof by coating it with roofing compound when it is still sound but is just beginning to show signs of weathering. Warning signs are slight flaking of a dry surface.

> YOU WILL NEED Extension ladder, spade, stiff broom, tough plastic bag, small trowel, bituminous mastic crack filler, bitumen-rubber roofing compound, cheap or old coarse paintbrush about 125 mm (5 in) wide.

Secure the ladder as for any roof work (see 'Working on a roof safely'), with at least three rungs above roof level to provide a hand grip when getting onto the roof.

Use a spade to scrape loose any stone chippings, then sweep them up with a stiff broom and put them in a bag.

Check for minor cracks and gaps. Dig out any dirt with the point of a trowel, and fill the gaps with bituminous mastic crack filler.

Then liberally coat the whole of the roof with a bitumen-rubber roofing compound. Start at the far end and work back towards the ladder as you go. Use a brush that can be thrown away afterwards.

When the coating has dried (the can will give drying time details), replace the stone chippings on the roof. They will help to dissipate the heat during summer.

Re-covering a flat roof with sheeting

Rather than replacing roofing felt that has worn out, it is possible to cover it with an EPDM rubber sheet. The sheet can be ordered to the correct size from a specialist supplier such as DIY Plastics (Tel. 01367 242932). It comes in one piece, with extra to turn over the edges of the roof and fixing instructions are supplied with it.

Take off stone chippings from the roof, but any other irregularities can be absorbed by first covering the roof with a padded underlay that can be bought with the sheet.

Rotten wood (SEE ALSO DRY ROT)

Wood that is continually damp will eventually be attacked by wet rot. The wood becomes soft and the paintwork discolours and blisters. Outdoor woodwork is most commonly affected though damp indoor areas are also at risk. If it is caught early and the source of the damp is removed, the rot will die off before it affects too much of the timber.

Repairing a small area of wet rot Time: ½ a day or less

> YOU WILL NEED Chisel and mallet, hot-air gun, wood hardener, old paintbrush, cellulose thinner, hand or power drill and twist bits, preservative tablets, two-part wood filler, flexible filling knife, sandpaper and block. Possibly: general-purpose saw.

First deal with the cause of the damp (if wet rot is caught early enough and the source of the damp is removed, it will die off before it affects too much of the timber). Then remove any existing paint (see *Paint stripping*).

Using a chisel and mallet or a general-purpose saw, cut out the damaged wood down to firm wood fibre. Dry the area with a hot-air gun. When the wood is dry, brush the rotten area liberally with wood hardener. This penetrates the fibres and eventually dries hard, providing a firm surface for filling. Clean the brush with a cellulose thinner.

Drill holes around the affected areas and insert preservative tablets to protect the wood from further attack.

Mix some two-part wood filler and apply it to the damaged area until it stands just proud of the surface. If you want to stain the filler to match the wood around it, check on the packet that it is suitable. Some fillers will not absorb stain, so they can only be painted. Work quickly, because the filler will start to harden in about 5 minutes, and it will be solid in 20 minutes.

Leave the filler to cure – some types change colour when they are ready for sanding. When it has cured, sand the filler back level with the surrounding area.

Repairing a rotten door frame Time: depends on area

External door frames often rot near the sill. The most satisfactory way to repair them is to replace the timber.

> YOU WILL NEED General-purpose saw, chisel and mallet, replacement wood, hammer, 38 mm (1½ in) oval nails, power or hand drill, twist bit, masonry bit, countersink bit, wood preservative, old paintbrush, waterproof wood adhesive, wood screws, screwdriver, try square, hardwood dowels, hammer.

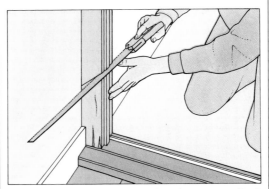

Make a sloping cut into the timber about 7.5 cm (3 in) above the rotted wood. Angle the cut at about 45 degrees. Prise the rotted part away from the wall with a chisel.

PROTECTING UNTREATED TIMBER

Where damp puts timbers at risk, and treated timber has not been used, drill holes in the timber and insert a fungicidal wood preservative plug. Seal it in with waterproof filler. The fungicide is released when the wood gets wet.

Take the old piece with you to buy a piece of timber to fit into the space, and some wood moulding to replace the door stop. Cut the new wood to the right size, using the old piece as a template. If necessary, cut a new door stop and nail it to the replacement timber.

Treat the new wood and the newly cut edges of the recess with wood preservative and allow it to dry.

Drill holes in the wall and insert wall plugs. Then apply wood adhesive to the repair and fix it in place. Screw 9 cm ($3\frac{1}{2}$ in) No.12 screws through the wood and countersink the heads.

Where the old wood meets the new, drill 6 mm ($\frac{1}{4}$ in) holes through the joint at right angles to the cut. Spread glue onto 6 mm ($\frac{1}{4}$ in) dowels and tap them into the holes. Decorate the patch to match the surrounding area, if necessary.

Rucksack

Most rucksack manufacturers run a repair service, but you can easily fit a variety of replacement buckles, toggles and webbing which are available from camping shops.

Replacing a buckle

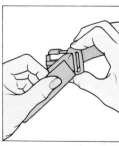

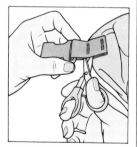

FREE-RUNNING Thread the webbing through a replacement buckle, in the same way as the original buckle.

SEWN-IN-PLACE Unpick the old webbing with a pair of fine, sharp scissors and discard the old buckle.

Loop a new length of webbing through the replacement buckle. Sew the webbing firmly in place. If you use a sewing machine, make sure to use the strongest needle available for the machine. Alternatively, a shoe repair shop may be able to stitch the webbing for you.

FRAYED STRAPS

Seal nylon straps by burning them with a match. If the straps are made of cloth, use antifray spray or double the strap over and sew it in place.

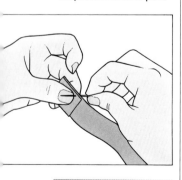

Rugs

How to stop rugs from slipping

Loose rugs and mats can be dangerous if they slip on polished floors. They are also inclined to 'creep' on carpeted surfaces. There are ways to prevent this.

RUBBERISED NETTING Available from most carpet shops. Cut a piece a little shorter and narrower than the size of the rug and place it underneath.

VELCRO STRIPS Available in self-adhesive strips. Fix one strip to the floor and the other to the base of the rug. Apply the strips just inside the edge of the rug.

ANTISKID TAPES Self-adhesive sponge-textured tapes. They are fixed to the back of a rug, and the sponge grips smooth floors and carpets, keeping the rug in place.

LATEX ADHESIVE Coat the back of a non-valuable rug with latex adhesive. Let it dry thoroughly before using.

CARPET HOOKS Known as Cat Claws. These are small plastic squares, each with dozens of tiny metal hooks embedded in it. They are fitted, one to each corner of the rug, to keep it in place and prevent it from creeping across a carpeted floor.

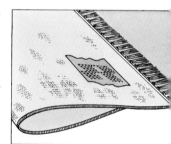

Cleaning a rug Time: depends on method and size

WASHABLE RUG Vacuum or shake the rug to remove loose dirt. Then remove individual stains using the correct method for the stain (see *Stains*). Then wash the rug in a bath, using carpet shampoo diluted with warm water.

Rinse the rug well, straighten it out and lay it to dry over a clothes horse or clothes line on a breezy day. If rinsing is difficult, use the garden hose.

Cotton tumble-twist rugs without a rubberised backing can be cleaned in a washing machine and tumble dried.

WOOLLEN RUGS Woven wool rugs can be cleaned with a sponge loaded with only the foam of frothed-up carpet shampoo. (Follow the shampoo maker's instructions.)

Before starting to clean the rug, try cleaning a section of the underside, to see if the colours run. If they do, take the rug to a specialist cleaner. Look in *Yellow Pages* under 'Carpet & upholstery cleaners'.

ORIENTAL OR HANDMADE RUGS To clean, use only a cylinder vacuum cleaner as the beater in an upright cleaner will damage delicate fibres. Alternatively, shake the rug outdoors and then lay it face down and tap the back gently with the back of a brush. Brush the surface gently.

FRINGES To prevent a rug's delicate fringe being sucked up into a vacuum cleaner and possibly damaged, cover the cleaner head with an old stocking.

Rust (SEE ALSO CAR BODY)

Preventing rust

The best way to prevent rust forming on steel and iron surfaces, such as hand tools, is to stop water and air from coming into contact with them. To do this apply a thin layer of oil or grease to the bare metal. Water-repellent oils are available in aerosol form, but the fine oil evaporates quickly and will have to be renewed regularly.

Painting metal protects it from rust, but the paint must be kept in good condition. If scratches penetrate a protective coating, apply a rust inhibitor immediately.

Treating light rust Time: depends on area

YOU WILL NEED Emery paper, dusting brush, paintbrush.
Possibly: rust inhibitor, cold galvanising paint.

If the metal is painted, as on a window frame, be sure to scrape the paint back until all the rust is exposed, otherwise the rust may continue out of sight until more paint is pushed off. Use emery paper to remove surface rust.

Dust the surface with a dusting brush and treat it with rust-inhibiting fluid, which converts the rust into a harmless black coating.

Coat unpainted metal with a cold galvanising paint, which applies a layer of zinc to prevent further rusting.

Finally, touch up the metalwork with a primer, undercoat and topcoat, or use a rust-inhibiting enamel which needs no primer or undercoat.

Treating heavy rust Time: depends on area

YOU WILL NEED Wire brush, safety spectacles, cotton gloves, emery paper, dusting brush, paintbrush, two-part epoxy repair paste, rust inhibitor. Possibly: power drill, cold galvanising paint.

Metal items that are used and kept outdoors are particularly prone to rusting. However, it is possible to treat fairly heavy patches of rust on items such as a wheelbarrow.

Wearing safety spectacles and cotton gloves, remove the rust scales with a wire brush, either by hand or with a power-drill attachment.

Rub down the surface with emery paper then dust with a dusting brush.

Then apply a two-part epoxy repair paste to fill the pitting caused by rust. Mix only as much as you can use in 5 minutes. Fill to just proud of the surface, then when the paste has hardened, sand it with emery paper until it is flush with the surrounding surface. Treat the surface with rust inhibiting fluid. Then apply paint or enamel.

Filling rust holes

If rust has eaten right through metal, such as an up-and-over garage door, it may be possible to repair it.

YOU WILL NEED Aluminium mesh (from a car accessory shop), scissors or tinsnips, repair paste, emery paper. Possibly: paint.

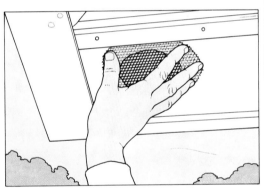

Working inside the door, use dual-purpose scissors or tinsnips to cut a piece of mesh about 2.5 cm (1 in) larger than the hole all round. Apply repair paste round the edge of the mesh and press it onto the back of the holed metal so that the mesh covers the hole. Leave it to set.

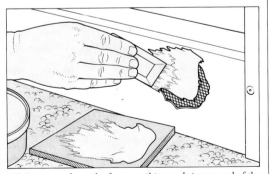

Fill the repair from the front until it stands just proud of the surface. The mesh will support the paste and add strength to the repair. Once the paste has set, sand it back with emery paper. Paint it to match the rest of the door.

Sandpapering (SEE ALSO OVERLEAF)

Sandpapering can be done in two ways – hand sanding and power sanding. Hand sanding is the safest way to achieve a fine finish on furniture, because it is slower and gentler.

If you are sanding a flat surface by hand, wrap the sandpaper round a sanding block made of cork or wood. Work in the same direction as the grain of the wood.

Power sanding requires careful control as the surface is removed quickly. Always follow the manufacturer's instructions when using a power sander.

If a surface needs a considerable amount of smoothing down, start with a coarse grade of abrasive, and gradually work down to a fine one.

When sanding any type of timber surface, whether flat or shaped, always work with the grain because scratches across the grain are very hard to lose or disguise, especially when a clear finish such as varnish is to be applied.

THE RIGHT WAY TO STRIP PAINT Abrasive paper is not intended for stripping paint. It will just clog up. Start with a hot-air gun or a chemical paint stripper, and then finish with an abrasive paper to give a smooth surface suitable for redecorating (see *Paint stripping*).

STORING PAPER Even the slightest damp will cause the glue on abrasive paper to fail, and the abrasive coating will fall off, so always store unused paper in a dry place.

THROW OUT USED PAPER Do not keep old abrasive paper to use for a smoother finish. Worn abrasive paper has microscopic projections which can cause serious scratches.

Sandy soil

Testing for sandy soil Time: a few minutes

Take about half a handful of soil from your garden and dampen it. Then roll it in your hand to make a ball. If the soil makes a rasping sound when you squeeze it close to your ear and feels slightly gritty, but leaves your fingers clean afterwards, you have sandy soil.

Improving sandy soil Time: depends on area

The advantages of sandy soil are that it drains very well, so you never have to worry about plants becoming waterlogged. Also, it is easy to work, and it warms up quickly in spring, which means you can start to work on it earlier than you can with clay soil.

The disadvantages of sandy soil are that nutrients are washed out rapidly, especially in high-rainfall areas, which can cause the soil to become progressively more acid (low pH). Sandy soils suffer more during a drought because they do not retain moisture.

When working on improving the structure of sandy soil, allow about half an hour for every 3 m² (3 sq yd).

> YOU WILL NEED Garden spade, wheelbarrow, organic soil conditioner (see below), garden fork. Possibly: seaweed meal, garden lime, fertiliser.

Use a bulky, organic soil conditioner such as well-rotted horse manure, or mushroom or garden compost. It should be added at least once a year, preferably in winter.

MANURE Vary the source of the manure you use (horse, cow or poultry) every time you apply it, so that you supply your soil with slightly different nutrients.

Apply a barrow-load to every 3 m² (3 sq yd), spreading it about 7.5 cm (3 in) thick and forking it in. After several applications, you should be able to apply it as a mulch and leave the worms to take it down into the soil.

GARDEN COMPOST Put on as much as you can make at any time. For more about making compost, see *Compost*.

MUSHROOM COMPOST If the soil has become acid (see *Soil testing*), mushroom compost will supply extra lime.

GARDEN LIME If the soil has become acid (see *Soil testing*) add some garden lime as well – particularly if you are not using mushroom compost.

SEAWEED MEAL Add 50-70g (1¾-2½ oz) of seaweed meal per square metre (or square yard) to add to the effect of the manure or compost used. It also helps to bind the soil.

FERTILISER In the early stages of your soil improvement programme, before the organic materials have had time to take effect, your soil may need fertiliser.

Signs of nitrogen and potassium deficiency are poor growth and yellowing leaves. Add a general fertiliser, such as blood, fish and bone, and a slow-release fertiliser such as hoof and horn (high in nitrogen), and rock potash (high in potassium).

It is important to treat sandy soil with organic soil conditioners such as manure and compost, because synthetic fertilisers will wash out very quickly.

WINTER CARE Keep flowerbeds planted during winter, rather than clearing them completely, because dead or dying plants help to bind the soil and prevent excessive loss of nutrients through drainage.

On vegetable beds, sow bitter lupins, alfalfa or crimson clover as a winter cover, and then dig the plants into the soil or compost them at the start of spring.

Choosing the right plants for sandy soil
Some plants enjoy the free draining and the loose structure of sandy soil, but they also need the 'body' and nutrients of well-rotted manure or compost.

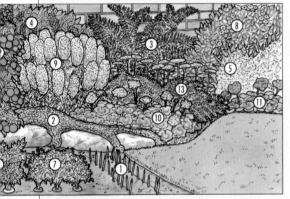

PLANTS THAT THRIVE IN SANDY SOIL

1	Asparagus	8	*Elaeagnus pungens*
2	*Aubrieta deltoidea*	9	*Euphorbia characias*
3	*Cotoneaster horizontalis*	10	Regal pelargoniums
4	Blackberries (*Rubus*)	11	Zonal pelargoniums
5	Broom (*Cytisus*)		(geraniums)
6	Parsnips	12	Tomatoes
7	Carrots	13	Yarrow (*Achillea*)

PLANTS THAT DO POORLY IN SANDY SOIL

- Bleeding heart (*Dicentra*)
- Clematis
- Columbines (*Aquilegia*)
- Leeks
- Lupins
- Potatoes
- Snowdrops
- Stone fruits
- Sweet peas

Check your soil's pH every year
The pH of your soil (the acidity or alkalinity) can change as a result of heavy rain, as well as your own soil improvement programme. So use a simple test kit (see *Soil testing*) to check your soil every year.

Loss of lime can be much more severe in sandy soil than in any other type. Over-liming can harm plants, so add a little each year as necessary.

Saucepan

Seasoning a new, nonstick pan

Read the instructions supplied with a new, nonstick pan. Many require some form of 'seasoning' before use, which may involve washing with a mild detergent solution, or wiping with cooking oil.

Removing burnt food Time: depends on amount

Keep pan-care instructions handy in a kitchen drawer, and refer to them when food is burnt in a saucepan.

Usually, burnt food can be removed by filling the saucepan with a warm solution – about 40°C (104°F) – of biological detergent and water. Leave the pan to soak for several hours or, preferably, overnight.

Then bring the water to the boil, carefully scraping away the food deposits with a wooden spoon or plastic spatula. Never use a metal utensil, as it could scratch or damage the surface of the saucepan and cause it to attract more food the next time you use it.

Discard the water, but if it contains a lot of burnt food, don't allow it to clog your drains. If you do not have a waste disposal unit in your sink, strain the solids into a sieve and discard them in the waste bin. Alternatively, tip it all into the lavatory and flush it away.

Don't use abrasives, such as soap-filled pads, unless the care instructions for the saucepan recommend them.

Cleaning saucepans in a dishwasher

Many saucepans can be cleaned in a dishwasher, but first soak off any large quantities of food stuck to the bottom of the pan, to prevent it clogging the dishwasher's filter.

Wooden handles and some plastic handles may be damaged by the very hot water used in a dishwasher, so check the saucepan's care instructions first.

Continued on page 294

SANDING

The word sandpaper is widely used for some types of abrasive paper, particularly glasspaper — which is coated with glass, not sand. Other minerals are also used to make abrasive papers for different purposes. They are available in many grades of coarseness. Sanding (or smoothing) can also be done with steel wool and abrasive metal plates. Various abrasive attachments can be used with power tools.

STEEL WOOL Special decorating grades can be used to fine-smooth wood. It is graded in 'O's — the more 'O's, the finer the grade. Synthetic steel wool can be used on walls, and can be rinsed and reused many times.

GARNET PAPER
A better quality abrasive than glasspaper. The open-coat grain resists clogging. Coarse and medium grades are used to prepare wood for painting; fine grades are ideal for fine finishing.

SILICON-CARBIDE PAPER
Also called wet-and-dry, it is backed with waterproof paper so that it can be used wet on paintwork or dry for an extra-fine finish on hardwood.

TUNGSTEN CARBIDE Pieces of tungsten carbide are fused into a metal plate or disc. Its main advantage is that it can be cleaned by scrubbing with a wire brush. It comes as hand-sanding blocks or as sheets or discs for power sanding.

SANDING BLOCK To make sanding easier on the hand, wrap abrasive paper round a block of cork or wood.

GLASSPAPER
The cheapest of the abrasives, glasspaper is coated with glass particles and is indispensable for sanding walls and wood, especially softwood. However, it is not suitable for fine finishing.

ETCHED METAL
A range of abrasives with fine projections etched onto a metal sheet which is attached to a handle. The tools are available in a number of forms, including files and hand sanders.

POWER FILE
A small power sander which has a thin belt of abrasive, designed to reach into awkward areas. It can be used on a variety of materials including wood, metal and ceramic tile.

ALUMINIUM OXIDE
Available with a paper or fabric backing, this tough abrasive is associated with power sanding of timber, metals and plastics. Also used for hand-sanding wood and painted surfaces.

WIRE BRUSHES
Power drill attachments which are used to clean up metal, usually to remove rust and provide a key for painting.

DRUM SANDER An abrasive belt fits round a foam drum which is fixed to a power drill. It is ideal for sanding with the grain of the wood, and it can also be used for shaping.

DISC SANDER
A power-drill attachment used with abrasive metal and paper discs. Mainly for rough sanding, as it makes score marks across wood grain. It can also be used for shaping.

FLAP WHEEL
Flaps of abrasive paper are mounted on a central core and fitted into a power drill. Ideal for removing paint from awkward areas and cleaning off rust.

BELT SANDER A powerful hand-held machine which can remove wood very quickly when used with coarse belts. Little pressure is needed. Choose a model with a dust-collecting bag.

ORBITAL SANDER
A hand-held tool with a sanding plate which moves in tiny circles, to give a fine finish to flat surfaces. Also known as a finishing sander.

EMERY PAPER AND CLOTH
Used mainly for smoothing metal. It is available with paper or fabric backing — the paper is best for flat areas; the cloth can be torn into strips and used on curved surfaces by pulling from each side in turn.

The right way to clean your saucepans

ALUMINIUM Always wash an aluminium pan immediately after use. Never leave food in the pan, as it may cause pitting. Aluminium pits easily and tends to be discoloured by the minerals in water.

Remove any discoloration by boiling up an acid solution such as apple peelings, lemon juice or rhubarb in water. Then rinse the pan and dry it.

Tomato stains can be removed by filling the pan with a solution of laundry borax — 20 ml (1 tablespoon) borax to 570 ml (1 pint) water.

Do not put aluminium utensils and saucepans into a dishwasher as the detergent solution and prolonged washing action can cause permanent discoloration.

NONSTICK Some nonstick surfaces are much tougher than others, so read the maker's instructions regarding the use of scouring pads and metal utensils.

If grease builds up on the surface, use a sponge cleaning pad with neat washing-up liquid on it.

Stains can be removed by pouring a solution of 2 tablespoons of bicarbonate of soda, half a teacup of liquid bleach and a full teacup of cold water into the pan then bring the solution to the boil in the pan.

Then rinse the pan well and dry it.

ENAMEL Stains on pans coated with vitreous enamel, which has a glassy surface, should be removed with a nonabrasive cleaner, such as Jif cream cleaner, recommended by the Vitreous Enamel Development Council. Look for their symbol on the pack (see *Enamel*).

Clean nonvitreous enamel-coated pans with a mild cream cleaner. Soak away stains with a weak solution of household bleach — use 5 ml (1 teaspoon) bleach to 570 ml (1 pint) water.

STAINLESS STEEL Do not soak stainless steel pans for any longer than is necessary in order to remove any burnt-on food, because stainless steel pits easily.

Wash normally with washing-up liquid and use a cream cleaner for stainless steel on the outside.

Alternatively, they may be washed in a dishwasher if the handles are dishwasherproof.

COPPER Copper pans must be lined with tin or nickel, as copper reacts with certain chemicals in food and produces an adverse reaction. Have the inside relined when it begins to show signs of wear. Take it back to where you bought it, or contact the manufacturer.

Clean the outside of a copper pan with a paste made from salt and vinegar, or a metal polish wadding (see *Copper*). Rinse the pan well and dry.

Repairing the loose handle of a saucepan

Act promptly if you detect looseness in the handle of a saucepan. It is extremely dangerous to continue to use the pan, as it could result in the boiling contents being spilled or splashed on someone.

In many cases the handle will be held in place with a screw which can be tightened with a screwdriver.

Some saucepan handles are held in place by rivets, and if these come loose, it may be possible to remove the old rivet and put in a new one (see *Riveting*: 'Removing an old rivet' and 'How pop riveting works').

If you are unable to tighten the screws or rivets because they are inaccessible, and if the saucepan is otherwise in good condition, send it back to the manufacturer for repair. If it is still under guarantee, they might replace it.

Saws, electric (SEE ALSO OVERLEAF)

Cutting with a circular saw

Use a multipurpose blade for cutting normal softwood or man-made boards. Use a blade with tungsten-carbide tips on abrasive materials such as chipboard; it stays sharp for longer, but is easily damaged by misuse. Other blades are available for cutting metal, masonry and ceramics.

Set the soleplate so that the blade will cut about 3 mm ($\frac{1}{8}$ in) deeper than the thickness of the wood.

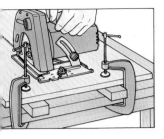

Because circular saws cut upwards, clamp the wood to a workbench with its decorative face down. Allow a space beneath it for blade clearance. Rest it on battens each side of the cutting line and, if the board is wide, under each edge.

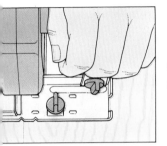

Line up the blade on the waste side of the cutting line, using the sighting guide.

GUIDING THE BLADE Provided that the edge of the wood has been factory-cut – and so is straight – use the saw's fence guide to help you to keep a straight cutting line.

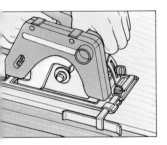

Set it to fit the distance between the edge of the wood and the cutting line.

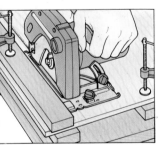

For cuts too far in for the fence, clamp or nail a straight batten to the wood to provide a guide for the soleplate. Position it so that the blade cuts just on the waste side of the cutting line. Check the position at both ends.

Hold the blade away from the wood and then press the trigger. When it is turning at full speed, start cutting.

Cutting with an electric jigsaw

Different types of blade are needed for cutting different materials. Look at the descriptions on the packaging before you buy. A jigsaw is not as accurate as a circular saw for cutting straight lines, but it will cut curves. Mark the cutting line clearly and guide the saw by hand. When cutting straight lines, clamp a batten to the wood as a guide for the saw's soleplate, or use the saw's fence guide.

Like a circular saw, a jigsaw blade cuts on the upstroke, so always make sure that the side of the board which will be on show is underneath.

When cutting thin material, such as plywood, you can prevent it whipping by clamping it between sheets of old hardboard or plywood and cutting through the sandwich.

Cutting a circular hole in a board

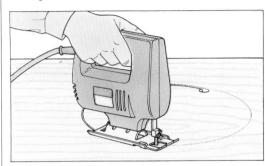

Draw the shape to be cut out on the board, drill a hole large enough for a jigsaw blade in the part that will be removed, then cut along the inside of the line with the jigsaw.

Cutting an angle with a jigsaw

It can be difficult to cut a board – particularly one which has a plastic coating – on an angle, using a jigsaw.

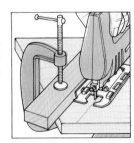

Clamp a straight batten to the board at the required angle. It will act as a guide for the jigsaw's soleplate.

Safety with electric saws

- Keep children right away while using the saw.
- Plug the saw into an RCD (residual current device) adapter. It will cut off the power if you slice the cable.
- Wear safety spectacles. Flying sawdust can cause severe injury to your eyes.
- Use a vice or clamp to anchor the item to be cut so that both your hands are free to use the saw.
- Keep the cable well away from the blade.
- Do not put the saw down until it has stopped.
- Pull out the plug whenever the saw is not in use – even for short periods.
- Make sure that the blade will not cut into anything under the material that you intend to cut.
- Make sure that you have no loose clothing, such as a tie, which can catch in the saw blade.
- Pull out the plug when replacing the blade.

SAFETY FIRST WITH ELECTRICITY

Before starting any work on an electrical fitting or appliance, make sure to cut off the electricity supply – either by switching off at the main fuse box, or by unplugging the appliance.

CHAIN SAW: A DANGEROUS TOOL

For cutting through trees or trimming branches. A chain saw is highly dangerous and should never be used by anyone without first receiving instruction. Safety gear in the form of goggles, face mask, ear defenders, gloves, reinforced overalls and helmet are recommended, and can be obtained from a tool-hire shop. An Alligator saw is a safer alternative when fitted with log-cutting blades.

S A W S

Manual saws are made in many shapes, each designed for a specific use. Around the home, a panel saw, a general-purpose saw, a mini hacksaw and a tenon saw will cope with most jobs. You can add more specialised saws as you need them. The blade of a saw is defined by the number of teeth to each inch. For example, '8 point' means 8 teeth per inch. The higher the number, the finer the cut you can achieve. Electric saws are faster and easier to use but care must be taken as their high-speed action can inflict injury or damage the object being cut if they are not kept under control.

GENERAL-PURPOSE SAW The blade cuts both wood and metal, so it is ideal for secondhand timber that may contain nails. The blade may have a nonstick coating and can be set at different angles.

PANEL SAW For general DIY use, buy a saw with a 55 cm (22 in) blade and universal teeth for cutting both along and across the grain of the wood. If it also has hardpoint teeth, it will never need sharpening.

TENON SAW (ALSO CALLED BACK SAW) A strip of steel or brass along the top edge improves rigidity. The saw has up to 20 teeth per inch and is designed to cut joints accurately. It is not suitable for cutting sheet material, because the strengthening strip prevents it from going through.

LOG SAW (ALSO CALLED BOW SAW) The tubular frame holds a blade that cuts logs or branches. A lever on the handle releases the blade.

COPING SAW The U-shaped frame holds a disposable blade. Use it to make curved cuts in wood, metal or plastic.

TILE SAW Similar to a coping saw, but with round-section blades coated with tungsten carbide chips. It is designed for cutting shapes in tiles. As the blade is circular the cuts can be made in any direction.

CIRCULAR SAW For straight cutting only. The saw can be fitted with a wide variety of blades, so read the instructions on the package before buying one. The cut is made from the underside, so the decorative surface of the wood should be placed downwards.

ALLIGATOR SAW Two blades move in opposite directions to give a smooth cut. Blades are available for rough and fine timber work, masonry-block cutting and log cutting.

HOLESAW An attachment to an electric drill for cutting an accurate circle. Different blades are made for wood, metal and even ceramics. A central drill bit makes a start hole, then ensures that the saw is kept steady.

MINI HACKSAW Used to cut metal and for general DIY work. Disposable blades fit onto the frame.

PADSAW
The thin tapered blade is for cutting out enclosed areas, such as holes in a door to take new door furniture. A hole has to be drilled first to allow the saw to be inserted. The handle is slotted to take a variety of blades. Care is needed not to bend the blade. Short, steady strokes are best.

ELECTRIC JIGSAW Probably the most versatile electric saw, as it can be used for both straight and curved cuts. The blade cuts on the upstroke, so boards with a veneered or laminated surface should always be cut with the decorative face downwards. Blades are available to cut wood or metal.

Saws, hand (SEE ALSO PREVIOUS PAGE)

Cutting a piece of wood by hand

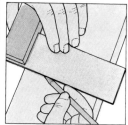

Place a try square firmly against one edge of the wood and use a pencil to draw a line across it where you intend to cut.

Then use the try square to continue the pencil line across both edges of the wood.

To hold the wood firmly as you cut it, clamp it to a workbench or hold it in a vice. Another method of holding it is to use a bench hook (see margin, left).

To start the cut, make a small V nick with a trimming knife on the waste side of the pencil line. Place the saw in the nick and draw the blade smoothly towards you a couple of times to establish the cut.

Hold the saw with your index finger along the side of the handle, and apply light pressure on the forward stroke only. As you saw, follow the pencil lines on the face of the wood and the edges. Make the last few strokes gently to avoid splitting the wood and leaving a ragged edge.

Avoiding a ragged edge on veneered chipboard

A plastic coating or wood veneer on chipboard will chip on the underside when sawn by hand, leaving a ragged edge. So mark the cutting line on the side of the wood that will show. The rough edge will then be on the unseen side. (The opposite applies when using an electric saw.)

To get the neatest result, score the cutting line all round the board, using a trimming knife held against a straightedge (right).

Use a saw with the greatest number of teeth and hold it as flat as possible to the board you are cutting.

HOW TO CUT THIN METAL

If you want to cut a thin piece of metal, sandwich it between two pieces of scrap plywood and cut right through the sandwich with a hacksaw.

Bench hook

Using a bench hook, you can saw wood on a kitchen table. Hook one of the end blocks on the edge of the table, and hold the wood firmly against the other while it is sawed.

Keeping a saw sharp

Panel or tenon saws with hardpoint teeth do not require sharpening. However, standard panel and tenon saws will become blunt with use. When you find that the saw is hard to push and that the teeth tend to tear rather than cut, a tool shop will be able to have the saw sharpened for you.

Coping saws, fretsaws and hacksaws use disposable blades which can be bought at DIY shops.

PROTECT A BOW-SAW BLADE
If the saw does not have a plastic tooth guard to stop the teeth getting damaged or injuring anyone, you can make one. Cut a slit along a cardboard tube (from inside a roll of wrapping paper) and fit it over the blade.

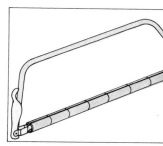

Scales

Using coins instead of weights

Lost weights can sometimes be replaced with coins. A 2p coin weighs $\frac{1}{2}$ oz and a 1p weighs $\frac{1}{8}$ oz. A 20p coin weighs 5 g and a £1 coin just under 10 g.

How to make a small weight Time: $\frac{1}{2}$ an hour or less

> YOU WILL NEED Thin wire, scales, weight, needle-nosed pliers.

To make a weight half the size of an existing one, put a piece of wire on one side of a set of scales and the weight, say 1 oz, on the other. Cut off small bits of the wire with a pair of pliers until the scales balance.

Then fold the piece of wire exactly in two and cut it at the bend. Wrap one piece of wire round a pair of needle-nosed pliers to make a neat coil weighing $\frac{1}{2}$ oz. Using this technique, you can make any small weight.

Scissors

Sharpening blunt scissors Time: $\frac{1}{2}$ an hour or less

If you have a multipurpose sharpener that is used with a power drill (see *Drills & drill bits*), it can be used to sharpen scissors. If not, sharpen them by hand.

First, use a fine file to remove any nicks from the blades. Then put some drops of oil on a slipstone.

Hold the scissors firmly (right) and steady the back of the blade against a solid surface. Run the slipstone along the scissors' cutting edge, keeping the slipstone at the same angle as the edge of the blade. Work in smooth strokes to get an even finish along the blade.

Finally, run the stone over the inner face of the blade to remove the tiny burr that will have formed.

Repeat with the other blade, then test the scissors on the type of material they would normally cut.

Fixing wobbly blades Time: 1 hour or less

Scissors (particularly small ones) may work loose at the pivot point. To tighten them, place the scissors over a block of metal so that the underside of the pivot is in firm contact with the metal. For small scissors, place a nail punch on the rivet section of the pivot and tap gently.

For larger scissors, use the ball pein of a hammer and tap the rivet head to tighten the pivot point. Test the scissors frequently to avoid over-tightening them.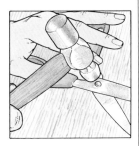

Screwdrivers (SEE ALSO OVERLEAF)

Squaring off a screwdriver blade Time: ½ an hour

Single-slot screwdriver blades can become rounded and worn with use, and will need to be squared up again.

Apply a little oil to an oilstone and rub the sides of the screwdriver tip on it to get them straight. Then run a flat file across the tip of the screwdriver to give it a flat surface. The tip must not be sharpened to a V as this would make it slide out of the screw slot.

Screws

Sizes of screw

The thickness of a screw is expressed as a gauge number: the higher the number the thicker the screw. For normal DIY work No.6, No.8 and No.10 gauges are the most useful.

Within these gauges, lengths that are commonly available range from 1.3 cm to 7.5 cm ($\frac{1}{2}$ in-3 in).

Types of slot

A single-slot screw is the most common, but the easiest screw to use has a cross-slot which gives a positive lock between screw and screwdriver (see overleaf).

Newly bought cross-slot screws will probably be the Supadriv pattern which gives a more positive fit with the screwdriver than the earlier Phillips cross-slot.

Shapes of screw head

COUNTERSUNK HEAD Designed to be recessed in the wood or metal so that the top of the head is flush with the surface.

RAISED HEAD Partly recessed but with a domed top. It can be set in a screw cup to spread the pressure and give a better appearance.

ROUND HEAD The underside of the domed top lies flat on the surface. It may be used with a flat washer to spread the pressure.

MIRROR SCREW Used to fix a mirror to a wall. The removable dome covers the slot and provides a decorative top.

CLUTCH HEAD The slot has two sloping surfaces. After the screw is driven in, it cannot be removed. Used for fixing a hasp and staple on a shed, when screws are exposed.

SCREWS FOR USE WITH METAL

Self-tapping screws are designed for making fixings in metal. Use an HSS twist bit to drill a hole in the metal, the size of the screw's core, not counting the thread. As the screw is driven home, it cuts its own thread into the metal.

SCREWDRIVERS

Several screwdrivers are required for DIY work around the house. They need to cope with screws of various sizes and different head patterns. If there is a lot of work to be done, use a battery-powered, rechargeable cordless screwdriver. Because its movement is reversible, it can also be used to remove screws.

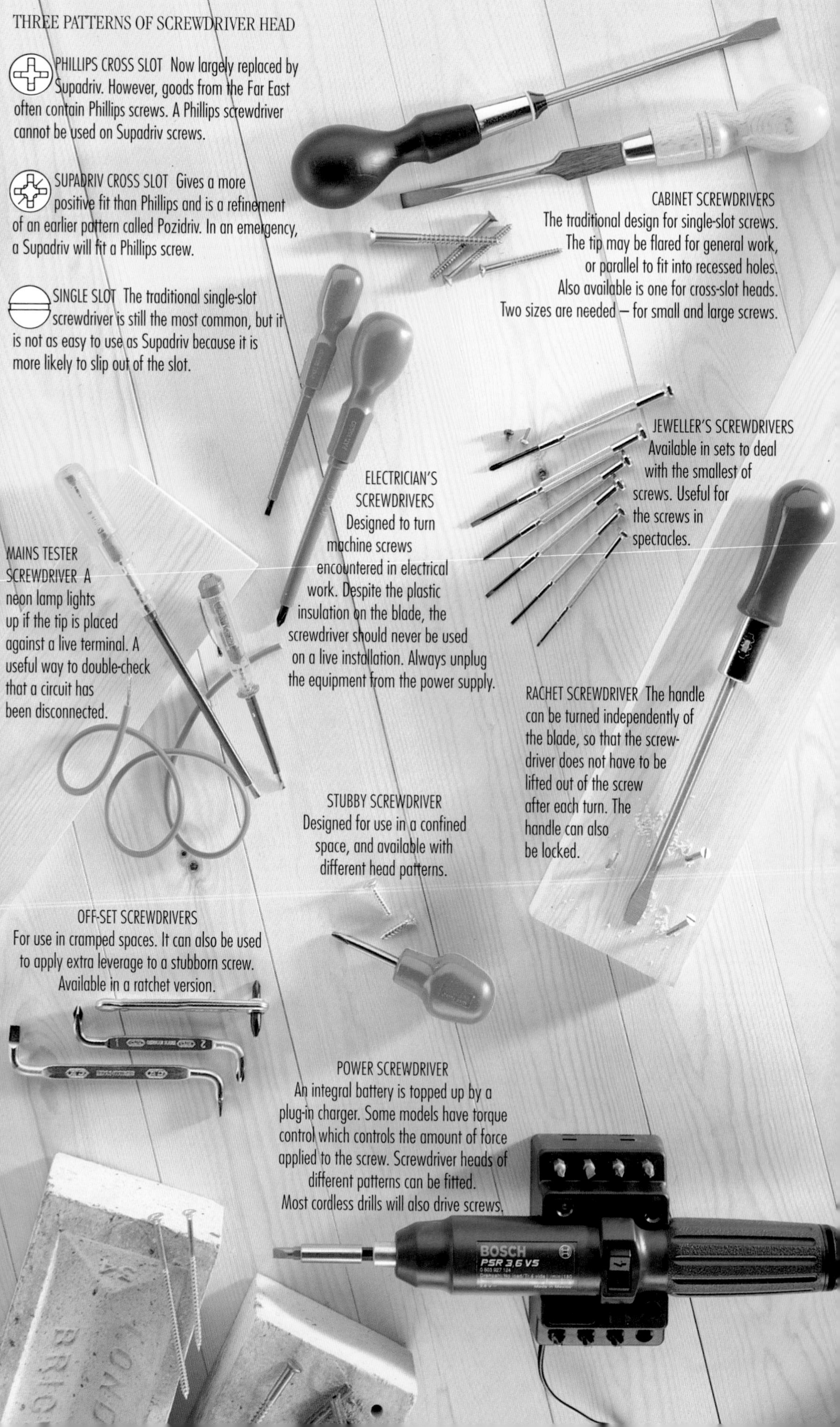

THREE PATTERNS OF SCREWDRIVER HEAD

PHILLIPS CROSS SLOT Now largely replaced by Supadriv. However, goods from the Far East often contain Phillips screws. A Phillips screwdriver cannot be used on Supadriv screws.

SUPADRIV CROSS SLOT Gives a more positive fit than Phillips and is a refinement of an earlier pattern called Pozidriv. In an emergency, a Supadriv will fit a Phillips screw.

SINGLE SLOT The traditional single-slot screwdriver is still the most common, but it is not as easy to use as Supadriv because it is more likely to slip out of the slot.

CABINET SCREWDRIVERS
The traditional design for single-slot screws. The tip may be flared for general work, or parallel to fit into recessed holes. Also available is one for cross-slot heads. Two sizes are needed — for small and large screws.

JEWELLER'S SCREWDRIVERS
Available in sets to deal with the smallest of screws. Useful for the screws in spectacles.

ELECTRICIAN'S SCREWDRIVERS
Designed to turn machine screws encountered in electrical work. Despite the plastic insulation on the blade, the screwdriver should never be used on a live installation. Always unplug the equipment from the power supply.

MAINS TESTER SCREWDRIVER
A neon lamp lights up if the tip is placed against a live terminal. A useful way to double-check that a circuit has been disconnected.

RACHET SCREWDRIVER
The handle can be turned independently of the blade, so that the screwdriver does not have to be lifted out of the screw after each turn. The handle can also be locked.

STUBBY SCREWDRIVER
Designed for use in a confined space, and available with different head patterns.

OFF-SET SCREWDRIVERS
For use in cramped spaces. It can also be used to apply extra leverage to a stubborn screw. Available in a ratchet version.

POWER SCREWDRIVER
An integral battery is topped up by a plug-in charger. Some models have torque control which controls the amount of force applied to the screw. Screwdriver heads of different patterns can be fitted. Most cordless drills will also drive screws.

BOSCH
PSR 3.6 VS
0 603 927 104

The right size holes for common screws

The clearance hole fits the shank of a screw. The pilot hole is narrower so that the screw grips the wood.

Softwood

SCREW GAUGE	CLEARANCE HOLE	PILOT HOLE
No.6	4 mm	1.5 mm
No.8	4.5 mm	2 mm
No.10	5 mm	2 mm

Hardwood

SCREW GAUGE	CLEARANCE HOLE	PILOT HOLE
No.6	4 mm	2 mm
No.8	4.5 mm	2.5 mm
No.10	5 mm	2.5 mm

How to drive a screw

A screw should go into the wood easily. If it is too tight it may split the wood, particularly hardwood, such as oak which is more brittle than softwood, such as pine.

If you are screwing two pieces of wood together you will need to drill two holes – a 'clearance' hole in one piece and a 'pilot' hole in the other.

Before drilling, clamp wood to the workbench with a piece of scrap wood beneath it to protect the surface.

> **YOU WILL NEED** Drill, drill bits, bradawl, insulating tape, screwdriver, screw. Possibly: countersink bit, Vaseline.

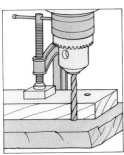

In the piece of wood to be fixed, drill a clearance hole equal in size to the screw shank (see chart above).

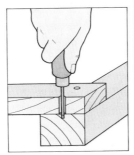

Hold the drilled piece above the second piece and mark with a bradawl where the second piece is to be drilled.

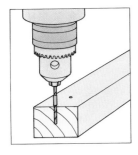

In the second piece, drill a pilot hole narrower than the screw shank (see chart above). Mark the drill bit with insulating tape (left) so that you drill to the required depth of the screw.

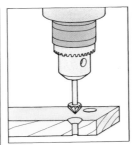

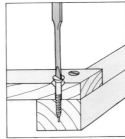

If a countersunk screw is being used, first drill the top piece with a countersink bit to accommodate the head.

Using a screwdriver that fits snugly into the screw head, drive in the screw to join both pieces of wood.

To ensure a smooth drive, apply a little Vaseline to the screw's thread. It will also make removal easier. Do not use soap; it attracts moisture and can lead to rusting.

Removing a jammed screw

REMOVING PAINT If the screw you want to take out is painted over, carefully cut through the paint around the screw head with the point of a trimming knife. This will help to release the screw and also prevent damage to the paint. Then use the tip of the screwdriver to clear the slot completely before trying to undo the screw.

USING A SOLDERING IRON If a screw refuses to move, apply the tip of a hot soldering iron to the head. The expansion of the heated metal will often release the screw.

TAP AND TURN If the screw is large, put a screwdriver in the slot and repeatedly tap the handle with a hammer while you turn it with the other hand.

RELEASING RUST If the screw has rusted in place, apply a little penetrating oil and allow half an hour for the oil to break the hold of the rust. Then try again to remove the screw. If it still won't turn, allow more time.

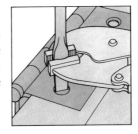

APPLYING LEVERAGE Clamp a self-grip wrench to the shaft of a screwdriver, then use the wrench to apply the necessary leverage.

For a large screw, use a carpenter's brace with an appropriate screwdriver bit. If the screwdriver has a square shank, turn it with a spanner.

USING AN IMPACT SCREWDRIVER You may be able to hire an impact screwdriver which exerts a powerful turning action that should be able to loosen most jammed screws.

USING A NAIL AS A DRILL

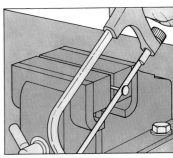

If you don't have a fine drill bit for making a screw hole, you can use a nail or a panel pin. Find one the right size and cut off the head with a mini-hacksaw, or file it off. Fit it in the chuck of a power drill and drill gently so that the tip does not overheat.

SCREWING INTO END GRAIN

The end grain of wood offers a poor grip for screws.

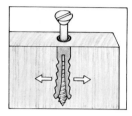

To improve the grip, drill a hole to take a small wall plug, insert the plug and screw into it.

WORKING WITH CHIPBOARD

When you are fixing something to chipboard, use special chipboard screws which are designed to grip well without causing the board to disintegrate. To screw into the edge of chipboard, drill a hole and insert a wall plug (see above). Locate the plug so that the two halves open along the length of the board – not across it.

The impact screwdriver is fitted with the appropriate screwdriver bit. Then it is struck smartly with a hammer and the impact is transformed into a powerful turning action, which will release the screw.

DRILLING OFF THE HEAD If all else fails, or if the screw slot is badly damaged, select an HSS twist bit equal in diameter to the apparent screw shank size.

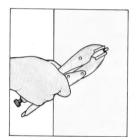

Use the bit in a power drill to drill off the screw head. Remove the fitting that the screw was holding.

Then use a self-grip wrench to grip the exposed screw shank firmly and turn the screw out of the hole.

This technique will not work with case-hardened screws, which are almost impossible to drill out.

Awls and bradawls

Awls and bradawls have round or square-section blades which can end in either a flattened or pointed tip. They are used for making small pilot holes in softwood and also for making tiny holes in needlework.

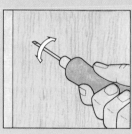

A flattened-tip awl is placed across the grain of the wood, pressure is applied, and with swift twisting movements a small starting-hole is created.

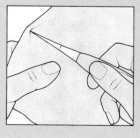

A small pointed-tip awl, also called a stiletto, is used in dressmaking for making eyelets or keyhole buttonholes.

Tightening loose screws in wood

Screws fixed in wood can become loose because the wood shrinks in a dry atmosphere or because of the pressure exerted on a doorknob or a hinge.

FILLING THE HOLE First try using a thicker screw. If a metal fitting is being attached, such as a door handle, and the hole in the fitting is too small, try a longer screw.

If this is not possible, as in the case of a brass drawer knob with its own screw shank, cut a sliver of softwood (or use a matchstick if the hole is small enough). Apply wood glue and tap the wood into the screw hole.

When the glue has dried, break off any surplus wood. Then make a new pilot hole with a bradawl and replace the screw.

GLUING SPLIT WOOD If the wood has split, remove the screw, open the split and insert wood glue. Then bind up the repair with masking tape – or use a G-cramp – until the glue has set. Drill a slightly larger pilot hole for the screw to avoid further splitting, and replace the screw.

MOVING A HINGE If a whole hinge is affected by loose screws, it may be best to remove the hinge and reposition it, so that new holes can be made in fresh wood.

Dealing with loose screws in solid walls

MAKE A NEW HOLE If a hole in a wall crumbles and becomes too big for a wall plug, try to make a new hole a short distance away and fill the first one with interior wall filler.

LARGER PLUG AND SCREW If you can't make a new hole, try using a larger wall plug with a thicker screw. Or push a small wall plug inside a larger one, and insert the screw down the middle.

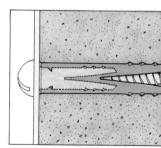

USING PLUGGING COMPOUND If neither of the above options is possible, clear the hole of debris and fill it with plugging compound. Follow the instructions on the packet carefully, as compounds vary. When the compound has set, make a pilot hole with a bradawl and drive in the screw. Take care not to overtighten it.

Screwing something to a cavity wall

PLASTERBOARD WALLS Plasterboard, which is used on most cavity walls, is not tough enough to hold screws firmly. If a screw has pulled out, fit a cavity fixing, but don't try to hang a heavy weight, such as a cupboard, from plasterboard alone (see *Wall fixings*).

LATH-AND-PLASTER WALLS Like plasterboard, lath-and-plaster is too weak to support a heavy weight, but it is possible to put up a light shelf unit using spring toggles. Use toggles with a long screw, because lath-and-plaster is much thicker than plasterboard.

Sealants (SEE ALSO FILLERS & STOPPERS)

Because door and window frames are made of materials that shrink or expand at different rates from the walls that surround them, gaps and cracks will appear around the frames over the years. Wood swells when it gets wet and shrinks when it dries; aluminium and other frame metals expand and contract with temperature changes.

To prevent draughts and damp from entering the house and warmth from escaping, it is necessary to seal the gaps. A flexible sealant is best, because it allows for the seasonal movements of wood and metal.

What kind of sealant?

Sealants are a relatively new type of filling material and are more durable and flexible than many of the older fillers. Some are used in a gun that must be bought separately, others have a screw cap at the base. They have nozzles which must be cut at an angle to the required size. A third group of sealants is available in an aerosol can. There are sealants for both interior and exterior work, so choose one that is appropriate to the job.

ACRYLIC SEALANT A flexible filler for indoor or outdoor use, filling fine cracks and draughtproofing round frames.

SILICONE-RUBBER SEALANT Even more flexible, and more adhesive than acrylic sealant. Some makes contain a fungicide, and are used for sealing gaps round baths, basins and shower trays. Another type is used in place of putty when fixing glass into frames.

OIL-BASED SEALANT A general-purpose sealant that is used mainly to fill gaps round doors and windows. It is not as flexible as acrylic or silicone-rubber sealants.

BITUMINOUS-RUBBER SEALANT A flexible sealant, used for gutters, downpipes and sheet roofing materials because it offers very high resistance to weathering.

EPOXY-BASED METAL SEALANT A two-ingredient pack. A chemical reaction takes place when they are mixed, and setting times vary with temperature, so mix only what can be used in 5 minutes. This type of sealant is used for repairing fine cracks in metal gutters and downpipes, and could be used in wood that is to be painted, in place of an epoxy-based wood filler (see *Fillers & stoppers*). There is a choice of rigid and flexible finishes.

Sealing gaps round baths Time: depends on area

Filling a gap between the bath and the wall or tiles that surround it is a straightforward job. Acrylic baths, however, can present a problem, because they flex as they are used. So before repairing gaps round the edge of an acrylic bath, fill the bath in order to weigh it down and open the gap to its maximum or else work from within the bath.

> YOU WILL NEED Silicone-rubber sealant. Possibly: razor blade, silicone-rubber solvent, old paintbrush, trimming knife, strips of expanded polystyrene, hair dryer or hot-air gun, masking tape, flexible plastic bath strip.

If the area contains old sealant, remove as much of it as possible with a razor blade and clean away the rest with a silicone-rubber solvent.

If the gap between the bath and the wall exceeds 6 mm ($\frac{1}{4}$ in), pack in a strip of expanded polystyrene and press it below the surface. Cut strips from an old ceiling tile or a piece of unwanted packaging with a trimming knife.

Make sure all surfaces are clean and dry. Use an old paintbrush to clear away dust, and a hair dryer or hot-air gun to get rid of moisture if necessary.

! Do not fill an acrylic bath with water until you have finished using an electric appliance, in case you drop it.

Run two parallel strips of masking tape, one along the wall and the other along the rim of the bath, on each side of the area to be sealed.

Fill the space between the strips with sealant, and peel them off while the sealant is still wet. Smooth the surface with a wet finger.

Sealants vary, so follow the maker's directions closely. Fill gaps between a basin and the wall in the same way.

If the flexing of the bath, when it is used, is enough to be visible to the eye, cover the sealant with a flexible plastic bath strip, available in most DIY stores.

Filling gaps round window and door frames
Time: depends on area

> YOU WILL NEED Small trowel, old paintbrush, appropriate sealant. Possibly: hot-air gun, lint-free cloth.

INTERNAL FRAMES Rake out any loose material with a trowel and brush the gap with an old paintbrush. Fill the gap with acrylic sealant and smooth off with a wet finger.

EXTERNAL FRAMES Dig out all loose material from cracks, and dry with a hot-air gun. Fill the gaps with an exterior-grade acrylic or silicone-rubber-based sealant, and smooth with a wet finger or a damp, lint-free cloth.

Sealers: SEE VARNISHING

Seam

Repairing a seam Time: depends on length

> YOU WILL NEED Needle, thread. Possibly: sewing machine.

Turn the garment inside-out. Unpick the thread at both ends of the split seam, until there is enough for you to thread into a needle, and fasten it off securely with a couple of back stitches.

Pin the open section of the seam. Check the right side to make sure you have followed the original seam line. Machine-sew or backstitch the seam (see *Stitches*), overlapping the old seam by about 1.3 cm ($\frac{1}{2}$ in) at each end. Secure the loose threads by hand as before.

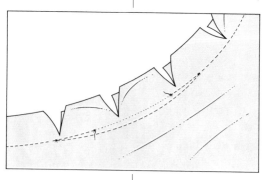

When you have to repair a curved seam that has been clipped, it may be necessary to stitch the new seam a little way inside the original stitching line. This ensures that the new seam is not weakened by the clips.

Secateurs

Use secateurs to cut only plants, never to cut garden wire. Clean the blades after use to keep them free from rust.

Oil the pivot occasionally. If wood gets trapped between the blades, the pivot screw may come loose. Remove the cap covering the tightening nut, and tighten it gradually, checking that the secateurs don't become too stiff to use.

Smooth out slight nicks in the blade by rubbing a fine slipstone lightly across the damaged blade.

Sharpen the blades, when necessary, with a secateur sharpener, available from a DIY or garden centre.

Security lights

A house that appears occupied, with lights and a radio turning on and off during the night, can deter thieves. Prowlers can also be deterred by a light outside the house.

OUTDOOR LIGHTS The most simple security light fittings are switched on and off by hand from inside the house.

Some light-sensitive security lights automatically turn themselves on at dusk and off at dawn.

Infrared sensors, which are activated when anyone comes within ten paces of them, can be connected to your existing outdoor light fittings but should be positioned a small way from them. This will give a better detection field.

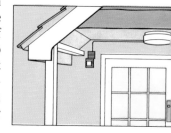

Alternatively you can buy a unit that combines the sensor and the light in a weatherproof casing.

When you are fitting a light with passive infrared sensors take care to follow these guidelines:

● Make sure you know the best height to fit the detector unit, so as to ensure adequate coverage of the area.
● Mount the detector on a stable base, which will not be affected by high winds which could change the direction of the detector and cause it to neglect a vital area, and be triggered instead by harmless stimuli such as neighbours or even passers-by in the street.

● Don't angle the sensor towards tree branches, water, air vents or any other object that may change temperature rapidly, as this could activate the sensor unnecessarily.

- Avoid placing the unit where foliage is in its field of view, as moving plants can switch on the light.
- Outdoor wiring is best carried out by an electrician.

TIMED LIGHT SWITCHES Time-controlled light switches are connected to the indoor-lighting circuit in place of normal switches and are wired in the same way (see *Light switch*: 'Replacing or repairing a switch').

Some can be set to turn on and off many times during their cycle. Others switch only twice in a cycle – for example on at dusk and off at dawn. Both types may also be operated as normal switches.

Light-switch timers cannot be used with fluorescent lamps or with energy-saving light bulbs.

LAMP TIMERS They fit into the bayonet socket on any ceiling, standard or table lamp, and the bulb fits in the other end.

The lampshade can be attached above or below the fitting and the lamp operates normally until you turn the wall or lamp switch on-off-and-on quickly. This activates the light sensor, which will turn the light on at dusk, and the interval timer, which will then switch the light off and on in a random sequence over a four or eight-hour cycle. This is repeated until the programme is changed.

SOCKET TIMERS A plug-in timer will control any appliance that plugs into a 13 amp socket – a radio, lamp, electric blanket, television or washing machine.

Set the required programme on the timer. Electronic timers have a display that is adjusted by pressing buttons. They cannot be used with fluorescent lights.

Mechanical timers can be used with all types of light. They have pegs that are pressed into position to set the required times. Both mechanical and electrical timers come with either 24-hour or 7-day cycles.

Sewing machine

If you have a problem when using your sewing machine, phone the manufacturer (see margin). Many companies have demonstrators who can give you advice. Or look in *Yellow Pages*, under 'Sewing machines – domestic'.

Getting the tension right

Test the tension before starting a job by sewing a piece of scrap material. A sewing machine has a tension control for the top thread and may have another for the lower one.

On a normal stitch the top and bottom threads link between the layers of fabric. The link stitch is invisible.

When the top tension is too tight, the link stitch is pulled through the fabric. Turn down the tension dial.

If the tension is too loose, the link stitch shows on the lower layer of fabric. Turn up the tension dial.

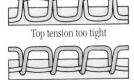

Normal stitch

Top tension too tight

Top tension too loose

If adjusting the top tension does not make the link stitch return to the correct position, you will have to increase the tension on the lower thread. There is usually a small screw on the side of the bobbin-holder for this purpose. Refer to your instruction booklet for details of how to increase the tension, because bobbins and their holders vary from make to make of sewing machine.

Choosing the right needle

For the best results, use the right type of needle for the fabric you are sewing and use a new needle every time you start making a garment.

The tip of a needle can become damaged quite quickly, especially if you are sewing coarse fabric, such as the header tape on curtains. Unless a damaged needle is replaced, it may catch threads in the next fabric you sew, particularly if the fabric is delicate.

Caring for your sewing machine

A machine should have an accessory box which holds basic maintenance equipment and other accessories, such as an oilcan, a screwdriver and spare bobbins.

- Remove the needle plate and clean the sliding parts in and around the bobbin before using your machine, brushing out dust, threads and bits of lint.
- If possible, remove the upper tension assembly and brush out any fluff that may have gathered there.
- If a needle breaks and part of it drops into the bobbin area, make sure you remove it.
- On some machines, the oiling points are marked with red dots. Refer to the instruction booklet if they are not. Oil these parts once or twice a year. (Most electronic machines do not need oiling.)
- Keep the machine covered when not in use, to stop dust gathering in its working parts.
- On an electric machine, take care that the electric power cord and plug are in good condition. Replace them at the first sign of wear or damage (see *Flexes & cables*: 'Replacing a flex').

HELPLINE NUMBERS

If you need advice on a sewing-machine problem call the manufacturer's hotline and ask to speak to one of their demonstrators or training officers who will advise you. Their helpline numbers are:
Elna: 0171 403 3011
Janome New Home: 0161 430 6011
Jones and Brother: 0161 330 6531
Singer: 0181 261 3230
Toyota: 0990 133 106.
Alternatively, contact the Sewing Machine Trade Association: 0181 995 0411.

SAFETY WITH SEWING MACHINES

Do not leave a sewing machine unattended when it is switched on if there are children about. Pull the plug out of the wall socket if you are going to be out of the room.

Sewing machine (cont.)

NEEDLE SIZES Needles range in size from 60 to 120, or 9 to 19, depending on the make. The lower the number, the finer the needle. As a general rule, use fine needles with fine, light fabrics and coarser needles with heavier fabrics.

Use Singer needles only in a Singer sewing machine, because they are slightly longer than other sewing-machine needles and they will not give good results if used in a different make of machine.

NORMAL NEEDLE An ordinary needle has a slightly rounded, sharp point. It is used for all woven fabrics.

BALL-POINT NEEDLE Has a slightly blunt, rounded end. Used for sewing knits and any type of 'stretch' fabric.

EXTRA-FINE-POINT NEEDLE Has a very sharp point and a larger-than-normal eye. For sewing heavy fabrics.

TWIN AND TRIPLE NEEDLES Used for decorative stitching. Consult your machine instruction booklet before use.

Choosing the right thread

There are many types of thread designed for specialist sewing tasks, but the three most commonly used threads are polyester, cotton and nylon.

POLYESTER THREAD A good general-purpose thread. It can be used for hand or machine sewing, and being slightly stretchy, is suitable for sewing woven fabrics, knits and other stretchy fabrics. It does not rot, snap, shrink or fray, and some polyester threads have a wax or silicone finish that allows them to slide through fabrics easily.

COTTON THREAD Often mercerised, a process which makes it smooth and lustrous. Although it is strong, it is not stretchy, so should not be used where 'give' will be needed. Cotton thread takes a dye successfully.

NYLON A transparent thread, made in two shades to blend with light or dark fabrics. It is used for hemming because it is stretchy, but it is difficult to end off satisfactorily.

Getting the right stitch length

For the best results, get the correct relationship between the type of thread, weight of fabric, size and type of needle and length of stitch that you are using.

Faultfinder guide: Sewing machine

Needle breaks

POSSIBLE CAUSE Needle was bent.
ACTION Replace needle.

POSSIBLE CAUSE Needle too fine for thick seams.
ACTION Use stronger needle. Sew slowly over seam.

POSSIBLE CAUSE Top tension too tight; distorting needle.
ACTION Reduce top tension (see previous page).

POSSIBLE CAUSE Fluff stops bobbin moving correctly.
ACTION Clean out bobbin area and remove fluff.

Link stitch is pulled through to bottom layer

POSSIBLE CAUSE Top tension is too loose.
ACTION Increase top tension.

Thread frays in eye of needle

POSSIBLE CAUSE Needle is too fine for thread used.
ACTION Use bigger needle or finer thread.

POSSIBLE CAUSE Eye of needle is damaged.
ACTION Replace needle.

Thumping noise as needle penetrates fabric

POSSIBLE CAUSE Needle is blunt.
ACTION Replace needle.

Needle damages fabric

POSSIBLE CAUSE Needle is too big or not sharp enough.
ACTION Use finer needle.

Skipped stitches or no stitches at all

POSSIBLE CAUSE The needle is not inserted properly.
ACTION Remove needle and reinsert it correctly — check in the manual.

POSSIBLE CAUSE Blunt or bent needle.
ACTION Replace needle.

Link stitch is visible on top of seam

POSSIBLE CAUSE Top tension is too tight.
ACTION Reduce the top tension (see 'Getting the tension right', previous page).

POSSIBLE CAUSE Bottom tension too loose.
ACTION Tighten bottom tension.

As a general rule, the finer the fabric, the finer the needle and thread you should use, and the shorter the stitch length should be. Conversely, a heavy, thick fabric requires a thicker needle, stronger thread and a longer stitch length. Before starting any sewing project, experiment with combinations of needle, thread and stitch length on a scrap of spare fabric.

Leathers and vinyls are prone to ripping, so they should be sewn with a relatively long stitch because a series of small stitches could weaken the seam area.

Inserting a new needle Time: a few minutes

Most sewing-machine needles are inserted in the same way. However, refer to the instruction booklet if in doubt.

YOU WILL NEED Replacement needle. Possibly: small screwdriver.

Loosen the needle clamp screw. On some machines this can be done by hand; on others, you may need to use the small screwdriver supplied by the makers.

Remove the old or broken needle and get rid of any small pieces which may have fallen into the bobbin.

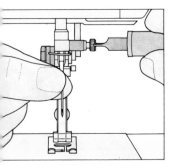

With the flat side of the needle shank facing away from you, insert the new needle. Push it right up into the clamp and tighten the screw, first by hand and then with the small screwdriver supplied with your sewing machine.

Gently turn the drive wheel by hand to check that the needle enters the hole in the needle plate correctly.

Shaver

There are two types of electric shaver: foil and rotary head.

Foil shavers have a very thin metal foil with tiny holes in it, and a vibrating cutter underneath it. Some models have two foils.

Rotary-head shavers are produced only by Philips. They have two or three fixed heads above rotating, concealed blades.

To ensure a good cut from your shaver, whichever type you have, keep it in good condition by cleaning it regularly, following the manufacturer's recommendations.

Cleaning a foil shaver Time: a few minutes

YOU WILL NEED Short-bristled brush. Possibly: special cleaning fluid (available from major chemists), light machine oil.

After using a shaver, switch it off and unplug it from the mains. Work over the bathroom hand basin with the basin plug in (not over the lavatory, in case the head drops in).

Remove the shaving head and give it a light tap to remove any hair in it, or blow out the hair. Then clean the cutter block with the special short-bristled brush which was supplied with the shaver.

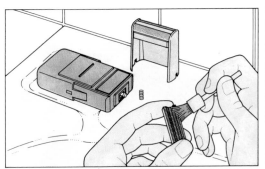

Every three weeks remove the cutter block and clean it thoroughly, following the maker's instructions.

Some instructions recommend that you spray the block with a special cleaning fluid which releases dirt and grease, and then brush it thoroughly. Lubricate the pivot with one drop of light machine oil.

Changing the foil and cutter block Time: a few minutes

The foil on a shaver should be changed once a year and cutter blocks every second year. Spare foils and cutter blocks can be obtained from the manufacturer or through major suppliers such as Boots and Argos.

Remove the old foil and cutter block, and insert the replacements carefully. These are precision-made parts and if wrongly assembled they can be permanently damaged. In particular, be careful not to crease or distort the foil, because this will prevent it from working properly and will shorten its working life.

Cleaning a rotary-head shaver Time: a few minutes

Every week, clean the shaving heads and the hair chamber which lies beneath them. Every three months include the guards and cutters in the cleaning routine, but if you use a preshave or have an oily skin, clean them every month.

YOU WILL NEED Short-bristled brush, long-bristled brush. Possibly: special cleaning fluid, light machine oil.

HELPLINES FOR SHAVERS

If you have a problem with your shaver, call the maker's helpline.
Braun: 01932 785611
Panasonic: 01344 853943
Philishave: 0181 689 2166
Remington: 0800 212438.

TAKING YOUR SHAVER ABROAD

If your shaver has automatic or universal voltage, there should be no difficulty in any country. If it has a dual voltage switch, you will not need to change the setting for European Union countries because 230 voltage electricity supply is standard. If you take it to the USA, change it to the 110-130 volt setting. You can use a travel adapter for the wall socket or buy a new flex abroad to fit the local sockets.

First, clean the shaving heads from the outside, with the special, short-bristled brush provided with the shaver.

Working over the bathroom hand basin with the basin plug in (not over the lavatory, in case you drop one of the parts), depress the button just in front of the shaving heads and lift off the head assembly.

Tap the hairs out of the hair chamber and use the long-bristled brush to clean it out thoroughly.

Each shaving head contains a cutter and a guard that have been ground at the factory in matched pairs. They are held in place by a retaining plate.

Lift off the retaining plate and carefully remove the shaving heads one at a time, to clean them.

Use the short-bristled brush to clean the cutter and the guard. Do not allow the pairs of cutters and guards to get mixed up; if they are mixed, it will take several weeks of use for them to become properly matched again, during which time the shaver will not give good results.

If the manufacturer recommends that you clean the shaving heads with a special cleaning liquid, apply one drop of light machine oil afterwards.

Electric shaving do's and don'ts

• Don't shave immediately after waking up in the morning. Your skin needs time to tighten up (from 10 to 30 minutes) if you are to achieve a close shave.
• Wash your face and dry it well before shaving, or the shaver will just slide over your skin.
• You will prolong the life of the foil if you apply only light pressure when shaving.
• After shaving, splash your face with cold water or an aftershave preparation, to close your pores.
• Don't let an electric shaver get wet. Although it is usually used in the bathroom, it is not waterproof.
• Do not connect a rechargeable shaver to the main power supply after its batteries have been removed.
• Before you throw out an old shaver with rechargeable batteries, remove and dispose of the batteries at your local refuse tip or shaver service centre. Never throw unwanted batteries into a fire.

Shears

Shears that are incorrectly sharpened and set will tear grass and plants rather than cut them.

The blades should bow way from one another very slightly along their length. The cutting edges should press together throughout the length of the shears during the cut. If they need to be reset, take them to an ironmonger, or send them back to the manufacturer.

BLADE TIPS If the blades are correctly positioned, the tips should overlap when the shears are closed.

If they don't overlap, lock each blade in a vice and file away the heel of the blade until they sit in the right position. Check their position regularly as you work.

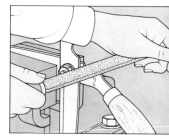

BLUNT BLADES To sharpen blunt shears, hold the blades of the shears apart and stroke an oiled carborundum stone along the cutting edge from pivot to tip. Keep the original angle of the cutting edge.

A more effective alternative is to get the blades sharpened by a local ironmonger.

LOOSE BLADES If the blades are loose, tighten the centre bolt until they cut cleanly. Do not tighten the centre bolt too far; the shears must be easy to open and close.

LOOSE HANDLE If a handle is loose, remove it altogether and clean out any debris from the hole.

Clean the metal shaft that fits into the handle with emery paper and apply epoxy-resin adhesive. Pour some of the adhesive into the hole in the handle of the shears and press all the pieces firmly back together. Tap the handle in place with a mallet if necessary.

If the handle works loose again, send the shears back to the manufacturer or take them to a local ironmonger.

Sheet

When a worn patch or a small tear appears in a sheet, repair it immediately. Otherwise it will quickly be made worse by the weight and movement of a sleeper.

Repairing a torn or worn sheet Time: depends on area

If the tears or holes are fairly small, a darn or patch will usually halt the damage (see *Darning*; *Patching clothes*).

However, if the centre of the sheet has become worn,

you can extend its life by turning the sides to the middle. Cut or tear the sheet down the middle, lengthways, then pin the outer sides together and stitch by machine. The sides of a sheet usually have selvage so they should not fray.

To make the seam lie flat, open and press it with a hot iron, and then stitch the edges to the sheet the full length of the join.

Fold over the raw outer edges of the sheet twice and stitch them by machine. And when making up the bed with the sheets, make sure that the smooth side of the seams is closest to the sleeper.

New uses for old sheets

DUVET COVERS If you change from using blankets to duvets, turn your flat sheets into duvet covers.

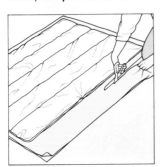

Lay the sheets, in pairs, on the floor and lay the duvet on top of them. Allow about 5 cm (2 in) all round for seams, and trim off the excess fabric.

Machine around three sides of the cut-down sheets and then add popper tape, press studs or Velcro fastening strips along the fourth.

PILLOWCASES If you still have excess sheeting after making a duvet cover, make matching pillowcases. Turn an existing pillowcase inside-out and use it as a cutting pattern and a sewing guide.

Very old sheets can be made into under-pillowcases to be used beneath new ones. Pillows will last longer and stay cleaner with under-pillowcases.

CURTAIN LININGS Old sheets can also be used to line curtains. To make sure that the lining does not show, trim them so that they are slightly narrower and slightly shorter than the curtains.

Stitch the curtain lining in place, using the original hem of the sheet as the hem of the lining. Sew the sheet sides to the sides of the curtain. Stitch the top of the sheet to the header tape at the top of the curtain.

Shelves

When you are planning to put up shelves, allow about 40 cm (16 in) between wall brackets, but put them closer together if the shelves will hold heavy loads such as large books or big jars of cooking ingredients.

What type of wall?

SOLID WALL In solid walls the brackets or supports must be screwed into wall plugs (see *Wall fixings*). Buy plugs to match the screw size. Select a masonry bit to suit the size of wall plug. Make the hole with a power drill.

HOLLOW WALL Use an HSS twist bit in a power drill or hand drill to make a hole through the plaster, applying light pressure. Then use hollow wall fixings to fix the brackets to the wall. If the shelf is to take a substantial weight, screw into the wooden studs behind the plaster (see *Wall fixings*).

Putting up a shelf with wall brackets
Time: 1 hour or more

> YOU WILL NEED Brackets, shelf, spirit level, bradawl, drill, drill bit, wall plugs, screws for brackets and shelves, screwdrivers.

Decide on the height of the shelf, and fix the first bracket in place according to the type of wall (see above).

Hold the second bracket up against the wall. Then get a helper to lay the shelf across both brackets. Place a spirit level on the shelf and move the free bracket up and down until the shelf is level. Mark the position of the screw holes on the wall with a bradawl.

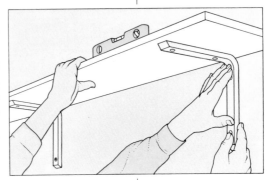

Drill and plug the wall, then fix the second bracket in place. Put the shelf on the brackets, then mark the position on the wall for any intermediate brackets.

Once all the brackets are fitted, put the shelf in place and use the bradawl to make pilot holes for screws in the underside, through the little holes in the brackets.

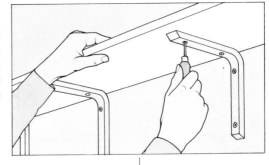

Check that the screws will not penetrate the top face, then drive them through the brackets into the wood.

Putting up a slotted-track shelf system

Brackets are fitted into slotted uprights so that the shelves can be adjusted to different heights.

> YOU WILL NEED Slotted track, spirit level, bradawl, drill, drill bit, wall plugs, screws, screwdriver, brackets, shelves.

Position the first length of slotted track, and check that it is vertical with a spirit level. Mark fixing points through the holes in the track with a bradawl, and fix the track in place according to the type of wall (see previous page).

Now position the second piece of track at a distance to suit the shelves, allowing for the shelf to overhang a short distance at each end. You may need help to do this. Slot a bracket into each piece of track at the same height. Rest a shelf on the brackets; place the spirit level on the shelf, then move the track up and down until the shelf is level.

Check that the second track is vertical, then mark the wall through the track for screw positions. Fix the second track in place in the same way as the first track.

Starting at the top, put the shelves in place and make pilot holes in the underside with the bradawl, through the little holes in the brackets. Screw the shelves to the brackets.

Putting up alcove shelving

In the alcove beside a chimney you can make up a simple shelf unit as illustrated, without drilling into the walls.

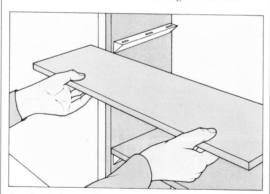

Cut the shelves to fit so precisely into the space between loose wooden uprights that the unit holds itself rigid.

Alternatively, you can screw wooden or angled aluminium supports (left) to the wall on each side of the alcove and rest the shelves on these.

If a shelf is to carry a heavy load, put another support along the back wall, and for extra strength, you could add a hardwood lip to the front of the shelf.

PUT A SHINE ON YOUR SHOES

If you are using polish rather than cream on leather shoes, use different brushes for each stage: a stiff brush for removing all dirt and mud, a medium one for applying polish, and a soft brush or buffing pad to work up a shine.

Saving space with shelves

- Adjustable shelving that can be altered to accommodate different-sized objects may be more useful than fixed shelves.
- When storing small items, several small shelves may be more useful than one or two large ones.
- Make your own simple shelves in the bottom of a cupboard to take your boots and shoes.

- Fit swing-out shelving into corner kitchen cupboards to hold vegetables or saucepans. Make sure the hinges of the doors are strong enough to take the extra weight.

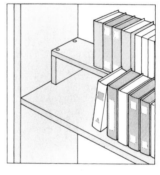

- Divide a wide shelf into two by building a mini-shelf for the back. You can use it to store videos, books or tapes. In a kitchen, use it for storing tinned foods.
- Attach fold-down racks or small drawers to the bottom of hanging kitchen units. They can be used for storing spices, knives or even cookbooks.

Shirt SEE COLLARS & CUFFS; SLEEVES

Shoes & boots

Shoes and boots will last longer if they are looked after well and not worn day after day. Put shoetrees or tightly packed newspaper into shoes that are not being worn. Clean shoes before putting them away so that they will be ready to wear when you need them.

Keeping shoes in good condition

LEATHER BOOTS AND SHOES Need regular polishing. For best results, apply polish and leave it overnight. Buff them in the morning before putting them on. Coloured renovating polish can help to disguise scratches.

Pack wet leather shoes or boots with newspaper to help them to keep their shape and to absorb moisture.

Stand them in a warm spot, but away from direct heat. Check the newspaper and change it as it becomes damp. Allow mud to dry before brushing or scraping it off so that it will come off more easily.

PATENT LEATHER Inclined to crack and must be kept away from direct heat. Polish them often with a soft, grit-free cloth and, to keep them from sticking together, wipe them occasionally with an instant shoe-shine pad.

Because patent leather is impermeable, shoes tend to trap foot perspiration, so allow plenty of time for them to dry out between wearings.

SUEDE AND NUBUCK Should be brushed regularly but gently, to prevent the nap from becoming shiny.

Remove mud immediately – do not allow it to dry on the shoes. Scrape it off gently with a blunt knife and then wipe the area carefully with a damp cloth.

Use a stain remover on oil or grease stains, but try it out first on an inconspicuous spot on the shoe, to make sure that it won't leave a 'high tide' mark.

Special rubber or wire brushes and different types of shampoo are available for cleaning suede and nubuck. Make sure you have the right shampoo for the type of leather, as they are not interchangeable.

Where colour has faded, use a proprietary dressing to restore it. Read the instructions well before starting.

FABRIC SHOES Range from satin to canvas. Shampoos and cleaners are available for many types of fabric. Follow the instructions carefully, allow the shoes to dry on shoetrees or stuffed with newspaper and then brush well.

Some cotton and canvas shoes can be washed in a washing machine. Look at the 'care' label, if there is one.

Wash them with other robust items, such as denim jeans. If you want to protect other items in the wash load, put the shoes into an old pillowcase.

If the shoes are being washed alone, put them in with old towels or sheets to cut down noise.

Prevent stains on new shoes by spraying with fabric protector, and treat stains that occur on untreated shoes with a stain remover appropriate to the stain. Change or restore faded colour with shoe whitener or shoe dye.

WORKING BOOTS Should be cleaned after each wearing. To keep the uppers flexible and prevent leather cracking, and stitches breaking, treat them with a waterproofing wax.

CREPE-SOLED SHOES Will become soft and sticky, and go out of shape, if they are left near a direct source of heat or exposed to sunlight for too long.

Do not wear crepe soles where grease, oil or paraffin have been spilled because it is absorbed by the crepe, which then turns soft and sticky.

SPORTS SHOES Must be allowed to dry thoroughly. Brush off dried mud. Scrub white shoes with a nailbrush and washing-up liquid before rewhitening them.

Leather riding boots need regular cleaning and feeding with hide food, applied in the evening and buffed up next morning. Use coloured renovating polish on scratches.

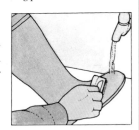

Rubber riding boots and wellingtons can be cleaned with an old nailbrush under cold running water.

New life for old boots and shoes

It is possible to have quite extensive renovation and repairs done to worn or damaged running shoes, rock-climbing boots and walking boots. They can be resealed and reproofed; new soles, inner back linings, inboards, lace rings and hooks can be fitted; and uppers can be restitched.

Take them to an outdoor-and-camping retailer who will give you the name of a specialist repairer.

GIVE NEW BOOTS THE TOE TEST

Sore toes and toenails at the end of a long walk could indicate that your walking boots are too short for you. When trying on new walking boots, kick the toes gently against a solid surface. If you can feel your toes touching the end of the boots, take a half-size bigger. You should also be able to wiggle your toes inside the toe caps.

DEALING WITH SMELLY TRAINERS

Trainers will smell if they are worn for too long without being aired. Ideally, the wearer should have two pairs and make sure that the pair that is not being worn is being aired thoroughly.

● To air trainers, turn them on their sides in a well-ventilated place. Do not fill them with newspaper or shoetrees. Loosen the laces or the tab, so that the maximum amount of air gets inside.

● The smell can be reduced by using special insoles which contain charcoal to absorb the smell, and antibacterial ingredients to prevent the development of athlete's foot. They are available from chemists and work most effectively if they are inserted when the trainers are new. When buying new trainers, allow for the space the insoles will take.

How to make your own shoe stretcher

If a shoe or boot is slightly too small, you can make your own stretcher, by following the illustration.

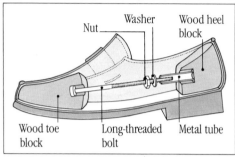

The two blocks of wood fit into the toe and heel of the shoe. To lengthen the stretcher, hold the bolt with Mole grips and turn the nut with a spanner. Leave the shoe with the stretcher in place for a week or more. Try the shoe on and stretch again, if necessary.

TRAINERS Can usually be washed in a machine. First brush off any dried mud and go over them with a damp cloth to remove any dirt which may harm the machine. When they are dry, apply a leather cream. (See 'Dealing with smelly trainers', margin.)

WALKING BOOTS Brush off any mud from soles and uppers and allow them to dry naturally. Regular applications of a waterproof boot wax will keep them supple and comfortable. Use a waterproofing spray for fabric or nylon boots. Protect new boots with a coat of wax before wearing them.

Renovating a scuffed toecap   Time: a few minutes

YOU WILL NEED Methylated spirit, very fine sandpaper, shoe colouring, soft cloth.

If the toecap on an otherwise good shoe becomes scuffed, remove all the polish with methylated spirit on a cloth.

Smooth the damaged area with very fine sandpaper. Brush off all dust and resurface the damaged area with a proprietary shoe colour. Keep on adding layers of colour until the damaged area matches the rest of the shoe.

Finally, buff them up to a high shine with a soft cloth.

Shower

Fixing a leaking shower head   Time: ½ an hour or less

If the shower head drips when the bath is being filled through the taps, the O-ring seal in the bath-and-shower mixer has probably failed. There is no need to cut off the water supply to fix this problem.

YOU WILL NEED Spanner, Vaseline. Possibly: new O-ring seal.

The control-knob mechanism diverts water from the taps of the mixer to the shower head.

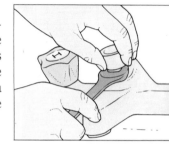

Lift and twist the control-knob. This will expose the spindle beneath. It has two flat sides to take the jaws of a spanner. Insert a spanner and unscrew the control-knob mechanism.

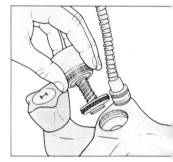

Remove the shower control knob in one piece to reveal the O-ring seal. The seal prevents water flowing up to the shower head when the shower is not in use.

Smear the O-ring with Vaseline and replace, and screw back the control-knob mechanism. If this does not cure the drip, remove the O-ring and take it to a builders' merchant to buy a replacement of the same size.

Smear the new O-ring with Vaseline and push it into its seating. Then screw the control-knob mechanism back in place and run the taps to test the seal.

Keeping a shower head clean

Remove the shower head from the flexible hose so that you can manipulate it more easily.

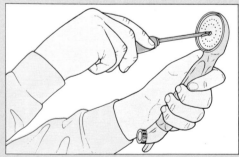

Depending on the type of shower, use a screwdriver to either prise the shower head apart, or to unscrew the retaining screw in the centre of the sprinkler.

Scrub the sprinkler parts with a nailbrush. If limescale is blocking the holes, use a chemical scale remover, following the instructions on the bottle.

Faultfinder guide: Shower

Problems with showers will usually require professional attention. But, by identifying the problem you may save time and money when you call a plumber.

Hot and cold water won't mix properly

CAUSE Unequal pressure from hot and cold supply.
SOLUTION The cold-water supply must come from the cold-water storage tank or an extra tank at the same level, not from the mains.

Inadequate pressure

CAUSE The distance between the shower and the cold-water tank is too small.
SOLUTION Raise the cold-water tank to at least 1 m (3 ft) above the shower head, or fit an electric pump.

Difficulty mixing the water to desired temperature

SOLUTION Fit a shower mixer which controls the temperature with a single control knob.

Water suddenly runs hot or cold

CAUSE Either hot or cold water is being drawn off in another part of the house.
SOLUTION Fit a thermostatic shower mixer.

Water drips from shower head when bath is being filled

CAUSE O-ring seal has failed.
SOLUTION Replace or improve seal (see facing page).

Deteriorating spray

CAUSE Sprinkler holes blocked by limescale.
SOLUTION Clean the shower head (see facing page).

Shredder

A shredder enables a gardener to recycle a wide range of garden rubbish that would otherwise be burned or taken to the local rubbish tip. Shredded waste composts faster and better than untreated waste.

Most shredders can turn fairly large prunings, hedge-clippings and even small branches into fine mulching and composting material. Some large machines can chop woody stems and branches into small, even-sized chips, and grind turf, clods of earth, bones and sea shells as well.

What to do when a shredder clogs up

Turn off the machine at once. Don't let it run on in the hope that it will clear itself. Damage may be caused if a stone or a large piece of wood is caught in the machine.

Disconnect the power source. If you have an electric machine, unplug it; if it is petrol-driven, disconnect the spark plug. It is advisable to do this even if your machine has an automatic cut-out. Make sure the blades have come to a complete stop before proceeding – they are very sharp.

Undo the handle or nut which holds the feeder funnel or hopper in place over the blades, and lift or open the funnel.

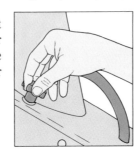

Remove the cause of the stoppage and check both of the blades for visible signs of damage.

Most shredders have double-sided blades which can be removed with an Allen key (right) or a screwdriver and reversed if one cutting edge is damaged.

Reassemble the shredder and turn on the power. Run the shredder empty for a few seconds to clear it out.

Sharpening shredder blades

Most shredders have removable blades that can be sharpened two or three times before you need to turn them round and use the other side.

To sharpen a blade, clamp it in a vice and file the cutting edge, keeping the original angle of the blade.

When blades need replacing, contact the manufacturer for the name of your nearest supplier.

If your shredder keeps clogging up

● You may be putting in branches that are too thick and tough. Try to break up the branches a bit before inserting them, by hitting them with a hammer or mallet.
● There may be too much moisture in the leaves and stems. Put them aside until they are drier, or alternate each handful of moist material with a handful of something dry, such as plain paper or straw, dry twigs or a newspaper rolled up tightly, like a stick.
● Check that you are putting in the material correctly. Refer to your instruction booklet. Some machines have two inlets – a narrow one for branches and sticks, and a wider one for weeds, foliage and twigs.

• Make sure that you do not put in stones, nails, plastic, colour-printed magazines or cooked food (it will attract rats). Smaller machines cannot handle bones or clods of earth, either – they will blunt or damage the blades.

Using a shredder safely

• Make sure the shredder is standing on even ground and won't fall over while it is in use.
• Always wear safety spectacles, ear muffs and gloves when using a shredder. Some makers supply them with the shredder. If not, buy your own.

• Hold branches firmly as you feed them in. The end of a branch can knock against you with considerable force while the blades are cutting. Use the narrow inlet if the shredder has one.
• Make sure that the shredder is clear at the end of a shredding session, by running it empty for a while.
• Use an RCD (residual current device) with an electrically powered shredder. Always turn the appliance off and unplug it when investigating a blockage.
• Make sure that the electric cable is long enough to reach the mains socket. The type of two-core extension lead that is adequate for use with a lawnmower will not be safe for a high-powered shredder. Instead, use a three-core cable classed as 1.0-2.5 mm² (15 amp) with a 13 amp fuse.

Silver & silver plate

Caring for silver plate

Silver plate, particularly valuable pieces such as Sheffield plate, should not be immersed in a silver dip. It could remove the plating, especially if it is damaged in any way.

Clean silver plate carefully, with one of the standard polishes, and try not to rub very hard.

Green corrosion, which occurs where silver plate has worn away, can be removed by rubbing with a lemon. Work on a small area at a time and rinse off as soon as the blemishes disappear. Dry the piece carefully with a soft cloth.

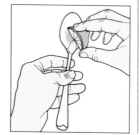

CLEANING INTRICATE SILVER PIECES

Use an old, soft toothbrush to apply silver polish to tiny spaces when cleaning intricate pieces of silver.
Wash and dry the toothbrush and then wrap a piece of soft, thin cloth over the bristles to polish the same area.

SILVER CUTLERY IN A DISHWASHER

If you wash silver cutlery in a dishwasher, put it into a separate cutlery basket, where it cannot touch other metal objects, because tiny particles of silver might be transferred to them through a chemical reaction.

Electrolytic method of cleaning silver
Time: a few minutes

It is possible to make your own electrolytic cleaner (using a chemical process known as electrolysis which causes dirt to loosen), but make sure that only silver items are immersed. Don't immerse any nonsilver attachments or knives with handles that have been cemented in place.

YOU WILL NEED Plastic bowl, aluminium foil, washing soda, hot water, soft cloth. Possibly: silver polish paste.

Line the bottom of a plastic washing-up bowl with a large piece of aluminium foil and lay the silver pieces on top of it.

Fill the bowl with hot water and dissolve a handful of washing soda in it. When the mixture stops bubbling, or when the tarnish disappears, pour the water away and rinse the silver in clear water.

Dry each piece and buff it with a soft cloth. If any marks remain, clean them with a silver polish paste. Do not rub too hard over hallmarks because they can be worn away easily, which would lower the value of the piece.

What kind of silver cleaner?

Silver cleaners and polishes come in various forms: liquid, paste, impregnated cloth and impregnated wadding. Do not be tempted to use brass polish on silver items, because it will damage them.

Some polishes are called long-term and include tarnish inhibitors. However, they are not as effective on badly tarnished silver as standard polishes.

Silver dips in which silver can be immersed are useful if you are cleaning a lot of pieces, such as a set of cutlery. But don't use it in a stainless steel sink as a chemical reaction between the stainless steel and the silver will cause the silver to discolour.

Another method of cleaning which involves the immersion of the piece is electrolysis (see 'Electrolytic method of cleaning silver', above).

When buffing silver after any method of cleaning, make sure the cloth is free totally from grit, which could scratch the surface.

Before using silver cutlery after any method of cleaning, wash and dry it thoroughly.

How to store silver

Silver that is not in constant use or on display should be stored in a dry place, and not exposed to the air.

Wrap silver objects in acid-free tissue paper which is usually available from cutlery shops and cutlery departments in large stores.

Alternatively, silver items can be kept in bags made of a fabric that has been impregnated with a tarnish-proofer (available from jewellery shops).

Silver cutlery which does not have its own canteen can be wrapped in a cutlery roll. This is a long strip of baize impregnated with an antitarnish treatment. Each piece of cutlery slips into an individual pocket in the roll. The whole piece is rolled up for storage.

Silverfish

Silverfish are wingless insects which do little damage in a home, but unless they are eliminated their long lives and copious reproduction could lead to an infestation.

They feed on starchy substances such as wallpaper paste and, where a wall is damp, they eat the paper itself. Silverfish also inhabit books, where they eat the paper and the bookbinding. They thrive in a damp, warm environment, such as a bathroom or kitchen.

How to trap silverfish Time: a few minutes

Silverfish are able to walk up vertical surfaces that are slightly textured, but they cannot walk up glass or ceramic surfaces. This makes them easy to trap.

> YOU WILL NEED Glass jar, masking tape or Pritt stick, flour.

Rub a Pritt stick over the outer surface of a small jam or honey jar, or stick several strips of rough-textured masking tape, such as Flexi-Mask, up its sides.

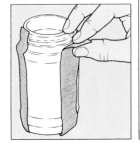

Spread flour-and-water paste round the lip of the jar and also put some inside as bait. Place the jar where the silverfish have been seen. The insects will be able to climb up the outside of the jar, but they will not be able to grip the smooth inside of the jar to get out again.

Close the jar and dispose of it.

Sink (SEE ALSO BATHS & BASINS)

Clearing a partly blocked sink Time: 1 hour or less

If a kitchen sink is slow to empty, there is probably grease trapped in the U-bend, partially blocking it.

> YOU WILL NEED Vaseline, borax or washing soda or chemical drain cleaner, rubber gloves, boiling water.

Once the water has drained away completely, smear Vaseline over the plughole to protect the chrome. Then pour a strong solution of borax or washing soda and boiling water down the plughole.

Alternatively, wearing rubber gloves, spoon chemical drain cleaner down the hole with a plastic spoon. Flush it down the waste pipe with boiling water. Repeat as needed.

A completely blocked sink Time: 1 hour or less

If water will not run away at all, a thick plug of grease or an object such as a bone is probably blocking the U-bend.

> YOU WILL NEED Sink plunger, damp cloth. Possibly: bucket, screwdriver, expanding curtain wire or sink auger, adjustable spanner, length of wood.

Hold an old, damp cloth firmly against the overflow. Then position the rubber cup of a sink plunger over the plughole.

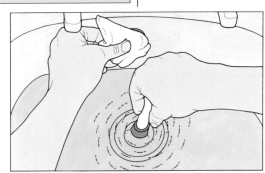

Press down firmly and sharply with the handle of the plunger four or five times in quick succession. Repeat a few times or until the water flows away. Once the blockage has gone, clean the waste pipe thoroughly with washing soda or a chemical drain cleaner (see above).

CLEANING THE TRAP If the sink plunger does not clear the blockage, you will need to remove the U-bend.

If you have already used a chemical cleaner, put on rubber gloves and pour about 1-2 litres (2-3 pints) of water down the plughole before removing the U-bend.

DISCOURAGING SILVERFISH

- Spray their favourite places with insecticide suitable for crawling insects.
- Eliminate damp from cupboards and floors (see *Damp*).
- Don't line shelves or drawers with ready-pasted wallpaper. The adhesive contains starch which may attract silverfish.
- Keep all starchy foods in airtight containers.
- Improve ventilation.

The waste outlet pipe may have either a conventional U-bend made of brass or plastic, or a plastic bottle trap.

To remove a plastic U-bend place a bucket beneath it and unscrew the two locking rings by hand. Clean it out and replace it, making sure it is firmly tightened.

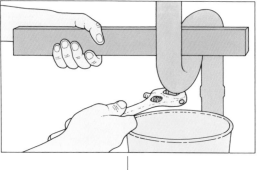

To clean a brass U-bend, place a bucket underneath it and undo the access nut with a spanner. To prevent the pipe buckling as you turn the spanner, steady the joint with a piece of wood held in the bend. Use a sink clearer or curtain wire to clean out the U-bend.

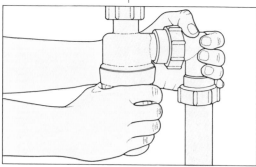

To clean a plastic bottle trap, simply unscrew the bottom reservoir of the trap by hand. Empty and clean it then screw it back in place.

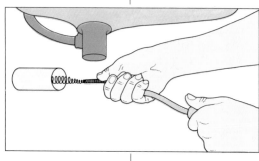

CLEANING THE PIPE If the blockage was not in the trap, use a piece of expanding curtain wire or a sink auger to probe the waste-outlet pipe to locate and dislodge the obstruction.

Replace the trap and test the system. Then clean the pipes with a chemical drain cleaner (see previous page).

If the sink is still blocked, call a plumber (see *Plumber*).

Skateboard

Almost all the parts of a skateboard can be replaced as they wear out. Specialist skateboard shops will often make repairs and modifications to your skateboard for you, but you can do some yourself.

The skateboard deck sits on two truck mechanisms and each of the trucks has two wheels on an axle.

Some models have plastic riser pads between the trucks and the board which act as shock absorbers; on others the truck is attached straight to the deck.

CARING FOR YOUR BOARD

If you use your skateboard regularly, check the nuts and bolts on your board every other week or so. Make sure they are moderately tight.

Replacing a skateboard deck   Time: a few minutes

YOU WILL NEED Spanner, new deck, nuts and bolts from the old deck. Possibly: new pads, power or hand drill, twist bit.

Detach the truck mechanisms from the old deck by undoing the bolts that hold them in place. If the new deck does not have holes drilled in it, place the trucks in position on the underside of the new deck and mark where the holes will go. Place the trucks in line with each other and parallel to the sides of the board, with the pivot cups (see facing page) next to the closest end of the board.

Then use a twist bit to drill new holes. Insert the bolts with the heads on the upper surface of the deck.

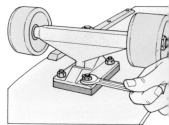

If you are fitting new riser pads, position them between the underside of the board and the trucks. Then screw on the nuts.

Replacing a worn kingpin, rubbers and pivot cup
Time: a few minutes

REPLACING THE KINGPIN The kingpin is the central bolt that runs through the truck mechanism into the board, holding all the parts of the truck in position.

It may become worn from scraping on the ground, but is simple and inexpensive to replace.

To remove the kingpin undo the nut holding it in place (right). If this does not release it, remove the whole truck mechanism by undoing the four bolts holding it to the deck.

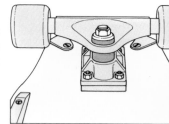

REPLACING RUBBERS Each kingpin has two rubbers threaded onto it – one each side of the axle.

The rubbers are an integral part of the truck mechanism. They are vital for steering and also act as shock absorbers. You can replace them if they get worn.

Undo the kingpin, remove the old rubbers and thread the new ones in place. Replace the kingpin and tighten the nut. If it is worn you may need to fit a new one.

REPLACING THE PIVOT CUP
The wheel axle pivots in a hole in the truck, which is lined by a pivot cup. The older rubber cups can wear. Prise out the old cup and replace it with the new one. Reassemble the truck.

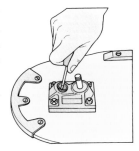

Replacing skateboard bearings Time: a few minutes

Older skateboards have open bearings under a cover. Keep them well greased with lithium-based grease. Modern skateboard wheels have bearings housed in a sealed unit. The better the condition of the bearings the smoother the skateboard will run, so change them regularly.

To remove a sealed-unit bearing, undo the wheel nut, and take off the wheel. Then slip the wheel back about three-quarters of the way onto the axle and prise out the remains of the old bearing by twisting the wheel to one side.

Push in a new set of bearings and replace the wheel. If the cover and bearings are missing, get them replaced at a specialist skateboard shop.

Skiing equipment

Patching a torn ski suit

If you tear your ski suit you should be able to patch it. For snowproof suits a stitched patch is adequate.

A waterproof suit on the other hand can be patched rather like a bicycle tyre. It is possible to make temporary repairs with waterproof sticking plasters.

Repairing worn boots

Boots mainly wear on the inside – at the tongue, the ankles and the uppers. You may be able to patch a worn boot with gaffer tape. If the inner is worn, you can either have the insides re-foamed, or insert customised silicon or polyurethane liners that are available from ski shops.

Replacing a ski-stick basket Time: a few minutes

If the basket breaks it can easily be replaced. Some have a metal flange which can be hammered into place, while others require a metal spring washer.

> YOU WILL NEED New ski basket, hammer.

Thread the ski basket over the end of the ski stick. Push it as far as it will go, then hit it with a hammer until it clicks into position.

Repairing a gashed ski Time: ½ an hour

There are two parts of a ski that can get damaged – the metal edges and the base material.

Blunt or burred edges can be resharpened by a ski shop or you can do it by hand with a file. But make sure that the edge is sharpened to a 90 degree angle.

If the underside gets damaged, as for example by hitting a rock in an area of light snow, you can repair it yourself. But if the metal gets torn out or badly dented, the ski will have to be replaced.

> YOU WILL NEED P-Tex stick, metal scraper, lighter or matches.

Follow the instructions supplied with the P-Tex stick. Melt the stick to fill the hole in the ski, holding it close to the ski to avoid carbon deposits. When the wax sets, scrape off any excess with a metal scraper.

The P-Tex stick that you carry is not as durable as that used by ski shops, so treat this as a temporary measure and get the ski fixed at a shop as soon as possible.

Storing skis safely

Don't tie skis together and do not store them lying down. Coat your skis with a layer of wax then lean them on their tips against a wall in a cool, dry place. If you do not have space to store skis, some ski shops will store them for you.

Waxing your skis

To prolong the life of your skis take 20 minutes or so every four or five skiing sessions to rewax them. Use special wax available from ski shops and an old iron.

Melt the wax onto the base of the ski, then iron it on so that it forms an even coat. When the wax has cooled, scrape it off with a plastic scraper until none is left on the surface. Then polish the ski with a piece of cloth.

The base of the ski is now impregnated with the wax. It will glide better over the snow and be less susceptible to damage, if it hits a rock for example.

AVOIDING DAMAGE TO BOOTS

Try to walk in ski boots as little as possible to avoid damaging the bottoms.

SKIING REPAIR KIT

Carry a few spares so that you can make any quick fixes necessary while you are on a skiing holiday.
- Spare set of buckles and ski baskets.
- Gaffer tape for temporary repairs to boots.
- Waterproof Elastoplast (to patch waterproof clothes).
- Rub-on wax and P-Tex stick.
- Matches or a lighter.
- Rubber abrasive block (to smooth sharp ski edges).

TRAVEL TIPS

● If a skirt is creased and you don't have an iron, you can use steam to make many of the creases fall out. Hang the skirt on a hanger over a bath and run hot water only. To create as much steam as possible keep doors and windows shut.

● To pack a permanently pleated skirt, roll it lengthways and insert it into an old stocking or one leg of a pair of tights. Pack the roll against the edge of the suitcase.
● When packing skirts of any type, fold them lengthways, not across the lap, as fold lines running from waist to hem will be least conspicuous.

Skirt (SEE ALSO ELASTIC; HOOKS & EYES)

Taking in a skirt waistband Time: 1 hour or less

If a skirt is too large – such as when you have lost weight – it is possible to take in the side seams, or put in darts where there were none, in order to achieve a better fit.

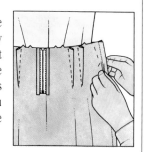

Unpick and remove the waistband. For a satisfactory fit, put on the skirt inside out and do up the zip. Pin the side seams and any new darts that are required (right). You may need a helper to pin the back darts.

Tack the new side seams and darts, and try on the skirt, the right side out, to make sure the fit is satisfactory.

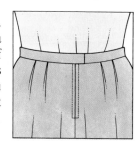

Reattach the waistband. Then either overlap the extra material (right) or trim it off and restitch the end. If it is likely that in the future you may have to let out the waist again, don't cut off the excess.

Letting out a skirt waistband Time: 1 hour or less

If a skirt becomes too small, it may be possible to enlarge it slightly by moving the button or hook-and-eye fastening at the top of the zip closer to the opening of the waistband.

Alternatively, if the zip was originally fitted with a large seam allowance, you can unpick and remove it. Reduce the seam allowance as much as you can, then reinsert the zip to give more room in the skirt (see *Zip*).

It is possible to make much larger adjustments if the skirt waistband has a large overlap which is sufficient to accommodate the increased waistline measurement. In this case, unpick and remove the waistband entirely. Then unpick the darts or loosen any gathers.

Put the skirt on, inside out, and pin new darts or adjust the gathers or pleats so that the skirt fits comfortably. If necessary, you may be able to loosen the side seams and pin them with a narrower seam allowance.

Stitch any new darts or seams, preferably by machine, for extra strength. Then reattach the waistband and move the fastenings so that it fits snugly (see *Hooks & eyes*).

Hanging a skirt to hold its shape

Always hang up a skirt after wearing it, especially if you have been sitting, to allow creases to drop out.

Avoid hanging it by its loops, as this can cause the skirt to droop or become baggy. Ideally, use the type of hanger that has two clothespegs fixed to the lower rail, especially if the skirt's waistband is elasticated.

A skirt with a firm waistband can be hung on an expanding hanger which holds the skirt by putting outward pressure on the inside of the waistband.

Avoid folding a skirt over the trouser-bar of a hanger – it may leave an unsightly crease across it.

Skirting boards

A skirting board protects the base of a plastered wall from damage by vacuum cleaners and brooms. It can become scuffed and damaged itself, and needs regular attention.

Wipe it down with a damp cloth or vacuum it, using the upholstery attachment, to remove dust. Scuff marks on a painted skirting can be removed with a mild household cleaner. If white paintwork is chipped, patch it with two or three coats of Tipp-Ex, taking care not get any on the carpet.

Sealing gaps above and below skirting boards

GAP ABOVE Before repainting a wall, fill all visible gaps and cracks between the wall and the skirting board with an acrylic sealant. Smooth it down, allow it to dry, and then paint it to match the wall (see *Sealants*).

GAP BELOW In some houses the gap below the skirting board has been designed to allow a fitted carpet to be pushed under for a neat finish. However, if the floor is left uncarpeted, or the skirting boards have shrunk, a gap at the bottom can allow draughts into the room.

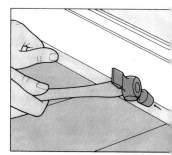

You can seal the gap by pinning lengths of quadrant moulding to the skirting board, so that they only just touch the floor.

At the corners, cut the moulding at 45 degrees. Use panel pins and a pin hammer to fix it to the skirting board. Do not fix it to the floorboards, which may move slightly as a result of expansion and contraction as the weather changes. Fill any small gaps with sealant. When it is dry, decorate the moulding to match its surroundings.

Replacing damaged skirting board Time: depends on area

Where a stretch of skirting board has been badly damaged, it is possible to replace it without damaging the wall.

> **YOU WILL NEED** Possibly: screwdriver, wrecking bar, scrap wood, cold chisel, club hammer, replacement skirting board, tenon saw, panel adhesive, acrylic sealant.

Methods of fixing skirting boards to walls vary greatly, so before you start removing the damaged board, examine the area to discover how it was fixed originally.

REMOVING THE BOARD If you find that screws were used, perhaps inset and covered with filler, clean out the screw heads and remove the screws. It will be easier than trying to lever the skirting board away from the wall.

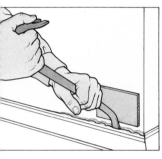

If you discover the skirting board was attached with nails, use a wrecking bar to lever it away from the wall. Rest the curved end of the bar against a piece of scrap wood to protect the plaster.

You may have difficulty getting the bar behind the skirting board, so use a cold chisel and club hammer to get you started. Try to avoid damaging the plaster.

This method is also suitable if plaster juts out onto the top of the skirting board. Insert the chisel through the plaster in one place only. You should be able to lever away the rest of the board without damaging the plaster.

GETTING NEW SKIRTING Take a piece of the old board to a timber supplier or DIY outlet. Modern skirting will be fairly easy to match, as standard mouldings are widely available.

Older houses often have unusual mouldings. If you have difficulty, try to make up the profile from various wooden sections. Fix them to a backing board (right).

As a last resort, ask at a timber yard for a length to be machined to match your sample, at an extra cost.

FIXING THE NEW BOARD Measure the new skirting board against the old one. Then cut the new board to the right length with a tenon saw. Use the old skirting board as a template to help you to get a mitred corner correct.

You may want to fix the new board to the wall in the same way as the original board. However, if you want to avoid making holes in the board, use a panel adhesive (see *Glues*). Fill any gaps between the wall and the skirting board with an acrylic sealant (see *Sealants*).

Hollow skirting boards to cover wiring

Unsightly electric cabling along skirting boards in a house can be covered by preformed, hollow skirting. The covers come off easily if the wiring should need to be changed, or if you are redecorating the wall.

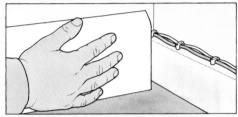

One system has melamine skirting covers, designed to fit over existing skirting boards and cables.

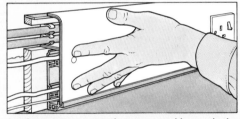

Another system carries the wires or cables inside the skirting board. Wooden battens are fixed to the walls, the wiring is laid along the carrying channels and then the skirting board is clipped into place.

These skirting board systems are usually available in DIY outlets and through most builders' merchants.

Sleeping bag

If a sleeping bag tears, you can use tent-repair tape, available from a camping shop, as a temporary measure to hold it together and stop the tear spreading. (Use nylon tape on nylon fabric.) A sewn repair will last longer (see *Patching clothes*: 'Making a sew-on patch').

It is possible to make a sleeping bag water resistant by soaking it in waterproofing solution or by applying spray-on waterproofer. Both are available from camping shops.

Sleeves

Converting long sleeves to short Time: 1 hour or less

Shortening long sleeves gives a blouse, shirt or dress a new look for summer, and will revive a shirt on which the cuffs are too worn to turn (see *Collars & cuffs*).

> **YOU WILL NEED** Scissors, pins, needle, thread. Possibly: sewing machine.

Decide on the new length and allow 2.5 cm (1 in) extra for a hem. Cut off the unwanted part of the sleeve. Then turn up the hem allowance on each sleeve and pin it.

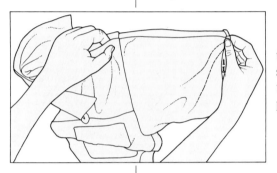

Hold both the sleeves together. Align the shoulder seams, and make sure that the new sleeves have been pinned to the same length.

Tack all round (see *Stitches*) near the fold, and press.

Turn the garment inside out. Fold the raw edges under again and pin them. Compare the two hems and, if they are the same depth, tack them.

Stitch the hem by hand, or use a sewing machine and stitch about 1 cm ($\frac{3}{8}$ in) from the edge of the hem.

Lengthening sleeves on a child's dress
Time: 2 hours or less

When a favourite party dress becomes too short in the sleeve, it can be given a few more years' wear by cutting the sleeves and adding a number of horizontal bands of ribbon (right) or insertion lace, which is daintier but not always easy to buy.

Insertion lace has two finished edges and does not need to be stitched into a seam. If you do find the right sort of lace, buy more than is needed, in case second or third additions need to be made as the child grows.

> **YOU WILL NEED** Tape measure, scissors, ribbon or insertion lace, pins, needle and thread. Possibly: sewing machine.

MEASURING Decide how many rings of ribbon need to be added to each sleeve to make them a comfortable length for the child. Take into your calculations a 1.3 cm ($\frac{1}{2}$ in) hem allowance on each of the cut edges of the sleeve.

Fold the dress and pin the sleeves together, aligning cuffs and shoulder seams. Then mark both sleeves with pins where the ribbon is to be inserted, making sure the sections match on each sleeve.

Cut through the sleeves at the marked levels.

INSERTING THE LACE Cut pieces of ribbon or lace the right length, allowing an extra 1.3 cm ($\frac{1}{2}$ in) for a seam.

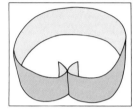

With either a needle and thread, or else with a sewing machine, stitch each band of ribbon to form a ring that will fit snugly over the open end of the sleeve.

With the right side of the sleeves facing, turn up a hem of about 1.3 cm ($\frac{1}{2}$ in), and pin it close to the fold.

Turn under the raw edge of the hem, repin and tack. Repeat this process on all the raw edges of the sleeves, keeping the hems as small and as neat as possible.

Position a ring of ribbon over the turned up hem on the sleeve. Pin it in place, making sure the fit is snug. If it is too loose or too tight, adjust the seam.

Repeat the process, pinning the bottom part of the sleeve to the lower edge of the ribbon. Make sure that the edge of the ribbon covers the small hem.

CHECKING Once all the rings of lace have been inserted into the sleeves and pinned in place, try the dress on the child, to make sure your calculations were correct. If necessary, add or remove one ring of ribbon.

With matching thread, stitch the rings in place by hand, using a small hemming stitch (see *Stitches*), or use a sewing machine. Take care not to catch up other parts of the dress when stitching the bands by machine.

Slides: SEE PHOTOGRAPHS & SLIDES

Smoke alarm

Fitting a smoke alarm Time: $\frac{1}{2}$ an hour or less

The best place to put a smoke alarm is between the sleeping area and the most likely sources of fire, such as the living room or the kitchen. Smoke rises and spreads out, so a central ceiling position is ideal.

Alternatively, mount the alarm on a wall, but not in a corner, where the air does not move quite so easily.

YOU WILL NEED Smoke alarm. Possibly: stepladder, cable-and-pipe detector, screwdriver, power drill, masonry bit, wall plugs.

Open the cover and hold the alarm where you want to fit it. If it fixes on with sticky pads, mark the position with a pencil, then expose the pads and press the alarm into place.

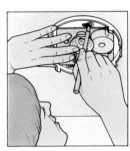

If the alarm screws onto the ceiling, hold it against the ceiling and use a pencil to mark the position of the screw holes on the surface.

Take care to avoid any wiring in the ceiling or wall by using a cable-and-pipe detector (see *Wall fixings*). Drill a hole through the centre of each pencil mark.

Insert the wall plugs and place the alarm in position. Insert the screws through the screw mounts on the alarm and screw them in firmly.

Fit the battery to the battery terminals. Push the battery into its holder and close the cover. Press and hold in the test button on the cover until the alarm sounds (this may take up to 10 seconds). The alarm will stop sounding when the button is released. If the alarm fails to sound, open the cover and check the battery connections and the battery.

Where alarms must be fitted

Building Regulations state that at least one smoke alarm, wired to the mains, must be fitted in every new property. Smoke alarms should comply with British Standard BS5446.

Smoke alarms should be fitted within 7 m (23 ft) of rooms where fires are likely to start, and also within 3 m (10 ft) of bedroom doors.

If the alarm is fitted to the ceiling it should be at least 30 cm (12 in) away from any wall and the same distance from any ceiling light fitting. If it is to be fitted to the wall, the alarm must be between 15 cm (6 in) and 30 cm (12 in) below the ceiling.

A fresh battery will last about a year. Some alarms have indicators to show that the battery is still working; others give an audible warning when the battery level is low.

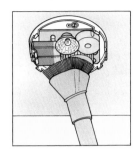

Clean your smoke alarm regularly because dust will impair its performance. Use the upholstery brush on the end of the extension pipe on your vacuum cleaner.

Snap fasteners

Also known as press studs or poppers, snap fasteners are two-part metal or plastic fastenings used for closing a gap on clothing or household linen. They work when one piece which has a protruding knob in the middle is pressed into a matching piece with a hole in the middle.

Snap fasteners do not close as strongly or smoothly as a zip, but they are lighter and usually more trouble-free.

They can be sewn on individually, or bought on a strip of tape which is then machine-sewn onto a large opening, such as the end of a duvet cover.

Positioning snap fasteners

To avoid creating a puckered closure, snap fasteners must be positioned and sewn on very carefully.

INDIVIDUAL SNAP FASTENERS When you intend using more than one snap fastener to close a gap, space them evenly along the gap, usually about 2.5 cm (1 in) apart.

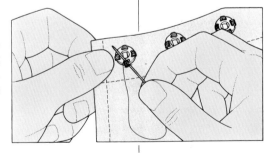

On one side of the gap, sew on all the halves with a hole in the middle, stitching two or three times through each of the four stay-holes and finishing off securely.

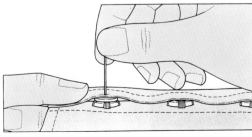

Starting at one end of the gap, smooth down the fabric of the other side, above the row of sewn-on halves and, with a pin, mark the centre of the first snap fastener.

CHECKING YOUR SMOKE ALARM

To help you to remember to check your smoke alarm regularly, try to do it on the same day every year, such as your birthday or some other anniversary.

Centre the other half of the snap fastener over the pin-point and stitch it into place. Check its position.

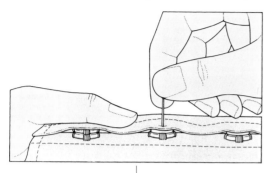

Leave that snap fastener closed, and move on to the next one, making sure that it closes the gap smoothly, without puckering. Mark it and stitch it in place, in the same way. Continue in this way until the entire gap has been closed.

TAPE-MOUNTED SNAP FASTENERS For large openings, tape-mounted snap fasteners should be machine-stitched into place with a line of stitching on both sides of the tape.

Machine-stitch one strip of tape to one side of the opening, and then do up the snap fasteners to fasten the loose tape to the stitched tape. Close the fabric over them and pin it to the unstitched tape, to get the positioning correct.

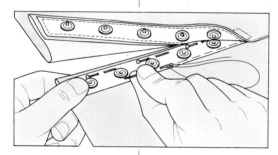

Then separate the tapes again and tack the second strip of tape into place.

Check that it will close the gap without puckering, then machine-stitch it into place, as before.

Soil testing

Treating acid soils Time: depends on area

To discover if your garden soil is suitable for most plants, measure its acidity with a pH testing kit. Soil pH can differ over small areas, so test in several places.

A pH reading of below 5.5 indicates acidity, 7 indicates neutral soil, and higher readings, of up to about 8.5, indicate alkaline soil that is unsuitable for lime-hating plants such as azaleas, heathers and rhododendrons.

Treat acid soils with lime, until you reach a level of about 6.5pH, which is suitable for most plants. Work the lime in with a fork in the autumn or winter, but if you have put manure into the ground during autumn or winter, delay liming until February.

Moderate the alkalinity of soil with a very high pH (around 8) and at the same time, improve its fertility, by regularly forking-in organic matter such as homemade compost, composted bark or well-rotted manure.

BUYING LIME

Get your garden lime from a garden centre. Do not use quick lime (also known as builders' lime) as it will damage plants.

Plants that thrive in alkaline soil

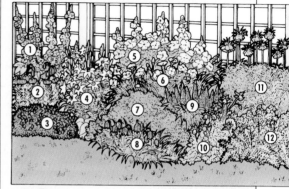

1	Mullein (*Verbascum*)	8	Snake's head fritillary (*Fritillaria meleagris*)
2	Pyrenean lily (*Lilium pyrenaicum*)	9	Sage (*Salvia officinalis*)
3	Daphne (*Daphne cneorum*)	10	Columbine (*Aquilegia*)
4	Madonna lily (*Lilium candidum*)	11	Crown imperial fritillary (*Fritillaria imperialis*)
5	Mallow (*Malva*)		
6	Pink (*Dianthus*)	12	Jacob's ladder (*Polemonium*)
7	Rue (*Ruta graveolens*)		

NOT SHOWN: False acacia (*Robinia pseudoacacia*), Lilacs (*Syringa spp*), Laburnum (*Laburnum spp*).

How much lime?

To bring the soil up to the ideal pH of 6.5, you can expect to use approximately the quantities of garden lime indicated below. Note that quantities over 250 g per m² (7 oz/sq yd) should be applied to the soil over several seasons, preferably being forked into the soil in autumn or winter.

A trowelful of lime weighs about 250 g (9 oz).

pH	PEAT SOIL OR ACID CLAY	SAND OR GRAVEL
6.5+	No lime required	No lime required
6.0	215 g/m² (6 oz/sq yd)	120 g/m² ($3\frac{1}{2}$ oz/sq yd)
5.5	260 g/m² ($7\frac{1}{2}$ oz/sq yd)	130 g/m² (4 oz/sq yd)
5.0	330 g/m² ($9\frac{1}{2}$ oz/sq yd)	155 g/m² (4 oz/sq yd)
4.5	400 g/m² ($11\frac{1}{2}$ oz/sq yd)	190 g/m² ($5\frac{1}{2}$ oz/sq yd)

If you apply hydrated lime, which is soluble and rather strong, use three-quarters of the suggested amounts.

Soldering

Soldering is used to join two pieces of wire or metal. Molten metal alloy runs between the surfaces to be joined, then cools to form a secure connection.

What model of soldering iron?

There are different types and sizes of soldering iron, ranging between 12 watts and 170 watts. Generally speaking, the higher the wattage, the larger the iron.

The iron supplies intense heat to a small area to melt the stick of solder. The temperature can be as high as 450°C (842°F) at the tip of the iron and it may be adjustable to suit different types of work.

For most DIY jobs, a simple pencil-type iron is adequate, but a gun-type with trigger action is fast, accurate and helpful for repetitive or delicate work.

Gas-powered versions are designed to be used where electric power is not available, and on larger jobs such as soldering pipes.

A bench stand is useful to hold the soldering iron while it heats up and also while you are not using it (shown below). Alternatively, hang it from a hook.

Fixing a handle to a kettle

Soldering is useful for metalwork repairs, such as refixing a handle to a metal kettle, where riveting is not suitable.

YOU WILL NEED File, emery paper or steel wool, flux and solder or resin-cored wire solder, soldering iron.

Use a file, emery paper or some steel wool to clean the two parts of metal to be joined, right down to the bright metal. Do not touch the cleaned surfaces with your fingers. Clean the tip of the soldering iron with emery paper.

If you are using a separate flux, coat both surfaces with it. Flux is not necessary with resin-cored wire solder. Then plug in the iron or turn on the gas, depending on the type of soldering iron that you are using.

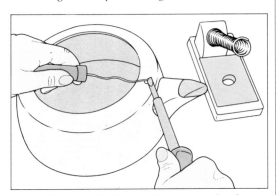

Apply solder to the tip of the soldering iron and melt some onto each side of the join. Rest the iron on a bench stand.

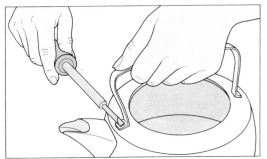

Then put the two parts together and apply heat from the iron to one surface, rubbing the iron over the surface. Hold the repair in place until the solder sets.

Soundproofing

It is easier to stop noise leaving your home than it is to prevent it entering. Sounds are vibrations, and when they meet a solid object such as a wall, they start the object vibrating too. Like ripples in a pool, the sound vibrations move outward from the source, through the solid structure and into the next room or adjoining house.

How far the vibrations will go depends on the materials that they travel through. Brick and stone do not vibrate easily, and so they deaden sound fairly quickly.

Soft surfaces such as acoustic tiles and curtains do not vibrate either, and they prevent sounds bouncing back, unlike harder surfaces such as mirrors and floor tiles.

Noise that comes from outside a house can be reduced slightly by sealing gaps around windows and doors.

Soundproofing windows

Apply a draught-excluding strip to window frames (see *Draughtproofing*: 'Sealing a window against draughts'). This will cut down on the amount of sound that comes through the gaps between a window and its frame.

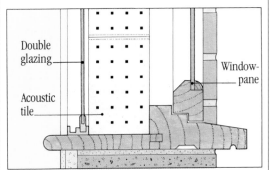

Double glazing

Acoustic tile

Window-pane

In addition, double glazing the windows will help to cut down incoming sound, provided the gap between the inner and outer glass is a minimum of 7.5 cm (3 in). For even better results, use panes of different thicknesses (because they vibrate at different rates and break up the sound), and also line the sides of the window with fibre-acoustic tiles.

NOISE ABATEMENT SOCIETY

Information and advice on all aspects of dealing with noise nuisance are available from the Noise Abatement Society, PO Box 518, Eynsford, Dartford, Kent DA4 0LL.

Soundproofing (cont.)

MEASURING NOISE

If noise is created regularly by troublesome neighbours, get your local environmental health officer to call round and measure it.

Anything over 80 decibels is above the acceptable level.

It is possible to relate the findings to other types of noise. A pneumatic drill at 5 m (16 ft) measures 100 decibels. 120 decibels is the threshold of pain. A jet engine at 152 m (500 ft) reaches 130 decibels. 180 decibels is a lethal level of sound.

If double-glazing is already in place, a third sheet of glass, of a different thickness, placed 7.5 cm (3 in) from the nearest sheet will make a difference.

Soundproofing doors

Clean the rebate in the door frame and apply a draught-proofing strip. Use either a self-adhesive strip of foam or a metal strip that holds a row of bristles.

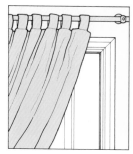

Hang a heavy curtain from a pole above a door, on the inside, to help to prevent sound created in the room from reaching and passing through the door.

Soundproofing floors

Uncarpeted timber floors allow the most sound to travel through them. You can reduce the noise from a timber floor by laying a good quality underlay and a thick carpet.

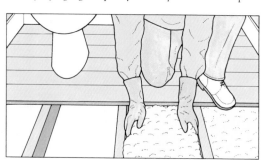

To reduce the sound of, say, a toilet reaching the room below, lift the floorboards and lay glass-fibre blanket or loose-lay vermiculite on the plasterboard below.

Alternatively, lift the floorboards and lay about 2.5 cm (1 in) dry silver sand on the plasterboard below – but have the joists checked for strength and suitability first.

Either of these treatments will absorb soundwaves more effectively than applying acoustic tiles to the ceiling of the room below, which will have little effect.

Soundproofing walls

Much of the noise produced in a room will be transmitted through the walls to other rooms and adjoining houses.

You may not be able to prevent the noise entering a room, but you can cut down how much leaves it by positioning noise-making appliances as far from shared walls as possible. Acoustic tiles or cork tiles can prevent noise leaving a room, but have little effect on how much enters.

In a bedroom, a built-in cupboard on a shared wall will deaden some sound, as the clothes absorb vibrations.

Soundproofing ceilings

If you live below a noisy neighbour who won't carpet the floor, consider installing a false ceiling in your own flat. You may need to employ a builder as it is a big job which involves fixing new ceiling joists across the room.

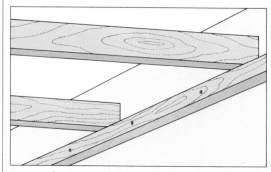

Support the joists with battens fixed to the walls, or by hanging brackets which are fixed to the existing joists.

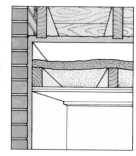

The new joists must be strong enough to take the weight of two layers of 12 mm ($\frac{1}{2}$ in) plasterboard as well as a layer of sound-insulating quilt.

The larger the gap between the new ceiling and the old, the more effective the sound insulation will be. In a house with fairly low ceilings, a gap as small as 2.5-5 cm (1-2 in) will make a noticeable reduction in the noise level.

Soundproofing eaves

To stop noise entering your home through the roof and eaves seal all the gaps with an expanding polyurethane foam (see *Sealants*), and fit strips of blanket insulation between the rafters. Work in daylight because the light shining through makes it easier to find holes.

Dealing with noisy neighbours

It is easier to control noise at its source than to try to reduce its effect. Most people will cooperate when they realise that their noise is affecting a neighbour, especially if you ask them to come and listen to the noise of, say, their hi-fi, from inside your home. An informal approach and practical suggestions for reducing the noise may solve the problem without any further difficulty.

For persistent, disturbing noise, write to the environmental health officer at your local authority or complain in writing direct to the magistrate's court under section 82 of the Environmental Protection Act.

Spade & shovel

The main difference between a spade and a shovel is that the blade of a spade is flat and sharp, sometimes with a turned over shoulder, to give a flatter surface for the foot to drive it into the ground. The blade of a shovel has slightly turned-up edges, which enable it to hold more when being used to move materials such as sand.

Spades are made in a number of sizes and weights, so choose one that suits your own strength. Remember that digging puts a strain on the back, and a smaller spade will make the work lighter. Consider buying a spade with a stainless steel blade – it is easier to use, as soil doesn't cling to the blade as much as it does to a standard blade.

Fitting a new handle Time: 1 hour or less

Do not use a spade or shovel as a lever. The strain could break the handle. However, if the handle on an otherwise sound spade or shovel does break, it can be replaced.

> **YOU WILL NEED** Replacement handle, tenon saw, vice, pencil, axe or chopper, trimming knife, sandpaper, wax polish. Possibly: flat file, electric drill, twist bits, nail punch, penetrating oil, screwdriver, mallet, screws, rivets, ball-pein hammer, rivet set.

Most wooden handles are a standard diameter, but to make sure you get the correct size, take the broken handle with you to buy a replacement.

To remove the stump of the broken spade handle from the metal socket, first take out the rivets or screws that hold it in place. Save one of the old rivets or screws and take it to a hardware shop to buy new ones of the same size.

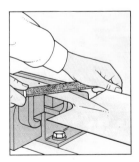

REMOVING RIVETS Fix the spade socket in a vice and file down the rivet head with a flat file until it is flush with the socket.

Select an HSS twist bit that is about the same diameter as the rivet stem and drill off the rivet head.

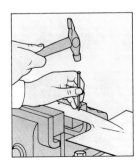

Use a nail punch (or a large nail) and a hammer to knock out the remains of the rivet. Remove any other rivets in the same way.

REMOVING A SCREW Fix the spade socket in a vice and unscrew the holding screw. If it is rusted or difficult to move, apply a drop of penetrating oil round the screw head.

REMOVING THE HANDLE If the wooden handle has broken off close to the metal socket, it may be more difficult to remove the stump, but it is not impossible.

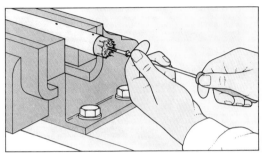

Screw a large wood screw into the exposed end, grip the head of the screw in a vice or self-grip wrench and pull.

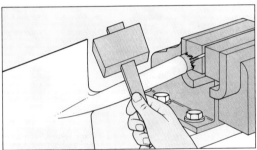

If the stump does not come out easily, tap the shoulder of the blade with a wooden mallet to force it out. Do not throw away the shaped wooden stump that comes out.

SHAPING THE NEW HANDLE Assemble all the pieces of the broken handle alongside the new handle to help you to get the length of the new one correct. If it is longer than you need, use a pencil to mark where to cut. Put the new handle in the vice and cut off the excess with a tenon saw.

Resting the end on a block of spare wood, use an axe or chopper to pare it down. Shape it more finely with a trimming knife until it fits snugly into the socket of the spade.

Maintenance of spades and shovels

- Clean the blade of the spade after use, rinsing off mud and drying it, if necessary.
- Keep the blades sharp. When they become blunt, restore the sharp edge with a flat file.
- To keep a spade in good condition, especially when putting it away for a while, fill an old bucket with sharp sand and pour roughly half a litre (1 pint) of engine oil into it. Mix it well, then thrust the blade of the spade or shovel into it a number of times.

FIXING THE NEW HANDLE Hold the spade with its blade pointing downwards and tap it two or three times on the block of wood to get the handle in as far as possible. Make sure the handle is parallel with the blade.

If the handle is held in place by a screw, drill a pilot hole in the wooden handle through the hole in the socket.

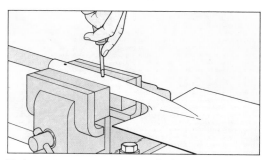

Fit the retaining screw so that it is flush with the outside of the socket. Smooth the head with a flat file if necessary.

If the handle is to be riveted, use the holes in the socket as guides and drill through the shaft. Tap in a new rivet, and lay the spade on the ground, placing the rivet head on something solid, such as a brick, to act as an anvil.

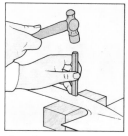 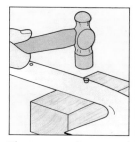

Place the narrow hole of the rivet set over the exposed bit of shank and hit the set to drive the rivet right through.

Then remove the set, and use the flat end of a ball-pein hammer to spread the shank of the rivet.

Shape the shank arms into a rough dome with the ball end of the hammer, then use the rounding depression of the rivet set to tidy up the head.

Remove any roughness with a flat file. Then lightly sand the shaft and apply a little wax polish.

Spanners & wrenches
(SEE ALSO FACING PAGE)

Using a spanner

Always choose a spanner that fits the nut or bolt head snugly. A loose-fitting spanner will round off the corners of the nut and the spanner itself could be damaged in the process. When using an adjustable spanner, set the gap to fit the nut as precisely as possible.

Take care when using a spanner with a long handle because it exerts great leverage and can strip the thread of the nut. If the nut is jammed or rusted, see *Nuts & bolts*.

When loosening or tightening a nut on a central-heating radiator with a large spanner, it is possible to distort the pipe below, so always brace the pipe by holding it with a pipe wrench (see *Central-heating radiators*), but don't use a pipe wrench to turn a nut; it will round off the corners.

How spanners are measured

Most spanners are measured 'across the flats' (AF), which means from one side of the bolt head to the other. So a $\frac{1}{2}$ in AF spanner fits a bolt measuring $\frac{1}{2}$ in across the head. Metric spanners are also measured across the flats so that a 10 mm spanner fits a metric bolt 10 mm across the head.

Whitworth spanners, however, are measured by the width of the bolt's shank. So a $\frac{1}{2}$ in Whitworth spanner fits a bolt with a head about 1 in across.

Spark-plug

All petrol engines use spark-plugs. Each plug produces an electric spark which ignites a mixture of petrol and air to drive the engine.

To work efficiently the spark-plug must be of the correct rating for the engine, its electrodes must be clean and the gap between the electrodes must be correct.

Cleaning and gapping a spark-plug
Time: 15 minutes or less

There are two types of spark-plug. One has a flat seat and a washer; the other has a tapered seat and no washer.

YOU WILL NEED Spark-plug spanner, feeler gauges, wire brush and emery paper or electric spark-plug cleaner, gapping tool or screwdriver.

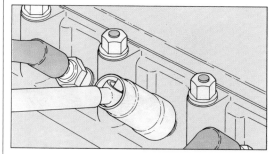

REMOVING THE PLUG Use a spark-plug spanner to remove the plugs so that you don't damage the ceramic insulation.

If there is more than one plug, the correct leads must be connected to the correct plugs when they are replaced. To prevent confusion, either mark the leads and plugs with coloured insulating tape or remove only one plug at a time.

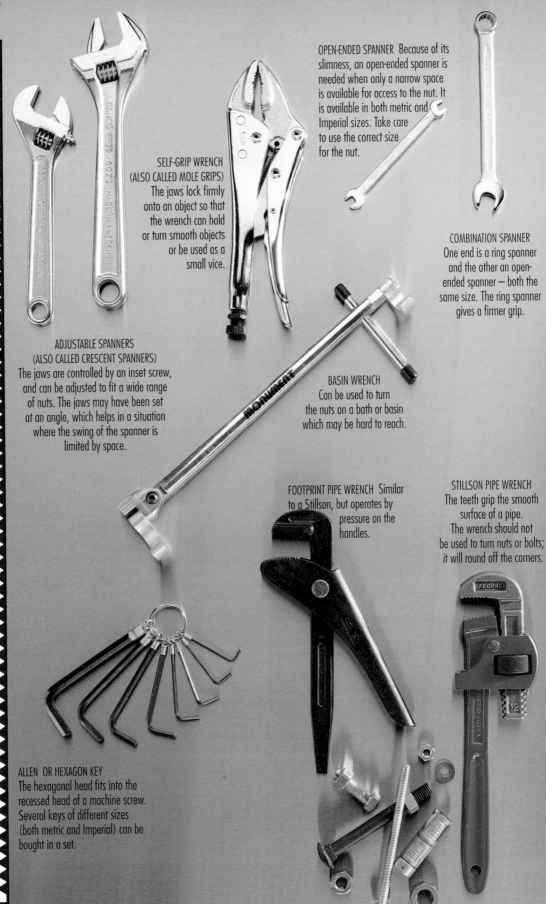

SPANNERS & WRENCHES

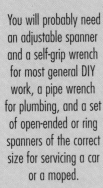

You will probably need an adjustable spanner and a self-grip wrench for most general DIY work, a pipe wrench for plumbing, and a set of open-ended or ring spanners of the correct size for servicing a car or a moped.

SELF-GRIP WRENCH (ALSO CALLED MOLE GRIPS) The jaws lock firmly onto an object so that the wrench can hold or turn smooth objects or be used as a small vice.

OPEN-ENDED SPANNER Because of its slimness, an open-ended spanner is needed when only a narrow space is available for access to the nut. It is available in both metric and Imperial sizes. Take care to use the correct size for the nut.

COMBINATION SPANNER One end is a ring spanner and the other an open-ended spanner — both the same size. The ring spanner gives a firmer grip.

ADJUSTABLE SPANNERS (ALSO CALLED CRESCENT SPANNERS) The jaws are controlled by an inset screw, and can be adjusted to fit a wide range of nuts. The jaws may have been set at an angle, which helps in a situation where the swing of the spanner is limited by space.

BASIN WRENCH Can be used to turn the nuts on a bath or basin which may be hard to reach.

FOOTPRINT PIPE WRENCH Similar to a Stillson, but operates by pressure on the handles.

STILLSON PIPE WRENCH The teeth grip the smooth surface of a pipe. The wrench should not be used to turn nuts or bolts; it will round off the corners.

ALLEN OR HEXAGON KEY The hexagonal head fits into the recessed head of a machine screw. Several keys of different sizes (both metric and Imperial) can be bought in a set.

USING A SPARK-PLUG CLEANER

An electric spark-plug cleaner usually runs off a 12 volt car battery. The threaded part of the spark-plug pushes into a hole in the top of the machine and a small fan inside blasts fine grit at the plug to clean off dirt.

Feeler gauges

Feeler gauges are used to check the distance between the spark-plug electrodes. They are simple strips of metal or wire marked with their exact thicknesses.

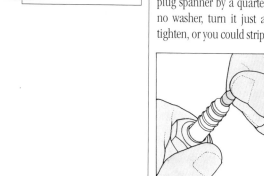

Check each plug for damage. If the ceramic insulation is damaged, the metal electrodes pitted or eroded, or if the outer electrode has worn thin, replace it with a new plug.

CLEANING THE PLUG If the plug is sound, clean any dirt and deposits off the electrodes with a wire brush and emery paper or a small file. Alternatively, use an electrically powered spark-plug cleaner. Wipe the ceramic body of the plug.

Check the owner's handbook for the gap between the electrodes. It will be in inches, millimetres or thousandths of an inch; for example, 0.0025 in, 0.6 mm or 25 thou.

Check the size of the gap using a feeler gauge of the right thickness (see margin).

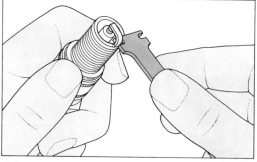

If the size is incorrect, gently bend the outer electrode with a gapping tool until the gap is correct; otherwise push against a flat surface to lessen the gap, or use a screwdriver to widen it. Be careful not to chip the porcelain.

REPLACING THE PLUG When the plug is clean and correctly gapped, replace it. First make sure the area around the hole is clean, then put a little light oil on the spark-plug's thread and screw it in place by hand until you feel resistance. If the plug has a flat seat and a washer, tighten it with the spark-plug spanner by a quarter turn. If it has a tapered seat and no washer, turn it just a couple of degrees. Do not over-tighten, or you could strip the threads in the engine.

Some plugs have a small threaded connector on the top which can work loose. Make sure it is screwed on tightly before reconnecting a push-on lead.

Spectacles

When buying a pair of spectacles, remember that glass lenses are less likely to scratch than plastic, but they will weigh more and can break. It is possible to buy tempered (or shatterproof) glass lenses, and also to have a scratch-resistant coating applied to plastic lenses.

Frames that won't go out of shape

Spectacle frames made from a lightweight alloy of nickel and titanium are available. They are so flexible that no matter how they are bent or twisted, they return to their original shape.

Repairing broken frames Time: a few minutes

If a spectacle frame breaks at the bridge piece, temporary repairs are possible. Get a new frame as soon as possible, because no matter how carefully the frame is repaired, it is possible that the angle of correction has been changed and will strain your eyes.

YOU WILL NEED Soft cloth, clear adhesive tape, craft knife.

Clean thoroughly all round the break with a soft cloth.

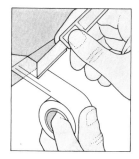

Pull out a 2.5 cm (1 in) length of clear adhesive tape and use a sharp craft knife to cut it lengthways into 6 mm ($\frac{1}{4}$ in) strips.

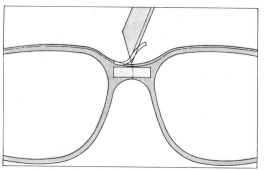

Hold the two frame parts firmly together, and lay strips of adhesive tape to straddle the break, across the back, front, top and bottom of the bridge piece.

Smooth down the adhesive tape with a fingernail to remove any air bubbles. Cut more strips of tape, if necessary, and use them to bandage the bridge piece with each layer slightly overlapping the previous one.

Living with lenses

- If a lens breaks cleanly, you can hold it together temporarily with two little pieces of clear adhesive tape, placed at both ends of the break.
- Clean your lenses with soapy water, or a drop of vinegar, vodka or surgical spirit. Always use a soft, clean cloth to wipe lenses, to avoid scratching them.
- If plastic lenses have become so scratched that they are unusable, try removing the scratches by polishing them very gently with Brasso.
- Before going out on a cold day, rub your lenses with a thin coating of soap. Then polish them until they are clear. This stops them fogging up when you walk into a warm room.
- If a lens pops out of your half-moon spectacles, use Plasticine, putty rubber (available in toy and craft shops) or any other sticky substance in the corner of the lens to hold it in place temporarily.
- Pushing your spectacles on top of your head when you are not using them puts a strain on the hinges.
- Do not wear spectacles with plastic lenses when using a perfume atomiser or hair spray. The chemicals in the spray may damage the plastic.
- To avoid scratching your lenses, rest your spectacles on their folded arms, with the lenses uppermost. Never rest them on their lenses.

Replacing a missing hinge screw   Time: a few minutes

YOU WILL NEED   Fine wire or paperclip, needle-nose pliers.

Cut a length of fine wire, or a small piece of paperclip, a little longer than the depth of the hinge on the spectacles.

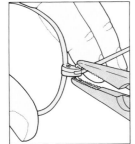

Hold the hinge together and insert the wire, using needle-nose pliers to bend it over at both ends.

Refitting a lens in half-rim glasses   Time: a few minutes

Lenses in glasses which are partly rimless, supported at the bottom by a nylon thread, can be refitted if they fall out.

YOU WILL NEED   Fabric tape or bias binding.

Fit the lens into the groove in the top half of the frame. Then turn the frame upside-down and run a short piece of fabric tape under the nylon thread.

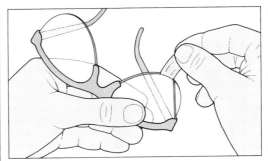

Hold the lens and frame firmly and, starting at one side, pull the tape along, lifting it slightly, so that it feeds the nylon thread into the groove at the base of the lens. With the thread back in place remove the tape.

Spin-dryer

A spin-dryer consists of a rotating, perforated drum, driven at high speed by a motor. Centrifugal force drives the water out of damp laundry through the perforated drum into an outer drum. From there it drains or is pumped out of the machine. The motor is controlled by a switch incorporated in the lid. It switches off when the dryer lid is opened.

Freeing a stuck brake cable   Time: 1 hour

When the lid of the spin-dryer is opened, the brake cable activates the brake. In time, the cable can stick, causing the brake to bind and the dryer to run unevenly. It is possible to free the brake, but as this involves turning the machine upside-down, you may need help.

Pull out the plug from the wall socket and turn the spin-dryer upside-down. This should expose the bottom of the drum and the drive pulley. On some models you may have to remove a base plate.

The brake assembly is beside the pulley and the cable extends from it. The brake cable is held in place by two locknuts, one on each side of the retaining bracket. An adjuster nut is fitted beside one of the locknuts.

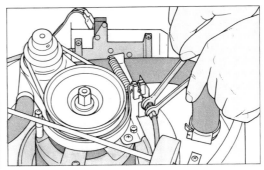

To adjust the cable, hold the adjuster nut steady with one spanner (shown in the left hand, above) and loosen the locknut beside it with a second spanner. Turn the adjuster nut until you can turn the pulley freely by hand.

Spin-dryer (cont.)

A typical spin-dryer

Spin-dryers vary from make to make, but most of them function in a similar manner. Water is removed from damp laundry by centrifugal force, and either drains or is pumped away.

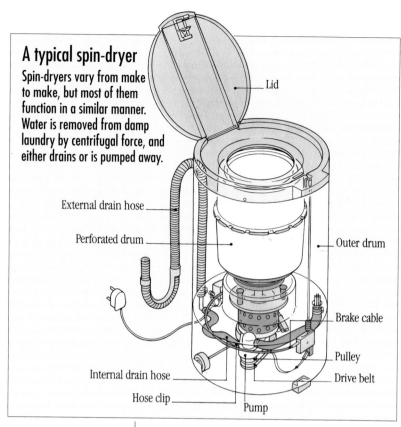

- Lid
- External drain hose
- Perforated drum
- Outer drum
- Brake cable
- Pulley
- Drive belt
- Internal drain hose
- Hose clip
- Pump

If you turn the adjuster nut too far, the brake will not operate when the lid is opened, so before tightening the locknut, turn the spin-dryer the right way up, plug it in and start it spinning.

Lift the lid, and if the brake does not stop the machine, pull out the electric plug, turn the machine upside-down again, and turn the adjuster nut a small amount in the opposite direction. Then test it again.

Once it is correct, tighten the locknut.

Removing an object from between the drums
Time: 1 hour or less

When something gets caught between the perforated inner drum and the outer drum of a spin-dryer, the inner drum will revolve noisily or with some difficulty.

> YOU WILL NEED Screwdriver. Possibly: wire coat hanger.

Pull out the plug from the wall socket and raise the lid.

Unscrew the moulding round the top of the spin-dryer. Some models have a rubber moulding which can be eased off by inserting a screwdriver under the edge – take care not to damage it.

Lift out anything within reach that has become caught near the top of the gap between the two drums.

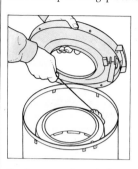

If it is too far down to reach, make a hook from an old wire coat hanger and pull it out. If this is impossible, call a service engineer who will strip the machine. Small objects such as buttons or coins may slide out if you turn the machine on its side and tilt it up.

Replacing a drive belt Time: 1 hour or less

> YOU WILL NEED Replacement drive belt. Possibly: screwdriver.

If the motor is working but the drum does not revolve or the pump is not working, the drive belt could be broken or may have become too stretched or worn.

Pull the plug out of the wall and turn the machine upside-down in order to expose the drive belt. In some models you may have to remove a base plate.

If the drive belt is worn or broken it should be replaced. Take the old belt with you when you buy a replacement.

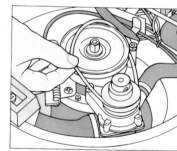

Stretch the new belt over the pulleys and if necessary, replace the base plate. Then turn the spin-dryer the right way up, plug it in and test it.

Clearing a blocked hose Time: 1 hour or less

If the pump is not pumping out water, the hose may be blocked or kinked. Before checking it for a blockage, make sure it is not bent or kinked. Straighten it out if it is.

> YOU WILL NEED Screwdriver, wire coat hanger, bowl.

Unplug the dryer from the wall socket. Drain any water out of it by lowering the drain hose into a bowl. If possible, remove the external drain hose and check it for a blockage.

If the external hose is clear, turn the spin-dryer upside-down to expose the internal drain hose (and if necessary remove the base plate). Unscrew the clip that connects it to the pump and if necessary disengage it at the other end from the external drain hose.

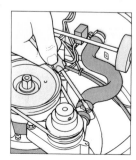

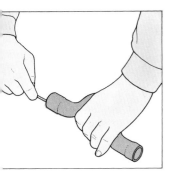

Remove the hose and, if it appears to be blocked, push a length of coat-hanger wire through it in order to dislodge the obstruction.

Run water through the hose to make sure it is clear. While the hose is disconnected, check the pump inlet for blockages and clean it. Rub a little grease or Vaseline round the joint and hose clip before replacing the hose.

While the machine is upside-down, take the opportunity to lubricate the wheels, if it has any, by trickling a little light machine oil onto the axles.

Turn the machine right side up and try it again. If it still does not pump out water, call a service engineer.

Faultfinder guide: Spin-dryer

Spin-dryer works intermittently or won't work at all

POSSIBLE CAUSE Faulty connection.
ACTION Check the fuse and the electrical connections at both ends of the lead. Replace the fuse or tighten the connections if necessary.

Check that the lead is not damaged and use a circuit tester (see *Toaster*) to locate breaks in the circuit. Replace the lead if necessary.

Drum revolves noisily or catches

POSSIBLE CAUSE Button, coin or small item of clothing is caught between inner and outer drums.
ACTION Remove object (see facing page).

Dryer runs unevenly

POSSIBLE CAUSE Brake cable is stuck.
ACTION Free the brake (see page 329).

Drum vibrates excessively

POSSIBLE CAUSE Clothes are unevenly distributed.
ACTION Stop the dryer and when the drum is stationary, redistribute the clothes more evenly, pressing them down into the drum. Tuck a tea towel over the top of the clothes to hold them in place.

POSSIBLE CAUSE The spin-dryer is not standing on a level surface.
ACTION Use a spirit level and an offcut of rubber-backed carpeting to get the dryer level.

Squash racket: SEE TENNIS RACKET

Stained-glass window:
SEE LEADED LIGHTS

Stainless steel

Despite its name, stainless steel can become marked if it is not cared for properly. Poor quality stainless steel will pit and scratch easily, so buy the best quality whenever possible.

Caring for stainless steel

WASHING Stainless steel can be washed by hand or in a dishwasher. If washed by hand, it should be dried quickly to prevent mineral salts in the water leaving white marks on it.

SOAKING Don't soak stainless steel dishes, cutlery or pans for longer than necessary, and avoid letting them come in contact with household bleach, salt or undissolved detergent, which can cause pitting of the surface.

Keeping a kitchen sink shiny

• Stainless steel sinks should be rinsed every time they are used, and dried with a soft cloth or sheet of paper towel, to prevent white marks forming, particularly in hard-water areas (see *Limescale & hard water*).
• Greasy marks can be removed by rubbing the sink with undiluted washing-up liquid applied on a soft cloth. Avoid using abrasive cleaners or scouring pads as they will scratch the surface of the sink.
• Polish the sink occasionally with a stainless steel polish, such as Shiny Sinks, to maintain the shine and remove very small surface scratches.

Stains

Try to remove stains as quickly as possible after they happen. If they are left, they tend to 'set' and can be more difficult, or even impossible, to remove.

Always test a treatment on an inconspicuous part of the item being cleaned, to make sure it doesn't cause more problems than it solves, such as bleaching or causing the colours in the item to run.

Most stain-removal treatments are more effective with several light applications. On carpets and upholstery, in particular, the treatment may leave a noticeably cleaner area, so you may need to use a carpet shampoo on the area around the stain to 'blend in' the cleaner patch.

USE A WASHING-UP BOWL

A plastic washing-up bowl inside a stainless steel sink will prevent the sink becoming scratched by contact with cutlery and crockery.

Stains (cont.)

Stain removal techniques

When removing stains, using the correct technique is almost as important as using the right preparation.

BLOTTING The amount of damage caused by most spills and stains can be reduced by quick action.

If liquid is spilled on a carpet or upholstery, blot it as quickly as possible with white paper towel, an old tea towel or any non-valuable white cloth. Keep turning the paper or cloth to a clean surface, and discard it and use fresh paper or a clean cloth as soon as it has absorbed the liquid. Do not blot up spills with coloured paper napkins — the dye in them could make the spill worse.

If the spill has gone deep into the carpet, blot up as much as possible, then lay a wad of white paper towel over the area and leave something heavy, but not metal, on it to aid the absorption of the liquid.

DABBING To avoid leaving a 'high-water mark' when using a liquid chemical or solvent, lay the stained section over a towel or other absorbent cloth.

Wrap a clean cloth round your finger, saturate it with cleaning fluid and, to prevent the stain spreading, dab in a circle round the stain, gradually moving in on the stain.

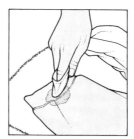

To avoid damaging the fabric and spreading the stain, dab the stain with a cloth rather than rubbing it.

DIPPING When a stain has to be dipped into a solution, hold the cloth by the stained area and twist the unstained parts. This should stop the solution spreading throughout the fabric. Take care if the fabric is fragile, as twisting could distort the fibres.

SOAKING Dissolve detergent thoroughly before immersing the fabric. Try to keep items completely immersed. Soak most fabrics for 15-20 minutes in hand-hot water. If you intend soaking the item overnight use cold water.

Don't soak coloured and white clothing together — the colours may run and discolour the whites.

Test coloured fabrics before soaking them by damping a small section on an inside seam or hem allowance. Then lay a clean white cloth such as a handkerchief over the damp area, and iron it. If colour comes off on the handkerchief, do not soak the garment, but have it dry-cleaned.

SPOTTING Minor stains can be treated without washing the whole garment by applying a prewash treatment such as Vanish, or a liquid detergent with no added dye.

Spray it onto the stain or apply it neat with an old toothbrush. Then remove it by sponging with a clean, damp cloth.

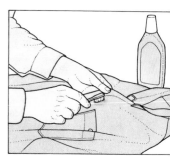

WHEN STAINS HAPPEN AWAY FROM HOME

- Grease: sprinkle the stain with talcum powder.
- Other stains: dip a clean cloth into water and sponge the area. Wash the garment properly as soon as possible.
- 'Dry-clean only' garment: soak up the stain with white tissue or handkerchief and take the garment to a dry-cleaner as soon as possible.

Removing stains from carpets, clothes and furniture

Most stains are either water based or grease based. Most water-based stains are treated with a shampoo or a detergent. Grease-based stains are treated with a solvent.

The following guide will help you to decide on the correct treatment for different stains. If you are at all unsure, it is safer to take the garment to a dry-cleaner as soon as possible because they may refuse to guarantee the removal of a stain if you have already tried to clean it.

Beetroot

SURFACE Clothing.

TREATMENT Rinse in cold water. White fabric: sprinkle laundry borax on damp stain. Stretch over a basin and pour boiling water over stain. Coloured fabric: soak whole garment in borax solution – about 15 ml ($\frac{1}{2}$ fl oz) borax to 500 ml (1 pint) water.

Blood

SURFACE Carpet.

TREATMENT Sponge with cold water or soda water. Blot firmly with paper towel. Finish with carpet shampoo.

SURFACE Clothing.

TREATMENT Soak in cold salt water. Launder as usual in biological detergent.

SURFACE Mattress.

TREATMENT Stand the mattress on its side while sponging it with cold water. Dry it with a hair dryer.

Candle wax

SURFACE Carpet.

TREATMENT Allow the wax to harden. Scrape off as much as possible with a blunt knife.

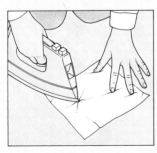

Place blotting paper or several layers of white paper towel over the spot and press with the tip of a warm iron. Repeat with clean paper until no more wax can be absorbed.

SURFACE Clothing.

TREATMENT Remove the wax in the same manner as recommended for carpets (above), and then dab with methylated spirit to remove any colour marks.

Chewing gum

SURFACE Carpet.

TREATMENT Wrap ice cubes in plastic and press onto the gum. Pick off as much as possible by hand. Rub residue with white spirit or meths on a cloth.

Alternatively, use a proprietary chewing gum remover, such as Stain Devils Chewing Gum Remover.

SURFACE Clothing.

TREATMENT As above, but dirty residue may need washing out with a detergent afterwards. Or, put garment in a plastic bag in the freezer overnight, then pick off gum.

Chocolate

SURFACE Carpet.

TREATMENT Scrape off excess. Use carpet shampoo.

SURFACE Clothing.

TREATMENT Soak in biological detergent, if washable. If the stain remains, dab white clothes with bleach solution.

Coffee

SURFACE Carpet.

TREATMENT Blot dry and treat with carpet shampoo. When dry, use grease solvent on milk or cream residue.

SURFACE Clothing.

TREATMENT Spray with prewash stain remover, then wash normally in a detergent that contains bleach.

If the stain remains, dab it with hydrogen peroxide 6% (20 vol). Or soak or wash it in heavy-duty detergent.

SURFACE Cups.

TREATMENT Fill with household bleach solution or denture cleaner. Leave until the stain disappears.

Continued overleaf

Continued overleaf

Removing stains from carpets, clothes and furniture (cont.)

Colour-runs

SURFACE Clothing.
TREATMENT Use a proprietary colour-run remover. Or soak white fabrics in diluted household bleach or hydrogen peroxide 6% (20 vol) for half an hour. Rinse and wash.

Cosmetics

SURFACE Carpet.
TREATMENT Dab with a grease-solvent fluid such as Dabitoff or K2r. Finish off with carpet shampoo.

SURFACE Clothing.
TREATMENT Remove grease with solvent fluid. Treat colour with heavy-duty detergent containing bleach.

Crayons

SURFACE Clothing.
TREATMENT Remove wax with grease solvent and colour with heavy-duty detergent containing bleach. Wash.

SURFACE Walls.
TREATMENT Various (see *Graffiti & scribbles*).

Curry

SURFACE Carpets.
TREATMENT Remove deposits. Rub mark lightly with borax solution – about 15 ml ($\frac{1}{2}$ fl oz) borax to 500 ml (1 pint) water. Treat persistent stain with neat glycerine, left in for 10 minutes. Sponge with warm water; blot dry.

SURFACE Clothing.
TREATMENT Treat the stain immediately, or keep it wet. Non-washable: sponge with warm borax solution, as above. If ineffective, have it dry-cleaned. Washable: rinse well in warm water. Apply equal quantities of glycerine and warm water, or neat liquid detergent. Rinse again after an hour. Launder with biological detergent. Or try Stain Devils Sauce and Spice Stain Remover.

Deodorant

SURFACE Clothing.
TREATMENT Sponge with solution of one part hydrogen peroxide 6% (20 vol) to six parts water. Then wash with heavy-duty detergent.

Egg

SURFACE Clothing.
TREATMENT Soak in biological detergent dissolved in tepid water. Then wash in biological detergent.

Glue

SURFACE Carpet and clothing.
TREATMENT Numerous solvents available (see *Glues*).

Grass

SURFACE Clothing.
TREATMENT Dab the stain with methylated spirit, then rinse in warm water and detergent. If a stain remains, soak it in glycerine, then wash it normally.

Gravy

SURFACE Clothing.
TREATMENT Soak in biological detergent dissolved in tepid water. Then launder in biological detergent.

Grease

SURFACE Carpet.
TREATMENT Dab with a grease solvent. Alternatively, place a sheet of blotting paper or several thicknesses of paper towel over the mark and apply heat with the tip of a warm iron. Keep repeating the action with clean paper until no more grease is absorbed.

SURFACE Clothing.
TREATMENT If washable, soak it in biological detergent. Check the care label first. Wash with heavy-duty liquid detergent in the hottest water the fabric can stand. Take non-washable garments to a dry-cleaner.

SURFACE Leather furniture.
TREATMENT Cover stain with rubber adhesive (e.g. from a bicycle puncture kit). First, test for 10 minutes on a hidden part in case it affects the colour.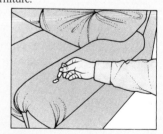
   Leave it on for 24 hours to absorb grease. Peel it off and apply hide food. Do not use a grease solvent.

Ink (also ball point and felt tip)

SURFACE Carpet and clothes.
TREATMENT Move fast to treat the mark before it sets permanently. Ball point: dab with methylated spirit on a cotton bud. Fountain-pen ink: blot with paper towel, and then sponge the mark with cold water. Alternatively, treat with Carpet Devils Ink Stain Remover. Felt-tip pen: use methylated spirit, then wash normally.

Removing stains from carpets, clothes and furniture (cont.)

SURFACE Vinyl.
TREATMENT Scrub the stain immediately with a soft nailbrush and warm liquid detergent solution.

SURFACE Leather.
TREATMENT If it is washable leather, swab the area with cotton wool dipped in milk.

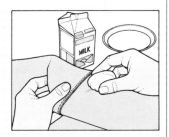

Then wipe it with a warm soap-flake solution, wetting the leather as little as possible. Make sure you remove all traces of milk to prevent odour from developing.

Lipstick

SURFACE Carpet.
TREATMENT Remove surface deposits with a blunt knife.

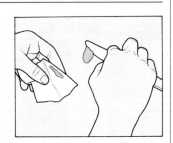

Treat with grease solvent. If colour remains, apply meths carefully on cotton-wool bud. Do not smear.

SURFACE Clothing and upholstery.
TREATMENT Nonwashable: use grease solvent. If colour remains, use methylated spirit on cotton-wool bud. Washable: Treat with biological detergent. Wash normally.

SURFACE Painted walls.
TREATMENT Rub wall with cloth wrung out in warm biological-detergent solution. Use cream-type household cleaner on a damp sponge for stronger stains.

Mildew

SURFACE Clothing.
TREATMENT The damage could be permanent. Try bleaching white fabrics, or soak and wash in heavy-duty detergent with oxygen bleach.

SURFACE Shower curtain.
TREATMENT Sponge with weak solution of household bleach. Treat area with proprietary fungicide for showers.

Milk

SURFACE Carpet.
TREATMENT Act fast, or the smell stays. Blot, then wet with soda water or warm water. Spot-clean with carpet cleaner.

SURFACE Clothing.
TREATMENT Rinse it in lukewarm water, then launder in warm detergent. Treat any remaining stain with a grease solvent, when dry. If the milk was very creamy, soak the garment in borax solution – about 15 ml ($\frac{1}{2}$ fl oz) borax to 500 ml (1 pint) water – then wash it. If garment is wool, sponge with the borax solution, but do not soak it.

Mud

SURFACE Carpet.
TREATMENT Leave it to dry completely before brushing or vacuuming. Use carpet shampoo to remove final traces.

SURFACE Clothing.
TREATMENT Let it dry, then brush off as much as possible. Wash in heavy-duty detergent containing bleach.

Paint

SURFACE Carpet.
TREATMENT Treat immediately. Oil based: dab carefully with white spirit on a cotton bud. Emulsion: sponge with cold water. Do not spread the marks.

If the paint dries, the mark is permanent. If it has dried on a cut pile carpet, use fine scissors to trim the paint marks off the surface of the pile.

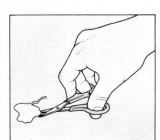

SURFACE Clothing.
TREATMENT Treat immediately, as for carpet above, but follow up with a wash in heavy-duty detergent.

Perspiration

SURFACE Clothing.
TREATMENT Dab with a solution of 1 tablespoon vinegar in a cup of water and leave for 5 minutes. Soak in biological detergent if washable, then wash in biological detergent. Old perspiration stains may not come out.

Continued overleaf

Removing stains from carpets, clothes and furniture (cont.)

Rust

SURFACE Clothing and table linen.
TREATMENT Rub with a cut lemon, then cover the stain with salt and leave it for an hour.

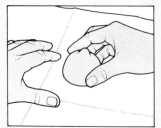

Rinse and launder as normal. Alternatively, use Stain Devils Rust and Iron Mould Stain Remover.

Scorch marks

SURFACE Carpet.
TREATMENT Loosen burnt fibres by rubbing them with the edge of a coin or with a suede brush.

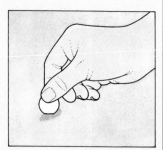

Trim off light scorch marks with fine scissors, but bad marks may have to be patched (see *Carpet maintenance*: 'Patching a damaged carpet').

SURFACE Clothing.
TREATMENT Washable: rub a light mark, fabric to fabric, under cold running water, then soak it in a warm borax solution – about 15 ml ($\frac{1}{2}$ fl oz) borax to 500 ml (1 pint) water. Launder as usual.

Nonwashable: Sponge with a glycerine solution – equal parts of glycerine and water – to loosen light marks; leave for an hour, then sponge with warm water. On heavier marks, dab with borax solution, as above.

Shoe polish

SURFACE Carpet.
TREATMENT Dab it first with a grease solvent and then with methylated spirit. Finish off with carpet shampoo.

SURFACE Clothing.
TREATMENT Treat as cosmetics.

Tea

SURFACE Carpet and clothing.
TREATMENT Treat as coffee.

SURFACE Cups.
TREATMENT Fill with a bleach solution and leave until stains disappear. Or use a denture cleaner.

Unknown stains

SURFACE Clothing.
TREATMENT Apply neat glycerine and leave for an hour. Then cool wash in heavy-duty biological detergent.

Urine

SURFACE Carpet.
TREATMENT Blot with paper towel, then treat with carpet shampoo, adding one egg cup of vinegar to about 500 ml (1 pint) shampoo. Then deodorise with a proprietary cleaner (e.g. Petstains).

SURFACE Mattress.
TREATMENT See *Mattress*.

Vomit

SURFACE Carpet.
TREATMENT Scrape up deposits and blot with paper towel. Treat with carpet shampoo and a little disinfectant.

SURFACE Clothing.
TREATMENT Shake off surface deposit then rinse under cold running water. Soak the garment in biological detergent and then wash normally.

SURFACE Mattress.
TREATMENT See *Mattress*.

Wine

SURFACE Carpet.
TREATMENT Blot fresh spills, then treat with carpet shampoo. Do not use salt because it stays damp and attracts dirt. Try glycerine on old stains: leave a solution of equal parts of glycerine and water on a spot for an hour, then sponge with water.

SURFACE Clothing and table linen.
TREATMENT Mop up excess, then apply salt to stain. Sponge the stain with a detergent solution as soon as possible. Or blot excess and then pour a little soda water or white wine onto stain. Blot again.

For dried stains on white fabric: apply glycerine, as above, then soak in heavy-duty detergent containing bleach. If the stain persists, dab with diluted hydrogen peroxide 6% (20 vol). Rinse well and launder as usual.

Stairs & staircases

(SEE ALSO BALUSTERS)

Timber expands and contracts according to its moisture content. Very often when central heating is installed in a house, the humidity drops and causes the wood in a staircase to shrink. Treads and risers in the stairs come loose, and creak when they are walked on.

Curing a creaking tread Time: depends on method used

Although creaks in stairs are often caused by loose treads, it is possible for an apparently secure tread to creak.

> YOU WILL NEED Possibly: Power drill and bits, countersink bit, screwdriver, wood screws, wood filler, sandpaper, old chisel, hammer, wood glue, panel pins, talcum powder or french chalk, epoxy resin wood repair paste, angle brackets.

TREAD SEEMS SECURE The problem may be that the creaking tread needs to be screwed to the riser beneath it.

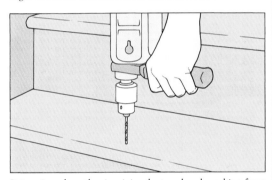

Determine where the riser joins the tread and, working from above, drill down (through the tread only) to make three clearance holes that will coincide with the top of the riser.

Then, with a finer drill bit, make pilot holes for the screws in the wood of the riser to prevent the screws from splitting the wood (see *Screws*). Countersink the three clearance holes and drive in the wood screws. The wood may groan as pressure is applied.

Fill the holes above the screw heads with wood filler, allow it to set and then sand them smooth.

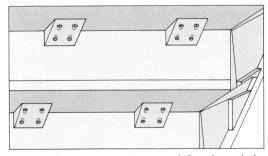

TREADS AND RISERS LOOSE Try to work from beneath the staircase, where you will find triangular blocks of wood screwed or glued into the angles between treads and risers.

If any are loose, tighten the screws, or prise off glued ones with an old chisel. Clean off any old glue that sticks to them and use wood glue to fix them back in place. Keep them secure with panel pins while the glue is setting.

Examine the slim wooden wedges that fit into tapered slots in the supports at each end of the treads and risers.

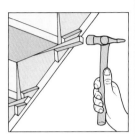

Remove any wedges that are loose, then apply wood glue to them and tap them firmly back into place.

If you cannot get underneath the stairs, try to force talcum powder or french chalk into any visible cracks.

Alternatively, you can use a chisel to force apart any gaps and squeeze wood glue or epoxy resin wood repair paste into them. In addition, screw the treads to the risers (see left).

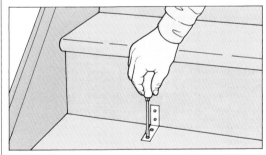

Another alternative is to screw on two or three small angle brackets to hold the tread to the riser, inset flush with the wood and positioned where they are least visible.

Repairing a cracked tread Time: 1 hour or less

Treads that become too dry may crack along the grain of the wood. If you can get underneath the staircase, you may be able to remove the tightening wedges and triangular support blocks so that the tread can be withdrawn and repaired or replaced. However, if this is impossible, you may still be able to mend the crack.

> YOU WILL NEED Spare timber, wood screws, screwdriver, wood glue, G-cramp, wood filler, sandpaper. Possibly: paint, wood stain, epoxy resin wood repair paste.

If the crack runs the full width of the tread, cut two wooden battens and screw them to the tread, parallel with the crack, one on each side of the crack.

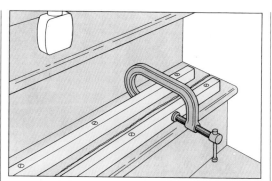

Insert wood glue into the crack and then fix a G-cramp to the two pieces of wood. This will apply pressure to the wood and pull the two sections of the tread together.

Once the glue has set, remove the cramp and the battens. Fill the screw holes with wood filler and sand them down. If necessary, paint or stain the wood filler.

If the crack does not run the full width of the tread, fill it with an epoxy resin wood repair paste. Allow it to set hard and then sand it smooth. Redecorate as necessary.

Tightening a loose newel post Time: 2 hours or less

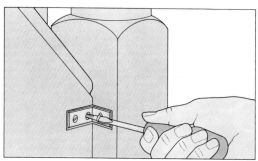

Movement in a newel post can be stopped by screwing small angle brackets to the base of the post on both sides, and fixing them to the wooden staircase beside it.

To make the repair less conspicuous, chisel out recesses for the brackets – about 3 mm ($\frac{1}{8}$ in) deep. Cover the brackets with wood filler, sand smooth and redecorate.

If it is necessary to reglue the handrail to the newel post, use a mallet to tap the post away from the handrail.

However, first you may have to drive out the dowel (right) which goes through both post and rail. Use a hammer and a steel rod just smaller than the dowel, or a short piece of smaller diameter dowel.

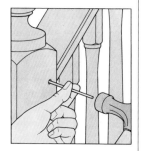

Apply wood glue to the section of the rail that fits into the post. Tap it back into place and then replace the dowel.

Handrails on a lightweight block wall

If a handrail has been fixed to a lightweight block wall, no standard wall plug is suitable for refixing it, as the block is too soft to give a good grip.

Instead, get professional help to install chemical anchors. They don't rely on expansion to grip securely, but consist of a resin which mixes with a hardener inside the cavity. Once set, they are very strong.

You can tell when a wall is made of lightweight building block by the grey colour of the dust produced when you drill. Building blocks drill more easily than brick, which produces red dust.

Securing a wall-mounted handrail Time: 2 hours or less

A loose handrail on a wall beside a flight of stairs should be fixed promptly, as people may put their full weight on it for support if they stumble when using the stairs.

It may be possible to make the handrail secure once more by tightening the screws that hold it to the wall, or by using slightly larger screws in the same holes.

However, if a number of fixing points on the wall are damaged or crumbling, it will be better to take down the entire handrail and repair the faulty holes.

YOU WILL NEED Screwdriver. Possibly: screws, electric drill, masonry bit, Rawlbloc wall plugs, interior filler.

SOLID WALL Remove one of the brackets from the handrail and take it to your hardware shop or DIY outlet to ensure that you buy Rawlbloc wall plugs which will fit through the holes in the bracket. Various sizes are available.

Try the Rawlbloc plugs in the holes in the wall, and if necessary, enlarge the holes slightly to get a snug fit. The holes must be just a little deeper than the plugs.

Pass the screws through the holes in the handrail bracket, press on the plugs and then insert the plugs and screws into the wall. You may need a helper.

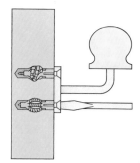

First tighten the screw in the upper hole with a screwdriver. The Rawlbloc plug is designed so that this action draws up the end of the plug to give a firm fixing inside the hole.

Then tighten the screw in the lower hole.

Alternatively, if the wall is too badly damaged to do this, repair the damaged area with interior filler (see *Fillers & stoppers*) and make a new fixing a little farther along the wall, using Rawlbloc wall plugs, as described.

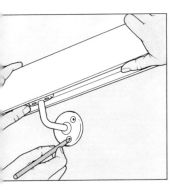

Fix the bracket to the handrail in a new position. Then get a helper to hold the handrail in place while you mark the new position of the screws on the wall. (If you fix the bracket to the wall first, it may not line up with the rail.)

Fix the handrail securely to the wall with Rawlblocs.

HOLLOW WALL If the wall is hollow, the brackets must be screwed directly into the wooden supports behind the plasterboard. To locate the wood, tap the wall with the handle of a screwdriver – a dull thud will indicate the position of supporting wood battens – or use a battery-operated wire, pipe and stud detector (see page 158).

Static electricity

Static is the name given to the small electric charge which causes clothes to stick together, dust to cling to television screens and unpleasant shocks when you touch a car door or a filing cabinet, specially in cold, dry weather.

Static usually arises from friction. Almost everybody has had the experience of picking up static by walking across certain types of carpet, or of finding their hair standing on end after pulling off a jumper.

If the charge in your body is big enough, a spark jumps the gap to earth itself, giving you a small electric shock.

Six ways to combat static

● Moisture in the air or sprayed onto surfaces can help. Try using a humidifier or putting bowls of water or potted plants in the room if static becomes very bad.
● Antistatic sprays and impregnated cloths are available which may help to cut down static on electronic equipment such as computers and TV sets. These sprays and cloths appear to work both by neutralising the charge and by lubricating the surfaces so that there is less friction.
● A few drops of vinegar in the final rinsing water may help to stop your hair rising to meet the brush or comb.

● If you get shocks from touching metal door knobs or office filing cabinets, try touching the wooden frame round the door, or the card label on the filing cabinet, before touching the metal.

● A generous handful of hand cream, rubbed over your legs and tights, will stop petticoats and skirts clinging. The cream appears to cut down the friction that causes static.
● It is claimed that ionisers can reduce static; however, it is not certain that the claims are justified.

Shocks from your car and how to prevent them

A number of factors – including what you are wearing – can determine whether you get a shock from your car.

TYRES The more tread on your tyres, the less static can escape harmlessly into the ground. So you are more likely to get a shock from your car when the tyres are new.

YOUR CLOTHES Freshly laundered clothes, especially those made of synthetic fibres, seem to give rise to more static.

YOUR SHOES You are more likely to get a shock when you are wearing rubber or synthetic soles than when wearing leather soles. Try driving in leather-soled shoes only.

PREVENTION To avoid getting shocks from a car, the static electricity that builds up needs to be discharged safely.

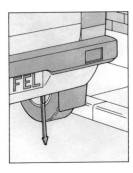

It is possible to buy a special strip made of granulated copper embedded in rubber, from car accessory shops. It is fixed to the back of the car and trails along the ground, earthing electricity safely as it builds up. Chains and wires that work in the same way are also available.

This technique is widely used by the drivers of petrol tankers who cannot risk a spark igniting their load.

Another method is to touch your car's metal framework before getting out of it. This allows the electricity in your body to disperse into the car's body and be earthed safely.

Steps

Never ignore damaged garden steps – they could be the cause of a serious fall, especially in wet weather.

Repairing concrete steps Time: depends on area

Where the steps have been made from concrete slabs, it may be possible to take out the damaged slab and turn it round so that a new edge is exposed.

If this is not possible, and the damage is minor, chip away all loose material and build up the damaged area with an epoxy-based repair concrete such as Febset NF. It sets quickly and is stronger than normal concrete.

Steps (cont.)

CLEAN AND PROTECT STEPS

Special cleaners are available for treating steps, patios and paths. Not only do they remove grime, but they discourage the growth of mould.

Where steps have been cast in concrete, and the damage to the edge of one or more steps is considerable, it is possible to rebuild the damaged area.

> **YOU WILL NEED** Cold chisel, club hammer, heavy-duty gloves, safety spectacles, mixing board, shingle, sand, cement, waterproof PVA adhesive, rubber gloves, bucket, paintbrush, bricks, heavy gauge polythene sheet, trowel, stiff-bristled brush.

Protect your hands with heavy-duty gloves and your eyes with safety spectacles. Then with a cold chisel and a club hammer, chip away any unsound concrete from round the damaged area.

On a wooden mixing board, make up a dry mixture of three parts shingle to two parts sand and one part cement. Then, in a bucket, make a liquid mixture of one part waterproof PVA adhesive to four parts water.

Put on a pair of rubber gloves to protect your hands, as working with cement will burn them. Moisten the dry mixture with the liquid one, adding a little at a time, until the mixture compacts in the hand like a sand pie.

With an old paintbrush, apply a generous coat of undiluted waterproof PVA adhesive to the damaged area.

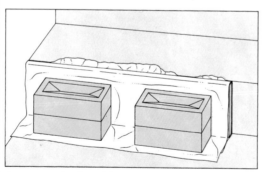

Cover a wooden board that is the same height as the step with heavy gauge polythene sheeting, to stop it sticking to the cement, and place it firmly against the riser of the damaged step. Support it with a couple of bricks.

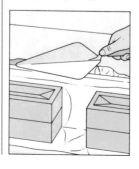

Use a trowel to apply the adhesive concrete mixture to the damaged edge of the step, pressing it down to compact it.

Smooth the surface and leave it to dry with the board in place for at least 24 hours. Then remove the board.

HOLLOW IN STEP Where concrete has crumbled away and left a hole or hollow in a step, brush away all the loose material with an old paintbrush and coat the damaged area with waterproof PVA adhesive.

Then make up a concrete mixture (or use Febset NF) and apply it to the damaged step, smoothing it with a trowel. If the rest of the step is textured, brush the damp mixture with a stiff-bristled brush before it sets.

Repairing brick steps

Where possible, pull out damaged bricks and turn them to expose a new face. In cases of serious damage, replace damaged bricks with new bricks of similar size and colour. Fix them in place with ready-mixed bagged mortar.

Slippery steps

Algae and mosses can form a dangerously slippery surface on steps when they are wet and should be removed.

> **YOU WILL NEED** Fungicide, watering can, stiff broom. Possibly: exterior grade PVA adhesive, silver sand.

Treat the affected steps with a proprietary fungicide, available at most garden centres. Use a watering can to apply it, but be sure to wash the can out well after use.

Allow time for the fungicide to kill the growth, then sweep away the debris with a stiff garden broom. Then apply a further coat of fungicide to act as a deterrent.

SMOOTH STEPS Make smooth steps less slippery by painting them with a layer of exterior grade PVA adhesive and sprinkling them while still wet with a fine layer of silver sand. This treatment will need to be repeated every year.

Repairing worn wooden steps

> **YOU WILL NEED** Tenon saw or panel saw, spare timber, pencil, waterproof wood adhesive, power drill and bits, countersink bit, wood screws, screwdriver, sandpaper.

Where the edges of wooden steps are worn, you may be able to turn a wooden step in order to expose new timber.

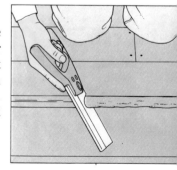

If you cannot remove the step, use a tenon saw or a panel saw to make a cut at a 45-degree angle at each end of the damaged area. Remove the worn piece and save it to use as a template.

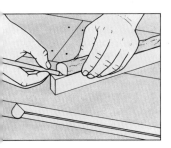

Choose a piece of timber of the same type and of very similar dimensions as the step, and use the template to help you measure and cut a matching piece.

Plane the new piece to size and make screw holes.

Then, using a waterproof wood adhesive and wood screws, glue and screw the new piece of wood to the old wood at the edge of the step. Countersink the screw heads.

When the wood adhesive has set, sand the join.

Stereo: SEE HI-FI

Sticky labels

Sticky labels and their adhesive residue can be difficult to remove. Different surfaces require different treatments.

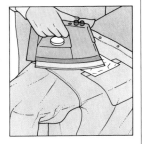

FABRIC Cover the label with aluminium foil and iron it with a warm iron to soften the adhesive. Peel off the label while it is still warm.

A stain remover designed for removing glue and chewing gum will get rid of the residue left when sticky labels are not properly removed from clothing (see *Stains*).

CHINA, GLASS AND VITREOUS ENAMEL Soak the label in warm water. If it won't come off, rub with methylated spirit, white spirit or cellulose thinners, which should remove the residue as well as the label. It may take a few minutes.

METAL Use nail-varnish remover or Mangers De-Solv-it, which is available in DIY stores. Wipe down and dry the surface afterwards. (Do not use this treatment on vitreous enamel, which should be treated as glass.)

PLASTIC CONTAINERS Fill reusable plastic containers with hot water to loosen stubborn self-adhesive labels.

PLASTIC AUDIO-TAPE BOXES Use dry-cleaning solvent such as Dabitoff to remove residue from unwanted sticky labels.

WALLS Rub or dab at the mark with a ball of Blu-Tack, or a similar reusable product to lift off sticky residue.

Stitches: SEE OVERLEAF

Stockings: SEE TIGHTS & STOCKINGS

Stonework

Much of the stone that is used in building is relatively soft and porous, so it collects dirt and grime. Because of its porous nature, it is best not to clean stonework with powders or detergents, as they can cause permanent staining. Some specialist products are available which don't stain, but there are also other options.

Cleaning stonework with a brush Time: depends on area

> YOU WILL NEED Stiff scrubbing brush, bucket, warm water. Possibly: newspapers or cloth, hose.

Using a stiff scrubbing brush and bucket of clean, warm water, start scrubbing at the top of the wall and work downwards, changing the water frequently.

If it is an interior wall, protect the floor with newspapers before starting, and if it is an exterior one, finish off by spraying the newly washed wall with a hose.

Pressure-cleaning a stone wall Time: depends on area

> YOU WILL NEED High-pressure water washer and lance. Possibly: large water container.

It is possible to hire a high-pressure cold-water washer with a lance. Some can be connected direct to the mains water supply. Others may require a reservoir of water, such as a water butt. Take care, when using the washer, not to direct a jet of water into gaps around window or door frames, or under the eaves, because water forced in under pressure can lead to wet rot.

Abrading stonework Time: depends on area

> YOU WILL NEED Power drill, wire cup brush, safety spectacles, simple face mask, garden gloves.

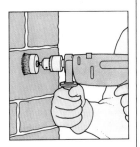

Where stonework does not respond to washing or pressure-cleaning, expose a new surface by abrading away the discoloured areas with a wire cup brush attached to a power drill. Apply only light pressure.

Protect your eyes and hands from flying bits of stone by wearing safety spectacles and garden gloves.

Continued on page 344

SMALL REPAIRS TO STONEWORK

Small areas of damage, such as a broken windowsill corner, can be repaired with an epoxy-based repair mortar and coloured to match with masonry paint.

STITCHES

Numerous stitches are used in sewing by hand, but those shown here are the ones you are most likely to need for the repairs explained in this book. All instructions are given for right-handed people. If you are left-handed, reverse the directions, left to right. A contrasting thread has been used, in order to show the stitches; normally, you would use a matching thread.

STARTING AND FINISHING
A small backstitch can be used to secure the thread at the beginning and end of a row of stitching.

BACKSTITCH
Used for making a strong, neat seam. Insert the needle half a stitch-length behind the point where the thread emerged, and then bring it out the same distance in front.

RUNNING STITCH
Used for fine seams, gathers, tucks and repairs on delicate fabrics. Weave the point of the needle in and out of the fabric several times, then pull the thread through.

SLANT HEMMING STITCH
Quick, but not durable, because a lot of thread is exposed and it can be snagged easily.

OVERCAST STITCH
Used for finishing the raw edges of a seam. Work from either side, taking diagonal stitches from back to front. Do not pull the stitches so tight that the edge of the fabric curls over.

TAILOR'S TACKS
Used for transferring fold lines, dart lines or centre folds, from a paper pattern to the fabric. For further details see *Collars & cuffs*.

WHIPSTITCH
Used to sew two finished edges together, picking up only a few threads in each.

TACKING (OR BASTING)
Used for holding two or more pieces of fabric together temporarily. To make identifying it easier when you come to remove it, use a thread of a contrasting colour.

OVERHAND STITCH
Used to join two finished edges, such as when attaching lace or ribbon to a garment or joining two folded edges. The exposed stitches, over the top of the sewing, should be vertical.

SLIP HEMMING STITCH
Strong and almost invisible. Bring the thread up through the fold. Take a one-thread stitch and take the needle straight back inside the fold.

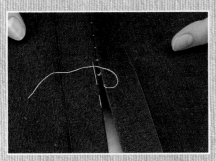

SLIP-STITCH An almost invisible means of joining two folded edges by running the thread back and forth between them, inside the folds.

BLANKET STITCH
Used for edging heavy fabric. Insert the needle in the upper side of the fabric. Keeping the point above the thread, pull it through, forming a stitch over the edge.

WORKING A BUTTONHOLE
Make the stitches very small, with no space between them.

BUTTONHOLE STITCH Make a loop with the thread, and insert the needle, from the underside. Pull it out towards you and then pull it away from you, to place the stitch at the edge of the fabric.

Sandblasting stonework

Sandblasting is another means of exposing a new surface on discoloured stone, but this is best left to experts. Look for a specialist in *Yellow Pages* under 'Blast cleaning'.

Repairing a stone wall Time: depends on area

You can repair a stone wall that has been damaged by severe frost, which attacks the surface, causing it to flake away.

YOU WILL NEED Cold chisel, club hammer, brick bolster, safety spectacles, face mask, heavy-duty gardening gloves, water, PVA adhesive, dry-mix mortar, small trowel, replacement stone.

Wearing safety spectacles and heavy-duty gloves, cut out the damaged stone with a cold chisel and club hammer, to form a rectangular hole in the wall.

Keep cutting until you reach stone that is healthy – you may not necessarily have to cut very deep.

Take a piece of the damaged stone to a garden centre that supplies stone, and look for replacement pieces that match its texture and colour. Choose pieces that are about as thick as the area you have chiselled off.

Protecting your hands and eyes, use a brick bolster to cut the new stone to roughly the right shape, and then shape it more accurately with the cold chisel.

Add one part PVA adhesive to ten parts water, and mix it into the dry-mix mortar to create a fairly stiff consistency – like a sand pie. Alternatively, use ready-mixed mortar.

Dampen both the new stone and the existing wall so that they don't absorb water from the mortar and weaken it. Then line the hole with mortar.

Insert the new stone and point around its edges to match the style of pointing in the surrounding area (see *Brickwork*: 'What style of pointing?').

If you cannot find replacement stone to match, buy a dry colorant of the nearest colour and mix it with the mortar. Fill the hole with mortar and smooth it over.

Stopcock

A stopcock works like a tap. It controls the flow of water through a pipe, but it is sited in the middle of a pipe rather than at the end. Each house has a main stopcock which controls the flow of water into the house. The main stopcock is usually under the kitchen sink or in the cellar.

Turning off the stopcock is the first step in just about any plumbing emergency. Every member of your household should know where it is and how to turn it off.

Closing the water company's stopcock

The water company's stopcock is in a purpose-made pit near the boundary of the property, or set into the pavement outside. Look for a hinged metal cover about 10 cm (4 in) across. You will see a stopcock just out of arm's reach at the bottom of the 'guard pipe'.

This stopcock may have a crutch handle that can be turned with an improvised key made by cutting a V-shaped slot in one end of a 1 m (3 ft) piece of strong scrap wood. The slot should be about 2.5 cm (1 in) wide at the opening and about 7.5 cm (3 in) deep.

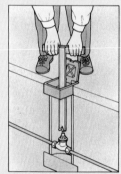

Fix another piece of wood as a crossbar handle at the other end. Slip the slot over the crutch handle and turn it clockwise to close the stopcock.

To turn a handle which has a tapered knob you will have to hire or buy a special key from a plumbers' merchant or the water company.

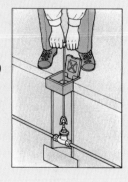

Fixing a dripping stopcock Time: 1 hour or less

YOU WILL NEED Adjustable spanner, penknife, screwdriver, wool, petroleum jelly.

If water is dripping from the spindle of a stopcock handle, the gland nut is probably the source of the problem. Deal with the leak immediately as water dripping onto a wooden floor may produce dry rot. Start by turning off the stopcock.

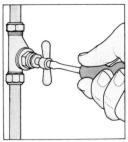

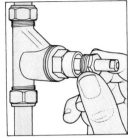

Then unscrew the tiny grub screw that retains the handle and either pull or tap the handle off its spindle.

Unscrew and remove the gland nut, which is the first nut through which the spindle of the stopcock passes.

Use a penknife or screwdriver to rake out the old packing material. Repack the space with ordinary knitting wool, steeped in petroleum jelly. Stuff the wool down hard into the space with a screwdriver blade. Continue until the packing material is caulked down hard.

Screw on the gland nut, finger-tight. Replace the handle and the grub screw. Turn on the stopcock and tighten the gland nut with the spanner until the dripping stops.

Rewashering a stopcock Time: ½ an hour or less

If turning off the stopcock does not completely cut off the cold-water supply to the kitchen tap, it needs rewashering.

> YOU WILL NEED Stopcock key, adjustable spanner or pipe wrench, bucket, new washer. Possibly: bowl.

To work on the stopcock, turn off its water supply by turning off the water company's stopcock (see facing page).

If there is a drain cock immediately above the stopcock, use it to drain the rising main into a bowl or bucket when you have turned off the water company's stopcock.

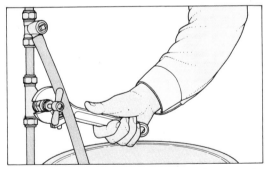

Use an adjustable spanner or a pipe wrench to grip the 'flats' of the stopcock's headgear and turn it anticlockwise. If there is no drain cock immediately above the stopcock, some water will flow out as you undo the headgear. Have a bucket and a bowl handy to catch it.

You will find the valve with the washer attached to it resting on the valve seating. Replace the washer, then reassemble the stopcock and restore the water supply.

Surfboard

Repairing surface damage Time: parts of 2 days

Surfboards are made of two symmetrical sides of polystyrene foam, joined together by a wooden backbone known as the stringer. The whole structure is coated in glass fibre. Most dents in the surfboard are repairable as long as the stringer has not been broken.

> YOU WILL NEED Glass-fibre resin, hardener, glass-fibre matting, thickening powder, sandpaper, spatula or brush, gloves, scissors.

Make sure that the inner foam is dry. Clean the surrounding area and roughen it with sandpaper.

Mix up the resin and the hardener strictly according to the instructions. If the gash penetrates the inner foam, add some thickening powder to the paste. This makes the paste lighter, to match the weight of the foam inside the board.

Use a spatula or a brush to apply the mixture of resin and hardener so that it is level with the surface of the rest of the board.

Cut a layer of glass-fibre matting to match the size of the repaired area or make it slightly larger, if necessary.

Lay the matting on the damaged area. Its surface will be slightly higher than the level of the board. Cover it with the mixture of resin and hardener.

When the repair is dry to the touch, sand it down so that it forms a perfect contour with the rest of the board's surface. Leave the repair to dry thoroughly overnight.

Repairing a torn-out leash plug Time: parts of 2 days

Sometimes the small metal plug that holds the leash can be pulled out of its fixing on the board. It is possible to replace the plug using the same materials and technique as for repairing surface damage (see above).

Repairing a torn-out fin

Replacing a torn-out fin is tricky and its position is important for the performance of the board. So take this type of repair to a specialist.

AN ALTERNATIVE TO THICKENING POWDER

If you cannot get hold of thickening powder, cut up the glass-fibre matting into small pieces instead and add it to the paste. Wearing gloves is advisable when you are handling glass fibre.

CARING FOR YOUR BOARD

If you wax your surfboard take care when scraping off the old wax not to damage the glass-fibre surface.

Table (SEE ALSO CASTORS)

A table may need to be repaired because of wear and tear or the drying effects of central heating. If it is very old or at all valuable, have it repaired professionally.

Levelling uneven legs Time: 2 hours or less

If a table appears to have uneven legs, make sure that it is the table and not the floor that is uneven. Place it on a flat level surface such as a sheet of hardboard or plywood. Use a spirit level to make sure that the board is level and adjust it if necessary.

> YOU WILL NEED Hardboard or plywood, spirit level, thin slivers of scrap wood, pair of compasses, fine-tooth tenon saw, fine sandpaper. Possibly: wood screw, drill, countersink bit, screwdriver.

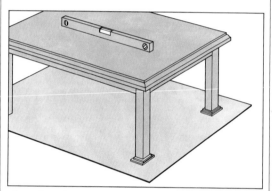

Place thin slivers of scrap wood under the short leg or legs of the table until it stands level and firm.

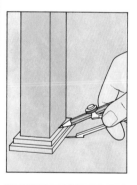

Choose the shortest leg (the one with most padding under it), and set a pair of compasses with the point touching the board and the pencil touching the bottom of the table leg.

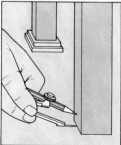

Mark all four sides of the other three table legs with the pencil in this position, keeping the point of the compasses on the board each time.

Saw the extra wood off the bottom of each leg so that they are even, and smooth the edges with fine sandpaper.

ONE SHORT LEG An alternative method is to cut a scrap of wood that fills the gap between the short leg and the floor, and attach it to the base of the leg with a countersunk screw. Smooth it with sandpaper to match the other legs.

Tightening loose legs Time: 1 hour or less

Look under the table to see how the legs are fixed in place. They may be held by glued joints, wing nuts which can be tightened by hand, or screws which need tightening.

Tap apart simple glued wooden joints with a rubber hammer or a mallet covered with a soft cloth. Remove old glue with a chisel and use wood adhesive to stick the joint back together. Clamp them in place with a sash cramp or use the tourniquet method (see *Chair*) to dry.

Strengthening corner joints Time: 2 hours or less

If the corner joints on a table come loose, it may be possible to strengthen them with metal braces.

> YOU WILL NEED Metal corner braces, pencil, bevel-edge chisel, coping saw or hacksaw, drill and twist bit, two nuts to fit the bolt supplied with the brace, spanner.

POSITIONING THE BRACES Turn the table upside-down on a surface that will not scratch it. Place a brace across the corner joint and mark where it touches the wood.

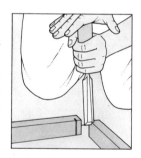

Remove the brace and use a bevel-edge chisel, coping saw or hacksaw to cut two small grooves in the side rails of the table to accommodate the brace.

Position the furniture leg between the side rails. Then hold the metal brace in place and use a pencil to mark on the leg where the bolt, which is supplied with the brace, will go through the hole.

Use the chisel to make a small flat surface at the mark then drill a start hole. Screw the bolt into the start hole by hand. Then screw two nuts onto the protruding end of the bolt so that they jam together. Use a spanner on the nuts to screw the bolt into the table leg. Remove the nuts.

FITTING THE BRACES Push the brace over the protruding bolt and slide the ends into the grooves cut into the side rails. Screw the wing nut onto the bolt. Repeat on the other corners. Then tighten all the wing nuts until the table is steady.

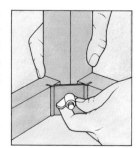

Repairing a loose or broken dowel joint

Time: ½ a day or less

YOU WILL NEED Screwdriver, rubber hammer or mallet, soft cloth, chisel, drill and twist bit, tenon saw, replacement dowels, sandpaper, wood glue, cardboard, sash cramps or sticks and cord for tourniquet. Possibly: luggage straps.

Turn the table over on a surface that will not scratch it and remove the screws that hold the top to the frame.

Hold the table frame firmly and tap apart the joint, using a rubber hammer or a cloth-covered mallet.

If possible, remove the dowels and use a chisel to scrape away any old glue that is left in the dowel holes.

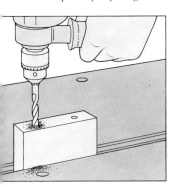

If a dowel has broken, cut the broken end flush with the rail. Drill out the remains of the dowel with a twist bit the same size as the dowel. Then blow the dust out of the hole (the dust will fly out of the hole so shut your eyes).

Cut new dowels to the correct length and taper the ends slightly with sandpaper to make insertion easier. Cover the ends with wood glue and push them into the holes.

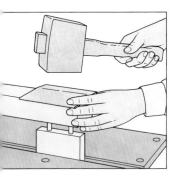

Tap the joint together, protecting the surface of the wood with a piece of wood or a thick piece of cardboard between the mallet and the wood.

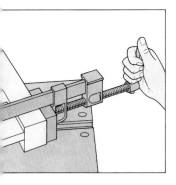

Wipe off any excess glue with a damp cloth, then clamp the joints together with sash cramps – or use the tourniquet method of clamping (see *Chair*). For the torniquet method luggage straps will do less damage than string or rope.

Allow the glue on the joint to dry completely then use the long screws to reattach the table top to the frame.

Repairing a split table top Time: parts of 2 days

A table top made from a single piece of wood may split part of the way across because of shrinkage. Once the split has released the pressure that caused it, it will not grow any longer. Rather than close the split and renew the pressure, it is possible to fill it with a strip of matching veneer.

YOU WILL NEED Coping saw or fret saw, strip of veneer, mallet, wood glue, sash cramp, plane, polish.

Because it is impossible to fill the tapering shape of this kind of split completely, saw down the length of the crack to make the sides parallel. If the split is curved, use a fret saw to follow its shape.

Cut a length of veener, slightly longer and deeper than necessary, and check that it will feed into the cut. Coat both sides of the piece of veneer with wood glue and use a mallet to tap it into place in the cut.

Clamp the table top with a sash cramp and wipe off surplus glue with a damp cloth. Allow the glue to set and when it is thoroughly dry, plane the veneer down to the level of the table. Then polish the repaired area.

Repairing a chipped table edge Time: parts of 2 days

YOU WILL NEED Wood batten, candle, edging cramps, putty knife, wood filler (epoxy filler is strongest), sandpaper, stain, varnish.

Rub candle wax along one face of a wood batten that is slightly longer than the damaged area, and clamp the waxed side to the edge of the table with edging cramps.

With a putty knife, force wood filler into the damaged area. If any section of the damage is greater than 6 mm ($\frac{1}{4}$ in) deep or long, do it in two or three coats, allowing each coat to dry before proceeding. Overfill the damaged area to allow for shrinkage.

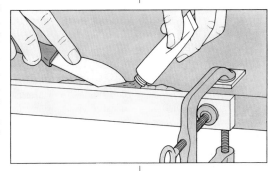

When the filler is dry, remove the wood batten and sand the edge smooth. Apply a stain and then varnish it.

Adjusting a drop-flap stay Time: 2 hours or less

Sometimes, with age, the drop flap on a table begins to sag. It is likely the stays that support it need adjusting.

YOU WILL NEED Slivers of hardwood, wood glue. Possibly: screwdriver, small hammer, electric drill, fine twist bit.

Turn the table upside-down on a smooth surface and examine the drop-flap stays. Tighten the screws, if necessary. When correctly positioned the stays should just touch the underside of the flap.

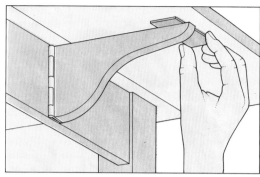

WOODEN STAYS If there is a gap between the stay and the table flap shape a sliver of wood so that it fills the gap. Glue it to the underside of the flap or the top of the stay.

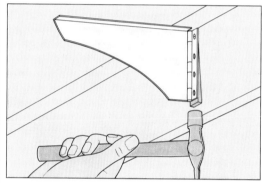

METAL STAY If the tip of the metal stay does not touch the the flap, remove the lower screws that hold the stay to the side rail of the table and slip in a wedge of wood, tapping it in until the stay touches the flap.

If necessary, drill fine clearance holes in the wooden wedges, then replace the screws.

CARING FOR YOUR BAT

Clean the rubber facing with soap and water, then dry the bat with a towel. Put on a bat cover immediately after playing.

Table tennis

If you cannot find a sports shop that specialises in table tennis, try calling the English Table Tennis Association (Tel. 01424 722525) who should be able to supply you with the name of a dealer in your area.

Cleaning a table tennis table

If the surface of your table becomes marked do not try to clean it with ordinary furniture polish as this can remove the nonreflective surface. Use a special cleaner.

Repairing a table tennis bat Time: $\frac{1}{2}$ a day or less

A common problem is that the rubber surface may come away from the wooden blade. Stick it down with a rubber-based glue. Follow the instructions on the tube.

Bats lose bits of rubber with age. Provided the chipped area doesn't encroach more than 6 mm ($\frac{1}{4}$ in) from the edge into the hitting surface, this is not a problem.

If you lose rubber from the middle of the bat, you should put on new rubber facing or buy a new bat. Most shops specialising in table tennis will fit a new rubber facing free of charge, but you can do it yourself.

YOU WILL NEED New rubber facing, contact rubber glue, craft knife. Possibly: fine sandpaper, scissors.

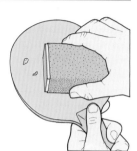

Peel off the old rubber. Use fine sandpaper if necessary to get it all off, leaving the wooden blade clean and smooth. Tidy up the edges with a pair of scissors, if they need it.

Spread glue evenly on both the blade and the new rubber and leave it until it is almost dry. Press the new facing onto the blade, starting at the centre, and leave it for about half an hour. Then trim off the excess rubber.

Official bat colours

The rules of table tennis state that bats used in official tournaments must have a red side and a black side. It may be best to fit these colours, in case you play in an official event.

Patching chipped table edges Time: 1 hour or less

If a folding table is stored with its outer edges touching the ground it may result in the edges getting chipped.

If you have to store a table in this way, make sure the hinged centre fold is on the ground. However, if the edge of a table gets chipped you can fix it yourself.

YOU WILL NEED Metal ruler, trimming knife, plywood, wood glue, sandpaper, paint, masking tape. Possibly: plastic wood.

Use a trimming knife and a metal ruler to remove a square from the table's surface. Cut the square a bit larger than the chip – don't remove any more than you have to. A square shape is much easier to fill.

Using the damaged piece as a pattern, cut an identical patch from plywood, so that it fits snugly into the hole.

If the patch is not level with the rest of the surface, use plastic wood to build up a flat base for it to sit on, until the patch makes a level top surface. Glue it in place and leave it to dry for about half an hour.

Sandpaper over the patch. Wipe it clean with a damp cloth, then dry it thoroughly. Paint it with a matching matt cellulose spray paint, protecting the surrounding areas with masking tape and newspaper.

Replacing the cord in a net Time: a few minutes

> YOU WILL NEED Large, thick needle or large safety pin, cotton thread, new net cord.

Pull out the old, damaged cord from one end of the net.

Feed a length of cotton thread into a large needle, double it and attach it to the end of the new net cord. Feed the needle through the net's cord channel, pulling the cord behind it (left).

Alternatively, pin a large safety pin to the end of the cord and feed it through.

If you have difficulty finding a replacement cord it may be better to buy a complete replacement net.

Tape recorder: SEE CASSETTE PLAYER

Tape, adhesive (SEE ALSO OVERLEAF)

Using masking tape

Masking tape has easy-release adhesive so it is useful for temporarily sealing, masking or holding objects in place.

● Dry and clean a surface before applying masking tape.

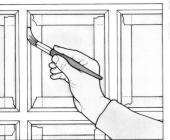

● Use it for masking off the glass in windows and doors before brush painting.

Position the tape so that a 2 mm ($\frac{1}{16}$ in) margin of paint is left on the glass, to stop condensation or rain seeping into the framework and causing rot.

● To get a very fine edge to the paint, run your thumbnail or a putty knife along the edge of the tape, to make sure that paint does not seep under it.

● Remove the tape as soon as painting is complete, so that it doesn't pull away any dried paint.

● Never leave masking tape stuck down for longer than 24 hours on surfaces that have been coated with polyurethane or varnish, because the adhesive will penetrate and leave a cloudy mark.

● If masking tape has been left on for too long, remove the stubborn residue by dabbing it with lighter fuel and lifting it with a craft knife. Take care you don't damage the surface, and be careful when working with the fuel – it is highly flammable.

● Masking tape can be used for holding down pieces of newspaper to mask off areas when spray painting.

● Before using any sort of dust-making machinery such as a floor sander, seal the doors of the room with masking tape to stop dust from getting into the rest of the house.

● Don't leave masking tape on the bodywork of a car for more than a few hours. It can be impossible to get off.

● When applying sealant around windows, sinks, baths and basins, create a very neat, straight edge by outlining the working area with strips of masking tape. Then squeeze the sealant into the gap, smooth it and remove the masking tape.

● Because you can write on masking tape, you can use it to number parts in the right order, specially when taking apart an appliance with many sections.

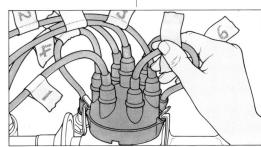

● When you need to take several measurements, stick a strip of masking tape on the case of your tape measure and write down the measurements on it as you work.

Making steps safer

Trusty Tread is a hard-wearing adhesive tape that can be applied to smooth surfaces, such as steps and the treads on ladders, to give a more secure grip and make them safer. It is available in DIY stores.

PREVENTING DAMAGE TO POLISHED FLOORS

Prevent tables and chairs from marking shiny floor surfaces by covering each foot with a self-adhesive Fuzzy Feet pad. The pads come in various colours and can be trimmed to the size of the foot to make them inconspicuous.

TAPES

Adhesive tapes provide a convenient, clean alternative to glues or pastes for many repair and maintenance jobs inside and outside the house, around the garden and in the garage. Choose the correct adhesive tape for the type of repair you have in mind: some tapes are suitable for only temporary repairs, but others are effective for considerably longer and can be used as a permanent solution. When not in use, they should be stored in a cool, dry place, because heat and humidity may reduce their effectiveness.

MASKING TAPE
A paper tape with a special release adhesive for masking off areas that are not to be painted. It should be removed as soon as possible.

ALUMINIUM WATERPROOFING TAPE
Used on conservatory roofs to seal joins. Can be painted.

CLEAR ADHESIVE TAPE
For simple household use, repairs and parcel wrapping.

DOUBLE-SIDED ADHESIVE TAPE
Used for various kinds of craftwork and for fixing photographs in albums.

ALL-WEATHER MASKING TAPE
Can be left in place for up to eight weeks, and still be removed without leaving a messy surface. Useful if bad weather holds up external painting jobs.

filmoplast ® P

BOOK REPAIR TAPE
A paper tissue coated with adhesive. It is thin and transparent, and used for mending tears in paper.

CLEAR ADHESIVE WATERPROOF TAPE
Useful for emergency repairs such as securing broken windowpanes until the glass is replaced, or for sealing cracks in plastic roofing, or for joining sheets of polythene. (No liquid adhesive will stick polythene.)

FLEXIBLE MASKING TAPE
Rougher textured than standard masking tape. It is used for masking off arches and other curved or irregular surfaces.

tesa
5696   25m 50mm
Flooring Tape
For Vinyl Flooring

tesa
5225   10m 50mm
Crack Cover

ALUMINIUM FOIL TAPE
Heat and water-resistant. Used as a decorative trim on metal, such as on a bicycle frame.

CARPET TAPE
A strong, double-sided adhesive tape used for anchoring carpet, sheet vinyl or floor tiles. Some tapes are permanent but others can be lifted, leaving a clean floor ready for a new covering.

CRACK-COVERING TAPE
Can be used to cover small cracks in walls before decorating. Because the tape is flexible, it can cope with a small amount of movement in the crack, unlike wallpaper which would tear.

GUTTER REPAIR TAPE
A flexible adhesive tape made of woven fabric and impregnated with a water-proofing sealant. It is used for sealing and rustproofing gutters and downpipes.

FLASHING TAPE
A heavy-duty adhesive tape, used with a special primer, for repairing or making new flashings, at such places as the joins between a chimney and a roof, or between a house wall and a lean-to shed.

CLEAR WEATHERPROOFING TAPE
Used for sealing gaps and joins on plastic roofing and plastic cloches.

HOUSEHOLD REPAIR TAPE (ALSO KNOWN AS GAFFER TAPE)
A weather-resistant cloth tape for repairing suitcases and sports bags, and protecting and reinforcing household items. Also suitable for temporary repairs to hosepipes and hot and cold-water pipes.

FOAM MOUNTING TAPE
Double-sided adhesive tape used for mounting light objects, such as mirror tiles, on walls or wardrobe doors and for fixing pottery and porcelain securely in a display cabinet.

PIPE-AND-HOSE REPAIR TAPE
A stretching repair tape suitable for emergency repairs to water pipes up to mains pressure, and for repairing hoses in the car or garden. One type is supplied in a two-part form — a reinforcing tape and an amalgamating tape.

INSULATING TAPE
Useful for binding together groups of wires and cables, preventing flexes from fraying and for colour-coding cables to identify them. It should not be used for making joins in electric flex (see *Flexes & cables*: 'Fitting a flex connector'). For extra safety, choose one that is flame retarding.

GLAZING TAPE
A special tape coated with non-setting putty-like material for waterproofing glazing bars on glazed roofs and for sealing gaps and cracks in pipes and in pipe joints.

PTFE TAPE
A joint-sealing tape that can be used on metal or plastic plumbing connections. It is very slippery (PTFE is used to line nonstick pans) and consequently makes the undoing and doing up of couplings very easy.

PACKAGING TAPE
Very strong, adhesive plastic tape, usually brown, used for sealing parcels and packages.

GRIPPING THE TAP

To guard against cracking the basin while you are trying to undo the headgear nut, you can make a gripping tool to hold the tap base steady.

Join two lengths of wood at one end with a bolt and use this to hold the body and nozzle of the tap steady while you apply pressure to the headgear nut with a spanner.

CERAMIC DISCS IN MODERN TAPS

In some modern taps, the water is controlled by two ceramic discs instead of a washer. The discs are designed so that they give an even better seal as they wear so they should never need replacing.

Taps & mixers
(SEE ALSO LIMESCALE & HARD WATER)

How to cut off the water supply to a tap

If a tap drips, its washer is probably faulty. You may need to cut off the water to the tap before replacing the washer.

KITCHEN COLD TAP The kitchen cold tap is fed by the rising main. Turn off the water at the stopcock, which is usually under the kitchen sink. Then open the tap to empty the pipe.

BATHROOM COLD TAP The bathroom cold taps may be supplied from the main or a cold-water tank. Cut off the water to a main-fed tap by closing the main stopcock. To cut off the water to a tap fed by the cold-water tank, turn off the gate valve to the tap, if there is one. Alternatively, tie up the ball-valve arm of the cold-water tank (see *Ball valve*).

Open the cold tap to empty the water from the pipes.

HOT TAPS May be fed by a combination boiler or a hot-water cylinder. If they are fed by a boiler, turn off the water at the main stopcock and turn on the faulty hot tap to empty the pipe. If they are fed by a cylinder that is fed direct from the mains, follow the same procedure.

For a hot-water cylinder fed by a cold-water tank, turn off the gate valve on the pipe between the two (if there is one). Turn on the faulty hot tap to empty the pipe. If there is no gate valve, tie up the ball-valve arm in the cold-water tank (see *Ball valve*) and drain it as follows.

If the bathroom cold taps are supplied by the cold-water tank, turn them on to empty it. When the flow of water stops, turn on the faulty hot tap to empty the pipe.

If the bathroom cold taps are fed by the rising main, drain the cold-water tank by turning on the hot taps.

Fixing a dripping handwheel (shrouded-head) tap
Time: 2 hours or less

> YOU WILL NEED Washer, adjustable spanner, pipe wrench and padding for its jaws, two pairs of pliers, penetrating oil.

Cut off the water supply (see above). Then remove the tap cover. On a handwheel tap the cover is also the handle and there are three possible ways of removing it. It may pull off. Or it may be held in place by a tiny grub screw on the side which must be undone.

Otherwise, look at the hot or cold indicator disc. If it has a serrated edge, it can be unscrewed. If not, prise it off with a screwdriver. Removing the disc will reveal a retaining nut – unscrew it and pull off the tap cover.

Unscrew the headgear underneath the cover to reveal the faulty washer and valve (see right, above). Replace the washer, then reassemble the tap. Ensure that the tap is turned off, then restore the water supply.

Dealing with a dripping pillar tap Time: 2 hours or less

> YOU WILL NEED New washer, pipe wrench and padding for its jaws, spanner, two pairs of pliers, penetrating oil.

Cut off the water supply to the tap (see left).

Turn the tap fully on and put in the plug to stop anything falling down the plughole. Then unscrew the tap cover. If it will not unscrew by hand, wrap padding, such as a cloth, round it and use a pipe wrench.

Use an adjustable or open-ended spanner to undo the hexagonal headgear nut by turning it anticlockwise.

If the nut is difficult to turn, apply some penetrating oil and wait for half an hour before trying again.

The valve, with a washer attached, will either be resting on the valve seating within the body of the tap or it will be in the removed tap headgear. The washer is secured by a small nut.

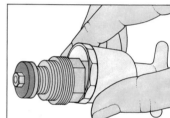

Hold the valve with pliers and unscrew the nut with a spanner (apply penetrating oil if necessary). Replace the washer. Grease the threads and reassemble the tap.

If you cannot remove the nut, remove and replace the complete washer and valve unit. If it is fixed in the head, undo the grub screw that holds it in place to remove it.

Turn off the tap and restore the water supply.

Fixing a dripping Supatap Time: 1 hour or less

It is possible to change the washer on a Supatap without first having to cut off the water supply to the tap.

> YOU WILL NEED Supatap washer-and-valve unit, adjustable spanner, screwdriver.

Use an adjustable spanner to undo the hexagonal retaining nut at the top of the nozzle (turning it anticlockwise, looking from above the tap).

Turn the tap on and keep twisting it in the same direction. At first the water flow from the tap will increase, but it will cut off just before the nozzle comes off in your hand.

Tap the base of the nozzle against a solid surface to release the antisplash device which holds the washer unit in position. Do not be tempted to tap it against the surface of the ceramic basin because it may crack.

Prise out the valve-and-washer unit by inserting a screwdriver under the washer plate and the antisplash device in the nozzle.

Snap the new valve-and-washer unit into position then reassemble the tap. Screw the nozzle back in place by turning it in a clockwise direction, looking from above.

Then tighten the hexagonal retaining nut by turning it clockwise, looking from above.

Curing a leaking pillar-tap spindle   Time: 2 hours or less

If a tap leaks from its spindle, or is too easily turned off and on, the gland nut may need adjusting or repacking.

> YOU WILL NEED Adjustable spanner, Vaseline, darning wool. Possibly: an O-ring seal, screwdriver.

Turn the tap off but do not cut off the water supply. Remove the bell-shaped cover and the tap handle. Twist the gland nut (the highest nut on the spindle) about half a turn clockwise. If this does not cure the leak, the gland probably needs repacking.

Use an adjustable spanner to undo the gland nut and note the type of packing below it. String or hemp packing can be replaced by darning wool, but graphite powder or a rubber O-ring must be replaced with the same thing.

If the old packing is string or hemp, rake it out with a penknife. Then replace it with darning wool that has been steeped in Vaseline.

Caulk it down hard with a screwdriver blade. Replace the gland nut and tighten it so that the tap spindle can be turned, but not too easily. Reassemble the tap.

Stopping a leak from handwheel-tap handle
Time: 2 hours or less

If water is leaking from below the handle of a handwheel tap, the O-ring seal probably needs replacing.

> YOU WILL NEED Screwdriver, new O-ring seal, Vaseline.

Turn off the tap and cut off the water supply (see facing page). Remove the tap handle (see 'Fixing a dripping handwheel tap', facing page). Unscrew and remove the headgear to reveal the washer and valve.

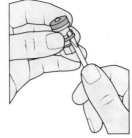

Hold the tap headgear and unscrew the spindle to remove the washer unit.

Use a screwdriver to prise out the O-ring at the top of the washer unit.

Take the old O-ring to a plumbers' merchant to buy a new one of exactly the same specifications.

Rub Vaseline over the new O-ring and put it in place of the old one, then reassemble the tap.

Dealing with a leak from a mixer tap
Time: ½ an hour or less

If a sink mixer tap is leaking from the base of its spout, the O-ring seal has probably worn. These wear quite quickly because of the swivelling action of the spout. You can replace the O-rings yourself.

> YOU WILL NEED Two replacement O-rings, screwdriver, Vaseline.

First turn off both taps that are connected to the sink mixer. Unscrew and remove the small retaining screw at the base of the swivel spout.

Then ease the spout out of the base of the mixer by lifting and twisting it from side to side at the same time.

Note the position of the old O-rings (there will probably be two) and remove them. Take them to a builders' or plumbers' merchant to get matching replacements.

The new O-rings must be the same thickness as the originals as well as the same diameter.

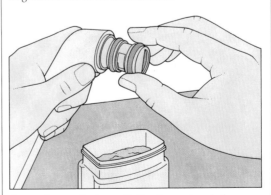

Smear the new O-rings with Vaseline and push them over the end of the swivel spout and into the channels that the old O-rings sat in.

Then ease the swivel spout into the base of the mixer and replace the retaining screw. Screw it up tightly.

REMOVING A HANDLE

If the handle of a tap is difficult to remove, unscrew the cover and open the tap. Insert pieces of wood between the base of the cover and the body of the tap. Turn the handle to close the tap, and the upward pressure of the cover will force off the handle. Remove the cover and push the handle on just sufficiently to enable you to close the tap.

Tea maker

Automatic tea-making machines need little maintenance apart from the removal of limescale that builds up round the element, particularly in hard-water areas.

Descaling the boiler unit Time: ½ an hour or less

If limescale builds up on the element or the water is taking longer than usual to boil, the boiler unit needs descaling.

> YOU WILL NEED Proprietary descaling solution, rubber gloves. Possibly: vinegar.

Put about 2 dessertspoons of descaler into the teapot. Pour in boiling water to the four-cup level and stir. Pour the solution into the boiler unit, taking care not to spill any on the surface of the tea maker in case it stains.

Replace the empty teapot. Stir the solution in the boiler unit and leave it to stand for about 30 minutes. Replace the lid and operate the tea maker in the normal way.

When the water has boiled and been transferred into the teapot, pour it down the sink. Run through the cycle with fresh water twice more before making tea.

Tea makers vary, so always read the descaling instructions carefully. Some makes recommend using vinegar in place of descaling solution. Use the vinegar-and-water solution twice and then boil clean water twice.

Faultfinder guide: Tea maker

No power

- Is it switched on at the socket?
- Check that the socket is working by plugging in another appliance such as an electric lamp.
- Check plug connections and fuse (see *Electric plug*).

Power light on but the tea maker doesn't work

- Check that the time is set correctly.
- Check that the boiler unit is in the right place.
- Make sure there is enough water in the tea maker.
- Remove the boiler unit and check that the tube connecting it to the teapot is clear. Remove any blockage with a piece of wire. Tape over the end of the wire first to avoid scratches.

Teddy bear

If you think that your teddy bear might be valuable, don't attempt to repair it yourself. Have it done professionally. The Bear Museum, 38 Dragon Street, Petersfield, Hampshire GU31 4JJ (Tel. 01730 265108) may be able to advise you. Or call The Bath Teddy Bear Clinic on 01225 445803.

Tightening a loose limb Time: ½ a day or less

> YOU WILL NEED Scissors, long-nosed pliers, kapok or cotton stuffing, needle and thread.

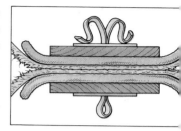

Most joints consist of two washers and a pin that goes through them. One washer is inside the limb with the pin protruding through it. The other washer lies inside the body, behind a leg hole or an arm hole.

If a limb has come off or is loose, the pin may have stretched and lost its grip, or the fabric of either the limb or the body may have torn away round one of the washers.

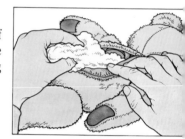

Open the main seam of the torso nearest the loose limb. Remove the stuffing and expose the joint.

FAULTY PIN If the fault lies with the pin, grip the joint and use a pair of long-nosed pliers to tighten the pin.

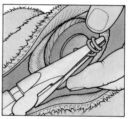 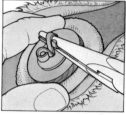

If the pin is a single piece of wire, grip the tip with the pliers, increasing the pressure and tightening the curl.

Where a split pin is used, tighten the curl on each end of the pin, and then flatten it with the pliers.

TORN FABRIC The limb may have come off because the fabric at the joint has torn. Carefully straighten the pin and remove the washer from the limb. Stitch up the worst of the tear in the fabric with matching thread.

Replace the washer and pin in the loose limb and stitch the fabric tightly round them, to hold them in position. The smaller the opening that is left around the washer and pin, the more firmly they will hold the limb to the teddy's body.

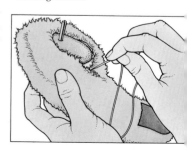

If the tear is in the body fabric, open the nearest seam and remove a good deal of the stuffing to expose the joint area. Repair the torn fabric round the hole.

Release the washer if it is attached to the loose limb, and replace it inside the body, centred over the hole for the limb. Reattach the limb to the teddy by passing its pin through the washer in the body. Tighten the pin as shown on the facing page.

Replace the stuffing if it is in good condition, or fill the body with new stuffing or kapok. Stitch up the seam, pulling the thread tight every three or four stitches.

Replacing an eye Time: 1 hour or less

> **YOU WILL NEED** Replacement eye, strong thread, long needle.

Glass eyes for teddy bears can be found in haberdashery departments and hobby shops. Lock-in eyes are safer, but eyes with a shank are commonly used.

Place the shank in the old site and sew the eye in position. Use strong thread the same colour as the bear.

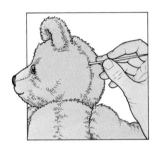

End by taking the needle right through the bear's head and fastening off the thread at the back with two or three firm stitches buried in the fur.

Cleaning a teddy bear Time: 1 hour or less

Bears can be brushed or vacuumed to remove surface dirt, or sponged lightly with a mild detergent solution. Never submerge a bear or wash it in a washing machine.

If there is any sign of insect infestation in a bear that is too precious to throw away, spray it with an aerosol moth-killer and seal it in a plastic bag for a month or so.

Telephone

A master telephone socket must be installed by the company that provides the service. Once this is in place you can install your own telephones and extensions.

Special connection kits are sold in most DIY stores and specialist telephone shops.

Fitting a telephone extension Time: about 2 hours

> **YOU WILL NEED** Screwdriver, trimming knife, telephone cable with socket converter attached, power drill, masonry bit, wall plug, small hammer, cleats.

Extensions must be no more than 50 m (55 yd) from the master socket. You may have more than one master socket in your home, and each one can supply up to four extensions at the same time. If you have any more than four extensions, it is likely that none of them will ring properly.

Telephone wiring works on a safe low voltage, but it must be kept at least 5 cm (2 in) from mains electric cable which could cause interference and damage.

Plan a route for the cable, avoiding laying it where it might be a trip hazard. Check that you have enough cable to cover the distance, with a little extra at each end.

Unscrew the cover on the extension socket and use a trimming knife to open the cable entrance gap marked on the inside of the cover at the bottom.

Pass the cable through the gap and hold the socket on the wall where it will go. Mark the position with a pencil and prepare the wall with a wall plug (see *Wall fixings*).

Use the trimming knife to strip about 3 cm ($1\frac{1}{4}$ in) from the outer sheath of the telephone cable. Fan out the conductors (plastic-covered wires) – there are usually six – and use the tool supplied in the kit to push each conductor into the correct space in the socket.

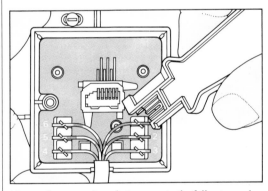

The conductors go into their spaces in the following order:

6 White/green	1 Green/white
5 White/blue	2 Blue/white
4 White/orange	3 Orange/white

If there are only four conductors, leave the numbers 1 and 6 empty or use a four-conductor socket instead.

Screw the socket into the prepared wall plug in the wall and fit the front plate onto the socket.

Plug the converter into the master socket and fix the nearest part of the cable to the wall with a cleat. Unplug the converter and fasten the cable along the chosen route, tapping in the cleats about 30 cm (12 in) apart.

Plug the converter into the master socket again. Fit the plug from the master telephone into the socket on the face of the converter. Then plug in the extension telephone.

Television

SAFETY FIRST WITH ELECTRICITY

Before starting any work on an electrical fitting or appliance, make sure to cut off the electricity supply – either by switching off at the main fuse box, or by unplugging the appliance.

ADJUSTING THE SIGNAL

If the signal on your TV set is not strong enough, fit a booster to the aerial. Symptoms are poor colour, poor contrast and an unstable picture. Also, if you have teletext, it will appear garbled on screen.

If the signal is too strong, fit a signal attenuator. Symptoms are over-saturation of colour and too much contrast, which do not respond to the controls on the set, and a loss of definition.

If you want the signal to go to several television sets, fit a signal splitter. Specialist aerial companies can advise on which to use to suit your circumstances.

Fitting a second extension

You can install a second telephone extension socket by running a cable from the first extension socket. No converter is needed. A third extension can be installed by running cable from the second and so on.

First, unplug the converter from the master socket.

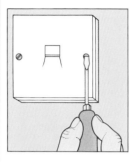

Unscrew the front plate on the first extension socket.

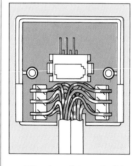

Connect the conductors from the new cable in the same order as those already in place.

Wire the other end of the cable to the second extension socket. Continue in this way for any further extensions – always fitting the new conductors on top of those already installed. Screw the front plates onto the sockets and plug in the converter on the master socket to connect them all.

Tracing faults in a new extension

- Unplug the converter from the master socket. Test each telephone in turn by plugging it into the master socket and dialling out. If none of them works, the fault is in the telephone company's wiring.
- If only one of the telephones doesn't work, it is probably faulty and will need to be repaired.
- If all the telephones work, the fault is probably in the new wiring. Check each socket to make sure that you have wired the coloured conductors to the correct numbers. Check that you have pushed them right in.
- If the conductors are wrongly connected, pull them out one at a time with long-nose pliers, cut off the used piece of cable and remake the connection.
- If the sockets are properly connected, check that the cable is not kinked, cut or squashed. If so, replace it.
- If the phones still do not work, return the sockets, joint box, converter and cable to the suppliers.

Television

Installing a loft aerial   Time: 1 day or less

YOU WILL NEED Aerial, fixing bracket, screws, screwdriver, 75 ohm coaxial cable, trimming knife, wire strippers, coaxial plug, pliers. Possibly: power drill, drill bits, portable television, surface-mounted wall socket, cable clips, hammer.

PLANNING AND PREPARING A CABLE ROUTE Select a position for the aerial in the loft as high as possible. The position must allow the aerial to rotate through 360 degrees. Plan the route for the cable from the aerial to the television set, making it as short as possible and avoiding sharp bends.

The cable may be run inside the house. In the corner of the rooms that it will pass through, drill holes about 1 cm ($\frac{3}{8}$ in) through ceilings and floors. Check first with a wire, pipe and stud detector (see page 158) that the drill will not damage any cables or pipes.

Alternatively, run the cable out of the loft through the eaves, then down the side of the house, and in through a hole drilled through a window frame. Drill the hole at an angle to prevent rainwater from running into it.

Secure the cable to the outside wall with cable clips and, before it goes into the house, let it sag in a small loop so that rainwater drips off and doesn't enter the house.

Once you have planned the cable's route, calculate its length and then add about 1 m (3 ft). Buy 75 ohm coaxial cable. A specialist aerial company can supply cable, plugs, sockets and cable clips, and also advise you. Alternatively, look under 'Electrical supplies' in *Yellow Pages*.

FITTING THE AERIAL Fit the aerial bracket to a joist and the aerial to the bracket. Tighten the fixing, ensuring that you are able to rotate the aerial with only a little force.

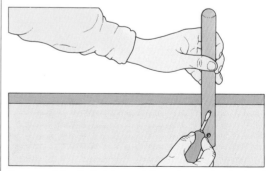

Some models of television aerial are designed to be fixed onto a pole. If you have one of this type, screw a length of broom handle to the joist and then slip the aerial onto it.

CONNECTING THE CABLE TO THE AERIAL On one end of the coaxial cable remove about 5 cm (2 in) of the outer plastic sheath to expose the braided copper mesh. Slide back the mesh and reveal the inner plastic insulation.

Use wire strippers to remove about 1 cm ($\frac{1}{2}$ in) of the insulation to expose the single thick copper wire inside.

Find the aerial's connector box, open it and loosen the connecting screws. Pass the prepared cable end under the cable grip on the connector unit. Make sure that the braided copper mesh makes good contact with the grip mechanism.

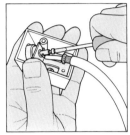 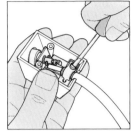

Introduce the inner, single copper wire into the one remaining connector and then hold it in place by tightening the fixing screw onto the wire.

Tighten the cable grip over the braided mesh, ensuring that no single strands of mesh come into contact with the inner copper wire or its connector.

POSITIONING AND ADJUSTING THE AERIAL Fit a coaxial plug to the free end of the lead (see 'Fitting a coaxial plug', right). Plug it into a television set to adjust the position of the aerial. If possible use a portable TV in the loft to check the picture as you make the adjustment.

If you cannot use a television in the loft, lay the aerial lead along its route and ask someone to watch the television while you adjust the aerial. In this case, you will have to fit the coaxial plug after running the lead.

Setting the aerial correctly can take some time, moving it round slowly until you get the best picture. As a guide, check in which direction your neighbours' aerials point. Once your aerial is in the position which gives the best picture, tighten all the brackets.

If you used a TV in the loft to adjust the picture, remove the coaxial plug, run the cable, then refix the plug in place when the cable is in position.

If a loft aerial does not give a good enough picture, try fitting a signal booster (see facing page). Otherwise, an outdoor aerial on a mast is necessary. You may be able to use the same aerial, though new fixings may be necessary.

Always have a roof aerial fitted by a professional.

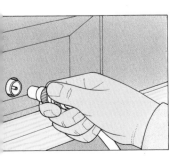

CONNECTING THE AERIAL LEAD TO THE TELEVISION SET The aerial can be connected to the television set by inserting the coaxial plug on the cable into the aerial socket in the back of the set.

Alternatively, connect the lead to a wall socket then make up a shorter lead with a coaxial plug at each end to run between the socket and the television.

Use a surface-mounted socket rather than a flush-fitting socket which will require a hole to be chased out of the wall. Screw the socket to the skirting board or wall behind the television, and connect the cable to the socket in the same way as it is connected to the aerial.

Fitting a coaxial plug Time: $\frac{1}{2}$ an hour or less

YOU WILL NEED Coaxial cable, trimming knife, wire strippers, coaxial plug, pliers.

Slide the plug cap over the coaxial cable then remove about 3 cm ($1\frac{1}{4}$ in) of the cable's plastic outer sheath to expose the braided copper mesh below.

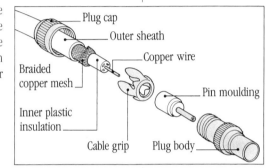

Slide back the copper mesh to reveal about 2.5 cm (1 in) of the inner plastic insulation.

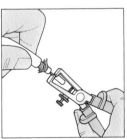 

Using wire strippers remove about 1.3 cm ($\frac{1}{2}$ in) of the insulation and expose the single thick copper wire.

Slide the cable grip down over the braided mesh and make sure that there are no strands of mesh protruding.

It is essential that the mesh does not come in contact with the single inner copper wire. Use pliers to close the jaws of the grip so that they clamp the mesh.

Insert the thick, single wire into the pin moulding, then fit the pin moulding into the plug body. Slide the cap up the cable and screw it to the plug body.

If any of the thick copper wire protrudes from the end of the pin moulding, cut it off flush with the end.

HIDING CABLES

A white conduit and a hollow skirting board are available which will hide cables (see *Skirting board*). Otherwise, clip the cable to the wall, running it unobtrusively along skirtings.

GETTING THE RIGHT AERIAL

Advice about the type of TV aerial to use and how to adjust it can be obtained from BBC Engineering Information, Villiers House, The Broadway, Ealing, London W5 2PA (Tel. 0181 231 9191).

FITTING A TV/FM AERIAL SOCKET

Your TV set and FM radio amplifier have separate aerials. To avoid running two cables from the aerials through the house, you can fit a TV/FM aerial socket in the loft and a second one in the living room and link the two with a single low-loss coaxial cable.

Faultfinder guide: Television

No power getting to the set

- Is the TV set plugged in?
- Is the wall socket switched on?
- Is the TV set switched on? Make sure that it is not in standby mode. Make sure that the remote control is not set to standby.
- If the TV set has a timer facility, check that it has not been set to start at a later time.
- Check the mains socket by plugging in another electrical appliance such as a lamp to see if it works.
- Check the fuse in the plug (see *Electric plug*).

If the TV still doesn't work, there is probably a serious fault. Contact the supplier or the manufacturer, or look in *Yellow Pages* under 'TV, video & radio' for a repairer.

Television set has no picture

- Do other channels give a picture?

    If so, the fault probably lies at the transmitter and there is nothing you can do except wait.

    If not, make further checks:
- Is the aerial lead securely plugged into the back of the television set? If not, push it in firmly.

- If the aerial comes into the television via the video recorder, unplug it from the video (left) and try plugging it directly into the back of the television.

- Plug the faulty set's aerial lead into another working television set. If no picture appears on the second television, either the aerial, aerial cable or aerial plug is broken or badly connected.

    If the second TV has a picture on all channels, then the fault lies with the first TV. Try retuning the set, following the instructions in the manual.
- If there is still no picture, the symptoms suggest a more serious fault and you should contact the supplier, the manufacturer or a television repairer. Look in *Yellow Pages* under 'TV, video & radio'.

Television picture deteriorates

- If there is poor picture quality on only one channel, the set may need retuning. Refer to the TV manual. Poor picture quality on all channels may mean that the connection between aerial and television is faulty.

- Check that all coaxial plugs are firmly in their sockets. Then check that they are firmly attached to their cable and rewire if necessary (see 'Fitting a coaxial cable').
- Check the connection between the cable and the TV aerial (if it is a loft aerial) and rewire it if necessary (see 'Installing a loft aerial').
- If there is still no picture, run a new cable between the aerial and television (see 'Installing a loft aerial').
- Call in a specialist TV aerial company to sort out the problem if it is a roof aerial.

Set has no sound

- If the sound goes but the picture remains, check the sound on the other channels. If the other channels are giving sound, the set may need retuning. Refer to the TV manual. If this does no good, the fault is probably with the transmitter and all you can do is wait.

    If there is no sound on the other channels make the following checks:
- Is the 'mute' switched on, either at the TV set itself or on the remote control? If so, turn it off.
- Make sure that the volume is turned up.
- Are headphones connected? If so, unplug them.
- Is the TV plugged in through the hi-fi? If so, make sure that it is switched on and turned up.
- If there is still no sound, the symptoms suggest a more serious fault and you should contact the supplier, the manufacturer or a television repairer. Look in *Yellow Pages* under 'TV, video & radio'.

Poor sound quality

- Check all the channels. If only one channel gives poor sound, try retuning it. If all stations produce poor quality sound there may be a more serious fault. Contact the supplier, the manufacturer or a television repairer. Look in *Yellow Pages* under 'TV, video & radio'.

Loss of satellite picture

- Check that all the normal 'land' channels (BBC/ITV/Channel 4) are still working. If not, your TV set may be at fault. Test it as already described, above left.
- If the land channels are working, check the test signal from the satellite receiver. If there is no test signal, the receiver may be faulty. Get it checked by the supplier or a television repairer.
- If land and test signals are all right, check that the lead connecting the dish to the receiver is firmly in place. Check that the receiver has not been moved by the wind. If it has, follow the maker's instructions for realigning it.

Tennis racket

The repairs and modifications that can be made to tennis rackets also apply to squash and badminton rackets.

Replacing a rubberised overgrip Time: a few minutes

Grips used to be made of leather and were replaced once a year, but most are now synthetic. Most players prefer to fit rubberised overgrips to the handle. They absorb sweat well and are softer on the hand. If you use them you may not have to replace the basic grip during the racket's lifetime. The disadvantage is that you have to replace the overgrip every four or five sessions.

Remove any old overgrip tape, and decide whether to leave the basic grip on the handle or not. Bear in mind that the new grip will add to the thickness of the handle.

Strip off the backing film on the new overgrip tape and place one end at the base of the handle. Some overgrips have the corner cut off at one end, which should go at the top of the grip. The rectangular end goes at the base.

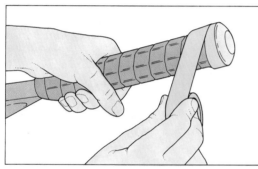

Hold the end in place with the thumb of one hand and wind the new overgrip round the handle. If you have left the basic grip in place, work in the same direction, overlapping by about 6 mm ($\frac{1}{4}$ in) on each turn.

Keep the tape as tight as possible while winding it on. If you don't get it right the first time, peel it off and start again. The cut-off corner at the top of the grip should allow you to level off the new grip, ready for the tape that holds it in place. All overgrips come with a piece of tape.

You can play with the racket immediately the new overgrip has been fitted.

Getting broken strings repaired

If a string snaps on your racket, take it to a professional stringer. Restrings can be done by most sports shops, but it may be cheaper through a club.

You will have to decide whether to get only the broken string replaced or to get the racket totally restrung. It is worth getting a racket restrung about once a year if you are a regular player.

Tent

Patching a tear Time: depends on area

You can patch a tear temporarily with waterproof tape (wait until the tent is dry or the tape won't stick), but for a lasting repair, stitch the damaged area.

YOU WILL NEED Tent-repair thread or strong cotton, tent-repair tape (use nylon on nylon and canvas on canvas).

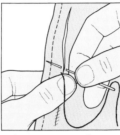 

Either put up the tent loosely or lay it flat. Make sure it is dry, then stitch up the tear using tent-repair thread or strong cotton.

Tape over the repair with tent-repair tape. Use a tape that matches the tent material – nylon on nylon or canvas on canvas.

Sealing leaking seams Time: depends on area

New tents often leak at the seams because the material has not yet shrunk enough to be watertight. Many suppliers recommend sponging a new tent or leaving it in the rain.

If seams start leaking with age you can apply seam sealer, available from camping shops. The bottle type is easiest to control and is more effective. Put up the tent and apply the seam sealer when it is dry. The seams can be resealed several times throughout the tent's lifetime.

Fixing a broken zip

Most manufacturers will repair tents for you and camping shops may also run a repair service. But there may not always be time to send a tent away.

YOU WILL NEED Possibly: pliers or a hammer, replacement zip, tent-repair thread, needle, Velcro, fabric ties, eyelets.

If the zip fastener isn't working properly try either squeezing the two halves together with pliers or hitting them sharply with a hammer against a hard surface.

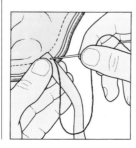

If the tent zip is damaged beyond repair, replace it with a new zip (see *Zip*) or sew fabric ties onto each side of the tent opening (left).

Alternatively, you could replace the broken zip with strips of heavy-duty Velcro.

(see *Zip*)

REPLACING A TENT EYELET

If an eyelet comes loose or is torn out of the canvas, replace it using an eyelet kit. Stitch any tears to prevent them from spreading.

CARING FOR YOUR TENT

● Do not pack up a tent if it is wet. If packing can't be avoided put the tent up again to dry as soon as possible.

● To prevent leaks, make sure that nothing inside the tent is touching the walls and that there is a gap between the fly sheet and the inner tent.

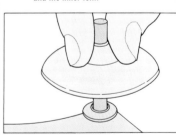

● Fit rain cowls (miniature plastic umbrellas) to prevent rain running down the poles into the tent.

● On some tents much of the strain is taken by rubber peg rings and the canvas loops round the base. Check the canvas loops regularly and replace them as soon as they start to wear. Fit a new rubber ring by looping it through itself.

FIXING A BROKEN POLE

If an upright pole breaks, you may be able to make a temporary repair, using a piece of metal tube to hold the two parts together. You can buy adjustable vertical poles from camping shops to replace broken ones.

Professional repairs to outdoor kit

If tents, rucksacks or waterproof clothing need repairs which you feel you cannot do yourself, consult an outdoor-and-camping specialist retailer who will be able to recommend a professional repairer.

New buckles and zips can be fitted, tears patched and restitching undertaken, in addition to cleaning and waterproofing services.

Replacing a broken pole spring   Time: a few minutes

Family frame tents have poles held together with springs. These can become loose or break with wear, but they are simple to replace.

> YOU WILL NEED Pliers, replacement spring, tent peg.

First pull the damaged spring out of the pole. Then compress the spring clip at the end of the chain on the new spring. Push it into the narrower of the two tubes.

Use a tent peg to push the spring clip down into the tube until the spring touches the tube.

Slightly compress the spring clip at the end of the spring between your fingers and push it into the other tube as far as possible. When you have finished reassembling the pole, the spring should be hidden.

Terracotta pots

Where a terracotta pot has broken cleanly, and you have managed to save all the pieces, they can be rejoined with PVA waterproof adhesive or epoxy-resin adhesive.

However, when a pot has broken into too many pieces to fit them all together again, or when pieces are missing, the resulting gap can be built up with a special terracotta-coloured epoxy putty which is available from The Milliputt Company (Tel. 01341 422562) and some DIY stores.

Patching a terracotta pot   Time: parts of 2 days

> YOU WILL NEED Terracotta epoxy putty, trimming knife, spatula. Possibly: rubber or disposable gloves.

Make sure the area to be patched is free from dirt and grease. If your skin is sensitive, wear gloves.

There are two different-coloured putties in the pack. Take slightly more of each part than you think you will need, and blend them until the putty is a uniform colour.

REINFORCING A CRACKED POT

If a fine vertical crack appears near the top of a terracotta pot, you can prevent it from getting worse. Tie a piece of garden wire under the lip of the pot, and tighten it with a pair of long-nose pliers.

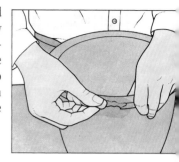

Moisten the damaged area and press the putty into it, allowing it to protrude a little on the surface which is most exposed to view and even more so on the surface which will be seen less.

Smooth the putty with a wet finger or spatula.

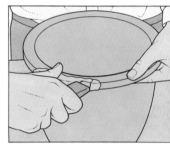

When it has hardened sufficiently to be cut (after about 2 hours) wet the blade of a sharp trimming knife and trim away the surplus on the surface that will be seen most. Create as perfect a finish as possible.

Scratch the protruding area on the less-seen surface with a trimming knife. Leave it to harden overnight.

Next day, make enough of the epoxy putty to cover the roughened area. Use wet fingers or a wet spatula to spread the putty over the area, feathering it outwards so that it covers the good parts of the pot that surround the damaged area.

Let it dry completely before filling and using the pot.

How to use epoxy putty

Before mending a broken terracotta pot, experiment with a small piece of epoxy putty.

Mix a small piece from each of the two sticks of putty in the pack, kneading them until the two colours have merged and there are no streaks.

Keep your hands and any tools moist while working with it. Wash hands and tools (and rubber gloves, if used) immediately after use.

It changes as it dries, starting off soft and sticky; after an hour it feels a bit rubbery; after 2 hours it can be cut into a shape with a pair of scissors or a knife; and after 3 hours it is quite hard with no trace of tackiness. Overnight it hardens completely.

Hardening can be speeded up with hot air from a hair dryer. Once completely hard, the putty can be sanded, sawn, drilled and painted.

Tights & stockings

Preventing a run Time: a few minutes

If you find a snag or the start of a ladder in tights or stockings while you are wearing them, you can prevent it from going any further by rubbing all round the area with a piece of wet soap. Alternatively, spray the snag with hair spray, or dab a little clear nail polish onto it.

Ease the repaired area away from your skin as soon as it is dry, and take care when removing the tights.

Wash them carefully (see below), and remember to apply the remedy again the next time you put them on.

Longer life for tights and stockings

- New tights will last longer if, before wearing them, you dampen them thoroughly, put them into a plastic bag and then into the freezer. Let them thaw and dry thoroughly before putting them on.
- A little laundry starch in the final rinse will help to prevent ladders in tights and stockings.
- If you wash tights and stockings in a washing machine, put them into a pillowcase first so that they are not damaged by zips or hooks and eyes on other clothes. Net bags, for keeping socks together in the wash, do not protect tights adequately.

Tiles: SEE CERAMIC; CORK; QUARRY; VINYL

Toaster

It is possible to do some simple repairs on a toaster, but if the element or the pop-up mechanism fails, get the toaster repaired by the manufacturer or a service agent.

Cleaning a toaster Time: a few minutes

Keep the toaster free of crumbs as they can clog up the pop-up mechanism, cause a burning smell, and even catch fire. Some crumbs can be removed by turning the toaster upside-down, but it may be necessary to remove the crumb tray to clean out all of them.

YOU WILL NEED Newspaper, pastry brush or old paintbrush. Possibly: screwdriver.

Unplug the toaster and, working over a sheet of newspaper rather than over the sink, loosen the bottom. In some models, the bottom of the toaster is hinged, to swing down for cleaning. Other models have a retaining screw that must be loosened before the base can be removed.

Shake out the crumbs and use an old, clean paintbrush or a pastry brush to remove the crumbs that have stuck to the inside of the toaster. Do not use a knife or other hard object when cleaning, as you may damage the elements.

Checking the flex Time: a few minutes

If the toaster works intermittently, there may be a broken wire inside the flex or a loose connection in the plug. First, check the plug's connections (see *Electric plug*).

YOU WILL NEED Screwdriver, battery-powered circuit tester.

If the plug's connections are secure, leave the plug out of the socket and open the base of the toaster.

This will expose the terminal block onto which the wires are joined.

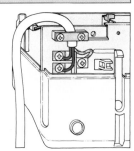

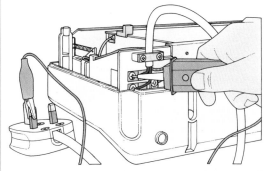

Attach the crocodile clip of a circuit tester to the Live pin of the plug (look for the 'L' beside it). Then touch the Live terminal in the toaster with the metal probe on the circuit tester and press the 'Test' button.

If the flex is undamaged, the light will come on and an audible signal will be heard. If the flex is broken or damaged, the bulb on the circuit tester will not light up, and the flex will need to be replaced (see overleaf).

Keep the cable short on a toaster

Some toasters have a cable storage slot in the side, or a cleat underneath, around which the cable can be wound. To prevent accidents, expose the minimum practical length of cable, especially if there are small children in the house who might pull at it.

REMOVING STUCK TOAST

Never use a knife or other metal utensil to hook out a piece of bread that has become stuck in a toaster. Instead, unplug the toaster and use a wooden spoon or spatula to dislodge the bread.

SAFETY FIRST WITH ELECTRICITY

Before starting any work on an electrical fitting or appliance, make sure to cut off the electricity supply – either by switching off at the main fuse box, or by unplugging the appliance.

Toaster (cont.)

Faultfinder guide: Toaster

Toaster doesn't work

POSSIBLE CAUSE Browning control is set wrongly.
ACTION Reset it correctly.

POSSIBLE CAUSE Fuse may have blown in the plug.
ACTION Test the fuse and replace if necessary.

POSSIBLE CAUSE Connections in the plug are loose.
ACTION Tighten the connections (see *Electric plug*).

POSSIBLE CAUSE Element failed.
ACTION Unplug the toaster. Remove the crumb tray. Examine the element. If broken, take to service agent.

Toast burns on even the lowest setting

POSSIBLE CAUSE Build-up of crumbs is preventing pop-up function.
ACTION Unplug the toaster. Clean the crumb tray and the inside of the toaster.

Toast doesn't brown

POSSIBLE CAUSE Thermostat or pop-up mechanism may have failed.
ACTION Take toaster to be repaired.

Toaster works intermittently

POSSIBLE CAUSE Loose connections to plug or toaster.
ACTION Unplug. Examine the plug and the connection to the toaster. Tighten connections.

POSSIBLE CAUSE Damaged or broken flex.
ACTION Unplug toaster. Check flex with circuit tester (see 'Checking the flex') and replace it if necessary.

Battery-powered circuit tester

This hand-held, battery-powered tool has a crocodile clip and an insulated metal probe. It is used to locate breaks in a circuit on an electric appliance, when the appliance is unplugged. If the circuit is unbroken, the bulb lights up and an audible signal is heard. It can also be used to test fuses.

Replacing the flex   Time: ½ an hour or less

YOU WILL NEED Screwdriver, masking tape, replacement flex.

If the flex needs replacing, unplug the toaster and remove the flex from the terminals in the toaster, checking that each terminal is clearly marked, so that you can reconnect them correctly when you fit the new flex.

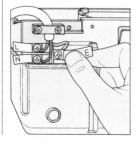

If the terminals are not marked, cut small pieces of masking tape, place one beside each terminal and label them all.

Open the plug and disconnect the old flex. Take the old flex with you when buying a new piece, to make sure you buy the same type (see *Flexes & cables*). Connect the new flex to the plug (see *Electric plug*: 'Wiring a plug').

Connect the other end of the new flex to the terminals in the toaster, making sure that each wire is connected to the correct terminal. Close the base of the toaster and screw the baseplate into position, if necessary.

Doing a safety check

After doing any sort of repair on a toaster, do a safety check. Use a circuit tester to make sure that the outer casing is earthed and that there are no short-circuits between the casing of the toaster and the flex wires.

YOU WILL NEED Battery-powered circuit tester.

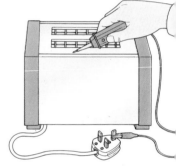

Unplug the toaster from the wall socket and attach the crocodile clip on the circuit tester to the 'Earth' pin on the plug (marked 'E'). Touch the outer casing of the toaster with the metal probe and press the 'Test' button.

Next, press down the bread carriage and touch the outer casing again, pressing the 'Test' button.

If the bulb does not light on either of these tests, the earth connection is faulty. Check that you have connected the wires correctly (see *Electric plug*: 'Wiring a plug'). If there is no obvious fault, take the toaster to be repaired.

Set the toaster to suit the bread

The commonest complaint about toasters is toast that is either burnt or not brown enough.

Different types of bread contain different levels of moisture, and it is necessary to remove some or all of this in order to toast the bread. Set the toaster to make allowances for this and for its freshness. There will be more moisture in a loaf of bread when it is fresh, so raise the setting slightly.

Bread that is taken from the freezer to be toasted will take longer to brown than the same type of bread kept at room temperature. Some toasters have a special button to compensate for this, usually marked with a star symbol.

If you are making a lot of toast, the toaster will get progressively hotter after the first few slices. To avoid burning later slices, lower the setting a little with each subsequent toasting.

Toggles & frogs

Toggles and frogs are decorative clothes fastenings and can work loose in time. They should be sewn back in place as soon as possible with a sturdy needle and strong thread.

Toggles should be sewn on like buttons, with a shank (see *Buttons*) that is long enough to take the frog (or loop), which is usually made of cord or braid.

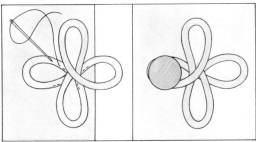

Restitch the frog onto the fabric in its previous position, making the stitches as small as possible. Make sure the loop will be large enough to accommodate the toggle.

Cleaning toggles and frogs

• Toggles are usually made of bone, plastic or wood. Wipe them occasionally with a little neat washing-up liquid, to remove grease from handling. Dry them with paper towel.

• Garments with frogging are usually dry-cleaned. The cleaner should know how to deal with frogging, which may need removing before cleaning and then replacing afterwards. Check how much this will add to the cost, as you may prefer to do the job yourself.

If you clean the frogging yourself, use an aerosol grease solvent. Allow the frogging to air thoroughly before stitching it back in place.

Military uniforms with metallic frogging should be cleaned by a specialist. The Dry Cleaning Information Bureau (Tel. 0181 863 8658) will recommend a cleaner.

Toilet: SEE LAVATORY

Torch

Repairing a torch with leaking batteries
Time: a few minutes

Batteries sometimes leak. When they do, they are useless and have to be replaced. To avoid this problem, use alkaline batteries wherever possible as they will usually last longer and are less liable to leak. And if a torch is to be left unused for any length of time, remove the batteries.

Even removing leaking batteries and replacing them with new ones may not make the torch work if acid from the batteries has covered the contacts in the torch. It must be removed before the torch will work.

YOU WILL NEED Coarse sandpaper, pencil or short stick, gloves, new batteries. Possibly: new bulb.

Wrap a piece of sandpaper around the end of a pencil and, wearing gloves, use it to rub away the acid deposits on the torch contacts. But beware – the acid deposits can burn the skin.

Make sure all the contacts are clean before reassembling the torch. You may also need to replace the bulb.

Recharging torch batteries

If your torch has rechargeable batteries, when the light weakens leave it switched on until it goes out completely then recharge the batteries immediately. Do not 'top up' batteries before it is necessary or they will cease to hold their charge correctly.

Towel rail

A towel rail may have to take a lot of strain, so fix it firmly to the wall. A long one may need a central support bracket.

Putting up a towel rail   Time: 2 hours or less

YOU WILL NEED Tape measure, paper, clear adhesive tape, masking tape, vice, hacksaw, spirit level, china-marker pencil, power drill, masonry or twist bit, wall plugs or cavity-wall fixings.

SHORTENING A CHROMIUM-PLATED RAIL If the rail is a chromium-plated tube that fits into two end-brackets, it can be shortened to fit the space available.

Wrap a strip of paper around the tube where the cut will be made and stick it down with adhesive tape so that the edge of the paper gives a cutting line.

Wrap a rag around the tube and clamp it in the jaws of a vice, then cut it to length with a hacksaw.

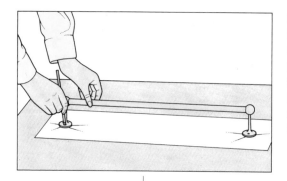

POSITIONING THE RAIL Lay the assembled towel rail on a strip of paper. Make a pencil mark through the screw holes in each bracket onto the paper. This will make a template to help you to drill the holes in the wall.

ON SOLID WALLS Position the template carefully, using a spirit level to ensure that the rail will be horizontal, and tape it to the wall with masking tape.

Drill through the hole marks with a masonry bit, then remove the paper template and fit the wall plugs.

ON TILED WALLS Position the template as above, then mark through the holes onto the tiles with a china-marker pencil.

Remove the template and stick strips of clear adhesive tape over the hole positions in the form of a cross, to hold the drill point in place until it penetrates the tile glaze.

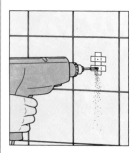

Drill deeply enough to ensure that the wall plugs are housed completely in the wall behind the tiles. A plug that is partly housed in a tile will expand as a screw is driven into it and will crack the tile.

Insert wall plugs in the holes and screw the first bracket in place. You may need a helper to hold the rail while you fix the second bracket.

ON HOLLOW WALLS Use a twist bit and heavy-duty metal cavity-wall fixings (see *Wall fixings*).

Tightening loose brackets Time: $\frac{1}{2}$ an hour or less

YOU WILL NEED Screwdriver, thicker and longer screws.
Possibly: long-nose pliers, thicker wall plugs, masonry bit.

Remove an existing screw and see if a thicker and longer screw will pass through the bracket hole.

If not, remove the bracket from the wall, pull out the wall plugs with long-nose pliers and insert fatter plugs. On a tiled wall you may have to increase the width and depth of drilled holes, to avoid splitting the tiles (see above). If the old wall plugs will not pull out, insert strips cut from new wall plugs. Replace the brackets.

If none of these measures works, you can move the towel rail along the wall slightly (see above) and fill any visible remaining holes with interior filler.

IF A HEATED TOWEL RAIL WON'T HEAT

Most heated towel rails are connected to a fused connection unit outside the bathroom. If your towel rail fails to heat, it is possible the fuse has failed. Test the fuse and replace it if necessary (see *Extractor fan*: 'If an extractor fan stops working').

Trees

When a tree is too large for the garden

REMOVING BRANCHES Best done by a qualified tree surgeon. Look in *Yellow Pages* under 'Tree work' to find one near you, or ask friends and neighbours to recommend one. Ask about the tree surgeon's previous work and get an estimate before having the job done. Also, make sure that the tree does not have a preservation order on it. Your local authority can tell you if it has.

COPPICING Suitable for younger trees in smaller gardens. For safety's sake, cut the tree down in stages, taking it down to just above ground level. New branches will sprout in a fountain shape from the stump.

This treatment can be repeated every six to eight years. Strip the cut branches of their leaves and use them in the garden as supports for beans or climbing plants.

Trees that will generally respond well to coppicing include ash, field maple, hazel and whitebeam.

TOPPING Usually effective with cypresses. If the tree or hedge is no more than 2 m (7 ft) tall, and you want to reduce its height or halt its further upward growth, cut off the top just below the level you want. Topping it in this way will force the tree to grow outwards rather than upwards.

A handsaw should be suitable for this.

REMOVAL Last resort for large conifers. If topping is not practical, get a tree surgeon to remove the tree. He will know how to do it safely. Doing it yourself with a chainsaw is dangerous unless you are very experienced.

If a tree has a preservation order

A local council preservation order on a tree means that it cannot be lopped, felled or seriously damaged without permission. Permission to fell a tree must be applied for in writing.

If a tree obstructs the view of traffic, the highway authority can insist that it is cut back or felled, despite any preservation order there may be on it.

There are heavy penalties for damaging a tree protected by a preservation order without first getting permission. The penalty can be a large set fine of up to twice the value of the tree. The tree is valued according to its position, its worth to the community and its price as timber.

If you live in a conservation area you must give the council six weeks' notice before working on any tree. The council will then decide whether or not to put a preservation order on it.

Neglected and overgrown apple tree

Old apple trees that have been neglected will need pruning and feeding to bring them back to fruitfulness.

PRUNING Best done in winter. Start by cutting out all the dead and diseased wood. Then remove all branches that cut across other branches or across the centre of the tree.

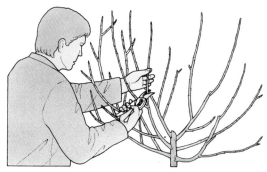

Aim at achieving a goblet shape by opening up the centre.

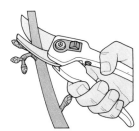

Try to cut just ahead of a good bud or spur (a short twig with buds on it).

Don't apply any sealant because trees are able to heal their own wounds.

When removing a branch use a lopper or a handsaw and make sure it is cut cleanly, to avoid encouraging disease. Do this by taking the branch back in stages, so that it doesn't fall and tear before you can cut right through it.

FEEDING Clear all grass and weeds away from the base of the tree and then give it a feed of well-rotted manure or garden compost, or a general fertiliser.

From early spring, use a hose-end feeder to give the foliage a feed of liquid seaweed once a month.

An apple tree that won't bear fruit

If the tree is overgrown, prune and feed it as described above. Alternatively, it may just be too young to fruit.

If it is in a windy position, give it some shelter by putting up a screen or wall, or move it to a sheltered spot.

If you have only one tree, check that it is a self-fertilising type. Consult your local tree nursery or garden centre, or ring Brogdale Horticultural Trust, Brogdale Road, Faversham, Kent ME13 8XZ (Tel. 01795 535286) about pollen partners. Your tree may require one.

Trees and neighbours

When a tree is planted close to a garden wall or fence, problems can arise with neighbours. Most can be resolved by informal discussions, but it helps to know your rights and responsibilities with regard to the trees in your garden.

DAMAGE TO FOUNDATIONS Trees can absorb large amounts of water from the ground and, particularly in clay areas, this can lead to the soil shrinking and causing subsidence to the neighbouring house. The tree's owner is responsible for the damage, provided that it can be proved that the tree was definitely the cause.

The house owner may be covered by an insurance policy for this type of damage, in which case the insurers will bring a claim against the tree's owner.

LIGHT AND SHADE If a neighbour's tree (or a wall) cuts out light from your garden, there may be little you can do. However, you can complain of loss of light to a part of your house or a structure such as a greenhouse in the garden.

ROOT AND BRANCH SURGERY A neighbour may be able to persuade the tree's owner to cut back the tree's roots and a few of the branches, without damaging or spoiling the look of the tree. If the roots and branches cross into your property you are entitled to cut them back, provided there is no preservation order on the tree.

Having cut them, you must offer them back to the owner. The same applies to fruit that may hang over your garden. If the fruit falls into your garden you are entitled to it, but fruit on the branch belongs to the tree's owner.

Trellis

A trellis is the ideal support for plants such as roses and jasmines which have no natural means of climbing. It can either be fixed against a wall or fence, stand free with supports at each end, or be used to add height to a fence.

There are three basic designs – square and diamond mesh in a frame and expanding diamond mesh.

How to get the best out of a trellis

● Wherever possible use preservative-impregnated wood. Otherwise treat the trellis and spacing blocks with wood preservative before assembling.
● Do not thread climbing plants through a trellis. As they grow and become stronger they may destroy the trellis or force it away from the wall. It is better to fix the plants to the front of the trellis with garden wire or reusable garden ties.
● Fix a rigid-plastic or coated-steel trellis in place with staples instead of screws. A staple gun can be used for thin sections, but for heavier trellis use heavy-duty U-shaped fencing staples.

Fixing trellis to a wall Time: 2 hours or less

> YOU WILL NEED Power drill, twist bits and masonry bit, spirit level, wall plugs, brass or alloy screws, screwdriver, steel tape measure, spacer blocks or wooden battens, wood preservative.

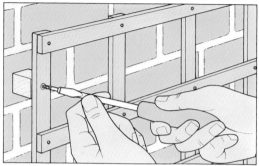

Never fix a trellis directly to a wall. Instead, use spacer blocks to leave a space behind. When fixing framed panels, the spacer blocks can be pieces of wood about 40 mm ($1\frac{1}{2}$ in) thick by 25 mm (1 in) square, or old cotton reels. For expanding trellis, use horizontal battens 40 mm ($1\frac{1}{2}$ in) thick by 25 mm (1 in). Use pressure-treated timber or coat the timber with wood preservative.

FRAMED TRELLIS PANEL Drill holes for screws through the four corners of the frame. Hold the trellis against the wall, check with a spirit level that it is level, and then mark the wall through the holes.

Drill holes in the wall and insert wall plugs. Drill through the spacer blocks if necessary (cotton reels have holes already). Hold the spacer blocks and the panel against the wall and screw them in place with non-rusting screws.

EXPANDING TRELLIS Open the trellis and measure its width. Cut the battens to length. Plan to place the battens horizontally, about 1 m (3 ft) apart.

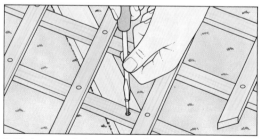

Drill clearance holes in the trellis and pilot holes in the batten and screw the two together (see *Screws*).

Then, drill clearance holes in the battens, and hold the trellis against the wall to check its position and ensure that it will be level. Use a nail or screw to mark the position of the clearance holes on the wall.

With a masonry bit, drill holes in the wall and fit wall plugs. Screw the battens to the wall with rustless screws.

Fixing trellis to a fence

> YOU WILL NEED Power drill, twist bits, brass or alloy screws, screwdriver, steel tape measure, tenon saw, set square, spirit level, wooden battens. Possibly: masonry bit, hammer drill.

Ideally, a trellis should be fitted when the fence is put up, so that posts can be used which extend high enough above the fence to take the trellis. If you are adding the trellis to an existing fence, you will have to add extension pieces to the posts. Choose framed trellis for this location.

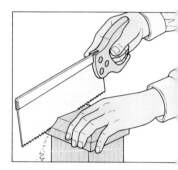

Trim fence caps on their front face with a tenon saw, flush with the post.

Use wooden battens that are about 25 mm (1 in) thick by 40 mm ($1\frac{1}{2}$ in) wide. Cut pieces the height of the trellis frame plus at least 25 cm (10 in) to create extensions for fixing the trellis to the fence posts.

Drill holes in the extension pieces and the trellis frame. Secure the extension pieces to the fence posts with rustless screws, then screw the trellis in place.

If, on close-boarded fence, the trellis is shorter than the distance between posts, join pieces of trellis together by screwing through the adjoining frames, and fix extension pieces to the posts as above.

If the fence posts are concrete, use a masonry bit in a hammer drill to make holes for the wall plugs and screws.

Trimmer, garden

Garden trimmers can be powered by electricity, batteries or petrol, and they use a rotating nylon line to cut rough grass, tall weeds or light woody growth.

Some models of trimmer are designed to be turned sideways and used to trim along the edges of lawns.

If a trimmer is not cutting effectively, check that the nylon line is feeding through correctly. The problem may be that the trimmer has run out of line. Refer to the instruction manual, if necessary.

Replacing the nylon line Time: a few minutes

> YOU WILL NEED Replacement spool or length of nylon line.

Check your manual before buying replacement line to make sure you choose the correct size and type.

If it is an electric trimmer, unplug it from the mains supply before attempting to replace the line.

In most models of trimmer, you will find the spool cover has to be twisted off in order to expose the spool.

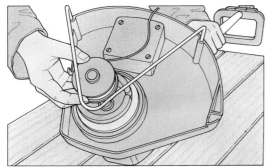

Some trimmers use a ready-to-fit spool, which slots in place.

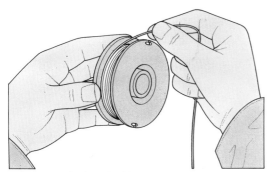

Others require a length of line to be wound onto an existing spool. Make sure it is wound on evenly, so that it will unwind without knotting or catching.

Safety with garden trimmers

- If your trimmer is electric, always use it with an RCD (residual current device) and unplug it before doing any repair, replacement or cleaning.
- Always wear sensible protective clothing when using a trimmer — closed shoes, long sleeves and trousers, and gloves. Trimming crushes some of the plant stems and their sap may contain irritants that cause burn-like blisters in sunny conditions.
- Wear safety spectacles in case the trimmer should flick up a stone (some manufacturers supply them with the machine). Take care when working near a glass door, a glass greenhouse, or a car, as flying stones could break glass panels.
- Protect the trunks of young trees and perennial plants with a piece of board when trimming nearby.
- If you have a powerful trimmer, take care not to cut the electric cable. Smaller trimmers are unlikely to damage the cable.
- For best results, use only the kind of nylon thread recommended by the manufacturer.

Maintaining a trimmer

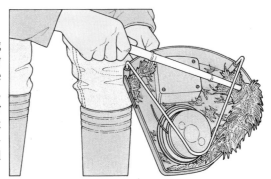

CLEAN THOROUGHLY Unplug the trimmer and thoroughly clean it and the nylon line after each use. Scrape wet, matted grass from under the trimmer with a stick and then brush the area vigorously with a stiff-bristled scrubbing brush.

DON'T STRAIN THE MOTOR Don't overwork the trimmer by trying to cut grasses and plants that are too tough for it. You may overheat the motor. If the trimmer appears to be straining, switch it off and let it cool. Cut down tougher growths by hand, or consider hiring a more powerful trimmer to complete very rough cutting.

AVOID GOOSE GRASS The weed known as goose grass or cleavers, which has leaves arranged in a starlike whorl up the stem, and very hairy clinging seeds and stems, should be avoided, because it can clog up a trimmer. Instead, pull it out by hand; it usually comes out quite easily.

Tumble dryer

Cleaning the fluff filter Time: a few minutes

The fluff filter is usually inside the drum, in front of the air outlet. In some models it may be in the door.

The filter cover varies from make to make, but most are removed easily with a twisting movement.

YOU WILL NEED Soft brush.

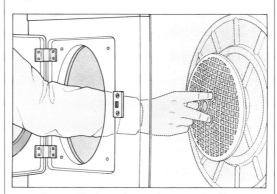

Open the tumble dryer door and remove the filter cover. The fine mesh filter behind it should come away as well.

If the fluff on the mesh is quite thick, it will peel off in large pieces. Brush the mesh and filter cover with a fine, soft brush to remove all the fluff, and replace them.

PREPARING CLOTHES FOR TUMBLE DRYING

- Check the care label on each garment. Sort laundry and dry it in groups of similar fabrics.
- Fasten zips and buttons and turn clothes inside out to stop zips damaging other clothes or buttons being twisted off.
- Wet clothes should be spun or wrung out first.

SAFETY FIRST WITH ELECTRICITY

Before starting any work on an electrical fitting or appliance, make sure to cut off the electricity supply — either by switching off at the main fuse box, or by unplugging the appliance.

THE DON'TS OF TUMBLE DRYING

- Don't put in clothes that have been washed with dry-cleaning fluid – wash them first.
- Don't tumble dry light-coloured towels with dark clothes – the dark clothes will pick up light fluff.
- Don't touch the metal drum if you empty it before the cycle is over; it may be very hot.
- Don't go out and leave the tumble dryer running. If the thermostat should fail, it could cause a fire.
- Don't tumble dry foam, rubber or rubber-type materials. The heat in a tumble dryer will damage them.
- Don't tumble dry glass fibre material, as it may contaminate other clothes and cause skin irritation.

Faultfinder guide: Tumble dryers

Machine stops or will not start

POSSIBLE CAUSE Door is not closed properly.
ACTION Close door properly.

POSSIBLE CAUSE No power supply.
ACTION Check the plug and the fuse. Tighten the connections, if necessary, and replace the fuse.

POSSIBLE CAUSE Air outlet is blocked.
ACTION Clean air filter.

Door sticks after long period of use

POSSIBLE CAUSE Heat has affected rubber door seal.
ACTION Wipe seal with non-scratch cream cleaner.

Clothes come out creased

POSSIBLE CAUSE Clothes dried for too long and probably at too high a temperature.
ACTION Soak clothes thoroughly, spin or wring, then tumble dry for a shorter time at lower temperature.

Machine stops in mid cycle

POSSIBLE CAUSE Door has come open.
ACTION Close door. If it recurs, get door catch replaced.

Dryer works but no heat created

POSSIBLE CAUSE Insufficient time set on selector dial. (Last 10-15 minutes of cycle are cool running.)
ACTION Set longer drying time.

POSSIBLE CAUSE Air filter is blocked.
ACTION Clean air filter.

Clothes not getting dry

POSSIBLE CAUSE Dryer overloaded.
ACTION Take out part of load and do in two batches.

POSSIBLE CAUSE Clothes too wet to start with.
ACTION Reset timer and give extra drying time. Spin or wring clothes first in future.

POSSIBLE CAUSE Insufficient fresh-air supply.
ACTION Open doors and windows.

Excessive condensation in room

POSSIBLE CAUSE Too much warm, moist air is being vented into room from the machine.
ACTION: Install temporary or permanent ducting to carry the moist air outside the room (see below).

Installing temporary ducting   Time: 1 hour or less

Tumble dryers which do not have a condenser give off a lot of hot, moist air, and unless this is ducted out of the room, severe condensation occurs.

If you do not wish to install permanent ducting, a temporary solution is to fit plastic ducting that carries the hot air out through a doorway or window. The hose can be disconnected and put away when it is not being used.

> YOU WILL NEED Flexible plastic duct hose, outlet connector.

Buy a length of flexible plastic duct hose with a diameter of 10 cm (4 in) and an outlet connector that fits your tumble dryer. The manufacturer will supply them.

Fit the connector and hose to the tumble dryer's outlet and lead the other end of the hose out of a door or window. It is possible to buy a right-angle connector (left), which makes this even easier.

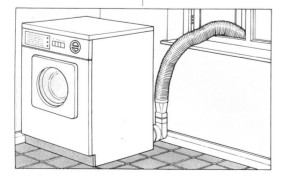

Wall and window venting kits

Complete tumble dryer venting kits, which are suitable for wall or window venting, are available from Oracstar (Tel. 01604 702181).

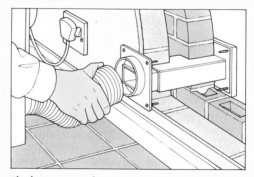

The kit contains a hose, a connector unit, an exterior vent, a cavity-wall duct, wall and window fixing plates and also an internal blanking off cap which prevents draughts when the tumble dryer is not in use.

Tyres: SEE BICYCLE TYRES; CAR TYRES

Umbrella

To prolong the life of an umbrella, always dry it open.

Many minor umbrella repairs can be done at home, but major repairs should be done by specialists. Look in *Yellow Pages* under 'Umbrellas'.

Rib has come away from cover Time: a few minutes

YOU WILL NEED Needle, strong thread.

With a strong, matching thread, doubled and knotted, take a stitch through the fabric cover at the point where it was stitched previously and then through the 'eye' of the rib. Bind the thread round the tip of the rib, to hold the cover as firmly as possible.

If the cover has torn, or the seam has come undone at the point where it joins the rib, restitch the seam neatly and strengthen it, before reattaching it to the rib.

Repairing a hole in the cover Time: a few minutes

YOU WILL NEED Matching nylon, clear adhesive.

Cut a piece of matching or toning nylon fabric, which will be large enough to cover the torn area adequately.

Following the manufacturer's instructions, apply clear adhesive to the patching fabric and position it over the tear, on the inside of the umbrella.

Smooth down the torn edges firmly onto the patch, and allow the adhesive to dry with the umbrella open.

Repairing a broken rib Time: $\frac{1}{2}$ an hour or less

YOU WILL NEED Wire cutters, wire coathanger, masking or insulating tape.

For an emergency repair to a broken rib in an umbrella, cut a length of wire from a wire coathanger and use it, like a splint on a broken limb, alongside the broken rib.

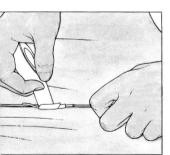

Wind some masking or insulating tape round both the splint and the broken rib. Make sure the ends of the wire are covered and will not tear the umbrella when it is open and taut.

Fixing a loose handle Time: a few minutes

YOU WILL NEED Epoxy-resin glue, cloth.

If the wooden or plastic handle comes off an umbrella shaft, it is possible to restick it. Wipe inside the handle to clean it, and also make sure the end of the shaft is clean.

Mix up a small amount of epoxy-resin glue and coat the shaft with it. Slip the shaft into the handle and wipe off any excess glue with a damp cloth.

Make sure the glue has set thoroughly before using the umbrella again (follow the glue instructions for timing).

Fixing a press-button release Time: a few minutes

YOU WILL NEED Very small screwdriver or nail file.

Telescopic umbrellas which are opened by a press-button release can sometimes refuse to close.

If this happens, check the shaft of the umbrella, just above the handle. It is possible that the little metal catch or catches, which should be protruding, have moved out of alignment and have become caught up inside the shaft.

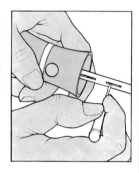

Insert the tip of a small screwdriver or nail file into the slot in the handle and apply pressure to the side of the catch, so that it aligns itself with the opening.

It should spring out.

If there are two catches, positioned one behind the other, releasing one will automatically release the other.

Upholstery

Caring for upholstery

Most modern upholstered furniture carries a care label which tells you how to clean it. Although many fabrics are stain-resistant, spills should be dealt with immediately to prevent permanent staining (see *Stains*). Silk, wool, tapestry and cotton velvets should be cleaned professionally.

Most other fabrics can be shampooed, but avoid saturating them. Many types of upholstery shampoo are worked into a foam, and then only the foam is applied. Dry foam products are easier to use.

Whichever cleaning method you use, always try it first on a piece of the fabric that is hidden from view. If colours appear to run, have the piece cleaned professionally.

Another method is steam cleaning (sometimes called hot-water extraction). It can be done professionally or you can hire the equipment and do it yourself – although the machine is heavy to use. Care must be taken not to over-wet the furniture. The machine produces a lot of moisture, so do it on a day when doors and windows can be left open.

Loose covers can be removed and washed or dry-cleaned, according to instructions on the care label.

Upholstery (cont.)

Re-covering the drop-in seat of a dining chair
Time: 2 hours or less

If the cover of a drop-in seat has worn through, or if you want to change the colour of the seat, it is possible to fit a new fabric cover. If the seat is in good condition, it may not be necessary to remove the existing cover – the new fabric can be fixed over it.

> **YOU WILL NEED** Pliers, screwdriver, flock or foam rubber, tape measure, replacement fabric, pin hammer, tacks, trimming knife, scissors. Possibly: staple gun.

Remove the seat from the chair, and lay it upside-down on a work surface of a convenient height.

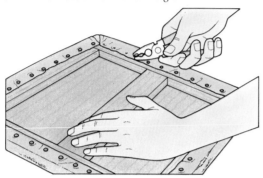

If you are going to remove the old cover, use a pair of pliers or pincers to remove the tacks which hold it down.

Pull off the cover and turn the seat the right way up. If the flock has become lumpy or uneven, pack in some new pieces to fill in the dents.

If the old flock is too badly worn to use again, cut two pieces of flock or foam rubber, one the size of the seat and one a little smaller all round. Lay the larger one on the seat and put the smaller one on top. This will make the seat look slightly domed and be softer to sit on.

FIXING THE NEW COVER Measure the seat, and cut the new cover 5 cm (2 in) larger, all round.

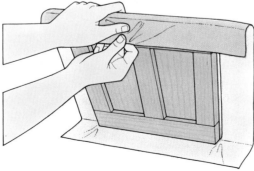

Place the fabric over the seat, and stand the seat on one edge, pulling the cover taut over the top. If the fabric is likely to fray, it is advisable to fold under the raw edge as you proceed, to keep it tidy and prevent it from fraying.

With a pin hammer, tap in a temporary tack in the centre, under the front edge. Then, making sure the cover is smooth, lightly tap in a tack at both the top corners.

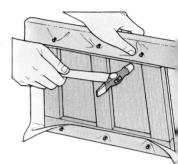

Turn the seat so that the opposite side is uppermost, and then pull the cover taut across it and hammer in three tacks as before.

With the seat the right way up, examine the edges and, if necessary, use the side of the hammer to tap away any unsightly lumps or ridges that may have appeared.

Turn the seat over again, and secure the remaining two sides with three temporary tacks in each.

An alternative method is to use a staple gun, which is quick and easy to use, but needs to be handled carefully.

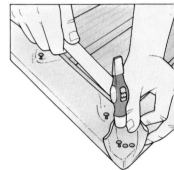

SECURING CORNERS Stretch the longest part of the corner fabric over the corner of the seat and then hammer in three tacks to secure it.

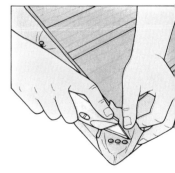

Slit the excess fabric just below the line of tacks, using a sharp trimming knife.

Lift the excess fabric at both ends of the line of tacks, and with sharp scissors, cut through to the nearest tack.

STAIN-REPELLENT SPRAYS

There are proprietary stain-repellent sprays available, designed to protect upholstery. They should be applied when the furniture is new, and again after cleaning.

370

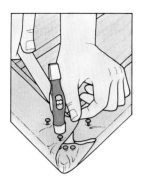

Fold in the cut end of the loose fabric and pull it taut so that it covers the line of tacks. Secure it with a tack. Repeat the action with the loose fabric at the other side.

Repeat this sequence on the three other corners of the seat, at the same time tapping the sides with the flat of the hammer, to keep the shape symmetrical.

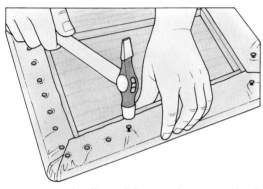

Hammer in tacks all round the seat, about 2.5 cm (1 in) apart, and hammer in all the temporary tacks, too.

If you have not been folding the raw edges of fabric under, trim away all excess fabric with a trimming knife, cutting as close to the tacks as possible.

Repairing a tear in an upholstered chair
Time: $\frac{1}{2}$ an hour or less

If there is a clean cut or tear in the upholstery of a chair or sofa, it is possible to repair it with a fabric adhesive.

> YOU WILL NEED Sharp scissors, patching fabric, old knife, fabric adhesive.

Trim off any loose threads with a pair of fine, sharp scissors, but take care not to cut the fabric any further.

Cut a piece of patching fabric that is longer and wider than the tear, trying to match the pattern, if there is one.

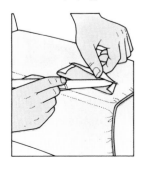

With an old knife, ease the patch into place inside the tear, taking care not to increase the tear at all.

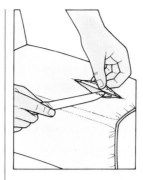

Use the knife to apply fabric adhesive to the top of the patch and the underside of the fabric. Be careful not to get it on any other part of the chair by mistake.

One at a time, press down the edges of the tear, making sure that they meet as evenly as possible.

Replacing decorative buttons on a chairback
Time: $\frac{1}{2}$ an hour or less

When a button comes off an upholstered chair, stitch it back into place with a mattress needle, which has sharp points at both ends, allowing you to sew in both directions.

> YOU WILL NEED 25 cm (10 in) mattress needle, strong thread or mattress twine.

Cut a length of thread or twine about twice as long as the thickness of the chair back. Thread it through the eye of the needle, so that one tail is only 7.5 cm (3 in) long. Do not knot the thread.

Stand so that you can see both the front and the back of the chair. Insert the needle into the front of the chair, where the button was before, and take hold of the point as it emerges behind the chair. Do not pull it right through.

When the eye disappears from the front of the chair, push it back to the front again, bringing it out as close to its original entry point as possible.

Push the needle right out, eye first, so that the short tail of the thread emerges from the second hole. Unthread the needle and pull the two threads even. Cut them off so that each tail is about 15 cm (6 in) long.

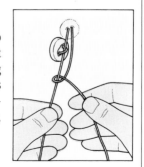

Thread the button onto one of the tails and knot both the tails once, pushing up the button into its recess in the chair. Then tie a second knot and pull it tight, securing the button firmly.

Cut both threads to about 5 cm (2 in) long and wind them round the shank of the button a couple of times, and then thread them into the eye of the needle.

Push the needle, eye first, into the seat and then pull it out at the back, leaving the ends of the threads completely concealed inside the upholstery of the chair back.

Vacuum cleaner

Clearing a blockage in the pipe Time: a few minutes

If a vacuum cleaner produces no suction when the motor is running, the dust bag may be full or something may have become lodged in the head or the suction pipe.

> YOU WILL NEED Wire coat hanger, wire cutters. Possibly: masking tape, sink auger.

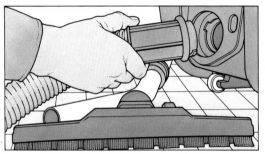

Remove the vacuum head and the hose, and pipe section from the vacuum cleaner. Separate the hose and pipe, and check each for a blockage. Some models have crushproof hoses that can be unscrewed from their plastic fittings.

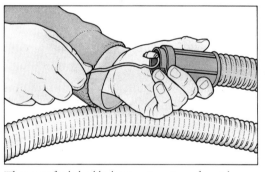

When you find the blockage, cut a piece of coat-hanger wire long enough to reach it, and twist the end into a hook. If the blockage is in the hose, wrap masking tape round the end of the hook to prevent damage.

Alternatively, you can use a sink auger (see *Baths & basins*) to remove the blockage from the pipe.
Pull out the blockage and reassemble the cleaner.

Replacing the drive belt on an upright cleaner
Time: 1 hour or less

> YOU WILL NEED Replacement drive belt, screwdriver, old nailbrush, soft cloth.

If the brush stops rotating, the drive belt may have broken or stretched, or threads may be tangled around the brush.
Switch off and unplug the cleaner.
To buy the correct replacement belt you will need to know the model number of your vacuum cleaner.

Some of the older types of upright vacuum cleaner have a small front cover plate. Remove it and lift the drive belt off the drive shaft, if it hasn't already come off.

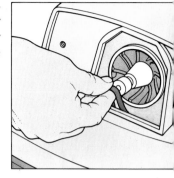

Most models have a metal base plate which holds the rotating brush. Remove the base plate to expose the brush assembly. (You may have to open a drive-belt cover as well.)

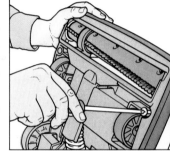

Remove the brush assembly. On older models, this may be quite difficult. Consult the instruction manual.
While you have the brush assembly out, give it a thorough cleaning with an old nailbrush and a soft cloth and cut away any entangled threads.
Depending on the model, the drive belt goes in a groove at the centre of the assembly or at one end. Loop the new belt over the brush assembly and stretch it over the drive shaft. In some older models, you may have to twist the belt clockwise before fitting it over the drive shaft.

Fit the brush assembly back into place and turn it a couple of times by hand, to make sure that it is running smoothly.

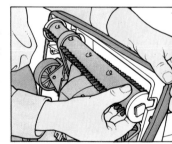

Replace the base plate or the front cover plate on the vacuum (and close the drive-belt cover if necessary).

Cleaning a filter Time: 1 hour or less

Most models of vacuum cleaner have two filters which must be cleaned or replaced regularly in order to keep the machine working efficiently.

> YOU WILL NEED Possibly: replacement filter, warm water, cloth.

The position of the filters may change from model to model, but their functions remain the same. They should be changed or cleaned at least twice a year.

UPRIGHT CLEANER Most makes have a central filter near the dust bag, which protects the motor from dust. Usually this filter can be washed and replaced when it is dry.

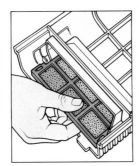

Another filter is usually located inside the dust-bag cover and it catches any small dust particles in the air that the cleaner blows out. It should be replaced about every six months.

CYLINDER CLEANER Most makes of cylinder vacuum cleaner have both motor and exhaust filters.

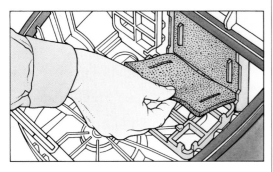

Some models of vacuum cleaner have two motor filters, held in place by a plastic grille. The front filter, which is located nearest the grille, should be replaced about once every three months (see above) – or according to the manufacturer's recommendation.

Replace the filter nearest the motor about once a year. The exhaust filter is usually located in the dust-bag compartment lid. Replace it two or three times a year.

THREE-IN-ONE AND WET-AND-DRY CANISTERS Depending on the make of the cleaner, there may be as many as four filters in addition to the dust bag. Never use the cleaner without the filters as they protect the motor.

Filters may be fabric, sponge or paper and heavy-duty cardboard. Some can be cleaned and reused.

Some fabric filters can be shaken, brushed or washed. If you wash a filter make sure it is dry before replacing it. Sponge filters can be washed and squeezed dry. You may need to reshape some types of sponge.

A paper filter can be shaken out and reused several times. Replace it when it gets too clogged to be effective.

A heavy-duty cardboard filter (or cartridge filter) can be brushed, shaken, or in some cases, washed gently and allowed to dry before being replaced.

Some models have different filters for use with wet or dry-cleaning. Always follow the manufacturer's instructions carefully when using your cleaner.

Faultfinder guide: Vacuum cleaner

Cleaner stops or won't start

POSSIBLE CAUSE Fuse in the plug has blown.
ACTION Replace fuse.

POSSIBLE CAUSE Loose connections in plug.
ACTION Replace and tighten wires.

Motor runs, but produces no suction

POSSIBLE CAUSE Dust bag is full.
ACTION Empty dust bag.

POSSIBLE CAUSE Head or suction pipe is blocked.
ACTION Clear head or inlet pipe (see 'Clearing a blockage in the pipe', facing page).

POSSIBLE CAUSE Filter is blocked.
ACTION Clean filter, following maker's instructions (see 'Cleaning a filter', facing page).

POSSIBLE CAUSE Sealed system (the system which circulates air) in a cylinder model is leaking.
ACTION Check for leaks in the hoses and bind any splits with household repair tape (see *Tape*). Replace a damaged hose as soon as possible.

Smell of burning rubber on an upright cleaner

POSSIBLE CAUSE Loose drive belt, or threads around the brush assembly.
ACTION Fit a new belt and clear the brush assembly (see 'Replacing the drive belt on an upright cleaner').

HOW TO AVOID SUCKING UP BITS OF METAL

Attach an adhesive magnetic strip along the front of your upright vacuum cleaner. It will attract paperclips, pins and nails, preventing them from being sucked up into the dust bag and damaging it. It will also rescue even smaller and more valuable metal objects dropped on the carpet, such as earring butterflies.

Varnish (SEE ALSO WOOD FINISHES)

Varnish enhances, protects and seals wood. It is available in gloss, satin or matt finish, either clear or tinted.

Buy varnish that is designed for the particular job you are doing. For example: floor varnish, such as Furniglas Floor and Stair Varnish, is resistant to scuffs, spills and domestic chemicals, and outdoor varnish may include an ultraviolet filter to prevent bleaching by the sun.

Varnishing techniques

PREPARING THE SURFACE Varnish must be applied to a clean, dry surface. If the old varnish is in good condition, wash it with a medium solution of sugar soap in water, then leave it to dry.

If the old varnish is worn, strip it off. Use chemical paint remover or a hot-air stripper on small areas. Hire an industrial sanding machine to strip wooden flooring.

Fill all gaps and cracks with wood filler. Use a waterproof filler for cracks in outdoor wood surfaces. Remove any nails, tacks or staples.

Smooth off the wood. For small areas, use medium sandpaper wrapped around a block, working with the grain of the wood and an industrial sander on large areas.

When the surface is smooth, dust it thoroughly.

APPLYING THE VARNISH Stir the varnish gently before you use it. Do not shake it, because fine air bubbles will develop, which will ruin the finish, appearing as pinholes.

Dilute the first coat of varnish with white spirit — use two parts varnish to one part white spirit. Work this into the wood with a lint-free rag, such as a piece of old sheet, to act as both a sealer and a primer.

When the varnish is dry, sand it down lightly with fine sandpaper, working with the grain, and dust it thoroughly.

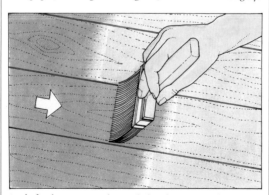

Apply further coats with a wide brush. First, work with the grain of the wood (above), then brush across the grain. Finish off by brushing with the grain.

Always apply thin coats of varnish, allowing each to dry overnight and sanding lightly between coats. It is usual to apply three or four coats of varnish.

SOFTENING THE SHINE OF VARNISH

To mellow the shine of varnish, wait a week until it is hard, then lightly rub it with steel wool. Dust it off, then apply wax furniture polish.

Veneer

Veneer is a thin surface layer of fine wood, glued to a base of less valuable wood. You can repair small areas of damage on veneered furniture yourself, but larger areas should be taken to a cabinet-maker. Look in *Yellow Pages* under 'Furniture repair & restoration'.

Flattening a small blister Time: ½ an hour or less

If the veneer has become slightly blistered, cover it with several sheets of blotting paper and press down on the paper with a hot iron. If this does not remove the blister, you will have to use glue.

YOU WILL NEED Craft knife, PVA wood glue, damp cloth, blotting paper or brown paper, iron, weight or clamp.

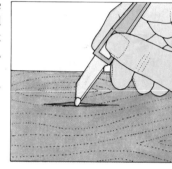

Cut the blister along the grain with a craft knife and use the blade of the craft knife to insert some PVA wood glue into the slit.

Wipe off any surplus glue with a damp cloth.

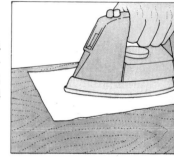

Cover the repaired area with several pieces of blotting paper or brown paper, and then press them with a warm, dry iron.

Then use a clamp or a heavy object to weigh down the paper over the repaired veneer until the glue has dried.

Refixing a loose veneered edge Time: ½ an hour or less

YOU WILL NEED Craft knife, PVA wood glue, damp cloth, brown paper, wooden batten, weight or edging clamp, fine sandpaper.

With the blade of a craft knife, carefully raise the loose area. Scrape out any old glue, then reglue both the wood and the veneer with PVA wood glue. Wipe away any surplus glue with a damp cloth.

Cover the area with brown paper and a piece of flat wood, and hold them down with a weight, if it is possible to turn the edge to face upwards. Alternatively, use an edging clamp (see *Table*: 'Repairing a chipped table edge') to hold the paper and wood in place until the glue has set.

When dry, sand lightly with fine sandpaper and finish the surface as appropriate (see *Wood finishes*).

Replacing a damaged piece of veneer
Time: 1 hour or less

If a small patch of veneer gets damaged, it is possible to remove it and replace it yourself. Try to obtain a new piece of veneer that matches the furniture as closely as possible. Some craft shops sell pieces of veneer for marquetry, or you can try a timber merchant.

> YOU WILL NEED Matching wood veneer, masking tape, craft knife, chisel, wooden spoon or small block of wood, PVA wood glue, brown paper, piece of flat wood, weight.

EDGE REPAIR Tape a new piece of matching veneer over the damaged area, matching the direction of the grain.

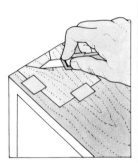

Using a craft knife and cutting through both layers of veneer (new and old), cut out a triangular patch.

Put aside the new patch and use the craft knife to carefully remove the damaged pieces of veneer. Then scrape off any remaining traces of glue with a chisel.

Make sure that the area is clean and dry, and then stick the patch of new veneer in place with a PVA wood glue. Wipe away any surplus glue with a damp cloth.

Press down the patch with the back of a wooden spoon or a small block of wood. Cut off any excess overhanging the edge of the furniture with the craft knife.

Cover the repair with brown paper and wooden batten and weigh it down. Allow the glue to dry, then trim and finish as appropriate (see *Wood finishes*).

CENTRAL REPAIR If the damaged area is not on an edge, lay the new piece of veneer over it and hold it in place with masking tape. Cut out a diamond shape through both the layers and continue with the repair as described above.

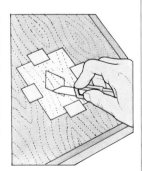

Venetian blinds: SEE BLINDS

Video cassette recorder

Faultfinder guide: Video cassette recorder

No power to the video

- Is the video plugged in?
- Is the wall socket switched on? Plug in another appliance, such as a lamp, to ensure that the socket is supplying power. If not, see *Electric socket*.
- Is the video switched on? Ensure that neither the television nor video is set to stand-by mode.
- Is there a child lock on the video? If there is, make sure that it is not switched on.
- Make sure the video is not set to 'timer record'.
- Has the fuse in the plug blown? (see *Electric plug*).
- If the fuse in the plug is not damaged, and the video still will not work, contact the supplier or the manufacturer, or look in *Yellow Pages* under 'TV, video & radio' for a television repairer.

Video won't play

- Is there a video tape loaded?
- Is the video tape rewound?
- Make sure the video is not set to 'timer record'.
- If the video still won't work, contact the supplier or the manufacturer, or a television repairer. Look in *Yellow Pages* under 'TV, video & radio'.

Poor quality video picture

- Is the video tape faulty? Try another tape.
- Clean the video head with a head-cleaning tape. Refer to the manual first and make sure that this will not invalidate the guarantee. Do not use a head-cleaner tape on a video recorder with its own built-in head cleaner – check in the manual.
- Is the picture jumping? Consult the manual and adjust the tracking on the video.

Video will not release the tape

- Condensation in the machine may be the cause of the problem. Leave the video recorder in a warm dry place for a couple of hours then try again. This should release the video tape.
- Make sure the video is not set to 'timer record'.
- If the video recorder still does not release the video tape, contact the supplier or the manufacturer, or look in *Yellow Pages* under 'TV, video & radio' for a television repairer. Do not attempt to prise the tape out of the video cassette recorder by force.

Continued overleaf

TESTING THE REMOTE CONTROL

Tune a radio to around 1300 kHz AM (medium wave), but make sure you cannot hear a programme. Move the remote video handset close to the radio aerial and push several of the handset keys. If you hear a pulsing sound then the remote control is transmitting a signal.

CARE AND CLEANING OF A VINYL FLOOR

- For normal cleaning, sweep or vacuum first, then mop with warm water and a floor detergent. Rinse the mop regularly in clean water to avoid leaving a dirty film on the surface as it dries. Once clean, polish a vinyl floor with a nonslip emulsion polish.
- Scuff marks, such as those made by shoes and boots, can be removed with an abrasive cream cleaner on a sponge pot scourer.
- Treat stains with fine steel wool and white spirit.
- Vinyl can be scratched easily, so avoid dragging heavy or abrasive objects across it.

Faultfinder guide: Video cassette recorder (cont.)

Video will not record

- Is the video tape rewound and in the machine?
- Are the time and date set correctly and in the correct format? Ensure that the programme end time has not been mistakenly set before the start time.
- If the programme starts after midnight make sure that the record day is set to tomorrow.
- Make sure the video is set to 'timer record'.
- Make sure that the programme details and times are transmitted to the video from the handset.

- Does the video tape have the record tabs in place? If not, cover the recess with a small piece of adhesive tape.

- If the programme still won't record, contact the supplier or the manufacturer, or look in *Yellow Pages* under 'TV, video & radio' for a television repairer.

Remote control will not operate video recorder

- Move closer to the video.
- Clear the path of the remote control beam.
- Ensure that the batteries are the right way round.
- Replace the batteries.
- Test the remote control unit (see previous page).
- If the remote control still won't work, contact the supplier or the manufacturer, or look in *Yellow Pages* under 'TV, video & radio' for a television repairer.

Vinyl flooring

Replacing a damaged tile Time: ½ an hour or less

> YOU WILL NEED Aluminium foil, electric iron, paint-stripping knife, replacement tile. Possibly: floor-tile adhesive, white spirit.

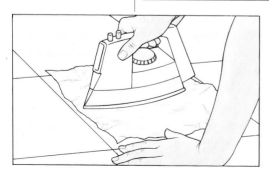

To remove a damaged vinyl tile, first lay a piece of aluminium foil over it. Then hold a hot iron on the foil for about a minute. The foil will stop the tile's surface from being burned.

When the heat has softened the vinyl and loosened the adhesive which holds the tile in place, a paint-stripping knife can be used to lift and remove the damaged tile and scrape away the old adhesive.

If adhesive is needed on the new tile, coat the back of the tile, using the notched spreader supplied with the adhesive. Then press the tile into place and wipe away the excess adhesive while it is still wet. Use a cloth dipped in white spirit or water, depending on the type of adhesive.

If the new tile is self-adhesive, just press it into place.

Patching sheet vinyl Time: 1 hour or less

> YOU WILL NEED Spare vinyl, masking tape, trimming knife, metal straightedge, floor-tile adhesive. Possibly: aluminium foil, electric iron, paint-stripping knife.

Lay a piece of new vinyl over the damaged area, making sure, if necessary, that it matches the pattern. Tape it in place with masking tape so that it cannot move.

Using a metal straightedge and a sharp trimming knife, cut a neat rectangular shape through both the new vinyl and the old.

Remove the masking tape and the top layer of vinyl. Then remove the lower rectangle, using the heat method if necessary (see 'Replacing a damaged tile').

Clean out any old adhesive and apply adhesive to the back of the new vinyl. Press it into place. Clean off any surplus adhesive while it is still wet, with a cloth dipped in white spirit or water, depending on the adhesive.

Violin

Cleaning a violin

- A violin should be cleaned every time it is used.
- Rosin from the bow comes off on the strings. Clean it off by wiping the strings with string-cleaning fluid on a soft cloth. Do not remove the strings to clean them.
- Regular dusting prevents a build-up of rosin which, if allowed to stay on the instrument, will affect the sound.
- Cleaning fluids and polishes are available from violin shops. Ensure that any polish you use does not contain linseed oil, which should only be applied by experts.
- Olive oil, used in moderation makes a good substitute for commercial polish.
- Never clean any part of a violin with methylated spirit.

Components of a violin

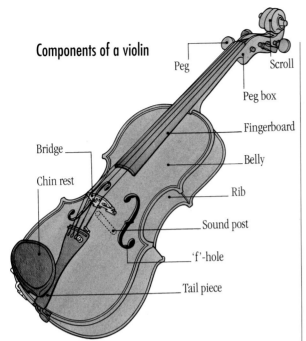

Peg
Scroll
Peg box
Fingerboard
Bridge
Belly
Chin rest
Rib
Sound post
'f'-hole
Tail piece

Replacing a worn peg Time: 1 hour or less

When a peg becomes so worn that it can no longer hold the string taut, replace it with a new one.

> YOU WILL NEED New peg, fine file, fine sandpaper, vice, pencil, tenon saw, bradawl, hand drill, 2 mm ($\frac{1}{16}$ in) twist bit.

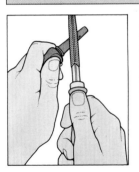

The new peg will usually be thicker and longer than required. Use a fine file to shape it then smooth it with fine sandpaper until it fits the hole in the peg box.

Turn the peg round a few times in the peg box to leave two shiny rings on it.

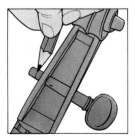

Mark the protruding end of the peg 3 mm ($\frac{1}{8}$ in) from the edge of the peg box.

Put the peg into a vice and saw off the surplus from the end. Smooth the exposed wood with fine sandpaper. Then replace the peg in the peg box and mark the centre spot on it between the two sides of the peg box.

Put it in the vice and make a start hole at the mark with a bradawl. Drill a fine hole with a 2 mm ($\frac{1}{16}$ in) twist bit to take the string. Sand the exit hole smooth.

Fitting new strings Time: depends on number

When you change a complete set of strings, deal with only one at a time. If all the strings are removed at once the reduced pressure on the belly may displace the sound post.

Gut strings do not last as long as steel strings.

> YOU WILL NEED Replacement strings, long-nose pliers.

FITTING THE E-STRING Fit the E-string first, following with A, D and then G, starting from the tail piece and working towards the scroll.

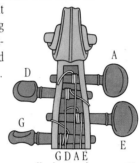

D
A
G
E
G D A E

The string comes with a small plastic sleeve on it. Position the sleeve so that it protects the bridge.

Catch the metal disc at the end of the E-string in the metal stay provided for it on the tail piece.

Catch the string in the groove of the bridge and then pull it up to the peg box.

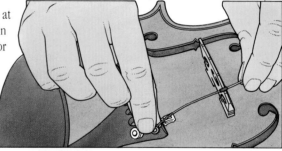

Fit the other end of the string through the hole in its peg. If necessary, use a pair of long-nose pliers to pull it through, until it protrudes from the hole by about 3 cm (1 in).

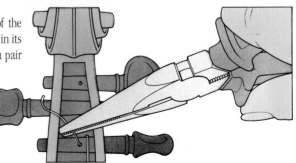

Turn the peg clockwise until the string is taut, making sure that it does not cross over itself as it is wound.

FITTING THE OTHER STRINGS The other three strings are fitted in the same way, but they may not have plastic sleeves fitted to protect the bridge.

DON'T ADJUST THE SOUND POST

The sound post is a thin stick of pine, wedged upright inside a violin, directly below the bridge. If it is dislodged when the violin is knocked or dropped, get it repositioned by a specialist.

Walkman: SEE PERSONAL STEREO

Wall fixings

The internal walls of a house may be either solid (made of brick or building blocks) or hollow (usually made of sheets of plasterboard nailed to wooden uprights).

What model of wall plug for a solid wall?

Screws cannot be driven direct into masonry. They need special wall fixings. With plastic wall plugs, first choose the screw, match it to a wall plug, then select a masonry bit the right size for the plug. All the information you need should be on the wall plug packaging.

PLASTIC WALL PLUG As the screw is driven in, the split body is forced apart, giving a firm fixing. Some have wings to prevent the plug turning.

PLASTIC STRIP PLUG Sold in long strips, this plastic wall plug is easily cut to the desired length. Used in hard walls, where holes are a perfect size for the plug.

LIGHTWEIGHT BLOCK FIXING A plug made of polyethylene for greater expansion, designed to give a good hold in solid lightweight block.

FRAME FIXINGS Their extra-long bodies can be inserted through a window frame then into the wall. Tightening the screw expands the plug in the wall. A hammer-in version expands as the nail goes in.

EXPANSION BOLTS A split metal body with a wedge is connected to the bolt. Tightening the bolt pulls the wedge up, forcing the leaves apart.

PLUGGING COMPOUND Powder is mixed to a paste then packed into a masonry hole to hold a screw.

Before fixing anything to a wall, discover which type of wall it is. Tapping the wall with your knuckles will usually give the answer, but if you are not certain, drill a hole with a fine masonry bit. A solid wall will produce masonry dust. On a hollow wall, the drill will suddenly meet no resistance. If by chance you drill into a wooden upright in a hollow wall, the drill bit will produce wood dust.

Decide whether the wall is solid or hollow, then choose the appropriate type of fixing (see left and opposite).

Drilling a hole in masonry

Select the correct size of wall plug for the screw, and the correct size of masonry bit for the plug. The wall plug packaging will give advice on the appropriate sizes.

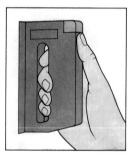

Decide where you want to make holes in the wall. Use a cable-and-pipe detector to check that no cables or pipes are hidden in the wall where you will drill.

Most cables run vertically or horizontally, so try to site holes out of line with light fittings or wall sockets.

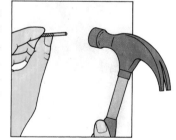

Mark the positions of the holes on the wall. Either use a pencil or, if the wall has a smooth surface, tap a small masonry bit against it with a hammer to make dimples where the holes will go.

Mark the length of the wall plug on the masonry bit, plus about 6 mm ($\frac{1}{4}$ in), by wrapping coloured adhesive tape round it.

Start drilling at low speed until the bit bites into the masonry. Withdraw the bit every 5 seconds to allow it to cool. For extremely hard materials such as reinforced concrete lintels, switch the drill to hammer action.

When the hole is complete, withdraw the drill slowly to allow the flutes in the bit to clear out the debris.

To drill a large-bore hole use a small masonry bit first, then change to a larger one to enlarge the hole.

What model of fixing for a hollow wall?

Many interior walls are hollow. They may be either plasterboard or lath-and-plaster. On a hollow wall, fix heavy loads, such as a coat rack or cupboard, directly into the wooden support battens (also called studs). Light loads such as pictures can be fixed to the plasterboard with special cavity-wall fixings.

HOLLOW-WALL PLUG As the screw is tightened, the metal, plastic or rubber casing flattens against the inside surface of the cavity. Plastic plugs are designed for lightweight fittings, such as pictures. The steel type can carry a heavier load, such as a small shelf unit.

SPRING OR WING TOGGLE There are numerous patterns. The fitting is inserted into a hole in the wall, then the metal wings spring open so that when the screw is tightened, they grip the inside of the cavity wall and anchor the screw in place.

TOGGLE AND COLLAR A nylon collar is linked by a notched nylon strip to a toggle. The toggle is inserted into the hole then pulled against the back of the plasterboard by pulling the nylon strip. The screw is screwed in and the nylon strip is cut off. If the screw is withdrawn, the fixing stays in place.

Finding timber uprights in a hollow wall

There are various ways in which to find the timber uprights (or studs) in a wall. The simplest way is to tap the wall to find the places where it sounds most solid, then push in a fine bradawl to pinpoint the position of the upright.

Where the wall is hollow, the bradawl will suddenly push through the plasterboard easily, but it will meet strong resistance from a timber upright.

PLASTERBOARD WALL Alternatively, if you do not want to make unnecessary holes in the plasterboard, use a battery-operated joist-and-stud detector (see page 158) which lights up or buzzes when passed over the densest part of a wall. Follow the instructions that come with the tool.

LATH-AND-PLASTER WALLS If you don't have a joist-and-stud detector, use a pipe-and-cable detector to detect the line of nails that holds the laths to each upright. When you run the detector along the wall, the light should come on or the buzzer sound about every 46 cm (18 in) to indicate the vertical line of nails in an upright.

A WIRE PROBE Another way to locate a wooden upright is to use a fine masonry bit to make a hole in the wall, angled sharply to one side. Then push in a piece of wire until it hits an upright. Hold it where it enters the wall and pull it out.

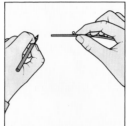

Transfer the measurement to the front of the wall and make a pencil mark about 2 cm ($\frac{3}{4}$ in) farther on.

Drill through the mark into the centre of the upright. Wood shavings will come out with the bit.

Fixing a cup hook

FIXING INTO WOOD Choose metal cup hooks, either painted or plastic coated. Make a small hole with a bradawl first to prevent the wood splitting, then screw directly into wood.

FIXING INTO MASONRY Choose a small wall plug that will grip the hook, then choose a masonry bit that will make the appropriate sized hole. Drill the hole and fit the plug.

FIXING INTO A HOLLOW WALL Use a cup hook designed to be held in place with a separate screw. Match a hollow-wall plug (see left) to the screw. Then match the wall plug with the appropriate masonry bit. The size to use will probably be given on the wall-plug packaging.

Putting up a hook for coats

HOLLOW-DOOR HOOK A small locating pin and an expanding plug are set into the back of a plastic hook. It is usually supplied with a plastic guide to give drilling positions.

Drill a hole in the door for the pin, then use the guide to position and drill a larger hole for the plug. Remove the guide and fit the pin into the lower hole and the plug into the upper. Insert the screw. It expands the plug when it is screwed in, securing the hook.

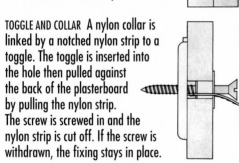

USING SELF-ADHESIVE HOOKS

Some plastic hooks are available with either a double-sided adhesive pad, or coated with glue that is activated by water. The glue type is the stronger. Only use self-adhesive hooks for hanging light objects. The adhesive grip will be only as strong as that of the paint underneath it. This type of hook is ideal for use on tiled surfaces, but do not use it on other wall coverings.

FIXINGS FOR A LATH-AND-PLASTER WALL

Hollow walls in a house built before about 1900 will probably be made of lath and plaster — plaster gripped between narrow strips of wood. As it is thicker than plasterboard, a standard hollow-wall plug will not be long enough to provide a grip on the inside of the cavity. Instead, use a type of spring toggle which has a longer screw than normal.

ON A CAVITY WALL Use a hollow-door hook, or a standard coat hook with a matching cavity-wall fixing and attach it to the wall as described on the previous page.

Alternatively, attach several hooks to a wooden batten and fix this to the wall, screwing it to the uprights.

Fixing a clothes line or a hammock to a solid wall
Time: ½ an hour or less

Expansion bolt hooks will take considerable strain — for example, the weight of a full clothes line or a person in a hammock. The hooks are available in a number of sizes.

Mark the position of the hook on the wall with chalk. Then use a masonry bit to drill the hole for the bolt.

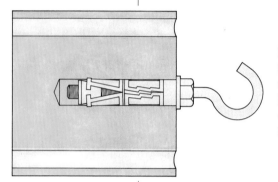

Fix each bolt into its hole. The action of tightening the hook draws a metal wedge up between two wings, locking the bolt firmly in the wall. Always drill into solid brick, not into the mortar.

Wallpaper fixes

Cleaning off grease splashes   Time: 1 hour or less

> YOU WILL NEED   Paper towel, warm iron.

If grease splashes onto wallpaper, act quickly or the mark will be permanent. Blot off the worst with paper towel. Then cover the spots with fresh paper and press with a warm iron (switched off) to draw out the rest.

Removing dust or fingermarks   Time: a few minutes

> YOU WILL NEED Bread. Possibly: very soft gum eraser.

Dark marks above radiators and around pictures can be removed with bread. Take some of the soft bread from the centre of a loaf, press it together and use it as a rubber. The bread will crumble, bringing the dirt away with it.

More persistent dirty marks can sometimes be removed with an artist's soft gum eraser.

Treating damp and mould stains   Time: depends on area

Find the cause of the damp and treat it immediately.

Mould stains associated with damp cannot be removed from wallpaper. Instead, remove the wallpaper and apply a fungicide to the exposed wall to kill off any mould spores, then repaper the area. Use a wallpaper paste containing fungicide to protect against further attack.

LOOK AHEAD!

When you hang new wallpaper in your home, put aside some spare paper against the day when you need to do repairs. When buying wallcoverings, bear in mind that good quality, heavier wallpaper usually resists damage better and is easier to repair.

DON'T USE VINYL NEAR A COOKER

Grease splashes can't be removed from vinyl wall coverings, so don't use them near a cooker.

Repairing a damaged patch of wallpaper
Time: 1 hour or less

> YOU WILL NEED Wallpaper paste, paste brush, matching wallpaper, sponge. Possibly: soft rubber, aerosol stain blocker.

If the wallpaper has been torn, or a small area has been badly marked, the easiest solution is to patch it.

First, prepare the area. For a tear, smooth the paper down and stick it with a little paste. For a pencil mark, remove as much pencil scribble as possible with a soft rubber. Cover wax crayon or a stain with spray-on aerosol stain blocker.

Match the pattern on a piece of spare wallpaper to the damaged area on the wall. Tear out an irregular-shaped piece large enough to cover the damage. Give it a feathered edge, with the white margin underneath.

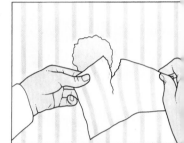

Paste the back of the patch and smooth it onto the wall with a sponge or wallpaper brush. If the wallpaper is textured, press it only lightly. The feathered edge should blend in to give an invisible join.

Repairing damaged vinyl wallcovering
Time: 1 hour or less

> YOU WILL NEED Spare vinyl wallcovering, masking tape, steel straightedge, trimming knife, wallpaper scraper, ready-mixed paste, paste brush, sponge.

Match a spare piece of vinyl wallcovering to the pattern on the damaged area, and fix it in place temporarily with masking tape. Do not use clear tape, which does not pull off as cleanly.

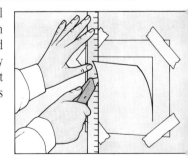

Use a steel straightedge and a trimming knife to cut a rectangular area through both layers of vinyl. Remove the patch and strip off the old vinyl with a wallpaper scraper. Then take off the masking tape.

Paste the patch and press it in place with a sponge.

Wallpapering

PREPARING THE ROOM Clear the room and remove fittings, such as wall lights and curtain rails. Remove carpet and underlay or protect them with cotton dustsheets over plastic sheeting. Place items which cannot be removed in the centre of the room and cover them with dustsheets.

STRIPPING OFF OLD PAPER Add washing-up liquid and a handful of wallpaper paste to a bucket of warm water and wet all the wallpaper in the room. Then wet the first four lengths again. Allow the paper to soak until it scrapes off easily, then use a wallpaper scraper to remove it. Or hire or buy a steam wallpaper stripper (see *Wallpapering tools*).

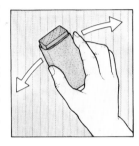

If the wallpaper is washable, it will not absorb water easily, so scour it with coarse sandpaper wrapped round a cork or wooden sanding block, to roughen the surface. Do not use wire wool or a wire brush as they can cause rust marks.

PREPARING THE SURFACE On freshly plastered walls or ceilings apply a stabilising solution. Wash down stripped or emulsioned surfaces with sugar soap and water.

Use a flexible abrasive block or coarse sandpaper to remove any small protrusions. Fill cracks in the plaster with interior filler. Let it set, then sand it lightly with medium sandpaper. Wipe the surface with a damp rag.

Bare plaster absorbs wallpaper paste, which stops the paper sliding and sticking properly. To prevent this, apply 'size' or diluted wallpaper paste to the plaster before papering – the paste packet should give instructions.

PREPARING THE PAPER Measure the height of the room from the skirting board to the ceiling (or picture rail) and add 5 cm (2 in) for trimming at each end.

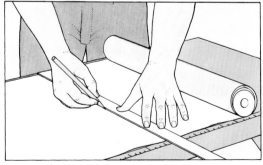

Mark a scale on the edge of the cutting table. Then unroll some wallpaper, pulling it along the table, pattern down. Measure off the required length against the scale on the table and cut it with wallpaper scissors.

Mark the top edge on the back of the paper. Turn the paper over and match the pattern of the second length against the top of the first piece. Cut several lengths.

Wallpaper paste comes as a powder to be mixed with water or premixed in a bucket. Check which type of paste is recommended when buying the paper. Make up the paste according to the instructions. Most types need to stand for a few minutes before you use them.

Brush the paste onto half of the first length of paper, working from the centre out to the edges, herringbone style. Work with as little of the table uncovered as possible. If paste gets onto the table, wipe it off immediately with a damp cloth to keep it off the right side of any paper.

Fold the pasted section of wallpaper over on itself, pasted side to pasted side, and draw more paper onto the table.

Finish pasting, then fold in the other end of the paper until it almost reaches the edge of the first folded piece.

Put the first piece to one side to soak and expand while you paste the second. Too little soaking time can result in bubbles when the paper is on the wall.

PAPERING A WALL Start hanging the wallpaper on a wall next to a window wall. Measure out from the corner at about head height. Make a mark about the width of the paper, less 2.5 cm (1 in), out from the corner. This allows for a turn of paper onto the window wall.

Hang a plumb bob down to just above the skirting board at the pencil mark. Allow it to settle, then check the distance to the corner all the way down. If the distance at

Wallpapering (cont.)

A GOOD TIME TO PAINT

The ideal time for painting all the woodwork in a room is when the walls have been prepared for papering. Take about 1.3 cm ($\frac{1}{2}$ in) of paint onto the wall in case the wallpaper does not fit exactly.

LADDERS AND SCAFFOLD BOARDS

A stepladder is necessary for decorating higher parts of walls. A scaffold board supported by two stepladders (or a stepladder and a trestle) makes a suitable platform for ceiling work. Always move the ladder or platform to an area that is just out of reach – if you stretch, you are likely to lose your balance.

SAFETY WITH ELECTRICITY

Before starting any work on an electrical fitting, make sure to cut off the electricity supply at the main fuse box.

any point is greater than the original measurement, there will not be enough paper to turn the corner, so shorten the original measurement and set up the plumb bob again.

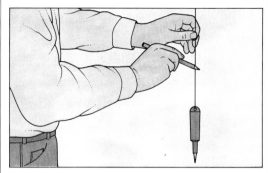

Make a second mark on the wall at about waist height immediately behind the bob string. Then draw a straight line between the two marks in pencil.

Hang the paper over your arm and carry it to the wall. Stand on the lower steps of a stepladder and take the top of the paper between your thumb and fingers. Align the paper at the top with the ceiling or picture rail, with about 5 cm (2 in) to spare, and butt it up against the pencil line.

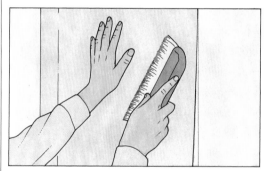

Smooth the top of the paper against the wall with a paper-hanging brush, pressing it into the corner until the turn of paper can be pressed against the window wall.

Release the lower half of the paper and smooth it into place with the brush. Then use the point of the scissors to crease the paper into both ceiling (or picture rail) and skirting. Pull it away and trim with scissors along the crease line. Thick papers and most vinyls can be trimmed on the wall with a knife and straightedge.

The second piece of paper should butt against the first. Clean off surplus paste with a damp rag as you go. When two or three pieces have been hung, run a seam roller lightly down the joins. Do not use a seam roller on textured wallpaper as it will flatten the pattern.

Dealing with tricky areas

WORKING ROUND CORNERS At a corner, measure the distance from the last sheet to the corner at the top, middle and bottom of the wall. Add 2.5 cm (1 in) to the widest dis-

tance. Cut a length of paper this width and save the offcut. Hang the length, taking the excess onto the adjoining wall.

Measure the offcut and use the plumb bob to mark a vertical line this distance away from the corner.

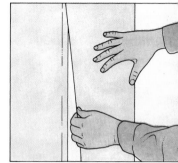

Paste and hang the offcut with the right hand edge aligning with the vertical. It will overlap the paper turned from the previous wall. Use special vinyl adhesive on overlapping vinyl.

CHIMNEY BREAST A paper with a bold pattern will look more balanced if you paste a first length centrally on the chimney breast, then work to the left and right of it.

SWITCHES AND SOCKETS Turn off the power at the mains. Hang the wallpaper from the top of the wall down as far as the switch or socket. Pierce the paper with the tips of a small pair of scissors and carefully cut a cross (or star if the fitting is round) to allow the fitting through.

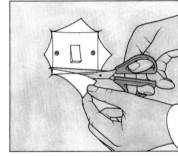

Press the cut sections against the fitting, then use small scissors to trim away the excess, leaving about 3 mm ($\frac{1}{8}$ in).

With a flush switch or socket, loosen the switch plate and tuck the extra paper behind it. Then tighten the screws.

WALL LIGHTS Turn off the power at the main fuse box, then unscrew and take down the wall-mounted light fittings.

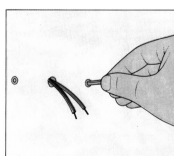

Press pieces of matchstick into the wall plugs that held the screws. Allow the matches to protrude so that they make a hole in the wallpaper when it is put in place. This ensures that you can find the holes later.

If the wall light cannot be removed, treat it as if it were a wall-mounted light switch or power socket (see above).

RADIATOR Feed the wallpaper down behind the radiator, making vertical cuts to fit around the holding brackets. Use a radiator paint roller to smooth the paper in place.

DOORS AND WINDOWS Crease the paper against the architrave and trim it so that about 3 mm ($\frac{1}{8}$ in) turns onto the architrave and hides any cracks between it and the wall.

Hanging ready-pasted wallpaper

Ready-pasted wallpaper does not expand in water so it is less likely that bubbles will form under the paper when it is on the wall. The paper does not have to be left to soak and you do not need a pasting table.

Cut a length of paper and dip it in the water trough supplied with it. Feed it into the water trough so that it rolls up loosely with the pattern facing inwards. Use both hands to lift the paper out of the trough. Hold it above the trough for a few seconds to drain off any surplus water.

Hang the length and smooth away air bubbles with a clean sponge. Work from the middle to the edge of the sheet. Wipe off any excess paste. Trim the edges as for standard wallpaper. Top up the trough with water as you work.

Curing wallpapering problems

BUBBLES Small bubbles should disappear when the paper dries out and tightens. But if the bubbles persist, the wallpaper was probably not left to soak long enough before it was hung, or it was hung over the top of old wallpaper.

Cut small bubbles with a craft knife and insert new paste behind the flaps with a fine paintbrush.

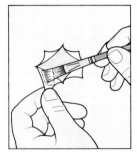

If a whole length of paper is badly affected, strip it off and hang another length, but remember to soak the paper for a bit longer before hanging it.

PAPER WILL NOT SLIDE Water in the paste is being absorbed too quickly. Either the wall has not been sized or the paste is too watery. Make sure you have mixed the paste as recommended by the manufacturer.

LIFTED SEAMS Most common with vinyl coverings. Lift the edge of the paper and apply seam adhesive. Press in place and wipe away any surplus adhesive while it is still wet.

PAPER COMES AWAY FROM THE WALL The paste is too weak, the wall has not been sized, condensation has formed on the wall, or the paper has been applied over distemper or gloss. It may be possible to paste small patches back in place, but if it is a large-scale problem, strip the walls and start again.

GAPS AT THE SEAMS Try painting the gap with watercolour and a paintbrush so that it is less obvious.

Wallpapering tools:

SEE OVERLEAF

Walls, rendered

(SEE ALSO BRICKWORK; GARDEN WALLS; PEBBLEDASH)

Patching cracks in rendering Time: depends on area

> YOU WILL NEED Small trowel, old paintbrush, PVA building adhesive, bag of mortar mix, mixing board.

HAIRLINE CRACKS Very fine cracks in rendering can be ignored if the wall is to be painted. To overcome the problem, choose a masonry paint with an additive designed to fill hairline cracks as the paint is applied.

LARGE CRACKS For larger cracks, use the point of a trowel to rake out loose and crumbling material, then brush the cracks clean with an old paintbrush kept for this purpose.

Apply a coating of neat PVA building adhesive to the cracks to bind any remaining loose material and make the new mortar grip better.

Make up a dryish mix of bagged mortar and apply it to the cracks with a trowel, smoothing it while it is soft.

Replacing missing rendering Time: depends on area

> YOU WILL NEED Small trowel, old paintbrush or dustpan brush, PVA building adhesive, bag of mortar mix, mixing board, straight wood batten.

Use the point of a small trowel to remove any remaining loose pieces of rendering, then brush the whole area clean with an old paintbrush or a dustpan brush.

Apply a coating of neat PVA building adhesive to the base of the hole and the edges of the area to be filled.

Continued on page 386

WALLPAPERINGTOOLS

Make wallpapering as easy as possible by collecting all the tools you are likely to need beforehand, and preparing the area thoroughly.
If you are hanging ready-pasted wallpaper make sure that you have a water trough.

WATER TROUGH For use with prepasted wall coverings.

COTTON DUSTSHEETS Used to cover furniture and floor coverings while preparing surfaces and wallpapering.

TRIMMING KNIFE For trimming and cutting vinyl wall coverings. You can use it with a straightedge to trim pasted paper, but make sure the blade is sharp and the paper is not too thin, to prevent tears.

PAPERHANGER'S SCISSORS Stainless steel blades, about 25 cm (10 in) long, are the best for most cutting work.

SMALL SCISSORS Used for fine-trimming round sockets and switches.

PLUMB BOB AND LINE A small weight suspended on a fine cord, used to mark the position of the vertical edge of a first strip of wallpaper.

STEEL STRAIGHTEDGE For marking off a length of wallpaper before cutting it, and for use with a trimming knife to trim heavier wall coverings at picture rail, ceiling or skirting.

PAPERHANGING BRUSH For smoothing out creases and bubbles. Do not use it for anything else; keep it clean.

SCRAPER
For removing softened, old wallpaper. A 10 cm (4 in) blade is the best for stripping wallpaper.

PASTING TABLE
For measuring, cutting and pasting wall coverings. An alternative is a flush door on trestles.

SERRATED SCRAPER Used to score impervious wall coverings so that water can penetrate, but be careful not to damage the plaster behind the covering.

STEAM WALLPAPER STRIPPER
For the easy removal of old wall coverings. A small model can be bought, or larger models hired.

STEEL TAPE MEASURE
For accurate measuring. Choose one that is at least 3 m (10 ft) long with a lock to keep the tape extended.

CHALKED LINE Fixed at one end, held taut and snapped against the surface to leave a guideline when positioning ceiling paper, coving or vinyl floor tiles. You can buy a chalked line ready-made, or make one yourself by rubbing coloured chalk along a length of string.

SEAM ROLLER
For pressing down the seams of newly hung wallpaper. Do not use it on embossed or relief wallpaper.

SPONGE For wiping away surplus paste from architraves and skirtings.

PASTE BRUSH
Use a 12.5 cm (5 in) or 15 cm (6 in) brush to apply paste to wallpaper or walls. Check that it is clean and free from old, hardened paste before use.

SOFT CLOTHS
Damp for wiping up spills and dry for final smoothing.

CAUTION STEAM

STEAMMASTER

WARNING
READ INSTRUCTIONS
MAXIMUM LOADING

STANLEY

Harris Classic

Make up a dryish mix of mortar – the consistency of a sand pie – and apply it with a trowel, pressing the mortar in place until it is just proud of the surface. Use a straight wood batten, applying a slight zigzag motion, to smooth the mortar to the level of the rest of the wall.

Filling gaps around window or door frames

If gaps develop around window frames or door frames, they should be sealed quickly to prevent rainwater getting in and rotting the wood (see *Sealants*).

Wardrobe:

SEE CUPBOARDS AND WARDROBES

Washbasin: SEE BATHS AND BASINS

Washing machine

Draining a machine and its outlet filter

Time: ½ an hour or less

If a machine stops during a washing cycle (see Faultfinder guide, opposite), you may have to drain it, but remember that the water and the washing inside it may be very hot.

> **YOU WILL NEED** Large bucket, pliers, shallow tray, sponge or old towels. Possibly: coin or screwdriver.

Switch off the machine and unplug it from the wall socket. Pull the machine away from the wall sufficiently to be able to gain access to the back of it. Protect the floor.

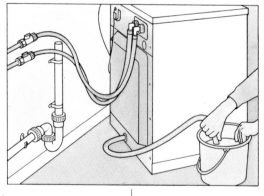

DRAINING THE MACHINE Lift the outlet hose from the outlet pipe on the wall and lower the end of the hose into a basin or bucket. The water will drain out.

If the bucket gets too full, raise the outlet hose and the water will stop draining while the bucket is emptied. Lowering it will start it draining again.

When no more water comes out, it is safe to open the machine and remove the clothes. On some models, you may have to reconnect the machine, switch it on again and set the control to 'off', before you can open the door.

DRAINING THE OUTLET FILTER The position of the filter can vary from make to make. Hoover and Hotpoint washing machines do not have an outlet filter at all.

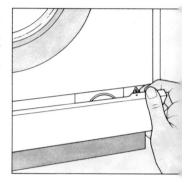

In some machines the filter is concealed behind a panel that simply pulls off (right). In others, the filter is behind a small hinged panel, visible from the front, which can be removed with a coin or a screwdriver.

The filter will have a handle or a grip-point which must be twisted, usually anticlockwise, to release it.

It may still have as much as a litre (1¾ pints) of water left in it, so place a container, such as a large, shallow baking tray under the filter opening before releasing it. You may also need a sponge or old towels to mop up any excess water that escapes.

Clearing a blocked outlet filter Time: 1 hour or less

> **YOU WILL NEED** Small, stiff brush.

Switch off the machine and disconnect it from the wall socket. Drain the machine and the outlet filter (see left).

Put the plug in the sink or basin, so that the fluff you will remove from the filter does not block the drain. Alternatively, work over a plastic bowl in the sink.

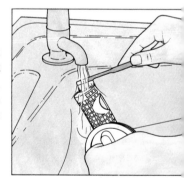

Remove the filter from the machine and wash it under cold, running water, cleaning it thoroughly with a small, stiff brush such as an old toothbrush.

While the filter is out, feel around carefully inside the filter chamber, to make sure that there are no objects, such as coins, buttons or paperclips, caught inside. Turn the drain pump vanes to make sure they are not being obstructed, but take care not to trap your fingers.

Replace the filter, checking that it is tightly in place, and then close the filter cover.

If you have a washing machine with a water pressure-operated valve to stop detergent wastage, you may need to operate the machine to reseat the valve. Refer to the manufacturer's instructions, as valves vary from make to make.

Faultfinder guide: Washing machine

Machine leaks

❗ Do not attempt to open the machine. Switch it off and unplug it from the wall socket. Drain the machine (see 'Draining a machine and its outlet filter', facing page). When it is empty, plug it in and switch on. You should be able to open the door and remove the clothes.

POSSIBLE CAUSE Door seal may have perished.
ACTION Call a service engineer to replace it.

POSSIBLE CAUSE One of the inlet hoses or the outlet hose may be loose or damaged.
ACTION Tighten joints on hoses or replace.

POSSIBLE CAUSE If the filter has been cleaned recently, it may have been refitted incorrectly.
ACTION Check that filter fits correctly (consult your owner's manual).

No hot or cold-water intake when machine is switched on

POSSIBLE CAUSE If there is no 'Power On' light, there may be a faulty electrical connection.
ACTION Check that the plug is pushed into wall socket correctly. If it still does not work, unplug it and check the connections and the fuse.

POSSIBLE CAUSE If the power light is on, suspect the programme set-up.
ACTION Check programme setting has not been changed and it is not on 'Rinse hold'. Is the door shut?

POSSIBLE CAUSE If the 'Power On' light is shining and the programme set-up is correct, the problem may be mechanical.

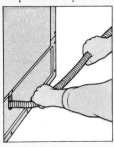

ACTION If outlet hose is kinked, straighten it. Check water supply tap is on. Check inlet hose for blockage (see 'Cleaning water inlet hose filters').

Machine takes a long time to fill

POSSIBLE CAUSE Low water pressure.
ACTION Check water pressure at sink or basin. If the pressure is low, check with your water company. Do not use the washing machine until the pressure has been restored.

POSSIBLE CAUSE Inlet filters may be blocked.
ACTION Clear inlet filters (see 'Cleaning water inlet hose filters', overleaf). Their position may vary from model to model, but they are usually situated near where the water inlet hose joins the machine – either between the hose and the tap, or the hose and the machine.

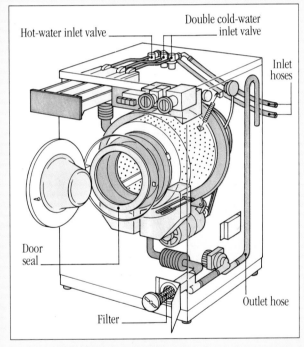

Hot-water inlet valve
Double cold-water inlet valve
Inlet hoses
Door seal
Filter
Outlet hose

Water will not pump away

POSSIBLE CAUSE The washing programme may be causing the problem.
ACTION Check that the programme is not on 'Rinse hold' or still at the water-heating stage. Has a power cut interrupted the programme?

POSSIBLE CAUSE The outlet hose has become kinked or may be blocked.
ACTION Straighten hose. If still blocked, drain the machine and clear the outlet hose (see 'Clearing a blocked outlet hose', overleaf).

Machine vibrates excessively when spin-drying

POSSIBLE CAUSE The washing machine may not be standing on a firm, level surface.
ACTION Check the top of the machine with a spirit level, and if it tilts, level it by laying off-cuts of carpet or a wad of newspaper on the floor under the machine. Test it again with the spirit level.

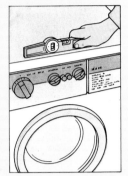

POSSIBLE CAUSE The load may not be distributed evenly.
ACTION If possible, stop machine, open it and redistribute load.

POSSIBLE CAUSE The load may be too heavy for machine.
ACTION Stop machine. Open and remove some items. Do not overload with towels or bath mats.

Machine stops during a washing cycle

POSSIBLE CAUSE If no 'Power On' light, suspect electrical fault.
ACTION Unplug the machine and check the plug for loose connections. Check and replace the fuse if necessary.

POSSIBLE CAUSE If the 'Power On' light shows, suspect faulty setting-up of the washing programme.
ACTION Check programme setting has not been changed. Check programme is not on 'Rinse hold'. Check the machine door is shut.

POSSIBLE CAUSE If the 'Power On' light shows and the programme set-up is correct, suspect a mechanical fault.
ACTION Check that the water-supply tap is on. Check the outlet hose for possible kink. Check the outlet hose and filter for a blockage (see 'Draining a machine and its outlet filter' and 'Clearing a blocked outlet filter', both opposite, and 'Clearing a blocked outlet hose', overleaf).

Wasps

CLEANING THE DISPENSER TRAY

If you use a powder detergent, the dispenser tray will need regular cleaning.

Some trays need to be lifted slightly after being pulled out as far as possible.

Follow the manufacturer's instructions for removing the tray and do not attempt to force it.

CUTTING DOWN LIMESCALE

If you live in a hard-water area, use a water-softening powder in your washing machine to reduce the build-up of limescale on the heating element.

If the heating element does become coated with limescale, it will be necessary to get a service engineer to change the element.

TREATING WASP STINGS

Treat a wasp sting with antihistamine lotion, spray or cream. A victim who is allergic to stings should be taken immediately to the nearest hospital's Accident and Emergency Department.

Clearing a blocked outlet hose Time: 1 hour or less

If the machine will not empty, and you have drained and cleaned the outlet filter without finding a blockage, it may be that the outlet hose is clogged.

YOU WILL NEED Screwdriver, long piece of wire, masking tape. Possibly: washing-up liquid.

Make sure that the machine is unplugged before proceeding. You may need to tip the machine onto its side to gain access to the outlet hose, which is attached at a bottom corner at the back. Be prepared for some more water to escape. In some models you may have to remove a panel from the back of the machine.

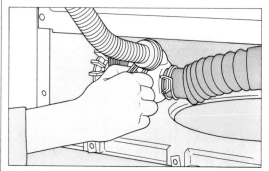

The outlet hose is fastened to the pump by a metal clip held in place by a screw or spring clip. Loosen the screw or clip, and you should be able to pull off the hose.

If the hose is tight, squirt a little washing-up liquid onto the joint, and wait for it to soak through.

Cut a suitable length of coat-hanger wire and bind the end with masking tape. Straighten the hose and carefully clear the blockage with the wire.

While the hose is off, check the pump for a blockage. When you put your fingers inside the pump, you should be able to feel the vanes of the pump. They should move freely. If not, it is possible that the pump is clogged. If you cannot clear the blockage by hand, call a service engineer.

When you have checked and cleaned everything, replace the outlet hose, making sure the metal clip is tight. Put the machine back on its feet, turn it on and watch for leaks. If it does not leak, push it back into position.

Cleaning water inlet hose filters Time: $\frac{1}{2}$ an hour or less

If a washing machine takes a long time to fill, and you are sure that the mains water pressure has not fallen, it is possible that the filters in the inlet hoses are partially blocked.

YOU WILL NEED Pipe wrench, long-nose pliers, vinegar, pin. Possibly: replacement hose.

On most makes of machine there is a water inlet filter between the inlet hose and the washing machine, or between the inlet hose and the tap. A few makes have both.

Unplug the machine and turn off the water supply at the tap. Remove one inlet hose from the back of the machine — you may need a pipe wrench. Save the washer in the plastic hose connection, as it will be needed again.

Use long-nose pliers to remove the filter from the back of the machine.

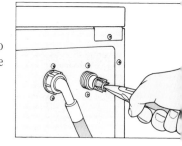

Remove the rubber seating that you find on the filter with the pliers, and keep it to use again.

Wash the filter under running water, and if any dirt sticks, soak the filter in vinegar and pick out bits of grit with a pin.

Replace the rubber seating and the filter in the back of the machine, and fit the washer into the hose connection.

Then disconnect the second inlet hose, remove the filter and clean it in the same way. While each hose is disconnected, examine it for surface cracks or signs of wear. If necessary, replace it with a new hose which can be obtained from the manufacturer.

Reconnect the hose, plug in the machine, restore the water supply and watch for leaks. If it leaks, tighten the plastic hose connections very carefully with the pipe wrench.

Wasps

When sitting or eating outdoors, you can keep wasps at bay by burning a citronella-scented candle. You can also make traps from jars a third full of jam and water and a little detergent. Cover them with paper lids perforated with wasp-size holes and held in place with an elastic band.

Indoors, fit insect screens over open windows and use a flying-insect aerosol. If wasps build a nest in your loft, spray the loft thoroughly with fly-and-wasp spray and close the hatch. Repeat the treatment two or three times until there are no further signs.

If you can see the nest — and it is small — treat it with powder from a puffer pack made especially for wasps' nests. Alternatively, contact the local authority and ask them to deal with it. A fee will probably be charged.

Waste-disposal unit

Waste-disposal units should be fitted only by professional plumbers or electricians. Use waste-disposal units with great care; never reach inside, and keep hard objects such as cutlery away from the unit. Always run water through the unit as it is working to flush away the waste.

Unblocking a waste pipe

If the waste pipe below the waste-disposal unit becomes obstructed you can probably clear the blockage yourself.

YOU WILL NEED Bucket. Possibly: screwdriver, sink auger.

Turn off the power to the waste-disposal unit. Then place a bucket under the unit and disconnect the waste pipe from underneath. It will be attached either with a plastic fitting held in place by a plastic retaining nut, or by a hose clip with a captive screw.

When the pipe has been removed, turn on the tap gently. If water comes through the waste-disposal unit, the blockage is in the waste pipe. This can be cleared with a sink auger (see *Baths & basins*).

If no water emerges, the blockage is in the waste-disposal unit. Call a service engineer to clear it for you.

Wheelbarrow

Mending a damaged wheelbarrow body Time: 1 hour

The short side of the wheelbarrow nearest the handles is often the first place to crack. However, the following fixing method will work on other parts of the wheelbarrow too.

YOU WILL NEED Plywood or acrylic-plastic sheet, hacksaw, bradawl, G-cramp, safety spectacles, power drill and HSS bit, 6 nuts and bolts, 12 soft fibre washers, screwdriver, spanner.

Cut a patch of acrylic (such as Perspex) or plywood to fit across the crack with at least 5 cm (2 in) overlap. Using a bradawl, mark positions on the patch for about six holes about 2.5 cm (1 in) from the edge.

Clamp the patch to scrap wood on a workbench, put on safety spectacles and drill the holes. Position the patch in the barrow, mark the position of the holes and drill.

Feed a fibre washer onto a bolt, push it through the patch and the body of the wheelbarrow. On the outside, put on another washer and finally the nut. Hold the bolt steady with a screwdriver and tighten the nut with a spanner. Repeat for the other bolts.

Repairing a ball wheel Time: ½ an hour or less

YOU WILL NEED Bowl of water, bicycle pump, matches or soldering iron, penknife or old screwdriver. Possibly: new ball.

REPAIRING A LEAK If the leak is hard to see, inflate the ball slightly, revolve it in a bowl of water and look for bubbles.

Apply gradual heat to the hole using a match or soldering iron, but take care not to use too fierce a heat. When the plastic has melted, smooth it over with a penknife or the blade of an old screwdriver. Allow the ball to cool, then pump it up with a bicycle pump.

REPLACING THE BALL If the ball needs replacing, deflate it slightly, and press on its sides to free it from the frame.

Deflate the new ball. There are two bearings, each in two parts. Place the small, domed bearings into each end of the barrow frame and the larger bearings into the ball.

Turn the barrow on its side and fit the ball onto the lower arm. Apply downward pressure on the ball and guide it so that the upper arm clicks into the uppermost hole in the ball. Turn the barrow upright and check that the ball is secure. Pump it up.

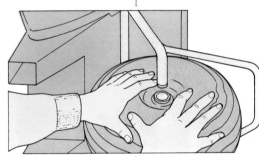

Windows

Removing broken window glass

If glass is cracked, but still in place, use clear weatherproof adhesive tape to make a temporary repair.

YOU WILL NEED Heavy gardening gloves, safety spectacles, hacking knife or old chisel, hammer, pincers, steel tape measure, hardboard or plywood, tenon saw, weatherproof tape, wood batten, screwdriver, screws, glue.

If any glass is missing, the pane must be removed completely. Lay newspaper on the ground on both sides of the window to catch the fragments of old glass. Put on leather gloves and safety spectacles. Also wear thick leather shoes to protect your feet from falling glass.

Remove the remaining pieces of glass by hand. Or tape over the glass, then score all round the edge and tap it out with a hammer. Remove the putty and any small pieces of glass with a hacking knife or an old chisel. Use pincers to remove holding pins or spring clips.

When the rebate is clean, cut a piece of hardboard or plywood to size and insert it in the hole. Tape it in place with weatherproof tape until the new glass is available.

Windows (cont.)

LOOSENING TIGHT WINDOWS

- Lubricate the frame by rubbing it with the stub of a candle or applying a dry powder lubricant.
  - If the window is stuck with paint, release it by cutting through the paint with a trimming knife.
  - If the problem is too many layers of paint, remove the paint to bare wood then repaint (see *Paint stripping*).
  - Damp can make the wood swell and cause the window frames to stick. If the paint is peeling remove it completely from the frame, then dry the frame with a hot-air gun. Repair any damage (see *Rotten wood*). Check it for fit, and sand off a little wood if necessary, then repaint.
  - With sticking sash windows, it may be necessary to remove the sashes completely (see 'Renewing a broken sash cord') in order to treat the wood.

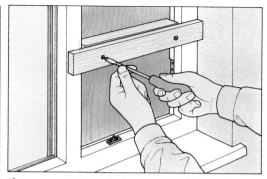

If more security is required, cut a piece of plywood at least 6 mm ($\frac{1}{4}$ in) thick to fit the frame. Working on the inside, glue and screw a batten of wood the same depth as the window frame to it from one edge to another. Then screw another batten in place so that it overlaps the frame.

Replacing a broken windowpane Time: $\frac{1}{2}$ a day or less

YOU WILL NEED Hacking knife or old chisel, paintbrush, wood or metal primer, steel tape measure, universal putty, glazing sprigs or panel pins, putty knife.

PREPARING THE FRAME Remove the broken glass and old putty (see previous page) and brush all the dust from the frame. Apply wood or metal primer to the frame.

BUYING NEW GLASS Working from outside, right into the rebate, measure the diagonals as well as the height and width. If they are equal, the hole is square. If not, make a template from cardboard and take it to the glass supplier. He also needs to know the location of the window in order to provide you with the correct weight of glass. He will deduct 3 mm ($\frac{1}{8}$ in) all round so that the glass is a loose fit. This will allow the bedding putty to cushion the glass in the frame. If the window is a security risk, as for example on the ground floor, laminated glass may be suitable. Although it can be cracked, it is virtually impenetrable.

FITTING NEW GLASS On both wooden and metal frames use universal or acrylic putty and work a lump in your hands until it is pliable. Then lay it about 3 mm ($\frac{1}{8}$ in) thick, to form a bed on the frame rebate. Press the new glass gently onto it. Always press round the outer edges of the new glass, never in the middle, to avoid cracking it.

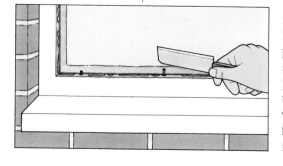

Use the back of a hacking knife or old chisel to tap in glazing sprigs or panel pins about 25 cm (10 in) apart, leaving the heads just proud enough to hold the glass firmly in place without showing above the frame. On metal windows resecure the spring clips.

Press more putty around the front of the glass, then use the flat edge of a putty knife to form a neat bevel.

Remove surplus putty from both sides of the window and use a paintbrush damped with water to smooth out any irregularities and ensure that the putty is in close contact with both glass and frame. Leave the putty to harden for at least two weeks before painting it.

Renewing a broken sash cord Time: $\frac{1}{2}$ a day or less

Cords in sash windows can fail with age, or become brittle and break if they have been coated with paint. If one cord on a window fails, replace all four cords.

YOU WILL NEED New sash cords, broad chisel or screwdriver, pincers or claw hammer, string, trimming knife, steel tape measure, galvanised clout nails.

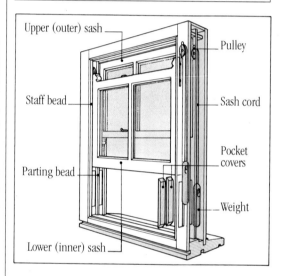

Upper (outer) sash — Pulley
Staff bead — Sash cord
Parting bead — Pocket covers
Lower (inner) sash — Weight

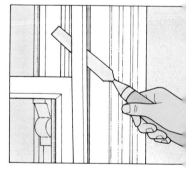

REMOVING THE OLD CORDS Work from inside the room and use an old chisel or a screwdriver to prise off the staff beads. Work from the centre outwards. Once the staff beads have been lifted at the centre, they can be sprung out of place. Use pincers to draw the nails out of the beading.

Lift the bottom sash out of the frame and into the room. Rest it on a table or a portable workbench.

Tie the end of a ball of string to the upper part of each cord (if the cords are not already broken). Hold each cord in turn and cut through it with a trimming knife below your hand. Gently lower the balance weights to the bottom of the box. This will draw the string up over the pulley. The string will be used to thread the new cord.

Prise out the narrow parting beads and lift out the upper sash. Tie string to the cords and cut as with the lower sash. If the sash cords have broken, tie a small weight such as a screw to a length of string and push it into the hole above the pulley, so that it lies over the pulley and drops down into the weight compartment and can be drawn out through the pocket.

Use pincers to prise out the galvanised clout nails that secure the cords to the sash.

Prise off or unscrew the pocket covers in the weight channels. Lift out the weights. Remove the old sash cord but leave the strings in place over the pulleys.

FITTING THE NEW CORDS To calculate the length of the new cords first measure the depth of the sash, then add two-thirds of this measurement again for each cord.

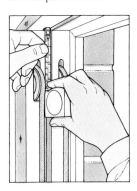

Attach the end of the new cords to the pieces of string and pull them up through the pulleys, then attach them to the weights using nonslip knots.

Place the weights back in their respective boxes and refit the pocket covers.

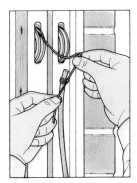

Measure the distance from the midpoint of the pulley up to the underside of the window frame and make a note of it.

Rest the upper (outer) sash on the window ledge. Then get a helper to pull down one of the cords so that the weight is just touching the pulley.

Nail the cord into the groove at the side of the sash using clout nails (see also margin, right). The top nail must be no higher than the distance from the midpoint of the pulley to the underside of the window frame. Cut off any excess cord. Repeat on the other side.

Then place the sash in position and check that it rises smoothly. Replace the centre beading. Fix the bottom (inner) sash to its cords in the same way.

Refit the inside beading, but before fixing it in place check for rattles in the bottom sash and if necessary, move the beading a little closer to the window frame.

Retensioning a spring-lift sash window
Time: 1 hour or less

Many modern sash windows have spiral springs instead of traditional sash cords. The springs can lose their tension with time, and they will need adjusting, using a special key supplied with the window.

First slide the bottom sash up and pull in the finger bolts. Tilt the sash toward you until it is horizontal, then push it up on the right and down on the left so that it is released. Repeat the process to release the upper sash, after which the spiral balances will be visible, set into the sides of the window frame.

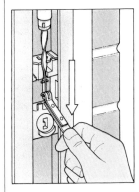

Hook the key over the bottom pin of the balance and pull down to release the upper pin. Turn the key to the right two or three times, then replace the balance in its anchor point. Test the window and repeat as necessary.

Windowsill

Repairing a rotten windowsill Time: about a day

If part of a wooden windowsill has started to rot, it is possible to repair it without replacing the whole sill.

> YOU WILL NEED Metal straightedge, general-purpose saw, chisel and mallet, replacement wood, pencil, power or hand drill, twist bit, countersink bit, wood preservative, old paintbrush, waterproof wood adhesive, wood screws, screwdriver, wood filler, sandpaper. Possibly: exterior grade paint.

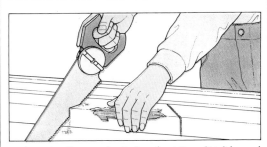

Mark cutting lines on the timber about 5 cm (2 in) beyond the damaged part. Angle them at about 45 degrees to form a wedge shape and cut them with a general-purpose saw.

If the masonry round the window restricts the saw's movement, finish off removing the rot with a sharp chisel.

STOP RATTLING WINDOW FRAMES

To cut down rattling, fit a draughtproofing strip to the main window frame (see *Draughtproofing*).

HOW TO HOLD A SASH-CORD WEIGHT IN PLACE

If you have no one to help you, nail the cord to the side of the sash, pull the weight up to the top of its compartment and wedge something like the end of a pencil into the pulley to hold the weight. Alternatively, wrap the cord around a screwdriver to keep the weight in place.

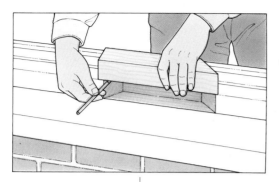

Lay a new piece of wood over the hole and mark the outline on the new wood with a pencil.

Cut the wood to fit the gap. When you have a good fit, which protrudes just a fraction from the frame, drill the repair piece to take wood screws and countersink the holes. Treat both the recess and the replacement piece of wood with clear wood preservative and allow them to dry.

Then apply waterproof wood adhesive to both the recess and the repair wood and fit the wood in place. Drive in the wood screws until their heads are well below the surface.

Fill any remaining gaps and the indent above the screw heads with wood filler. Allow it to set, then smooth it with sandpaper, working with the wood grain, until the patch is flush with the surrounding timber. Repaint the sill.

Fitting a drip bar to a windowsill Time: 1 hour or less

A windowsill should have a groove cut into its underside to act as a barrier to rain dripping down the wall. If there is a groove, clean it out whenever you repaint the sill. If there is no groove, fit a drip bar.

> **YOU WILL NEED** Hardwood strip as long as the sill and 6 mm ($\frac{1}{4}$ in) square, steel tape measure, tenon saw, drill, fine twist bit, waterproof wood glue, panel pins, sandpaper, paint.

Cut the hardwood strip to length. Drill pilot holes for the panel pins at about 5 cm (2 in) intervals in the strip.
Sandpaper the strip and clean the underside of the sill.

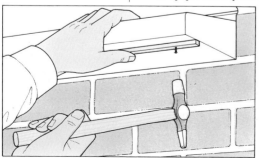

Then apply waterproof wood glue to the strip and pin it in place about 2.5 cm (1 in) from the edge.
If a concrete windowsill is too hard to drill, you can simply fix the wooden strip in place with a waterproof panel adhesive.
Paint the strip to match.

Windscreen wipers:
SEE CAR WINDOWS

Wood & board
(SEE ALSO OVERLEAF)

Softwoods

Softwoods are most often used for DIY applications around the house. Suppliers grade them by appearance and strength. Discuss with the supplier the application for which you are selecting wood and, when quality matters, choose from individual pieces of wood rather than buying a polythene-wrapped pack.

PINE Also known as deal or redwood. Pine is used for a wide variety of DIY applications, both indoors and out. It can range from creamy-white to reddish-brown and darkens rapidly when exposed to light.

PARANA PINE Tough, creamy-brown coloured, often with reddish streaks. It has an even texture and a straight grain. Available in wide, long boards, often without knots, Parana pine is often used for interior joinery. It tends to twist as it dries out, so use it immediately or store it in a dry place, weighted down evenly.

DOUGLAS FIR Also known as British Columbian pine or Oregon pine. Because it is strong and durable it is ideal for a wide range of applications including window and door frames, furniture and flooring.

WESTERN RED CEDAR A straight-grained wood with few knots. It is light reddish-brown with distinctive figuring. Its warm colouring changes to a dull grey with age. Although it is often used for external cladding and for sheds and greenhouses, this wood stands up to central heating well and can be used for radiator shelves without warping. However, it can be dented easily.

Hardwoods

Hardwoods are tougher and heavier than softwoods and consequently, harder to work. There are hundreds of species and they are more likely to be found at a timber merchant's yard than in a DIY store. Hardwoods for carving and turning can be bought from specialist suppliers.

OAK Rich, light brown, sometimes with attractive, silvery streaks. It is a hard, heavy wood which darkens with age. English oak is the toughest; European and North American oak are easier to work. It is used for flooring, external woodwork, boatbuilding, carving and for decorative veneers.

ASH Brownish-white wood with a straight grain and a coarse texture. It is tough, strong and flexible, and responds well to woodturning. Ash takes finishes such as varnish very well and is widely used in furniture-making, joinery and also for decorative veneers.

BEECH A range of colours from white to reddish-brown is available. This straight-grained wood is strong and easy to work and finishes well, but is not long-lasting. Its main uses are for furniture, toys, models and woodturning.

LIME This fairly soft wood has a whitish-yellow colour, turning to brown later. Its fine texture and straight grain make it ideal for wood carving and turning.

MAHOGANY A family of woods – which includes sapele, African mahogany and American mahogany – that is relatively easy to work and finishes well. The colour varies from medium brown to dark reddish-brown depending on the country of origin of the wood. It has attractive grain patterns. It is used mainly for furniture, fine interior joinery, decorative veneers and panelling.

MAPLE This hard and compact creamy-white wood has dark lines and a straight grain. It is strong and hardwearing and finishes well.

RAMIN Straw-coloured wood with an even texture and a straight grain. It is easy to work but it doesn't bend easily so it has a tendency to split. It is mainly used for furniture, woodturning, veneers, mouldings, handles and toys.

ROSEWOOD This extremely hard wood is dark rust-brown with some light markings. It doesn't take a good polish, but it turns well and makes good furniture. It is also used for interior joinery, handles and musical instruments.

TEAK Light golden-brown oily wood which darkens on exposure to light. It has a variety of grain and a coarse and uneven texture. Teak is easy to work and finishes well. It is mainly used for furniture, fine interior and garden joinery, decorative veneers and woodturning.

WALNUT A variety of colours is available, depending upon the source of the wood. It is greyish-brown with darker, brownish markings. The grain is straight to wavy. Walnut works easily and polishes well. Its main uses are furniture making, interior joinery, carving and woodturning.

Laminated boards

PLYWOOD Strong and pliable board made of three or more thin layers of veneer bonded together, with the grain of each layer running at right angles to its neighbour. Plywood is available in standard, exterior, WBP (weather and boilproof) and marine grades. In addition, it is possible to buy plywoods with decorative veneered surfaces on one or both sides, or with a plastic facing.

BLOCKBOARD A wood-strip core, faced on both sides with a plain or decorative wood veneer. It is extremely tough, but expensive. It needs edging with a thin batten or 'lipping' of wood. The core runs lengthways, so its resistance to bending is greater from end to end than it is from side to side.

SOLID PINE PLANK A solid board composed of strips of quality pine, bonded together with alternating grain to add stability. It can be treated as solid wood for furniture making, desk tops and shelving. No edging is needed.

Particle boards

STANDARD CHIPBOARD Wood chips bonded together to produce a coarse-grained board with a finely sanded face. Though chipboard is heavy, it has little structural strength. It is abrasive and blunts tools quickly. Internal grade is used for shelves and doors. External grade is used for cladding and flat-roof covering under felting.

FLOORING-GRADE CHIPBOARD A dense, smooth-finished, heavy board that is used as an alternative to floorboards or under carpeting. Square edged and tongued-and-grooved sheets are available.

VENEERED CHIPBOARD A core of chipboard, faced on one or both sides with a decorative wood or melamine veneer. Chipboard veneered with wood on both sides is used for shelves or as panels for furniture. Iron-on or roll-on edge strips to match the veneer are also available.

HARDBOARD A thin, tough board made from heavily compressed wood-fibre pulp. It has one textured and one smooth side and is widely available in standard and exterior (oil-tempered) grades. Oil-tempered is durable outdoors, even if it is not painted. Other varieties available include hardboard that is smooth both sides; a perforated hardboard suitable for mounting and displaying items (also known as pegboard); textured hardboards and boards with decorative faces.

MEDIUM-DENSITY FIBREBOARD (MDF) Made from wood fibres bonded together under pressure. A thick, smooth-faced board which cuts and works like timber but doesn't buckle. It is widely used for furniture and is designed to be veneered, painted or varnished.

INSULATION BOARD AND PINBOARD Softer forms of particle board, made from wood fibres lightly pressed together to form a lightweight board with little structural strength. It is ideal for insulation and for noticeboards.

WOOD & BOARD

Softwood comes from conifers, and hardwood from deciduous trees. Man-made boards include laminates in which materials are sandwiched together, and particle boards, where wood particles are compressed to form solid boards. Details of all these woods and boards, and how they are used, appear on the previous pages.

Softwoods

PINE

PARANA PINE

DOUGLAS FIR

WESTERN RED CEDAR

Hardwoods

OAK

ASH

BEECH

LIME

MAHOGANY

MAPLE

RAMIN

ROSEWOOD

TEAK

WALNUT

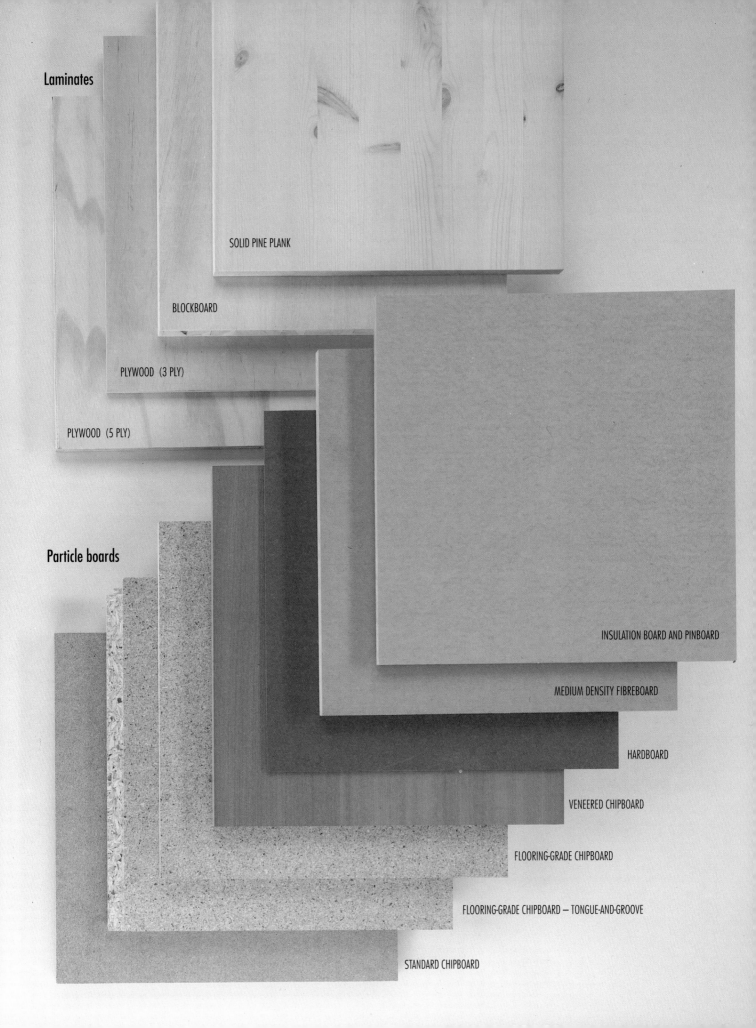

Laminates

SOLID PINE PLANK

BLOCKBOARD

PLYWOOD (3 PLY)

PLYWOOD (5 PLY)

Particle boards

INSULATION BOARD AND PINBOARD

MEDIUM DENSITY FIBREBOARD

HARDBOARD

VENEERED CHIPBOARD

FLOORING-GRADE CHIPBOARD

FLOORING-GRADE CHIPBOARD — TONGUE-AND-GROOVE

STANDARD CHIPBOARD

Wooden furniture

(SEE ALSO CHAIR; TABLE; WOODWORKING JOINTS)

Most furniture will be scratched and knocked at some time. In most cases, something can be done to repair the damage, but do not try to restore antique furniture yourself. Specialist antique furniture restorers can be found through a reputable antiques dealer or in *Yellow Pages* under 'Furniture repair and restoration'.

Repairing scratched wood

Disguise a fine scratch by painting on matching wood stain with a fine artist's brush. A patch of scratches can often be disguised by gently rubbing it with fine garnet paper, moistened with linseed oil, and then polishing it.

Alternatively, rub along the scratch with the kernel of a brazil nut (left), or with a shoe polish that matches the wood closely.

On deep scratches, use a wax filler stick or a liquid scratch filler to fill up the scratch. Leave it to dry for about an hour, then gently remove any surplus with fine garnet paper that has been moistened with linseed oil.

Buff up the treated area until it matches the rest.

Dealing with dents and bruises

On solid wood surfaces (but not on veneers) dents can often be filled successfully with a wood filler.

Raise deeper dents slightly before filling. Remove the wood finish on the affected area with wood restorer-and-cleaner (see margin, left). Then dab on some water to swell the wood grain and lift the compressed fibres.

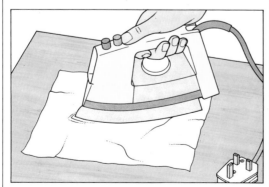

If this fails, lay a damp cloth over the area, then heat a domestic iron. Unplug the iron and apply the tip to the area. The steam will help to expand the wood fibres.

If a cavity remains when the wood is dry, fill it with a matching coloured beeswax or wood filler. Sand the area lightly, then apply the filler until it stands a little proud of the surface. When it is set, sand it smooth with fine sand-paper, working with the grain of the wood. Stain it with wood dye to match the surrounding wood.

DENTED VENEER Damp the surface of the damaged area, then cut and lift the veneer with the tip of a craft knife.

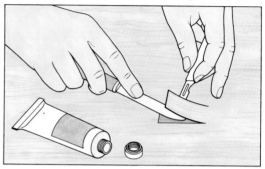

Fill the recess with wood filler until it is flush with the surface. Apply a little PVA wood glue to the underside of the veneer and clamp it down firmly until the glue has set. Lightly smooth the veneer with the handle of a table knife.

Disguising burns

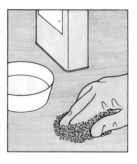

Scrape away any loose bits of charred wood, and then lightly rub the burn with some steel wool and wood restorer-and-cleaner (see margin, left), working with the grain of the wood.

When the finish has dissolved, wipe it off with a clean cloth. Allow the wood to dry, then sand it until the burn mark has disappeared. Work with the grain of the wood.

Wipe the surface with a cloth moistened with white spirit to remove all traces of dust and grease. Polish or varnish the area to match the surrounding wood.

If the burn is deep, it may be better to seek expert help.

Repairing cracks in wooden furniture

FINE CRACKS Use a matching wax filler stick to fill the crack. Remove any surplus with fine abrasive paper which has been moistened with linseed oil.

LARGER CRACKS Fill the crack slightly proud of the surface with a matching wood filler. When it has set, sand it smooth, working with the grain of the wood. If there is a strain on the wood that may cause a crack to open again, use a two-part epoxy wood filler, which is much stronger.

Removing white rings

If the white ring mark has affected only the finish on the wood, you may be able to remove it yourself – various methods are suggested below.

However, if the mark penetrates to the wood, the only satisfactory solution is to strip and refinish the wood.

BASIC TREATMENT Rub the white ring vigorously with a cloth dipped in metal polish such as Brasso. The abrasive in the polish will help to erase the mark.

Alternatively, try a commercial ring-remover, finish-reviver or burnishing cream. Follow the instructions.

FRENCH POLISH If a hot plate or cup is placed on french-polished furniture a white ring will form. As an alternative to using metal polish, try rubbing in a mixture of one part turpentine to four parts boiled linseed oil.

Leave it overnight then rub it off with a soft cloth.

WAXED SURFACE Try a paste made from salt and olive oil. Spread it over the ring and leave it overnight. Next day, wipe it off and rewax the affected area.

TEAK Lightly sand the surface with fine sandpaper or fine steel wool, working with the grain of the wood until the ring has disappeared. Then apply teak oil with a soft cloth.

Wood finishes

(SEE ALSO FRENCH POLISH; VARNISH)

The colour of hardwoods such as oak or ebony are enhanced by clear finishes, and wood dyes are often used to alter the shade. The colour of softwood, such as pine, can be altered with wood stain, dye or tinted varnish, to mimic the colour of hardwood.

Dyes are absorbed completely into the wood and make softwood darker than hardwood. On pine, dye is absorbed differently by the sapwood and heartwood.

Tinted varnish sits wholly on top of the wood and so is prone to chipping. Each extra coat darkens the wood.

Wood stains are partly absorbed into the wood, and partly coat the surface so they tend to mask the grain.

Wood stains of the same brand can be mixed to produce a wide range of colours. To lighten water-based stains wipe them with a damp cloth as soon as they are applied.

Many products that are called wood stains are intended for exterior woodwork only and because they leave a film on the surface they cannot be used prior to french polishing or varnishing.

Applying a wood stain

Remove any old finish right back to bare wood (see *Paint stripping*). Wood stain will not take on paint or varnish.

Also remove any traces of glue from around the joints of the furniture, because glue acts as a barrier to the wood stain, resulting in light patches.

Fill all cracks and gaps with a wood filler of the type which will absorb stain. This should be stated on the pack. Some epoxy-based fillers are unsuitable for staining.

If you are using a water-based stain, first apply clean water to the wood to raise the grain. Then lightly sand the surface until it is smooth. If you are using a solvent-based stain, simply sand the wood surface smooth.

Shake the wood stain well, then pour a little into a small container such as a saucer. Dip a new washing-up sponge or a non-fluffy cloth or a brush into the stain and apply it liberally, quickly and evenly over the surface. Work in the direction of the grain.

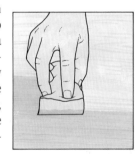

Let the whole area dry before applying a further coat. If the wood surface feels rough to the touch when the stain has dried, sand it lightly with fine sandpaper. Otherwise, wipe the surface with a clean cloth. Finish off with wax or varnish, bearing in mind that these will darken the wood.

Oiling wood

DANISH OIL Gives an almost clear, durable satin finish and seals the grain. It takes between 4 and 8 hours to dry. It is usual to apply at least two coats.

TEAK OIL Developed for finishing teak, it gives a quick-drying finish to hardwoods. Applied in the same way as Danish oil (see overleaf), but it gives more of a sheen.

PURE TUNG OIL Can be raw or heat-treated and both types give a soft film that is resistant to water, heat and mildew.

FINISHING OIL Can be used on its own to revive old woods, or it can be used before wax polishing.

LINSEED OIL It was once a popular finish for natural timbers, but it takes 3 days to dry. Modern oils are better.

BLEACHING WOOD

If various coloured woods are encountered on one piece of furniture you can use wood bleach, available from a decorator's shop, to even the tone. Follow the instructions on the pack.

SANDING WOOD SUCCESSFULLY

Always sand wood in the same direction as the grain. Working across the grain produces scratches which are difficult to disguise or remove.

WHAT TYPE OF WOOD STAIN?

● Water-based stains are easy to apply, but they raise the wood grain so the wood must be lightly sanded after the stain has been applied. They can be diluted or mixed to vary the depth of colour, and take about half a day to dry. Brushes used to apply water-based stains can be cleaned in water.

● Solvent-based stains take about an hour to dry. They have the advantage of not raising the grain of the wood.

Applying Danish oil to wood

Apply a liberal coat of oil over the wood surface with a brush or a cotton cloth and leave for a few minutes.

When half of the area looks drier than the rest, redistribute the surplus oil by wiping the surface with a clean cloth.

If, however, the oil is being applied to an absorbent soft wood such as pine, leave it to soak in.

Apply a second coat of oil, working with the grain.

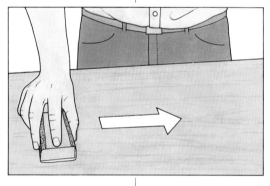

Leave it to dry and apply a third coat if necessary. If the last coat has 'pips' on the surface, sand it lightly. Alternatively, apply more oil with a Scotchbrite scouring pad or fine steel wool, then wipe it off immediately with a clean rag or paper towel.

Use white spirit to clean the brushes used to apply the oil. But it you used rags either burn them or store them in a sealed metal container because in unusual circumstances they may self-ignite.

Waxing wood

Wax polishes come in a number of formulas. The most common is beeswax, carnauba wax, paraffin and turpentine. A quick-drying brushing wax is also available.

It takes frequent applications of wax over several years to develop the patina associated with old furniture. A good compromise is to seal the wood with Danish oil or sanding sealer, then apply wax.

> YOU WILL NEED Soft cloths and dusters, fine sandpaper, tack rag, Danish oil or sanding sealer, wax polish, shoe brush. Possibly: wood restorer-and-cleaner, wood-reviver, finishing wax.

The wood surface must be clean and dry before waxing. Wax polish can be applied over a previously waxed or varnished surface as long as it is in good condition.

For the best results, remove the existing finish with a wood restorer-and-cleaner. Then apply a coat of wood-reviver to feed the wood. Smooth with fine sandpaper, working in the direction of the wood grain. Use a tack rag (see *Painting tools*) to remove any remaining fine dust.

Apply a coat of Danish oil. On porous wood you may need a second coat to provide an even seal.

When it is dry, rub with fine sandpaper. Then, with a clean, lint-free cloth, apply a generous coat of wax over the whole surface and rub it into an even coating.

Leave the wax to dry for at least 24 hours, then burnish the surface using a clean cloth or a shoe brush.

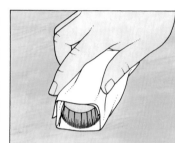

Wrap a duster round the brush to give the surface a final shine. If the finish is patchy, apply a second coat.

If a bloom (a milky-white appearance under the finish) develops after a day or so, wipe it off with a polishing cloth. This is caused by solvents evaporating from the polish.

Wood-mosaic floor

Fixing a loose wooden block   Time: 1 hour or less

> YOU WILL NEED Wood chisel, bitumen-rubber flooring adhesive, club hammer, white spirit.

Lever out the loose wooden block with a wood chisel. Use the chisel to remove all old adhesive from the back of the block and the floor underneath.

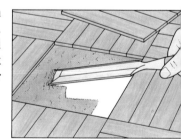

Butter the back of the loose block with bitumen-rubber flooring adhesive and press it back into position.

If necessary, tap the block into place with a club hammer, but protect it with a piece of scrap softwood.

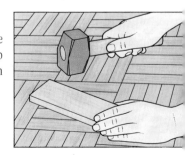

Remove any surplus adhesive while it is still wet with a rag dipped in white spirit. Polish the area when it is dry.

Cleaning a scuffed parquet floor Time: a few minutes

A floor in generally poor condition is best stripped and refinished (see *Floorboards*), but light scuff marks can be cleaned off. Rub the marks gently with fine steel wool lubricated with white spirit, working with the grain of the wood. Wipe away the debris with a clean cloth.

Wood preservative

Preservative prevents the natural decay of wood and keeps destructive insects at bay. Preservatives fall into two main categories – solvent based and water based. Some preservatives are purely functional, others are also decorative.

There is a range of timber which has been pressure-impregnated with preservative. It is more expensive, but will last almost indefinitely, so it is the best choice for construction work or for replacing old timbers. However, if untreated wood has been used already and you want to protect it, there are several options available.

What kind of preservative?

GREEN WOOD PRESERVER For use indoors and out. Ideal on structural timbers. Suitable for use near plants.

CLEAR WOOD PRESERVER A colourless preservative used to protect bare timber, such as window frames and doors, prior to painting, staining or varnishing.

INTERIOR PRESERVATIVE STAIN Combines a penetrating preservative with a natural wood colour. It can be varnished or polished. Useful on beamed ceilings and panelled walls.

EXTERIOR WOOD PRESERVATIVES These combine protection against rot, fungal growth and the effects of sunlight. Moisture trapped in the timber can escape, though the wood is protected from rain. The preservative may be clear or coloured.

WOODWORM KILLER Available as a fluid to be brushed on, or as an aerosol to be sprayed into the exit holes.

WET AND DRY ROT KILLERS Kills the fungi which cause rot. You can treat wet rot yourself, but dry rot should be left to specialist companies.

CREOSOTE A traditional wood preservative for outdoor use derived from coal tar. It is cheap and effective but should not be used near plants.

Applying the preservative

Soaking is the best way of applying preservative. For timbers such as fence posts, make a simple trough using bricks or timber and heavy-gauge polythene sheet. Fill the trough with preservative, insert a post and weight it down with bricks. Allow it to soak for 24 hours.

Alternatively, apply the preservative with a brush. Pay particular attention to the end of the timber, which is particularly vulnerable to rot.

Where timbers are difficult to reach, preservative can be applied by spray. In a confined space such as a loft, wear an industrial respirator and safety spectacles.

Preservative is also available in pellet form to be inserted into drilled holes in the timber. When the pellets become damp the preservative is released.

Woodworking joints

Joining wood with a butt joint

A butt joint is the simplest way of joining two pieces of wood. One piece of wood (A) is joined by its end grain at right angles to the other (B) to form a corner or a T.

> YOU WILL NEED Try square, pencil, tenon saw. Possibly: screws, nails, drill, twist bit, hammer, screwdriver, pencil, steel straightedge, clamp, vice, wood glue, wood block, corrugated fasteners, flat drill bit, chisel, bolts, spanner.

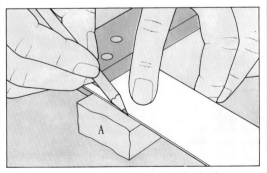

The piece being butted (A) must be absolutely square. Mark its end with a try square and pencil, and continue the line down the side. Use a tenon saw to cut it accurately.

The two pieces may be nailed or screwed together and for an even stronger joint, glued as well. In some cases it is better to use corrugated metal fasteners and, if the joint may have to be dismantled again, use bolts (see overleaf).

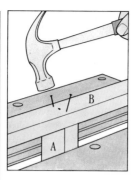

JOINING WOOD WITH NAILS
Secure piece A vertically in a vice. Hold the crosspiece (B) in the correct position and drive a nail into the centre of the overlap. Drive in two more nails on each side at an angle of about 30 degrees to the upright nail.

If you need to nail a butt joint into position from the inside of a frame, mark the position of the join on piece B and make a positioning guide by clamping or temporarily nailing a block of wood to it, butting up to the line.

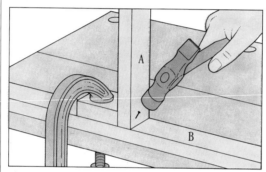

Then hold piece A against the block and drive the first nail diagonally down through both pieces.

Remove the positioning block and nail it on the other side of piece A. Working from the other side, drive in a second nail, in the same way, through both pieces.

USING SCREWS TO SECURE A JOINT Choose screws that will be long enough to penetrate all the way through piece B and at least 3.2 cm ($1\frac{1}{4}$ in) into piece A.

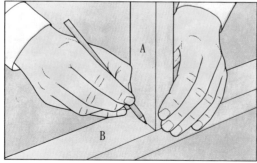

Hold the pieces of wood together and mark the location of the joint on the crosspiece (B).

In piece B, drill clearance holes that are the same width as the shanks of the screws you have chosen. Butt the two pieces of wood up against each other and, with a pencil or nail, mark the position of the holes on piece A.

Drill pilot holes in piece A, then apply wood glue to both meeting surfaces. Hold piece A in a vice, butt piece B up against it and screw it into position. With a clean, damp rag, wipe off any surplus glue while it is still wet.

HOW TO USE CORRUGATED FASTENERS TO MAKE A JOINT
If you are building a light frame that needs only a little strength, use corrugated fasteners to hold it together. Simply hold the two pieces of wood in position and hammer in the fasteners across the joint.

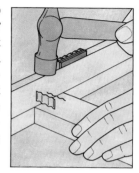

Corrugated fasteners are specially shaped to hold the two pieces of wood together tightly, with no movement.

USING BOLTS If you are likely to need to dismantle the frame in the future, bolts are useful fasteners.

Hold the pieces of wood together and mark the position of the joint on piece B (see below, left).

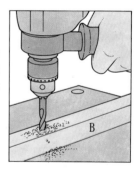

Drill a hole that will be large enough to take the bolt body, through the middle of piece B.

Reassemble the joint and mark the position of the hole on the end grain of piece A and drill a corresponding hole.

Use a drill and flat bit to bore a large hole in the flat surface of piece A so that a nut can be inserted. Position the hole so that it will be centred over the end of the bolt when the bolt is inserted, with at least 3.2 cm ($1\frac{1}{4}$ in) of wood between the edge of the hole and the end of the wood.

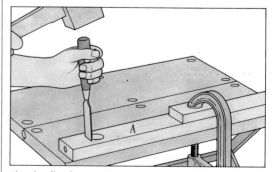

Chisel a flat face on the side of the hole nearest the end of the wood, where the nut will be exposed.

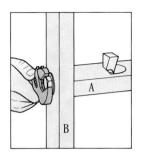

Insert the bolt through piece B into piece A, with a washer at each end. Put on the nut inside the hole, then wedge it with a piece of scrap wood while the bolt is tightened with a spanner.

Strengthening a butt joint

Drill a hole at right angles to the end grain and insert a piece of dowel. The screws will then grip in the dowel. This is a particularly useful technique for strengthening joints in chipboard.

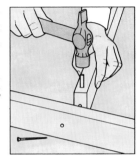

Alternatively, drill holes and sink wall plugs into the end grain. Position the plug so that it expands along the widest part of the wood to avoid splitting.

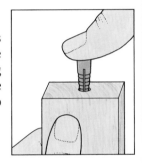

Mitre joint

This is a common form of butt joint, most often seen in the making of picture frames. The ends of two pieces of wood are cut to 45 degree angles, and butt against each other to create a joint at 90 degrees.

Carefully mark the lengths of wood required, then roughly draw the cut line on the wood to ensure that you make the cut in the right direction. Position the wood in a mitre box with a piece of scrap wood underneath it.

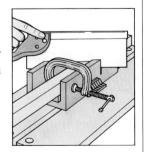

Clamp the wood firmly in place then use a tenon saw to make the cut.

Do not attempt to smooth or shape the cut end with sandpaper. The rough cut will give a better surface for the glued joint. Repeat the operation for the other mitre cuts.

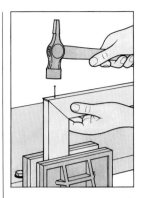

With one piece of wood fixed vertically in a vice, apply wood glue to both meeting surfaces. Position the second piece so that it is fractionally higher than its intended final position, and tap in panel pins.

As the pins are driven home, the horizontal piece will move down a fraction, giving a perfect joint. For an even neater finish, sink the pins into the wood with a nail punch and fill the holes with wood filler.

A picture-framer's tip is to find a block of metal with a perfect right-angle corner, and hold it inside the corner while you are pinning the joint.

Joining wood with an overlapping joint

One piece of wood is laid on top of the other, checked for position with a try square then nailed or screwed together.

If one piece of wood is thicker than the other, nail or screw the thinner piece to the thicker piece.

USING SCREWS Make clearance holes for the screw shanks in the top piece of wood and smaller pilot holes in the lower. Use screws that are shorter than the combined thickness of the two pieces to avoid damaging the surface.

USING NAILS To add strength to rough frames, use nails about 1.3 cm ($\frac{1}{2}$ in) longer than the combined thickness of the wood, then hammer the protruding ends over.

Joining wood the easy way

Various accessories are available to cut down the amount of work needed to form joints.

METAL BRACKETS L-shaped brackets or flat metal T brackets can be used to make rough butt joints. Fix them in place with screws that are shorter than the depth of the wood.

JOINING BLOCKS Plastic joining blocks, either fixed or in two parts to be separated, are available for simple unit construction. Alternatively, make your own from square or triangular wood mouldings.

Mitre box

A mitre box is an open wooden box with slots on two sides into which a saw blade fits at 45 degrees. The wood to be cut is placed in the box, raised on a piece of scrap timber to protect the bottom of the box. It is then sawn accurately to a 45 degree angle.

AN ALTERNATIVE TO USING A MITRE BOX

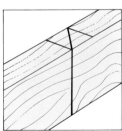

If the wood is too wide to fit in a mitre box, draw a square on the edge, then draw a diagonal. Continue the diagonal line down both faces of the wood. Cut to the diagonal line. If your tenon saw is not deep enough to cut the wood, use a fine-toothed panel saw instead.

Making a halving joint

Build stronger frames by cutting away half of each piece to be joined. This can be done to form corner joints or to join two pieces crossing or meeting each other.

CORNER JOINT Mark half the thickness of each piece of wood, then mark the depth of cut to equal the width of the wood being fixed. Use a tenon saw to cut out the waste.

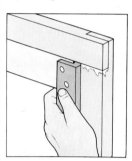

Glue the joint and then nail or screw it. Check with a try square to ensure the corner forms a perfect right angle before the glue sets.

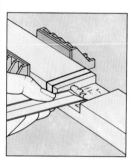

CROSS HALVING For T or cross halvings, use a tenon saw to make the vertical cuts, and then make three or four extra cuts in the waste part of the wood, down to the halving line. Then use a chisel to remove the waste wood.

Woodworm

Woodworms are actually the larvae of beetles. The beetles lay their eggs on the surface of timber. The eggs hatch into grubs, which then bore into the wood. Eventually the grubs pupate within the wood and change into adult beetles, which emerge and start the cycle again.

There are four or five main varieties of beetle which are known to attack timber in Britain.

Identifying the problem

COMMON FURNITURE BEETLE The most common of the pests that attack the wood in houses in Britain. It attacks most wood and thrives in plywood.

The adult beetle is a small brown insect, about 6 mm ($\frac{1}{4}$ in) long. It lays as many as 60 eggs in cracks in timber, usually between May and September.

Look for round exit holes about 2 mm ($\frac{1}{16}$ in) across, plus fine droppings and debris round the holes. The holes indicate that the beetles have left, but they may have laid eggs elsewhere in the area. Check roofwork, floorboards, under staircases, skirting boards and also your furniture – particularly furniture with plywood back panels.

CONTACTING THE EXPERTS

The British Wood Preserving and Damp-proofing Association will answer queries about infestation of wood and supply a list of members. Contact them at PO Box 894, London E15 4ED. Tel. 0181 519 2588.

DEATH WATCH BEETLE Rarely found in houses, as it prefers old hardwoods such as decaying oak. It is mostly found in church timbers, where it leaves circular holes about 3 mm ($\frac{1}{8}$ in) across and coarse, rounded pellets. If this pest is discovered, seek professional help.

POWDER POST BEETLE Attacks only certain hardwoods including oak, ash, walnut, willow and elm, within the first few years after felling. There are no distinctive tunnels. The wood is destroyed in layers, leaving a thin veneer of sound wood on the surface. Look for circular holes, about 2 mm ($\frac{1}{16}$ in) across and fine dust, like face powder, near the holes.

HOUSE LONGHORN BEETLE Attacks only the sapwood of softwoods, and is usually found in rafters in attics. The longhorn beetle is rare, but it appears in parts of Surrey and Hampshire. In these areas building regulations may demand the pretreatment of susceptible timber.

A few oval holes about 6 mm ($\frac{1}{4}$ in) across indicate the presence of the grub. It burrows near the surface of the wood, but the internal damage may go unnoticed as a thin veneer of sound wood is left. The grub of the house long-horn beetle may stay in the wood for up to six years and cause serious structural damage. If you discover this pest, notify your local authority and seek professional help.

Check for woodworm before buying

If you plan to buy a house more than 20 years old, ask for a check for woodworm to be included in the survey. If it has been treated for woodworm in the past, ask to see the certificate, in order to know how much longer the guarantee has to run. Specialist woodworm insurance cover is available.

Solving the problem

Cut away and burn all badly attacked wood and expose infested wood as far as possible – for example lift floor-boards and take down affected panelling.

Remove any surface coating such as paint or varnish (see *Paint stripping*). Clean the timber thoroughly and remove surface dust with a vacuum cleaner. Then apply a woodworm killer. It is available as liquid, spray or paste.

Treat all replacement timber with woodworm killer or, preferably, use pressure-impregnated timber.

LOFT SPACE Clear and clean the loft. Because you will be working in a confined space, wear an industrial respirator. Hire it, along with an industrial spray-and-lance, from your local hire shop. Alternatively, apply the woodworm killer with a paintbrush. Pay close attention to corners and crevices. Ventilate the space as much as possible, and do not smoke because the solvent fumes are flammable.

FLOORBOARDS Lift affected floorboards if possible and check for infestation in the joists. If it is not possible to remove the floorboards, thoroughly spray or paint the surfaces with two applications of a woodworm killer.

FURNITURE Paint all surfaces with two coats of woodworm killer, especially backs, undersides, drawers and runners. For extra protection, inject some holes with a proprietary woodworm killer with a special nozzle. Use an insecticidal polish on all furniture you feel may be at risk of infestation. This will discourage the laying of eggs.

Worktop

Repairing damage to plastic laminates

CLEANING Use a cream cleaner such as Jif, or hot soapy water to clean the surface immediately after a messy job.

REMOVING STAINS Rub stains quickly with bicarbonate of soda, or cream cleaner on a damp cloth. If the stain persists, apply lemon juice and leave for half an hour before rubbing again with bicarbonate of soda.

REMOVING BURN MARKS Rub burns with a little methylated spirit on a cloth. If this doesn't work, try a car-body cleaning compound on a cloth.

HIDING SCRATCHES Scratches can be touched up with matching enamel paint. Apply layer on layer with a fine artist's brush. Formica also supply a range of repair fillers which match their standard colours.

Replacing a laminate worktop

If a laminate is badly damaged, don't try to remove it. It is better to lay a new laminate surface on top, instead.

> YOU WILL NEED Hand-sanding block, steel tape measure, tenon saw or trimming knife with a laminate-scoring blade, steel straightedge, contact adhesive, notched spreader, sheet of brown paper or drawing pins, file or block plane. Possibly: edging strip.

Roughen the surface of the old laminate with a hand-sanding block. Clean and dust the surface.

Measure the new piece of laminate, allowing about 3 mm ($\frac{1}{8}$ in) extra all round for trimming. Use a tenon saw, held at a shallow angle, or a trimming knife with a laminate-scoring blade, to cut the laminate.

To cut with a trimming knife, lay the laminate with its patterned face up, and hold the straightedge along the proposed cutting line. Run the blade along the straightedge until it has scored through the patterned surface to the brown backing. Keep the straightedge in place and lift the laminate up, so that it snaps along the scored line.

Evenly coat both laminate and worktop with contact adhesive, using a notched spreader. Leave them until they are touch-dry, to allow the solvent to evaporate – otherwise the laminate may bubble up when it is in position.

When both surfaces feel dry, lay a sheet of brown paper over at least half of the worktop. Carefully position half of the laminate over the paper, while holding the rest of it well clear of the glued worktop. You may need a helper.

Lower the laminate so that one half sticks, then slide out the paper from under the second half. Press down all over the laminate with the ball of your fist.

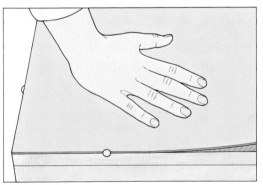

Alternatively, press drawing pins into the edges of the worktop so that the pin heads project above the surface. They will act as guides to help you to get the edges of the laminate lined up correctly with the edges of the worktop.

Let the adhesive dry for at least an hour, then trim off the surplus laminate along the edge, using either a file or small block plane. Work along the length of the laminate, from the corners towards the middle.

Finish off the edge by painting it or covering it with strips of laminate. Alternatively, cover it with a hockey-stick-section plastic edging strip, available in DIY stores.

Transforming a worktop with tiles

If you are redecorating a kitchen, consider sticking worktop-grade ceramic tiles over a laminate surface, using waterproof tile adhesive and grout (see *Tiles*).

AVOIDING DAMAGE ON A LAMINATE WORKTOP

- Hot pans and dishes will crack laminates, so stand them on a heat-resistant mat.
- Some liquids such as fruit juices and strong dyes will stain the surface. Mop them up immediately if there is a spill.
- To avoid scarring the surface, use a cutting board when working with sharp knives.
- Do not use metal scouring pads on the laminate surface.

Zip

Replacing a zip Time: ½ an hour or less

For a neater result when putting a new zip into a garment, make sure that its teeth are concealed by the fabric.

> YOU WILL NEED Stitch ripper or fine scissors, needle and thread, replacement zip, sewing machine. Possibly: electric iron.

Remove the damaged zip, using a stitch ripper or fine scissors. Pull out any loose threads along the opening.

DECREASING THE WAISTLINE If the garment was too loose, make new fold lines, taking more fabric into the seam allowance (see also *Skirt*). Press the new fold line.

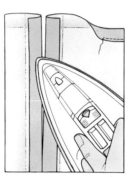

INCREASING THE WAISTLINE If the garment was too tight previously, iron out the old fold lines, and iron in new ones, leaving a smaller seam allowance (left).

INSERTING THE ZIP With the wrong side facing, align the new fold lines and tack them together with a needle and thread, taking very large stitches. Open out the seam and press it flat.

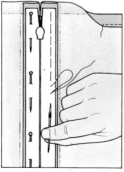

Close the new zip and centre it on the inside of the garment, so that the zip teeth follow the line of the tacked seam. Pin and tack the zip into place, making sure that the slider and tab (handle) will be facing outward when you unpick the tacking stitches.

Stitch the zip into place, either by hand with a fine backstitch, or using a sewing machine with a zip foot. Unpick all tacking stitches and check that the tab runs up and down the zip freely, without catching the fabric.

Reattaching a zip's slider Time: ½ an hour or less

When the slider comes off one side of a zip, it is possible to reattach it and continue to use the zip.

> YOU WILL NEED Sharp scissors, needle and thread.

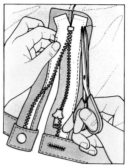 

Unpick the stitching at the bottom of the zip for about 2.5 cm (1 in) on both sides.

Prise off the metal stop at the zip bottom (or cut it off a plastic zip, if necessary).

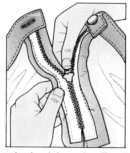 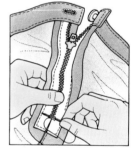

Take the slider right off and then feed both the raw ends of the zip into it. Make sure they are even, then pull it upwards, closing the zip.

Pin and tack the bottom of the zip back in place. Make a new bottom stop by stitching across the closed teeth, three or four times.

Restitch the bottom of the zip, either by hand, using a fine backstitch, or by machine, with a zip foot attachment.

Tips with zips

- If a zip is sticking, rub the edges of the teeth with pencil lead, lip salve, soap or candle wax. Then wipe off the residue with a tissue.
- To make a secure holder for money, passport or a season ticket, stitch a short zip across the top of an inside pocket in a jacket, or a hip pocket in trousers.
- Before sewing a new, cotton-sided zip into a garment which has already been washed and is unlikely to shrink any further, preshrink the zip (by soaking it in hot water for three minutes) and allow it to dry.
- If the tab at the top of a zip comes off, replace it temporarily with a small safety pin or a paperclip.

INDEX

EMERGENCY ACTION

Car emergencies 56
Chimney fire 83
Chip-pan fire 84
Gas leak 170
Pipe, burst 264
Pipe, dripping overflow ... 12
Pipe, frozen 264
Pipe, leaking 264
Power failure 275

SAFETY FIRST

! Before starting any work on an electrical fitting or appliance, make sure to cut off the electricity supply, either by switching off at the main fuse box, or by unplugging the appliance.

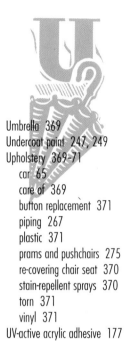
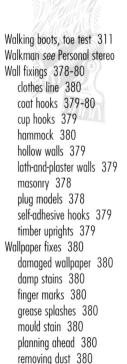

ACKNOWLEDGMENTS

The publishers appreciate the help given by the
following organisations in the preparation of

HOW TO FIX JUST ABOUT ANYTHING

A.O.C. Ltd • AEG (UK) Ltd • AL-KO Britain Ltd • Amstrad plc •
Appliance Care Ltd • Applied Security Design Ltd • Armitage Shanks Ltd •
ATCO Ltd • Automobile Association (AA) • BEG Bruck Electronic Ltd •
Beiersdorf Ltd • Black & Decker Ltd • Blue Hawk Ltd • Robert Bosch Ltd •
Bostik Ltd • Canon UK Ltd • CeKa Works Ltd • Citizen Europe Ltd • Creda Ltd •
Crown Berger Ltd • Cuprinol Ltd • DR Cooker Hoods Ltd • Duckbill Anchors Ltd •
Dunlopillo UK • Dylon International Ltd • Artur Fischer (UK) Ltd •
Flamco Brefco Ltd • Flymo • Frigidaire Consolidated Ltd • Gardena UK Ltd •
Glass & Glazing Federation • Globe Organic Services • Goblin Ltd •
Heatrae-Sadia Heating Ltd • Hepworth Building Products Ltd •
J Hewit & Sons Ltd • Hewlett-Packard Ltd • Hitachi Ltd • Holt Lloyd Ltd •
Hotpoint Ltd • Hozelock Ltd • ICI Paints • IMI Santon Ltd •
International Paints Ltd • Jemp Engineering Ltd • E L M Le Blanc • John Lewis
Partnership • Lexmark International Ltd • Loctite (UK) Ltd • Martek Ltd •
Mason Accessories Ltd • Merloni Domestic Appliances Ltd • MK Electric Ltd •
Monument Tools Ltd • National Bed Federation • Neff UK Ltd • Oracstar Ltd •
Osram Ltd • Panasonic (UK) Ltd • Philips Domestic Appliances &
Personal Care Division • Philips Lighting Ltd • Pifco Ltd • Polycell Products Ltd •
Procter & Gamble Ltd • Rapitest Ltd • The Rawlplug Company Ltd •
Redring Electric Ltd • Safety Tools Ltd • Sandvik Saw & Tools UK •
Sealmaster Ltd • Silentnight Beds • Sir Galahad plc • Slumberland plc •
Sturmey Archer Ltd • Superswitch • The Sylglas Co • Thorn Lighting Ltd •
3M United Kingdom plc • UHU (UK) Ltd • Vent-Axia Ltd • Whirlpool (UK) Ltd •
John Wood: Freelance journalist & Photojournalist • Xpelair Ltd • Zanussi Ltd

ORIGINATION Graphic Facilities Ltd, London, England
PRINTING AND BINDING Grafica Editoriale Srl, Bologna, Italy
40-444-4